# YACHT DESIGN
## ACCORDING TO
# PERRY

**INTERNATIONAL MARINE / McGRAW-HILL**
Camden, Maine | New York | Chicago | San Francisco
Lisbon | London | Madrid | Mexico City | Milan | New Delhi
San Juan | Seoul | Singapore | Sydney | Toronto

# YACHT DESIGN
## ACCORDING TO
# PERRY

## My Boats and What Shaped Them

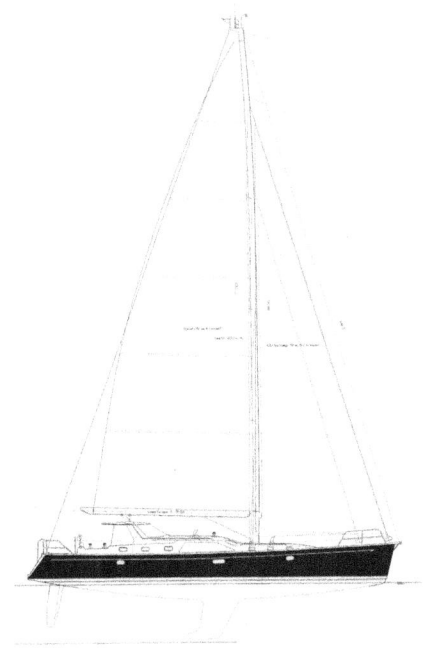

### Robert H. Perry

**The McGraw·Hill Companies**

1 2 3 4 5 6 7 8 9 CCW CCW 0 9 8 7

© 2008 by Robert H. Perry
All rights reserved. The publisher takes no responsibility for the use of any of the materials or methods described in this book, nor for the products thereof. The name "International Marine" and the International Marine logo are trademarks of The McGraw-Hill Companies.

*Library of Congress Cataloging-in-Publication Data*
Perry, Robert H.
   Yacht design according to perry : my boats and what shaped them / Robert H. Perry.
       p.  cm.
   Includes index.
   ISBN 978-1-265-80792-4 (pbk)
   1. Yachts—Design and construction.   I. Title.
   VM331.P47 2007
   623.8'1223—dc22                       2007033665

ISBN 978-1-265-80792-4
MHID 1-26-580792-2

Questions regarding the content of this book should be addressed to
International Marine
P.O. Box 220
Camden, ME 04843
internationalmarine.com

Questions regarding the ordering of this book should be addressed to
The McGraw-Hill Companies
Customer Service Department
P.O. Box 547
Blacklick, OH 43004
Retail customers: 1-800-262-4729
Bookstores: 1-800-722-4726

Unless otherwise noted, all photos and illustrations are courtesy of the author.

*This book is dedicated to all my clients,
past, present, and future.*

# Contents

| | | |
|---|---|---:|
| | INTRODUCTION | 1 |
| 1 | FROM SYDNEY, AUSTRALIA, TO BALLARD, WASHINGTON | 3 |
| 2 | THE APPRENTICE | 7 |
| | *According to Perry: Comparing Sailboats* | 10 |
| 3 | VALIANT DAYS | 19 |
| | *According to Perry: The Hull-Lines Plan* | 37 |
| 4 | ISLANDER YACHTS OF CALIFORNIA | 44 |
| | *According to Perry: Sheerlines and Bow Profiles* | 60 |
| 5 | CT YACHTS AND THE TA CHAIO STORY | 64 |
| | *According to Perry: Transoms* | 73 |
| 6 | AN EXTENDED FAMILY OF DOUBLE-ENDERS | 75 |
| | *According to Perry: Stability* | 84 |
| 7 | THE TA SHING FAMILY OF DOUBLE-ENDERS | 88 |
| | *According to Perry: Thoughts on the Cruising Keel* | 99 |
| 8 | CHEOY LEE | 102 |
| | *According to Perry: Full Keels* | 118 |

| | | |
|---|---|---|
| 9 | PASSPORT YACHTS | 123 |
| | *According to Perry: Draft* | 146 |
| 10 | *NIGHT RUNNER* | 149 |
| | *According to Perry: Rig Dimensions and Types* | 158 |
| 11 | *LOON* | 164 |
| | *According to Perry: Shortening Sail* | 172 |
| 12 | *YONI* | 175 |
| | *According to Perry: Masts* | 185 |
| 13 | A PAIR OF CHICKENS | 188 |
| | *According to Perry: Rigging* | 202 |
| 14 | TWO CALIFORNIA CRUISING SLEDS: *STARBUCK* AND *FOXFIRE* | 209 |
| | *According to Perry: Thoughts on Bows* | 221 |
| 15 | *AMATI* | 226 |
| | *According to Perry: More on Bows* | 232 |
| 16 | THREE CRUISING SLEDS: *WHITE EAGLE, MOBISLE,* AND *ICON* | 235 |
| | *According to Perry: Real-World Bow Evaluations* | 251 |
| 17 | DESIGNING *JAKATAN:* A CUSTOM 40'6" SCHOONER | 254 |
| | ACKNOWLEDGMENTS | 268 |
| | INDEX | 269 |

# Introduction

In 1972, when I was 26 years old, I received my first published design review, a full-page critique of a 47-foot ketch in *National Fisherman* magazine. That review led to my first design commission, which ultimately became the CT 54, a story told in this book.

That was 380 designs and more than 6,000 launched boats ago. When my Seattle office opened in 1974, my boyhood dream became a reality. From that point on, my hobby was my occupation. So far it has been a good ride. I've weathered a few squalls along the way, but when I survey my collection of designs, I'm proud of my productivity and durability.

Now, more than 30 years later, it's time to get down on paper some of the stories behind those boats. I've had the pleasure of working with remarkable clients, and their contributions to my designs have at times been profound. The real richness of the design experience rests in working with such people. The challenge is to match the boat to the individual. I want the boat to reflect the client's approach to life on the water. It's as personal as it sounds, and it's the central premise that has shaped my production designs as well as my custom boats.

I'll explain what worked and why, and I'll explain what failed to work and why. In addition, I have inserted between the chapters of this book a fistful of essays discussing my approach to specific design elements. I hope these diversions will outline a productive approach to dealing with the range of technical and aesthetic challenges a designer confronts.

Still, this book is not intended to be an instructional treatise, but more a way of understanding how the design process unfolds both in human and technical terms. I try to keep things as simple as possible. If yacht design were solely a matter of formulas, tables, and charts, all boats would look pretty much the same. Yacht design is instead one of those wonderful blends of art and science, and that's what makes it so rewarding.

Chapter 17 is the culmination of the book, a design case study. By retracing the design process for a 40'6" custom schooner, my aim is to bring together the book's two elements—human and technical—and show how they work together to shape a design.

If I've mixed the right ingredients in the right proportions, this book—I hope—will be something any sailor can chew on and find nutritious. It will also serve as a road map of sorts for an aspiring yacht designer. I know one thing—if I'd found a book like this in 1972, I would have gobbled it up.

Over the years I've had a lot of office help and some highly skilled people working with me. Suffice it to say that my work would not be the same without their contributions. I thank them all sincerely.

Now let's talk about boats and the people and factors that shape them.

## Chapter One

# FROM SYDNEY, AUSTRALIA, TO BALLARD, WASHINGTON

In 1957, when I was 12 years old, my dad returned from a visit with his parents in the United States to tell us that we could live better if we moved to America. I don't think my mum, a native Australian, was too keen on the idea, but it sounded good to my sister and me. My parents auctioned off our furniture, and we left our flat with a few suitcases of belongings. Boarding a tired World War II Liberty ship, the *Lakemba*, we prepared to set off from Sydney for Vancouver, British Columbia.

Dad had enticed us with brochures of majestic ocean liners like the *Mariposa* and the *Lurline*, the ship that had carried our family to Australia from the United States when I was just a year old. In the end, however, those wonderful ships were beyond our family's budget in 1957. A Liberty ship carrying 90 passengers in addition to its cargo turned out to be the right ticket, and we even managed to travel second class, with opening portholes in our two staterooms. (Third-class staterooms had no portholes at all.) Even better, we pretty much had the run of the *Lakemba*, although the captain would not let us on the bridge and the Fijian crew preferred that we stay off the fantail, where they relaxed and sang beautiful Polynesian harmonies to the bosun's guitar.

Off we went toward Fiji, where we were to pick up a load of sugar. Leaving Sydney Harbour and the Sydney Heads astern, we lumbered into the open sea at a steady nine knots. The ship rode high with empty holds, rocking and rolling like crazy. On the first morning out I found myself one of the few passengers willing to face breakfast. It turned out that I had been born with a forgiving stomach, and seasickness was never on the menu for me.

Fiji had been shut down by a sugar worker's strike, and the ship could not be loaded. We sat for two weeks waiting for the strike to end. It was heaven. Each morning the ship would lower a lifeboat, and off we'd go to a remote beach or village where the locals would dote on us. Unfortunately, I think this extra two weeks in Fiji sapped my parents' budget, and we landed in Vancouver broke. My dad had to borrow my life savings of $20 so he could buy train tickets to Seattle, where his sister was waiting for us. But what did I care? We were going to America!

Looking back, I think this month-long voyage played a seminal role in my obsession with boats. I enjoyed every day of it, including the three days we spent riding out a typhoon in the North Pacific. We averaged less than two knots during the storm while the skipper struggled to keep our ship's head to the wind. I vividly remember the feeling of the prop shaking the entire ship whenever it broke free of the water. Loaded with sugar, we were riding low, and water ran through the passageways. Mom, a non-swimmer, was always terrified of boats. She woke us one night in the middle of the storm, made us put on life jackets, and herded us into their stateroom.

I took it all in stride, finding ways to entertain myself as the miles slowly receded astern. I think the adults played cards during the day, then sat in the tiny bar at night where my dear old dad entertained the others on a rickety old piano. Dad was a great musician. I spent a lot of time playing "deck tennis" by myself, and when that got old I made paper airplanes and launched them off the rail. I also whiled away the hours sketching. I fancied myself an artist and enjoyed drawing parts of the ship.

America! It was everything I had hoped for. Dad landed a job as an accountant and, with some help from my grandparents, bought us a house. Imagine that. I got my own bedroom with four walls instead of the breezy, open porch on which I'd slept in our flat in Australia. I even got a dog! You can't have a dog when you live in a flat. The dog ran away, but then I got my own bike. We had a car, a phone, a refrigerator—and if that wasn't enough, we even had a TV. America was cool.

At the beginning of my ninth-grade year my parents decided to move us to a section of Seattle renowned for its school system. This was Mercer Island, smack in the middle of Lake Washington, a ritzy neighborhood with lots of waterfront homes and boys my age who wore Pendleton shirts to school. "Thirty-five dollars for a shirt? Over my dead body," my mom kept saying.

I don't know how or why, but something clicked that year, and I found myself drawn to boats. I began cutting pictures of yachts out of magazines and reading everything I could get my hands on about the old clipper ships. I kept imaginary ships' logs with detailed accounts of my routes across the ocean, which I tracked on a large map pinned to my wall. I made record-breaking run after record-breaking run. I drove my ship under full canvas when every sane skipper was shortening sail. I was the fearless captain of the balsa schooner I carved and rigged with whatever scraps I could find. Gee, I wished I could *really* try sailing.

Then several things happened. Halfway through the semester I was kicked out of the school band for twirling the cymbals overhead after clashing them, just as my eighth-grade band director had taught me. The technique elicits a jacked-up, gratifying sound, as every marching band member knows, but my high-school band director didn't see it that way. He ordered me to stop, which to a 15-year-old boy is a challenge to continue. You could say we had creative differences.

The only class my teachers thought they could slot me into midterm was mechanical drawing, so into that class I went, half a semester behind. I was given a small drawing board and a few drafting tools, and within two weeks I owned that class. I really took to mechanical drawing. My teacher's name was Mr. Kibby, but we called him "the walrus" due to his many chins. He was a big, good-natured man with a pragmatic and effective way of handling energetic boys and a pedantic approach to the discipline of mechanical drawing. He was a great teacher, and I owe him a lot. "It's all about line weight, line weight!" he thundered, and I took the lesson to heart.

Through Mr. Kibby I ordered a drawing board and drafting equipment that I could take home. Sitting at home before my little drafting board, I pondered what to draw and knew it had to be a boat. I did not yet own any ship's curves—the plastic drafting tools with smoothly curved edges for drawing curves of varying radii—so I designed what I thought was a model of the Civil War ironclad *Merrimack*, the straight, slab sides of which suited my abilities and tools. I kept drawing boats. I bought curves. I worked in a meat market after school and spent almost all my money on drafting gear. I was focused.

That year, too, I was babysitting for a family who had a waterfront home and a nondescript 17-foot daysailer. I begged them to take me sailing, and eventually they did. They were not good sailors, but the dad was content to let me steer. I just strapped in the sails and let the boat tip on its ear while we labored along. Boy, this was fun.

But school was not so much fun. I was earning straight As in mechanical drawing but paid little attention to anything else. In geometry class I learned how to calculate the area of a triangle, and that was good for sail plans, but the rest was of no interest. Luckily my geometry teacher, Don Miller, was an active sailor. "So you want to draw boats. Why don't you go visit Bill Garden?"

Nervously I called Bill Garden and made arrangements to visit, and my dad dropped me off at Garden's office, right across from the Ballard Locks, early one Saturday morning. Today when a kid comes to my office, I try to remember how it felt meeting Bill for the first time, and I try to be as encouraging and honest as Bill was with me. I remember standing transfixed in that small office, surrounded by stacks of drawings, half models, and photos of beautiful boats. I want to do this, I thought.

Bill took me to lunch at a local restaurant. I was acutely aware that the 35 cents I had in my pocket was my bus fare home. The only thing on the menu for 35 cents was french fries, so I ordered french fries. I could always hitchhike home or walk. Bill could not believe that a few french fries were all I wanted for lunch, so I explained in detail how I loved french fries. When the bill came, of course, Bill paid it and I felt foolish. I left his office that day loaded down with old spare prints he had lying around. They were treasures to me.

Don Miller was also the adult adviser for the Corinthian Junior Yacht Club. "Why don't you join the yacht club?" he suggested. It cost only $10 to join, and I could come up with that.

"Mom, Dad," I announced, "I'm joining the yacht club."

"That's nice, dear."

Soon, with encouragement from Don, I was sailing regularly, sometimes three days a week. At the yacht club I was surrounded by kids my own age who were totally immersed in sailing. They all wanted to be yacht designers—Scott Rohrer, Brian Wertheimer, Joe Golberg, Dennis Clark—and they all would go on to become highly competent racing sailors. None of the others became yacht designers, though. We would take turns trying to steal the yacht club's collection of Uffa Fox books, which would work only until one of the other junior members figured out who had the collection last. I think Scott Rohrer and I had that collection memorized by the time we were 16 years old. Today Scott is an invaluable repository of yachting lore and trivia. I had a strong sense that I was not "yacht club material," but somehow I didn't let that stop me from enjoying the experience.

When my other high-school teachers had given up on me, Don Miller hung in there with constant encouragement (even though I got a D in geometry). I was always racing. I would walk the five miles from our house to the marina on Lake Washington, where the races were held. If I did not have a crew position, I would show up at the docks anyway and walk from boat to boat asking if anyone needed a crew member. Someone always did, and I always got a ride. I sailed on almost every small boat imaginable: Penguins, Lightnings, Geary 18s, OK dinghies, Snipes, International 14s, 110s, 210s, PCs, Evergreens, Flying Scots, Cougar cats, Ravens, Thistles, Dragons, Blanchard juniors, Blanchard seniors, six-meters, Stars.

Before long I was skippering one of the club's Penguin dinghies and doing fairly well in local races. My best finishes were in the winter frostbiting series, when nobody else bothered to show up as regularly as I did. A trophy is a trophy. Before long I was walking the docks of Shilshole Bay Marina and crewing on big boats. I raced with Bill Garden aboard *Oceanus*. Sailing and drawing boats was my life. My parents never related to what I was doing, although they did give me a welcome set of foul-weather gear one Christmas.

I maintained contact with Bill Garden through high school and college, but I never worked for him (although several articles in sailing magazines have stated that I did). Bill finally agreed to let me apprentice for him one summer, but he would not have paid me, and I needed a paying job for college. So, to set the record straight, I never worked for Bill Garden. I just hung around him when I could and sailed with him when he needed crew members. I consider myself very lucky to have had the opportunity to get to know Bill when I was young. Looking back, Mr. Kibby, Don Miller, and Bill Garden combined to give me the skills, opportunities, and self-confidence I needed to pursue my dream.

When I graduated from Mercer Island High School in 1964 with a 1.69 GPA, the acknowledged universities for naval architecture were beyond my finances and my academic record. Seattle University was the only local college that would accept me—although only on a probationary status—so I matriculated there as a mechanical engineering student and finally outlasted my academic probation after two years of respectable grades. Meanwhile, I continued to draw boats while playing bass guitar in a locally prominent rock band, The Springfield Rifle. The Vietnam War kept growing, but I stayed in the ROTC for two years; this prevented me from being drafted.

I quit college at the end of my fourth year, and soon the draft board called. When I reported, however, the board decided that my childhood history of petit mal seizures made me unacceptable for military service. I had not had a seizure since I was eight years old, but I was not one to quibble with the military over details. I was elated. Vietnam was not part of my plan. Today I carry pangs of guilt, but back then all I knew was that I did not have to go to Vietnam, and that was good.

Should I have stayed in college and finished my degree? Of course. Every father knows that. The problem was that after four years I had more credits toward a degree in English literature than I had for engineering. I wasn't keen on cold calculations, I was keen on Shakespeare, Milton, and Spencer.

Seven years later, though, I would be hired by Evergreen State College at a full professor's salary to teach college kids the basics of yacht design in a course called Marine History and Crafts. In that course we designed and built a 38-foot wooden sailing research vessel. Today students come to my office from the most prestigious engineering and yacht design schools in the world, including Southampton University and The Webb Institute, to earn credits in work-study programs. I enjoy this immensely. It's rejuvenating to work with students. They put in their three months and go back to school to get their degrees. Me? No degree.

At the age of 21, I read a help-wanted ad in the paper for a draftsman with a company called Marine Weight Control. I was broke, playing in the band at night, and my days were free. The company did what is known as "interference control" for large ships, mostly navy vessels. They got paid to tell the shipbuilders how to route pipes and ducts through bulkheads without weakening the structures and without creating a rat's nest of tangled ductwork and piping.

I drove to their offices and was sent to a room where I sat for 20 minutes while employees walked by to gawk and chuckle at the "longhair" who wanted a job. Finally an executive handed me an application and told me to take it home, fill it out, and mail it in. Right. I knew a brush-off when I saw one. I went home, had my girlfriend cut off most of my hair, bought a white shirt and a tie, and returned the same day with the completed application. I was hired immediately.

For the first time, I was getting paid to draw boats. Well, not boats exactly, but parts of ships—holes in parts of ships to be precise. If it wasn't yacht design, at least it was a kissing cousin. Along with another new hire, I was assigned to take out the garbage on Thursdays. We were partners in crime. Once we found out we could drop trash bags into the Dumpster from our third-floor window, Thursdays became the highlight of the week. My buddy started a chain made of pop-tops and told me that when it got long enough to reach the ground from our window, he was quitting.

This job lasted a little more than a year while I continued to play in the band at night. But things went south for Marine Weight Control when the company tried to integrate computers into the world of plotting holes in bulkheads. It was the early days of punched-card computers, and we found ourselves turning up more "unreal" interferences than real ones. As work slowed, I was the first to be laid off. I told them, "I am outdrawing my 50-year-old work partner three drawings to his one." My bosses said they were aware of that, but as I had the band to fall back on and no mouths to feed except my own, the impact on my life would be minimal. Six months later they called me back and asked me to prepare a sample of their work so they could present it with a bid for a big job. I was their best draftsman. I said OK, but I wanted my own work space and a radio. They put me at a drawing board in the hall, told me that was my office, and gave me a radio. A month later I completed the sample study and left once again, this time for good.

The band wasn't doing very well either. After years of playing packed weekend teenage dances, our gigs were generally playing bars and taverns six nights a week for the same money we'd once made playing two nights a week. I hated it.

Bored and broke, one morning in 1969, I took stock of my talents. I'd haunted the local temp agency, I'd tried selling my blood—if nothing else, I was refining my notions of the sorts of careers I *didn't* want. I picked up the phone and called Jay Benford, the only yacht designer in Seattle at the time. It was a call that would begin to change my life.

## Chapter Two
# THE APPRENTICE

Jay Benford told me to come on over. Armed with a pile of drawings, I went to his houseboat office. He looked at the drawings and asked if I could start after lunch. "Of course," I said, my heart leaping, then I asked what he was going to pay me. "I'll pay you 10 percent of every design job we finish," he said. In a year's time we "finished" one job and Jay paid me $100. Still, working with him kept me off the street and introduced me to the business of yacht design, and I earned enough playing with the band to eat. You have to start somewhere, and Jay gave me a start. I left his office after a year.

I drew two boats on my own, a 50-foot ketch for a man from Arizona and a 38-foot ketch for a Seattle owner. Both boats are still around. The 38-footer still looks pretty good. The 50-footer still floats—I just wish it would float away from Seattle. What I learned designing those two boats was that I had a lot to learn, so in 1970, when I saw a help-wanted ad for a marine draftsman with yacht experience, I called immediately. It was Jay Benford, but I was getting desperate and, apparently, so was he. He reluctantly offered me the job, and I reluctantly accepted—this time at a guaranteed hourly rate, which I think was $4.50 an hour with time-and-a-half for overtime.

I began working five days a week in Jay's office, designing the ferro-cement boats he was promoting at the time. It was steady work, if not lucrative, and I loved the job. I didn't like the types of boats we were designing, and I didn't like being confined to ferro-cement while the boats that excited me were being built with fiberglass, but I was getting paid to draw yachts, and that was a dream come true.

The ferro-cement craze was cresting, fueled by *Whole Earth Catalog* readers with visions of "seasteading" in the South Seas on a homebuilt boat. A cement hull was cheap to build alright, but finishing it was not, and the hulls that most of these dreamers were building were destined to have no resale value. In 1970 and 1971, however, ferro-cement looked like a growing niche, and Jay's ambition was to create a ferro-cement designing and building empire. He moved his offices from his houseboat on Lake Union to more expansive digs in a building in Ballard, close to the Ballard Bridge, and then to a still bigger space on the shores of Lake Union, next door to boatbuilder Vic Frank.

One day I looked out the office window to see an old, battered Volvo wagon, loaded down with belongings, pull into the parking lot. It was Nathan Rothman, "New York" Nathan, lured from the Big Apple by Jay to be the business manager of the new empire. Nathan had some experience building cement boats and thought Seattle was where the trend would really take off. In no time he was working for Jay as a manager. I happily stayed in the design office. Nathan and I were the same age and shared similar interests. We soon became fast friends.

Not long after I began working for Jay, I had my first design published—a 47-foot ketch that received a full-page review in *National Fisherman*. When Jay saw the review he issued a directive that any inquiries I received from it should be forwarded to him. I didn't have the luxury at the time of disagreeing with him. Soon I received a letter from a gentleman in California asking whether I would be interested in designing a 47-foot ketch to his specifications. With great reluctance I gave the letter to Jay, who put it on a stack of other letters, most of which were from would-be amateur boatbuilders—who, it turned out, were the most demanding clients.

Two weeks later my letter was still sitting on Jay's pile, unanswered. It beckoned to me like an open door, calling me to walk through. Finally I went into Jay's office when he wasn't there and retrieved the letter. It was addressed to me and it required a response, and if Jay wasn't going to answer it, I would.

The prospective client was a high-school shop teacher from Long Beach, and he had the idea that he could take a set of plans to Taiwan and get a boat built cheaply. "Where?" I asked him. "Taiwan," he repeated. His name was John Edwards, and he flew to Seattle to meet with me. We began sketching a 47-footer in the corner of my dining room, where I had my drawing board set up. I already knew that my job with Jay wouldn't last forever. Sooner or later Jay would get a bellyful of me, if I didn't get a bellyful of the job first.

By 1972 the ferro-cement boat movement was winding down, and Jay's attempts at establishing his own ferro-cement boatbuilding yard were proving unsuccessful. Jay moved his offices again, this time into the basement of the building on Lake Union, where the rent was cheaper and the writing was on the walls. "Here's your paycheck," he'd say, "but don't deposit it until I tell you it's OK." That doesn't work when you're living hand-to-mouth. I began looking for and getting other design work outside the office. When Jay found out I was doing drawings for his neighbor, boatbuilder Vic Frank, he was justifiably angry. I was called on the mat to answer for my moonlighting. Nathan sat across the table with Jay and Jay's wife, Robin. I was the bad guy undermining the work of the office, but for me it was simple self-preservation, and I knew that Nathan knew that. It was time for a change.

In the *Yachting* magazine classifieds, I saw that Dick Carter was looking for a draftsman for his Nahant, Massachusetts, office. Dick was renowned for his cutting-edge racing boats, and I applied for the job. When Dick said he was nervous about hiring

*Here I am at 28 years old.*

someone from clear across the country, I volunteered to fly out and work for him for two weeks gratis if he would cover my expenses. He said OK, and when my two-week vacation from Benford's firm arrived, off I went to audition for Dick Carter.

I got off the plane at Logan Airport with no money and grabbed a map from the Hertz counter, intending to walk to my hotel in Swampscott. It was night, and I didn't know that Captain Jack's Inn was at least nine miles away. I headed north, keeping the Atlantic Ocean on my right. Two hours later I stumbled into a bar in Lynn to ask directions, and a few patrons gave me a lift the rest of the way.

The audition must have gone well enough, because at the end of the two-week tryout Dick offered me the job.

This was an exciting time. The 47-footer I'd started sketching with John Edwards had morphed into the Hans Christian 54, and it was going to be one of the very first Taiwan-built boats with a specific designer's name on it—Robert H. Perry. Back in Seattle, I was paid $350 for my work thus far, and Edwards promised another $350 when I completed the design plus a $350-per-boat royalty. I enlisted Ted Brewer to assist me with the structural details. In Taiwan, work on the prototype began, while in Seattle I raced to finish the detail drawings. One day I opened a letter from Taiwan and saw the first photos of the boat. I was ecstatic to see a design of mine getting built and looking really good.

Jay had long since forgotten about the inquiry letter I'd given him, but when John Edwards first advertised the Hans Christian 54 in *National Fisherman* magazine, Jay called me into his office. "Is this yours?" he asked. "Yes," I confessed. I explained that I had felt it necessary to answer the letter if he would not, and not to bother firing me as I had already accepted a position with Dick Carter and would be leaving in 30 days.

I packed up and moved to the Boston area, North Beverly to be exact, from where I could commute the 15 miles to the office on my bicycle, weather permitting. I started working for Dick on April 1, 1973. I will forever be indebted to Jay for the start he gave me in this business, but I earned it.

Carter's office was a dream come true. We worked in a 13-foot-square, concrete, five-story World War II submarine watchtower on the shore of Nahant. My workmates were Yves-Marie Tanton, Mark Lindsay, and Chuck Paine. I suppose we were a motley crew, but we were effective and efficient and fired up with the fun and thrills of designing racing yachts to the International Offshore Rule (IOR) for some of the world's most prestigious clients. I was low man on the totem pole, working directly under Yves-Marie. Dick did not draw. He spent his time flying to Europe to massage new projects out of his clientele. He'd return from a trip, give us a 30-minute-or-less description of the boat we were to design, then disappear until the drawings were finished. Then he'd scoop up the finished drawings without much more than glancing at them and fly out again to meet the clients. One day Dick walked into the office and said, "I can just feel the horsepower in here." If he only knew.

I'd taken Doug Peterson's position. After working for Dick for about a month while living out of the back of a Volkswagen van, Doug had simply left one Friday and never showed up again. The next Dick heard of Doug was when Peterson's one-tonner *Ganbare* won the One-Ton North Americans in San Diego.

Before long, Dick's boats were getting beaten regularly by the designs Doug was drawing in his San Diego office, and our clientele started drifting away. When 1974 rolled around, I was working on two designs of my own—the Valiant 40 (Chapter 3), in addition to the remaining work on the Hans Christian 54, which by then had been rechristened the CT 54 (Chapter 5)—and I had a third one, the Islander 28 (Chapter 4), starting up. I was also doing drafting work for Ted Brewer at night to make ends meet. It occurred to me that if I was ever going to make it on my own, now was the time to try. I dis-

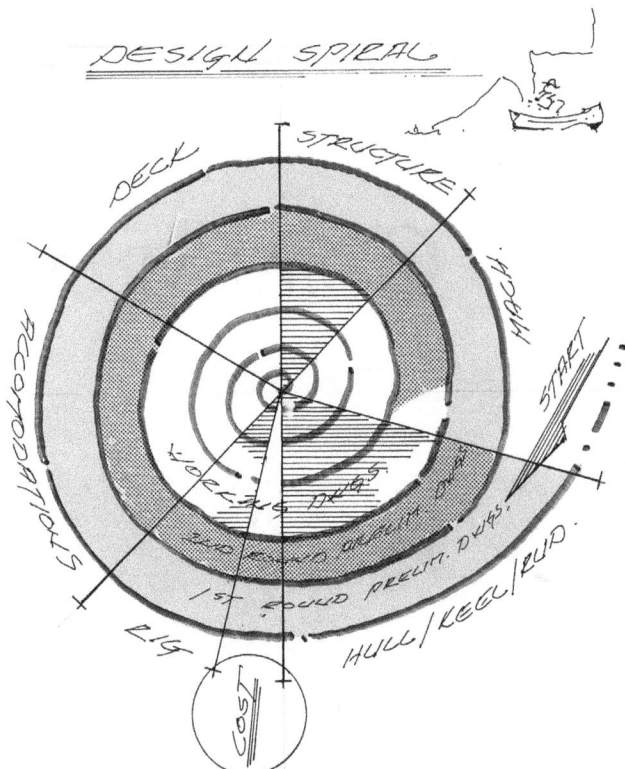

*I learned about the classic design spiral with my first boats. As designer and client spiral in toward the target—the finished design—each round begins with the hull and appendages, followed by a gut check on cost, and then by the rig, accommodations, deck, structural issues, and machinery. First-round preliminary drawings are followed by second-round prelims and then, in later spins around the target, by working drawings of increasing refinement.*

cussed my options with Mark, Yves-Marie, and Chuck. They laughed and said that if I tried to quit, Dick would just raise my pay until I couldn't afford to leave. Dick paid well, relatively speaking. Heck, I was making $157 a week take-home.

Chuck, Mark, and Yves-Marie got a pool going for how much Dick would offer me to stay. I asked Dick for a meeting. He led me into his house, 15 feet from the tower, and asked what was on my mind. I told him I was thinking of quitting, moving back to Seattle, and starting my own office. He pondered what I had said for 30 seconds, then said, "Well, good luck." That was that. I was gone.

I loaded a rental truck with my belongings, drove back to Seattle, rented an office, and got to work finishing the Valiant 40, the CT 54, and the Islander 28. I was poor but busy, full of myself and happy.

## *According to Perry*
# COMPARING SAILBOATS

The terms and ratios that help to characterize a design constitute a language of their own—the most efficient and descriptive one there is for conveying the particulars of a boat. The language is nearly universal throughout the yacht design world, but different designers use terms differently. I believe my method reflects mainstream usage. If you become a collector of design data, the important thing is to use the same definitions consistently so that you compare "apples to apples" over the years.

The ratios listed here provide a quick and fairly easy way to compare dissimilar boats over a range of sizes. The validity of the comparisons may not hold when one of the boats being compared is shorter than 25 feet or longer than 75 feet, but within that range, valid comparisons can be made. The ratios are nondimensional, which simply means that they have no units. The technical term for such comparisons is parametric analysis, but that makes it sound more complicated than it is.

## Length-to-Beam Ratio (L/B)

This ratio is useful for determining whether a boat is beamy or narrow. You simply divide the boat's length overall (LOA; see below) by its maximum width. A narrow boat will have a L/B of 4.00 or more. A moderate-beam boat will have a L/B of around 3.30 to 3.65. A beamy boat will have a L/B of 3.00 or less. A 40-foot boat with a 10-foot beam is narrow, but couple that 10-foot beam to a 30-foot LOA and you've got yourself a fairly beamy boat.

## Displacement-to-Length Ratio (D/L)

The D/L can ascertain how heavy a boat is relative to its waterline length. Divide the displacement of the boat in long tons (one long ton being 2,240 pounds) by the cube of 1 percent of the waterline length (in feet). Suppose, for example, that a boat has a waterline length of 32 feet and weighs 15,680 pounds, which is (conveniently!) 7 long tons. Then $32 \times 0.01 = 0.32$, and $0.32^3 = 0.032768$, and $7 \div 0.032768 = 214$.

Heavy boats will have a D/L greater than 300 and sometimes higher than 400. Most full-keel boats, by virtue of the volume in their keels, have D/Ls over 325. A moderate-displacement boat will have a D/L of around 220 to 280. I consider a D/L of 260 the "middle" of the overall displacement range. Light boats will have D/Ls from 200 down to 100. Boats with D/Ls less than 100 should be considered ultralight-displacement boats, or ULDBs.

## Sail Area–to-Displacement Ratio (SA/D)

The sail area–to-displacement ratio is a sailboat's version of horsepower to weight. The ratio is calculated as sail area in square feet or square meters divided by

*Profiles and plan views of three boats, showing length overall (LOA), which I consider equivalent to length on deck (LOD); designed waterline (DWL, also known as length waterline, or LWL); and maximum beam (B max). Top to bottom: A) A 48-foot keel-centerboard yawl showing the long overhangs encouraged in the 1960s by the Cruising Club of America (CCA) rating rule (L/B = 3.68; D/L = 275); B) A modern 66-foot cruising sled (Icon, see Chapter 16) with reverse transom, high-aspect keel, and beam carried aft (L/B = 4.45; D/L = 68); C) A 45-footer with canoe stern and low-aspect keel (L/B = 3.18; D/L = 230). Note: LOA includes a reverse transom but does not include a bowsprit, overhanging bow pulpit, or any other non-integral overhanging gear; and DWL in my lexicon does not include a surface-piercing rudder blade.*

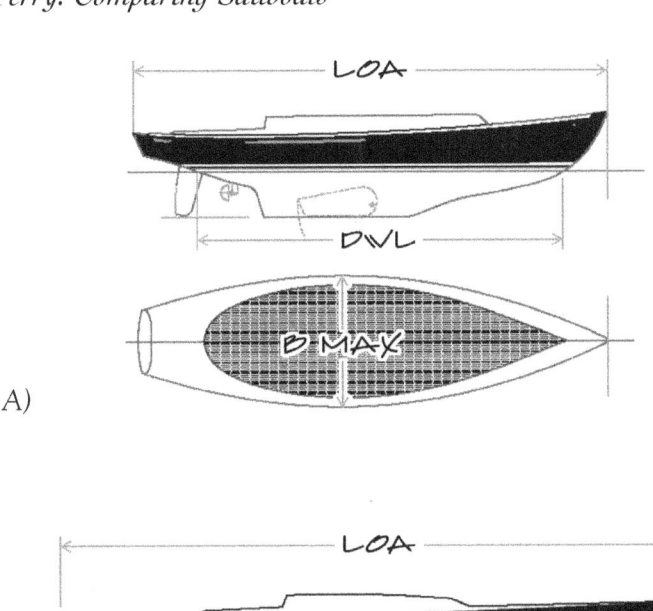

A)

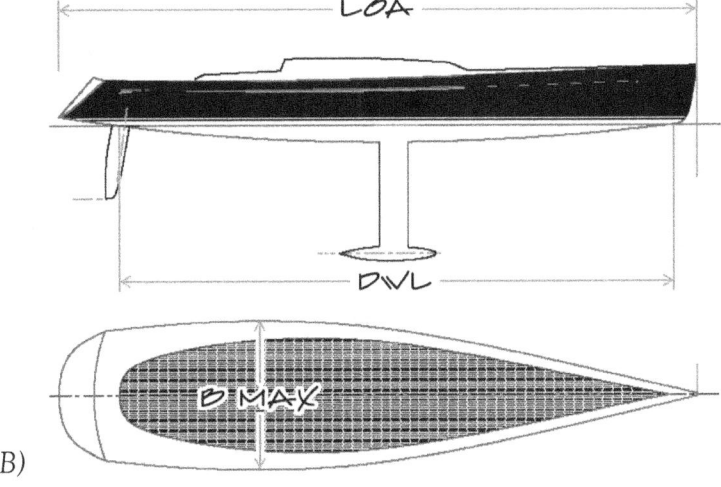

B)

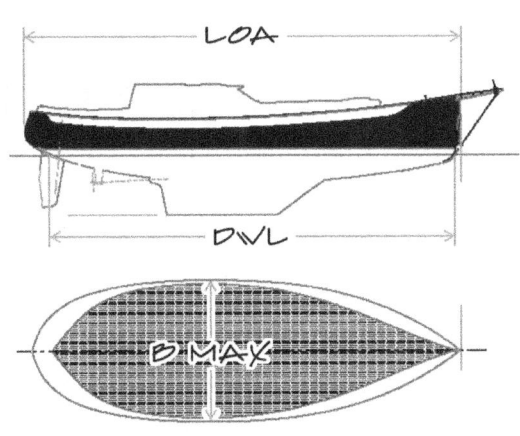

C)

the displacement in cubic feet (pounds divided by 64) or cubic meters to the two-thirds power. The boat from the previous example has a displacement in cubic feet of 15,680 ÷ 64 = 245, and 245 raised to the two-thirds power is approximately 39.1. If the boat has 704 square feet of sail area, its SA/D is 18.0.

It's important early in the design scheme to define just how powerful the rig will be. SA/D numbers range from a low of around 11.00 for motorsailers to 40.00 for an extreme racing type. Clearly, one set of numbers needs to be used for racing designs and another for cruising designs.

# Yacht Design According to Perry

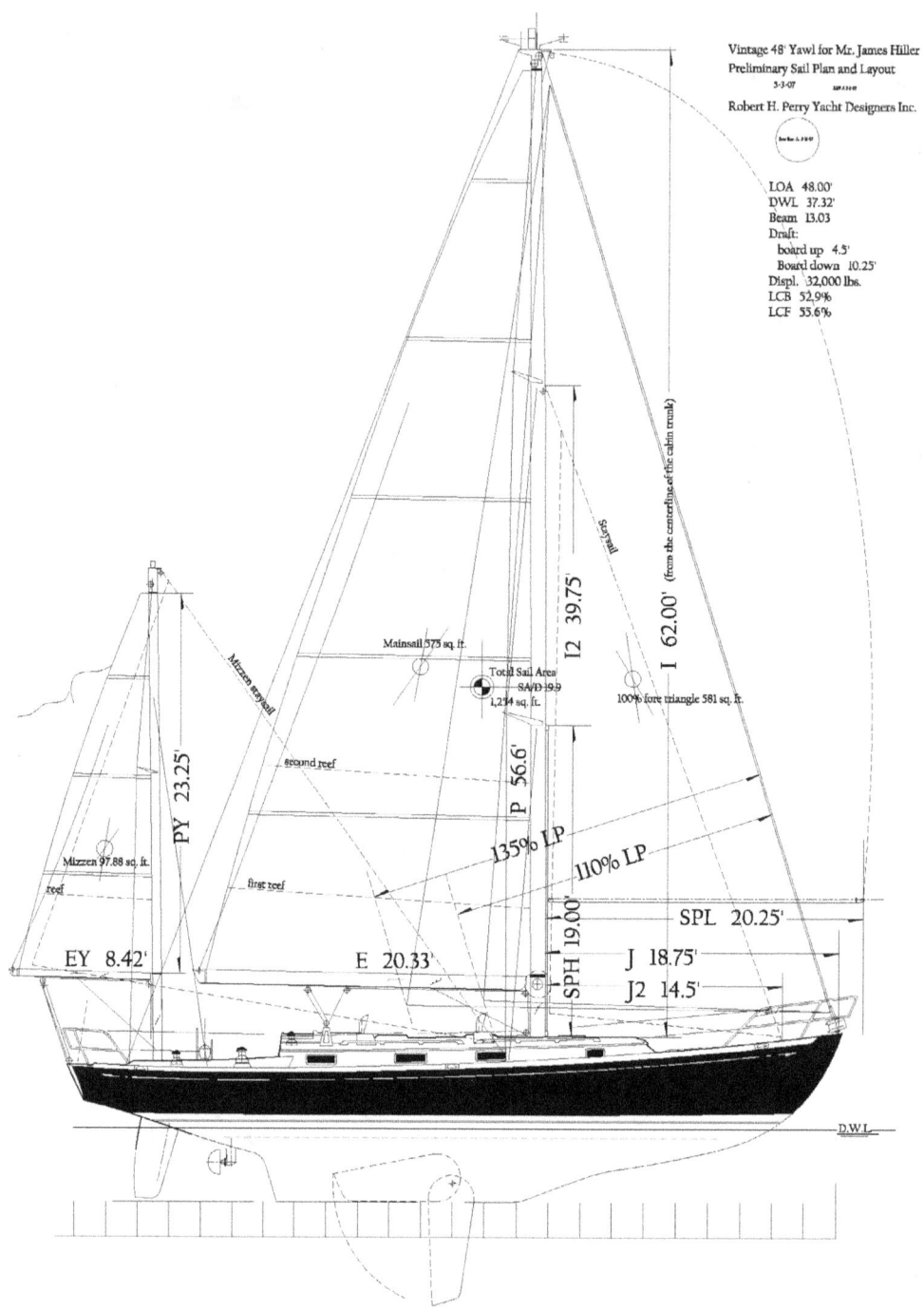

This sail plan for the classic yawl shown in the previous illustration gives the principal rig dimensions (see page 11) and lists design data from which to calculate comparative ratios. The LOA is 48 feet and the maximum beam is 13.03 feet, so the L/B is a moderate 3.68. The displacement is 32,000 pounds or 14.28 long tons, and the waterline length is 37.32 feet, so the D/L is 275—which, again, is moderate. The total sail area (main + mizzen + 100 percent foretriangle) is 1,254 feet; note that headsail overlap is not counted, and neither are such light-weather sails as a spinnaker or mizzen staysail. This makes the SA/D 19.9, which is a bit higher than you might expect for a traditionally inspired cruising sailboat, but the split rig makes a higher total area desirable as well as feasible. The mizzen doesn't generate a lot of drive, and when it's lowered the operative SA/D drops to 18.3. Finally, note that the LCB (see page 15) is 52.9 percent of the DWL aft of the cutwater, while the LCF (see page 15) is just aft of that at 55.6 percent.

To calculate the SA/D, you need the sail area of the boat as derived from its I, J, E, and P rig dimensions (see "According to Perry: Rig Dimensions and Types," page 158). I do not include genoa overlap area or the additional area that a staysail might provide. Sometimes marketing hype will include anything and everything that can be called "sail area" in order to inflate this number, but I do not support this practice. I also do not include in the mainsail any area added by roach, which is modest in most modern cruising boats. You can make a strong case that the exaggerated roach of a multihull or high-performance monohull should be added to the (E ÷ 2) × P area, although this is a judgment call. If I think that the roach area is a significant part of the mainsail area, I will add it, but I always note that in the review.

To get an accurate SA/D you also need an accurate displacement. This can be problematic, as displacements are frequently low-balled in order to make the SA/D and D/L ratios look more attractive. Whenever possible, the displacement you use should reflect the true weight of the boat in cruising trim.

A typical cruising boat today will have a SA/D of 17.5 to 18.5. This is enough power to drive the boat reasonably well in light air while not overpowering it too quickly when the breeze picks up. Of course, a boat with a powerful hull form and good stability characteristics can carry more sail, but hull shape aside, a SA/D of 18.00 will do nicely for most cruising sloops and cutters. A sailor looking for a benign and forgiving rig will want to stay closer to 17.5 or lower, while a sailor who might like to race his or her boat once in a while should look for a SA/D around 18.5 or more. Smaller cruising boats can get by with lower SA/Ds, while larger boats with more stability can use a higher SA/D.

High-performance racing boats and even boats that will see an active PHRF (see page 62) racing life should have a SA/D of at least 21.00. A boat with a lower SA/D will get a lower (slower) PHRF rating, but a slow boat isn't much fun to race no matter what its rating is. At the extreme end of today's high-performance boats, classes such as the Open 40 have SA/Ds around 40.00, but 25.00 to 30.00 is a more typical high-performance SA/D.

Several months after buying my current 26-foot boat, I calculated its SA/D and came up with 15.6. That number seemed too low to satisfy my need for speed, yet the boat sails well, so I did the calculation again, certain I had made a mistake. I had not. After years of pushing for SA/Ds in cruising boats of 17.5 or better, I ended up with a boat having a surprisingly low SA/D. While my boat was designed for the Baltic and is no light-air rocket, it is not a light-air pig either. This is just another indication that we should use these ratios as guides and starting points, not as absolutes.

## Ballast-to-Displacement Ratio (B/D)

To get this ratio, divide the weight of ballast by the overall displacement, using the same units in both numerator and denominator. The calculation is simple if you have accurate numbers for both components, but using the ratio to assess a boat's potential performance is not so simple. It might be best when considering the B/D ratio to treat race boats and cruising boats separately.

Let us use as an initial example of two racing boats with an LOA of 40 feet. One displaces, or weighs (the two words mean the same thing), 12,500 pounds, and the other displaces 9,500 pounds. If they both have B/Ds of 40 percent, the heavier boat will have 5,000 pounds of ballast, leaving 7,500 pounds for all other components of the boat's structure, machinery, gear, and rig. If these other components weigh more than 7,500 pounds, the boat will float below its designed waterline.

Our lighter boat, displacing 9,500 pounds, has 3,800 pounds of ballast, leaving just 5,700 pounds for essentially the same components of structure, machinery, gear, and rig. This tells us that the lighter boat must have a lighter structure, in this case 2,000 pounds lighter, which might be achieved with a carbon-fiber hull and deck. The weight difference would typically be reflected through the other components as well, but the structure absorbs the greater part.

Does the B/D tell us anything about race-boat stability? It would if all the comparative components of the two boats were equal, but they will not be. Obviously a high B/D with the ballast low would indicate a stiffer boat than one with a low B/D and its ballast high, but there is not enough information in a simple B/D to make reliable judgments about a boat's stability. We need to know where that ballast is before we can make a stability judgment. If both boats draw 8.5 feet and carry their ballast in a bulb at the keel tip, the boat with the higher B/D should be stiffer provided both hull forms are reasonably normal.

When reviewing a racing boat design, I prefer to use B/D as an indication of relative structural weight rather than stability.

Cruising boats are different. Let's compare, for example, a long, light cruising boat—say 59 feet LOA, displacing 30,000 pounds—with a heavy 50-footer weighing 50,000 pounds. Both boats are set up for long-distance cruising, and both carry full complements of cruising gear and accessories. To simplify this, let's assume that the cruising gear and accessories are the same—and therefore weigh the same—for both boats. Both have gen sets, A/C, refrigeration, copious batteries, an inverter, big tanks, extra anchors, a dodger, solar panels, a wind generator, a dinghy or two, an all-chain anchor rode, and so on.

Our light 59-footer loaded down with all this cruising gear can carry 10,000 pounds of ballast and still hit its designed displacement target of 30,000 pounds—and therefore float on its designed waterline. That gives it a B/D of 33 percent. The heavy 50-footer carrying the same cruising gear is able to carry 20,000 pounds of ballast, for a B/D of 40 percent. Though 9 feet shorter than the lighter boat, its bigger hull displaces 20,000 pounds more water when it floats on its designed waterline, and 10,000 pounds of that is allocated to additional ballast. The other 10,000 pounds goes to heavier construction, bigger tanks, and most probably heavier machinery.

Generally speaking, if the weight of all the cruising gear is more or less the same, some portion of the additional displacement of a heavier boat can be assigned to ballast for a higher B/D ratio. You simply cannot design a fully found, long, light cruising boat with a high B/D. This is why you see more radical fin and bulb keels on light cruising boats. The stability has to come from getting a relatively small amount of ballast as low as possible, whereas a heavy boat has the luxury of a high B/D and can carry that large amount of ballast in a relatively shoal keel and still hit its stability parameters.

All else being equal—displacement, rig size, keel configuration, draft, accommodations, and gear—the boat with the higher B/D would be the stiffer boat. But I have never seen an example like that.

A B/D less than 30 percent is low, whereas one higher than 40 percent is high. Typical grand prix racing yachts can have B/Ds approaching 50 percent, but a modern, medium-displacement cruising boat will have a B/D from 40 percent down to 35 percent. Generally speaking, the lower the D/L of a cruising boat, the lower its B/D.

## Prismatic Coefficient (Cp)

You seldom see the prismatic coefficient (Cp) published. It's a little difficult to comprehend. This ratio measures the distribution of volume in a boat from its most voluminous immersed section toward the bow and the stern. In short, the prismatic coefficient tells us if the boat has full ends or fine ends.

Picture a boat in which the most voluminous immersed section (usually, though not always, the midship section) is carried without shrinking right to the forward and after ends of the designed waterline (DWL). In other words, this improbable-looking boat has no taper either forward or aft. Its ends are not pointed—they are not even pinched. This boat—*this barge*—would have a prismatic coefficient of 1.00.

In the real world, all boats have a prismatic coefficient less than 1. To get this ratio for a given design, you multiply the area in the greatest immersed section (in square feet or square meters) by the DWL (in feet or meters) and divide the product into the boat's displacement (in cubic feet or cubic meters; since a cubic foot of seawater weighs 64 pounds, a displacement of 25,000 pounds would be 390 cubic feet). You can use imperial or metric units provided you use the same units consistently in the numerator and denominator.

You will get a number for most sailing boats between 0.50 and 0.56. The textbook "medium" Cp is 0.54. The lower the Cp, the finer the ends of the boat. The higher the Cp, the fuller the boat's ends will be. A low prismatic will give you an easily driven hull, and a high prismatic will give you a hull that is harder to push through the water. The catch is that a low-Cp boat will have a lower hull speed (i.e., a lower speed-to-length ratio) than a high-Cp boat. If you wanted a boat that was fast in light air, you would want an easily driven hull with a low Cp. If you sailed in an area where the winds were consistently strong, you would want a boat with a higher

Cp. I generally target a Cp for my cruising boats in the 0.54 to 0.55 range.

## Vertical Center of Gravity (VCG)

The vertical center of gravity is the most important number there is for determining the stability of a boat. Combined with the hull shape and its contribution to form stability, the VCG will determine the length of the boat's righting arm—i.e., the distance between the VCG and the transverse center of buoyancy. The length of the righting arm at a given heel angle times the displacement of the boat will give you the righting moment at that heel angle.

In technical terms, the VCG is the centroid of the sum total of all the weights in the boat on a vertical axis. In a typical cruising boat with modest draft, the VCG will be just above the DWL, say four to six inches. In a modern light-displacement racing boat with a deep fin and bulb keel, the VCG can be as much as 12 inches below the DWL, or even lower in some cases. The lower the VCG, the greater the righting arm and the stiffer the boat. This reinforces the importance of draft.

## Longitudinal Center of Buoyancy (LCB)

The longitudinal center of buoyancy (LCB) is a function of hull shape and the distribution of underwater volume. The typical location for a modern boat's LCB is at about station 5.4—that is, about 54 percent of the DWL aft of the cutwater (see "According to Perry: The Hull-Lines Plan," page 37). I will accept up to 57 percent, but anything more than that makes me suspicious of the shape I am developing. The LCB must be vertically aligned with the boat's longitudinal center of gravity (LCG). If the LCB is aft of the LCG, the boat will trim bow-down. If the LCB is forward of the LCG, the boat will trim stern-down.

## Longitudinal Center of Flotation (LCF)

The longitudinal center of flotation (LCF) is the center of a boat's flotation plane, otherwise known as its waterplane, which is simply the boat's footprint on the water surface. Imagine taking a horizontal slice through a hull right at the water's surface. That's the waterplane. LCF has nothing to do with immersed volume, and it is always aft of the LCB. I will generally place the LCF at about station 5.6 to 5.75 (that is, 56 to 57.5 percent of the waterline length aft of the cutwater). The boat will trim around the LCF, not the LCB.

If you multiply the waterplane area by 64 and divide that product by 12, you will get the "pounds-per-inch immersion." This number will tell you how many pounds of additional weight would be required to sink your boat 1 inch—or, conversely, how much the boat will sink in the water for every pound of weight that is added. Of course, as the boat sinks, the waterplane will increase and the pounds per inch will also increase.

## Length Overall (LOA)

This seemingly simple term causes all kinds of trouble, as most boats carry some type of gear or extension beyond the bow and stern. On any given boat a bowsprit, a stern pulpit, davits, or the main boom might overhang the bow or stern. I do not include any such items in a boat's LOA. LOA should be confined to the extent of the hull itself, from the tip of the bow to the aftermost projection of the transom (or the stern, in the case of a double-ender).

If the boat has a wooden caprail that extends beyond the hull, I measure the LOA from the joint between the caprail and the hull. If the boat is made of fiberglass, I measure its LOA between the forward and after extents of the molded fiberglass hull.

While I think of a boat's length as the length of the hull itself, a marina operator may include the bowsprit. It's hard to ignore a seven-foot-long, six-inch-diameter bowsprit with its whisker stays and bobstay when your income is based on linear dock footage rented. The same applies to a dinghy suspended by davits six feet aft of the stern. When a boat has a bowsprit or other protrusion from either end, the more descriptive term for its length might be length on deck (LOD).

When I measure LOD, I measure it as described above for LOA. Here, too, there can be complications. If the boat has a reverse transom, I do not measure the deck length per se; depending on the transom angle, the LOD I measure may be several

# Comparative Dimensions for Representative Sailboats

| BOAT NAME | LOA | DWL | BEAM | DRAFT | DISPL. (LBS.) | D/L | SA/D | L/B |
|---|---|---|---|---|---|---|---|---|
| WESTSAIL 32 | 32' | 27'6" | 11' | 5' | 20,000 | 435 | 13.89 | 2.9 |
| FRIENDSHIP 40 | 40'11" | 29'7" | 12'10" | 10'3"/3'11" | 22,500 | 388 | 17.24 | 3.18 |
| ISLAND PACKET 370 | 37'10" | 31' | 13'1" | 4'3 | 21,000 | 315 | 17.1 | 2.89 |
| CATALINA 387 | 39'10" | 32'5" | 12'4" | 7'2"/4'10" | 19,000 | 249 | 16.15 | 3.23 |
| ISLAND PACKET 420 | 44'7" | 37'4" | 14'3" | 4'4"/4'1" | 28,400 | 244 | 18.9 | 3.16 |
| MOODY 47 | 47'8" | 39'4" | 14'5" | 6'9"/5'3" | 32,890 | 241 | 14.25 | 3.22 |
| VALIANT 42 | 40' | 34'10" | 12'4" | 6'3" | 24,500 | 240 | 16.5 | 3.24 |
| HALLBERG-RASSY 40 | 40' | 34'9" | 12'6" | 6'3" | 22,000 | 234 | 16.44 | 3.23 |
| SABRE 426 | 42'6" | 36 | 13'5" | 6'10"/5' | 24,000 | 230 | 17.7 | 3.22 |
| ISLANDER 28 | 28' | 23' | 10' | 5'3" | 6,000 | 229 | 15.89 | 2.9 |
| SOUTHERLY 110 | 36' | 30'3" | 11'10" | 7'2"/2'4" | 13,750 | 221 | 16.05 | 3.04 |
| SABRE 386 | 38'7" | 32'6" | 12'8" | 6'10"/4'10" | 16,950 | 220 | 118.5 | 3.05 |
| TARTAN 3700 | 37' | 32'6" | 12'7" | 7'3"/4'5" | 16,150 | 210 | 18.2 | 2.92 |
| TARTAN 4400 | 45' | 44' | 14'1" | 5'6" | 24,000 | 203 | 18.13 | 3.19 |
| FARR 50 | 50' | 43'10" | 15'5" | 7'6" | 37,400 | 198 | 18.27 | 3.25 |
| HALLBERG-RASSY 37 | 37'2" | 33'6" | 11'8" | 6'3" | 16,500 | 196 | 18.07 | 3.19 |
| OUTBOUND 44 | 44'11" | 40'5" | 13'4" | 6'4" | 28,000 | 189 | 18.44 | 3.37 |
| SAGA 48 | 47'10" | 43'7" | 13'9" | 6' | 30,000 | 188 | 19.98 | 3.47 |
| OYSTER 62 | 63'3" | 55'1" | 17'8" | 8'6"/6'6" | 70,550 | 188 | 17.28 | 3.49 |
| BENETEAU FIRST 36.7 | 36'7" | 30'4" | 11'7" | 7'2"/5'11" | 11,552 | 185 | 20.6 | 3.1 |
| BAVARIA 36 | 37'5" | 30'10" | 11'10" | 6'5"/5'1" | 12,100 | 184 | 18.6 | 3.04 |
| HYLAS 66 | 66'5" | 58'1" | 18'0" | 9'2" | 76,060 | 173 | 18.21 | 3.69 |
| C&C 99 | 32'6" | 29'1" | 10'10" | 6'6"/5'3" | 9,265 | 168 | 20.38 | 3.01 |
| SWAN 75 | 75' | 64'0" | 19'0" | 9'2" | 83,800 | 165 | 22.1 | 3.9 |
| J/109 | 35'3" | 30'6" | 11'6" | 7' | 10,900 | 165 | 21 | 3.06 |
| J/46 | 46' | 40'6" | 13'10" | 6'2" | 24,400 | 164 | 19.4 | 3.33 |
| BENETEAU 323 | 32'10" | 29'2" | 10'8" | 5'11"/4'9" | 8,448 | 152 | 18.93 | 3.08 |

| BOAT NAME | LOA | DWL | BEAM | DRAFT | DISPL. | D/L | SA/D | L/B |
|---|---|---|---|---|---|---|---|---|
| Swan 601 | 60'1" | 52'11" | 14'10" | 11'10" | 39,700 | 120 | 28.79 | 3.7 |
| J/145 | 40'1" | 42'6" | 13' | 8'11"/7' | 19,000 | 110 | 29 | 3.7 |
| Farr 52 | 52' | 45'6" | 14'7" | 10'8" | 20,277 | 96 | 34.19 | 3.17 |
| Ultimate 24 | 24' | 21'2" | 8'6" | 5'6"/2'11" | 2,040 | 96 | 35.3 | 2.88 |
| Santa Cruz 63 | 63' | 54' | 16'5" | 9'1" | 32,640 | 93 | 27.6 | 3.8 |
| Columbia 30 | 30' | 26'6" | 9'6" | 7'/2' | 3,400 | 82 | 30.6 | 3.18 |
| Synergy 1000 | 32'10" | 29'2" | 9'9" | 7' | 4,400 | 79 | 33.96 | 3.36 |
| Open 40 | 40' | 40' | 14'4" | 11'10" | 7,260 | 51 | 56.2 | 2.78 |

When two drafts are given, the shoaler of the two is with centerboard up or a shoal-keel option.

feet more than the deck length. Here, as elsewhere, the key is consistency. However, a boat with a reverse transom probably would not have a bowsprit anyway, so, with reverse transoms, LOA is the more appropriate and descriptive number.

## Designed Waterline (DWL)

The designed waterline is sometimes called the length at waterline (LWL), or occasionally the load waterline. All these terms are synonymous. The DWL is measured on the boat's flotation plane, from the cutwater forward to the aftermost end of the waterplane.

Even here there is room for interpretation. What do you do if the top portion of your rudder breaks the waterplane aft? This feature is common on modern designs. Maybe you have a transom-hung rudder or an outboard rudder like that on a Westsail 32 or on my own boat, the Cirrus 5.8. I do not include a rudder in the DWL, but designers occasionally do so in order to make a DWL appear longer and the boat's hull speed (on paper at least) correspondingly higher.

There is no point in deceiving yourself that a rudder adds to the DWL. There is simply not enough volume in the rudder to make it an effective extension of sailing length. I can think of only one exception to this, and that would be a boat designed under the old meter-boat rule—America's Cup 12-meters, for example. These designs have short, stubby, thick rudders that are fully faired into the run of the boat. I could make a good argument, just for the sake of argument, why the chord of these rudders should be added to DWL. However, even the meter-boat rule does not count the rudder as an addition to the DWL.

If there is room for argument when measuring the DWL, it has to be in what flotation condition you measure the waterplane. A boat right out of the manufacturer's box will float light, and if the boat has an overhang in either or both ends, it will have a shorter DWL floating light than it would in a loaded or even a half-loaded condition. If the counter aft has a long overhang, changing the load condition can add feet to the DWL measurement. On the other hand, if the boat has a plumb or near plumb bow and a truncated stern overhang, the load condition will have little effect on DWL.

Most racing handicap rules specify how a boat must be loaded when determining its waterplane and DWL. Consider also that measuring a boat with overhangs in fresh water will yield a longer DWL than you will get when measuring it in denser salt water, because the boat will float deeper in the fresh water.

## Beam at the Waterline (BWL)

The BWL is measured roughly amidships, where the topsides cut the waterplane at its widest point. This dimension is not often listed in boat specs. Some designers use DWL and BWL to get L/B—and this is probably the more accurate method—but it's more common to use LOA and B max (maximum beam).

## Righting Moment (RM)

I could spend the entire book talking about stability, but I'm not going to. (I do return to the subject in "According to Perry: Stability," page 84.) Here I'll just say a word or two about righting moment, which is a measure of stability.

A *moment* is a quantity—generally a weight—multiplied by a distance. If the weight is measured in pounds and the distance in feet, the resulting moment will be given in foot-pounds. For the righting-moment calculation, the weight is the boat's displacement and the distance is its righting arm, which is the distance from the boat's vertical center of gravity (VCG) to its heeled center of buoyancy (CB). While the VCG stays static, on centerline, the heeled center of buoyancy will change with each shift in heel angle as the shape of the immersed hull changes. Righting moment is calculated at various heel angles by multiplying the displacement of the boat by the righting arm, and it describes how much the boat will resist further heeling.

At zero degrees of heel, the CB is vertically aligned with the VCG and there is zero foot-pounds of righting moment. Yet at just one degree of heel, a 24,000-pound boat may have a 0.05-foot righting arm and therefore develop a righting moment of 1,200 foot-pounds. If you increase the heel angle to 15 degrees, you immerse more hull to leeward, the center of buoyancy moves farther from the VCG, and the righting arm increases to, say, 1.00 foot, raising the righting moment to 24,000 foot-pounds.

Sparmakers often use the righting moment at 30 degrees to calculate the maximum load a rig will see. If you calculate RM for every heel angle, you will produce an entire stability curve showing where the righting moment turns negative and the boat begins to capsize. (See page 87 for an example.)

Ratios and coefficients are fine to study, and a good designer will look at them all. But each is only a small glimpse into a boat's personality and no one number will define the character of a design. Today, if the designer's eye is working and his or her computer is turned on, there's no excuse for out-of-the-ordinary hydrostatics. Computers give the designer the freedom and power to play almost endlessly with the variables until all of the numbers fall into their target ranges. With the exception of weight studies, calculations that 20 years ago took several days can now be done in a few minutes.

## Chapter Three
# VALIANT DAYS

Although the Valiant 40 design came after the CT 54, I consider the Valiant 40 the real start of my career as an independent yacht designer. The seeds for the design had been planted when I was working for Jay Benford.

By the time I sat across the table from Jay, his wife, and Nathan Rothman to receive a tongue-lashing for moonlighting, Nathan and I had been daydreaming out loud for a year about starting a company and becoming our own bosses. I'd be the designer and Nathan would be the builder and business manager. The chances of this actually happening seemed slim to none, as Nathan and I shared one pot to piss in and had minimal financial resources.

Nathan left Jay's business after I did, but he remained in Seattle. While I worked for Dick Carter, Nathan and I kept talking and dreaming about "our boat." This was when Nathan's true talents and skills emerged. He began talking to other people—people with money. A Seattle attorney, Jeff Brotman, one of the later founders of Costco, connected Nathan with some venture capitalists, and the idle chatter about building a Perry/Rothman boat began to get serious. I drew preliminary lines.

One day Nathan called me in Boston and asked me to start preparing the working drawings.

"Fine," I said.

"How much do you want for the design?" Nathan asked.

I said, "Twenty-five hundred dollars. But you don't have to pay me now. Wait until you get everything worked out—then you can pay me." Hell, I was making $157 a week. I didn't need money, and I was certain Nathan had none. I know now that he had enough backing by then to pay me, but in truth I was happy just to be asked to design a boat. The prospect of getting it built still seemed remote.

I soon began work on a 40-footer. It would be a double-ender. The Bill Crealock/Bill Atkin–designed Westsail 32 had taken off after a huge spread in *Time* magazine in early 1973, and it was clear that the sailing world, reality notwithstanding, thought that blue-water cruisers should be double-enders. That was no problem for me. I had grown up with the Atkin double-enders and those designed by Bill Garden—strong images for offshore cruising boats. I loved Albert Strange's canoe yawls, and K. Aage Nielsen had done some nice double-enders too. In fact, one Nielsen design, *Holger Danske*, had graced the cover of several magazines the previous year. *Holger Danske* was a marvelous-looking boat, exuding strength and blue-water capability.

My idea of a perfect canoe stern had been Bill Garden's *Bolero* design, but while *Bolero*'s stern reduced the bulk of the buttocks and volume aft, *Holger Danske*'s stern extended the buttock lines aft and added volume to the boat's fanny. The two shapes were at odds with each other, but my work with racing yachts told me that the *Holger Danske* direction was better for my purposes. There was every advantage in carrying the buttocks aft as flat and far as possible, delaying that sweep up into the canoe stern as long as possible. Flat buttocks were the key, and this would require a stern that, while based upon the Scandinavian-inspired stern of *Holger Danske*, would take the shape to a new extreme. The result was the Valiant's tumblehome canoe stern, in which the buttocks carried way aft before being tucked and rolled abruptly upward into the sheer. ("Tumblehome" is an old design term for a sectional shape that rolls back inboard as it rises.)

Did I "invent" that stern? No, it was there from the days of the Vikings. I just massaged it. I rolfed it. Aage Nielsen was angry with me, convinced I had stolen "his" stern, but yacht design is no different in that respect from any other creative pursuit. Like dramatists, scientists, and songwriters, designers take their inspiration wherever they can find it.

I was not a cruising sailor. I was a racer, a waterfront rat who'd grown up crewing on other people's boats. The closest I'd come to cruising was delivering a boat to a race or when I managed to scrounge a boat for a weekend or a week. Once, when I was working for Benford, a local boatowner named Dooley Pierce had advertised his Haida 26 for charter. I called him. "How long do you want the boat for?" he asked. "One day, Saturday," I said. It was all I could afford. There was silence on the other end of the line. "OK, Saturday it is," Dooley said. Later I called him back and asked if I could sleep on the boat Friday night in order to get an early start on Saturday. Again there was silence on the other end of the line. Finally he said, "Sure you can. Just have the boat back by Sunday night."

I'll never forget that. Plagued as I was with hay fever, a weekend on the water meant I would breathe freely for almost three days while enjoying a good little ship. A couple of years later I was elated when Dooley became part of the Valiant family.

The bottom line was that I knew racing boats far better than I knew cruising boats. I also knew that racing boats were nice boats to cruise. They were fast, and in the 1970s their interiors were designed to work well for a crew. I just did not see any vital conflict between the racing boats of the day and what a cruising boat could or should be. The typical cruising boat of that time was a pig. Speed and weatherliness were not part of the cruising design equation. I had cruised a 42-foot staysail schooner, the quintessential cruising boat, and while it was fun and salty as hell, the racy little Haida 26 was a lot faster and more rewarding to sail. Almost by definition, cruising boats of the day were slow.

After reading an article by Ted Brewer about sail area–to-displacement ratios (SA/Ds) and displacement-length ratios (D/Ls), I became manic about those two dimensionless parameters, which within limits were independent of a boat's size. With these two numbers you can tell a lot about a boat or compare dissimilar boats. I calculated D/Ls and SA/Ds for every boat I could find and compiled the results. I knew my 40-footer would not be heavy.

I chose for the midsection a sectional shape from a Carter design. His boats *Aggressive* and *Airmail* had been very similar, successful IOR two-tonners back in the day before the IOR sectional shapes got angularly radical. Both boats had nice, deep-deadrise midsections and a hint of tumblehome. This shape provided a natural bilge sump and lent itself to a fine entry.

For a bow, I went back to Garden's *Bolero* design. This is where I probably went wrong. I liked the profile of *Bolero*'s bow with its hint of concavity, but when I adapted it to the Valiant I gave the sectional shape of the bow a lot of flare, maybe too much. The Valiant bow was always dry, but I think if I had made the bow finer, the boat would have been faster—even if wetter—on the wind in a chop. Still, this flare and fullness in the bow make the Valiant a fast-reaching boat when it heels and begins to immerse those meaty, high-volume forward sections.

With a D/L of around 260, the Valiant would be a radically light cruising boat compared with the D/L of 400 for the Westsail types. About five years after the first Valiant was built, California designer Ray Richards, writing for *Yachting* magazine, said the Valiant was "too light to be considered a serious offshore boat." Given the successful voyaging and offshore racing histories of numerous Valiants over the years, Ray was wrong.

The key to reducing displacement was to get rid of the full keel and replace it with a fin keel and a skeg-hung rudder. This was what we were doing with the Carter racing boats I was designing at the time. I had sailed several of them, and I knew them to be docile on the helm and very manageable. I kept asking myself, "Why can't this boat be a cruising boat?" The answer was obvious. That underbody shape could and would make a far better cruising

*Valiant Days*

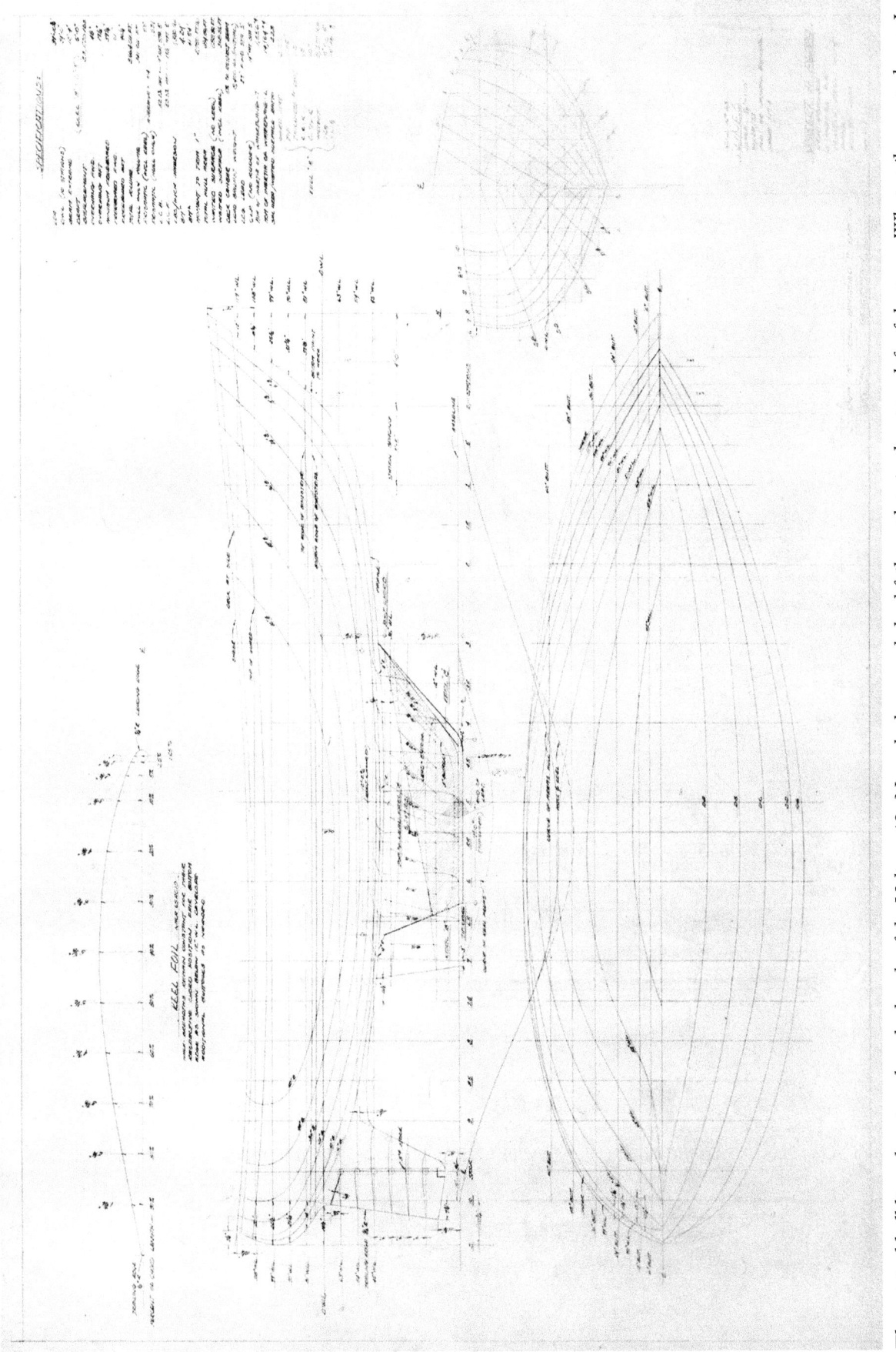

*The original hull lines drawing, done by hand, of the Valiant 40. Note the large-scale keel foil template in the upper left of the page. What strikes me today as I look at these lines is that though they were drawn at a time when overhangs were popular, the Valiant 40 has less than 6 feet of total overhang.*

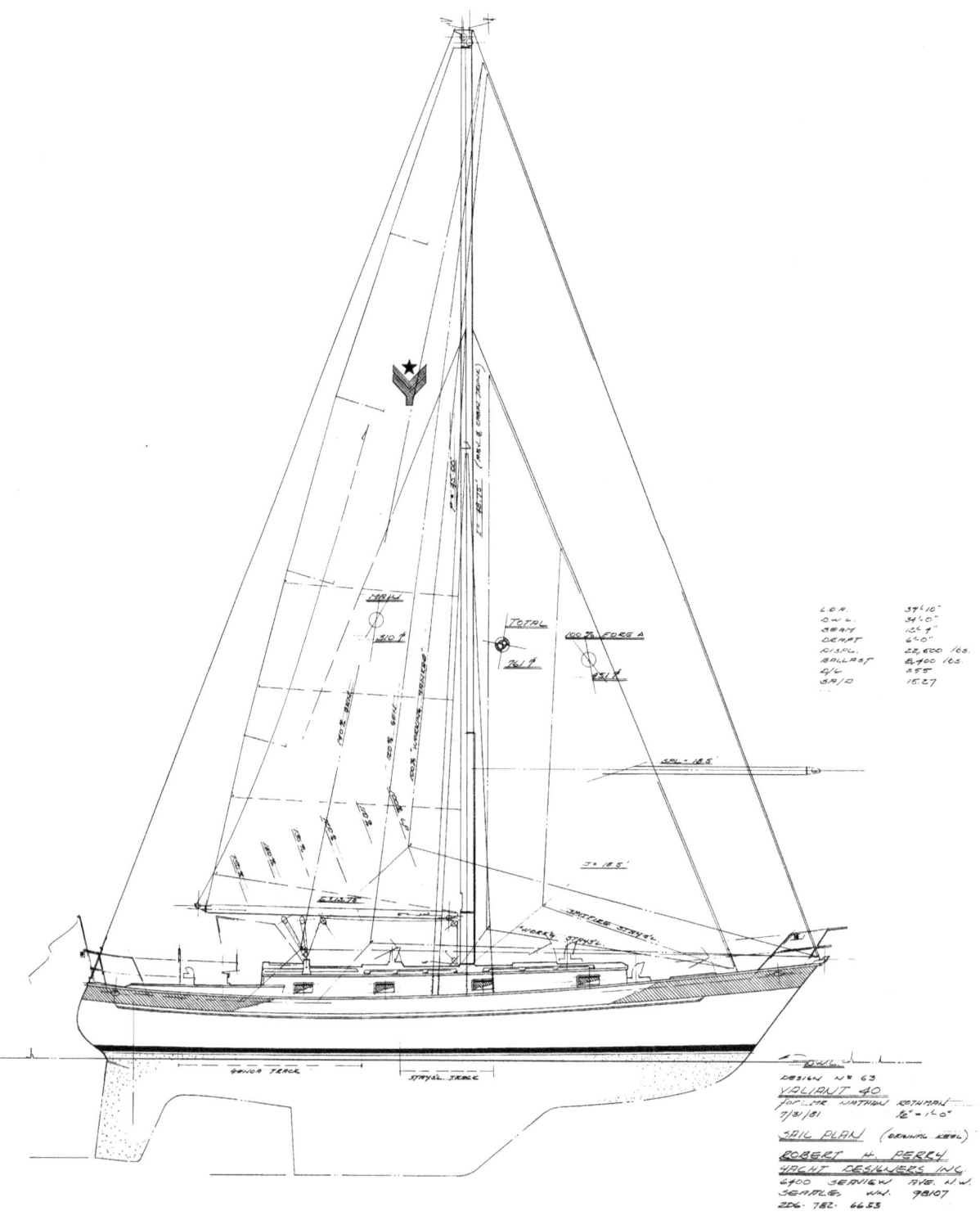

*This Valiant 40 sail plan shows the moving of the mainsheet system to the cabintop from its original position aft of the cockpit.*

boat than the currently accepted crop. I gave the Valiant's fin keel and rudder a little lower aspect ratio for structural and the ever-important marketing considerations. A split-appendage offshore cruising boat was going to be a tough sell to some sailors.

A diamond-shaped waterline was combined with the pointed stern to give the Valiant good balance as well as a relatively consistent waterline when heeled. You could drive a Valiant hard while maintaining consistent helm balance. In fact, the Valiant is one of those rare boats that reveled in being driven hard.

Was the Valiant 40 an innovative design? Some sailors think so, but I'm not among them. I knew exactly where every piece of the boat came from. I could trace each design element back to a boat from my past. I think I put the pieces together in a way that had not been done before, and the timing was right. The IOR's idiosyncrasies—including the contorted stern treatment that the handicapping rule encouraged—had offended a lot of racing sailors who had grown up racing the venerable and more moderate boats that had been designed according to the Cruising Club of America rule. The IOR was pushing sailors away from racing, but they were not ready for fat, heavy, full-keeled Westsail types. There was a hole in the market for a boat that would bridge the interests of racing and cruising sailors.

In addition to timing, we came up with an ideal marketing hook for the Valiant, dubbing it a "performance cruiser." I don't know where that term came from, but I do know we were the first to use it. I suspect I came up with it. The Valiant stood alone in its newly coined category. Accurate or not, the Valiant 40 is remembered as the first "performance cruiser."

The drawings for my fantasy 40-footer were progressing nicely when Nathan called me in Boston and said, "I have a builder."

"Who?" I asked.

"Uniflite."

"Well, you better send me some money then."

Uniflite was a highly successful Northwest powerboat builder, and I knew that if Uniflite was going to be involved, things had progressed to a point I had not imagined possible. Nathan had worked his magic and created something out of nothing. The original name we had chosen for the boat was Voyager, and our friend and graphic designer Dennis Burns designed a logo featuring a strong star and nestled VY to go with it. Soon after, however, we discovered that "Voyager" was already taken, so we searched for another name that started with V so we could keep the logo. The boat would be the Valiant.

It was October 1973. I had managed to finagle some vacation time from Dick Carter even though I'd only been there a few months, and Nathan had secured booth space at the Long Beach Boat Show in California. We had a builder and we had a price—$63,500 with pulpits and lifelines. It was time to unveil the Valiant 40 to the yachting world. Dennis Burns built a display for my drawings and the half model we had made. It was all very amateurish, but we didn't know any better at the time and we forged ahead. Nathan sent me a plane ticket and I packed what good clothes I had, hoping to look plausible. I had a lot riding on this. I was 28 years old, and already I'd been dreaming of this opportunity for 14 years.

Our booth was on the perimeter of the Long Beach convention center, right across from the restrooms, so we got plenty of traffic. We wore ties. We did our best to look like established yachting types. I did not own a blazer, but I faked one with a Pendleton shirt/jacket over a shirt and tie. Like carnival hucksters, we tried to lure people into our booth, where I would pounce on them with tales of displacement-to-length ratios, sail area–to-displacement ratios, and the fallacy of the full keel. Soon we were getting a lot of interest. We worked the show 12 hours a day, from 10 a.m. to 10 p.m., stopping only for toilet breaks. Mrs. Harvey Freeman from two booths down began to worry about us and started bringing us sack lunches. Nathan and I were having the time of our lives. We were kids in a candy shop.

While I was standing in the booth one day, a fellow asked, "What did Bill Crealock think of the design?"

I told the gentleman I had no idea. I told him I didn't think Crealock had seen the boat.

"He was just here in the booth," the fellow said. "In fact, that's him walking down there."

I bolted from the booth, caught up with Mr. Crealock, shook his hand, and mumbled something. Bill Crealock was as gracious as I was brash. He must have known by then that the thrust of my sales pitch was that the Valiant was the opposite of a Westsail, his fiberglass design adaptation of the Atkin Eric design.

# Yacht Design According to Perry

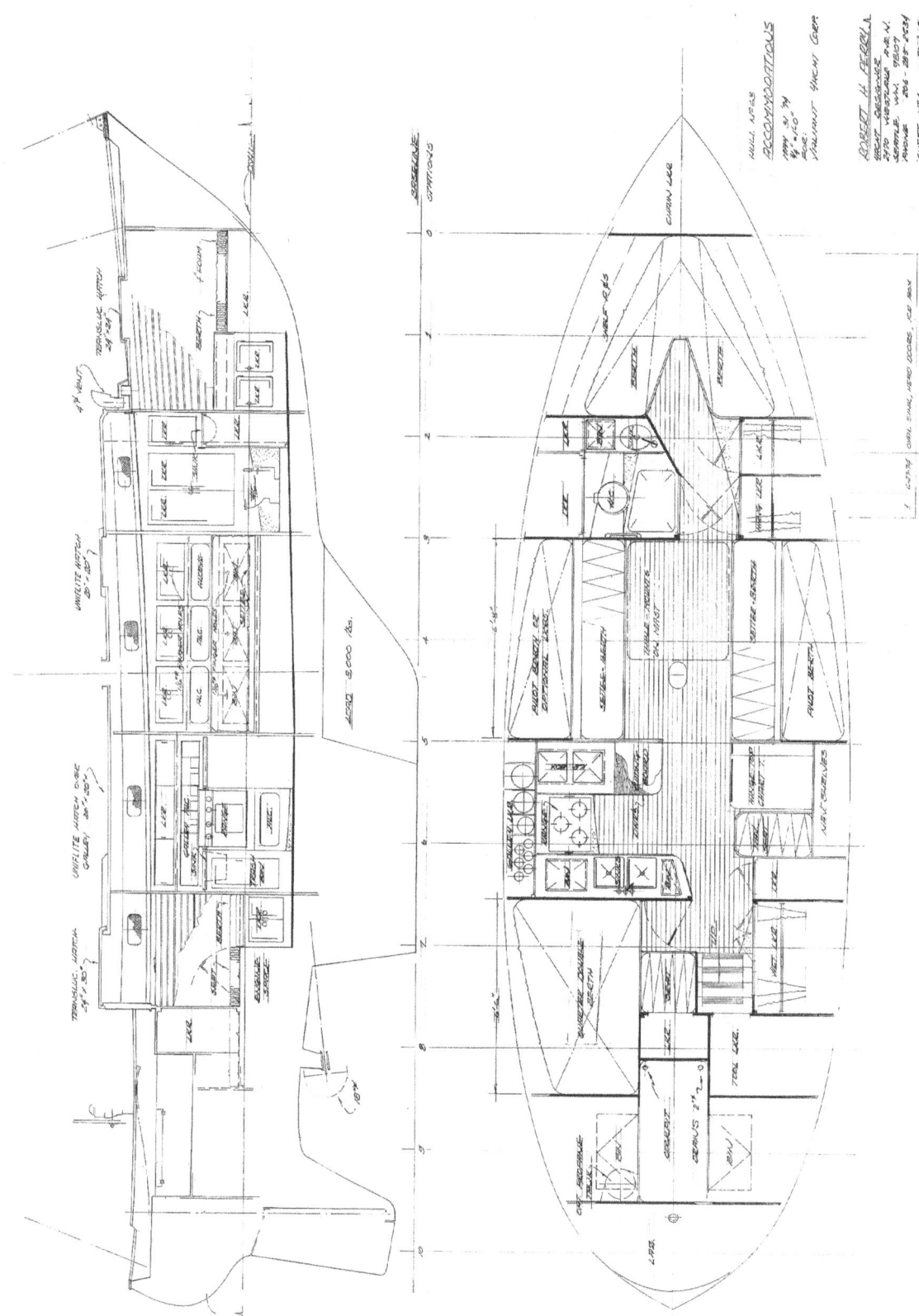

*Despite numerous subsequent revisions, I still think this standard Valiant 40 layout with its two pilot berths and large single head works the best.*

Nathan and I did not sell a Valiant during that show, but we made some noise. The sailing world knew we were coming, and soon, with help from Stanley and Sylvia Dabney, we were making a lot more.

Sylvia and Stanley had been Jay Benford supporters in Seattle, which was how Nathan had met them. Their storefront retail operation, The Magic Machine, was a half block from the University of Washington campus and featured the only publicly accessible photocopy machine in Seattle's University District. Their business was a runaway success. Stan was the consummate salesman. When you talked to Stan you were always right, and Stan managed to put a positive spin on just about everything. Stan owned an Islander 36. Sylvia was the counterpoint to Stan. She just loved pushing people's buttons, and she was darn good at it. Still, she was a lot of fun and it was hard not to like her. Together, the two of them made a powerful team, overflowing with energy, optimism, and confidence. They would become the sales backbone of the Valiant group and were integral to many of the early decisions regarding the boat and the company.

After returning to Seattle in April 1974, I attended one or two of the meetings at which those decisions were made, but I had little patience discussing boats with non-sailors.

"What do you mean by apparent wind?" a potential investor would ask. "Apparently the wind is coming from over there?" After a little of this, I stayed with the design work and left the business end to Nathan.

When the first Valiant was launched in the fall of 1974, we sea-trialed it extensively. We knew we had a great boat. We arranged an open house at Seattle's Shilshole Bay Marina in the late fall, reserving a slip on the guest dock.

The morning of the open house, Jay Benford showed up. By this time, Jay was not on cordial terms with either Nathan or me, to say the least. In retrospect, I understand his reasons, but I was young then. Jay toured the Valiant in silence, keeping his own counsel. When the intrepid Sylvia Dabney asked him what he thought of the boat, he could only manage a "hrumph."

Nathan and I were making enemies within the industry with a boat that seemed to make a lot of the competition look obsolete. An aggressive and imaginative advertising campaign drove home the

*A Valiant 40 with the apparent wind at about 34 degrees and the mainsail oversheeted. An in-the-mast furling mainsail like this is hard to trim properly.*

*Ruby is the only custom, backyard-built Valiant. I moved Ruby's mast forward to help improve helm balance. Note the tiller steering.*

message that this cruising boat was different. When people questioned the split-appendage underbody, our ads countered with the Valiant underbody superimposed over the body of a salmon and the headline "20 billion fish can't be wrong."

By late 1974, Valiants were rolling off the line at Uniflite, and by 1975, the boats were selling to prominent sailors. On the third day of the Annapolis Boat Show in October 1975, we noticed a bad smell on our boat. A short search led us to dead squid stashed in lockers around the boat. We figured it was the work of the Westsail people. Nathan and I were both 30 years old and proud fathers of a boat that would go on to become a modern classic.

After building 150 Valiants, Uniflite faltered and went out of business in 1984 due to a fiasco with its Hetron fire-retardant polyester resin. Hetron was the resin Uniflite had used in the boats it had built for U.S. military deployment on the Mekong delta in Vietnam. It was the resin Uniflite used in its powerboats, and it was the resin Uniflite wanted to keep on using. The company showed us documented instances of powerboats built with this resin actually stopping marina fires. It was a positive safety feature with an existing track record and no known downside, and we were happy to agree. It took several years before Valiants built with Hetron resin started blistering, and it was the subsequent class-action lawsuit against Uniflite—a suit in which, thankfully, neither side elected to involve me—that finally brought the company down.

At this juncture, a Texas Valiant dealer, Rich Worstell, stepped in and moved Valiant production to his yard on Lake Texoma on the Texas/Oklahoma

One of the later Valiant 40s, built just before we switched to the Valiant 42 model with the bowsprit. Note the boarding ladder obscuring my beautiful stern. This high-clewed genoa gives up too much sail area for my taste, but this is a good shot of a Valiant on a tight reach.

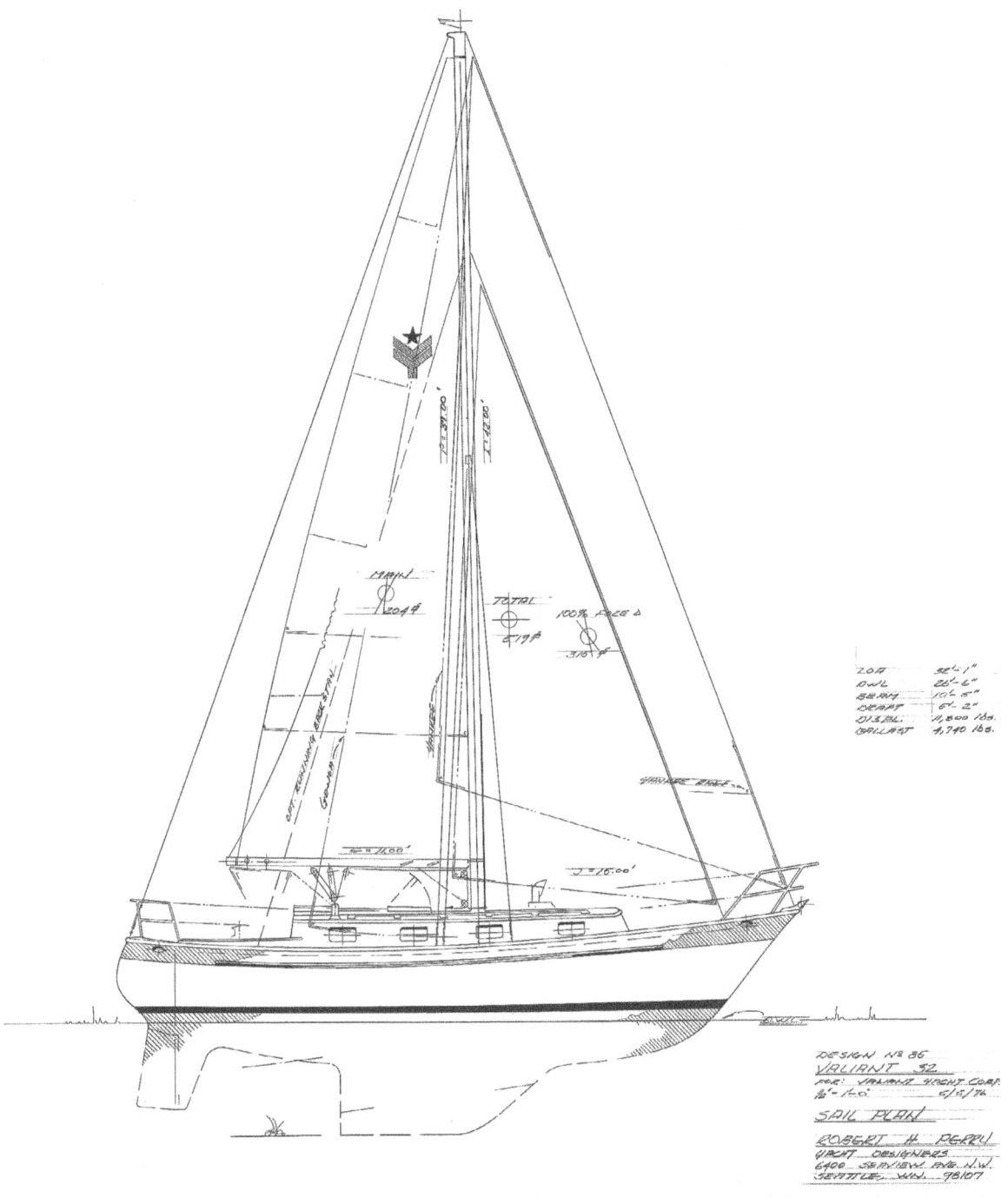

*The original sail plan for the Valiant 32. I should have reduced the J dimension and moved the mast about 12 inches forward.*

border, where it continues to this day. Under Rich's strict guidance, another 200 Valiant 40s have been lovingly built. Thanks to Rich and his crew, the fall of 2007 marked 33 years of unbroken Valiant 40 production.

Due to the generosity of my pal Daryl McNabb, who paid the bills while I sailed the boat, I was lucky enough to be a partner in a Valiant for three years. It's a marvelous boat, able to make any sailor feel confident. Sailing a Valiant 40 is a bit like pulling

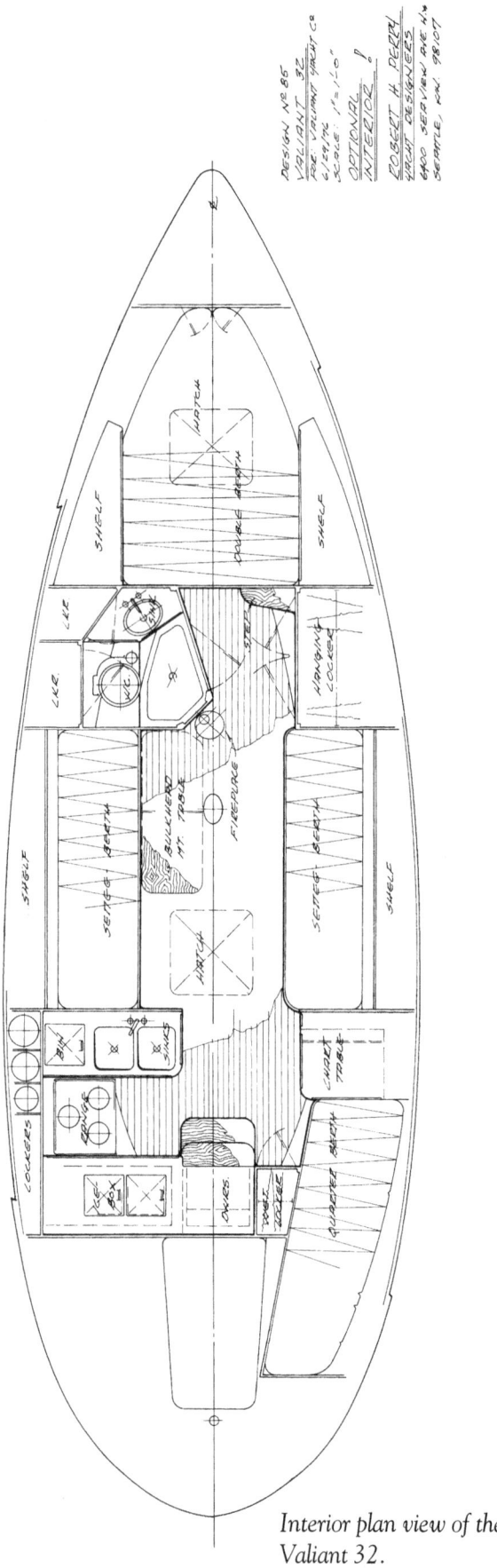

*Interior plan view of the Valiant 32.*

on an old, favorite pair of Levis. It just feels right. The boat has a good turn of speed, a wonderful, forgiving nature, and no bad habits.

Even before the first Valiant 40 was built, it gave birth to the Valiant 32, and it was this design that provided my ticket from Boston back to Seattle. I convinced Nathan, who was by this time president of Valiant Yacht Corporation, to pay me a $10,000 flat fee in lieu of royalties for the 32, and that money was in my hand, figuratively speaking, when the door to Dick Carter's design office closed behind me.

The 32 started as a 30-footer, but when Uniflite quoted a price for the new model, we decided to make the boat two feet longer. Length overall is cheap—it's everything else that's expensive. Having marketed themselves into a corner with the 40, Valiant was now compelled to offer all the same features on the new 32. This made the 32 both very expensive and very strong. We used the same keel and skeg construction arrangement as in the 40, the same tie-rod, the same topside stringers, and the same true cutter rig. It was a lot to put into a 32-footer, but today, Valiant 32s are still sailing the world, the epitome of the stout little offshore boat. For some reason, when *Practical Sailor* reviewed the 32, they called it a "coastal cruiser." I cancelled my subscription.

The 32 is a chunky little hooker, heavy and with a much harder turn to the bilge than the 40. The lead is all on the bottom of the keel fin, and this, along with the fin's generous thickness ratio, makes the vertical center of gravity (VCG) of the lead very low. Valiant 32s are nothing if not stiff. In fact, they may be a bit too stiff for my taste, but cruisers love stiff boats. The keel fin is long and, in retrospect, too far forward when coupled with a true cutter rig with the mast well aft. I should have moved that keel aft a bit and placed the ballast a bit higher in the fin. We would have sacrificed a small amount of stability but gained a better-balanced boat. Most owners of 32s love their balance, but the owners are not whom I want to please. I want *me* to be happy with a boat's balance, and I've always thought that the 32 has more weather helm than I wanted. A bowsprit could have corrected this, and some 32s have been retrofitted with sprits to move the center of effort farther forward.

While walking a dock a couple of years ago, I saw a fabulous-looking boat. It looked familiar, but

*Valiant Days*

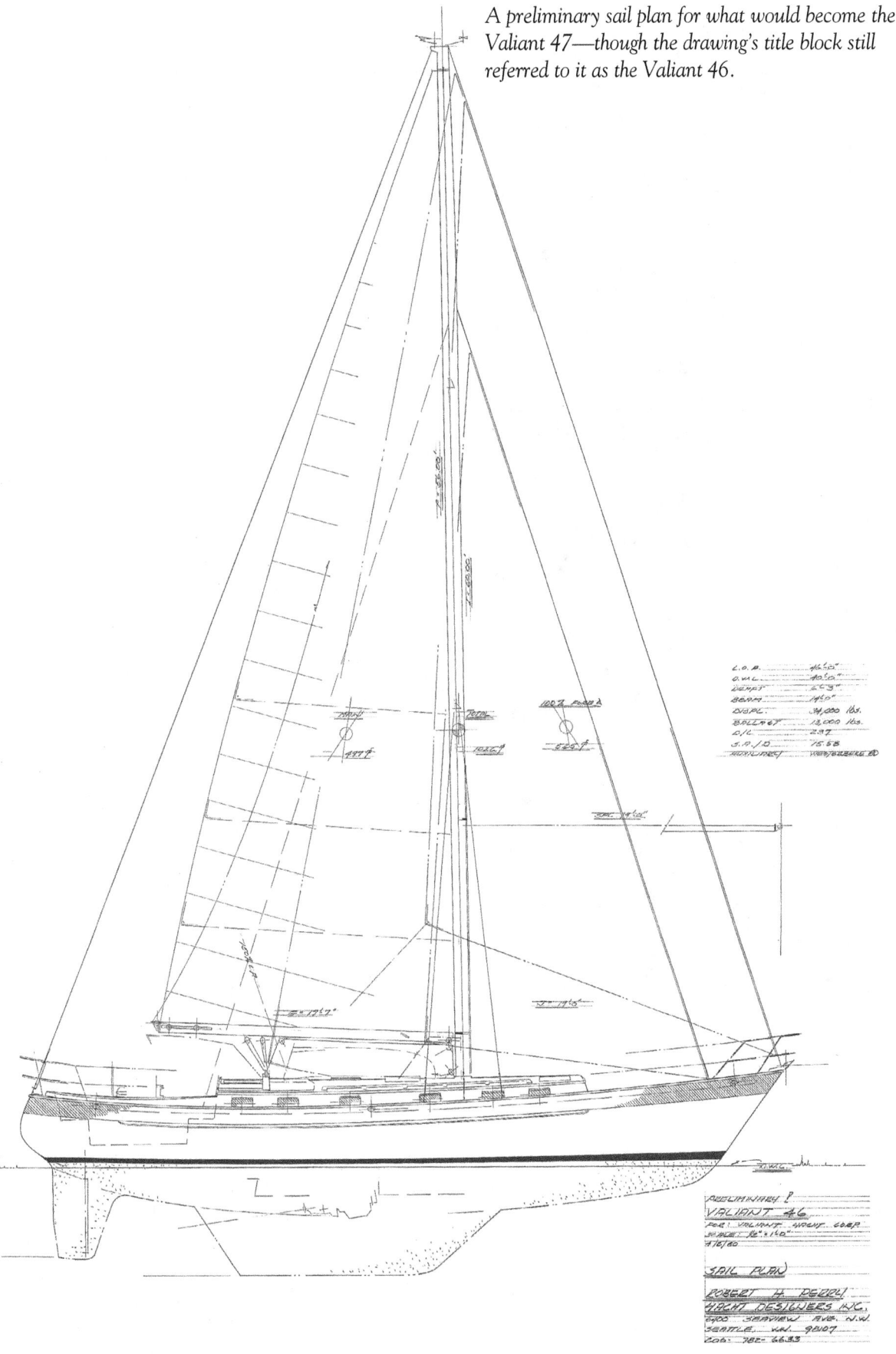

A preliminary sail plan for what would become the Valiant 47—though the drawing's title block still referred to it as the Valiant 46.

*A Valiant 47 on a close reach with all three sails pulling nicely.*

there was something strange about it. I knocked on the cabin side and called for the skipper, and when he appeared, I asked what kind of boat it was. "It's a Bob Perry design," he replied.

"Really. Well, I'm Bob Perry, and I don't remember this one."

The skipper explained that he had bought the strip-planked plug over which the female mold of the Valiant 32 had been formed, parked it in his driveway, and over a ten-year period finished it himself. That explained why the design looked familiar but the detailing did not. It was all custom and not to my design. Clearly the owner/builder was a master of metalwork, as the boat had marvelous fittings that could only have been custom made. That owner has brought his prototype Valiant 32 to the last two Perry Rendezvous. I get happy whenever I see it.

The 32 was followed by the Valiant 47. Today this model is still available as the Valiant 50, with a bowsprit added for the additional length. I must have been feeling daring when I drew the lines of the 47. I should have drawn a big, fat boat with the emphasis on interior volume, because cruisers primarily buy interiors. Instead I drew a lithe Valiant with a sharp entry, much less flare to the topsides forward than in the 40, minimal deadrise, and flat buttocks. The good news is that by this time I had figured out how to design a good-looking cabin trunk, so both the 32 and the 47 have shapely houses that avoid the "shoe box on a banana" look of the 40. Mark Schrader sailed his 47 *Lonestar* around the world single-handed in the 1986–87 BOC Challenge, competing successfully in a fleet composed primarily of boats designed and built especially for the race. Mark suffered no major structural problems. This was Mark's second circumnavigation in a Valiant. I'm indebted to Mark and his valiant efforts.

Valiant 50s are still available on a semi-custom basis and are still in demand. I can remember sailing a 47 with Nathan around Cape May in 1981 on a cold and blustery night en route to the Annapolis Boat Show. We hit 10 knots as we reached off the waves while dodging commercial ships.

We also created a pilothouse version of the Valiant 40, which gave me the opportunity to address the handling characteristics of the original 40 that I felt could be improved. I moved the mast almost two feet ahead, substituting a sloop rig for the original cutter and thereby removing any hint of excessive weather helm. I've always felt that the pilothouse version is easier to balance than the original 40.

In 1983 Nathan and I once more sailed a 40—this time a pilothouse model—from New York Har-

*A Valiant 47 in Valiant 50 mode with tubular bowsprit. This boat has a Leisure Furl boom. I was never fond of the all-one-color topside paint jobs on these boats. To my eye a Valiant's lines are set off better with a white wale stripe above the rubrail.*

bor to the Annapolis Boat Show. Motor-sailing down Chesapeake Bay in the dead of a cold night in order to make our scheduled docking time was an adventure for a Seattle boy used to deep water. Now I know what the running lights of a dredging barge look like.

With the pilothouse 40, I think I managed to draw the most difficult-to-build cockpit in the history of fiberglass-production sailboats. The seats featured a changing contour that drove the builder crazy. We had not taken into account the need for locker hinges to be in the same plane. Oops! That aside, the cockpit was amazingly comfortable.

By 1977 Nathan was getting concerned about having all of his eggs in the Uniflite basket, and he decided to build a new model with a Uniflite off-shoot company called Nordic. The new boat, which we named the Esprit 37, would be a more contemporary version of the Valiant series. I gave the 37 a more dishlike hull form with less deadrise than the 40, and terminated the buttocks in what is probably the most shapely tumblehome canoe stern I have ever drawn. The bow profile of the Esprit was convex, in contrast with the concave bow profile of the Valiant 40, 32, and 47. With its narrow, wedge-like cabin trunk, strong sheer spring, and shapely fanny, the Esprit 37 was a real looker. I wanted one of these boats, so I ordered hull number 1, and my wife, Jill, and I named it *Ricky Nelson*. In time we were introduced to the real Ricky Nelson at a concert, which gave me the chance to present him a poster of the boat showing his name on the stern.

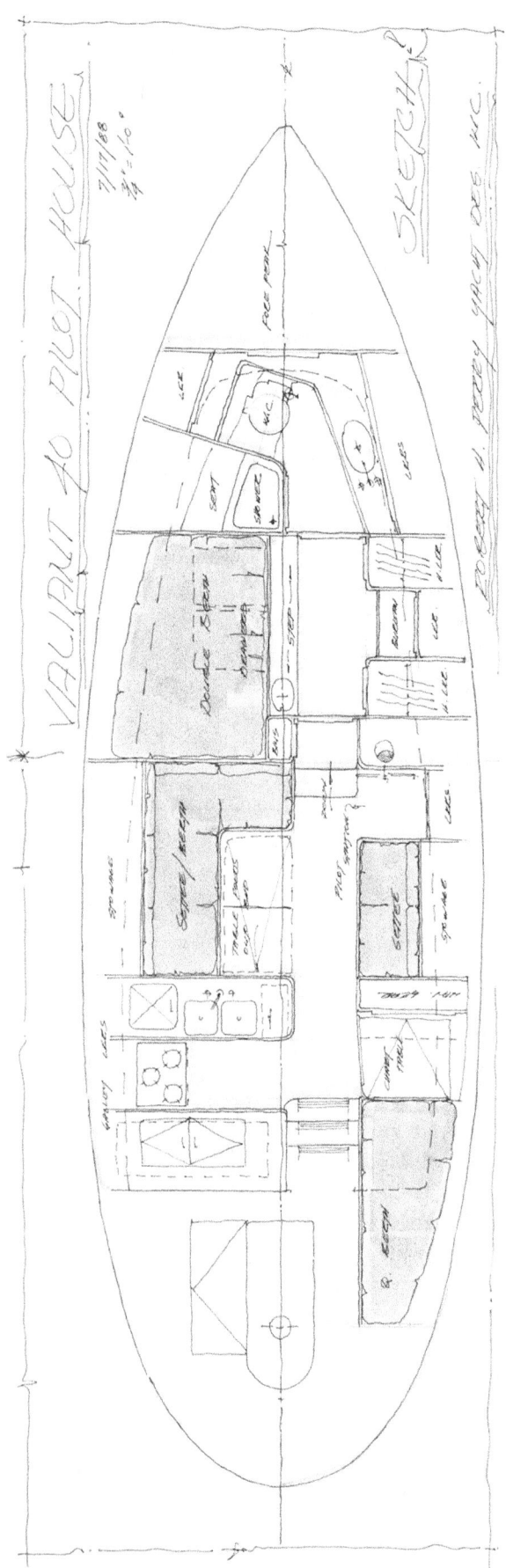

He had no idea what to make of it, but he quietly thanked me and died six months later in a plane crash.

The Esprit was initially built at the Nordic plant, but when Nordic's contract with Valiant expired, the tooling was moved back to Uniflite, which had signed a contract to build the boat for less than Nordic's price. This left Nordic with no model to build, so they commissioned the Nordic 44 and Nordic 40 designs from me. The Esprit 37 tooling ended up in Texas in 1984 with the rest of the Valiant molds, and with the addition of a bowsprit, it became the Valiant 39. To make the rechristened model a better fit with the existing Valiant line, I was commissioned to redesign the cabin trunk. Reluctantly, I replaced my svelte wedge cabin trunk with a blocky box similar to the trunks on the Valiant 40, 32, and 47. To my eye, it looked awful.

The Esprit 37 was the first "big" cruising boat that I owned. I was newly married, and my wife and I enjoyed a lot of cruising on it. It was a good boat, stiff and with generous beam. The keel of the 37 was too far forward, giving it too much weather helm, and I think the draft of 5′6″ is too little. Still, in most conditions, I could sail with the Valiant 40, and in fact I was a bit faster upwind. Off the wind, the 40 was considerably faster. It is my recollection (though some will argue the point), that the Esprit 37 was the first production boat less than 40 feet to have a separate shower stall.

I raced *Ricky Nelson* extensively for the first two years I owned it, winning the first race I entered, but I sold the boat after my second son was born. Sailing with a newborn and a toddler was too much work.

My enduring image of the *Ricky Nelson* is rowing away from it on a chilly morning with a layer of fog hanging over the water and looking up at that shapely stern. Now there was a stern.

*This sketch showed what I had in mind for the interior layout of the new Valiant 40 pilothouse model. Freehand sketches like this were crude, effective, and a lot of fun to do. My architect friend Ned Johnson taught me how to do them using flimsy beige paper, a drafting pen, and colored marking pens.*

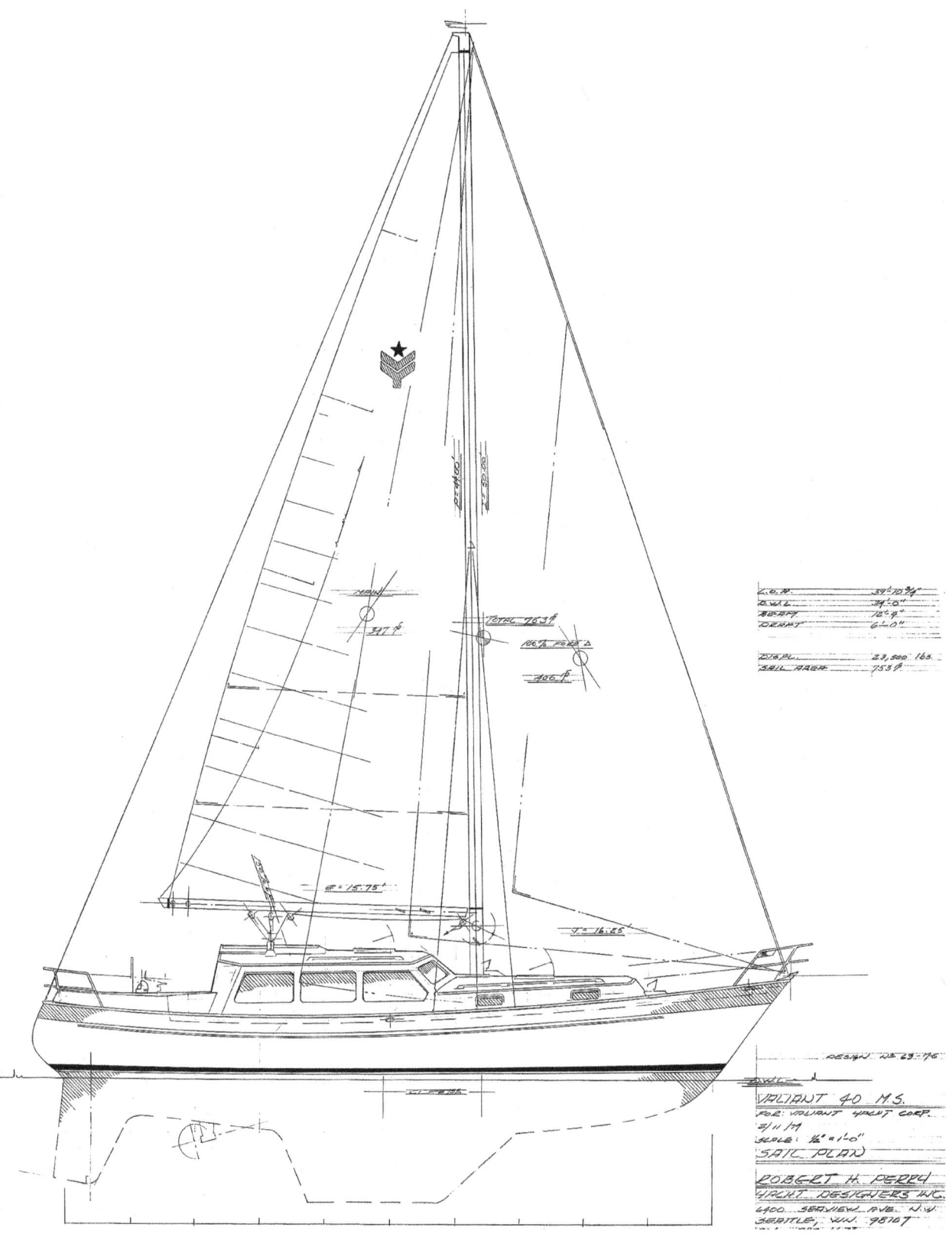

*The Valiant 40 pilothouse model gave me a chance to move the mast forward.*

*A pilothouse Valiant 40 in the Valiant 42 configuration, with short bowsprit and tall rig.*

*This is my Esprit, hull number 1. Hopefully I am indicating with my left arm to my crew that we need to do something about that baggy shape at the foot of the mainsail—perhaps "a little more main halyard, please." (Roy Montgomery)*

Today I have had the great good fortune of having my name inexorably joined to the name Valiant for more than 30 years. I feel lucky and proud. I doubt Nathan and I fully appreciated back in 1974 and 1975 that what we were doing with the Valiant 40 was like catching lightning in a bottle. That was a long time ago. Nathan went on to work for several years in China and Malaysia developing new businesses, and together we built the first eight-foot Perrywinkle dinghies in China. Now Nathan, married with two grown children, works in the energy-management field. We still see each other about twice a year and get together on the phone from time to time to argue politics and exchange life views. We seldom discuss boats, though. Boats go without saying between New York Nathan and me.

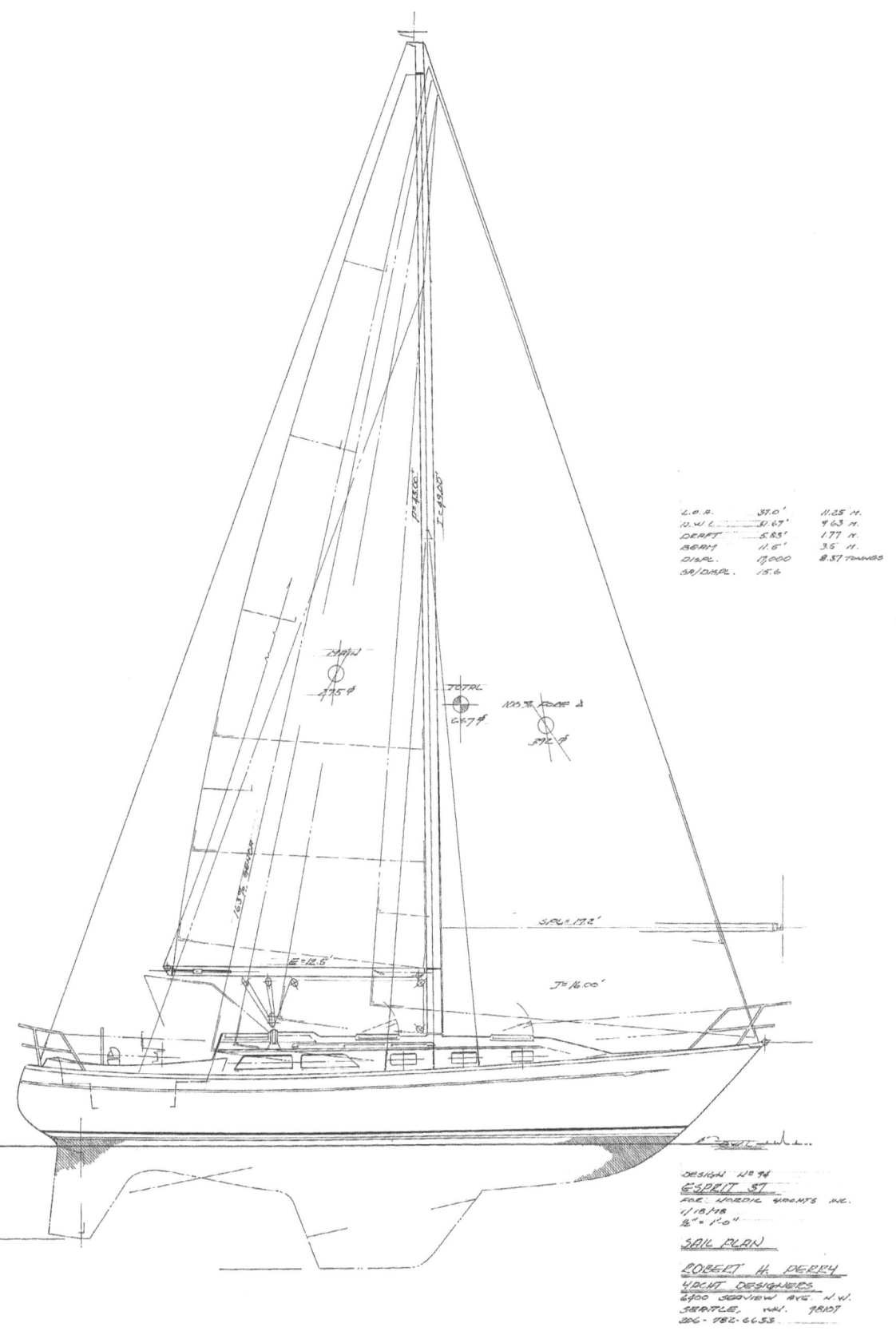

The Esprit 37 sail plan clearly shows the influence of the IOR rigs of the time. The foretriangle is too large, the mast too far aft, and the mainsail too skinny.

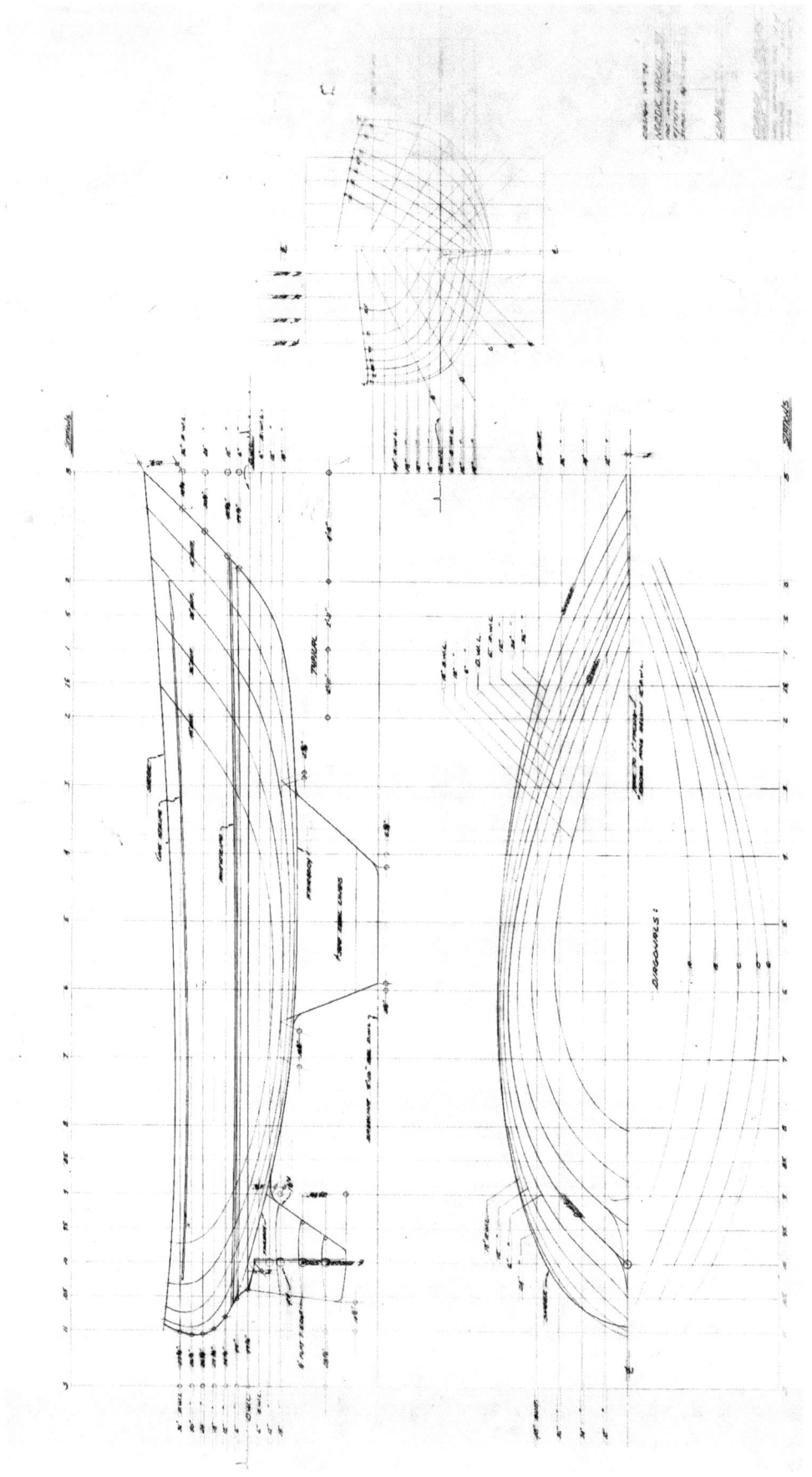

*The Esprit 37 hull shape is near and dear to me. It's a good design that could have benefited from more draft and a decent spade rudder. I have always considered this the prettiest stern I've ever drawn.*

## According to Perry
# THE HULL-LINES PLAN

Years ago, hull shapes were carved as models by their designers. The model was sawn into sections in the horizontal and vertical planes, and from these sawn-out shapes a drawing was made. Eventually designers switched to starting from a drawing and then building a model to check the drawing. Today, three-dimensional hull shapes are developed using computer programs.

Regardless of how you arrive at a final hull shape, the end result must allow the builder on the "loft floor" to expand the small-scale hull-lines plan to full-size patterns for the mold frames, over which the hull or hull plug is built. Today I have a computer-operated plotter with which to draw full-sized patterns on Mylar for builders. This eliminates the need for the builder to "correct" or make the small changes necessary to the designer's hull lines to bring the drawing from small scale to full scale. Other builders go straight from a computer file to a CNC machine—an 80-foot-long, five-axis milling machine that literally carves a hull or deck shape out of a block of foam—avoiding the lofting process altogether. Whether hand-drawn or computer-generated, however, the hull-lines plan is the heart and soul of the design. Anyone interested in hull shapes must be able to read a lines plan.

The hull-lines drawings include three or sometimes four views of the hull: the profile, the plan view, the body plan, and, in a hand-drawn set of lines, the diagonals. (For an example of diagonals, see the lines drawing of the Valiant 40 on page 21.) Each view is like a topographical map showing the contours of the hull in that particular view. These include the buttock lines (or simply the buttocks) in the profile, the waterlines in the plan view, and the sections in the body plan. An additional auxiliary view can show diagonals.

Buttocks are vertical, longitudinal cuts through the hull parallel to the centerline. Waterlines are horizontal cuts through the hull parallel to the waterplane. Sections are transverse vertical cuts through the hull perpendicular to the centerline, while diagonals are cuts sloping down and out from the vertical centerline.

We don't see many diagonals these days. In the old days of hand-drawn lines, diagonals were used as a final check for fairness, just to verify the other views. Early in my career, I used diagonals in the fairing process, as I found they were an easy way to fair an initial shape quickly. In the days of planked wooden yachts, the diagonals were laid out so as to cross the hull sections as much as possible at right angles, and in this way they simulated the run of the boat's planking. A builder would check diagonals to see how easy it was going to be to plank the boat.

Buttocks and waterlines are traditionally spaced evenly on the hull, although the exact spacing is not critical. Sections were generally laid out starting at station "0" at the cutwater and ending at station "10" at the aft end of the waterplane (or the "butt water," as I like to call it). Breaking the waterline into ten evenly spaced stations formerly made it easier to

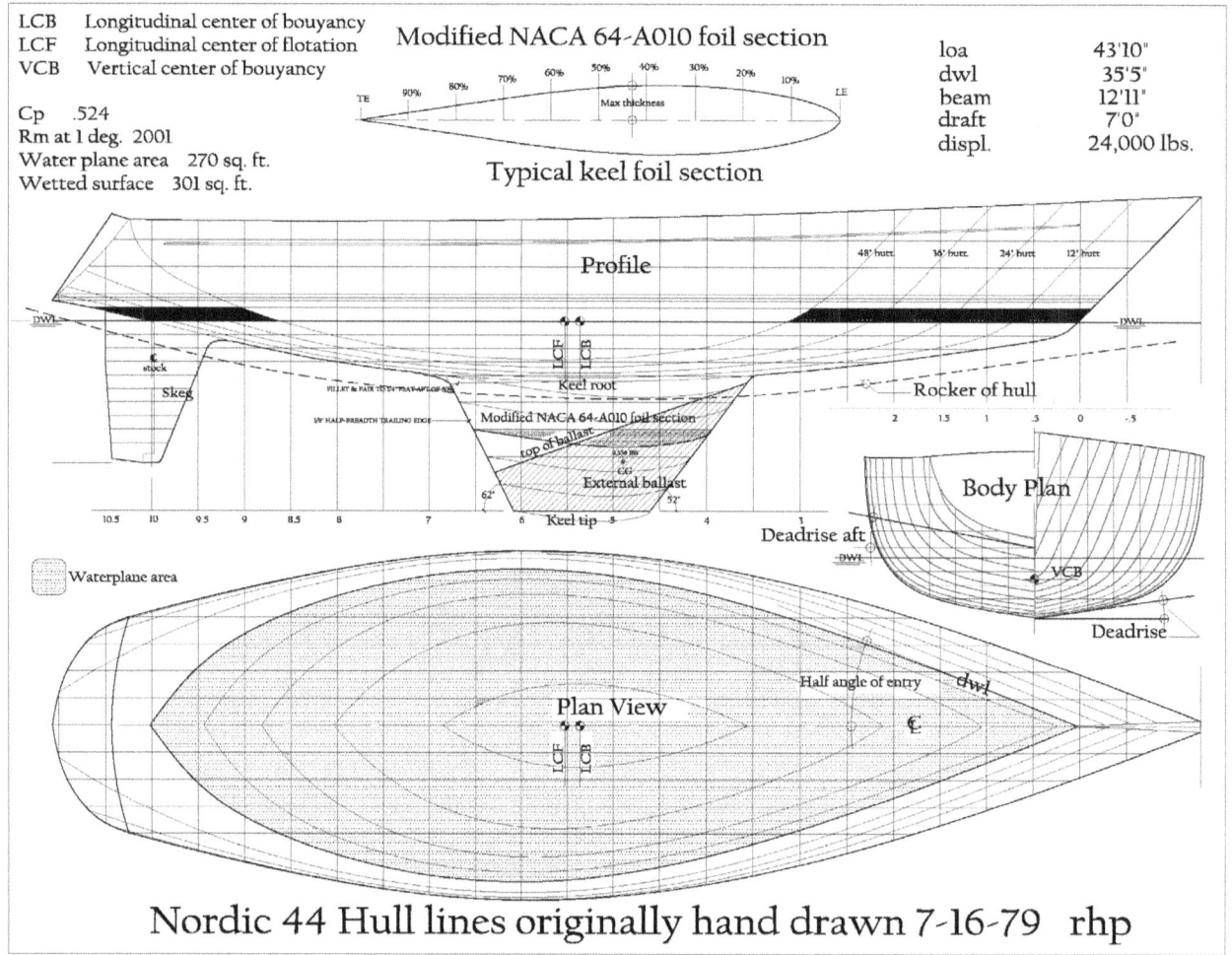

I drew the lines of the Nordic 44 by hand in 1979, but later we created the computer-generated lines shown here. The buttock lines are curved in the profile view, horizontal and parallel with the centerline in the plan view, and vertical and parallel with the centerline in the body plan or sectional view. The waterlines are curved in the plan view and horizontal in both the profile and sectional views. The sections are curved in the sectional view and vertical in both the profile and plan views. The sections aft and forward of the maximum beam are shown on the left and right sides, respectively, of the sectional view. The stations in the profile and plan views are numbered from 0 at the cutwater (the forward end of the waterplane, which is lightly shaded in the plan view) to 10 at the after end of the waterplane. The longitudinal center of buoyancy (LCB) is noted at about 53.5 percent, and the longitudinal center of flotation (LCF) is at just over 55 percent of the way aft on the DWL. Note the hull rocker in the profile view and the half-angle of entry in the plan view. In the sectional view you can see that there is more deadrise aft than amidships. The Nordic 44 has a L/B of 3.39 (see Chapter 1), a D/L of 241, and (given its ballast of 9,356 pounds) a B/D of 39 percent, all indicative of a moderate hull. The waterlines in the plan view and the prismatic coefficient of 0.524 suggest a hull with fine ends that is easily driven in a light breeze but has a lower hull speed than a boat with the same waterline length but fuller ends. The moderate rocker, moderate deadrise, and fairly soft bilges further reinforce the overall impression of a hull that emphasizes comfort over top-end speed, as does the skeg-hung rudder. With the right sail plan, however, this hull will give you good performance.

*According to Perry: The Hull-Lines Plan*

calculate the various hydrostatic data (i.e., the prismatic coefficient, the LCB, the LCF, the righting moment, etc.) that were needed to verify the validity and appropriateness of a hull shape. Designers would speak of hydrostatic centers in terms of station locations—for example, the longitudinal center of buoyancy, or LCB, might be at station 5.34, or 53.4 percent of the designed waterline aft of the cutwater.

Today a computer generates all the numbers, and it doesn't care where your stations are. I usually put my stations on whatever centers the builder wants for the mold frames during construction. For a metal boat that will incorporate the frames into the finished hull, I put the stations where those frames will go. I add intermediate stations—called half-stations—in the bow of a boat and in the stern of a double-ender, where there is a lot of shape change.

I don't want to give hard rules for evaluating the shapes of buttocks, waterlines, and sections. They vary as widely as types of boats. A designer shapes a hull to achieve a target D/L and the desired hydrostatic data. Light boats will have flat buttocks, as the hull will have little fore-and-aft rocker, or

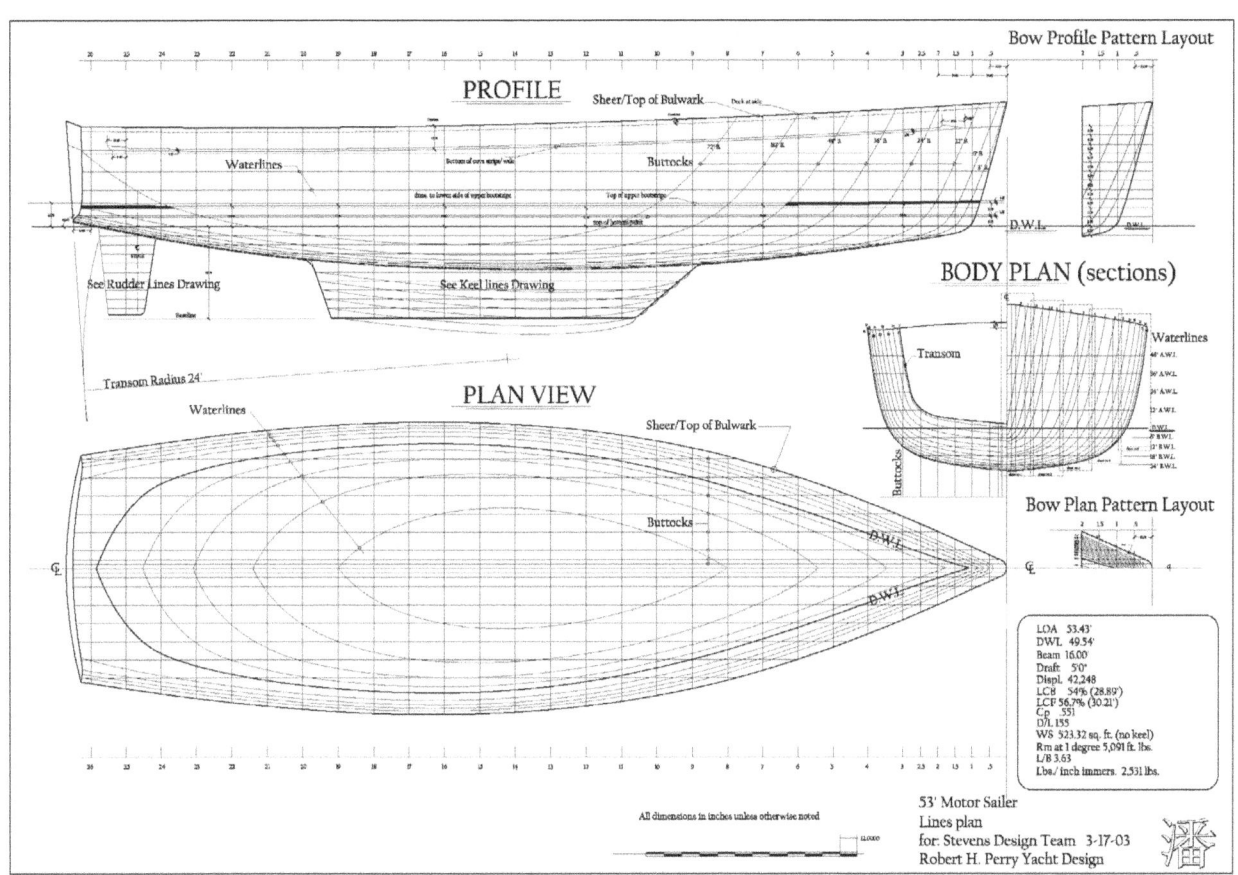

*Using full-size patterns developed from these hull lines, a boatbuilder in Xiamen, China, built frames for a plug over which the hull mold for the Stevens 53 motorsailer was formed. These lines reveal a quest for waterline length, volume, and stability combined with shoal draft. Upwind sailing performance will be less than optimal, but that's the price you pay for shoal draft. Note how flat the buttocks are aft—a function of extending the beam aft with a hard turn of the bilge. You can see this in the waterlines in the plan view, as well, with the waterplane carried almost all the way aft. This will give the hull excellent performance under power while preventing it from squatting at high rpm. The high Cp (0.551) is also indicative of high-end performance under power, and the hard bilges make the boat very stiff. The D/L of 155 might suggest a light, high-performance sailing hull, but the hull's other characteristics are telling us that this is clearly not the case. It would be more accurate to think of this as a medium-displacement boat with an unusually long DWL. If the boat had even moderate overhangs, its D/L would rise to 250.*

*The Stevens 53 under sail.*

fore-and-aft curvature on centerline. Heavy boats will have more rocker, and their buttocks will be more rounded.

The designer will usually begin with a midsectional shape. Beam will be determined by a number of factors, including a target L/B. I use LOA and B max for this ratio, but you could also use DWL and BWL. Again, the important thing is to be consistent. I like LOA and B max because I can always get those numbers from published literature for comparison boats, whereas I cannot always get beam at the waterline (BWL) from published data.

With B max determined, you can choose your BWL. Your choice may depend upon the stability characteristics of the boat you are designing, or it may be a function of the interior volume you want. More BWL generally means a boat with more initial stability. A narrow BWL will give you a boat with low initial stability, but if the topsides are flared, you will pick up stability as the boat heels.

Related questions include: How much deadrise (the angle of rise from the garboard to the turn of the bilge) should the midsection have? (For that matter, should the midsection have any deadrise at all?) Should the deadrise, or some portion of it, be carried to the stern? Should the bow sections be V- or U-shaped? Should the forefoot have a hard knuckle, or will the boat do better with a more softly rounded forefoot?

The answers to some of these questions will depend in part on the displacement and nature of the boat. Cruising boats might like deadrise because it gives a boat a nice, deep, natural bilge sump area, which prevents water in the bilge from slopping over the cabin sole. Racers and light boats may prefer a flat bottom with no deadrise for reduced drag. I like some deadrise at the transom for cruising boats, because it helps to prevent the counter area from slapping as waves hit it when you are tied to a dock. For racing boats, I think that a flat or gently rounded run is better for speed, although Bill Lee, the king of the ultralight displacement (ULDB) movement, always incorporated deadrise in the sterns of his Santa Cruz boats.

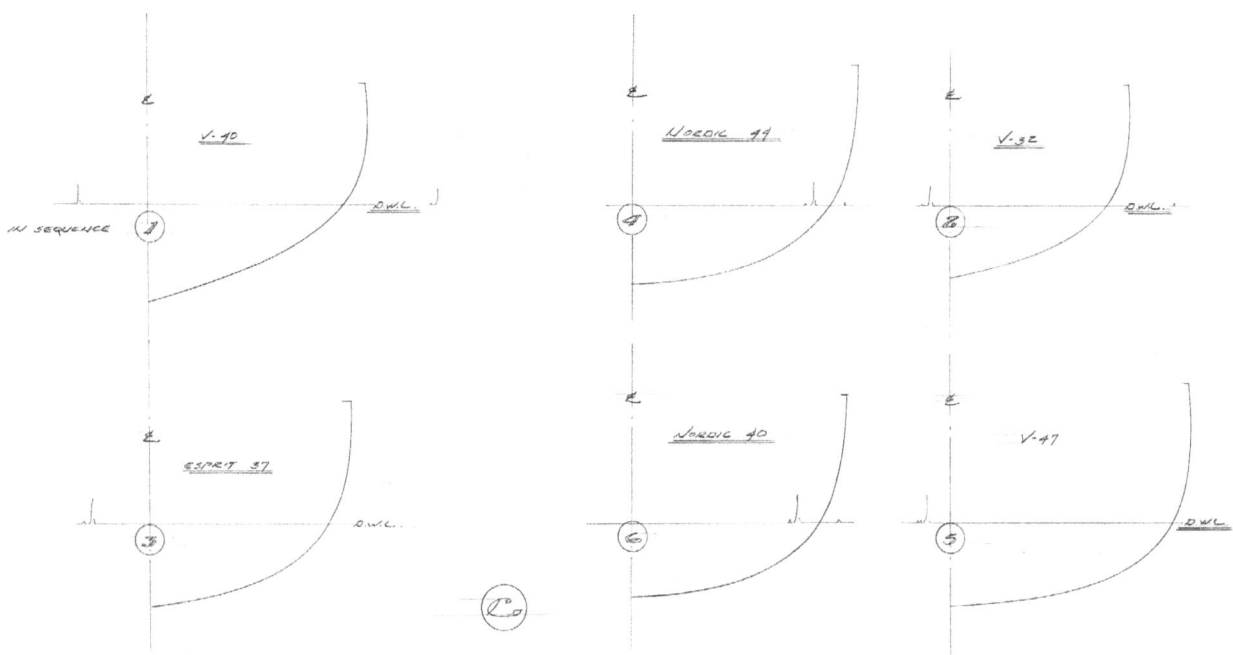

*A family of Perry-designed moderate-displacement cruising boat midsections showing variations in deadrise. Most designs begin with the midsection, which focuses the designer's attention on maximum beam, waterline beam, and deadrise.*

I like to see some V shape in the bow sections of a cruising boat, because it helps reduce pounding when you are motoring dead into a chop. I do not think this feature alleviates pounding under sail, however. Boats pound under sail when they are hard on the wind or almost hard on the wind, at which point they are well heeled over. When they come down onto a wave, they make the initial contact with their topsides, not their forefoot. Even a Valiant 40, sharply V-ed forward though it is, will pound from time to time in a steep chop.

Pounding, as I see it, is a function of wave frequency, wave height, boat speed, and D/L. I believe that a light boat with minimal fore-and-aft rocker will heave more of its forebody out of the water in a seaway, then drop it back in with a slam. A heavy boat such as a Westsail has tremendous fore-and-aft rocker, and when it lifts its bow free in a seaway, it creates a much greater angle between the hull profile and the waterplane, which makes for a much softer landing when the bow comes back down. I don't think anything you can do with the bow sections of a light boat will have any impact on its tendency to pound.

## Computer Design Software

About 25 years ago, I was approached at the Annapolis Boat Show by a fellow, George Hazen, who had written a computer program that would fair hull lines and reduce the time needed to produce a finished, fair hull shape. He made his pitch, then I attacked. How could a computer do the work of the designer's hand and eye? I stayed with my hand-drawn hull lines, convinced that doing everything by hand gave me ultimate control over the shapes I produced. I didn't yet realize that I was playing the role of John Henry and that the computer was the steam hammer.

About two years later, I was again approached by a developer of a hull-fairing program. Again I trotted out my objections, but this developer, designer Graham Shannon of Vancouver, British Columbia, was not so easily deterred. He was convinced that his way was the way of the future.

Months later, Graham showed up again at my office to deliver another sales pitch for his program. At the time, I was deeply immersed in the design of a boat with a difficult and complex hull shape, and in an effort to get rid of Graham, I said, "If your program is so good, why don't you fair this hull for me?" In five minutes, Graham had carried his computer up from his car and was busy inputting the hull shape I had developed by hand. In an hour we were done. I had the shape I wanted, and Graham had made a sale. I paid him $800 and was left with an early version of AutoYacht that would take about two more years to debug. But we stayed with it. In time, working with almost monthly updates and revisions to the program along with my constant complaints to Graham, I was a whiz at computer lines fairing.

I had already worked extensively with Dave Vacanti, developing programs that would work well with my hand-drawing approach to design. Dave designed programs that allowed me to evaluate existing foils and even design my own, and he wrote programs that allowed me to compare my designs in detail. Dave's programs were an immense help with keel design. I worked out a time-share computer arrangement with Boeing Computer Services before purchasing one of the early IBM computers.

There are several benefits to using a computer to fair hull lines. First, it is quick. Once you develop a library of "parent" hull forms, you can easily morph an existing hull into a new one of similar type. If the hull you're designing has no appropriate "parent," you can hand-draw a quick set of lines, then input these into the computer to further refine them.

Another benefit is accuracy. Hand-drawn lines—even when drawn at a 3/4"=1'0" scale and accompanied by an elaborate table of offsets—must be lofted full size on the shop floor in order to resolve the small errors caused by small-scale drafting and trace building patterns. This is a time-honored and established way of building boats. I loved lofting and admired the real masters of that art, but lofting a boat gave the builder an opportunity to change the hull shape, and this opened the door to possible problems. I always wanted to be certain that the boat lofted was the boat I had drawn. Even the most fastidiously hand-drawn lines left some room for deviations.

The computer does away with shop-floor lofting. After designing a hull shape on the computer, I print out full-sized Mylar patterns on my office plotter, and the builder lays those patterns on the floor and makes the building patterns from them. I can even deduct the skin thickness on the computer so the builder's patterns will be accurate to the inside of the skin or the outside of the frame.

A computer can also spit out in seconds the hydrostatic calculations a designer needs to fully understand the shape he or she has drawn. Deriving these data by hand used to take days. With the computer doing the hard computations, I can try hull shape after hull shape in a short time while looking for the perfect shape, and I can change it again the next day if I have an idea overnight. It is no exaggeration to say that the computer can fair hull changes in seconds that would take a skilled draftsman all day to do by hand.

My office uses a variety of hull-design programs along with a program called Rhino that develops three-dimensional shapes for deck design. Our hull-shaping programs interface with velocity-prediction programs (VPPs), which predict performance. Thus, before we even start the building process, we have a good handle on the performance of the boat. If we want to explore the effect of a different keel on a design, we can do it accurately with a VPP. A stability study of a new design that 30 years ago would take a skilled designer a week to complete can now be done in the blink of an eye.

For general drafting, I use AutoCAD (abbreviated ACAD). I fought this to the bitter end. I loved drawing, and I fell in love with my own drafting. I had good teachers. When I was working for Dick Carter, Chuck Paine worked on the floor above mine. One day he looked over my shoulder and said, "I just love your drafting. I try to make my drawings look like yours." "That's funny," I said, "I try to make my drawings look like yours." I worked hard at my drafting and I was damn proud of it—that is, until I sent off a package of beautifully hand-drawn lines to the New Zealand builder of *Icon* (Chapter 16), only to receive by way of response a curt e-mail asking me to "please send no more hand drawings, only ACAD." Although my staff was using AutoCAD exclusively, I had merely been fiddling with it while hanging on to my old 3H pencil. Clearly it was time to make the transition.

I'm often asked by people, "Don't you miss drawing by hand?" No, I don't. Once in a while I get an urge to sketch some design ideas on paper in the early stages of a new design, but I transfer those ideas to the computer as quickly as possible. ACAD has too many benefits to list, but accuracy and a tight tolerance for dimensions are worthy of special note. Another feature I appreciate more and more is the ability to zoom in on areas where a detail is needed. Of course, the ability to e-mail drawings from one workstation to another in my office is also convenient, and we also e-mail the drawings and revisions to the builder. Some builders will produce their own "shop drawings" from our e-mailed ACAD drawings.

I think of ACAD as a fancy pencil. I use the same drafting techniques with ACAD that I used when I drew by hand, and I think my ACAD drawings rival my hand-drawn work for beauty. It's just different.

## Chapter Four
# ISLANDER YACHTS OF CALIFORNIA

In 1973, when Nathan Rothman and I were on our mission to promote the Valiant 40 at the Long Beach Boat Show, three men approached the booth. Buster Hammond, Bob Babson, and Hank McCormick looked over our drawings and introduced themselves as being from Islander Yachts. I immediately said, "You need a new designer!" Buster, who was Islander's president, said that they had been thinking the same thing and would be interested in talking to me. When I got back to Boston, I called Buster and inquired what sort of boat he had in mind for the next Islander yacht. He said they wanted a 28-footer.

I started drawing. At the time, I was pedaling my bike the 32-mile round trip to Nahant from North Beverly, and the commute took me an average of 55 minutes each way. I would arrive home by 6 p.m. and be drawing by 6:01. I had nothing else to do, and there was absolutely nothing else I would rather do. I drew 28-footers for days until finally I was ready to send a drawing to Islander. They were clearly interested, but Buster was reluctant to give the final go-ahead.

Among all the components in my past that have led me to where I am today, Buster Hammond looms large. He was short, maybe 5'5", stocky, with droopy eyelids that had inspired his high-school nickname "Tojo." His real name was Roland, but everyone knew him as Buster. Buster would talk to you with his head tilted back so that he could see beneath his eyelids. I'm not sure I have ever met a better man.

Buster had a way of asking questions that I knew he had the answers to, and that he knew I didn't, but he never did so in a way that called my own inadequacies to attention. As a result, I never hesitated to tell him everything I knew about whatever was being discussed. It's clear to me now, looking back, that in 15 minutes on any topic, Buster would not only know exactly what I knew, he would know how best to use the knowledge. He made me feel valuable and up to the job. He knew all too well that he could fill in the blanks. Buster was a fiberglass pioneer; he had begun building fiberglass boats with the Schock family in California back in the days when Schock built production dinghies over male molds. Buster knew boats, he knew sailing, and he knew boatbuilding. Most of all, he knew people.

Buster worked with Islander's marketing manager, Hank McCormick. Hank was a tall, good-looking, archetypical Southern Californian with permed gray hair, and I'll always remember him wearing an awful olive-green, crushed-velvet leisure suit (it was the 70s) and driving his olive-green Mercedes SL sports car. Of course, Hank lived on the beach in Newport Beach. Hank had design ideas and they were good ones. It was he who conceived of woven-cane locker fronts and what I call the "California rococo" interior style. I think Hank may have owed some of this to California interior designer Joe Artese, who had worked with Islander on the super-successful Alan Gurney–designed Islander 36. To this day, I consider the Islander 36 the very first of the modern yacht interiors. In the hands of Joe Artese and Islander, the boat's interior was no longer the "boy's cabin in the woods." This new interior style looked good, especially to new sailors. Practicality may have suffered, but at the boat-show dock, these interiors were winners. Hank was clever with marketing issues. Bob Babson, Islander's sales manager, was a hyperactive nail-biter who traveled the country trying to keep Islander yachts in stock in every active dealership. He did it well. Later, when I was totally immersed in Islander work and visiting the plant in Costa Mesa frequently, Bob loved to pick me up in his private plane at LAX and fly me down the coast to the Irvine airport (now John Wayne Airport). It made me nervous as hell. Or he would pick me up at the Irvine airport in his Ferrari, which I could hear coming from blocks away. If I needed a car while I was in California, Bob would loan me his so-called beater car, a pristine Mercedes 450 SLC, the same model that the shah of Iran had driven. This Islander group knew how to make a young designer feel welcome.

Engineering and in-house design work at Islander was handled by Steve Mosely and Leif Beily, although Leif was eventually replaced by Phil Arnold. Steve and Leif would be responsible for transforming my design drawings into what are called "shop drawings." My drawings were vague in many areas and would have to be embellished before they could be handed to a mechanic installing an exhaust system or a carpenter building a bank of drawers. I provided hull, keel, rudder, and deck lines; the interior layout; inboard profiles and sections; and a deck plan and deck schedule. Islander did its own structural design and detail design work. I was happy with this arrangement, as it filled in what I did not know at the time. Steve taught me a lot about the engineering of production boats. It's one thing to draw shapes, but it's another to know where to get every piece or the most economical way to manufacture your own.

Steve had a strong Hungarian accent, and I can't think of him now without remembering the Hungarian three-hat cold remedy he prescribed when I showed up once with a heavy head cold. First you get a hat. Then you get a bottle of whiskey. You put the hat on a table in front of you and begin to drink the whiskey. When you can see three hats, you stop drinking, take a hot bath, and go to bed.

It was an exciting group with which to work. In future days, when I had moved back to Seattle and was working out of my own office, I would fly to Costa Mesa regularly. Costa Mesa was the heart of California's production boatbuilding industry. Islander shared its back fence with Ericson. Westsail was just down the street. It was heaven to me. I reveled in the personal contact with the projects and the men involved with Islander. I felt like a boy among men, but Buster Hammond's quiet confidence in me, deserved or not, reinforced my own faith in my strong design ideas.

That was all in the future, however, when I sent Buster my first drawing of a potential Islander 28. Before committing, he decided that we should do a trial project to see if we could work well together. I was up for anything. The project I was given was to transform the company's failing Islander 40 clipper-bowed, center-cockpit ketch, originally a Charlie Davies design, into a viable product.

This was a weird boat, straight out of the Charlie Davies/Hugh Angleman school of character boats. It looked like a little pseudo pirate ship. The Islander 40 was all displacement and full keel with a massive, squared-off stem that stayed square from the tip of the clipper "beak" to the rudder gudgeon. The boat was extremely full in the ends, with an exaggerated sheer that showed little sensitivity and a snubbed bow. I was used to Bill Garden's elongated, sweeping clipper bows and flowing sheerlines, and the Islander bow looked awful to me. The stern was punctuated on the quarters by what we began calling "Errol Flynn" casement windows. While there was nothing wrong with these windows, they made a powerful style statement, one that clearly was not finding many takers, and the first thing I did was to remove them.

Then I added a foot to the bow and made the stem more extended and graceful. Next I redesigned the rig, giving the masts some rake and a bigger foretriangle while adding to the overall sail area by heightening the masts.

I then tackled the interior layout, my primary objective being to provide standing headroom in the passageway from the saloon, or main cabin, to the aft cabin. It's hard to imagine today, but at that

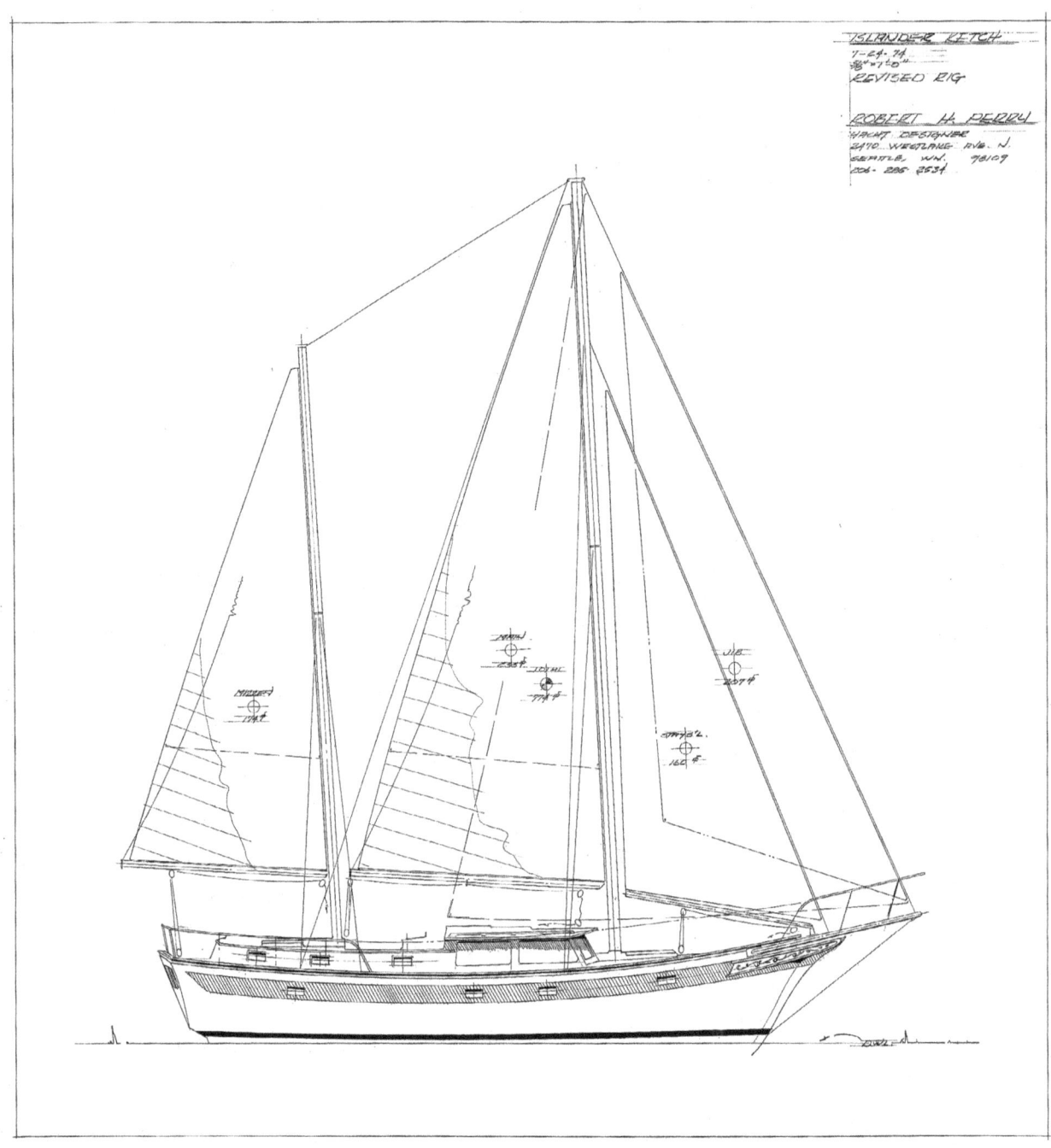

*I modified the Islander 40 sail plan to create this sail plan for the Freeport 41.*

time, center-cockpit boats were uncommon, so I had few models for reference. I could see no way, given the size of the cockpit, to fit a decent passageway, but Islander wanted to retain its labor-intensive cockpit tooling. I don't recall whose idea it was—it may have been mine—but someone in a moment of genius said, "Why don't we just shove the entire cockpit off to one side of the centerline?" This allowed us to make one cockpit coaming narrow and the opposite one wide enough to provide full headroom in the passageway aft. This successful detail was almost invisible on the finished boat.

The Islander 40 thus became the Freeport 41 in August 1975, and it sold well—about 65 boats, I think. In Islander's eyes, this was success. I had passed the first test. I received no royalties for the redesign,

*Hull number 1 of the new Freeport 41s, at anchor in Newport Beach.*

but I did get a $1,500 fee and the green light to design the Islander 28. This was one of the key elements in my decision to move back to Seattle. I had the Valiant contract, and the CT 54 (Chapter 5) was already in production. The Hans Christian 34 (Chapter 6) was well underway, and I felt that with that much work, I should surely be able to make a start with my own office. It was now or never.

The idea behind the Islander 28 was to produce a good, all-around family racing/cruising boat. The IOR had taken hold, and Islander Yachts had suffered a dismal failure with its Gurney-designed Islander 41, an IOR freak with an exaggerated beam pulled too far aft, a tucked-in fanny, and way too much J dimension in the rig. There was nothing unique about these problems—all were endemic in the early IOR days as designers tried to find the magic combination of minimal measured length with maximum sailing length. I'm not sure why Islander Yachts gave up on Gurney. I do know that after a series of super-successful boats, including the revolutionary Windward Passage, Gurney retired to an island in Scotland to become an author of outdoor adventure books. Maybe I still have a chance to be the conductor of the San Francisco Symphony.

Islander wanted its 28 to pay attention to the IOR's scheme of proportions but not be "wrapped around" the IOR measurement points. The IOR might come and go, as all measurement rules do, but the Islander 28 would be more enduring. It was an excellent decision, and I suspect it was Buster's idea. Mom-and-pop sailors of the day were justifiably suspicious of the overly complicated IOR and the complex and confusing shapes it encouraged. The gap between racers and cruisers was widening. The Islander 28 would bridge that gap. Boy! If only we could have looked into the future and seen the complexities of the International Measurement System (IMS) rule and its descendants. By today's criteria, the IOR was child's play. Unfortunately, while it did produce some close and exciting racing, it did not produce what I think of as "wholesome" boats.

My work with Dick Carter had made me keenly aware of the IOR and how to wrap shapes around the measurement points. That's all we did at Carter's office. The predominant IOR midsection shape of the day featured tumblehome, as described in the previous chapter. A boat with tumblehome had its maximum beam below deck level. It was a comely shape with its origins in the sailing ships of old—Nelson's *Victory* had pronounced tumblehome—but I could see the value of wider side decks and a more dish-shaped hull section. I had seen this shape in sketches that Yves-Marie Tanton had been working on at Carter's. We didn't have the chance to use it there, but the shape struck me as a good one.

I tucked in the stern, IOR fashion, but didn't exaggerate it. We needed beam aft for the cockpit. I incorporated the typical IOR bustle in the aft sections, as we still believed then that pulling down the run into a distended bustle shape (a bit like a pregnant trout) would gain us back the sailing length we were giving up with the tucked-in stern. That was an easy decision. In those days, every boat had a bustle. The Valiant 40 had a bustle. Years later, when I finally had the nerve to draw a boat without one, the client got nervous and made me put one on, but that's another story.

The underwater profile of the Islander 28 was much like the IOR boats of the day, with little rocker in the profile and a deep forefoot to take advantage of the IOR's forward depth station (FDS)

# Yacht Design According to Perry

*The original Islander 28 sail plan. This boat to this day looks good to my eye. I like the way I cut off the stern overhang, and I like the general proportions of the design.*

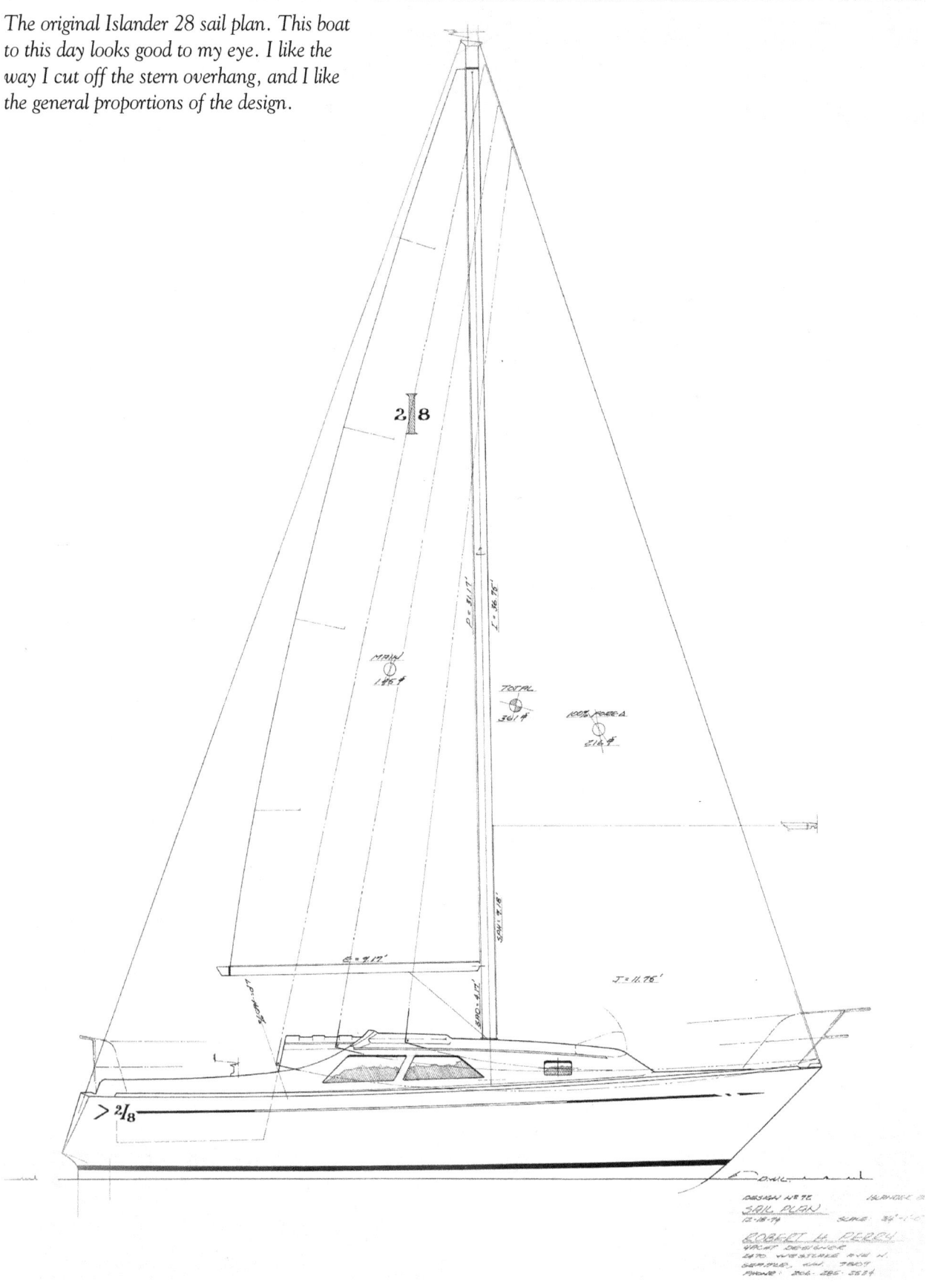

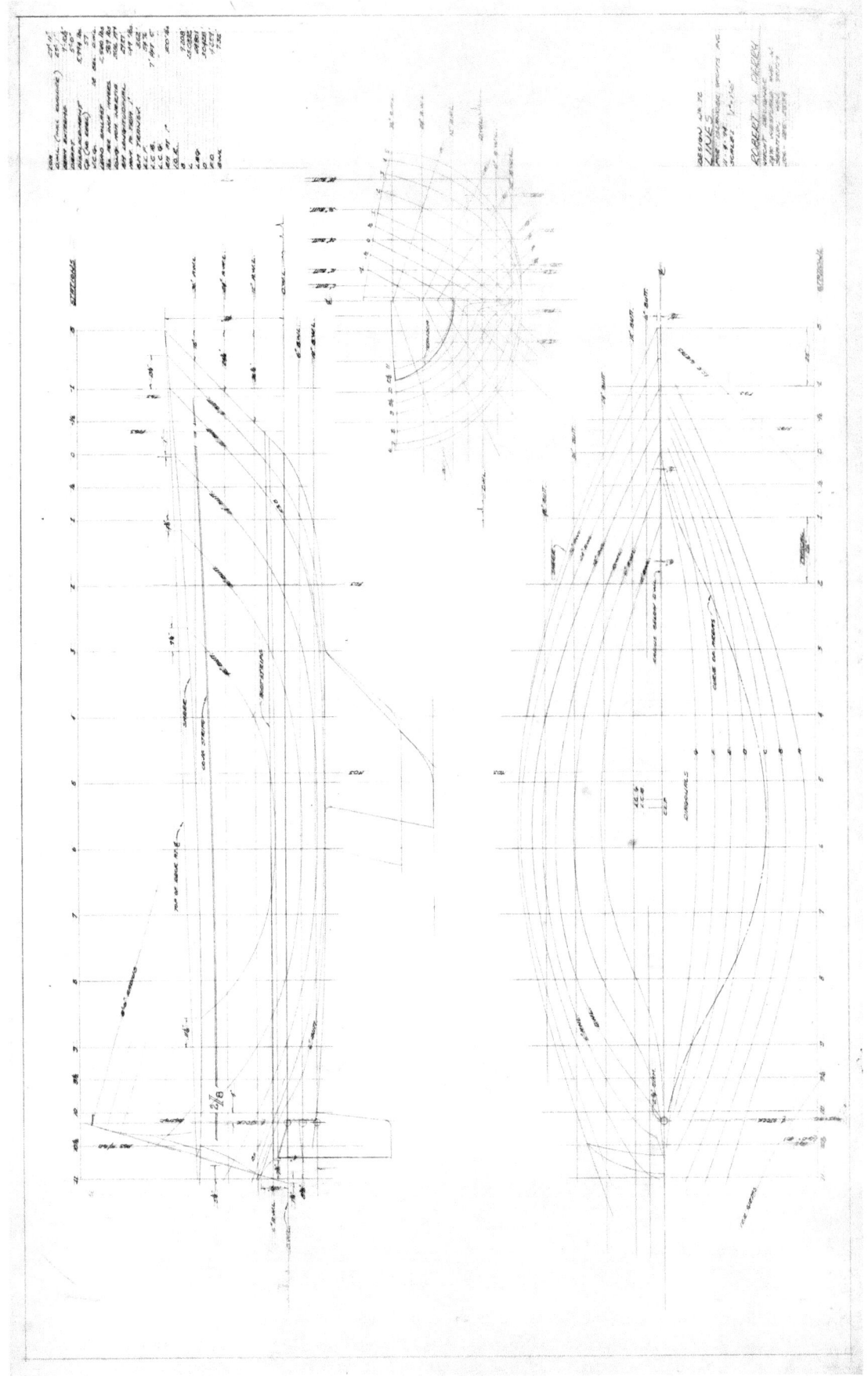

The hull lines of the Islander 28 show the beamy, dishlike sectional shape I used at a time when most boats had some degree of sectional tumblehome. I was inspired to draw this shape after seeing a quarter-tonner that Yves-Marie Tanton was doodling with.

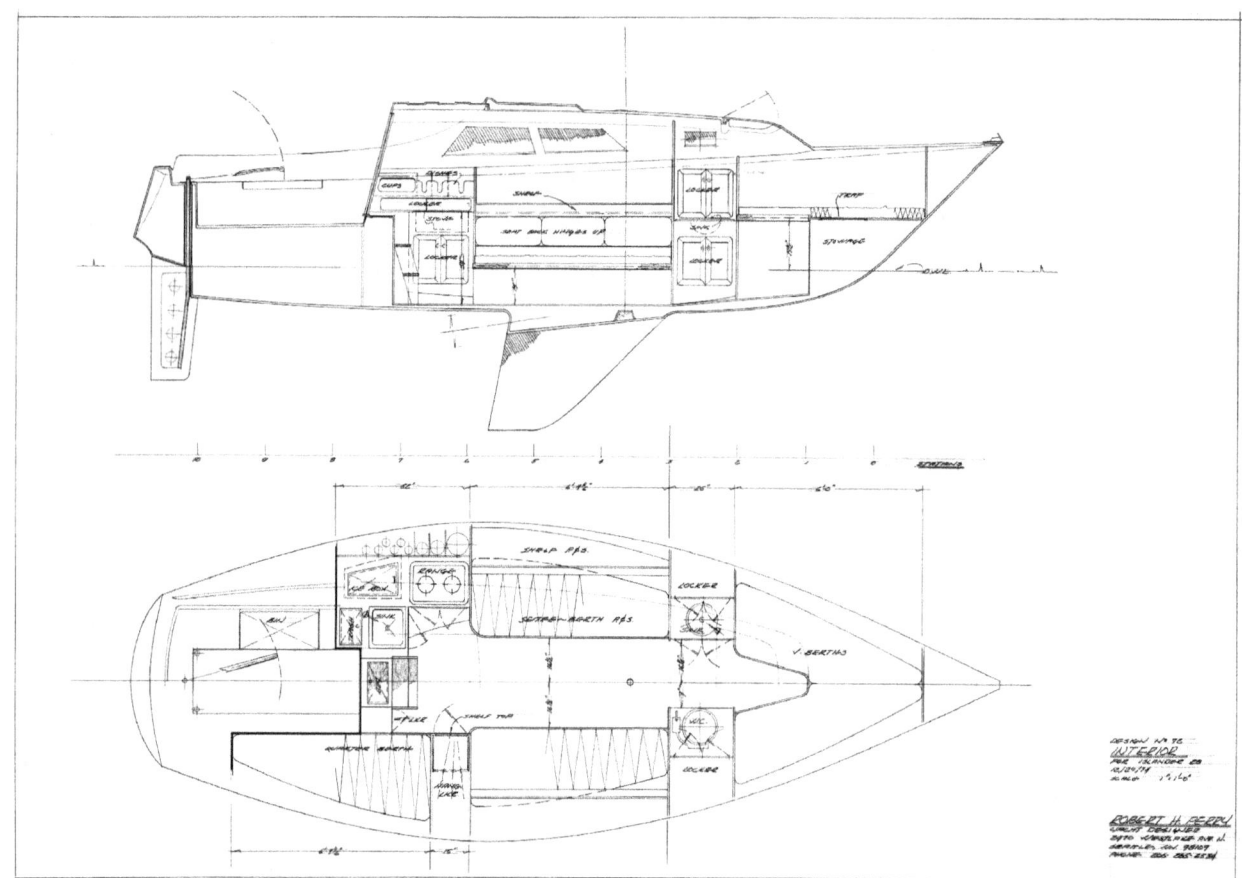

*The Islander 28 interior shows the prop shaft exiting the trailing edge of the keel, as if I was intending a hydraulic motor to be housed in the keel, the way we did it at the Carter office. I'm sure Buster got a chuckle out of that idea. This was changed to a straight-shaft arrangement.*

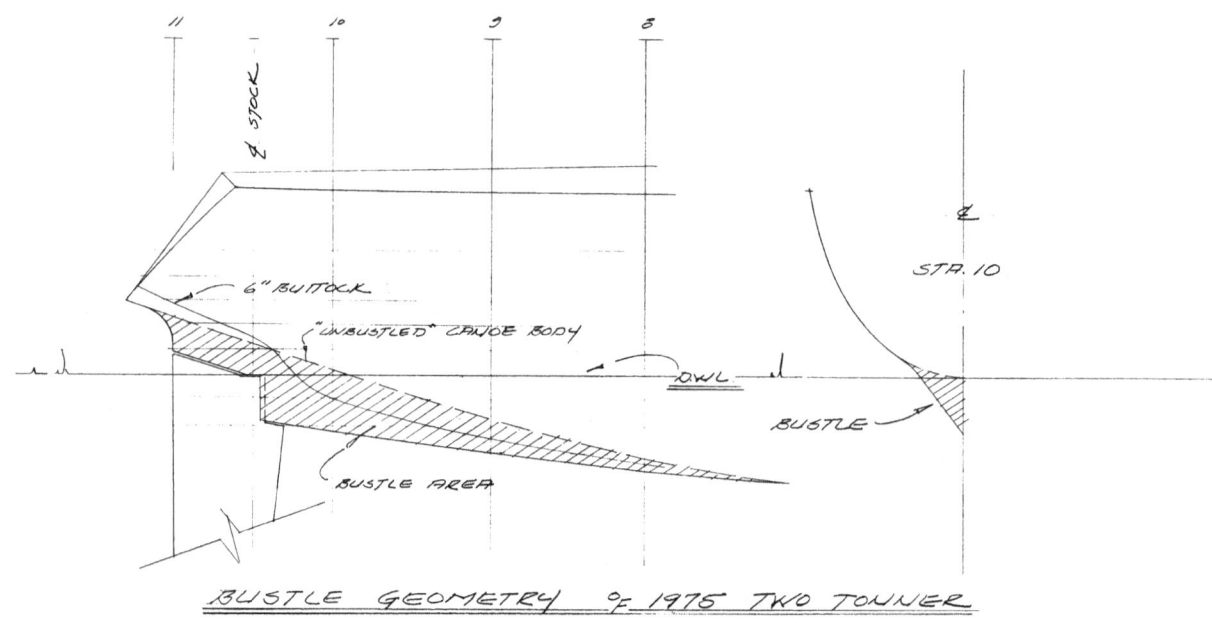

*Bustles added volume aft, thus increasing the prismatic coefficient, but more important they were used in the IOR era to help squeeze the aft girths (AGS and AIGS) together and increase the slope of the aft buttock. This created a shape that the rule treated as having less sailing length than a boat with a flatter run and no bustle.*

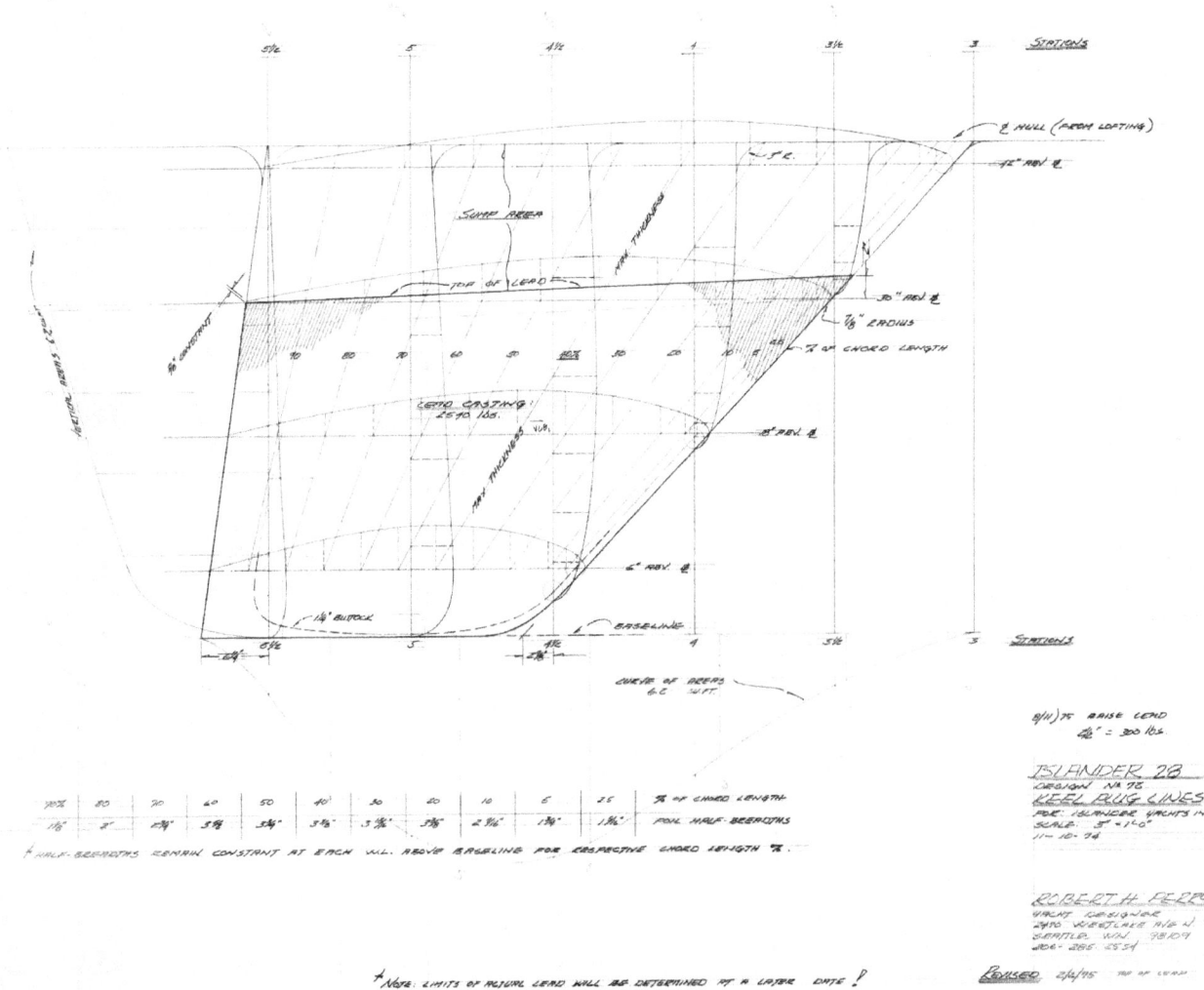

*The original hand-drawn keel design for the Islander 28. Keel designs required demanding drafting and careful geometry, and it took two or more days to draw what computers would later do in 15 minutes. But I miss those days when a dry detail like a keel could result in a handsome drawing.*

measurement. We molded the keel fin into the hull so that the lead could be internal in an effort to save money during construction by eliminating keel bolts and the fairing required with external ballast.

I had a scheduling conflict when the prototype 28 was to be launched in July 1975. I had committed to race with a friend in the Chicago-Mackinac Race. The boat we raced was the slowest-rated boat in the fleet, so my chances of finishing in time to get back to Newport Beach for the launching seemed remote. As luck would have it, the race that year was one of the slowest on record, and my skipper decided to drop out at Frankfort, Michigan, two-thirds of the way up Lake Michigan's west shore. This allowed me time to hop a bus, get back to Chicago, and fly out to Los Angeles just in time for the launching. I can remember vividly parking my rental car, walking through the parking lot to the launch area, and seeing the little 28 sitting in its cradle. I was amazed. It looked exactly like my drawings. When we launched the boat, it floated perfectly on its lines and looked beautiful. How could you not say your own baby is beautiful? My baby was gorgeous.

Islander 28s began to sell. The Seattle dealer, Chuck Buffiou, was selling them like crazy. Furthermore, they were being raced and doing well. I placed first overall in Seattle's Point Hudson race in a friend's 28. Islander 28 owners ordered custom,

*An Islander 28 with a medium-sized genoa, as it appeared in one of the very early Islander 28 brochures.*

*A trim little Islander 28 belonging to my friends Elisa and Mark.*

*Another shot of Elisa and Mark's Islander 28, showing the boat's truncated stern and broad beam. The narrow cabin trunk and overall proportions still look great to me after 30 years.*

tapered, two-spreader rigs to "turbo" their hot little boats. Soon, Islander's production line was dominated by the 28s with a few Freeport 41s and Islander 36s thrown in. We had a good boat, and we all knew it. It was time for another new Islander.

This is where the story begins to follow what would become a recurring theme in my office. A boatbuilder asks a designer for a new boat to reenergize his faltering business. The designer prepares a trailblazing design, and the boat is a success. A second project is commissioned to follow up that success, but the builder now believes he has seen into the heart of things and knows exactly what it will take to make the new design as successful as the first one. Whereas the designer created the first project with a relatively free hand, now he is swamped with dictates, and the new boat suffers. This, at least, is my perspective on the Islander 32.

If you count the number of boats sold—more than 500—and owner satisfaction, the Islander 32 was a tremendous success. But I see it differently. Islander Yachts wanted interior volume for this boat. If the 28-footer could get away with 10 feet of beam, they reasoned, why couldn't the 32-footer have 11? This gave the 32 a length-to-beam ratio (L/B) of 2.9, which is fat by any standard. The 28's L/B was even lower at 2.8, but the 28 had a dramatically different midsection shape, one with a narrow BWL and consequently low initial stability.

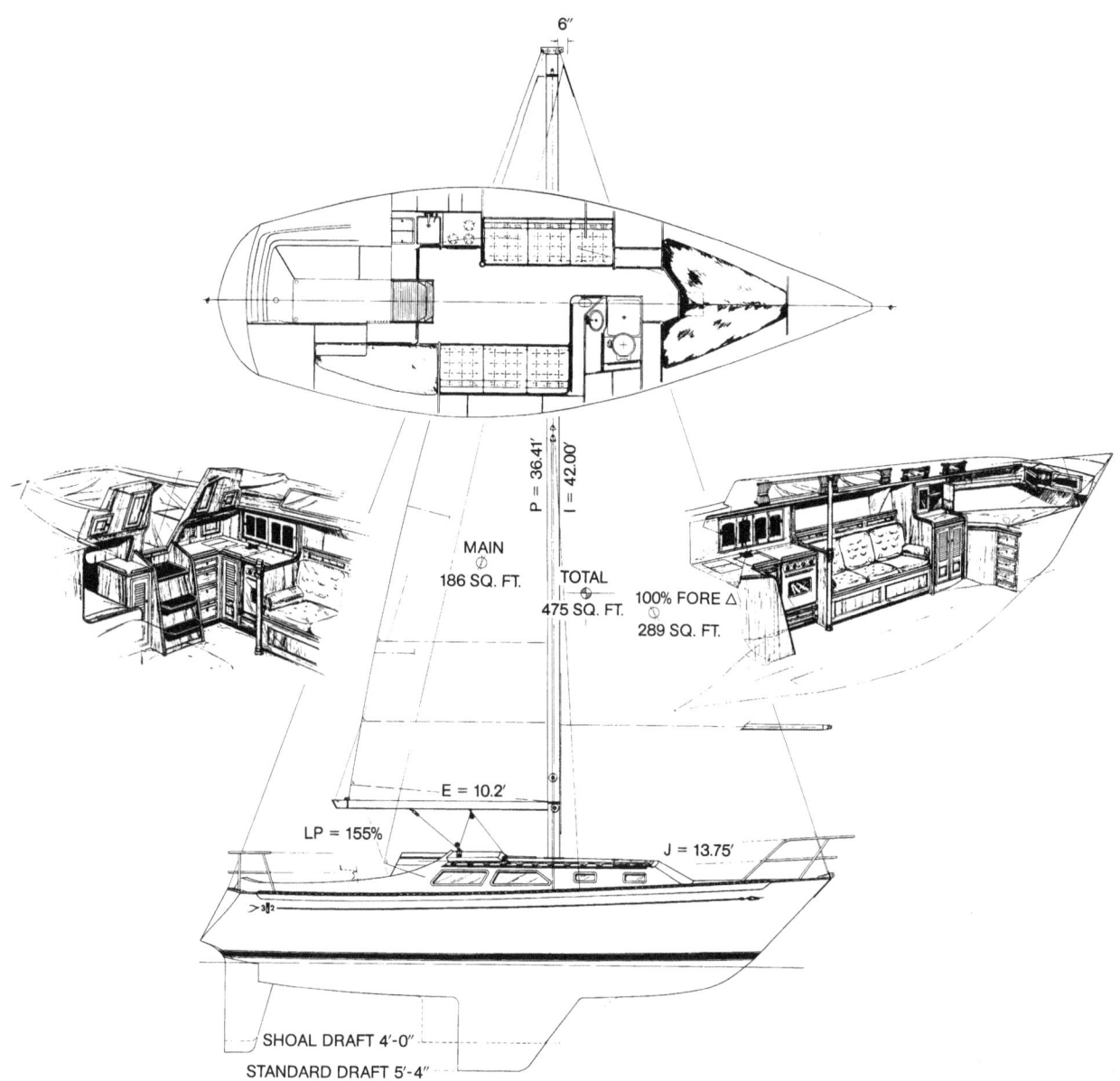

*This factory drawing of the Islander 32 shows the "California rococo" interior. The mast is probably about 10 inches too far aft for ideal helm balance, but this location worked great for the interior layout.*

The IOR rule promoted low initial stability in order to optimize a boat's center of gravity factor (CGF) measurement. It was just one more of the IOR measurement factors around which a designer had to wrap his boat. The 28 was a fat boat if you measured at deck level, but its dish-shaped midsection made the waterline beam fairly narrow, thus reducing initial stability. Unfortunately, low initial stability has never been high on any buyer's list of wants. Everyone loves a stiff boat. Islander Yachts wanted the 32 to have better initial stability than the 28, and initial stability is almost exclusively a function of waterline beam. Therefore, I broadened the waterline beam and incorporated a harder turn to the bilge, reshaping the 28's dish-shaped section into something boxier. The result was more interior volume and a stiff boat, two things everybody loves. Probably this was why Islander sold so many 32s. Still, I never felt that the boat sailed as well as the 28. I didn't like its overly stiff feel, and its IOR-proportioned, large J-dimensioned rig gave it a little too much weather helm for my taste. Because the

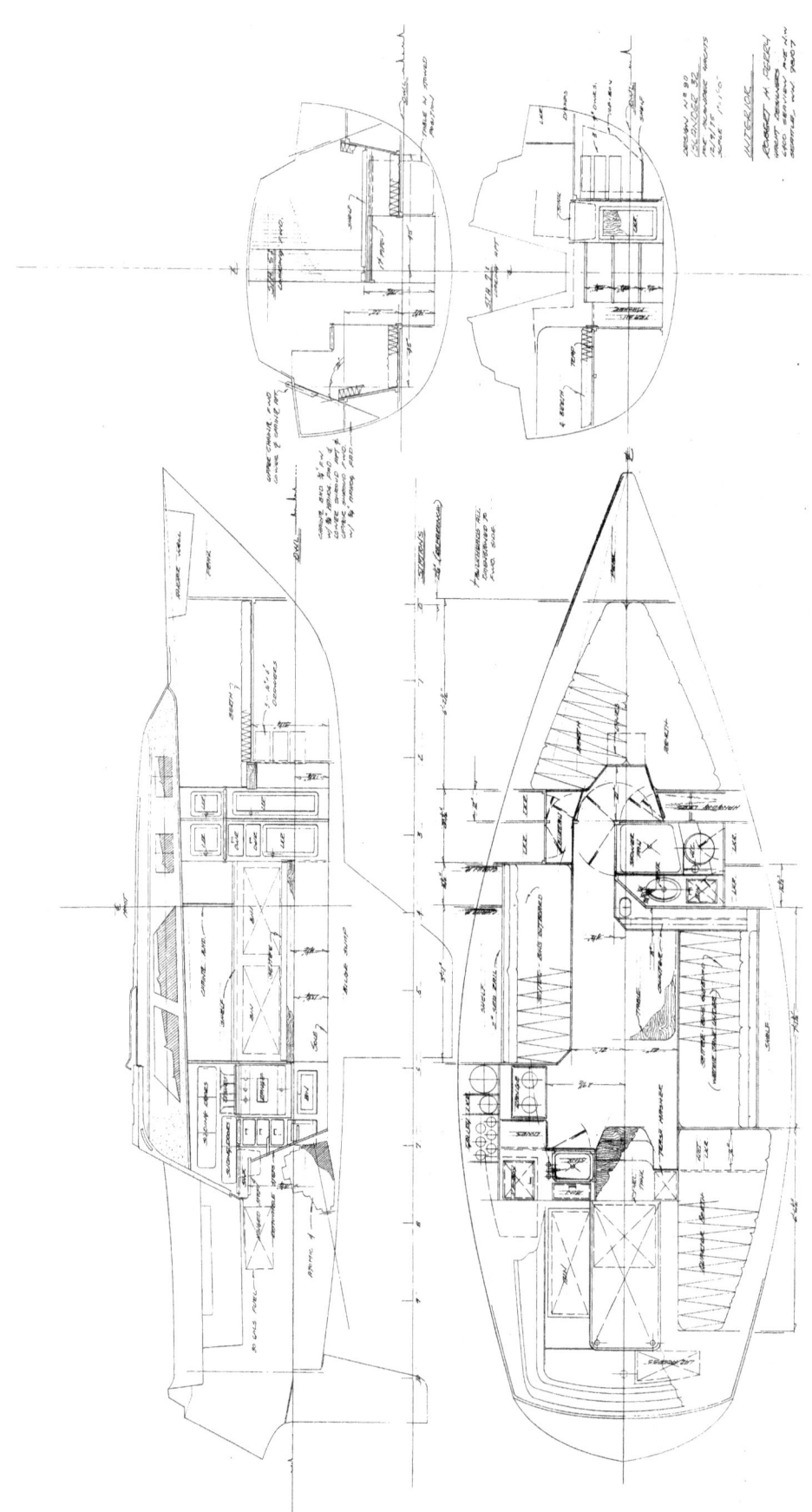

*Looking at my drawing of the Islander 32 interior reminds me how much fun I was having with the drafting process.*

boat had so much stability, there was little impetus to reduce sail. As a result, the weather helm would get worse when the wind blew.

I could have made a better boat if I'd known then what I know now. I could have moved the mast forward, but in those days the IOR encouraged small mainsails and big genoas. I simply put the mast where everyone else was putting theirs. Maybe I could have pulled the keel aft a bit while maintaining the desired longitudinal flotation. Instead, I gave it the "Peterson" profile keel that had been so successful on Doug Peterson's one-tonner *Ganbare*. It was the keel du jour.

I'll say this about the Islander 32: When you opened the huge companionway hatch and looked below, you saw a voluminous saloon finished in the classic California rococo style that Hank McCormick loved. When I was preparing the drawings for the boat, Hank insisted that I raise the freeboard two inches to give us even more interior volume. Marketing people are always after interior volume. Designers are always after speed. At that time, I didn't think I was in a position to argue, so I raised the freeboard.

When we launched the prototype 32, we all stood on the dock to get a look at our new baby while the crew put the boat through a big, lazy circle in front of us. As the boat made its way slowly back to the dock, Hank turned to me and said, "We should have taken two inches out of the freeboard." I exploded, albeit quietly and courteously.

I still think I could have designed a better boat if I'd been left alone with the design decisions. Would it have sold as well? Probably not. Over time, a designer has to come to grips with these things. Islander 32 owners love their boats, and that should be good enough.

I was involved in the earliest meetings that determined the next Islander model, and by this time I was clearly their established "out-house" designer (as opposed to being an in-house designer like the staff at Catalina and Hunter). When we had examined all the model possibilities and marketing targets, the boat was to be a new Freeport model in the style of the old Freeport 41. The new Freeport would be a 36-footer, traditional in styling but with modern design advantages.

Hank had in mind a 35-foot Bill Lapworth design that Cal had produced in modest numbers. The head would be forward and there would be a

*This photo from Islander's first brochure for the Islander 32 shows a genoa that is way too large by today's standards, but that's the way we did it back then. The genoa lead car is way aft, adjacent to the sheet winch.*

Pullman-style double berth off to one side. I don't remember much about the Lapworth boat except its handsome profile, but Hank had an idea that would revolutionize the interiors of boats less than 45 feet, and that still persists today. Pullman-berth staterooms and head-forward arrangements are commonplace today. Good old, crushed-green-velvet, leisure-suited Hank.

The first design challenge with the Freeport 36 was that there simply was not enough room beneath the large, deep cockpit for an engine. The solution was to put the engine beneath the saloon sole. However, if I gave the boat the displacement and midsection I wanted, there would be insufficient room there for a Perkins 4-108, which was the automatic choice for an auxiliary in those pre-Yanmar days. So I backed up, put my pencil down, and gave it a thought or two. Then I started drawing again.

This time I drew a midsection with no regard for the required engine volume. When I had the

*The Freeport 36 has always been a good sailer despite its conservative shape and style. It would have been even better if I'd pushed the mast 12 inches forward, but this design was done when big foretriangles were the rage.*

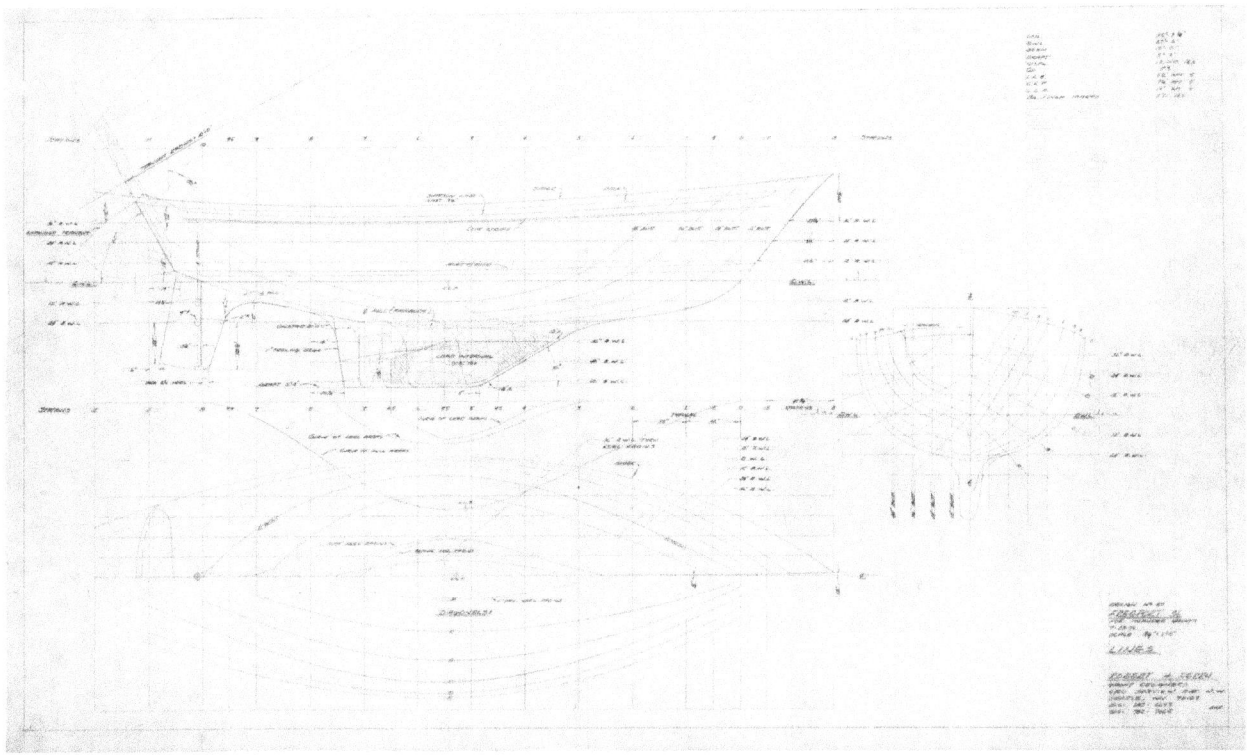

*These hand-drawn lines for the Freeport 36 show the integrating of the keel shape with the hull, making an almost wineglass section. This allowed sufficient volume in the bilges for a Perkins 4-108 diesel.*

midsection the way I wanted it, accommodating the displacement and prismatic I had in mind, I drew in the engine. Of course, the engine section pierced the midsection and stuck out the sides of the bilge. Then I added a preliminary low-aspect-ratio keel shape with a large garboard radius to fair it into the midsection. If I made this "tuck" radius large enough, it provided enough volume to enclose the Perkins 4-108. The result was a traditional-looking section, almost wineglass-configured, and it worked. I designed the rest of the hull around that midsection.

The Freeport 36 featured another innovation, too, but I have no idea who came up with the idea. Buster, Hank, and Steve have died, and Bob Babson is missing in action, so I'll take credit for it. We decided to incorporate in the transom a drop-down door with a boarding ladder built into its inboard side. With the door down and half filled with water, it required some effort to raise, but despite that, it worked well. Today transom doors are commonplace.

Amazingly, the Freeport 36 sailed very well. I had tried hard to make the hull a good shape, but I had been concerned that the large-radius garboards would reduce the apparent aspect ratio of the keel fin and hurt performance. I'm certain it did to some extent, but still, the boat speed and balance were good. I raced an early Freeport 36 against a Gurney-designed Islander 36, and we ran boat for boat throughout the race.

Islander eventually produced a Freeport 37 model that was the Freeport 36 with a tubular bowsprit added. This further improved the boat's helm balance and provided a convenient home for double anchor rollers.

The head-forward layout was a winner, but Islander soon decided to make a V-berth model with the head aft. I had nothing to do with that layout, but it became the layout of choice. Today, however, I think that the Pullman version is the more sought-after layout among buyers of used Freeports. Likewise, without consulting me, Islander tried to cut some costs by replacing the heavy and expensive Perkins 4-108 with a lighter and cheaper Volkswagen Rabbit marine adaptation called the Pathfinder diesel. It was half the weight of the Perkins, and that weight, given the location of the engine, was in effect taken out of the keel. At the same time, Islander replaced the original lead ballast with a smaller amount of iron ballast. I was unaware of the modification until I got a call one day from an owner.

"My Freeport 36 is very tender," the owner told me.

"Well, I've sailed the boat and I don't think it's tender at all," I said.

The caller went on to tell me he had a Freeport 36 with iron ballast and a Pathfinder diesel. I assured him there was no such beast, but he just as firmly assured me there was. Clearly it was time to call Islander and ask a few questions. Yes, Islander said, they had used Pathfinder diesels in all the most recent boats, and yes, they had produced some boats with iron ballast instead of the lead ballast I had designed into the boat. Lead weighs 700 pounds per cubic foot but cast iron just 450, and there simply was not enough volume in that molded fiberglass keel to make up the difference. Therefore, Islander had gone light on the ballast. Coupled with an engine that weighed 350 pounds less than the Perkins, the result was a tender boat. Builders commonly modify their boats without talking over the changes with the designer, and this is a prime example.

Islander built a lot of Freeport 36s—about 350, I think—including a handful of center-cockpit models that went into the charter trade. I can remember standing on the Islander shop floor when almost every boat under construction was my design. (Islander also built the Peterson 40, a very nice boat.) Royalties poured in, and I felt good about the connection in every way. In the early 1980s we even started on a new line of models to replace the old Islander 36, 28, and 32.

The first of the new Islanders was a 34-footer that we produced in both deep-draft and winged-keel versions. Hulls number 1 and 2 included one of each version, and we sea-trialed the two boats extensively over two days to see which keel was superior. The differences were minimal. Both boats sailed great, with neither able to earn a distinct and consistent advantage over the other.

The Islander 34 was a well-balanced, well-behaved boat with a great feel and a good turn of speed, but it was quickly eclipsed in the market by the big, fat-fannied French models that soon became the dominant type, once again proving that buyers put interior volume ahead of performance. My pal Joe Golberg, who ran the Seattle North Sails loft,

*With help from Dave Vacanti I designed a wing keel for the Islander 34 to provide a shoal-draft option. This configuration worked exceptionally well in two days of boat-on-boat testing against a deep-draft version.*

called me early one Monday morning to rave about the way the Islander 34 sailed. Joe knew boats, and his opinion was good enough for me. But for Islander it didn't matter anyway.

After building a half dozen 34s, Islander abruptly shut its doors in 1985 or 1986. The company was owned by an East Coast conglomerate called Fuqua Industries, and rumor has it that Fuqua decided the prime Orange County real estate that Islander occupied was worth more to them than a boatbuilding company. With little or no notice, the doors were shut one Friday and the workers sent home for the last time. Poor old, crushed-velvet Hank was on vacation at the time, and he pulled into the parking lot Monday morning to find the place deserted. Nobody had told him.

The Islander 34 tooling was sold to Nordic Yachts of Bellingham, Washington, where another half dozen 34s were built. Then Nordic fell victim to the villainous luxury tax, which had been imposed on yachts by the federal government and drove up the retail cost of a typical boat by more than 7.5 per-

The Islander 34 was designed as the IOR was on its way out, and thus owed its shape to no particular measurement or handicap rule. I think that is one of the reasons, along with modest beam, it turned out to be such a nice, well-rounded boat.

cent. Before it was lifted, the luxury tax drove a lot of builders out of business.

I had calls from builders who were interested in buying the rest of the Islander tooling, but nothing came of them.

Still, I had the pleasure of working with Islander for 10 years. It was one of those team efforts in which all the members clicked. I was lucky. Islander Yachts was critical to establishing my credibility early in my career. Today, the Islander 28 looks as fresh to my eye as ever. I think of it as a little gem.

I only wish I could send a copy of this book to Buster.

## *According to Perry*
# SHEERLINES AND BOW PROFILES

No line influences the aesthetic appeal of a design more than its sheerline. This can appear to follow the top of the bulwark in some boats, although by definition the sheerline is the intersection of the hull with the deck. The curvature of the sheerline is referred to as *spring*. A conventional spring gives you a sheer that, in the profile view, is lower in the middle than at the bow and the stern. In a boat with "reverse" sheer spring, the sheer appears to be higher in the middle than in the ends. Today most boats have conventional sheer spring, but you do see reverse sheer on some racing and high-performance boats. Many catamarans are designed with reverse sheer to maximize the headroom in the hulls.

Although practical factors such as a need for freeboard or interior volume will sometimes play a role, the degree of sheer spring incorporated into a design is generally an aesthetic choice. There are no hard rules for how to draw a sheer, but there are several things to keep in mind. First and foremost, sheer spring has to be a function of the designer's intended style of boat. Second, it is to some extent a function of the three-dimensional, actual linear length of the sheerline. In short, the sheer you see in a two-dimensional profile or sail plan is not the sheer you will see in real life. Think of laying a flexible tape measure along the top of the caprail. Double-enders have a longer sheerline because they have no transom to truncate the sheer, and a beamy boat has a longer sheer than a narrow boat of the same length because the beamy boat's deck edge has to follow a more pronounced outboard curve (when viewed from overhead). Thus, both a beamy boat and a double-ender need more sheer spring than a narrow boat with a transom stern. A very narrow boat, such as a meter-class boat, can get by with almost no sheer spring.

In fact, you can simply use a straight line for the sheer on almost any boat. That straight line may look awkward on paper and may not suit your aesthetic goals, but due to the contour of the hull, once the boat heels your way, you will see a concave, conventional-looking sheer.

A straight-line sheer is the ultimate "planar sheer," which is any sheer that can be described by a single plane cutting through the topsides of the boat. Usually, with a conventional sheerline that plane is higher in the bow than in the stern, and it slopes downward and outboard from the boat's fore-and-aft centerline. If you were to tilt the plane upward from the centerline, you would get a reverse sheer spring. If you use software such as AutoYacht to draw your sheer, you can choose the "planar sheer" command, then choose the coordinates to describe your plane, and the computer will do the hard work. Back in the days when hull lines were drawn by hand, the easiest way to get a planar sheer without a long and drawn-out geometric calculation was to carve a half model of the hull. Then the designer would hold the half model deck-down on the drawing board and try to make contact with the board top along

## According to Perry: Sheetlines and Bow Profiles

*Here I'm demonstrating planar sheer with a half-hull model. A sheer is planar if (and only if) the model can make contact with the tabletop along its entire stem-to-stern sheer simultaneously, as here, almost. (Jill Perry)*

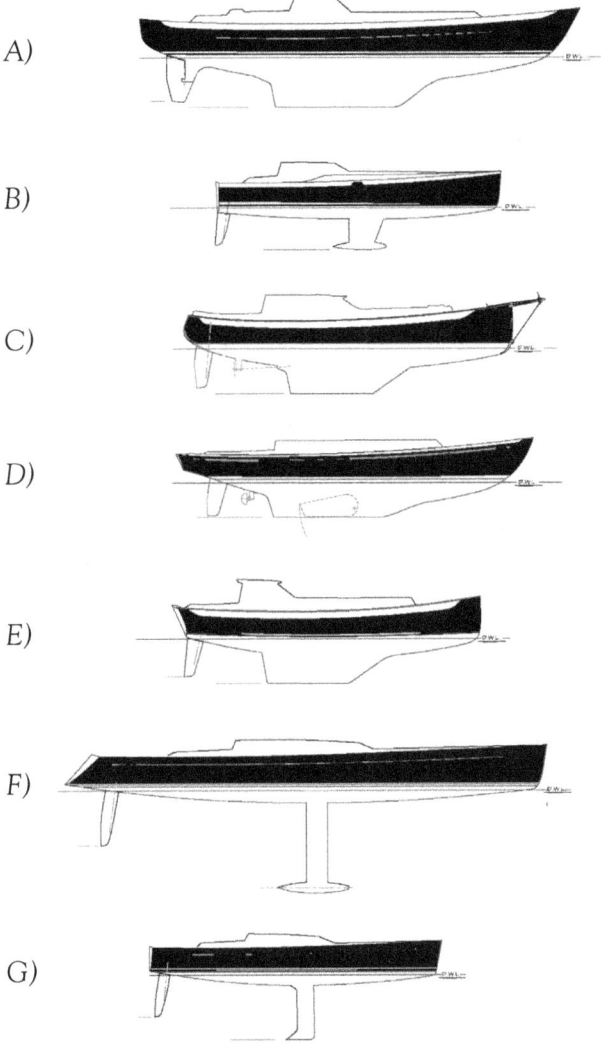

*An assortment of sheerlines with their associated bow and stern profiles. Top to bottom: A) A 60-foot double-ender with a Crealock-styled stern and spoon bow (L/B = 3.53; D/L = 226); B) Bernie's "boat-for-a-box" showing a raised sheer forward and an almost plumb bow and transom (L/B = 5.25; D/L = 102); C) A 45-footer for Ken showing generous sheer spring, a tumblehome canoe stern, and tumblehome in the bow profile (L/B = 3.18; D/L = 230); D) Jim's 48-footer with a strong sheer and traditional transom rake, right out of the late 1960s (L/B = 3.68; D/L = 275); E) Matt's new boat showing pronounced sheer spring to go with its full ends and traditional transom rake. This bow, too, shows slight tumblehome in profile (L/B = 3.23; D/L = 229); F) Dick's Icon has a subtle sheer spring; a shapely—not quite plumb—straight bow; and a reverse transom (L/B = 4.43; D/L = 68); G) Paul's Amati shows a very straight but not flat sheer, a dead plumb transom, and a straight stem (L/B = 3.73; D/L = 96).*

the entire sheerline simultaneously. If and only if this was possible, the sheer was planar.

On the other hand, the designer may not want a planar sheer. Lots of famous designers have ignored planar sheers, and many of my own designs lack them. My double-enders would all look like mallards in heat if they had planar sheers. Typical beamy cruising boats can have pleasing nonplanar sheers if the designer has a good eye for springing the batten, whether it's an old-fashioned plastic spline held down by spline weights or a computer-generated nonuniform rational B (NURB) spline. Here the eye is king. Some designers are much better at it than others. I love the sheers of Philip Rhodes, Bill Garden, German Frers, Rob Humphreys, and K. Aage Nielsen.

A nonplanar sheer may be just right for a particular design, but it will not look fair from every perspective. The advantage of a planar sheer is that it will always appear fair, no matter your viewpoint. The next time you walk through a boatyard, glance up at the decks of the hauled boats. If the sheer on a boat tends to wander from a concave to a convex shape toward the bow as you look up at it, that's a surefire sign that it's not planar.

The bow profile will have a big effect on what type of sheer should be used. Thirty or more years ago, most boats had spoon bows, which are convex in profile. The Bermuda 40 and the Cal 40 are good examples. These boats were designed to the Cruising Club of America (CCA) rule, which encouraged fullness forward as an easy way to pick up sailing length when the boat heeled, and a spoon bow is a good way to get that fullness. Spoon bows carry a lot of reserve buoyancy, and they do increase the sailing length by a small amount as the boat heels. However, they pay for that with an increase in drag. To reduce drag, the angle of entry (usually measured as the half-angle of entry) has to be sharp. My Nordic 44 (see "According to Perry: The Hull-Lines Plan") has a moderate half-angle of entry at 21 degrees. *Amati* (Chapter 15) has a fine half-angle of 17.5 degrees. The stocky little Baba 30 (Chapter 7) has an entry half-angle of 25 degrees.

During the days of the International Offshore Rule (IOR) in the 1970s and early 1980s, forward girth measurements were taken in the bow. Girths of a length determined by B max had to fit on the bow. The farther forward these girths fit, the fuller the bow, and the rule saw this as indicative of more sailing length and penalized accordingly. Under the IOR, therefore, bows got finer and sharper in order to bring the forward girths aft, and bow profiles were almost always straight lines with considerable overhang to accentuate the girth-length difference from the forward girth station (FGS) to the after bow girth station (FIGS). Straight, raked stems were in. Spoon bows were out.

The IOR rule fell from favor when it resulted in distorted and misshapen boats, and it was supplanted by the International Measurement System (IMS) by about 1990 in the United States. This time, the rule makers kept their measurement formulas under wraps in order to prevent designers from drawing hulls to beat the rule. Needless to say, designers soon discovered that the IMS penalty for bow overhang was inconsistent with actual gains in boat speed. Immersing skinny bow sections does not result in much additional sailing length. For a bow overhang to contribute to sailing length, the bow has to have some fullness. The next time you see an America's Cup Class boat, notice how fine the angle of entry is, then note how full the U-shaped bow sections are. These boats are trying to minimize pitching while gaining sailing length through immersed volume.

Thus, one result of the IMS was to get us used to seeing plumb or nearly plumb stems. If you want to maximize boat speed for a given LOA, you will maximize waterline length—that much is obvious. The easiest way to do this is to eliminate the bow overhang and go with a plumb or nearly plumb stem. (You do need some overhang aft to clean up the flow at the stern when the boat heels.) If you eliminate the bow overhang of a typical IOR-influenced, 40-foot cruising boat from the 1970s, you may gain as much as five feet of DWL. The boat will be faster. You see this not just in IMS boats, but also, dramatically, in any of the "box rule" boats, such as the TransPac 52 or the International 14s. These boats are designed to a maximum LOA, and they have no bow overhang at all.

## Box Rules

*A "box rule" is a measurement system that enables yachts to compete on a boat-for-boat basis without any time-correction factor. The most famous box rules are those for the International 14 dinghy class, the much newer TransPac 52 class, and the radical Open 40 and Open 60 classes.*

*Imagine a box in which the boat must fit, and this box controls LOA, maximum beam, displacement, draft, and sail area. That's a simple box rule. However, rules like that for the TransPac 52 are actually a box within a box, controlling minimum as well as maximum dimensions. The result is that the boats within a class will be of very similar design and can race essentially as one-designs without actually being one-designs.*

Some bow overhang may be good for a cruising boat, however. Overhang helps, for example, if you want to keep the anchor and chain away from the stem of the boat, and it also buys you more space on deck and a drier boat in a seaway due to the bow's flare. Bow overhang may also work aesthetically for you and produce a more classically styled, elegant look.

As of 2007, the IMS has gone the way of the IOR, since it, too, eventually encouraged contrived hull shapes. Today it seems that any measurement-based rule is doomed to failure. Only the empirically based Performance Handicap Rating Fleet (PHRF) rule has endured. A boat's PHRF handicap is based on the historical performance in local waters of boats of its type, and the handicap is modified as fresh race results are compiled. The PHRF eliminates rule-beating advantages for wealthy boatowners, and it eliminates a lot of work for designers, but it also works well for casual cruiser-racers.

The remaining relevance of the IMS for cruising boat design is that the velocity-prediction programs designers use are based on the IMS. If you are not working to a measurement rule, however, your choice of bow style becomes a matter of picking a shape that enhances the look of the boat, then fine-tuning that shape so that you get the most efficiency and the longest sailing length.

## Chapter Five
# CT Yachts and the Ta Chaio Story

In Chapter 2 I introduced the 47-foot ketch I began drawing for John Edwards in 1972 after retrieving an unanswered inquiry letter from Jay Benford's office. The narrative in that earlier chapter veered off in another direction, but now it's time to finish that story. When the preliminary plans were complete, Edwards took the drawings to Taiwan and met with the Ta Chaio yard. Upon returning to the United States, he called me with the startling news that building a boat there was even cheaper than he'd anticipated, which meant that we could make the boat bigger. He flew to Seattle again, and we spent another two days at the drawing board in the corner of my dining room.

With me drawing and Edwards directing the pencil, we produced a 54-foot clipper-bowed ketch that John called the Hans Christian 54. It was to be the first in a line of Hans Christians that John planned to build in Taiwan and sell in America. I enjoyed working with John, who could have passed for Wally Cox in *Hollywood Squares*. John is gone now. Business associates would later describe him as a dreamer and an eccentric, and I guess that's right, but he had an excellent eye and a good command of aesthetics. I did the drawing, but he knew what he wanted drawn.

I was familiar with the type—I'd been sketching it for years. The boat John wanted was right out of the pages of Bill Garden's design portfolio. My job was to make it my own and try to wrench my style away from Garden's influence so that I could feel

"original." The basic hull form would include a clipper-bowed, long-keeled, traditional profile with a heart-shaped transom and plenty of tumblehome. The boat would have wineglass sections and internal iron ballast.

This design was well underway a year before I began the Valiant, and the idea of a performance cruiser had not yet entered my mind. Still, I did not want the boat to be a dog, so I used what meager skills I had at the time to design a shapely hull that would sail well. I gave its bilge a firm turn and cut back the leading edge of the keel as far as I dared.

For construction details I called Ted Brewer, who agreed to design the structure for a modest fee. Ted produced some quick drawings, and I translated them into a laminate schedule and structural layout. Ironically, the yard used none of this, and to this day I do not know where their laminate schedule came from. My structural scheme called for multiple hat-section longitudinals, but the yard used a beefy single-skin laminate with no longitudinals. In those days, especially in Taiwan, there was no structural problem that could not be overcome with more mat and roving.

In the early 1970s, drawings were all done by hand, and I was proud of my hull lines, but Ta Chaio had trouble deciphering exactly how I wanted the top of the transom to be shaped. Their solution was to mail me, in a big box, a 3/4"=1'0" cedar model of the hull, completed except for its transom crown, along with a letter asking me to finish the model and send it back. I have a skill or two in my repertoire, but woodworking isn't one of them, and the thought of having to carve on this model terrified me. I bought a Surform plane—really just a flat wood rasp—thinking that with this tool I would not be able to take off too much wood at a time. It worked, and I managed to carve one half of the transom perfectly. I sent the model back with a note telling them to make the other side the same. I knew there was no way I could get both sides to match.

When the design was nearly finished and the prototype was under construction in Taiwan, I left Seattle to go to work for Dick Carter. I was the only designer in Carter's office at the time who had an "outside" project going, and I was inordinately proud of that, but the other designers couldn't relate to what looked to their eyes like a distinctly West Coast type of boat. "Plank lines! Why would anyone want to see plank lines on a fiberglass hull?" To me, plank lines were salty, straight out of the West Coast workboat tradition. In Carter's office, surrounded by one-tonners and custom Admiral's Cup racers, there was nothing about my 54-footer that made sense.

I finished the design. My fee was to be $700, and I had been paid half of it. The other half was overdue. I don't know the details of the problem that ensued between Edwards and the yard, but I can speculate. In the early days of yacht building in Taiwan, taking advantage of the Taiwanese builders was part of the game. Of course, these builders were in most cases good, honest, and clever businessmen, and while they might sign an unfair contract written in English, they would not honor it once they realized they had been taken advantage of.

It was a frigid winter's day in Boston when I got a call at the office from C.T. Chen, the president of Ta Chaio—which in Mandarin means Big Bridge. In halting English, C.T. wanted to know how much I had been paid and who really owned the design. I explained that Edwards had not paid me the entire amount, and in my naïveté, I said that if C.T. paid the remainder of the design fee, he could own the design. I had started another design with Edwards, a 34-foot double-ender, but that project had gone sour when Edwards turned it into a 36-footer and refused to pay me anything for my work. All things considered, I did not feel it was in my best interest to back Edwards in his battle with C.T. A few days later, I received via Express Mail a check from C.T. for $750. I ran out and bought a warm coat, then I wrote a letter to C.T. saying that he was now the sole owner of the design rights to the 54-footer. C.T. produced the letter in court in Taiwan and took over the project. The boat that was to have been the first Hans Christian was now the CT 54. John Edwards went on to produce hundreds of Hans Christian yachts, but never a Hans Christian 54, and he and I never spoke again.

About three months later, I received a package in the mail from the Ta Chaio yard with photos of my 54-footer finished and rolled out of the shed. I was amazed. It looked great. By early 1974 boats were being sold in the United States, and I sea-trialed the first one. Blasting around San Francisco Bay on my very first design was something I'll never forget. The boat sailed well. It had a good turn of speed, and the helm balance was perfect, as far as I could tell with the boat's hydraulic steering. Ted Brewer had convinced me to increase the size of the rig, and this turned out to have been a good move. It was a great-looking boat, salty as hell. The yard would go on to build 100 CT 54s. I chartered one for two weeks in the British Virgin Islands and had a great time on it. It was a real pirate ship.

It was while designing the CT 54 that I came to know Ted Brewer. Ted's design office was in Maine at the time, and he was doing well. At one point during our discussions about the CT 54, Ted remarked that I was a "yacht designer." I thought to myself, "Heck, if *Ted* thinks I'm a yacht designer, I must be one." I had no degree to tell me I had made the grade, but Ted ought to know. I started putting "yacht designer" after my name instead of the more humble "boat designer" I had been using.

The CT 54 was built in two versions, one with my deck and layout and one modified by the yard. I had nothing to do with the yard's modifications, but apparently this was their answer to a headroom issue in my version. I, of course, considered my deck better looking, but the yard's deck was not all bad and did offer some interior options that helped the boat sell. I think about three-quarters of the 54s had the yard's deck.

In May 1976, when I went to Taiwan for the first time, I met C.T., S.T., C.S., and Wayne Chen, the owners of the yard. It was a little difficult keeping the initials of the first three brothers straight, but Chinese and Taiwanese builders always (and correctly) assumed that Americans could not pronounce their names, so they reduced them to initials. Or,

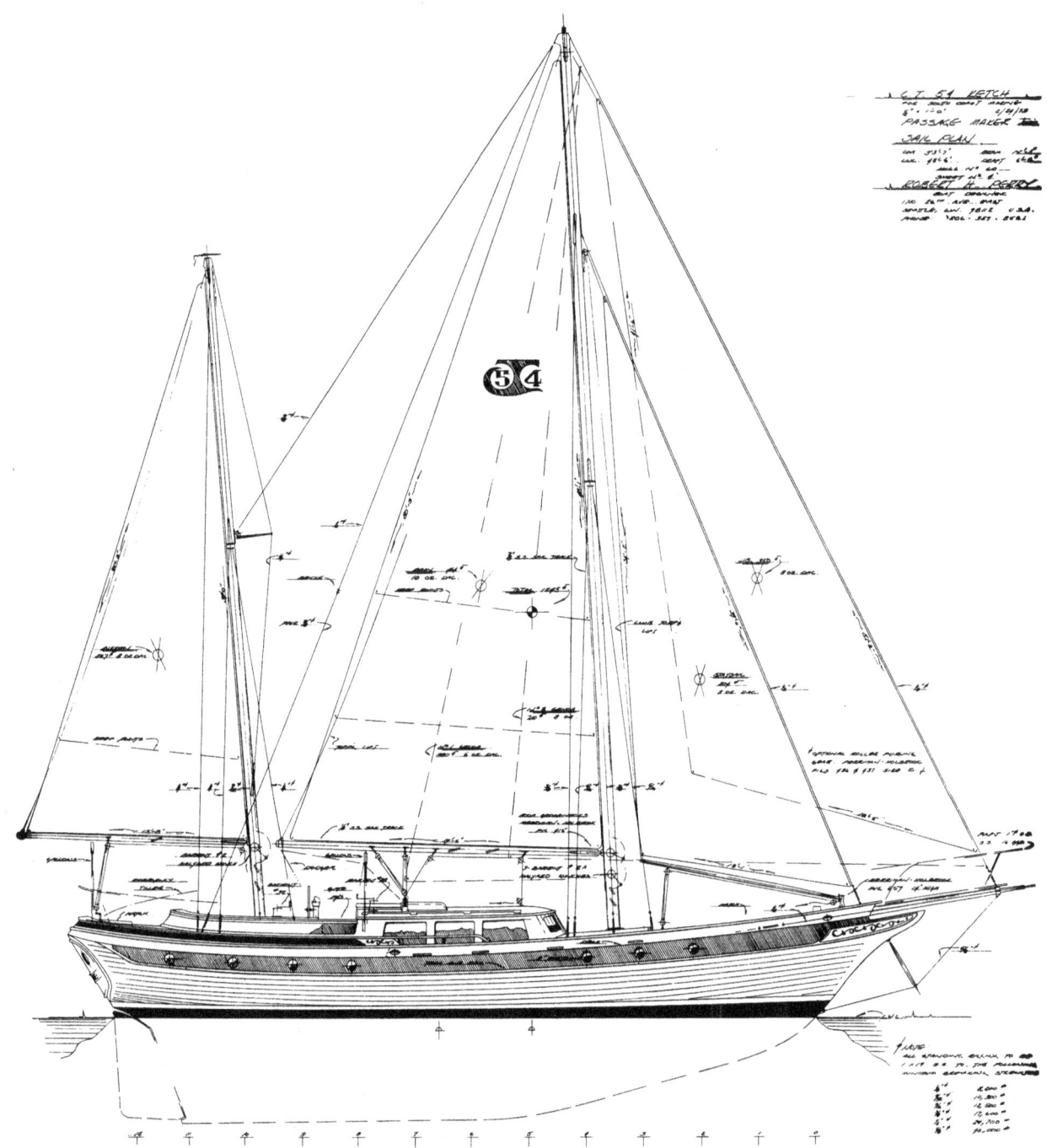

*This old sail plan for the CT 54 brings back a lot of memories—among them, how heavily I was influenced at the time by the drafting style of Bill Garden.*

like Wayne Chen, they adopted an English name with a vague phonetic similarity to their given Chinese name. C.T. was the oldest Chen brother and ran the yard. S.T. was the yard's "designer." I never did figure out what C.S. did, but Wayne ran the sailboat end of the yard's business. Wayne and I would become good friends. C.T. is dead now, but he was a good man and treated me well. He was immensely proud of his Volvo, a rare car in Taiwan at that time.

Seven years of good CT 54 sales prompted the American importer, Don Gibson, of Seabrook, Texas, to propose that we introduce a bigger boat, a 65-footer. In February 1982, Wayne Chen and I joined Don in Texas to get the new project rolling.

*The first photograph I ever saw of one of my own designs near completion.*

By this time I was well into my efforts to design fast cruising boats, so the new 65 was to be a very different beast from the old long-keeled 54. This time I would go with a long fin keel and a skeg-hung rudder.

This was my biggest project to date and an exciting one. The tooling of the 65 was complex, demanding that I make several trips to Taiwan before the molds were built. Taiwan and I bonded effortlessly. I loved Taiwan. I would meet Don Gibson there and we would spend our days at the yard, with Don in the office and me crawling over the plugs to fine-tune design details on the fly with a small army of Chinese carpenters who spoke no English. Although almost all the workers at Ta Chaio were in fact Taiwanese (meaning that their families had moved to Taiwan before Chiang Kai-shek was driven there from mainland China in 1950), I worked hard to learn to speak Mandarin. The yard workers spoke mostly in the Taiwanese dialect, but Mandarin was considered the official language of Taiwan. I may have offended some of the workers by speaking Mandarin, but learning it made sense in the long run, and I could pull out a few Taiwanese phrases when I needed them. One day one of the workers put me on the back of his little motorcycle and off we went to his home for lunch, a rare privilege for a foreigner.

I worked mostly with Sea Dog Deng, the yard foreman. In Mandarin he was Deng Hi Gou, with Hi Gou meaning Sea Dog, or seal. The Chinese believed that eating seal meat made you tough, and Sea Dog had been the tough guy in his school, hence the name. Sea Dog had taught himself to read

*I was so proud to be able to take my family to the Caribbean and enjoy two weeks of carefree cruising aboard* Windwalker, *a CT 54. This is the pilothouse version produced by Ta Chaio to provide more headroom. Had I been on board when this shot was taken, I might have suggested some changes to the way the asymmetrical chute was hoisted.*

*The first CT 54 at the old Ta Chaio yard alongside the Tamsui River in Pali, just outside Taipei. Often I would shoot off to lunch clinging to the back of one of those little motor bikes. I kept this photo on my office bulletin board for 30 years.*

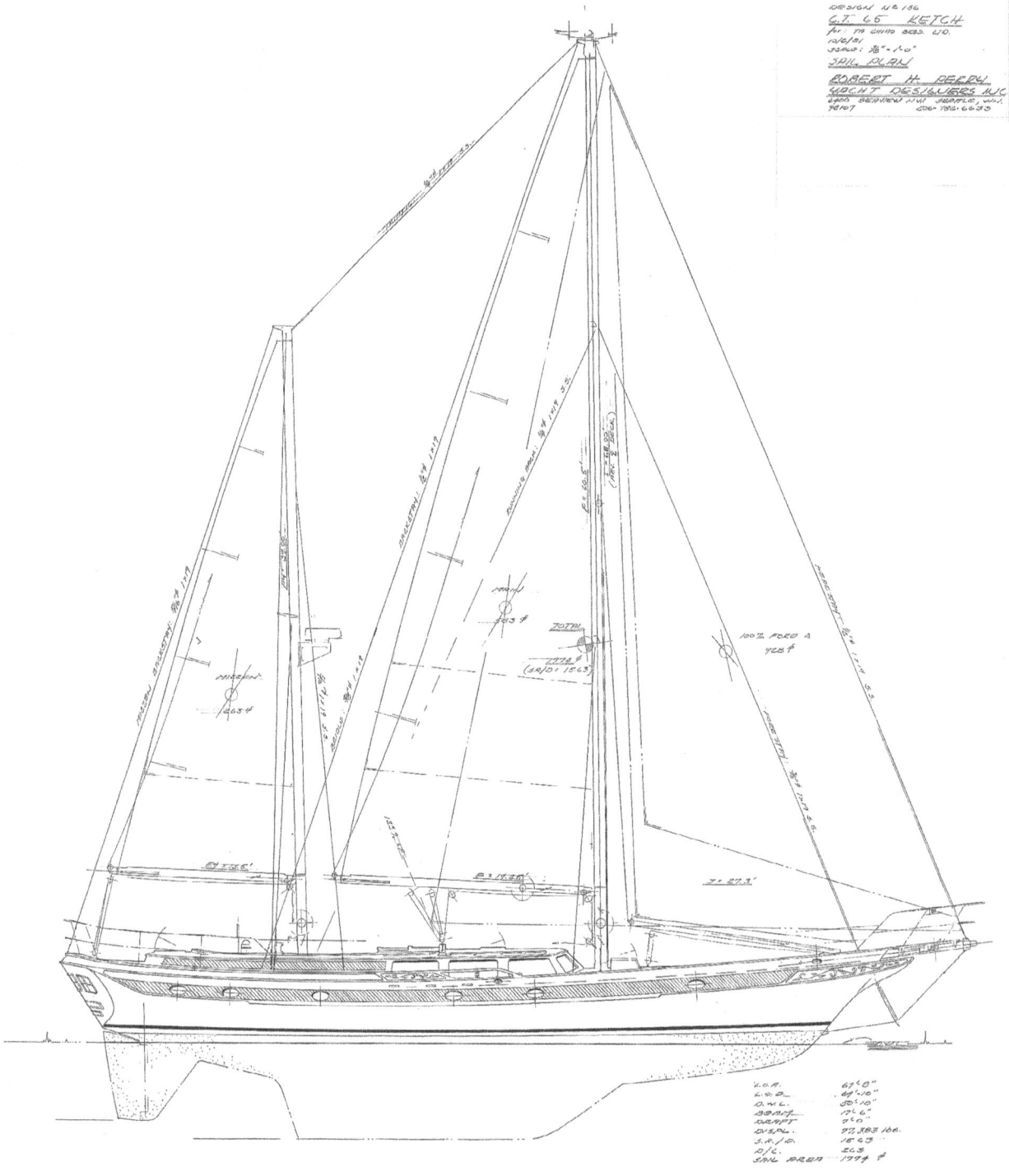

*The CT 65 sail plan shows a split-appendage underbody—a real break from the full-keel CT 54.*

and write English, German, and Spanish. He was amazingly smart, and it was impossible to slip anything by him.

When most Chinese took an American to lunch or dinner, they would order sweet and sour pork or cashew chicken, dishes they knew Americans were accustomed to. Not Sea Dog. Sea Dog reveled in ordering the strangest things when we ate: big fish heads—just the heads—baby eels, raw sea snails.

"What's this?" I would ask.

"Don't ask. Just eat," said Sea Dog.

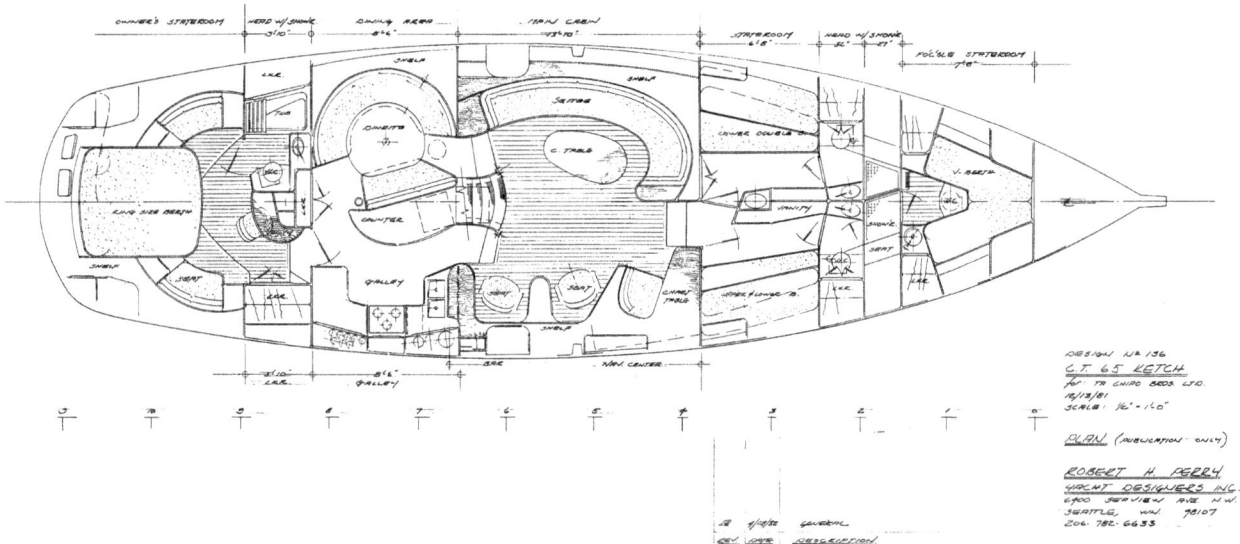

*In the CT 65, I echoed the curves and shapes of the deck layout with more curves below decks. We did a wide variety of layouts.*

He knew exactly what he was doing, but he refused to humor me. In a world where saving face is everything, it was hard to get people to correct my attempts at Mandarin. Sea Dog corrected me endlessly, laughing at my mistakes.

"What you have for lunch?" he asked.

"I had *shiatze*," I said in an effort to say "shrimp."

"You have blind person for lunch!?" said Sea Dog.

I owe him a lot. He saved my butt on many design and construction details. The last I heard of Sea Dog, he had started a boatyard in Puerto Rico. Recently I searched a Puerto Rican phone book but could not find him.

One Saturday at the yard, Wayne asked me if I wanted to come to his house for lunch. He was hosting a "small get-together," he explained. I said fine, and off we went. Wayne lived in an apartment block built around a common courtyard area that was essentially the Chen family "compound," and the small get-together turned out to be his mother's eightieth birthday party. Among the 75 people there, I was the only non-Chinese. That was a memorable afternoon. I felt honored to sit at a big table

*Wayne Chen of Ta Chaio is on the right, with Don Gibson, the U.S. importer for Ta Chaio, in the middle. The bags under my eyes were caused by several nights of aftershocks after a 7.2 magnitude earthquake.*

*A CT 65 ready for launch on the Tamsui River. The jumbled mess of the yard was typical. I spent many a happy day wandering around this yard, trying to be of help.*

*A CT 65 in the Scorpio 72 or European configuration for charter in the Mediterranean.*

with Wayne's male relatives, eating all manner of unusual things. To this day I can't get the taste of dried fish eggs out of my mouth.

I think Ta Chaio built about 40 CT 65s, which made it a markedly successful big boat and a good moneymaker for Don Gibson and the yard. Many were sold in Europe as the Scorpio 72 and entered the charter trade with a company called Stardust Charters. Most of the 65s were delivered right at the yard and sailed away by professional delivery crews.

The 65 is a big, heavy boat with an interesting two-cockpit-well deck design. Due in large part to all the time I spent crawling around on the deck plug, I think I did a masterful job with that figure-eight cockpit configuration. I still find the 65 to be a handsome boat, and I know it sails well. The interiors were mostly custom, some drawn by me and some by the yard.

The CT 65 was followed by the CT 56, which was meant to replace the tired tooling for the CT 54. It was a far better design, in my eyes. I fined up the bow, decreasing the angle of entry considerably to make the boat faster on the wind. I also made the keel more distinct from the canoe body and thus more efficient, and I flattened the buttocks to give the 56 better overall speed. Don Gibson, however, preferred the old 54, which had more usable interior volume forward. The 54 was slower, but Don sold these boats based on accommodations and so naturally preferred interior volume to performance. I think the yard only built a dozen CT 56s.

We also did a CT 48, but by that time there was trouble at the yard. The French importer of the CTs was Michel Tissier, who was responsible for selling the CT 65 (aka Scorpio 72) in Europe. This gave him clout with the yard. He felt that he should be the one to dictate to the yard what the next project should be, while Don Gibson felt that was still his responsibility, and the two men clashed over the CT 48. After the drawings were well underway, Michel Tissier demanded changes to make the boat more appealing to the European market.

I think he was right. The old pirate-ship aesthetic that Don Gibson promoted was no longer being as well received. Boats were getting more contemporary, and the CT line needed an updated appearance. I preferred Tissier's approach but was caught between Michel and Don. In the end, Michel prevailed at the yard. The CT 48 would have a flatter sheer and a cleaner deck than the boat Don wanted. I changed the drawings. Don was irate and refused to import the CT 48 into the United States.

Michel soon went out of business due to difficulties in managing the CT 65s he had put into charter for private owners. With Michel out of the picture, the CT 48 died after a brief run. Meanwhile, because Don Gibson was at odds with Ta Chaio, the entire CT sales effort in the United States petered out.

I have fond memories of working with Ta Chaio. Sometimes I imagined I was the fifth Chen brother, and I felt much at home in that yard. The Chens treated me very well. I spent many happy hours walking the mile down along the Dan Sui riverside on the dusty country road that separated Ta Chaio's two plants, smoking my pipe, practicing Mandarin, and keeping an eye peeled for cobras. We built a lot of boats. I got a real kick out of directing efforts during the plug-building stages.

It is often suggested that my design career began with the Valiant 40, but it was really the CT 54 that got me started. I still talk to the yard, and they keep threatening to build a CT 85 or revise the CT 65. For some reason they think a schooner rig for the CT 65 might sell. But Don Gibson, CT, CS, and ST are dead now. Taiwan is a changed place, and I am a lot older. I can't stick my toe in that river again.

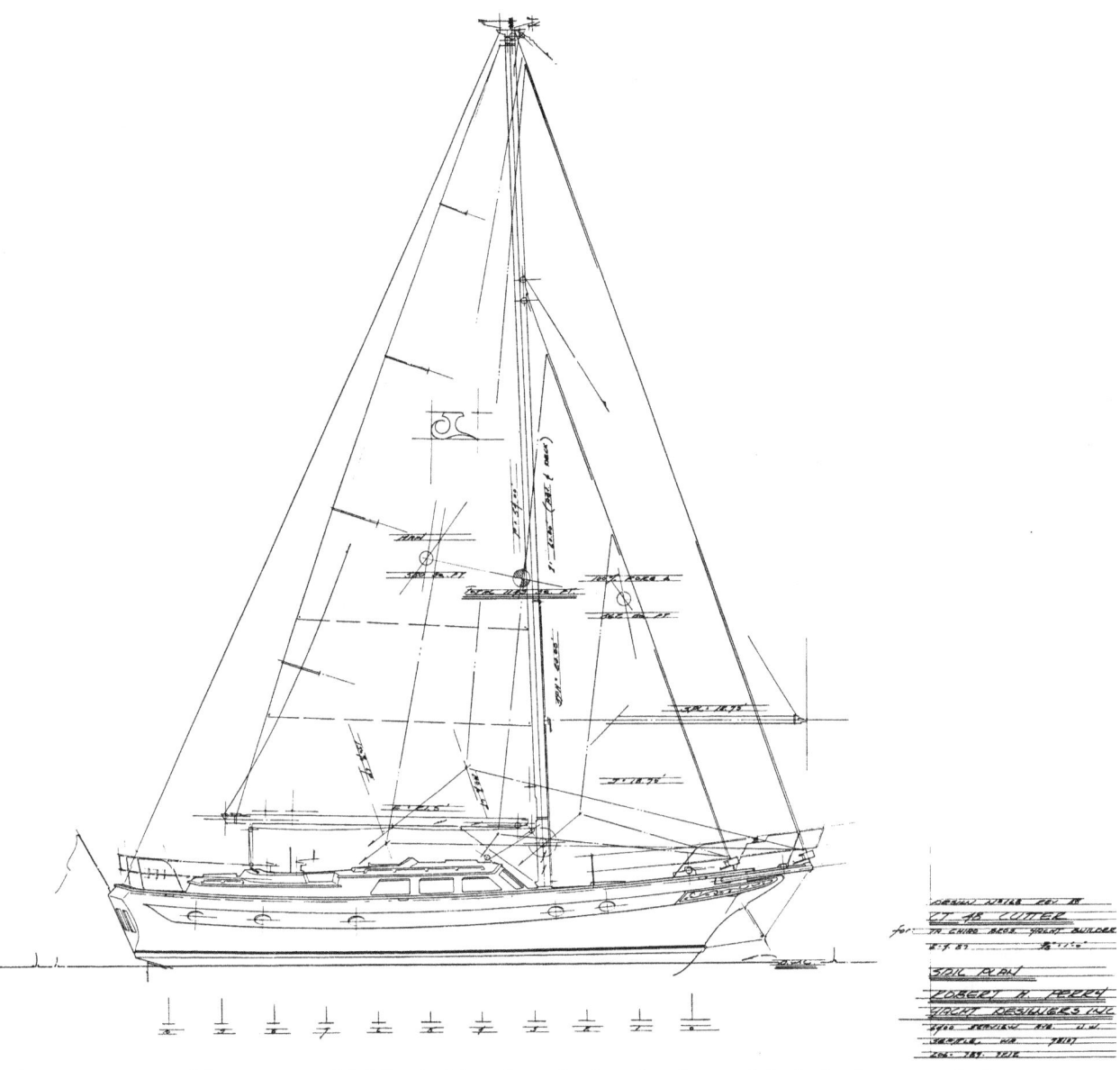

*The Euro version of the unsuccessful CT 48. Note the unbroken sheerline and the lack of a quarterdeck.*

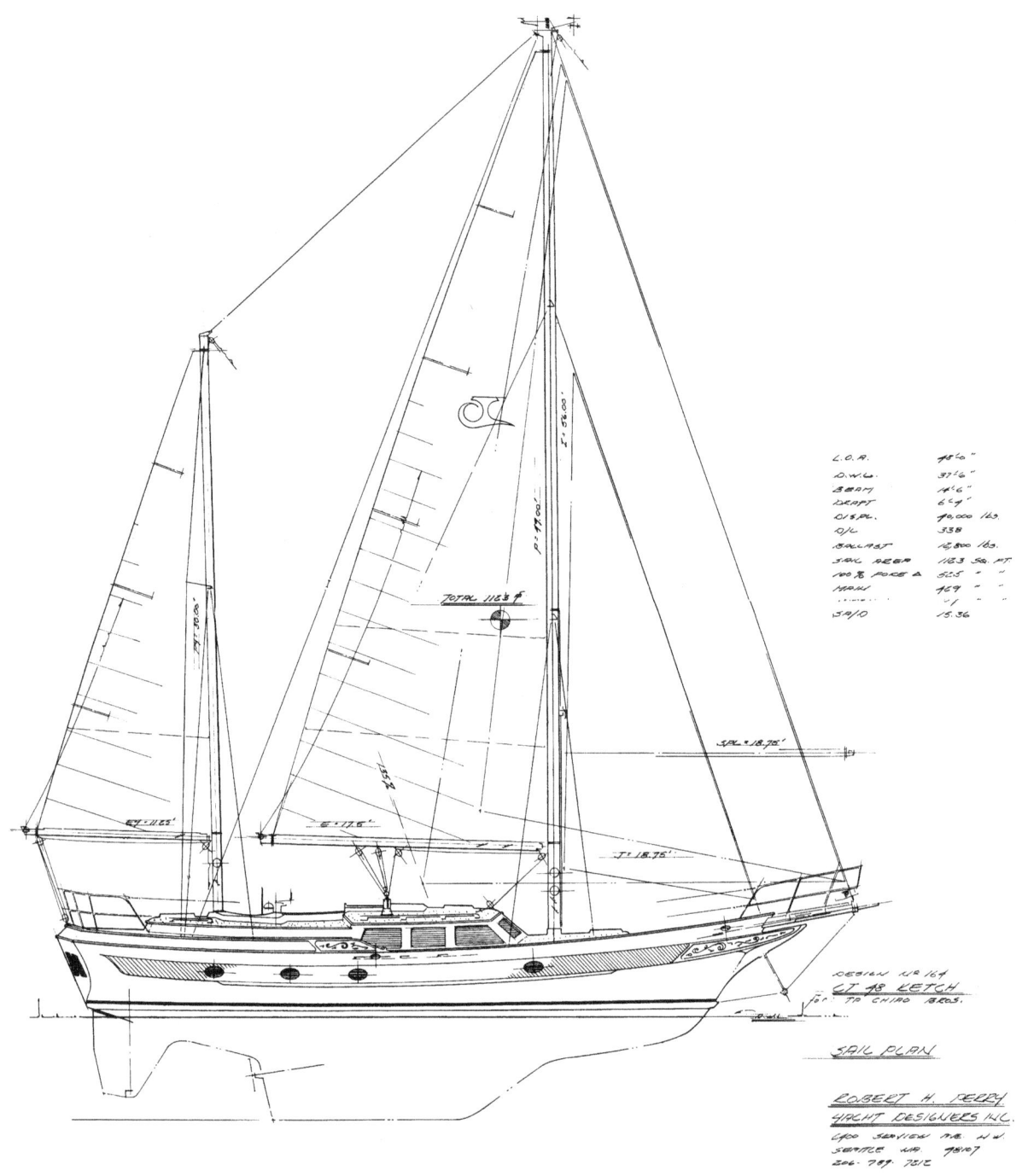

*The CT 48 as Don Gibson envisioned it, with a raised sheer aft and a quarterdeck. Don refused to import the flatter-sheer version.*

## *According to Perry*
# TRANSOMS

In order to lay out the plan view of a boat with a transom, I first need to know how wide the transom should be. Today we see wide transoms on two very different boat types: high-performance racing boats and family cruisers.

Light, beamy racing boats with shallow hulls can get away with wide sterns because when they heel, they present narrow heeled waterlines to the waves. While immersing the transom causes some drag, these boats have huge rigs and the horsepower to drive their radically light hulls efficiently despite the drag. In fact, at the super hull speed these boats attain, immersing some of the transom raises the prismatic coefficient, which, in turn, raises the hull speed.

The family cruisers mass-produced by major production yards such as Hunter and Beneteau, on the other hand, employ a wide stern for interior volume and cockpit space. Some might argue that such sterns are "fast" because they resemble racing-boat sterns, but it doesn't work that way for a family cruiser. You do not want the corner of a cruiser's transom dragging when the boat heels, because that creates drag. Ideally, you want the wake to peel off the edge of the transom cleanly and not wrap around in a drag-producing eddy.

Making a cruiser fat aft can also create helm-balance problems. As the boat heels, its waterlines become asymmetrical, and this can increase weather helm. Combine a broad stern with a beamy boat and you can face a real problem in a breeze. Still, I favor a moderately broad transom for a cruising boat because beam aft enhances stability, permits more room in the cockpit, and adds useful interior volume aft.

Beam aft has to be determined in conjunction with overhang aft. If you watch an America's Cup class yacht from leeward while it sails to windward, you might almost imagine that someone has hung over the stern with a piece of chalk, outlined the shape of the quarter wave, and said, "Cut here." The trick is to use as much of the stern as you can for extending the sailing length. The problem is that production boats are usually designed to an LOA parameter for marketing purposes. Adding overhang aft may not be an option if it adds to LOA. You could create aft overhang by shortening the waterline aft, but that would decrease interior volume, and boat buyers love volume. It would also shorten the sailing length, and designers love sailing length.

There is no absolute way to measure speed factors against comfort factors. The designer just has to intuit how the two elements should be balanced.

Transoms can be traditionally raked, sloping forward from the deck toward the water, or they can be "reverse transoms," sloping aft from the top. Reverse transoms predominate today because they allow you to carve a handy swim platform out of the transom. I like the look of a traditional transom on some boats, but there is no denying the value of a well-designed swim platform.

Aesthetically, a traditional transom requires some deadrise through the stern sections if it is not to look awkward. I even like to enhance the sectional shape of a traditional transom with a hint of hollow as it approaches the centerline.

In an effort to maximize both sailing length and length on deck, I gave *Amati* (Chapter 15) a dead-vertical transom. At the time, I thought this was bold, but today I am seeing it more and more on racing yachts. Bill Tripp, Sr., one of my favorite designers when I was young, designed several boats with vertical or near-vertical transoms. It's a strong look and it works.

## Chapter Six

# AN EXTENDED FAMILY OF DOUBLE-ENDERS

I don't recall a time as a young sailor when double-enders did not appeal to me. I once fell in love with a converted whaleboat that was for sale on the shore of Lake Union, and I imagined buying it and sailing off. I would walk miles just to sit aboard that boat at the brokerage where it was on display. In high school I was attracted to Seattle's fleet of converted Bristol Bay double-enders, remnants of the days when salmon fishing in Bristol Bay was under sail only. They made nice little cruising boats, and because most had been converted by Bill Garden they looked just right. My favorite was *Gull*, because *Gull*'s freeboard had been left original and was not raised like the rest of the conversions. I did like boats with points on both ends.

Perhaps the real epiphany came when I was walking the docks of Shilshole Bay one day. I was probably 15. I was stopped dead in my tracks by a boat unlike any I had ever seen. It was 60 feet long, narrow, pale greenish-gray, and had an extended, overhanging, pointed stern. No feature of this boat was like any other feature on any other boat I'd seen. From the bow to the cabin trunk forward, to the raised saloon house with its overhang aft, to the deep cockpit, and to that amazing stern—this boat was an expression of original design thought. It was Bill Garden's own boat, *Oceanus*. I didn't know much about boats yet, but I knew enough to recognize that this one was special. Recalling that day, I'm reminded of the scene in *Close Encounters of the Third Kind* where Richard Dreyfuss is at the dinner table mounding up the platter of mashed potatoes into a replica of the desert basalt spire. "This means something. This is important," he says.

To a 15-year-old boy interested in yacht design, *Oceanus* meant something. Today I can acknowledge that *Oceanus* is a weird boat design. Its shape makes little sense at all. There was simply less science available to most yacht designers in those days. The distribution of hull volume and beam is all wrong by today's standards. The keel is bizarre, as is the rudder. The rig is in the wrong place, and I know that the boat had helm issues. It was not fast for a 60-footer. When I raced on *Oceanus*, we had a hard time beating an old, tired eight-meter boat for boat. And yet, blemishes aside, it was a fabulous-looking boat and remains my all-time favorite design. Double-enders became one of the foundation stones of my appreciation of yacht design.

Twelve years later, while working in Boston and just completing my work on the Hans Christian 54 (which was soon to become the CT 54), I was asked by the head of Hans Christian, John Edwards, to draw a 34-foot double-ender. It was a time when the Westsail ruled as the premier offshore cruising boat and when sailors accepted, without question, that any "real" offshore boat would be a double-ender. No one, including me, asked why. We just accepted it.

It probably had something to do with the workboat mythos originating with Colin Archer and his famous double-ended Norwegian lifeboats. This myth had been perpetuated in the attractive design work of William Atkin, with several designs done in this style, and Bill Garden's *Seal*. These designers did not adopt Archer's trochoidal waveform theory that his hull shapes were based on, but they borrowed heavily on the general aesthetics of his boats. It was a strong look, with deep bulwarks cut down at the ends, long bowsprits, heavily curved stems and sternposts, and massive outboard rudders with tree trunk tillers. Who could resist a look like that? It said, or at least implied, "seaworthy."

To help me get started with the new design, John mailed me a copy of the front page of *Soundings* magazine. There was a picture of K. Aage Nielsen's *Holger Danske* sailing away from the camera with one of the most shapely pointed sterns I had ever seen. I was just beginning work on the Valiant 40 design at the time, and days later Nathan Rothman mailed me the exact same picture. Rothman and Edwards both offered the same advice: "Make the stern like this." I did, basically. I added my own touch to it, but the basic stern shape was that of K. Aage Nielsen. Of course, he had copied the stern from someone else, too.

This type of canoe stern made a lot of sense because it allowed the designer to stretch out the buttocks and avoid tucking them up until the last possible moment. It pulled a lot of volume aft compared with the squeezed-in, pointed stern of Atkin's Eric or a Westsail 32. This improved the sailing length, stability, and lazarette volume.

My design for Edwards was to be the Hans Christian 34. I eagerly accepted the design job and drew hull lines and rig, but as I proceeded with the rest of the design, I began hearing rumors of a 36-footer being built to my design in Taiwan. Few boats were being built in Taiwan at the time, so it was impossible to get projects confused. I told people that the boat was really 34 feet, but the rumors persisted. Finally I picked up the phone and called Edwards in Taiwan.

Yes, he said, the boat is 36 feet long, and it's just a bigger version of your 34-footer, and we'll build the 36 first and then your 34. I told him that was great and that I could certainly use the royalties from both boats, but Edwards said he had no intention of paying royalties on both. I countered that there would have been no 36 without my 34, but he was adamant. It was hard for me at the time, making $157 a week, to watch a project that I had set my hopes and dreams on go sideways and disappear. My retaliation was to back Ta Chaio in their dispute with Edwards over the Hans Christian 54, and then to drop all involvement with Edwards as related in Chapter 5. Angry about losing the 54 project, Edwards wanted nothing more to do with me either.

The 36-foot double-ender was first marketed as the Hans Christian 36. Then Edwards had a falling out with the Union yard, where the 36 was being built, just as he'd had a falling out earlier with Ta Chaio. It was common in those days for the marketing entity, in this case Edwards, to own the design, while the yard, Union, would own the molds and tooling. In the event of a disagreement between the marketing group and the builder, the marketer was sent packing and the yard maintained its ownership of the tooling.

The Union yard had no intention of halting production of the Hans Christian 36. They just had to find another name for the boat. The design was eventually sold as the Union 36, the Union Mariner 36, the Mariner Polaris 36, the EO 36, the Universal 36, and other names I have no doubt forgotten. It was a popular boat and remains so today, although a Hans Christian 36 always sells for more money than its identical but less prestigious sister models despite the fact that all the boats came out of the same yard.

The Union yard kept using my name in conjunction with this boat, and eventually I met with Bengt Ni, who ran the yard. He offered to pay me for the use of my name, but I told him that it would be unethical for me to claim that the design was all mine. We settled on the locution "based upon a design by Bob Perry," but that soon reverted to "designed by Bob Perry," and I withdrew from the arrangement. Still, my name has been forever linked to the boat, and you seldom see one of the 36-footers go up for sale without "designed by Robert Perry" appearing in the ad. I have almost given up trying to explain that the design is not really mine. I told this story on the dock one day to a young couple who owned a 36, and the woman started to cry.

"But we thought we were buying a Bob Perry design," she whimpered.

"OK, OK, OK!" I said. "It's sort of a Bob Perry design. Just don't cry."

The problem continues today, but I have learned to treat the 36-footer as an adopted child. I work with proud owners, most of whom have become aware of the boat's true origins. They still call it a Perry design and I don't mind.

One version of the 36, called the Mao Ta 36, is a different boat built at a different yard. It's the same design but with one small change. It came about like this. I was wrapping up a hectic visit to Taiwan and was scheduled to leave Sunday at lunchtime. I received a call Saturday from a Willie Ma, asking for a meeting. I explained that I had no time to spare unless he could meet me for breakfast Sunday morning at my hotel. This was fine with Mr. Ma. Over breakfast he explained to me that he worked for Bengt Ni and that they had decided to modify the 36 to increase its sales appeal. He wanted me to design a change in the keel profile—a Brewer bite, as I call this feature. It was a small, arc-like bite taken out of the keel profile directly ahead of the rudder. This "divot" would not help much in a big, full-keel underbody, but it wouldn't hurt much either and it would give the boat a more contemporary look.

I told Mr. Ma I could do this easily for $400. He said that was fine, but as it was Sunday, he could not get into the Union factory to get a company check, so would I please accept his personal check? He made an effort to explain to me that this check "represented" a factory check, and I said fine. To me a check was a check, and I loved flying home from Taiwan with a bag full of checks. I returned home, drew the keel change, and sent it to the address Mr. Ma had provided me.

The next thing I heard was that Willie Ma had started a new yard, Mao Ta, and was building the 36 with the Brewer bite keel modification. The boat was marketed as the Mao Ta 36. Apparently Mr. Ma had left Union to start his own yard and had taken the drawings for the 36 with him. (I have no idea what drawings there were.) Now he was producing the same boat, with the keel change, under a new name. When Bengt Ni found out about the copy of his 36 and asked Willie Ma to stop production of a design he owned, Willie Ma said that he had bought the design from me and produced the cancelled check for $400 as proof that I had sold the design. Years later I had the opportunity to tell my side of this story to Bengt Ni. The Mao Ta model had not been a success, and we both had a good laugh over the whole thing. It remains the only time a Taiwanese builder ever tried to cheat me, at least that I know of.

The little Hans Christian 34 went on to become reasonably successful, but the 36 in its various incarnations outsold it. I would guess that more than 100 of the 36s were built. The 34-footer had some deadrise in its hull, similar to that of the Valiant 40. This was a feature I would soon drop and then later come back to. In fact, this deadrise shape was right, and the 34 was an able sailer and a handsome boat.

I struggled for years with these "full keel" designs. The 34 had a true full keel, as the leading edge of the keel grew right out of the forefoot of the stem. There is nothing to indicate where the forefoot ends and the keel begins. I knew from my work with Dick Carter that the keel needed to be a National Advisory Committee for Aeronautics (NACA) foil to work correctly, but in those early days I had some difficulty blending the NACA foil sections with what I wanted in a big keel envelope. Another factor that hindered strict use of NACA foil shapes in the keel was that the trailing edge of the keel had to maintain a constant width to fair properly with the rudderpost, which was mounted on it. Add to this the fact that my drawings lacked a little precision with respect to keel shapes, and the early keels for my family of full-keel double-enders were in some cases a little crude in terms of foil definitions and leading-edge geometry. I'd like to blame the yard's loftsman, but I'm sure I played a role in this too. I was young then.

The Young Sun 35 is another design to which my name is always attached, but I have no idea where this boat came from. At one time I assumed the Young Sun was the "residue" of the Hans Christian 34 project, maybe my 34 stretched a foot and with some freeboard added. But the more I studied the design, the less I was able to find any element of the hull form that matched a shape I would draw. It's a fine boat, but it's just not mine. I get calls from a lot of owners, and to save grief, I have decided to add the Young Sun to my list of "adopted children." To their credit, the Young Sun Company suggested an agreement with me whereby they would pay royalties for the use of my name, but it just did not make sense. It was not my design.

The big step forward in the development of this double-ender family was my interaction with a Seattle dealer for the CT 54, Will "The Flying Dutchman" Eickholt. Will, a consummate salesman, was eager to introduce the Taiwanese builders to the

*Basil Lin, of Ta Yang, working with me over the plans for the Tayana 48.*

yard, he said, would do the structural detailing. This sounded OK to me. I was young, and it would give me a chance to strike back at Edwards.

I designed a 37-footer that was almost a sister ship to the Hans Christian 36. By this time I had soured a little on Edwards's aesthetic approach to some design features. He had a great eye, but to me his boats looked like cartoons. His approach turned out to be highly successful, but I preferred a cleaner look to the cabin trunk and general lines of the boat. Partly this reflected my inability to shake the notion that a designer should minimize the man-hours of labor required to accomplish certain details. Builders like Edwards knew that labor was so cheap in Taiwan as to render this consideration irrelevant. I learned this later.

Notwithstanding these minor aesthetic differences, my design for the CT 37 started to sell, and then it really started to sell. Seattle sailor Bob Berg got hull number 1, a ketch, and the boat sailed fabulously. It was fast, close-winded, and perfectly balanced. I remember a 37-foot trawler yacht, used as a photoshoot chase boat, barely being able to keep up with us. Soon CT 37s were rolling past my office window at a remarkable rate. The boat was so successful so quickly that the yard decided they did not need the CT name. Thereafter the boat was

Seattle marketplace. Knowing the Edwards/Union 36, he asked me if I would like to design a similar boat for him to market. The boat would be built at a brand-new yard, Ta Yang, in which C.T. Chen was a partner. C.T.'s involvement meant that we could use the Ta Chaio and CT names to get the boat established. Will was frugal, and he asked for only a basic set of plans to keep down the design cost. The

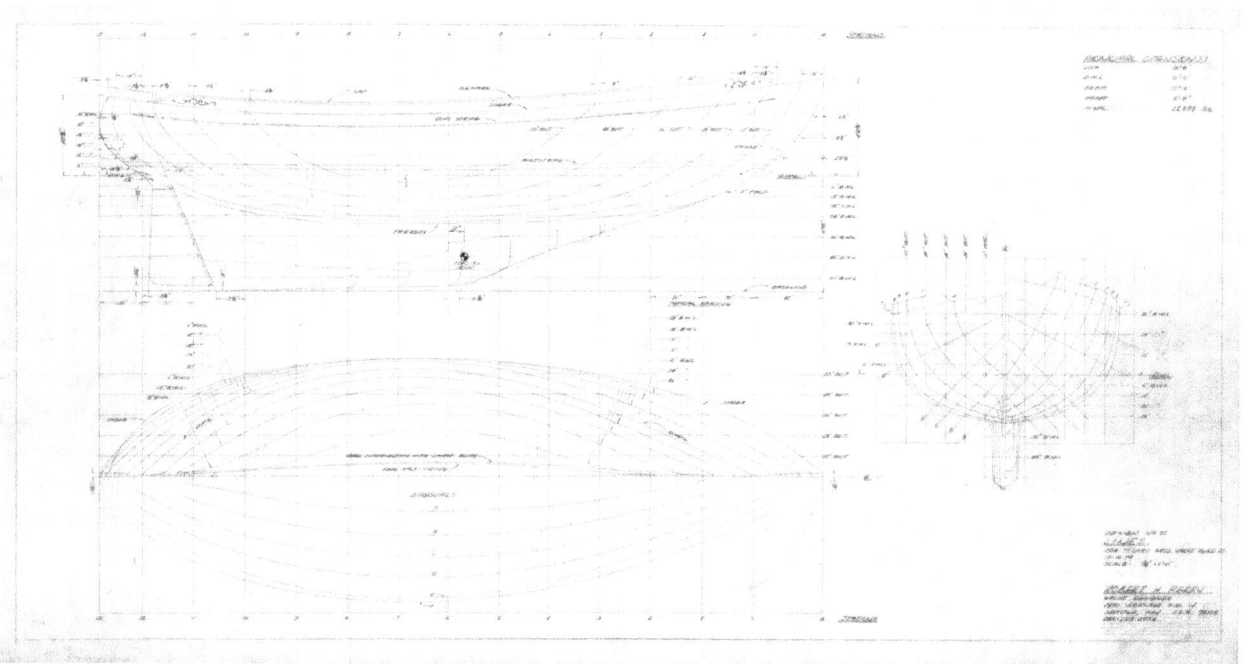

*These carefully hand-crafted hull lines of the Tayana 37 show the round sectional shape and the distinct break between the hull and the keel envelope.*

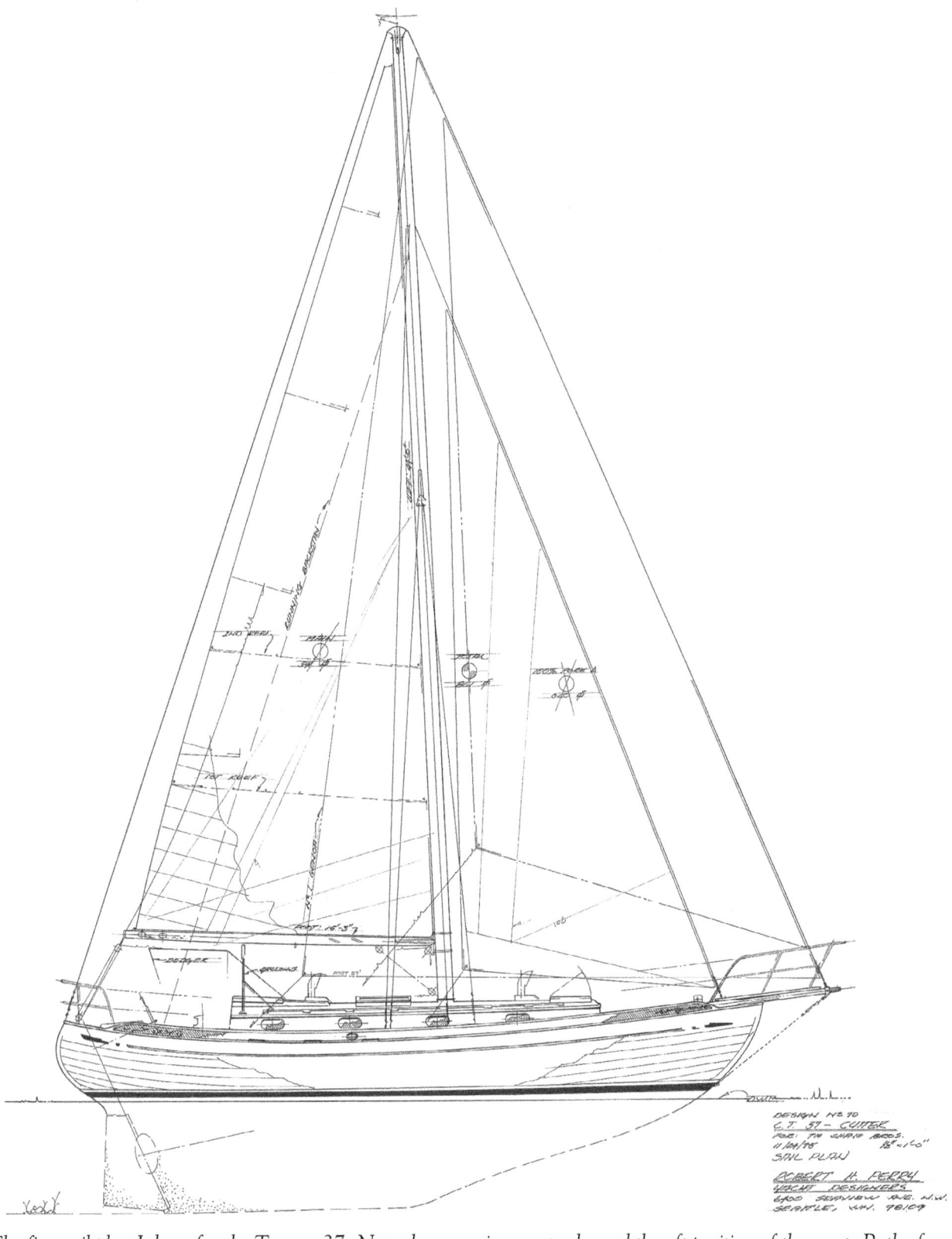

*The first sail plan I drew for the Tayana 37. Note the excessive mast rake and the aft position of the mast. Both of these features made the Tayana 37 cutter a demanding boat to balance. Once mast rake was reduced, helm pressure was greatly reduced.*

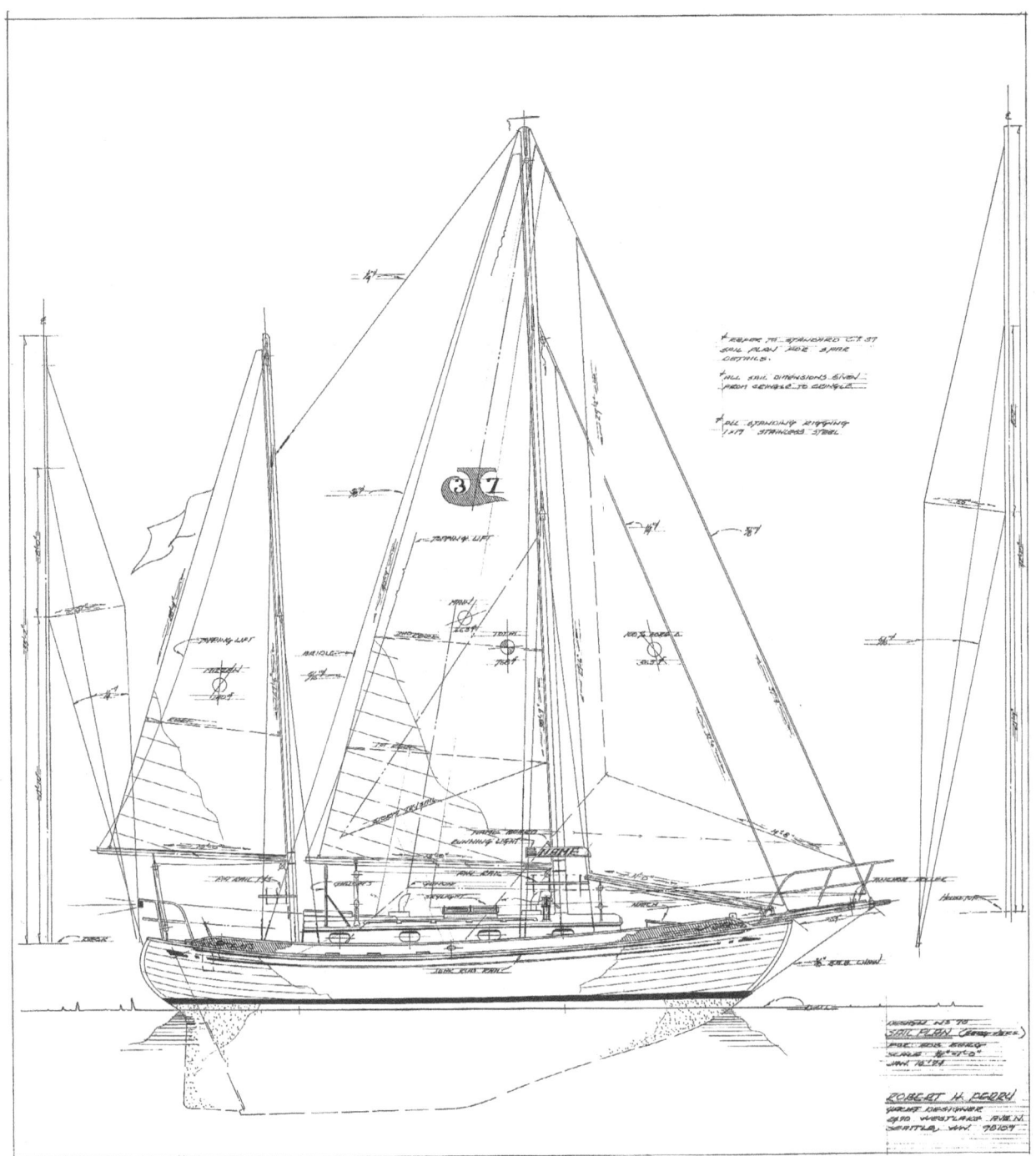

*The ketch version of the Tayana 37 was always my favorite. It was quite fast and well balanced. Nonetheless, the cutter outsold the ketch twenty to one.*

marketed as the Ta Yang 37, then later as the Tayana 37. I waited eagerly for my first royalty check, and eventually I mentioned to Will Eickholt that I should be getting some good royalties soon.

Will looked at me and said, "What royalties? Your contract, which you wrote, makes no mention of royalties."

My heart sank. I checked the contract, which I had indeed written, and he was right. There was nothing there about royalties. I had simply forgotten the royalty clause. Will and I discussed this, and he mentioned that the yard had been having some problems with areas of the design in which the yard had done the engineering. These included the hull-to-

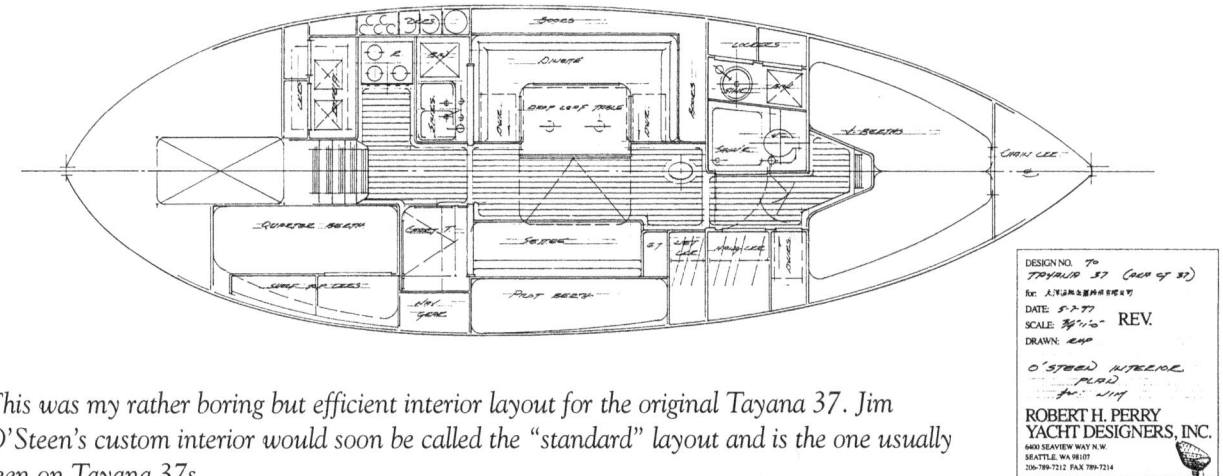

*This was my rather boring but efficient interior layout for the original Tayana 37. Jim O'Steen's custom interior would soon be called the "standard" layout and is the one usually seen on Tayana 37s.*

deck joint, for which the yard had devised a bizarre solution. Will thought the yard might be interested in getting some more design help from me, and perhaps that would be a good way to reintroduce the idea of royalties.

Y.P. Chen, the president of Ta Yang, soon visited Seattle, and Will brought him to my office to discuss the 37. To date they had built 40 boats, and there was no end in sight. Y.P. said he would like me to finish the design and to help them with the structural issues. I said I would, and that I'd like a royalty in exchange, whereupon he reached into his coat pocket and produced a royalty check for the first 40 boats. I almost fainted. I had not expected that. I would have been happy with royalties starting at hull number 41. I was so happy that I said I would accept only half of the proferred royalties, and I wrote him back a check for the other half. Later, Will always insisted that he had stuck that check into his own bank account.

Today Ta Yang is run by Y.P.'s son Peter, and the yard has built at least 600 Tayana 37s. George Day, a circumnavigator and editor of *Blue Water Sailing*, says there are more Tayana 37s cruising the oceans of the world than any other single design. I love that.

The 37 has slack bilges, very little true deadrise amidships, and short ends. It displaces the same as a Valiant 40 and shares the same laminate schedule. I had seen what the Westsails were doing, and I knew that if we were going after that Colin Archer look, we should do so with a faster boat. So I flattened the rocker on the 37 and tried to get the shape closer to what we were doing at Carter's. One very distinct departure from the Atkin-designed, Crealock-modified Westsail was to draw the hull and keel as distinctly separate entities. I designed a canoe body, then stuck a keel on it while trying to keep the hull and keel as separately defined as possible. This gave the 37 a tightly radiused garboard tuck instead of the typical big, wineglass, hollow garboard area, and the result was a lot of clean foil span on the full-length keel. It also reduced unneeded displacement through the garboard area and helped me flatten the buttocks. I was looking for speed in a boat type that was famous for being slow.

The ballast of the 37 is internal cast iron. The boats are heavily built, and the first few even had wooden spars, so their vertical center of gravity (VCG) was high. The round, slack-bilged hull makes for a boat with low initial stability and a nice, slow motion in a seaway. That easy motion is a nice feature for an offshore boat, but in retrospect, the 37 should have had more form stability. With its big rig, it's tender, and you need to know just when to reef. Fortunately the helm of the 37 lets you know quickly when that time has come. I would enjoy seeing what a lead keel version of the 37 sails like, but lead was expensive in Taiwan and we almost always worked with cast iron.

I knew from studying SA/D ratios that the Tayana 37 needed a big rig. Today SA/D is common design vernacular for almost any sailor, but in 1973 it was not well known, and many of my contemporaries viewed it with suspicion. I did not invent it. I first read about D/L and SA/D ratios in a Ted Brewer article, and he didn't invent them either. While sick

A *Tayana 37* nestled to the shoreline in Desolation Sound.

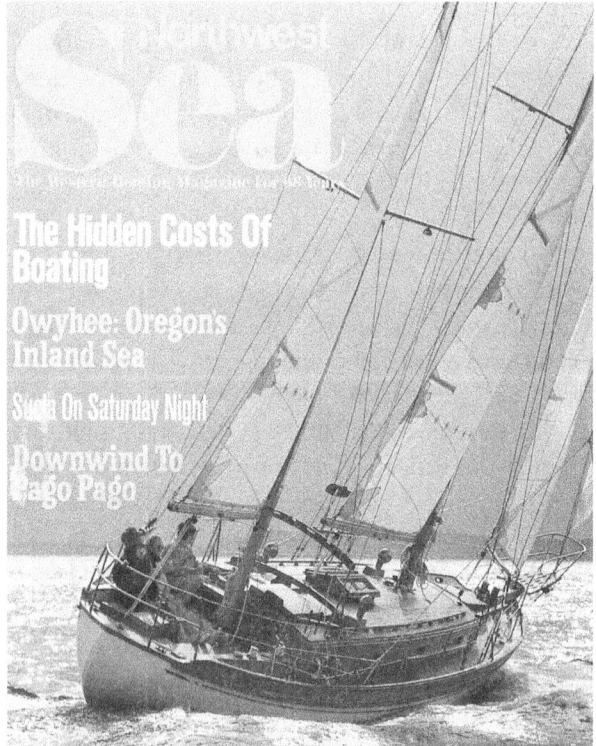

Bob Berg's very early Tayana 37 ketch being sailed for the first time. I'm at the wheel, hat on head and beer in hand. Forward of me is my old engineer Craig Goring, with Bob Berg forward of him. The boat was doing everything well and almost outrunning the pudgy little trawler yacht the photographer was using as a chase boat.

in bed one day, I took a pile of old yachting magazines and my six-inch slide rule and began deriving ratios for every boat on which I could find numbers. The ratios began to make a lot of sense and correlated directly with what I knew about boat performance. I gave the Tayana 37 a SA/D of 16.55, which was quite high for the type. The Westsail SA/D, by comparison, was just 13.89. Living on Puget Sound had taught me that light-air performance is important. Over the years I drew a variety of shorter rigs for the 37, but the owner preference has always been for the original tall rig.

My design error in the Tayana 37 was giving the boat a true cutter rig with the mast too far aft. This worked great with the bowsprit and let the 37 set a staysail with good proportions in addition to a Yankee jib, but it also introduced a problem. When I first sailed the 37, I was shocked at the weather helm developed by the cutter rig in comparison with the perfect balance of the ketch. I immediately called the yard and suggested we move the mast forward, but this suggestion met severe opposition from an East Coast dealer who had been selling a lot of the 37s. He would not hear of changing the design. This was the same dealer who decided it was a great idea to increase the fuel tankage by adding a 100-gallon tank under the V berth. I've been led to believe that the yard actually built a few boats with the mast moved forward, but I have never seen one of these.

One day I dropped in on Hugh Jones, the Oakland, California, Tayana dealer, and he said he'd been having a lot of luck selling the Tayana 37 to local San Francisco Bay sailors. I said I couldn't imagine how, considering how much weather helm the 37 carried and how hard it blew in San Francisco.

"Oh, we fixed that," Hugh said. "We just took all the rake out of the mast and the helm balances fine." That was great news to me. It's not enough to know that the buyers of my boats think they are good designs. I need to be convinced myself. If you are a student of yacht design, study the sail plan of the Tayana 37 (aka Ta Yang 37). That mast should be 24 inches farther forward. The rake looks sexy as drawn, but it is incompatible with a well-balanced boat. Today when I talk to people looking to buy a 37, I encourage them to look for the ketch-rigged model or, at the very least, to make sure the rake of the mast is minimal.

Ta Yang went on to produce a Mark II deck for the 37. I have no idea where this deck came from, but it looks much like the Hans Christian deck and cockpit shapes, and it's a better deck design than the one I provided. It not only looks better, it works better. But my original design remained the deck of choice for more than 90 percent of Tayana 37 buyers.

I don't think the yard will build new 37s anymore. Six hundred seems a logical place at which to stop, and the yard is preoccupied with much larger models now. It's too bad. There is no doubt in my mind that the Ta Yang yard was built on the success of the Tayana 37. We get at least a half dozen of the boats at every Perry Rendezvous.

## According to Perry
# STABILITY

Entire books have been written about stability. I'll touch on the basics here. The best way to understand stability is to think of it as a sum of parts, and those parts include the sail plan and rigging; the hull shape and displacement; the keel shape, draft, and ballast; and hull construction (i.e., heavy construction will reduce ballast weight and raise the vertical center of gravity). You must consider all these when you set out to balance the heeling force of the wind against the righting moment (RM) of the hull. Righting moment is influenced by the boat's vertical center of gravity, VCG, and the shape of the hull.

The heeling force is the easy part to grasp, at least in a simple, two-dimensional model of the rig. It is a vector resolution of the sail force vectors, which result from sail area, sail shape, the vertical center of effort (or pressure) of the sail plan, wind speed, and heel angle. For simplicity's sake, the center of pressure for the sail plan is generally taken as the sail plan's geometric two-dimensional center of areas.

There is no quick way to determine a boat's VCG. To get an accurate VCG from drawings, you need to do a weight estimate for each component and keep track of vertical weight distribution. At the same time, you'll need to track the fore-and-aft weight distribution in order to determine the boat's longitudinal center of gravity (LCG), which is used to determine ballast location and to control fore-and-aft flotation trim.

To calculate the vertical center of gravity, moments (distance times weight) of components will be taken around the boat's waterline. The VCG for a typical cruising boat is generally right around or just above the designed waterline (DWL). For a 40-foot cruising boat with modest draft, for example, a VCG at four inches above the DWL is considered normal. A modern 50-foot racing yacht with a deep fin-and-bulb keel may have its VCG two feet below the DWL.

Consider that adding 20 pounds in the rig, 25 feet above the DWL, will result in a vertical moment of 500 foot-pounds. In order to maintain the boat's previous VCG, you will have to add 500 pounds one foot below the DWL or 250 pounds two feet below the DWL.

Stability is measured as righting moment. Again, a *moment* is a weight times a distance, and in this case, the weight is the displacement of the boat and the distance is the righting arm, which is the distance from the boat's VCG to the center of buoyancy of the immersed hull. The center of buoyancy of the immersed hull—and thus the righting arm—will change for every heel angle as the shape of the immersed hull changes. Therefore, the righting moment is measured at various heel angles to generate a stability profile or curve for the boat.

A hull's center of buoyancy (CB) is a function of its sectional shape. Stability created by hull shape is called "form stability." Hull shape rarely affects

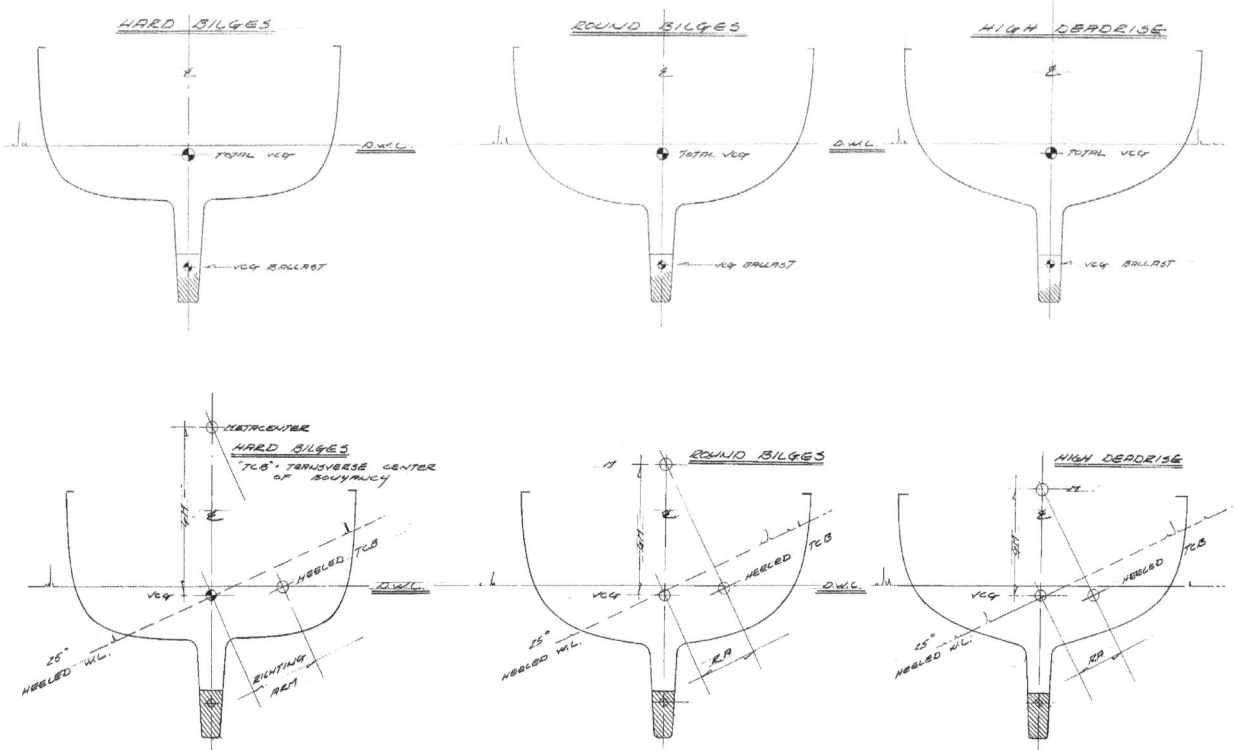

*These three midsections show the effect of hull shape on initial stability. The boats have equal beam, draft, ballast VCG, and total VCG, yet the righting arm developed by the hard-bilged midsection at 25 degrees of heel is significantly greater than that of the round-bilged midsection, which is in turn greater than the high-deadrise midsection.*

the VCG, although obviously a boat with very high freeboard will have a higher VCG than a boat with low freeboard, all else being equal.

When a hull is at rest and upright, its transverse center of buoyancy (TCB) is on centerline, which means there is no righting arm and thus no righting moment. When a boat begins to heel, the TCB moves to leeward with the immersed hull sections, creating a righting arm. This resistance to the first increments of heeling is called *initial stability* and is almost purely a function of hull shape and the moment of inertia of the waterplane. Nothing helps initial stability more than beam. All else being equal, a beamier boat will always have more initial stability.

As the boat heels beyond five degrees, the shape of the immersed hull comes more into play. The more hull you immerse, and the farther outboard of the centerline you immerse it, the farther your TCB will move to leeward. This will increase the length of the righting arm (i.e., the distance between the TCB and the boat's VCG, which is always on centerline unless you have water ballast, a canting keel, or movable crew weight). As the righting arm grows longer, the righting moment becomes larger.

Because a righting moment is weight times distance, all other things being equal, a heavier boat will have more RM. Stated differently, a heavy boat with a relatively high VCG can have the same righting moment as a light boat with a low VCG, because the heavy boat doesn't need as long a righting arm as the lighter boat. This is why today's light racing designs all have very deep keels with big lead bulbs at their tips. They need a long righting arm, and you can create that righting arm with hull form, a low VCG, or both.

Over the years, I've learned that cruisers like stiff (i.e., initially stable) boats, but stiffness comes at a price. A boat with a lot of form stability can give a jerky, quick ride in waves. A boat with low initial stability (i.e., low form stability, like a Valiant 40) can be initially tender but gives a soft ride with a slower heeling motion, and this is the preferred motion for a boat intended to spend a long time at sea. The boat with high initial stability works hard

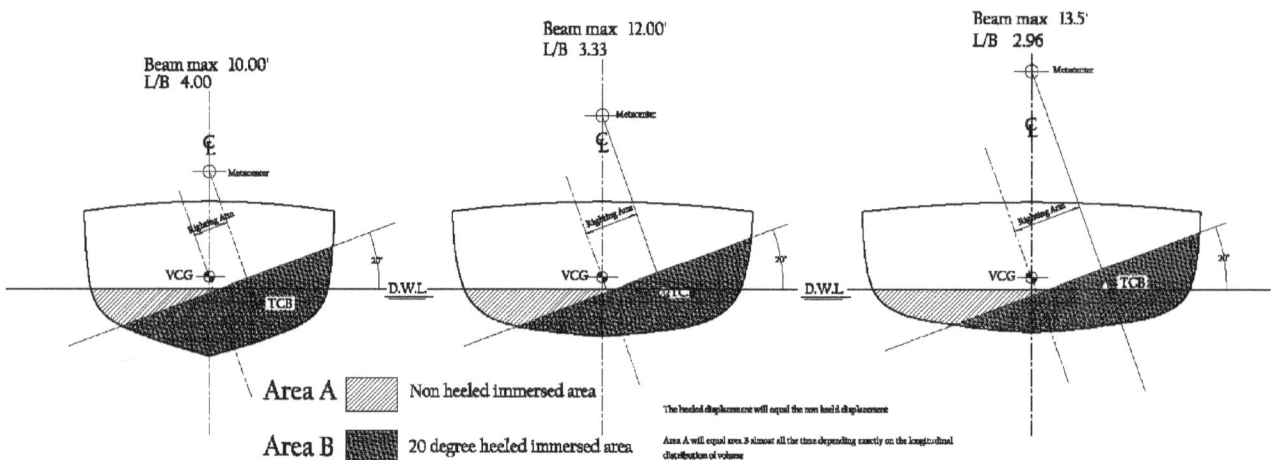

*The effect of beam on initial stability is evident in these midsections of three hypothetical 40-foot boats, each displacing 18,000 pounds. The boat on the left has 10 feet of beam (L/B of 4.00) with deep bilges, while the boat on the right has 13.5 feet of beam (L/B of 2.96) and shallow bilges. At 20 degrees of heel, the transverse center of buoyancy (TCB) of the boat on the right moves farther outboard, and the righting arm is substantially longer. In other words, the boat on the right has greater initial stability and is said to be stiff. Note that the immersed midsection area will remain more or less constant regardless of heel angle, since the boat's displacement doesn't change.*

to remain perpendicular to the wave surfaces at all times, and it is this that creates that quick, jerky motion.

Also, although it sounds counterintuitive, boats with low initial stability often have greater *ultimate stability*, which is the ability to resist rolling over in extreme conditions. Technically speaking, ultimate stability is the heel angle at which the righting moment becomes a negative number and the boat will no longer right itself. Once you reach this *point of vanishing stability*, the boat may continue over. This is the point where a knockdown turns into a true capsize.

However, caveats are required regarding ultimate stability. Rodney Johnstone of J-Boat fame did an exhaustive search of rollover case studies about ten years ago. His findings showed that the boats with the consistently best static stability numbers were more likely to roll over than some boats with poor static stability. I think that the key word here is *static*. It's one thing to assess the stability profile of a boat in the office with a three-dimensional model, and it's another to be confronted with a multidimensional storm sea and 80 knots of wind. A lot of variables, subjective and objective, could be identified in Rod's study, but the main thing I took from it is that numbers don't tell the whole stability story.

Extensive tank-test studies in Australia recently came up with only one hard conclusion: the bigger the boat, the more it resists rolling over.

So how should a designer balance initial with ultimate stability? To most of us who spend our sea time racing around the bay or cruising near-shore waters on sunny afternoons, a boat with good initial stability is probably the higher priority. The bottom line is that most sailors prefer a stiff boat. Ultimate stability can be determined easily on the computer, and more is always better if it doesn't have to be bought at too high a price in the boat's proportions and performance.

I consider a limit of positive stability (LPS) of 120 to 130 degrees to be a safe and conservative range for a cruising boat. In other words, if the ultimate stability—the heel angle at which the righting moment turns negative—is 120 to 130 degrees, the boat will take anything likely to be encountered by a cruising sailor. Valiant 40s have been measured with LPSs of 112 to 128 degrees in incline experiments. This range can only be attributed to measurement errors and the way the trial boats were loaded. I'm inclined to think that the true LPS for most Valiants is around 124 degrees. History has proven the Valiant to be an able and safe offshore boat.

*According to Perry: Stability*

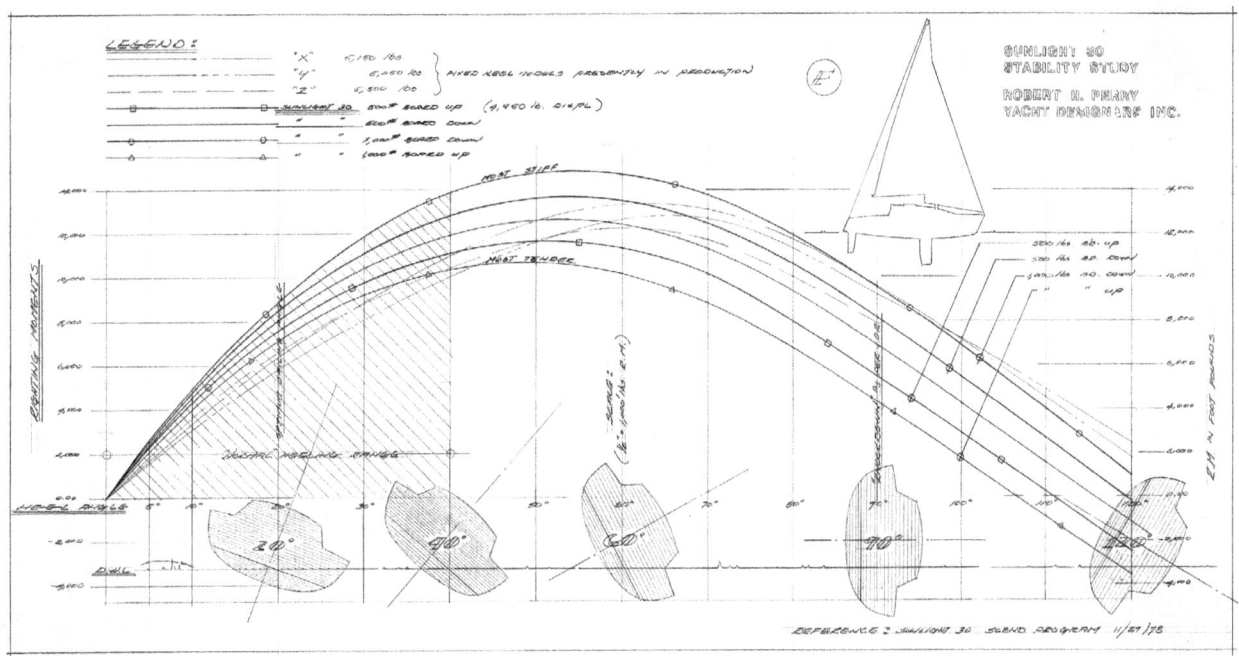

*The results of a stability study I conducted in 1978 for the Sunlight 30. A prototype of this boat was built, but it never went into production. The sail plan sketch shows an IOR-influenced fractional rig with short, high main boom. The lighter curves are fixed-keel variations, and the darker curves show the effects of moving 500 or 1,000 pounds of ballast into a lifting keel, with keel-up and keel-down positions shown. In this graph of righting moments (RM) versus heel angles, the lifting-keel versions are stiffer through the normal sailing range (up to 40 degrees of heel), but the stability advantage begins to evaporate at higher heel angles. With a 1,000-pound lifting keel in the up position, the boat reaches its point of vanishing stability (where RM turns negative) at 106 degrees of heel, whereas the fixed-keel models still retain positive stability at 120 degrees of heel.*

## Chapter Seven

# THE TA SHING FAMILY OF DOUBLE-ENDERS

No sooner had Bob Berg taken delivery of Tayana 37 hull number 2, *Chatelain*, than he quit his job as a technical director for a TV network and joined Will Eickholt and Jim Heg in the booming Flying Dutchman dealership, mid 1976. I liked Jim Heg. He always called me "maestro." The Tayana 37s were selling very well, and Bob thought the line could be expanded with a new, smaller model. Bob had found a new builder in Taiwan, Ta Shing, a yard with which I was unfamiliar, and he commissioned a 30-foot double-ender from me.

I met Bob in Taiwan in early 1976, and, along with his inspector Tim Ellis, we drove to inspect the new yard in T'ai-nan, one of Taiwan's oldest cities. T'ai-nan was a compact town with narrow streets and some very old buildings, about an hour's interesting drive north of Kao-hsiung. Tim parked the car and we walked down a narrow alley, nudging chickens out of our way as we walked. At the end of the alley, nestled into the jumbled collection of buildings, was a small boatyard. It did not look like much, and I expected the worst. But Bob was all optimism, and I was introduced to the management in the "office." We walked out into the yard, and there, about two-thirds complete, was a beautiful little Japanese-designed quarter-tonner. I was surprised. It was unusual for the Taiwan yards to try their hand at a racing boat, and it was immediately evident that this yard was doing a very good job. It was the best quality I had seen to date in Taiwan. Ta Shing started from humble beginnings and would go on to become the premier yacht-building company in Taiwan.

Back in Seattle, I started to work on the new 30-foot design. Bob wanted a stout little ship in the Norwegian double-ender style with a full keel. The selling point to this small boat would be its interior, so I had to give the hull a lot of volume. It would be a heavy boat with a displacement of 12,500 pounds and a D/L at the top of my acceptable range, 379. But I would not let the fact that we had to work with a heavy hull restrict me to a slow boat. I therefore took the basic hull form of the Tayana 37 and reduced it with a L/B of 2.9 and a modest draft of 4.75 feet. The sections show an arc-like shape similar to that of the Tayana 37, and I did my best to flatten the buttocks and reduce the angle of entry. There was no escaping the fact, however, that this would be a pudgy (robust sounds better) little version of the Tayana 37.

As with all five boats that I eventually did in conjunction with Bob Berg, the interior was Bob's concept, and I was reduced to an almost-draftsman level as I drew the layout to Bob's directions. Bob would not let one cubic inch go without using it to enhance the layout. The office joke was that when you opened a drawer on a Bob Berg boat, inside would be another little drawer. But Bob was very good at this, and I had no problem at all following his instructions. Bob was aware that labor hours meant nothing at that time in Taiwan. "If you can draw it, they can build it" was his motto. The interior of the Tayana 30 was essentially the layout of a typical 36-footer compacted into 30 feet. The boat would be called the "something 30." We needed a catchy name for the new model.

The Taiwanese liked Bob Berg. Bob had a gentle, easygoing manner, and he quickly became sensitive to the best way to deal with the Taiwanese culture and business practices. Bob did not try to speak Mandarin or Taiwanese, but neither did he accidentally insult his Taiwanese hosts with overly loud, dumbed-down English accompanied by profuse waving. Bob just spoke quietly and slowly and knew when not to push his point and threaten loss of face. "Always leave them a graceful way out," he would say. He was always pleasant to work with. But the Taiwanese had a problem with his name. Bob Berg did not roll off the Taiwanese tongue. They shortened it to "Baba," Mandarin for "father." They all called him Baba, and soon we were all calling him that. The new boat would be the Baba 30. I designed a sail logo as Ba squared.

Ta Shing did not stay long in that cramped, crude yard. The company had plenty of financial backing and soon had a gleaming new, huge yard on the edge of T'ai-nan. Baba 30s rolled out of there at a good pace and sold very well in the United States.

I did not have high expectations for the performance of the Baba 30. Fast boats did not have those proportions. It was just so pudgy. To my surprise, though, the boat sailed very well. It had excellent helm balance and a nice feel. While not a rocket at 12,500 pounds, it sailed smartly. I can remember leaving the dock late one Saturday and trying to catch up with the rendezvous fleet "racing" to the anchorage for the Perry Rendezvous. I was under power in a Valiant 40, and I could see the fleet spread out over the Sound up ahead. I soon caught up with the last boat. It was a Baba 30 under a main and a big, multi-colored drifter. I told my wife that there was no way I could just motor on by the Baba, so I cut the engine and raised the sails on the Valiant. I had beautiful, new North sails with a 135 percent Norlam genoa, my pride and joy. I trimmed the sails and prepared to blow by the little Baba. It took a lot longer than I expected. The skipper of the Baba knew we were in a race and held me off for quite a

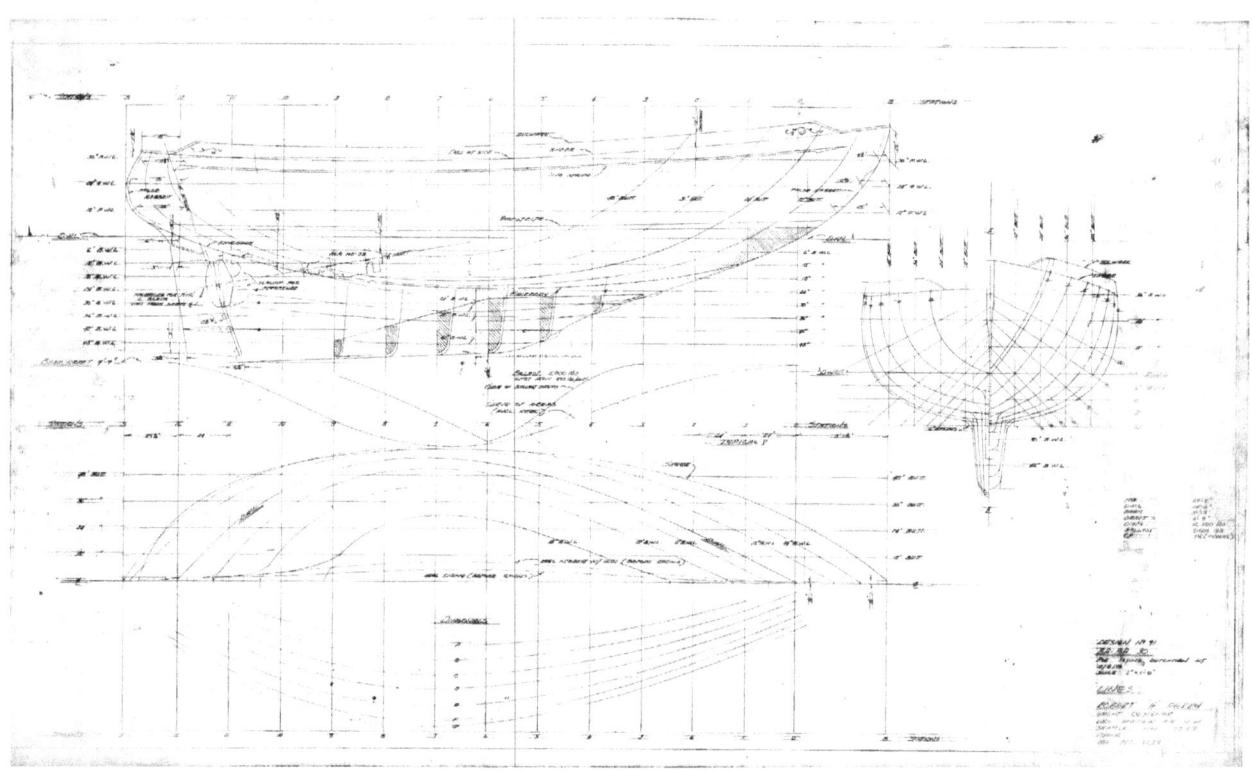

*The Baba 30 hull lines pack a lot of displacement into a small package, but I tried to make the shape pleasing and the result was a boat with surprising performance. The midsection is similar to that of the Tayana 37.*

*The Baba 30 sail plan shows the mast farther forward than that of the Tayana 37. The intermediate backstay is a useless but traditional piece of rigging, and I was not yet ready to abandon it when I drew this.*

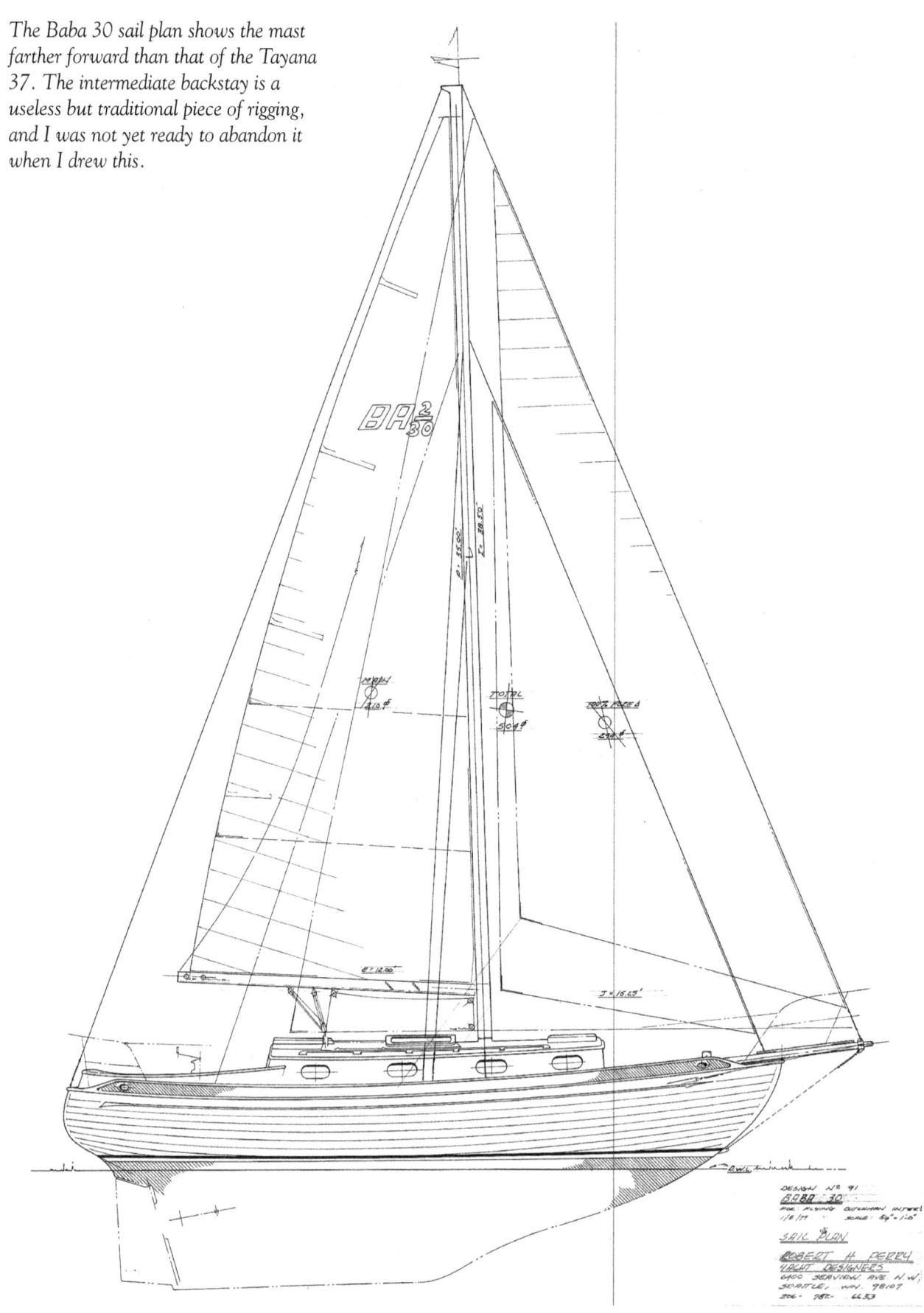

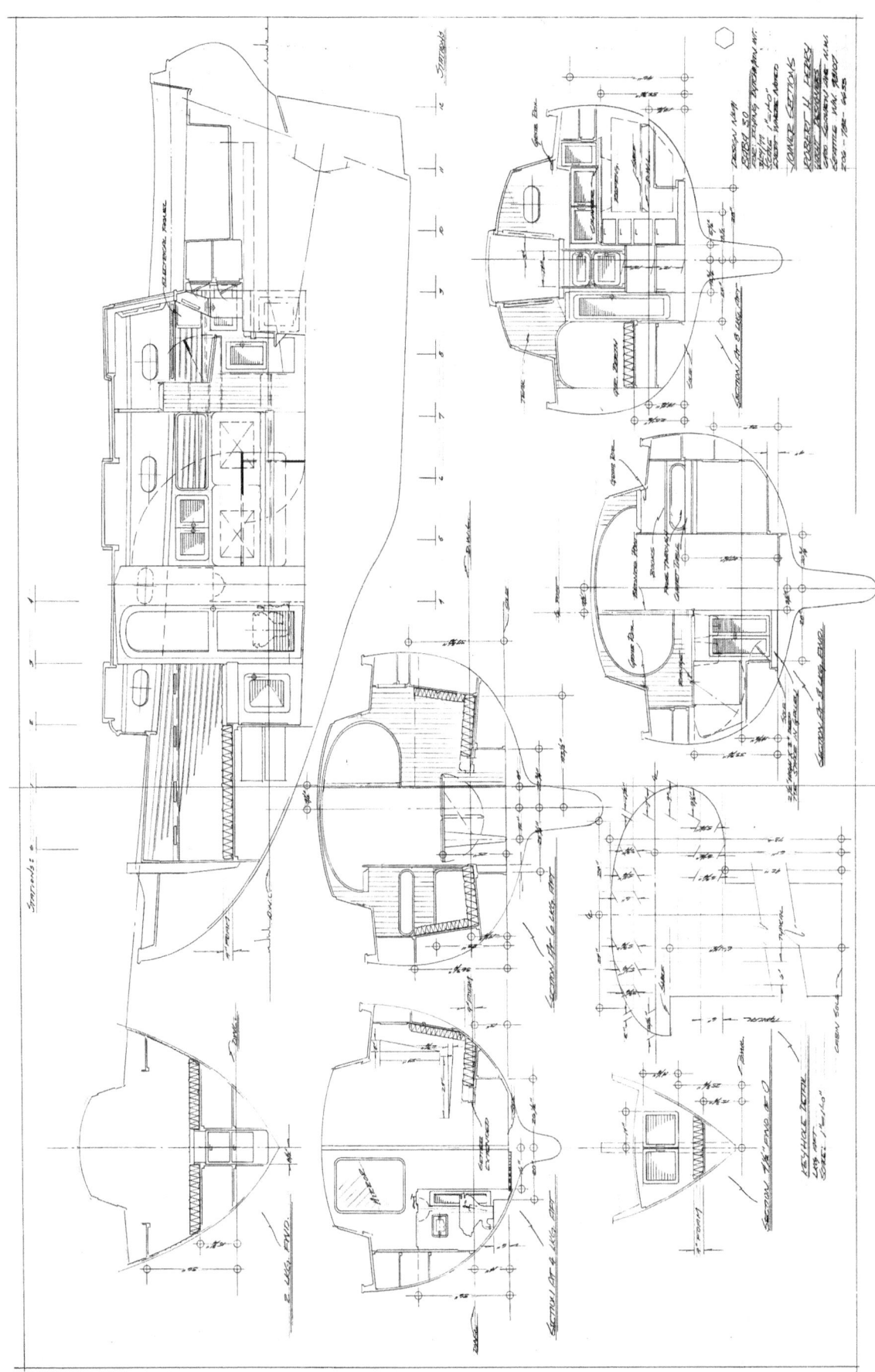

*I had a lot of volume to work with on the Baba 30, and Bob Berg made certain I used every cubic inch.*

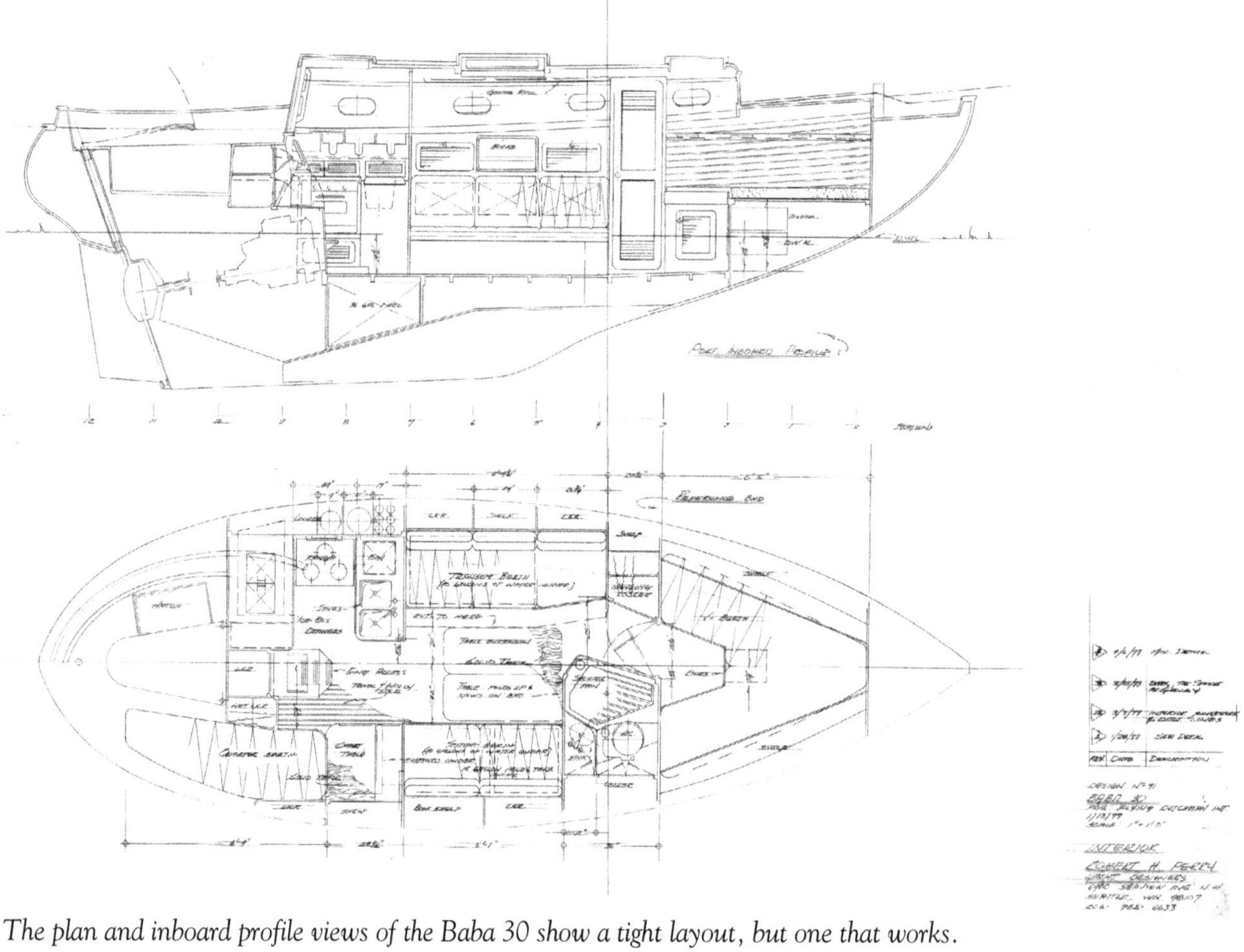

*The plan and inboard profile views of the Baba 30 show a tight layout, but one that works.*

*A Flying Dutchman 35 on a close reach.*

while. I felt really good about that. Say what you will. Yes, it's a fat little boat, but it can sail. One of the reasons for the Baba 30's good performance in light air was its low prismatic coefficient of 0.5. The hull was easily driven despite its bulk. Babas have several circumnavigations to their credit, including one done single-handed by a retired Baltimore bricklayer.

Ta Shing was in high gear in June 1979 and was starting another of my designs, the Norseman 447 project. Bob thought we should do a bigger version of the Baba 30, something that could compete with the Tayana 37. This design should have been the Baba 35, and in the office we have always referred to it as the Baba 35. But that was not to be. For reasons never explained to me, the model name would be the Flying Dutchman 35.

The new 35 was just a big brother to the Baba 30 in hull form but with the luxury of more length overall (LOA)—34.85 feet. I could stretch out the shape and lower the D/L to 325 plus reduce the L/B to 3.12. This is still on the fat side of moderate beam, but I needed beam for interior volume and stability. This hull shape, with its rounded sections combined with iron ballast, is also initially tender. Heavily built and with every cruising amenity available at the time, the ballast-to-displacement ratio for the Flying Dutchman 35 is 36 percent. Ta Shing did an excellent job with this design, and the boats came in on weight. I retained the hull's molded-in plank lines. These were essential to the overall aesthetic style and consistent with the type. I would not use the Hans Christian trick of molding in rabbit line and a big, flat stem and sternpost facing, simulating the look of a heavily built wooden boat. It was just too contrived for me. I did not like the idea of pushing or pulling flat surfaces through the water—it was slow. I gave the 35 a hint of that stem facing, but today that feature just looks odd to me.

Sailing in Puget Sound, I appreciated light-air performance, so the 35 had a big rig—maybe too big in some areas. Over the next couple of years I did several shortened versions of that rig, and I think they may have been all-around better boats than the original tall rig. The Tayana 37, the Baba 30, and the Flying Dutchman 35 all shared the same stability characteristics. They stiffened up when they got to 20 degrees of heel, but they got there quickly. Of course, this initial tenderness gave the boats a nice, soft motion at sea, and they all had good ultimate stability. The Flying Dutchman 35 sailed almost exactly like the Tayana 37 but was slightly faster in light air and an easier boat to balance. In true Ta Shing style, the boats were built beautifully, but they were more expensive than the Tayana 37 and never reached the same hull numbers.

The deck design of the Flying Dutchman 35 borrowed more from the Hans Christian line with its wraparound cockpit coaming; and is a big improvement over the Tayana 37. The side decks are broad, and the house narrow. The housetop has a strong camber to it. The sides of the house roll gently inboard as you go forward. I had learned this trick after doing too many boxy-looking houses. The rake of the house sides established aft could not be carried forward at the same angle. This angle had to be increased as you moved forward if you wanted a trim look to the house. The Flying Dutchman 35 had a great-looking deck. I did a very shapely version of the Flying Dutchman 35 deck with a small pilothouse and inside steering. This remains one of my favorite designs, but only a handful of this model was sold. I think this version is one of the best-looking small pilothouse boats you can find.

Bob Berg came to me next with an idea for a 40-foot Baba. Bob was still working with Ta Shing, and they had asked him to develop a new 40-foot model. When I started this design in August 1979, the first thing I did was to pull out the original Valiant 40 hull lines I had done years earlier. After sailing the Flying Dutchman 35, it was apparent to me that while the 35 was a fine boat, it was not an improvement over my earlier efforts with the Tayana 37. I had been developing a hull form that I felt was right, but I was not getting the performance improvements I was after. I studied the Valiant 40 lines and decided that the new Baba 40 would have a hull shape based more on the hull form of the Valiant 40.

This meant that the new Baba 40 would have firmer bilges than the Flying Dutchman 35 and

*A Baba 40 romping along on a beam reach offshore. The partial reef in the genoa, I was told, was to try to slow the boat down so the buddy boat on this passage could keep up. I like those stories. I think the staysail would have worked nicely on this point of sail, but of course it would have added to boat speed.*

some deadrise to the midsection similar to but not quite as pronounced as in the Valiant 40. I kept the new Baba 40 beamy with a L/B of 3.1. I knew that Bob Berg would be after interior volume. I flattened the buttocks as much as I could, gave the forefoot knuckle more definition, and reduced the angle of entry compared to that of the Flying Dutchman 35. I also took volume and flare out of the topsides forward to maintain this sharper angle of entry farther up into the topsides for better upwind speed. You can see this easily in the stem profile of the Baba 40. The stem of the Baba 40 has much less convexity than my previous boats in this aesthetic family. A rounded stem profile almost always and should mean more fullness or convexity "flam" to the topsides sections. Fullness buys you interior volume, but the boat is not fast when you are punching through waves and trying to squeeze it up to weather.

I also pulled the leading edge of the keel as far aft as I could. There is always a design battle between trying to get the lead forward and the center of keel pressure aft. This battle must be resolved in order to get the boat to float on its lines and at the same time have a nice, gentle helm. I remain convinced that most cruisers need a near-neutral helm, for convenience if nothing else. It's just handy to be able to let go of the wheel and not have your boat round up hard. Trim considerations want the keel/lead forward, and helm-balance considerations want the keel aft. If you look at the hull lines of the Baba 40, you will see that there is a marked distinction where the leading edge of the keel meets the canoe body/hull. When you compare this area to the same area on the Flying Dutchman 35, you will see that the leading edge of the keel of the 35 is faired into the hull profile with a sweeping fillet or curve. If you go back further and compare the same feature on the Baba 40 with the Tayana 37 and the Baba 30, you'll see that in these designs there is no distinction as to where the forefoot ends and the leading edge of the keel begins. Attempts at "blending" the keel shape with the hull shape with big-radius, hollow garboards, while standard practice 40 years ago, have now proven to compromise the function of both shape entities. I consider these earlier designs true "full-keel" designs and the latter Baba 40 a modified full keel. The distinction is subtle but important.

Ta Shing was doing the deck plug of the Baba 40 at the same time it was building the deck plug of the Norseman 447. The two styles of boats were at odds with each other. The Norseman 447 was all facets and angles, while the Baba was all soft-rounded contours. I wanted a highly traditional look for the deck of the Baba 40, and I wanted a very nontraditional look for the deck of the Norseman 447. The workers in the shop were confused when I arrived at the yard. The two deck plugs were side by side in the shop, and the workers needed direction despite the fact that my deck-plug drawings were always well detailed. My decks were always very difficult to build, as I tried hard to control all the aesthetic elements and I never let difficulty of construction stop me from drawing a detail and insisting on its execution. You only build the plug once. But I found the key to solve their problem.

"The Norseman is a diamond," I explained. "The Baba 40 is a pearl."

They understood immediately. The Baba 40 deck is beautiful. Unfortunately, or fortunately depending upon your viewpoint and height, some dealers thought that the early Baba 40s needed more headroom and a wider cabin trunk. This change was made without consulting me. It's a subtle change; even I have to look hard to tell the difference, and the revised deck still looks great. However, my orig-

*One of my favorite sailing shots of the Baba 40. This was taken on San Francisco Bay and shows near perfect trim for a cutter on the wind.*

inal deck, with its broader side decks and more pronounced cabin-top camber, looks better to my eye.

Working with Bob Berg, I produced an interior for the Baba 40 that to this day I consider one of if not my best. This layout just feels right the moment you go below. The detailing is impeccable, and the layout shows no apparent compromise. You often hear that all yacht design is compromise, and that may be true. The trick is to deal with the compromises so that the buyer is never aware that any compromises were made. To me, saying "it's a compromise" is an excuse for bad design.

My new hull form proved a huge step forward. The Baba 40 had an entirely different stability personality. It was stiffer initially, beautifully balanced, and much faster than its older siblings. The Baba 40 had a wonderful feel to the helm and was a fun boat to sail, especially in a breeze. I had opportunities to race my Valiant against Tim Roth's tall-rigged Baba 40, and it was always a tough race. I added five feet to Tim's rig when he told me he intended to race the boat in Seattle's PHRF fleet. Over the years, Tim had accumulated a lot of trophies, and his boat, the *Airloom*, had earned the nickname the "Furniture 40." I owe Tim a debt of thanks for showing Seattle sailors that boats with long (full) keels really can sail well. It was clear to me that the hull of the Baba 40 was a dramatic improvement over the older designs.

Standing at my Ballard dining room window one blustery fall afternoon, I noticed a boat beating southward. This boat was cleaving its way through the steep Puget Sound chop and appeared to be making very good boat speed. I see a lot of boats from that window, but this one caught my attention. I got my binoculars so I could identify the boat. It was a Baba 40. It probably had the tide with it, but nonetheless, I was impressed even before I knew it was one of mine.

I designed a pilothouse version of the Baba 40. This model had a great layout with two very comfortable staterooms. I raised the dinette to get good vision when seated. I also sunk the galley down a step to get better stowage volume in the lockers under the side decks. Pilothouse boats usually suffer in this respect, because raising the coach roof means raising the cabin sole. When you raise the cabin sole with a given freeboard, you reduce the height under the side decks. When you add counter height into this formula, you end up with only a sliver of available locker height under the side decks. The pilothouse Baba 40 with its sunken galley had the same galley stowage capacity as the non-pilothouse version. With its comfortable inside steering position, the pilothouse Baba 40 became a very popular model.

Today, people shopping for a used Baba 40 often get confused because the Baba 40 was built using three different names: Baba 40, Panda 40, and Tashiba 40. When Bob Berg first started marketing the 40, it was a Baba. Then, in one of those weird legal situations, Bob left the Flying Dutchman dealership and lost the right to use the Baba name. It was his nickname, but he did not own that name. For a short while Bob marketed the 40 as the Panda 40. However, as Ta Shing became a real force in Taiwanese boatbuilding, the company decided it did not need outside help and that it would do the marketing of the boat. Ta Shing took the project away from Bob—the man who had conceived it. Ta Shing marketed the boat as the Tashiba 40. I did not like this name—it was just too close to Toshiba, the Japanese electronics giant. But Ta Yang had gone with Tayana for marketing its boats, and Ta Shing must have taken Ta Yang's lead and decided upon Tashiba. Maybe the "ba" part of Tashiba was a tribute to the Baba origins of the project. If there is any thread you can follow as the 40 went through its progression of marketing identities, it is that, as more boats were produced, Ta Shing made an effort to reduce the cost of the boat. The early Baba 40s with their butterfly saloon hatch had far more teak trim, more port lights, and intricate Bob Bergesque interior detailing than the later less-detailed Tashiba 40s.

With the Tashiba in full production, Ta Shing decided it needed to add to the family, which was good news to me. I was commissioned to design a new 36 and a new 31. B.K. Kuo, manager of Ta Shing, flew to Seattle and stayed in my house for a month while we produced those two new designs. My sons were excited about having a Chinese man living with us. B.K. was an intelligent and affable man with a good grasp of English—affable to a point, but I always had the sense that he only tolerated the Western mentality. He knew what he wanted in the new designs, and he hovered over the drawing boards. We worked well together.

The new designs were produced side by side. Both drew on the progress in hull form that I had made with the Baba 40. However, knowing what the improvements had meant to the Baba 40, I went

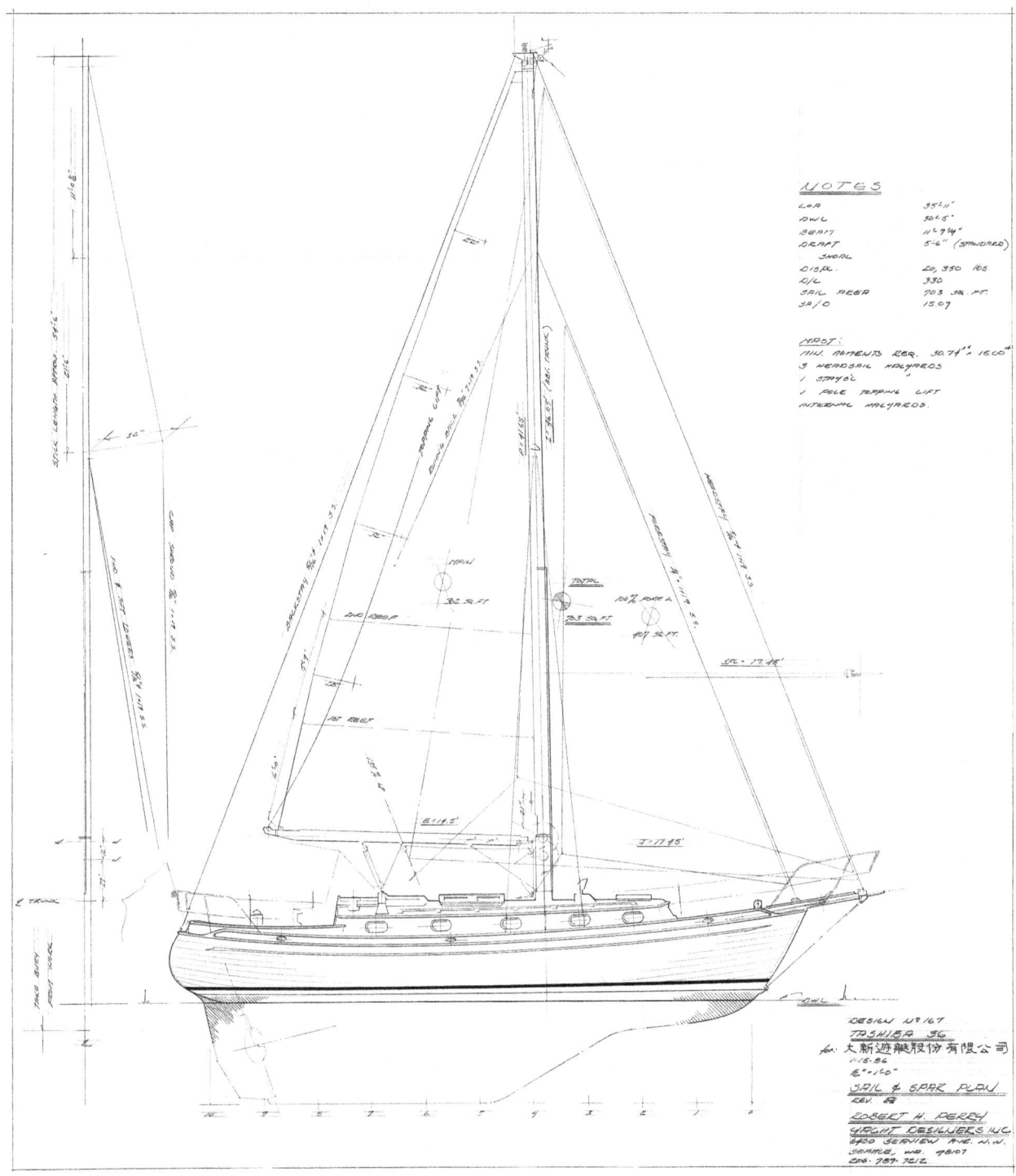

*The sail plan and profile of the Tashiba 36 show what I'd learned in 20 years of designing this style of boat. The mast is farther forward than on the Tayana 37.*

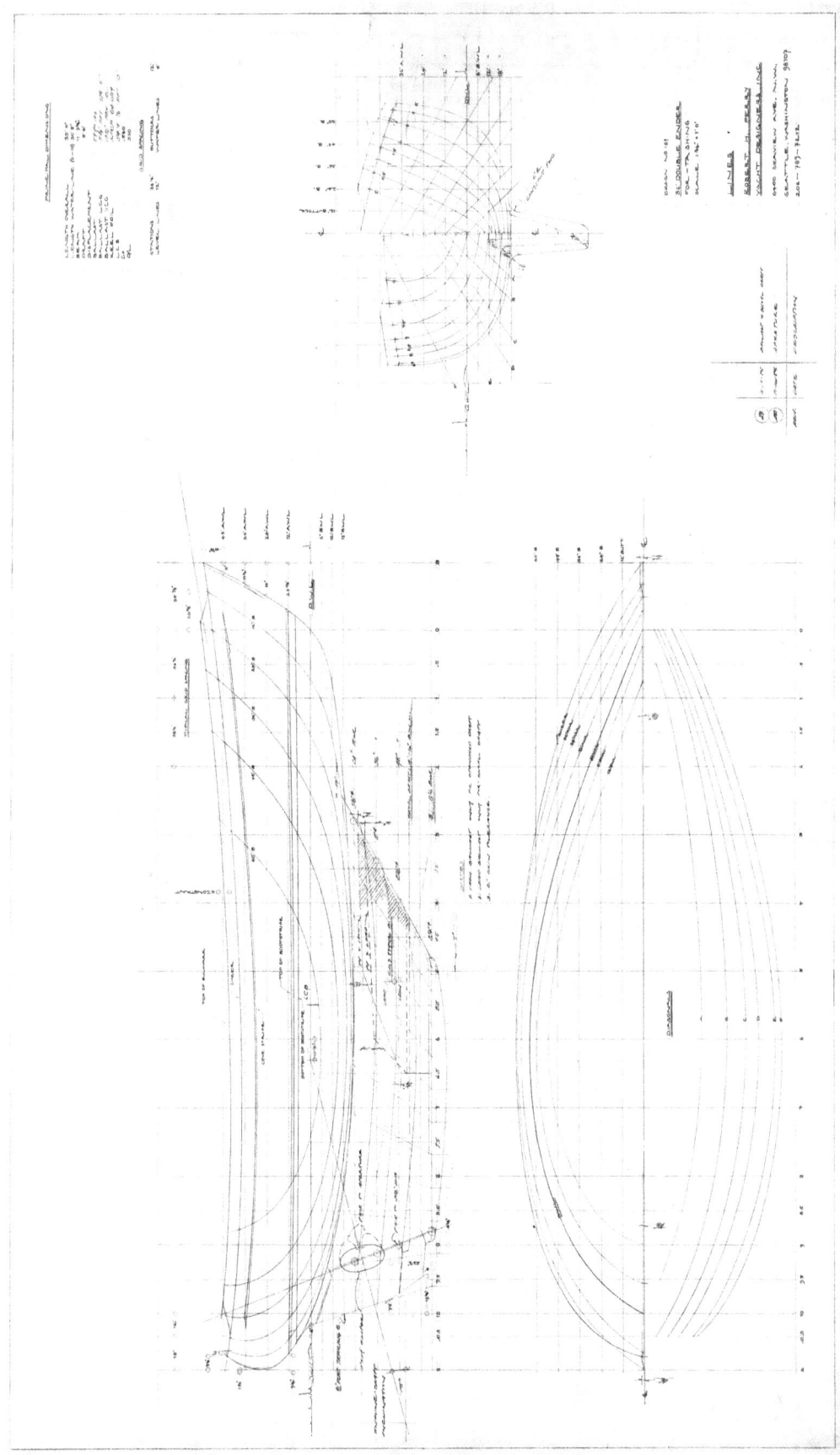

The lines of the Tashiba 36 show a harder turn to the bilge, a finer entry, and flatter buttocks than on my earlier double-enders in this style. I pulled the leading edge of the keel as far aft as possible.

even further with these same design elements. The turn to the bilge got even more firm for increases in stability. The bows were finer. All trace of faux wooden construction styling was avoided, except for the de rigueur plank lines. The leading edges of the keels were pulled farther aft, and I stuck strictly to NACA foil sections for these long keels. I reduced the chord length of the rudder tip with a kink in the tailing edge to shorten the tip chord and reduce drag on the Tashiba 36. This feature may not amount to much of an advantage in drag, but on paper it worked theoretically and it looks right. I moved the masts forward in both designs in order to ensure good helm balance. I think that the Tashiba 31 and 36 mark the best boats I ever designed with modified full keels. The boats were fast, close-winded, stiff, and well balanced. I constantly got calls from owners telling me how they had "beat" a local contemporary design. Every cruiser has those stories, but these two models were consistently capable of delivering good boat speed. If I run into sailors who are skeptical of the performance potential of full-keel designs, I just tell them to reserve judgment until they've sailed one of the Tashibas. People often think that the Tashiba 31 is just a rehashed Baba 30 and that the Tashiba 36 is a revised Flying Dutchman 35, but despite a similar approach to the aesthetic elements, the Tashibas have totally different hull shapes and are entirely new designs.

I also drew pilothouse versions for both the Tashiba 31 and the 36. Not many of either model were built. Ta Shing was going on to bigger things with more contemporary designs, and the appeal of the double-ender was waning. Both were very handsome designs with pilothouse shapes and geometries similar to those of the Tashiba 40 pilothouse model. I'm partial to these models. I think they should have sold better, and they may have if they had been marketed with more zeal and exposure. It's hard to draw small, handsome pilothouse boats, but I think that the pilothouse versions of the 31 and 36 are pleasant-looking boats. Today, both versions are hard to find used and are much sought after. I think there are only two pilothouse 31s in existence.

The compact and intricate Tashiba boats were expensive to build, and Ta Shing was developing its line of Taswell boats. The Norwegian double-ender was seen as a sailing cliché, no longer marketable in the coming age of Eurostyling. This perception was helped along by an overabundance of "me-too" mediocre boats designed and built to the same styling aesthetic. The form is classic. All it takes is for the aesthetic elements to be married to modern hull-form technology. However, boat appreciation and market vitality are more functions of advertising dollars than they are of excellence in design. The one objective drawback to a modern double-ender is the difficulty in incorporating a swim step into the design. It's only a difficulty and not an impossibility. There is a strong possibility that I have designed and been responsible for more built double-enders than any other designer. The type remains a favorite of mine. *Oceanus* will forever loom large in my memory. It would be a long time before someone asked me to draw another double-ender.

## According to Perry
# THOUGHTS ON THE CRUISING KEEL

I don't think there is any more misunderstood part of a cruising sailboat than its keel. We see every conceivable geometry presented as a "cruising keel," with accompanying terminology and justifications as varied as the shapes themselves. The only universal definition of a cruising keel is "a keel on a cruising boat," and because a "cruising boat" is any boat you can take cruising, keels vary accordingly. To accept this premise is to realize that there is no perfect, one-size-fits-all cruising keel.

Despite this great latitude, however, we should also accept that some cruising keels are "wrong." The keel must be matched to the hull, the rig, the projected performance envelope of the boat, the type of construction, and the owner's style of sailing. And we can add to those considerations what is probably the most important factor of all: Where are you going to sail the boat? The ideal keel for deep Puget Sound would be inappropriate for the shallow waters of Chesapeake Bay or the Bahamas. Conversely, a keel optimized for a shoal area would cripple a boat in Puget Sound. If you intend to voyage around the world, where do you draw the line on draft? Pragmatic considerations are often at odds with technological ones when it comes to keel design. The clever designer will work out appropriate compromises to produce a good all-around keel.

The accompanying art provides a list of terms and definitions.

The keel has several functions. In being or in many cases housing the ballast, it balances the boat so that it will sit on its designed fore-and-aft lines. If the keel ballast is too far forward, the design will be down in the bow; if it is too far aft, it will be down in the stern. A correctly designed keel also acts as a "wing" that will create lift and limit leeway. The keel ballast will lower the boat's overall VCG and contribute to the boat's righting moment for stability. In a fore-and-aft sense, the keel balances the rig forces such that the boat will have a manageable and predictable helm. If the keel is too far forward, you may experience too much weather helm. If the keel is too far aft, you may have lee helm, although lee helm is rare.

I am not going to get into the area of specific foil sections (i.e., the longitudinal sectional shape of a keel fin). This is a complex subject burdened with conflicting data and opinions. Suffice it to say that the thickness of a typical keel foil will be about 9 to 12 percent of its length, which is what we call its *thickness ratio*. The thickest part of the foil will usually be about 40 percent of the chord length aft of the leading edge. This is usually referred to as "max thickness." Foil type and thickness ratios need not be the same for the entire keel fin, as is starkly apparent when the keel is a bulb type. Most keels are thicker proportionately at the tip than at the root in order to lower the VCG of the ballast. The foil I have used for 80 percent of my keels over the years is the

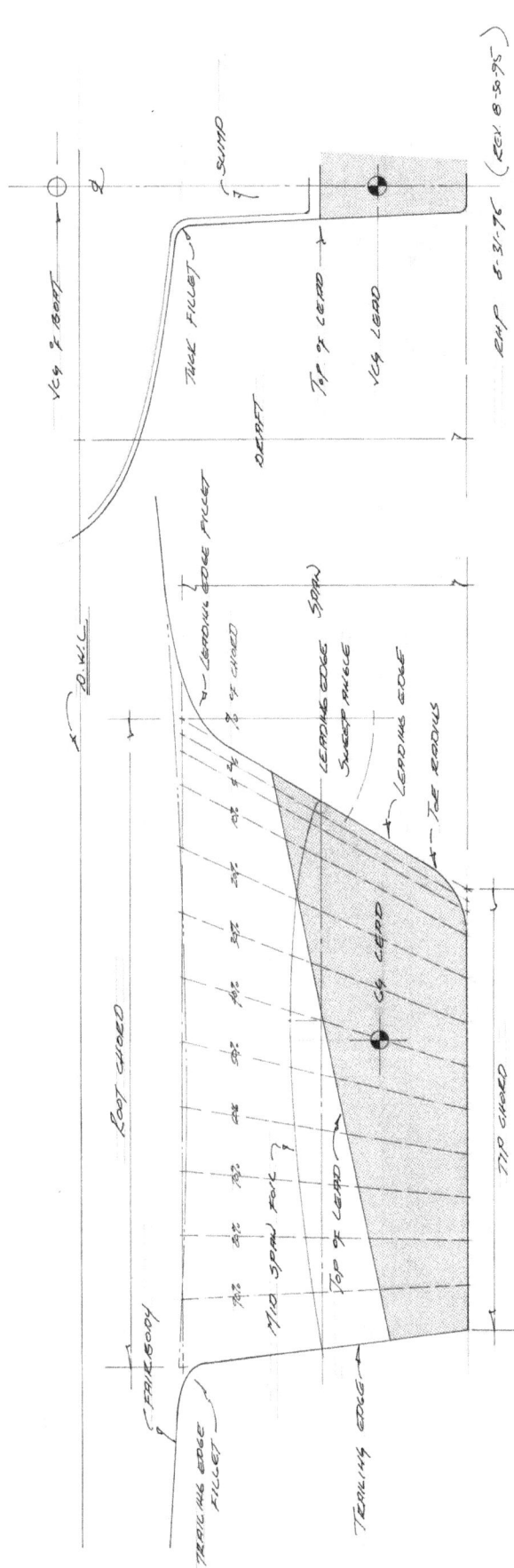

A representative medium-aspect fin keel with outside ballast, showing the primary points of comparison.

**Draft**—the depth of the boat from its load waterline (LWL) to its deepest point, presumably the bottom of its keel

**Planform**—the profile shape of the keel

**Root**—the uppermost foil section, where the keel fin joins the hull

**Tip**—the lowest foil section, at the bottom of the keel

**Span**—the depth of the keel from root to tip

**Chord**—a horizontal line from the leading edge to the trailing edge at any point along the span

**Thickness**—usually expressed as a ratio of foil thickness to chord length

**Sweep**—the angle of a keel from the vertical, usually measured on a line that runs down the keel through each quarter-chord (which is 25 percent of each chord length aft of the leading edge)

**VCG**—vertical center of gravity

**LCG**—longitudinal center of gravity

**Bulb**—I apply this term liberally to any distension or bulge at the tip of the keel

**Tuck**—the area in a sectional view where the keel meets the hull; often called the garboards in older boats

**Fillet**—the radius of the tuck or the turn where the edges of the keel meet the canoe body of the hull

**Aspect ratio**—the ratio of the mean chord length to the span

NACA foil 64-A010, modified to the thickness ratio I am after.

Keep in mind that, unlike the asymmetrical foils of an airplane, the symmetrical foil of a keel requires leeway in order to develop an angle of attack. In other words, without leeway, there is no lift.

The one term not used in this book is *modified fin*. I hear this term frequently—often in reference to my own designs—but I have no idea what it means. A fin is a fin. It may be a low-aspect fin or high-aspect fin, but it's still a fin. A Valiant 42 has a low-aspect fin, while *Amati* (Chapter 15) has a high-aspect fin.

## Chapter Eight
# CHEOY LEE

When I was in high school, it was my habit to send for brochures for the boats I admired. I didn't try to disguise the fact that I was a kid trying to learn yacht design, so most of my letters included the line "please send me all your brochures." That, at least, should have been a dead giveaway, but nonetheless, my collection of brochures was impressive and growing. After sending away for the Cheoy Lee brochures, I was surprised one night to get a phone call from the Seattle Cheoy Lee dealer, Gary Horder. I didn't know Gary personally, but I had seen him on the racecourse racing his Cheoy Lee 35 Lion class sloop designed by Arthur Robb. *Dandelion* was not a fast boat but it was handsome, with long overhangs, a narrow beam, and pleasing proportions artfully executed in all-teak construction. In 1964, Cheoy Lee was the major Asian boatbuilder. Other boats were being built in Asia, but they were usually custom yachts like Garden's *Teak Bird* and *Walloon*, or they were limited-series boats like the Calkins 50s. Cheoy Lee was producing a range of boats that included its version of the famous Scandinavian folkboat, the boat of my boyhood circumnavigation dreams.

It was 1978 when I received an inquiry from Cheoy Lee for a new 35er. I was very honored, having been an admirer of Cheoy Lee boats for years. My working arrangement with Cheoy Lee was to be unusual, and in time I learned some valuable business lessons from this arrangement. Cheoy Lee wanted to own the designs outright with no royalties attached. This meant a one-time payment for the design. One of my mistakes throughout my career was undervaluing my design work. This plagued me for years. I was just happy to be asked to design another boat, and I really had no benchmarks for how much to charge. Still, I made ends meet and had fun doing it. I have few regrets in this area.

Cheoy Lee did not want the "normal" design package. The company wanted the basic drawings: hull, keel and rudder lines and offsets, deck lines, deck plan, sail plan, and rig layout and the standard interior layout, inboard profiles, joiner sections, and tank layout. They did not want any structural drawings. Their builders would do these themselves. Cheoy Lee also wanted a weight study. It's not easy to do a weight study when you do not have structural drawings. My office staff members went through our regular system of specifying scantlings so that we had something to work with for structural weights. The family that owned Cheoy Lee included sons who had all graduated from the University of Michigan with degrees in engineering and naval architecture, or so I was told, and I have no reason to doubt it today. They were confident that they could handle the structural side of the design without my help. Given the pedigree of the Cheoy Lee factory, I had every reason to believe them.

My first design for Cheoy Lee was the CL 35. I chose a traditional look that drew inspiration from one of my very favorite Rhodes designs, the Chesapeake 32. The CL 35 had moderate overhangs, a

## Cheoy Lee

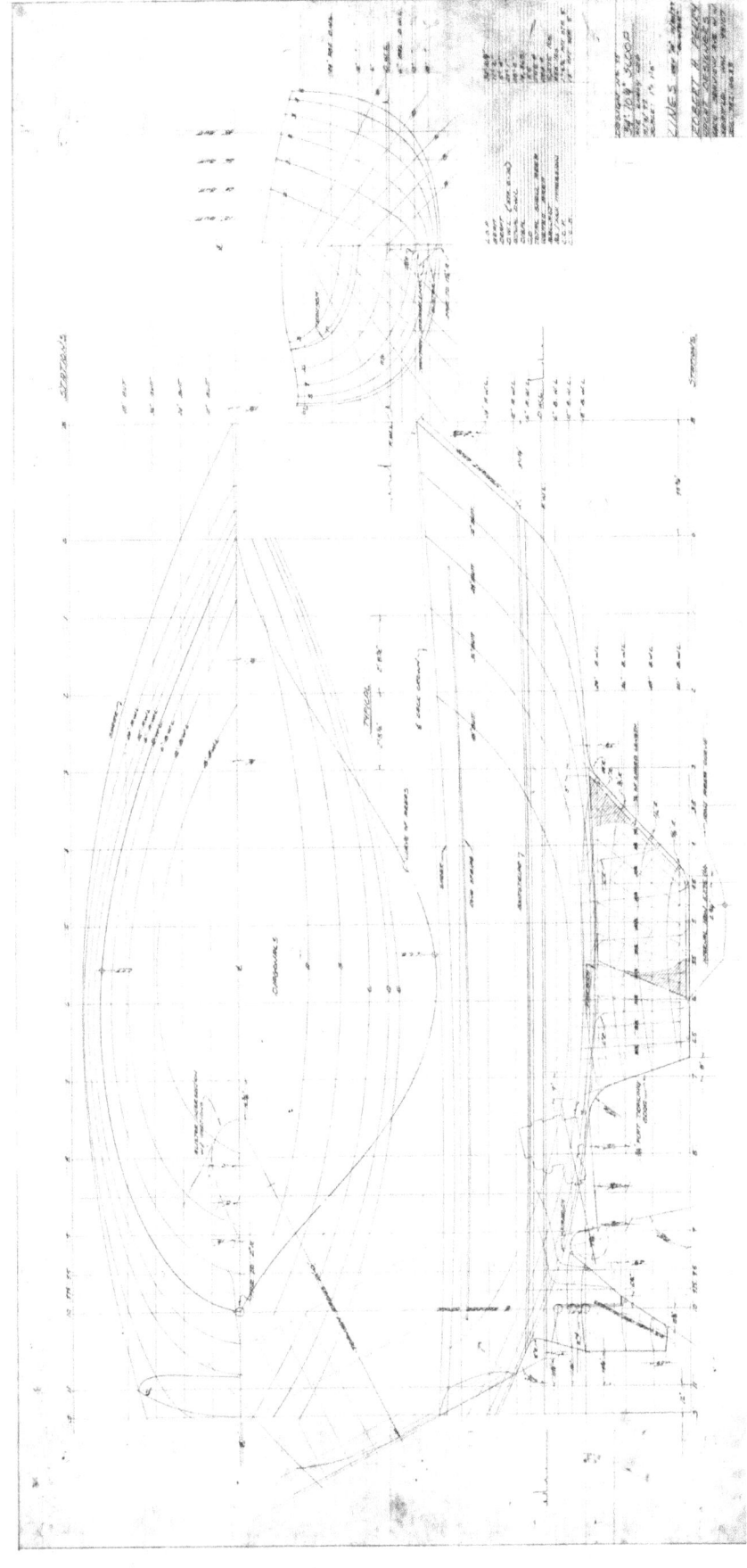

*The hull lines of the Cheoy Lee 35 show the distended bustle-like region aft of the keel fin to keep the prop shaft enclosed. I think this was my first design with a partial skeg. Looking at it now, I wonder why I did not take the opportunity to balance the rudder a little more.*

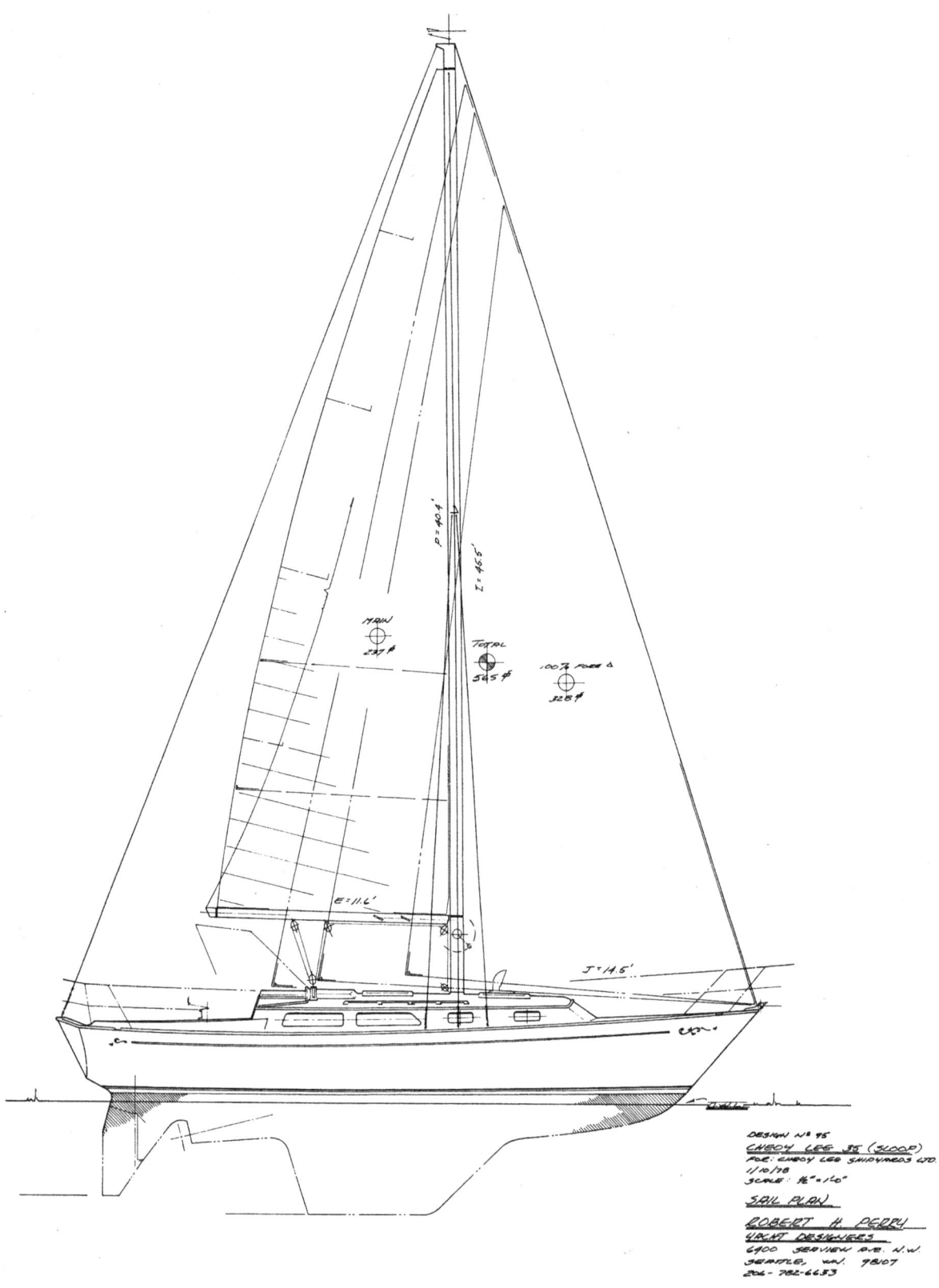

*The CL 35 sail plan shows the mast nicely forward. The profile owes some of its appeal to the designs of Philip Rhodes and Bill Luders.*

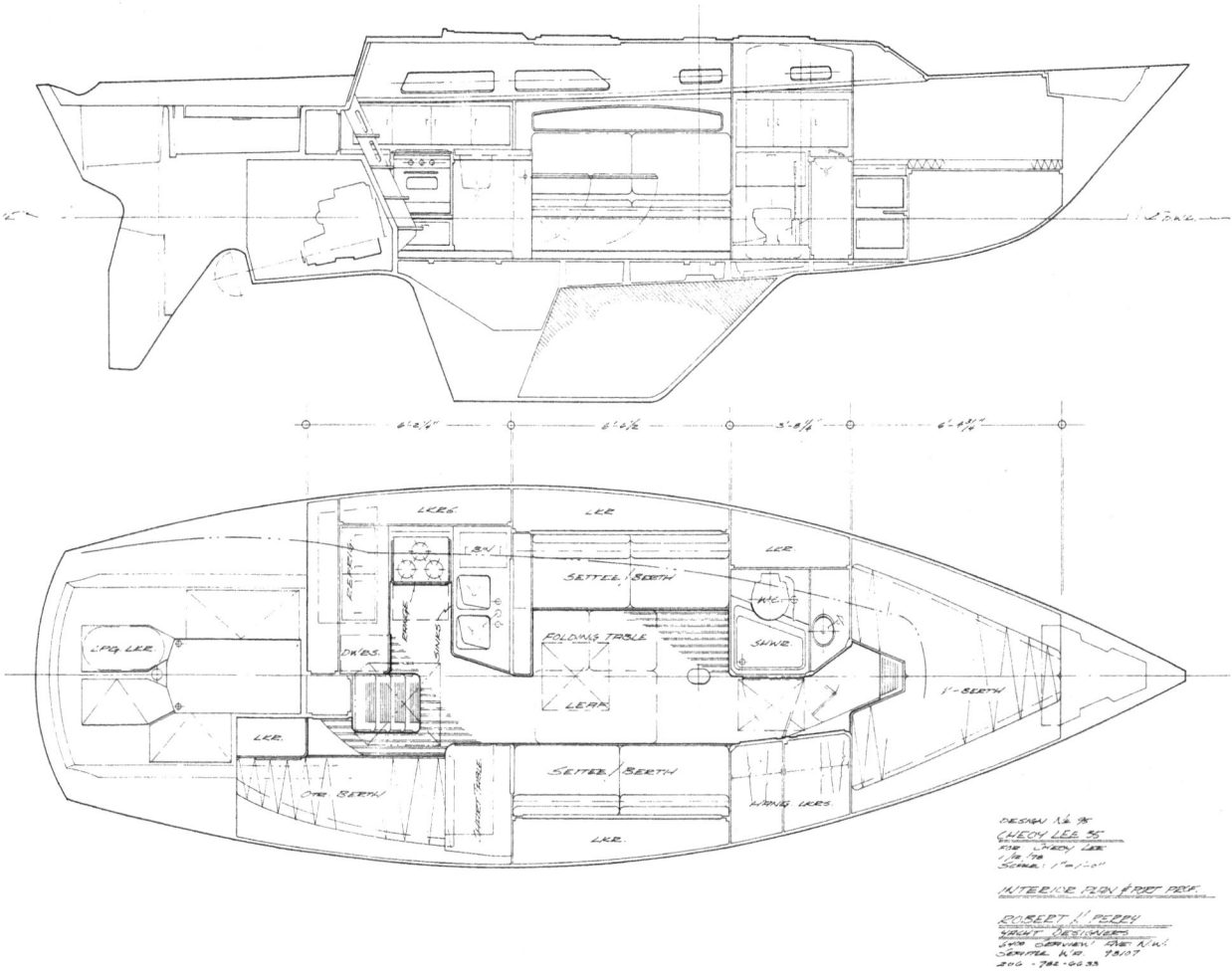

*This drawing of the CL 35 interior clearly shows how I used the bustle area, at Cheoy Lee's request, to capture the entire pop shaft and avoid a bracket aft of the stuffing box. Note also how much volume the cast iron ballast takes up inside the integral keel fin.*

strong spring to the sheer, and a very conventional and trim cabin trunk that I copied directly from the work of the Rhodes office. The hull form was my own and included my first use of a half skeg with a semi-balanced rudder. Cheoy Lee insisted that the engine be located in the bilge and that the hull canoe body be distended to avoid the use of a prop strut. This resulted in a bit of a bustle shape to the hull starting at the trailing edge of the keel, but the bustle was cut short to leave room for the prop and the appropriate clearance in front of the rudder.

Cheoy Lee built spruce spars, and we spec'd the scantlings for the spars. Unfortunately, I designed keel-stepped spars and Cheoy Lee built deck-stepped spars. This was no problem in most cases, as the designer would just adjust the moments of inertia required for a strong stick to account for the lack of support at the partners. It was done all the time, and deck-stepped spars had distinct advantages. However, you cannot simply take the scantlings for a keel-stepped mast and use them for a deck-stepped spar. This proved to be a problem later on.

I had little communication with Cheoy Lee. I sent the company the drawings, and they sent me the money. For months I would hear nothing until I received a package in the mail with photos of the finished boat under sail in Hong Kong harbor. I was used to continuous communication with the yards building my designs, and this almost always included at least one trip, usually more, to the yard to inspect the progress of the design while the first boat was under construction. By the looks of the photos I

*The first CL 35 undergoing sailing trials in Hong Kong harbor.*

received Cheoy Lee had done a good job building my 35-footer. A local Seattle doctor bought one of the first 35s, and I ran into him and his wife as we both cruised the Puget Sound area. He loved the boat. I was proud.

Cheoy Lee must have been happy with the boat, too, because in January 1977, the company asked me to design a 44-footer for them. For this project I had the advantage of being in the middle of what would turn out to be a string of 44-footers: the Lafitte 44, the Norseman 447, and the Nordic 44. I got to know what you could do with 44 feet quite well. I did make one trip to the Cheoy Lee yard. I had just spent ten days in Taiwan working on various projects and I scheduled a stop in Hong Kong on my way home. My goal was to spend time at the Cheoy Lee yard and buy an expensive watch that I presumed I could get cheaper in Hong Kong.

As usual, due to my ongoing problem with the international dateline, I arrived in Hong Kong a day earlier than I had told Cheoy Lee. We had arranged that I would be picked up at the airport, but after standing at the curb for an hour, it became apparent that I was on my own. This was disappointing, but I was not one to be intimidated by the vagaries of international travel. It was just another adventure to me. As I stood there at the curb musing about my new expensive watch, I felt a tapping on my wrist. I turned to see an old Chinese man pointing at my watch, an Eddie Bauer "camp watch" I bought through their catalog for much less than $100. He said as he pointed to the watch, "American military watch—very high quality."

"Oh, really?" I said, and all of a sudden the lure of the expensive Hong Kong watch began to fade. I had in mind a watch called the Royal Oak by Piaget.

Obviously I was not going to be picked up, so I called my hotel and was sent a limo. Well, actually it was a Peugeot station wagon. I could not get a reservation at the Peninsula so I booked into the Holiday Inn. It was fine and my room was spacious and comfortable. It was mid-afternoon and I cleaned up and went out for a walk, thinking maybe I'd find the watch. After several blocks and an unusual number of jewelers all with displays of expensive watches, I began to get scared that I would buy a knockoff, a fake expensive watch. Reluctantly, I abandoned the watch mission, satisfied that I was wearing an American military watch of "very high quality." The crowded sidewalks were getting to me. I was intimidated with the bustle and population density of Hong Kong. I stopped long enough to buy a bottle of wine then hightailed it back to the safety of my hotel room, where I ordered lamb chops from room service and drank my bottle of Beaujolais while watching an American football game on TV. My new skill with Mandarin did me little good in Hong Kong, where the population spoke Cantonese, a seven-tone dialect compared to the simpler four tones of Mandarin.

I had no idea what had happened to Cheoy Lee, but I knew I did not want to spend my time in Hong Kong alone. I picked up the phonebook. I had once had a phone call from a Hong Kong owner of a CL 35. He was a lawyer, and his name was Hebtee Hoosenally. Somehow I had never forgotten that name. It just rolled off the tongue and stuck in the mind. Voila! There he was in the phonebook. So I called the number and asked for Mr. Hoosenally and the lady on the other end said he was not at home. He was out sailing. Drat! But I left my number and Mr. Hoosenally called me later that night. We arranged to meet the next evening at the Royal Hong Kong Yacht Club, where we would rendezvous with some friends of his and go out to dinner. Sounded like a good plan to me.

I did contact Cheoy Lee the next day and toured the yard with the owner's son, But Yang Lo. We went to lunch, where he made a point of telling me the price of everything I ate. The meeting was quite formal, the lunch uncomfortable, and the yard quite crude by Taiwanese standards. I was dropped back at the hotel with the feeling of "well, that's that."

With directions in hand, I headed off to the ferry at 5 p.m. for the trip across the harbor to the yacht club to meet Mr. Hoosenally. I made it across the harbor, but because it was rush hour, I could not get a taxi to stop for me. I tried everything but it was not going to happen. I started to walk in the direction I knew the yacht club to be. But I wasn't going to give up on a taxi. I stood on a corner and tried again. I noticed another Westerner on the opposite corner also trying to get a cab. I crossed the street and asked him for advice on getting a cab. He asked where I was going, and to my surprise he said he was also going to the yacht club. He was English and his name was Roger Mudd. He was the editor of the *Asian Medical News* (as I recall), and he knew who I was! That felt pretty good. Small world. We rendezvoused at the yacht club as planned, and after a few rounds of drinks, I was whisked off to an exciting night of Hong Kong dining with a group of friendly sailors. I spent the next day shopping, spending most of my money on crazy, expensive Italian clothes for myself and my wife. I knew at the time it made no sense, but I was bored and I had my watch money burning a hole in my pocket. After the relatively quiet and structured life I led during my trips to Taiwan, my introduction to Hong Kong was frantic and quite intimidating. I never returned to Hong Kong.

My CL 44 was a good design—all Perry ideas based upon what I had done with the Lafitte and the Norseman. I gave the CL 44 a traditional transom with a bit of hollow to the garboards at the stern to help with the aesthetics of the big, broad transom. If you don't introduce some hollow there you can get a big, bland, fat-looking transom, and we wouldn't want that for the sake of a few tenths of a knot. Ballast was to be internal iron, so the keel envelope had to be voluminous enough to get the iron low. No problem—I had been working with internal iron ballast with almost all of my Taiwanese-built designs. We used a National Advisory Committee for Aeronautics (NACA) 64-A010 foil with its maximum thickness at 40 percent of chord. I played with the thickness ratio of the foil to give the fin positive draft. This would allow it to be removed easily from the mold while increasing the thickness ratio at the tip for better volume low in the fin. I often went as high as a 14 percent thickness ratio, but in most cases I liked to stay around a 12 percent maximum thickness ratio to keep the frontal area of the fin as low as possible.

We produced this design in both cutter and ketch rigs with either center-cockpit or aft-cockpit-layouts. The cabin trunks were well defined and were low and angular, with a sloping forward face to give the new CL 44 a contemporary look. To my eye this is still a very good-looking boat. Cockpit seats and seat backs were highly contoured for comfort.

We followed the CL 44 with a new CL 48 in November 1978. This hull was similar to that of the CL 44, with modest beam and a traditional transom with the same degree of hollow in the garboards at the stern as the CL 44. I have always tried to keep beam minimized. It's easy in the usual quest for interior volume to let beam get out of hand; however, beamy boats with a L/B of, say, less than 3.3 can have dual personalities. They may be well balanced and docile up to around 16 degrees of heel, but when that beam gets immersed, they can quickly develop weather helm and be bears to steer. My first question when deciding the beam for a new design is just how narrow can I make this boat while satisfying the client's needs for interior volume and layout particulars. The relatively long bow overhang of the CL 48, coupled with the short stern overhang, gave the boat, to my eye, a muscular look. The CL 48 was a big, stiff boat with good sailing length and it sailed very well. Years later this was the hull on which I based my design for the Passport 47.

The CL 48 was again produced in ketch or cutter rigs with center-cockpit or aft-cockpit deck configurations. The interiors were well laid out and paid attention to the growing trend away from the "boy's cabin in the woods" approach and toward the

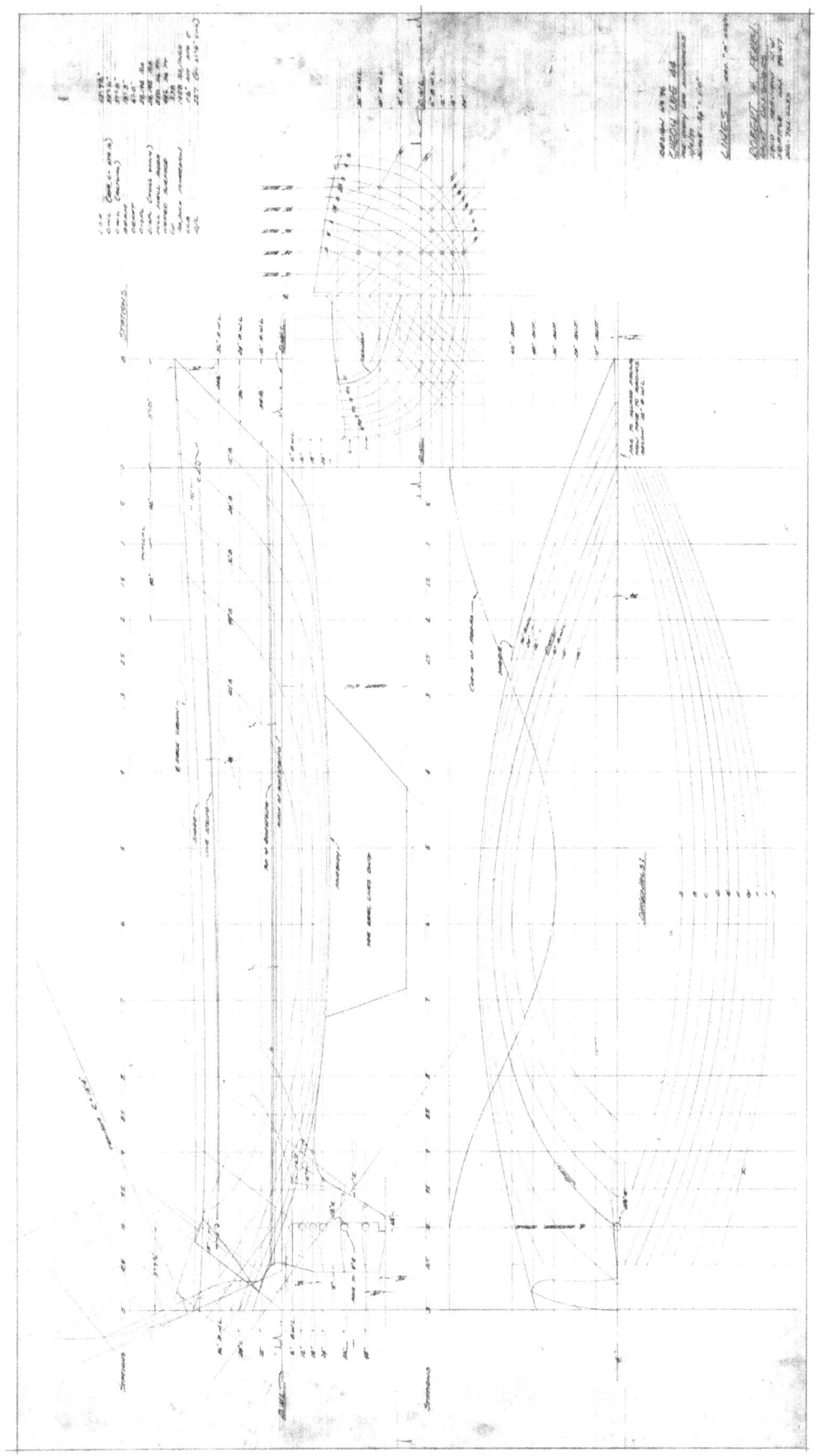

*You can see if you look carefully a reverse transom drawn on these hull lines for the CL 44. That transom was never built, and now I'm not sure why it is even on the drawing. The stock boat had the traditional transom also shown here.*

# Cheoy Lee

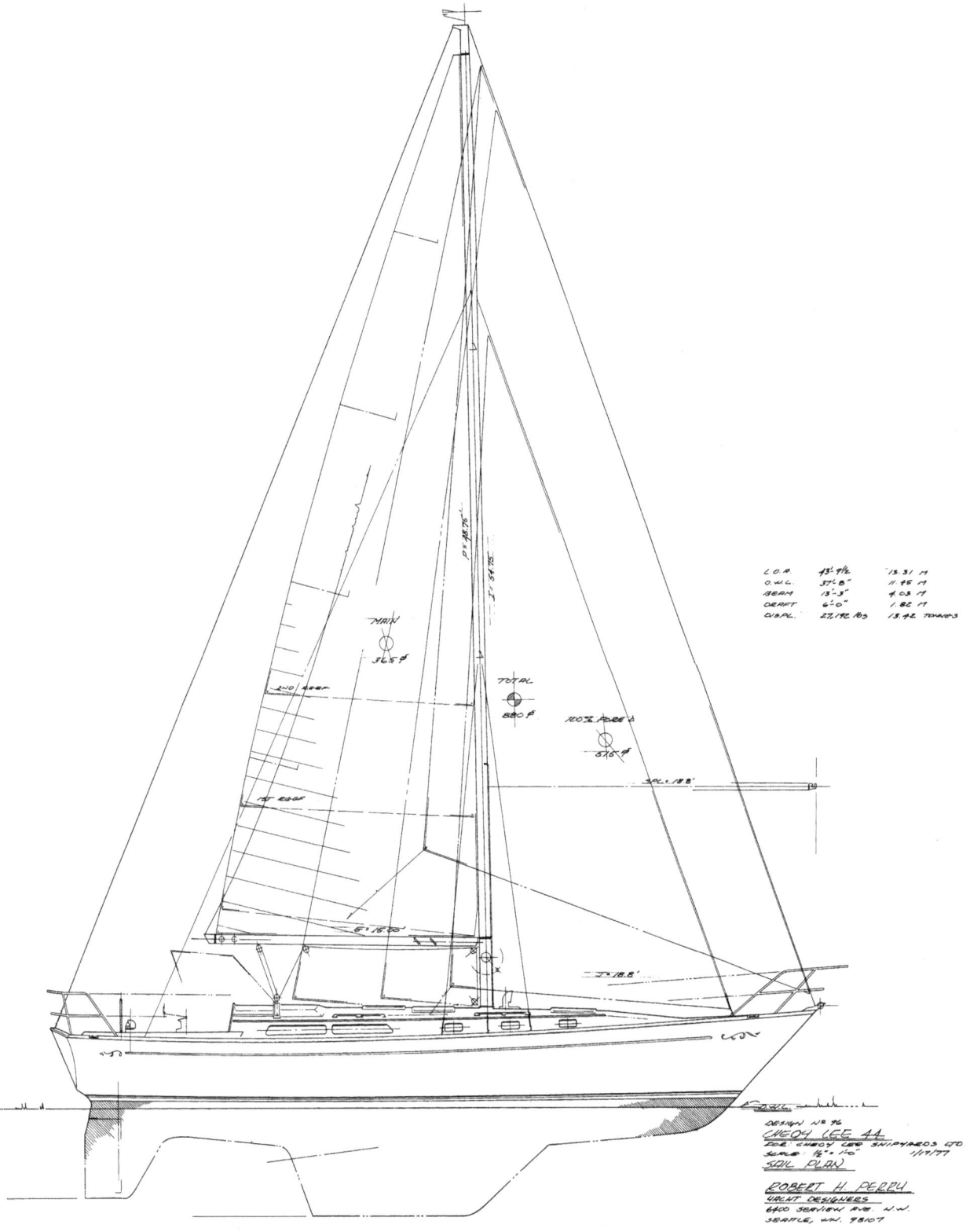

I liked the look of the CL 44. It was aggressive yet traditional, combining a rakish cabin trunk with fairly conservative hull lines.

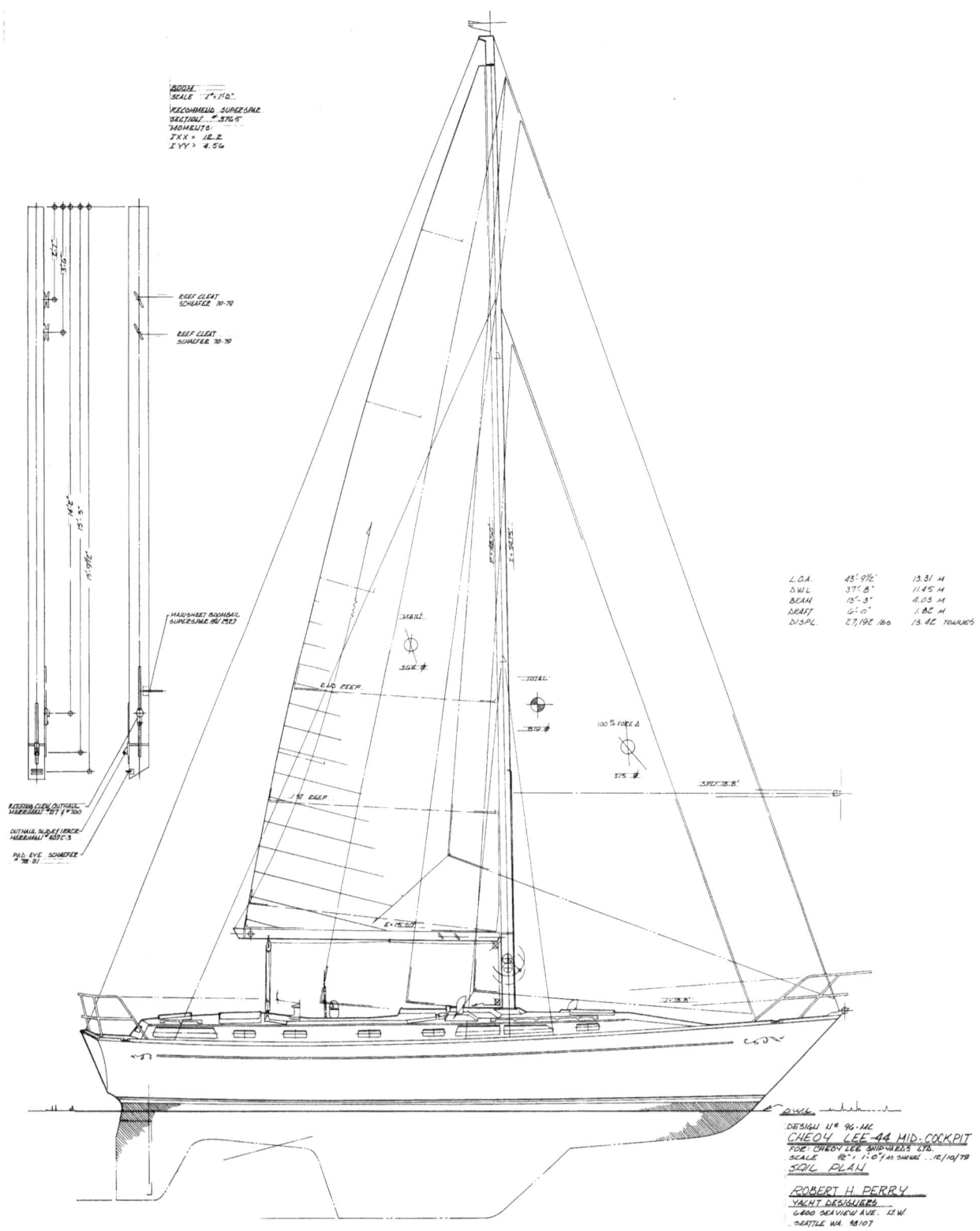

*In the center-cockpit version of the CL 44, I worked hard not to let the profile pile up, wedding-cake style, around the cockpit.*

## Cheoy Lee

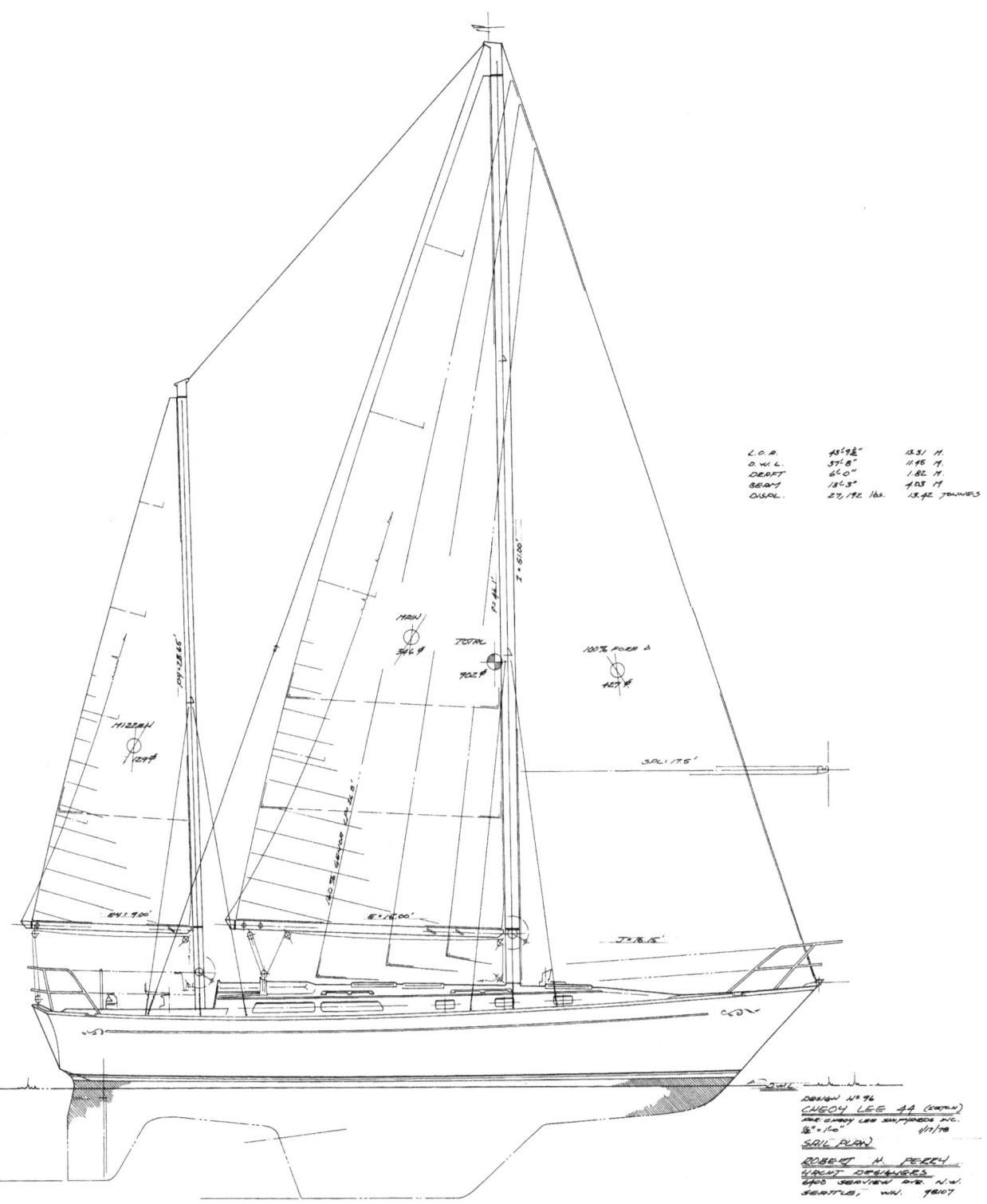

A handsome ketch version of the aft-cockpit CL 44.

*The CL 44 in cutter configuration, undergoing sailing trials in Hong Kong harbor.*

"home on the sea" approach. Heads had shower stalls, galleys were expansive, and berths were designed to be more comfortable at the dock and on the hook rather than serving as narrow sea berths. Settee berths could be rigged with lee cloths if you needed sea berths. Again, 90 percent of the time, interiors sell cruising boats.

The CL 35, 44, and 48 were my best attempts at all-around cruising boats, but my next commission from Cheoy Lee was to be entirely different. It came as a surprise, but the next letter I received from Cheoy Lee asked for a long-range motorsailer. Cheoy Lee spelled out exactly what engine the company wanted to use for this 43-footer, and they specified tankage at 600 gallons of fuel. This was a lot for a 43-footer. Clearly, this design was to be heavy on the "motor" and light on the "sailer." But that was fine. I had always admired the motorsailers of William Hand, and this new design would give me the chance to show what I could do with this type of challenge.

Of course, you could start with a hull shape then cram in the machinery and tankage, but that seemed backward to me. Instead, I started this design by drawing a cross section of the engine, adding the wing tanks to get the required fuel tankage. Then I drew a midsection shape around the engine and tanks. The result was a deep midsection with soft bilges. I gave the CL 43 a long keel. You could call it a "full keel," but there is still a distinction between the forefoot and the leading edge of the keel. In my book, that qualifies this keel as a "modified" full keel. I pulled the leading edge of the keel as far aft as I could to help with the keel shape and maneuverability. I gave the bow short overhang, and I put a stubby canoe stern on the boat in order to keep the designed waterline (DWL) as long as possible for speed under power.

With a D/L of 319, the CL 43 was a heavy boat, but the canoe body had minimal fore-and-aft rocker for its displacement. I endeavored to keep the buttocks as flat as possible to keep the quarter wave squashed down, again to help with speed under power. Years later, when cruising Bob Cole's CL 43 up to Tinsley Island with Frank McClear and Dave Pedrick aboard, they were both amazed at the speed of the CL 43 under power. We could do nine knots easily, and the only boat that passed us all day on the way to the island was a Santa Cruz 70. I didn't have any clear answers to their queries other than to explain that I had done the best I could. After the cruise, I mailed them both copies of the CL 43's hull lines. Maybe they could figure it out. All of the calculations and ratios are fine, but sometimes the designer needs a "holistic" vision of the finished boat that defies breakdown into a series of nondimensional ratios. Ratios are just pinhole glimpses into the overall personality of any design.

I really like this design. It has the look of a small ship. I have modified the rig for a couple of owners to add sail area to improve sailing performance. Two owners of the CL 43 were impressed enough to become subsequent custom-boat clients. In fact, one of these clients, Bernie Blum, had me design a new boat for him, but there is no way he would ever part with the CL 43. He loves his CL 43 enough to have put a carbon-fiber rig on it. Bernie's impeccable

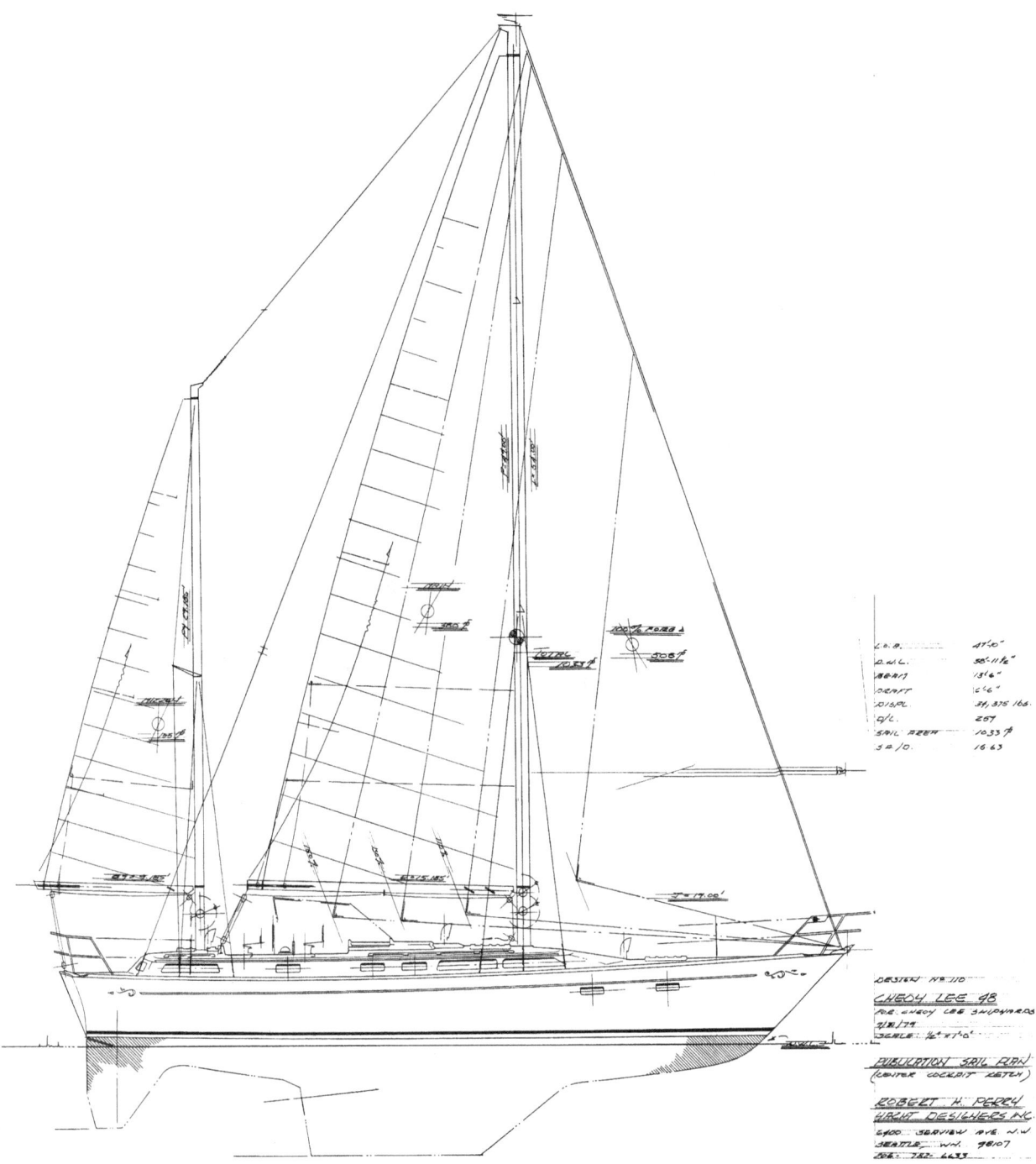

*The CL 48 has a muscular look with its high freeboard and short stern overhang.*

maintenance of his CL 43 makes me look good and proud to be the designer of the boat.

My relationship with Cheoy Lee ended on a sour note in 1981. The builder asked me to design a new 42-footer that would be their entry into a higher-quality level in the marketplace. This was to be the Golden Wave 42, and I would style it to be Cheoy Lee's version of a Swan with a low, wedgelike cabin trunk and hull lines close to the racing boats of the day. It was a good hull, and it's a very good boat in light air. However, the internal ballast in a narrow fin resulted in a high VCG for the ballast, and the boat was tender in a breeze—beautifully

# Yacht Design According to Perry

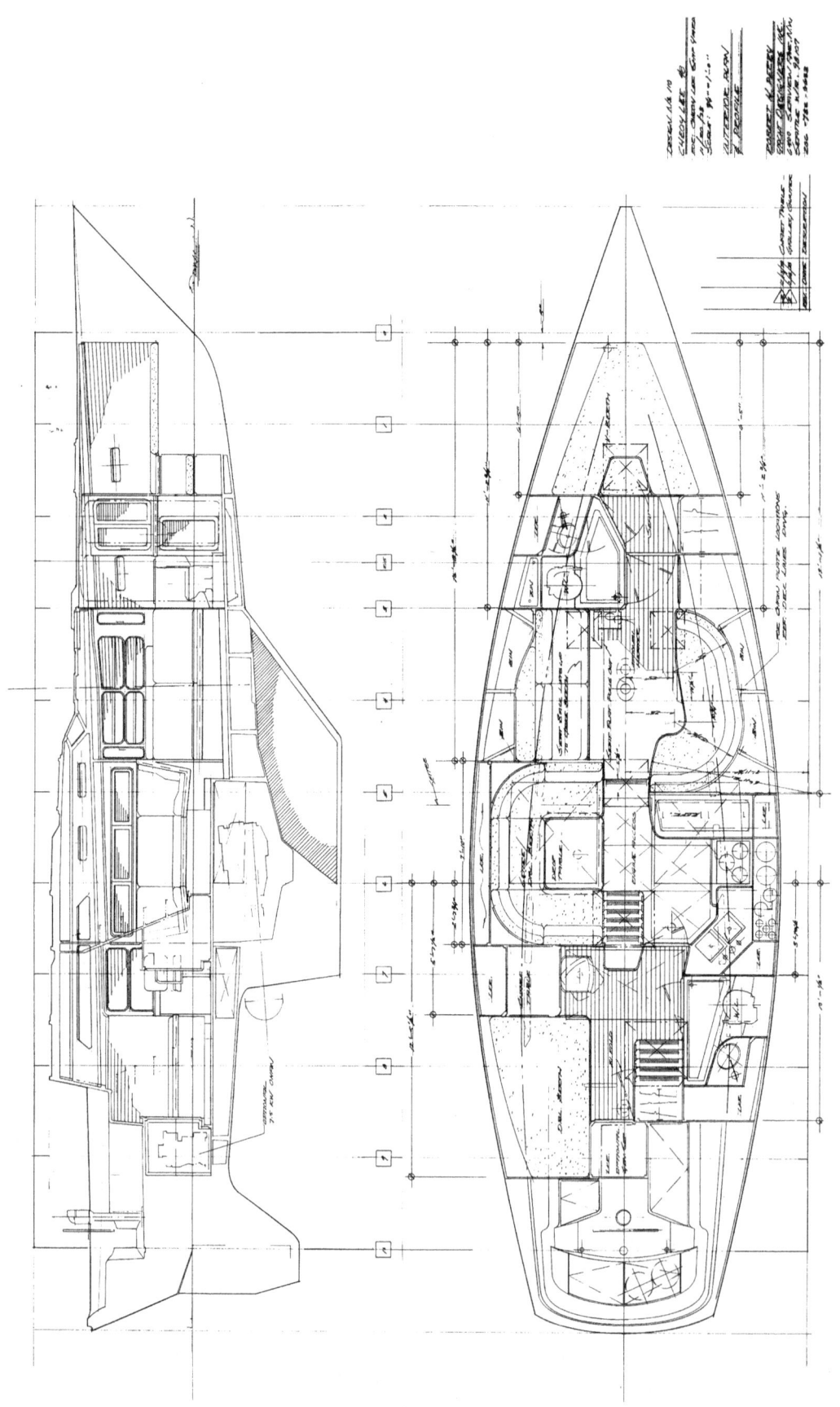

Interiors have changed since this CL 48 layout was drawn. Note that you walk through the owner's stateroom from the cockpit to access the rest of the interior. You could not sell that idea today. In my defense, if you look closely, you can see a second companionway adjacent to the galley.

*Hull number 1 of the CL 48s undergoing sailing trials in Hong Kong harbor. A vang would have helped the mainsail shape.*

*Bernie pushing his CL 43 hard off the coast of Florida.*

balanced but tender. Still, owners love this boat and I have seen them all over the world.

True to the time, the Golden Wave 42 features a big foretriangle and a small mainsail. This makes the Golden Wave easy to convert to a cutter. My problem with Cheoy Lee started when I got a call from an owner who had lost his rig. This concerned me, as you can imagine, so I questioned him about the rig and how he had it set up. In the discussion, the owner mentioned the fact that the rig was deck-stepped.

"What?" I said. "I designed it to be keel-stepped." The mast moments matched my specs, but my specs called for the rig to be stepped on the keel so that a given mast section would be stiffer and stronger.

For now the problem was solved, and I contacted Cheoy Lee to go over the rig specs. Then I got a call from another owner who said he had lost his rig while motoring, with no sails up. The mast had just buckled. This was very unusual, and I defended myself by telling the owner that the rig was not to my design. My design was keel-stepped. I soon received a letter from Cheoy Lee asking me to stop telling owners that the rig of the Golden Wave was not to design specs. They told me that I was undermining their marketing efforts. I sent a return letter telling them that they, by changing the rig design, were undermining my design efforts. That was the last we ever spoke. The next Golden Wave was designed by Britton Chance. He lasted for one design, then Cheoy Lee went to Dave Pedrick to design a couple of models of the Golden Wave series. These proved to be very good boats. I can't say I was entirely free from jealousy of his success with Cheoy Lee.

In retrospect, the Golden Wave I designed should have had a more form stable hull. I should have given the boat a bigger, fatter keel envelope to get the iron ballast lower. I could have designed a better (i.e., stiffer) boat for Cheoy Lee. But today's owners of the Golden Waves like the boat and it has proven itself a durable, capable performer with a very user-friendly interior layout.

All that aside, today I am proud to have been one of Cheoy Lee's designers.

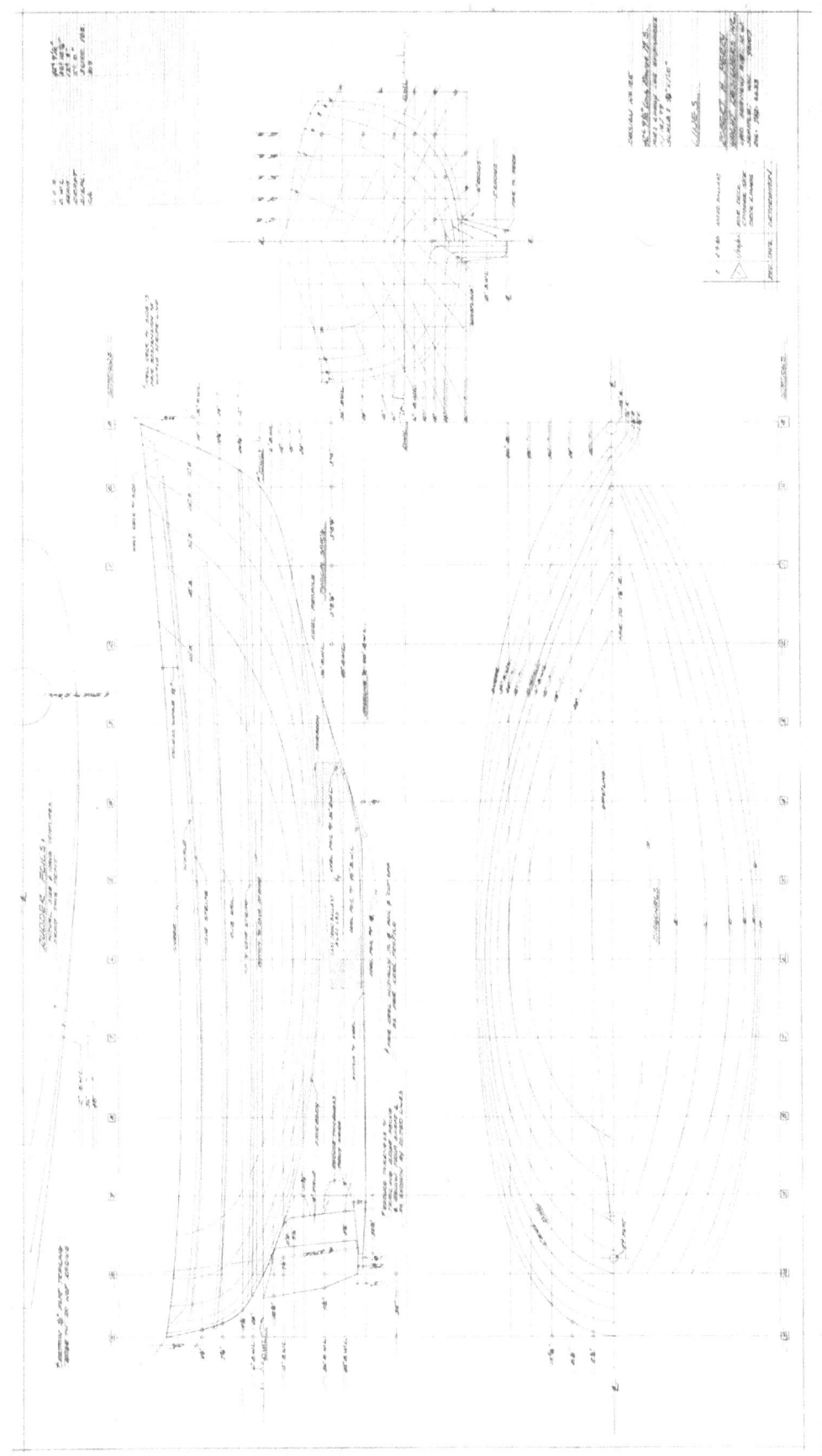

*I like this hull of the Cheoy Lee 43 long-range motorsailer. It was literally wrapped around fuel tanks to get the shape started. Once I'd accommodated the fuel requirements I did my best to design a heavy but slippery shape. It may not be a rocket under sail, but this design has proven itself a capable motorsailer.*

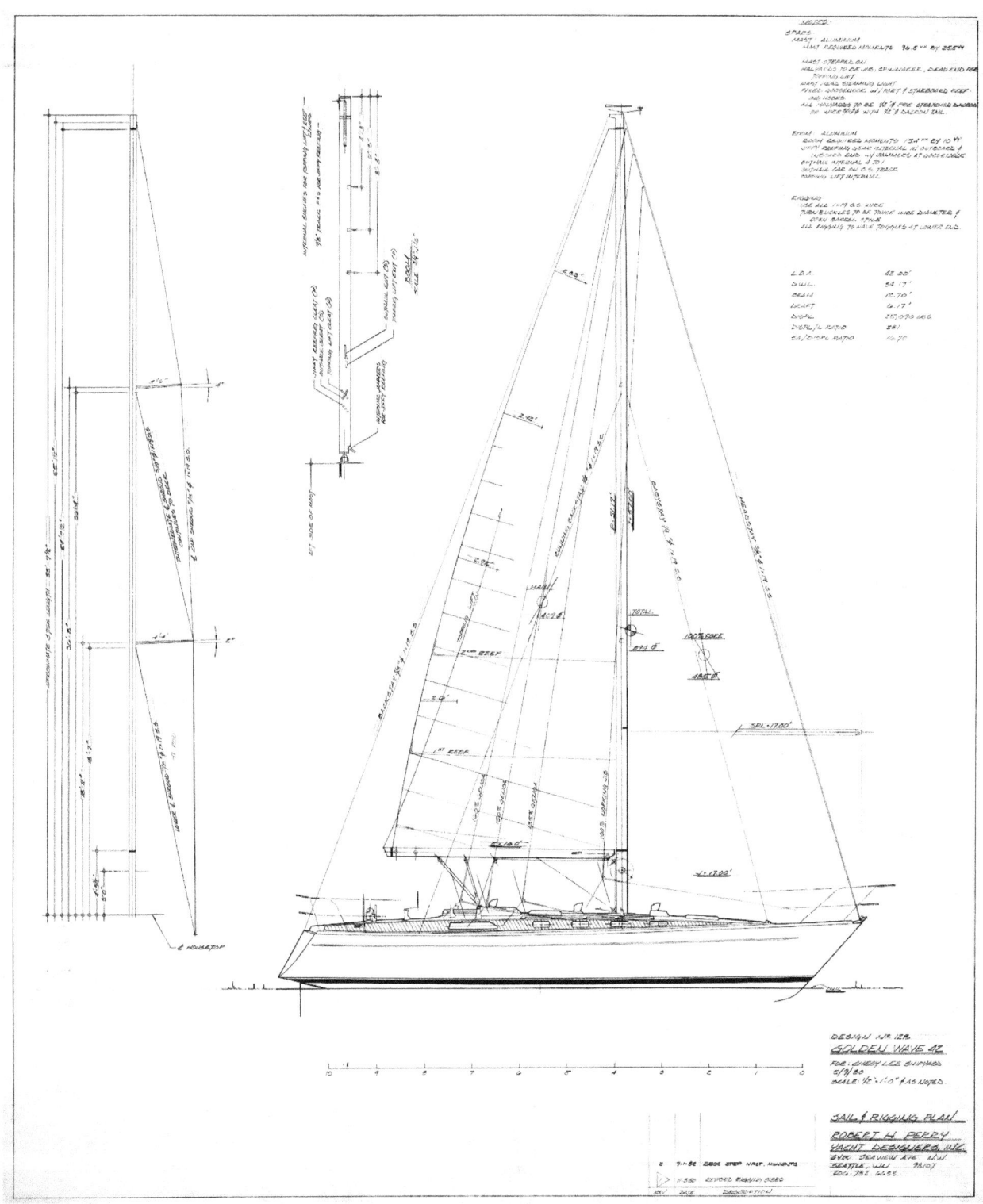

The Golden Wave 42 was Cheoy Lee's try at a higher-quality boat with more contemporary styling and performance.

## According to Perry
# FULL KEELS

On a true full-keel boat (e.g., a Westsail 32), the forefoot in the profile view flows without discontinuity or differentiation into the leading edge of the keel, and the keel extends aft to terminate at the rudderpost. From forefoot to rudder, you can't tell where one part ends and another begins. Full keels are common on older designs.

In today's full-keel boats, the forefoot is usually defined, and the leading edge of the keel is pulled aft rather than being a fair extension of the forefoot. This approach can be called a modified full keel and is typified by the keels I designed for the Tashiba series of boats (Chapter 7). Chuck Paine has placed similar keels on many of his cruising boats, notably the Cabo Rico series. In an effort to reduce wetted surface, shorten chord length, and reduce the displacement of the keel, you can move the leading edge aft. You might also move the trailing edge and its attached rudder forward, but I would avoid this at all costs. It generally results in a boat that has poor directional stability and is hard to steer, especially when pressed off the wind. I always keep the rudder as far aft as reasonably possible.

A full or modified full keel has several disadvantages, one of which is that it lacks the aspect ratio to develop good flow across the chord for lift. In order to achieve an appropriate thickness ratio on a long-chord keel, you have to make it excessively thick, which gives you too much added displacement and frontal area. If you reduce the thickness ratio to achieve acceptable displacement and frontal area, the keel may become too thin to keep flow attached and will stall at early angles of attack. Stalling eliminates the keel's lift and causes drag. The good news is that when a full keel stalls and loses lift, you're still left with all that planform area to prevent the boat from being shoved sideways. I use a 7 to 9 percent foil thickness ratio for my modified full-keel designs.

All other things being equal, I always want to optimize keel lift and minimize keel drag. Also, there is obviously far more wetted surface in a full keel than a fin keel, and wetted surface has a severe negative effect on boat speed in light air. Therefore, an effort should be made to reduce wetted surface. From my perspective, though, the biggest disadvantage of a full or modified full keel is the additional displacement it adds to the canoe body compared with a far less bulky fin keel.

On the other hand, there are pragmatic benefits to a full or modified full keel. (I'll let the term *full keel* apply to both from here on.) A full keel has enough internal volume to house the ballast, with room left over for a tank or two. This gets the weight of the tanks low in the boat and contributes to a lower VCG for the boat. Unfortunately, this means that the tanks often wind up sitting in a chronic puddle of bilge water. Also, and ironically, due to the abundant internal volume for ballast, most full-keel boats use cast iron at 450 pounds per cubic foot (or even less dense materials) rather than cast lead at 700 pounds per cubic foot, and in doing so fail to

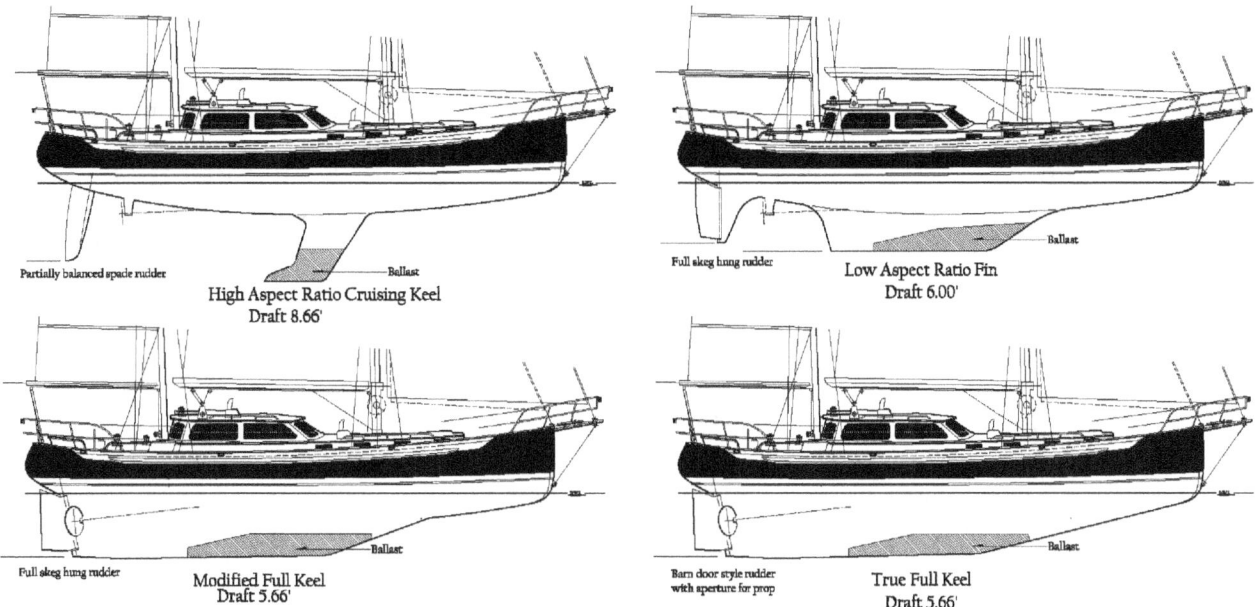

*A comparison of cruising keel types using a custom 48-foot double-ended ketch.*

take full advantage of their keel volume to lower the VCG. Lead is always better.

It's nice to have a big, long keel on which to rest your boat when you haul out. People also say that a full keel protects the rudder, but I wonder. Most full-keel boats still have the heel or gudgeon of the rudder at the lowest point, so there is still a chance of damaging the rudder when you hit bottom. I design the rudder bearing or "gudgeon" to be at least 4″ above the lowest part of the keel to help prevent damage.

I do not regard having the propeller in an aperture in a full keel as being an advantage. On the contrary, I want my prop out in the open where it can get clean flow. The worst boats to operate in reverse are full-keel boats. If you drop a light line over the side near your prop while your engine is running and in gear, you may see that line being pulled inexorably to the prop aperture. (I don't advise this experiment.) I have wrapped lines around the prop shaft twice this way (unintentionally). This directional flow through the aperture acts like a stern thruster and hinders the boat's ability to back up with any grace or panache.

Of course, you may sail in waters littered with lobster and crab pots, or maybe your boat sits on the mud at low tide. These are good arguments for a full keel, and a prop in an aperture may also be desirable in this case. A full keel is also a strong shape to have in a catastrophic grounding or if you are pounding on a beach. Haulouts in marinas with crude gear may be easier on a full-keel boat, whereas a boat with a short fin keel might suffer damage to its prop strut and shaft from sling placement.

A sailor must balance these virtues against the full keel's performance vices. To me, performance is paramount. This is not to say that all full- or modified full-keel boats are slow. Starting with the Tayana 37, I made an effort to separate the full-keel shape as much as possible from the canoe body by reducing the garboard radius and increasing the span. My Tashiba series boats all sail beautifully, and I'm sure that Chuck Paine's similar full-keel boats do also. Look, for example, at the new Cabo Rico 45. This design shows a highly refined full keel that approaches a low-aspect fin. In fact, I'm not sure if this is an example of a modified full keel or the very elusive modified fin keel.

Let's talk about keels and stability. I hear all the time, "I want a full-keel boat for stability." But given the amount of volume in a full keel, all else being equal, a full-keel boat will be less stable through the normal sailing range, 0 to 30 degrees of heel, than a fin-keel boat. Picture the midsections of a full-keel boat and a fin-keel boat with both boats heeled 20 degrees. The immersed portion of the fin-keel midsection is almost entirely to leeward of the centerline, where it contributes to righting moment via buoyancy. The windward portion of the hull is mostly out of water, where it, too, contributes to righting moment via gravity. The immersed portion of the full-keel midsection, on the other hand, is still perhaps 40 percent to windward of the centerline, where it contributes to further heeling. Volume immersed to windward becomes heeling moment, while volume immersed to leeward contributes to righting moment. Technically expressed, the volume of a full keel reduces the righting arm (the distance from the VCG to the transverse center of buoyancy).

Thus, not surprisingly, I get a lot of calls from owners of older full-keel boats complaining about lack of stability. They want to know if they can add ballast or an external lead shoe to cure this tenderness. The first thing I tell these people is that they are going to be fighting the shape of their hull, and that relatively minor changes in ballasting may have little if any effect on stability through the 0- to 30-degree range. It can be done if you are willing to put your boat through major surgery and replace internal iron with internal lead, but I don't recommend it.

The stiffest boats are those with deep, high-aspect fin keels with some type of bulb at the tip. It's all about getting the VCG low. In many cases, the fin is of a less dense material (commonly stainless steel or cast iron) than the bulb (commonly lead), further lowering the VCG of the keel. In *Amati*'s case (Chapter 15), the keel is a hollow, welded steel fin that is used as a fuel tank, and the lead ballast is all in the bulb at the tip. Combine this with generous draft and you have a recipe for excellent stability.

You can even argue that, in some cases, the right bulb shape will help increase the apparent aspect ratio of the fin by acting as a quasi-end plate. (An end plate works by keeping the flow over the keel from ducking under the tip toward the low-pressure side of the fin, creating large tip vortices.) On the other hand, it's important to remember that bulbs in themselves are not hydrodynamically desirable. A clean fin has far less drag than a fin/bulb combo. It is only the contribution of the bulb to lowering the VCG and increasing the stability that adds to the speed of the boat.

A relatively thin, high-aspect fin will have less frontal area than most other keels, which can reduce drag and add up to a downwind speed advantage, but this thinness comes at a price. A high-aspect fin poses a structural challenge due to the short chord where the fin attaches to the hull. A short fin makes it difficult or impossible to spread the fin loads over a big section of the hull. You wouldn't want to bounce a fin like that off a reef for a day or two, nor would you want to sit the boat's entire weight upon it when you haul out. Short-chord, high-aspect fins are unsuitable for most cruising boats, which hold durability as a primary desirable feature.

Remember, more stability means a boat that will stand up to its sail better and present a more efficient keel shape to the water. People like stiff boats. *Amati*'s keel is obviously a radical solution for a cruising keel, one made possible because a deep draft is no hindrance in Puget Sound. Yes, it does catch kelp, but this can be remedied with a standard leading-edge, groove-mounted kelp cutter. These are almost common on the kelp-infested West Coast. Yes, it would be a disaster in the lobster-pot-riddled waters of Maine, but this is a custom boat designed to specific owner requirements, preferences, and objectives.

As Frankenfurter said to Janet in *The Rocky Horror Picture Show*, "I didn't build him for you!"

While a radical keel like this one is often considered dangerous by cruising sailors, it can produce a far greater limit of positive stability than do the typical cruising boat keel/hull combinations.

It's often argued that a full- or modified full-keel boat has better directional stability, which is often referred to as "tracking ability." My experience is just the opposite. I have found that the farther I can separate the keel from the rudder, the better a boat tracks. Some full-keel boats like to go in a straight line because they just don't want to turn, which is great only until you *need* to turn. The best combination is a highly maneuverable boat that also likes to track. I'm a believer in the "feathers on the end of the arrow" theory. In other words, keep the rudder as far aft as possible. The reduced planform area of the fin keel, combined with a good rudder well aft, will give you a boat that maneuvers beautifully at low speed around marinas. This is important to me. For sterling performance when maneuvering under power, a fin keel and spade rudder combination is hard to beat.

Keep in mind that many full-keel boats are, by today's standards, grossly underpowered, with small sail plans, copious displacements, and full entries. A modern split-appendage boat may have much more

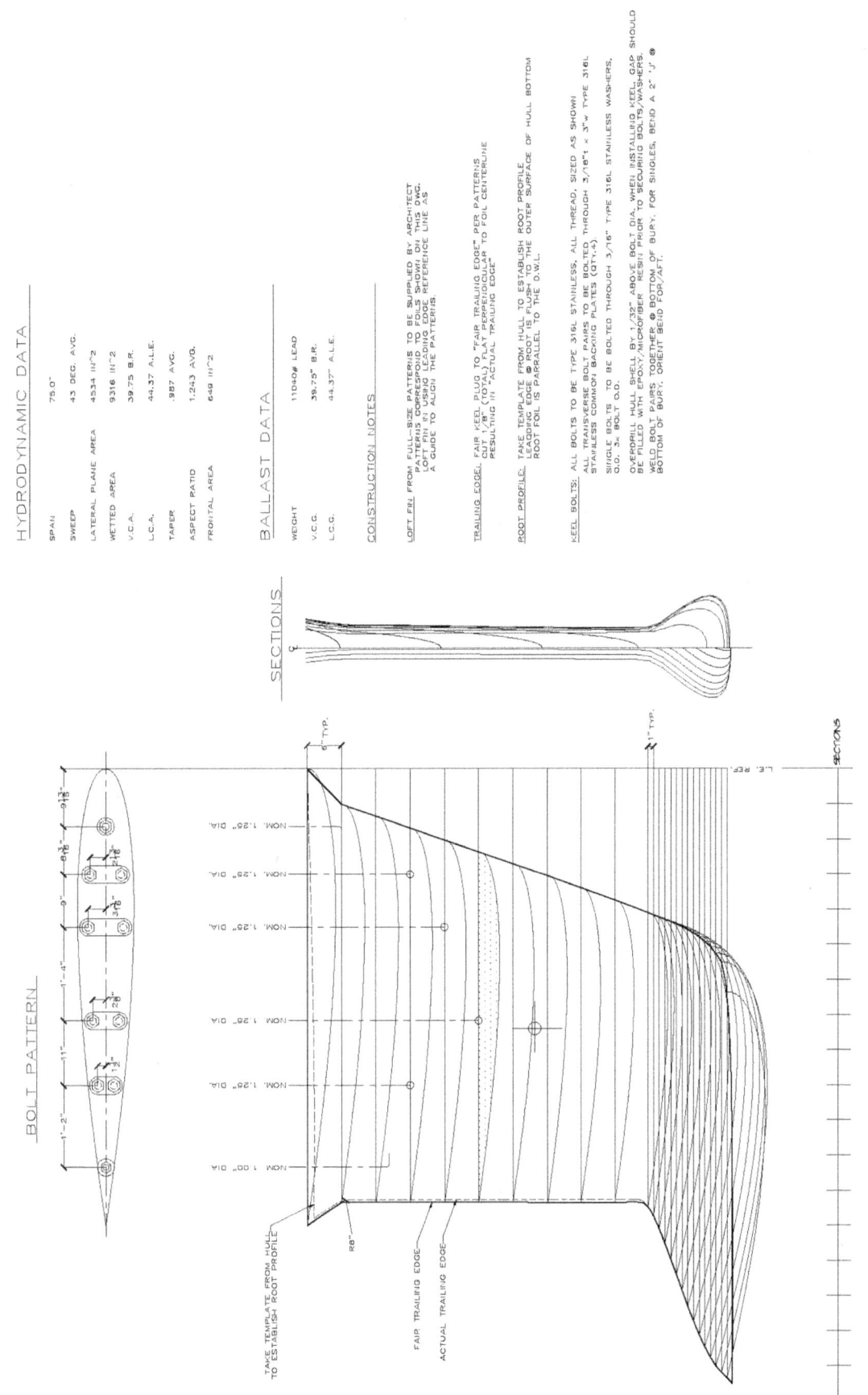

Mobisle's hybrid keel confers a lower vertical center of gravity (VCG) than the typical cruising fin but is not as deep or skinny as Amati's (see Chapter 15). This keel has a 75-inch span with a long root chord and a 43-degree sweep angle.

sail area per pound than its full-keel cousin, and for this reason alone may require more attention to its helm when pressed hard. It's prudent to line up and assess all the sailing characteristics before deciding that such-and-such a boat "doesn't track."

I have designed far more fin-keel than full-keel boats, and I'm convinced that, all things considered, a well-designed, well-built fin-keeler is the better all-around boat.

Putting aside the radical *Amati* approach and limiting yourself to more "normal" cruising keels, you arrive at hybrid keels like those in the accompanying illustration. This is an external lead keel for the 57-foot cruising sled *Mobisle*. The challenge is to get the VCG low while maintaining a long root chord for structural durability and—on the West Coast—achieving a sweep angle that won't make this keel a kelp harvester. That last goal is a tough one. It is generally assumed that it takes about 40 degrees of leading edge sweep to get a keel to shed kelp, but my experience has been that kelp will stick quite well to a keel with 40 degrees of sweep. I have chosen in my cruising designs not to be concerned with kelp.

I have used this hybrid keel shape on three of my "cruising sleds" (Chapters 14 and 16) with good success. These keels might perform better with a higher-aspect ratio and a shorter root chord, but pragmatic cruising considerations (including draft restrictions) and cost ruled against that. A one-piece, all-lead keel fin saves money over a two-part lead bulb and steel fin configuration. Obviously you want to limit draft on any cruising boat, and this severely ties the hands of the designer. In my office, we have been incorporating 6.5 to 7.5 feet of draft on boats up to 45 feet, and 8 to 8.5 feet on our 50- to 60-foot cruising sleds. People who say that they are looking for "shoal draft" are usually looking for draft less than 5.5 feet, regardless of the size of the boat. In a perfect world, all keels would have infinite span and be all fin with no bulb. Then again, in a perfect world I would look like Gregory Peck and sing like Ben Heppner.

Pragmatic considerations are likely to dictate the keel design of any boat except for an all-out racer.

## Chapter Nine
# PASSPORT YACHTS

It was 1978. The office was going great guns and we were getting very familiar working with the Taiwanese builders. A letter arrived one day, handwritten on stationery that read, "Yacht Builders, Frozen Foods, Eel Farms." It was an inquiry for a design of a 40-footer for a group that was unknown to me at the time. The eel farm part was not unusual. I would see crates marked "live eels" being loaded onto the 747 each time I left Taiwan headed for Narita in Japan. Still, the juxtaposition of eel farms and yacht building was a stretch for me and it gave the letter a less-than-credible feel. Over the years I have asked people involved early with Passport about that letterhead, and I have never received an answer as to its origins. I have come to the conclusion that it was just a random piece of stationery that was on hand at the time. But at the time, it did little to impress me that this was a legitimate inquiry.

I shot off a quick reply, intending to get rid of this yard or would-be yard. I demanded a one-time payment of $10,000, and in return I would deliver the design of a 40-footer. Simple as that. In about a month, I received a letter back with a check enclosed for $9,500 and a note saying I would get the other $500 when the design was finished. I was surprised. The design brief was for a 40-footer with an interior based upon the successful Freeport 36 we had designed for Islander Yachts. The key was the Pullman-style double berth with the head forward.

The origin of the design is important here, because in most cases we are asked to take a layout from a larger boat and condense it down into a smaller hull. This is hard and seldom works well. You just end up with the "two pounds of marbles in the one-pound sack" situation. However, with the new 40-footer, we would be taking the layout of a 37-footer and allowing it to expand and grow into the hull of a 40-footer. This would work nicely as time would prove, and well over 150 Passport 40s were built.

At the time, Passport Yachts was Peter Hoyt and Wendel Renkin. Both were California sailors who had bought early Taiwanese 37-foot ketches and had then been lured to Taiwan with the idea that they could build themselves larger boats there. Their first boat was the Stan Huntingford–designed Passport 42, originally called the Solar 42, a double-ender that was involved with some design-rights issues with another yard that produced virtually the same design under the name Slocum 43. The Passport 42 was built at the Tamsui Miracle yard. The only distinguishing external difference between the Passport 42 and the Slocum 42 was that the Passport model had a raked rudderpost while the Slocum had a vertical rudderpost. Both of these models sold well, with more than 100 being built under the Passport name alone. They are good boats and are still sought after as used boats.

By the time work began on the Passport 40 at the King Dragon yard just outside of Taipei in a town called Tamsui (pronounced "Dan Sway"), Peter Hoyt had left Wendel Renkin to pursue his own line of boats in another Tamsui yard. Wendel was married to a Taiwanese woman named Caroline. She was cute, vivacious, and very smart. Wendel made no attempt to even try to speak Chinese beyond the obligatory hello, good-bye, and thank-you. Caroline did all of Wendel's talking for him at the yard, and this caused problems with the workers as they were not comfortable taking orders from a woman. Wendel would walk around a boat in progress essentially ranting, and it was up to Caroline to translate the rant to the yard owner, Big Lo. Big Lo was about 5'3", but he was the oldest of the family's brothers, so he had earned the name Big as in big brother (*da gege* in Mandarin). Big Lo spoke English quite well, but when details were discussed, it was best to speak in both languages so there was at least the impression that confusion was reduced.

Before long, the Passports were selling very well and there was not enough room at the King Dragon yard to increase production. A second yard was built a couple of miles away. This was the Hai Yang yard, and it exclusively built the Passports while the King Dragon yard built for a number of other contractors, including Hans Christian.

Working with Wendel was a real challenge for me. Wendel fancied himself a designer of sorts, and he certainly had his own ideas as to how the boats should be built. The office provided structural drawings and laminate specifications, but these were used as "guidelines," and Wendel changed details and specs as he saw fit to "improve" the boats and make construction easier. In that the Passports were offered with a variety of interior options, Wendel changed structural details so that they could be common to any and all interior options. This included chainplates and structural bulkheads. Wendel had a unique hull-to-deck joint detail he insisted on using, and I'll grant him that it was very watertight. However, it involved burying steel into the laminate so that stanchions and other fittings at the deck edge could be tapped into this plate instead of being throughbolted. This type of detail can be great when the boat is new, but over the years it can make retrofitting new components difficult.

There is no doubt that Wendel was doing his best to build the best boat he could. When he showed me an almost two-inch-thick cutout from the aft end of the cabin trunk where the instruments were being mounted, I exclaimed that this was way too thick and way too heavy. Wendel's reply was that it was strong and the owners loved it. Passports were built heavy. But to Wendel's credit, they have proven very durable.

When Caroline would object to something Wendel wanted, Wendel's standard reply was, "Caroline, are you going to be Chinese all your life?" And Caroline's reply to that was always, "Oh Wendel, you so funny."

Wendel clearly saw tremendous irreconcileable differences in the Western and Chinese cultures. In

*Big Lo, owner of the King Dragon yard, studies Wendel Renkin's wife Caroline as she, no doubt, expounds on a nuance of yacht construction.*

*Here Wendel Renkin no doubt expounds on a nuance of yacht construction for my benefit at the King Dragon yard.*

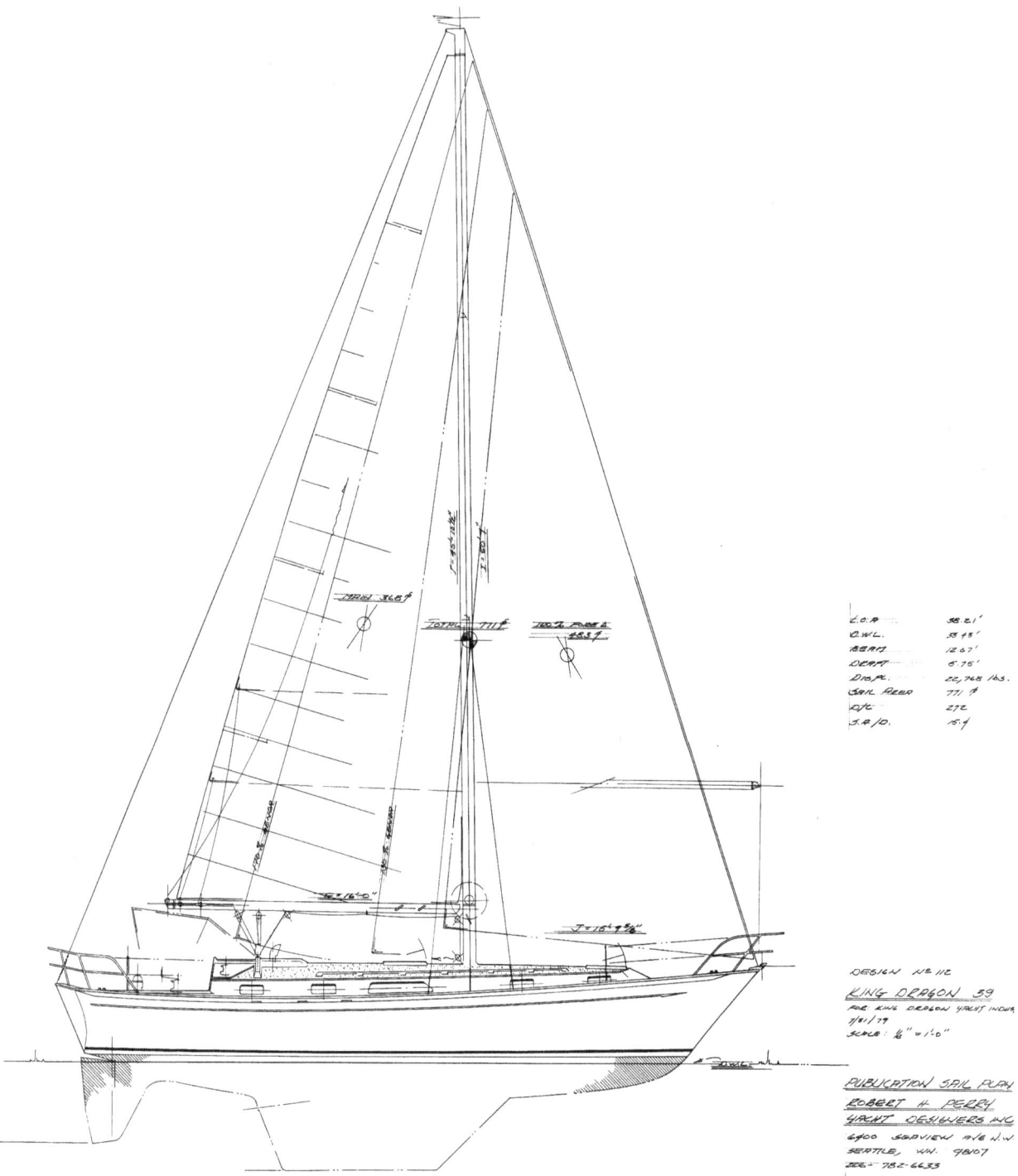

*The original sail plan of the Passport 40 places the mast forward and makes no provision for a cutter's staysail. With short ends and a strong sheer spring, this is a good-looking boat despite its overly long cabin trunk.*

most cases I think he was right—he just had that "ugly American" way of conveying it that often left me uncomfortable. Wendel wanted me in Taiwan a lot as we did subsequent boats. I got to spend a lot of time with Wendel. He enjoyed reminding me that what would have been my royalties for the Passport 40 went under the table to Big Lo, and that's how Wendel kept the skids greased at the yard. Wendel made a lot of money building Passports. He quickly established a potent network of very effective dealers

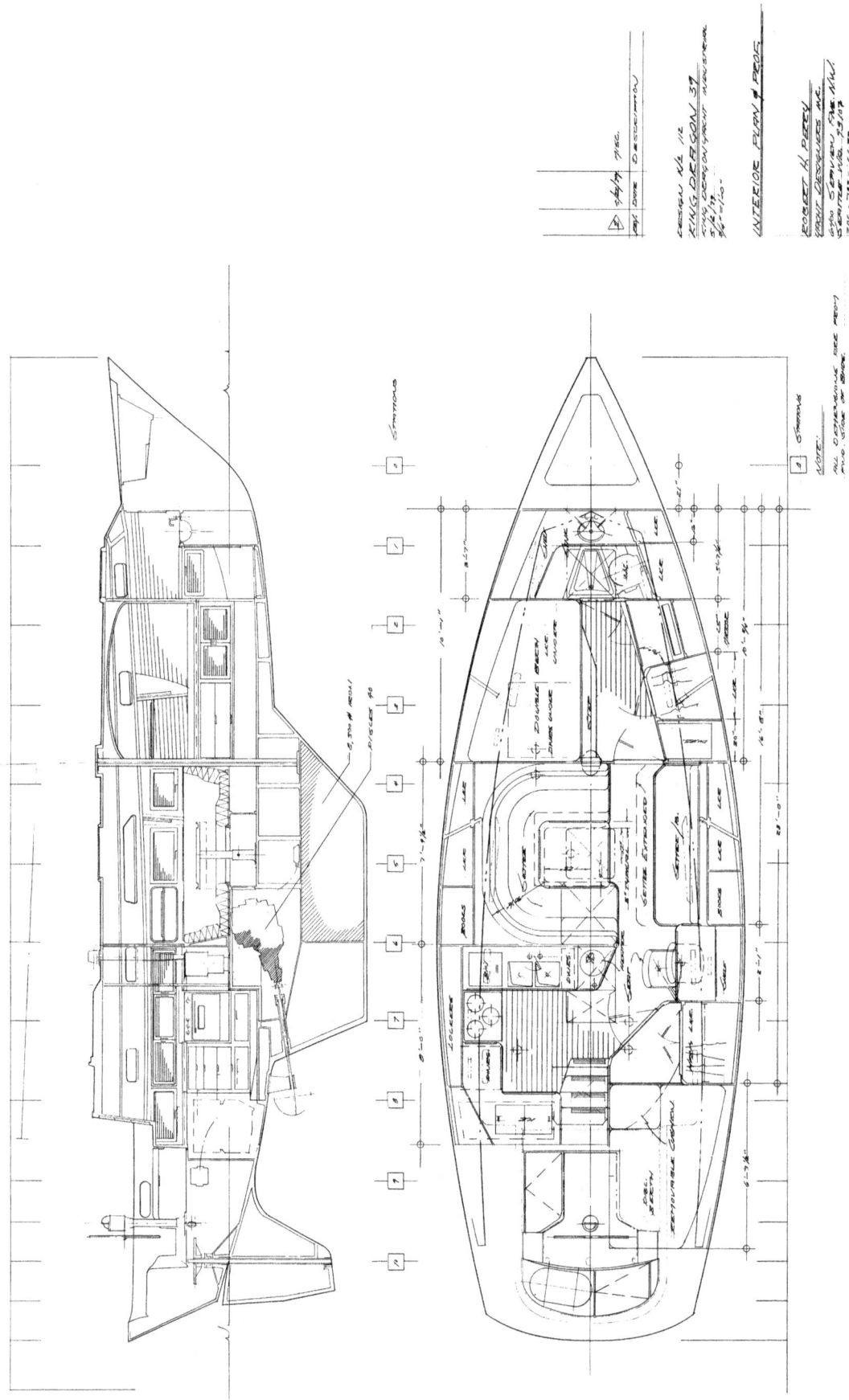

The port inboard profile of the Passport 40 shows how the long cabin trunk provided headroom in the forward head. Over time this has proven one of my best layouts.

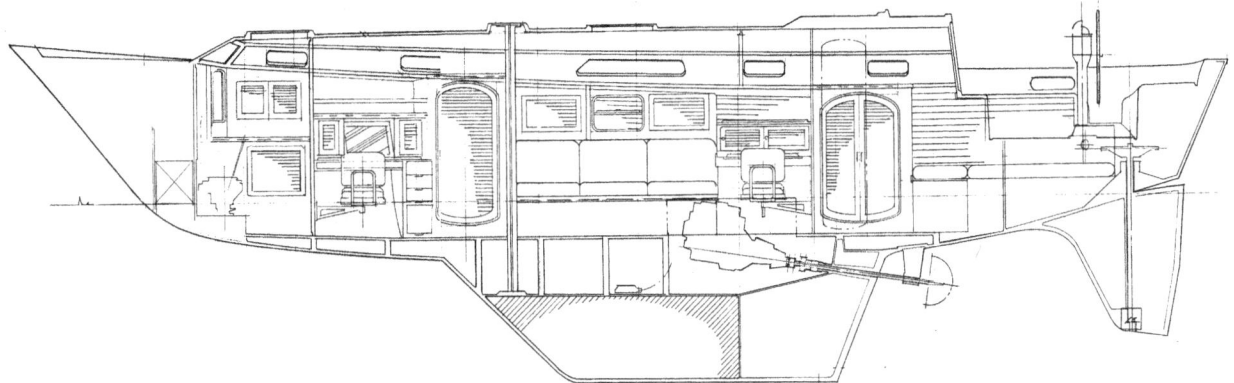

*The starboard inboard profile of the Passport 40 shows the engine tucked in the bilge, where access would be a challenge.*

in the United States, including Thom Wagner in Annapolis and Ben Oldham in San Francisco at Passage Yachts.

The hull of the Passport 40 is actually 38.21 feet, and features plenty of beam, with a L/B of 3.12. While by today's standards the stern does not look too broad, it was certainly broad by the acceptable proportions of 1979. The ends were short with almost no overhang aft. The bow had a very slight concavity to it, allowing the forward stations to show some gentle flare. In an effort to maximize cockpit size, we chose a conventional transom rake. This would later be changed in the Passport 41 and 43 models when a reverse transom was added so that a swim step could be incorporated. The bilges had a firm turn for good initial stability, and the ballast was internal in a long fin with a 12 percent thickness ratio at the root tapering to a 10 percent thickness ratio at the tip for good mold release. The real beauty of these thick fins was that the internal iron ballast could be fitted low in the fin for a better vertical center of gravity (VCG).

The Passport 40 would prove very popular on San Francisco Bay, where its stability won it a lot of advocates. Looking back at this hull form now, I believe that the wide-beamed, broad stern put this design ahead of its time. It was certainly a high-volume hull shape that allowed a wide variety of interior options.

Aesthetically, the Passport 40 was a challenge. In order to get the head all the way forward, we had to carry the cabin trunk far more forward than I was comfortable with. We softened this detail aesthetically with a wedge-like front to the cabin trunk and considerable camber to the top. When I look at a well-kept Passport 40 today, I see a good-looking boat. They are all heavier than designed, but this just lowers the freeboard and makes them even better looking to my eye.

This rig was never intended to be a cutter. By the time I designed the Passport, I had begun to think that a true cutter was not the best rig for most cruisers. Pushing the mast aft, as was required in a no-bowsprit true cutter, produced a boat with a helm that required careful adjustment of the main in order not to build up too much weather helm. This technique was often beyond the skills of non-racing cruising sailors. I felt that they would be better off with the mast pushed forward and a more neutral helm. This closed up the foretriangle and made it impossible to get a staysail in there with any reasonable proportions. Today, you will find that half of the Passport 40s have been converted into two headsail rigs. I won't call them cutters. They are just sloops with a staysail.

The rig is short. I designed the Passport 40 to weigh 22,738 pounds, but I would guess that the average weight of a Passport 40 today would be closer to 28,000 pounds. So while even my initial SA/D was low at 15.4, the actual SA/D of an original Passport 40 is closer to 13.00. Again, this may be one of the reasons why the boat was so popular on windy San Francisco Bay. You could sail the Passport 40 in 25 knots steady with full main and a 100 percent jib. Once a year we would assemble a fleet of a dozen Passport 40s for a day of racing on the bay. You would have thought it was the America's Cup, the way some owners prepared their boats. But at the end of the

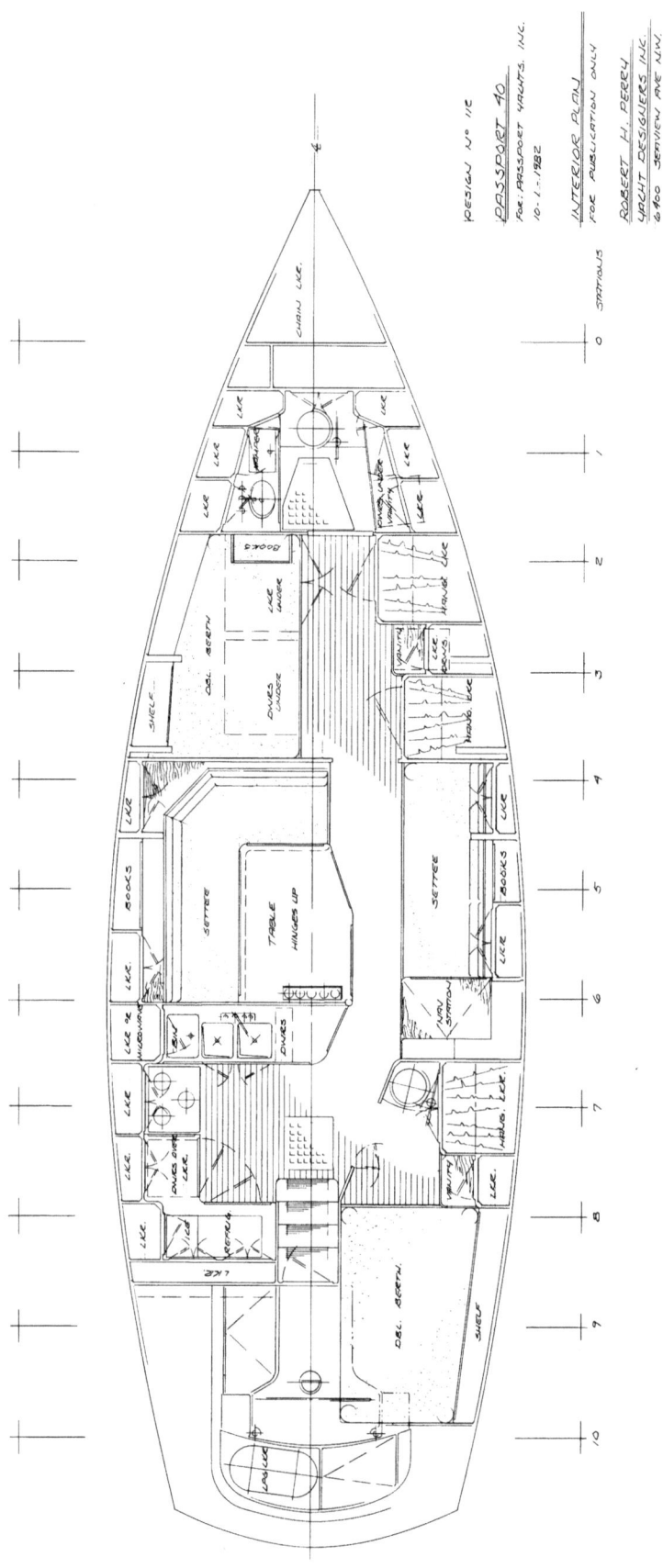

This layout for the Passport 40 would prove the most popular. Note the head aft, the athwartships chart table, and the L-shaped dinette.

## Passport Yachts

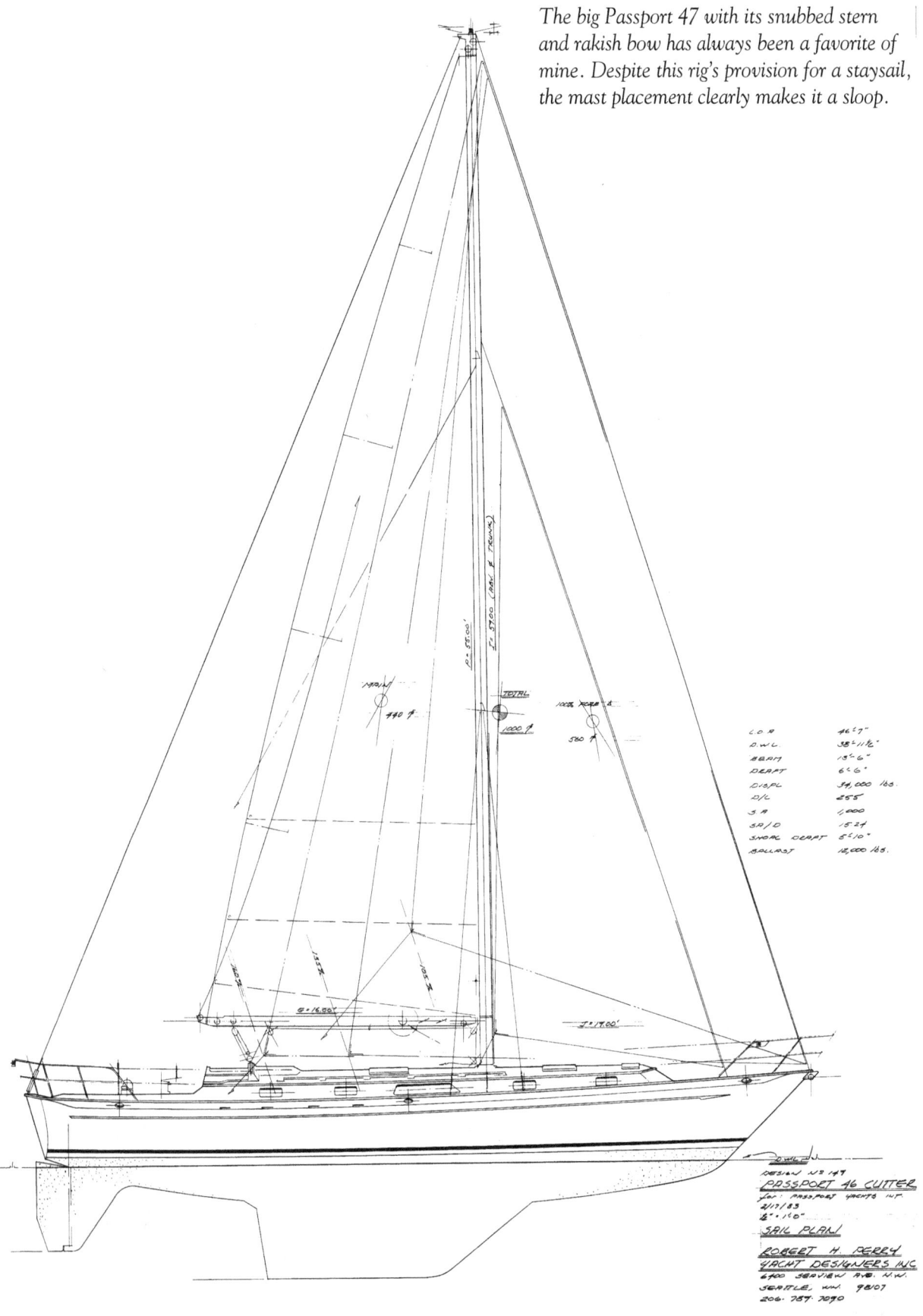

*The big Passport 47 with its snubbed stern and rakish bow has always been a favorite of mine. Despite this rig's provision for a staysail, the mast placement clearly makes it a sloop.*

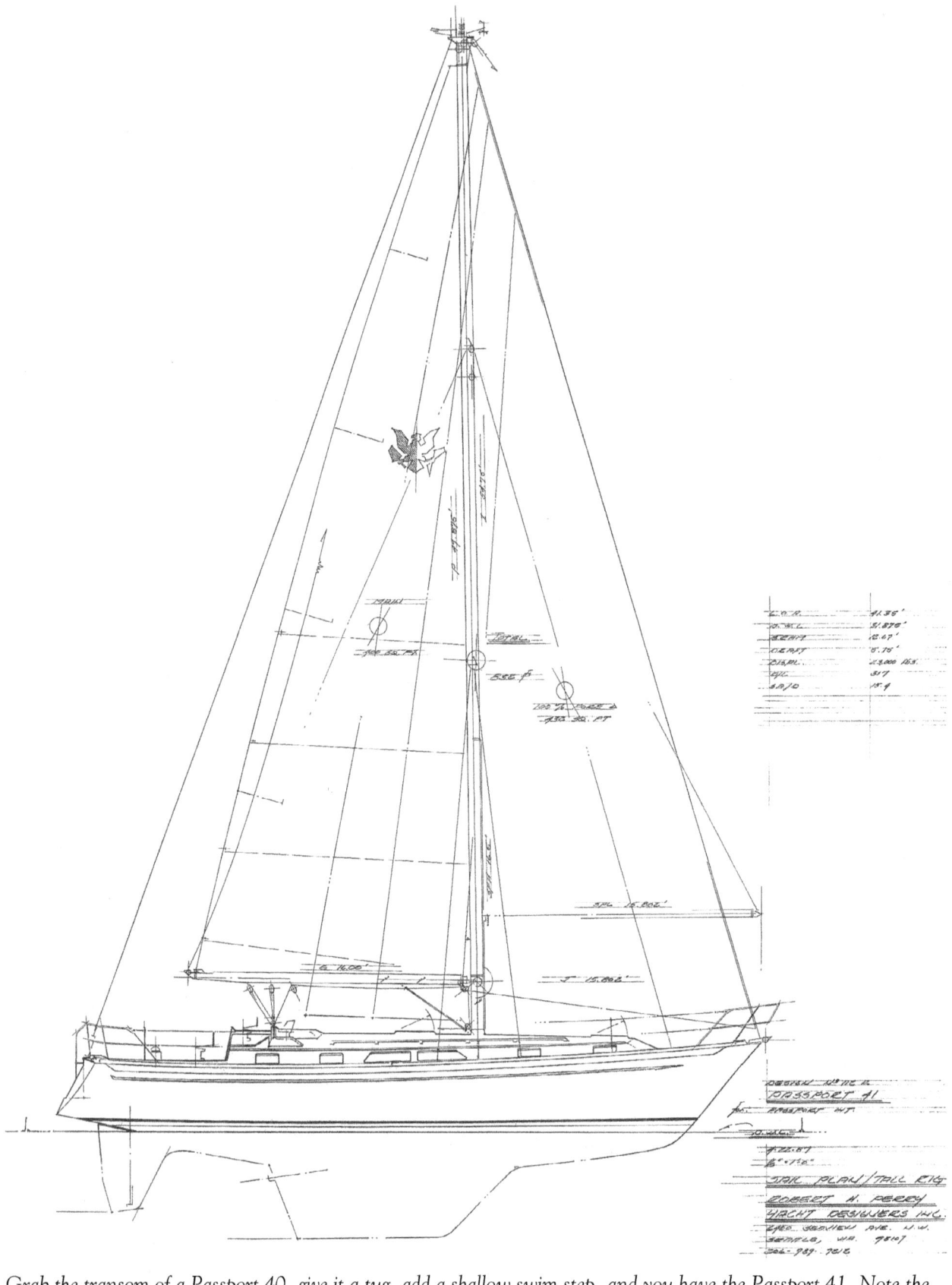

*Grab the transom of a Passport 40, give it a tug, add a shallow swim step, and you have the Passport 41. Note the taller rig on this version.*

day, the order of finish was almost an exact reflection of the overall weight of each boat. The one owner who emptied all of his tanks and took his cushions ashore won. Dueling tubas. In time, with the addition of the reversed transom, making the Passport 40 to a 41, and then with even more extension to a 43, we did add five feet to the rig, going from a single-spreader rig to a double-spreader rig. This greatly improved the sailing speed of the boat and even won over "the wizard" Bill Lee as a fan of the "turbo'd Passport." We even produced a 44-foot version of the Passport 40 with an extended conventional transom, but this was not my idea, and my eye never adjusted to the long overhang aft and the way the longer length overall (LOA) distorted the balance of the sheer spring. Sometimes these changes are driven by dealers, and they are determined to get their way with or without the help of the designer. When push comes to shove over these details, it just comes down to who is placing the order with the yard. They will do it with or without my blessing. Including extended stern versions of the 40/41/43, a total of 163 Passport 40s were built. In 1996 the Passport 41 won the *Cruising World* Boat of the Year award, 18 years after the original lines were drawn.

With the Passport 40 doing very well, two new models were developed between 1983 and 1986—the 37, followed by the 47. The Passport 37 was a great little boat and beloved by its few owners today. The problem with the Passport 37 was that it was too close in overall size to the Passport 40 and too expensive to build compared to the 40. This problem has plagued many models of production boats. Why buy a 37-footer if you can pay $25,000 more and get a 40-footer? Twenty-four of the Passport 37s were built.

The Passport 37 was a sweet little boat. It was more performance oriented than the Passport 40 and had a finer bow, a lower D/L, and a bigger SA/D. The L/B was still low at 3.1 in order to produce another stiff boat. Keel and rudder configurations were almost identical to those of the Passport 40. The biggest difference in the two Passport models was that the new 37 was a lot finer forward on the DWL and at the deck to make the boat faster to weather.

We did a tall rig and a short rig for the Passport 37. The first 37 was delivered to Passage Yachts on San Francisco Bay, and the local dealers were disappointed that the 37 could not carry full main in 25 knots like the Passport 40. The 37 needed a reef in that much breeze. But Ben Oldham knew his market, and he wanted a shorter rig that was more manageable in the San Francisco Bay area. In light-air areas, owners love the sprightly performance of the original tall-rig model. The Passport 37 is a great-looking boat to my eye. It has all the shape and appeal of the Passport 40 but more refinement and a better hull form. It's a shame that it priced itself out of the market. Today, this boat is rare and highly sought after.

The Passport 47 was to be the Passport 40's big brother with the same look and the same interior features, including the head-forward layout that had by now become an industry standard thanks to Wendel Renkin. I made the Passport 47 proportionally narrower with a L/B of 3.45, but I kept the stern overhang very short, with a near-vertical transom-rake angle. I really liked the way this abrupt angle played against the highly raked bow profile. I thought it was aesthetically exciting and it afforded the boat a long sailing length.

However, as time progressed the Passport 47 gradually changed. The stern was constantly extended to the point where the last models built were 49 and 50 feet on deck! Of course, to an owner or a broker, this was an attractive addition. It gave the boat a nice deck space aft of the cockpit, and people seem to love overhangs. But once again, to my eye it upset the balance of the sheerline I had labored over to get perfect. The sectional shape of the Passport 47 was rounder amidships with more deadrise aft than the Passport 40 or 37. I was always trying my best to produce a faster cruising boat while striving to avoid that flat run that can pound while you sit at the dock.

The original aft-cockpit Passport 47 was a big, muscular-looking boat. I was at a meeting at a yacht club on one of the Great Lakes. It was almost sunset and we were out on the waterfront lawn enjoying our toddies when a gleaming white Passport 47 cruised into the harbor and did a series of slow turns while looking for a spot to drop the hook. We all stood and stared at this beautiful boat. I felt really good. I knew the boat looked great. And damn it, a lot of it had to do with that chopped-off fanny. The Passport 47 sailed well, too. It was stiff and weatherly and came in closer to the designed displacement. The Passport 47 was to be Wendel's own boat and, in fact, he did build one for himself.

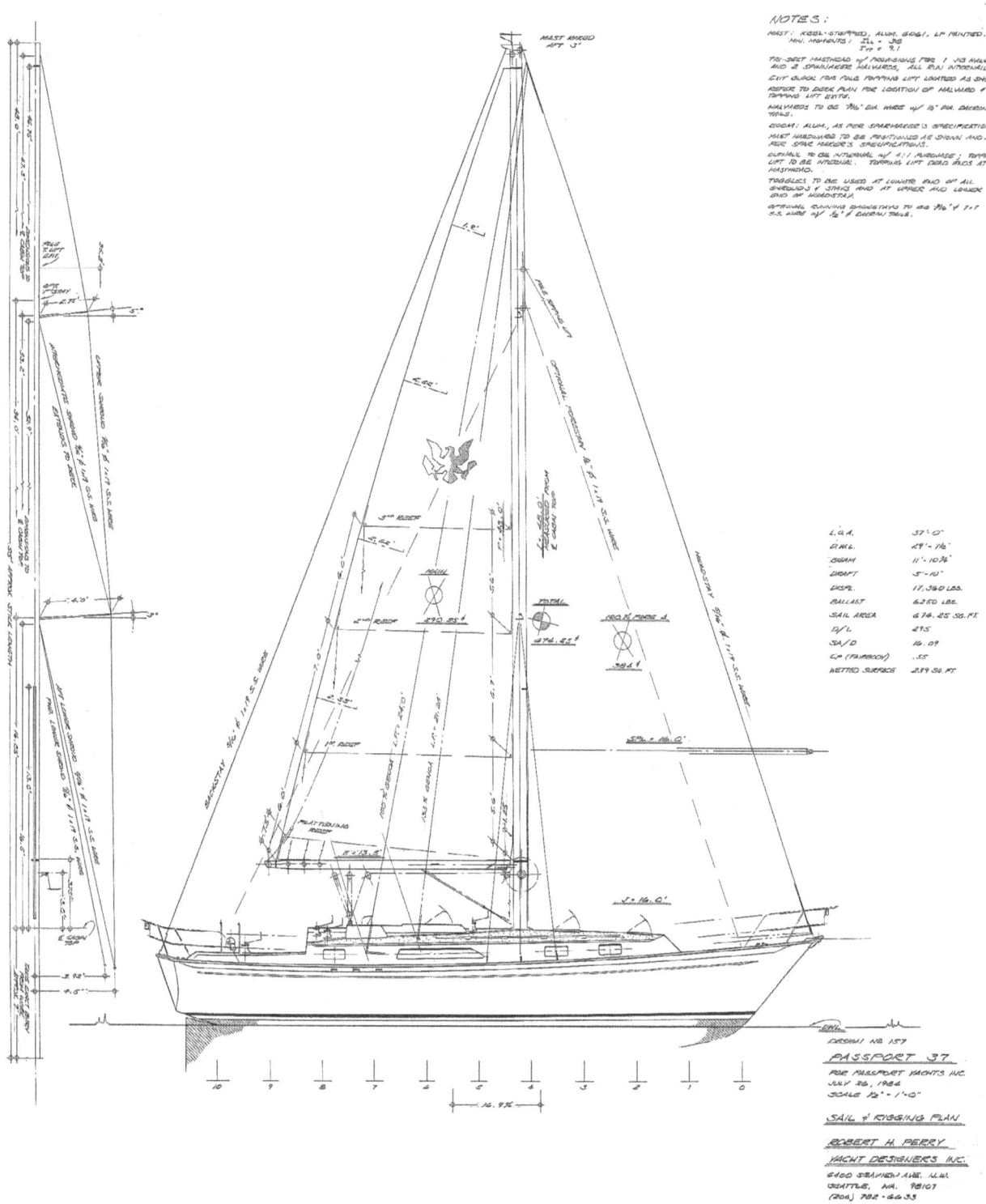

The Passport 37 is clearly the little sister to the Passport 40—and to my eye the more graceful and prettier boat. When I drew this sail plan I had bowed to pressure to add a staysail option.

We also did a center-cockpit model of the Passport 47. This was a difficult challenge for a designer. If you know you are going to do both aft- and center-cockpit models from the start, it's no big deal, but if you design an aft-cockpit model first and then find out the client wants a center-cockpit model, you have some problems. You need more freeboard for a good center-cockpit model. The headroom issues around the cockpit in the passageway to the aft cabin require height. You can do this by piling up cabin trunk and coaming structure, wedding-cake style. It works. We have all seen it. It's just not an elegant way to achieve the end. If you have generous freeboard with which to work, you can disguise some of this height. In the Passport 47 I had specifically worked to keep the freeboard modest. Freeboard is windage, and windage is slow. But we pushed ahead in the office, never willing to admit we could not do it, and in fact we produced a nice-looking if not svelte center-cockpit 47-footer. I sent the carefully crafted deck lines to Wendel in Taiwan.

The office phone rang. It was Wendel. "You've got to get over here right away. We are having problems with the deck." My buddy and fellow sailor John Bristol, who worked for Northwest Airlines, had graciously upgraded me to first class a couple of times, so I was well aware of the benefits of flying first class and I did have the air miles to upgrade. (Remember the days when they would slice roast beef at your seat following the caviar appetizer?) "No problem, Wendel, I'll be right there."

I arrived at the King Dragon yard where the Passport 47 was being built to find a deck plug that had been altered so much from my drawings that I could not even find a benchmark on the plug to begin taking my dimensions. This was clearly not the deck I drew. Wendel had gone creative on me and had totally screwed up the cockpit, and he was very well aware of it by that time.

The mistakes were classic. To get sheets up to center-cockpit mounted winches, you need clearance around the coaming. Wendel had it on one side, but winches all wind clockwise and not symmetrically port to starboard. There were no fairleads on the starboard side winches. However, working with two non-English-speaking Taiwanese carpenters of amazing skill and focus, we fixed the deck plug in three days without a single drawing other than sketches scrawled on the plywood of the deck plug. I grouse now about it, but at the time I was in heaven.

Together with the Taiwanese carpenters, we literally sculpted that deck right on the spot, me puffing on my *yendo* (pipe) and the Taiwanese carpenters puffing on their so-called Long Life Taiwanese cigarettes, surrounded by wood chips and shavings. We finished our work on the plug around 1 p.m. on the third day. The two carpenters invited me to lunch. We ate at an outdoor "restaurant" about eight feet from the side of the busy dusty road. I remember that the water buffalo was particularly tasty there. We drank 14 big bottles of Taiwanese beer between the three of us. I treasure those times. There is a picture-perfect example of the breed in my marina in Seattle. If you include the extended versions of the Passport 47, 14 were built.

But Wendel was tired of building boats and wanted to move back to the United States. So while Thom Wagner had a client and a deposit for a new Passport 49, Wendel assured him that the boat was "in progress," but in reality nothing was being done. The client began calling the new boat "*Godot*." (He was always waiting for it.) When push came to shove, Wendel agreed to sell the tooling for the 47 to Thom, and Thom proceeded with the new Passport 49. In fact, he sold two more 49s and two of the 50-foot models. These 49/50s were built at the Grand Harbor yard in Kao-hsiun, Taiwan.

Wendel went back to California a wealthy man, by my standards. Thom Wagner was now a very active dealer of Passports in Annapolis in partnership with Curt Stevens, and they became Passport Yachts. Wagner-Stevens bought the existing Passport 40 tooling from Big Lo, who had maintained ownership of the Passport 40 tooling all along. Curt has gone on to other yachting endeavors, but Thom is still the owner of Passport today.

Now for some pragmatic issues. U.S. "builders" in Taiwan were really not builders. They were contractors who would find a Taiwanese yard and contract with them to build the boats. Oftentimes this meant that a given yard was producing boats for more than one U.S. builder. Each U.S. group would compete for the full attention of the yard, and this was best done by ensuring a constant stream of boat orders. If your orders fell behind and the yards were left fallow, another "builder" would move in and take over production while your tooling would be moved out into the adjacent rice paddy or field. The biggest threat was always powerboat builders. Face it, there is just more of a demand for powerboats, and while

# Yacht Design According to Perry

*The need for a swim step was greater than my need for a distinctive transom, and soon length was added to my Passport 47 to give it a reverse transom with swim step.*

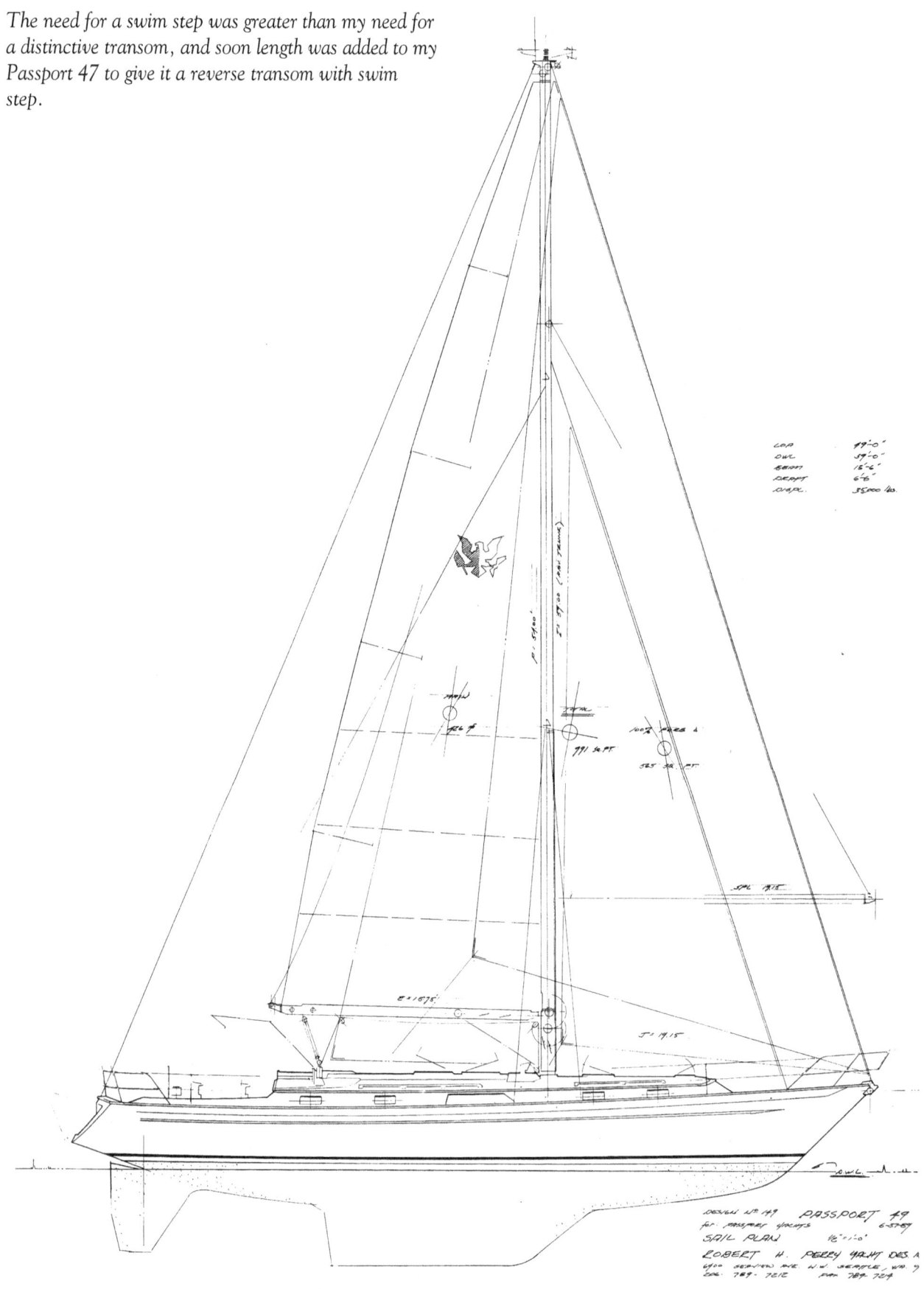

# Passport Yachts

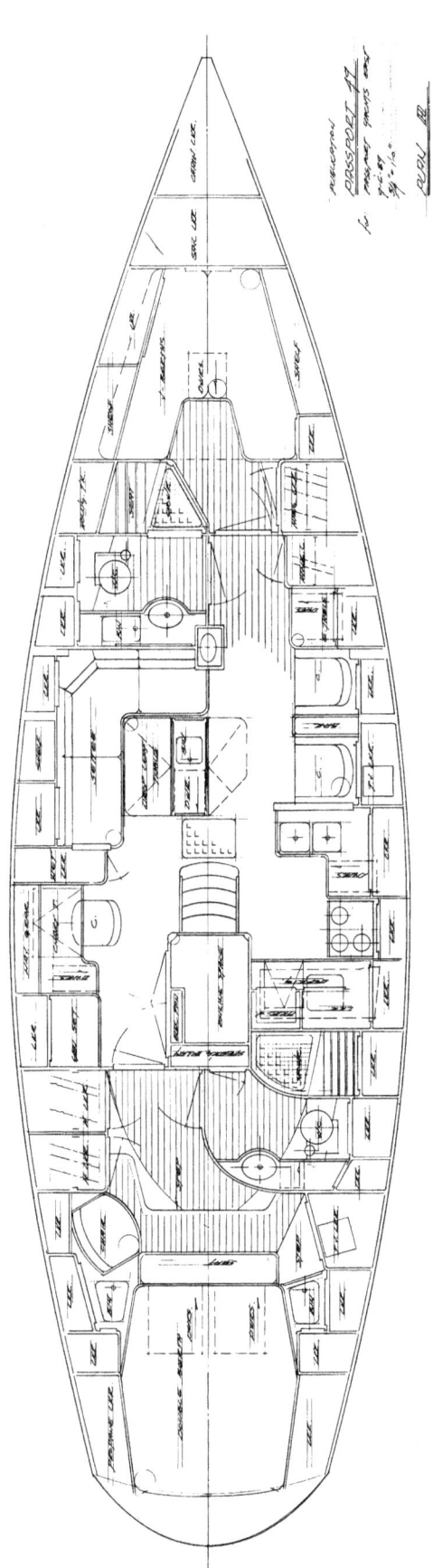

This shows a typical Passport 47/49 center-cockpit layout as requested and choreographed by Thom Wagner. Thom knows how to use very inch of a boat's interior, whereas I like to leave some cubic inches unused. Just in case.

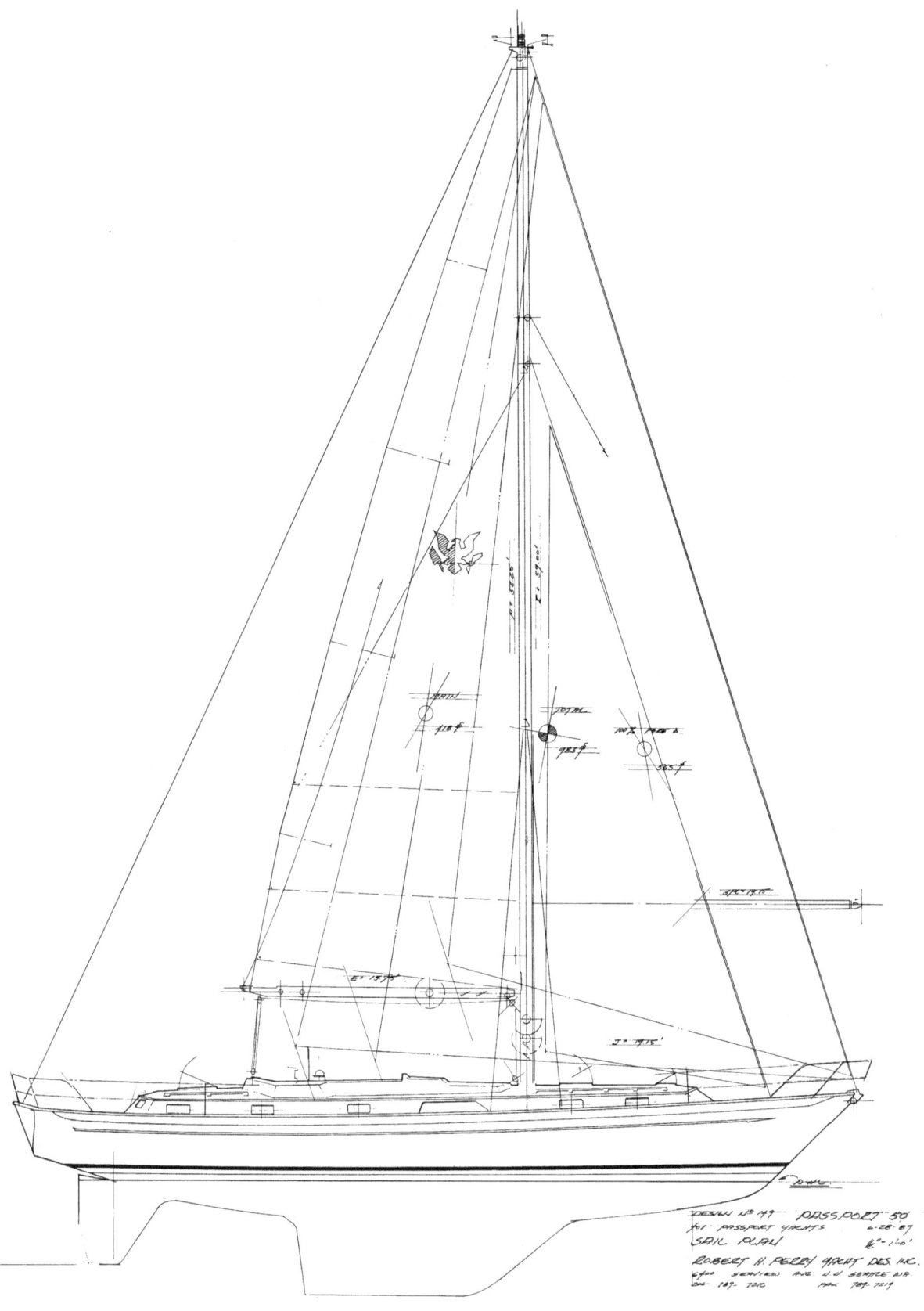

*If you add even more LOA to the Passport 47, you get the Passport 50 with traditional transom. This model is loved by its owners and has great deck space aft, but I always preferred the original short-ended 47.*

*This photo of the Passport 50 shows why owners like its look.*

U.S. contractors tended to be purist in their approach and loyal to their sailing roots, the Taiwanese builder was after the bottom line and could just as easily have produced powerboats if the dollars were there. Having your tooling moved out of the covered yard into the harsh Taiwanese tropical climate was strong incentive to keep the yard active.

Passports were eventually built by the South Coast Marine yard in Taipei. South Coast also built the Nordhavn powerboats, and it was a very good yard. It was soon decided that Passport needed a new model, and we began design work on the Passport 44/47. You could get this boat with a reverse transom at an LOA of 44 feet, or you could go with the conventional transom for an LOA of 47 feet.

The new boat featured modern lines with a fine entry, a firm turn to the bilge, and the tried and proven skeg-hung rudder with a long, low-aspect-ratio fin keel. In hull form it was a classic Passport with flatter buttocks and the typical Passport broad stern. Once again I was after an even faster Passport. From the start, the design was intended to be produced as both aft-cockpit and center-cockpit models. This was not a volume-oriented hull form, but given the lengths that Passport has gone to in order to vary and elaborate the accommodation plan, it probably should have been more voluminous. We have seldom designed two 44/47s with the same interior layouts. Part of the appeal of a new Passport was that you could have the interior any way you liked it, and we drew each and every new layout.

The 44/47 proved to be a very good boat. It sailed well and had extremely good helm balance when pushed hard. Several owners still actively race their Passport 44s. I'm partial to the aft-cockpit version, because to my eye it's just a big brother to the first Passport 40s.

Nordhavn, however, was quickly starting to dominate the production of the South Coast Marine yard. Yard owner Tsai Wan Chu had the idea that they could mold hulls and decks at the yard, then ship them to mainland China for finishing. Several 44/47s were built this way before the Chinese yard established its credibility. Not only was the finishing work up to the Taiwanese standards, it was better. Thom Wagner decided to move all production of the Passport 44/47 to China and the Han Sheng Yacht Building Company in Xiamen. A total of 38 Passport 44/47s have been built, with 16 of them built at the Xiamen yard.

By 2005, Thom Wagner and I had worked together on countless semi-custom Passports. We had developed a feel for what the Passport line should represent in terms of the balance between comfort and performance. It was time to develop a new Passport that carried this theme further. We wanted a volume-oriented hull form, because Passports were being sold primarily based upon accommodations. However, we also wanted to maintain high-performance targets with a form-stable hull shape and a long sailing length. With design targets firmly established and a long line of previous hulls

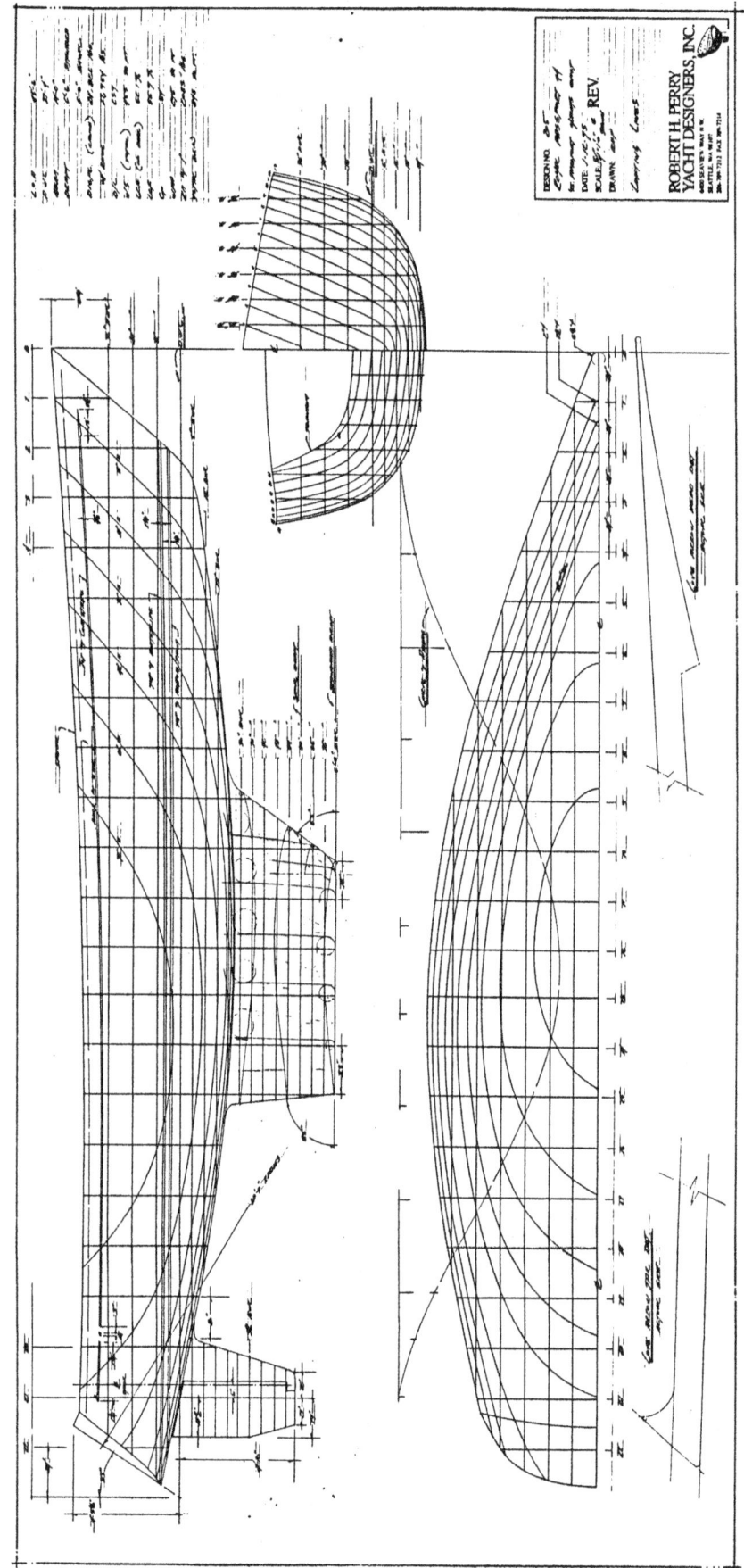

The Passport 44 came to be designated a "456" with the reverse transom and a "470" with the traditional transom. This was one of the last designs I did with a full skeg.

## Passport Yachts

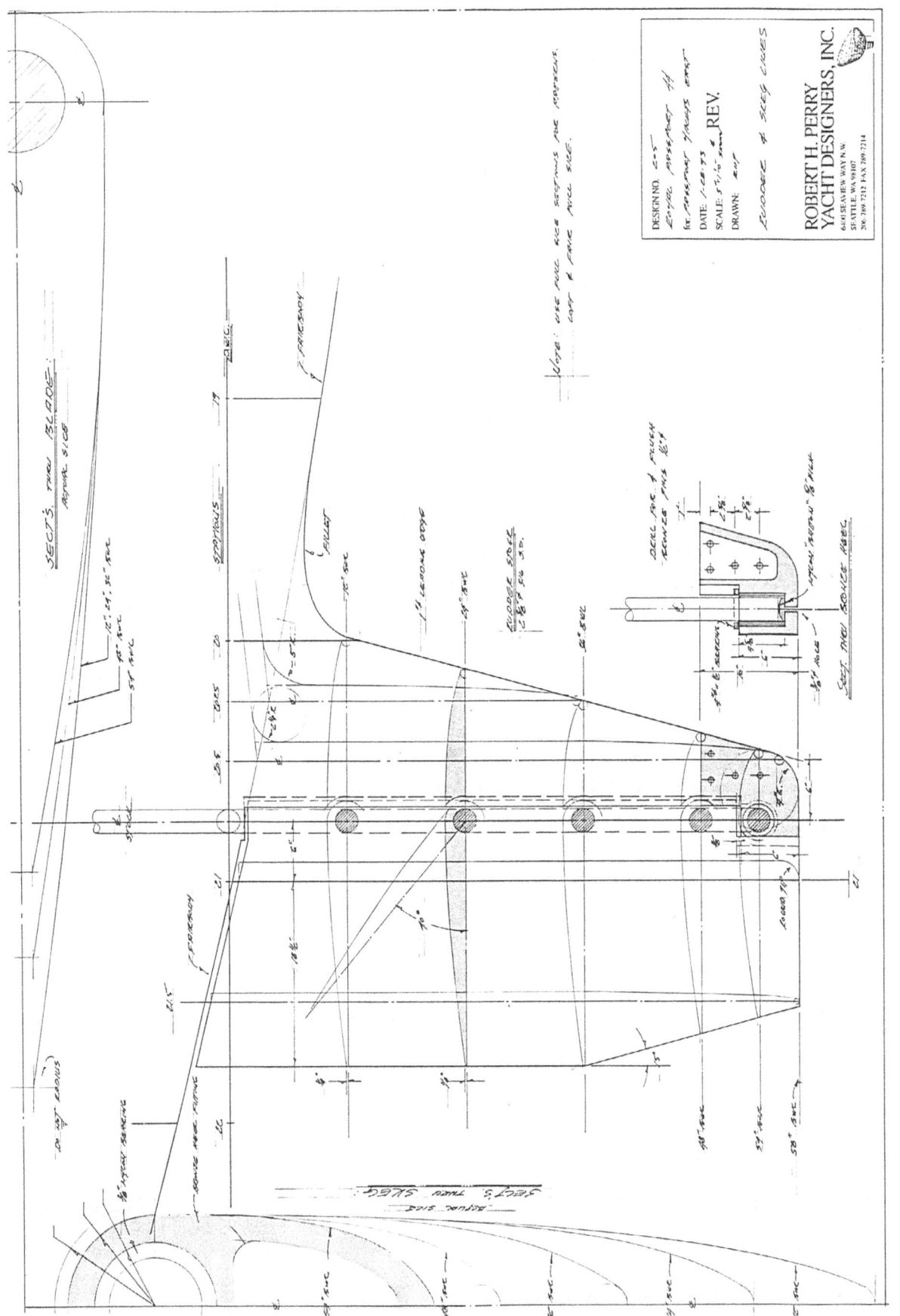

*I enjoyed drawing these details by hand and tried to make each drawing graphically interesting so the builder would be more inclined to follow my design.*

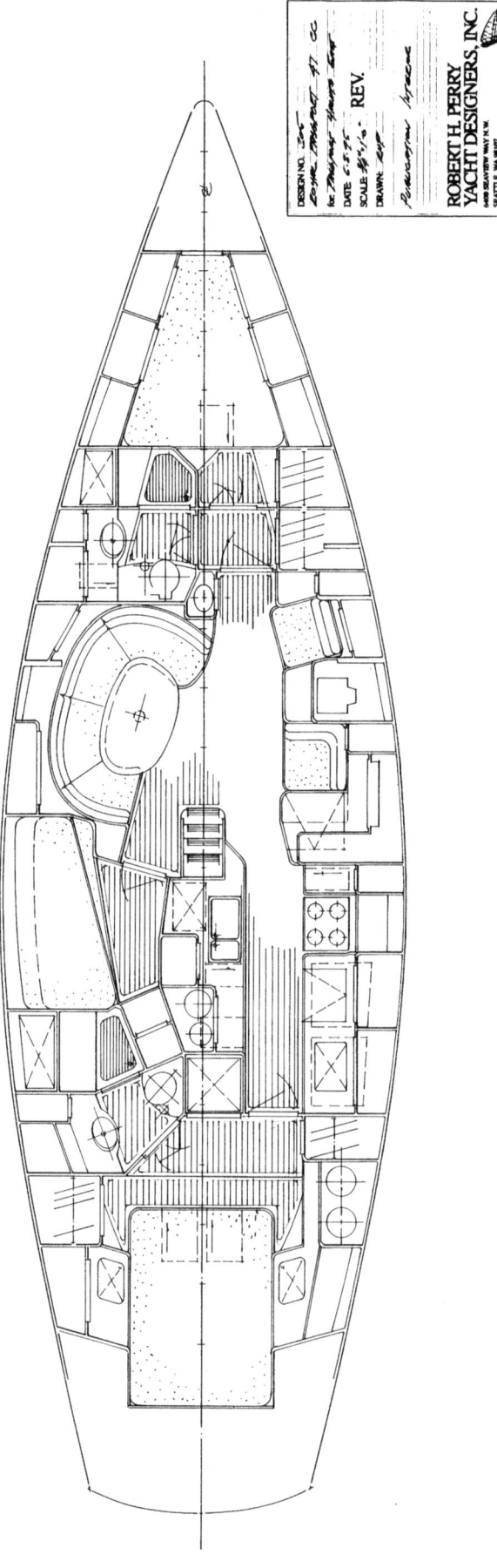

A typical Passport 470 center-cockpit layout. We never did two interiors of this popular design the same. Each was designed as a custom layout for a particular client.

*Thom Wagner looking satisfied at the helm of a beautiful Passport 456. I'm not too keen on the high-clewed genoa and in-mast furling, but the boat in this photo appears to be rolling along nicely.*

*This center-cockpit Passport 470 shows off Passport's excellent interior finishing work.*

in the series, the designer's job is easier. I just needed to take the Passport concept to the next level.

We knew that we needed a boat that would be able to be both aft-cockpit and center-cockpit models, so this meant a bit more freeboard than you might choose for an exclusively aft-cockpit model. We also knew that we needed to reduce the bow overhang to extend the waterline and bring the new boat more in line with current performance-oriented designs. While a plumb or near-plumb bow is faster than a bow with overhang in a cruising design, some overhang is beneficial in that it keeps the ground tackle away from the stem.

I gave the new model, the Passport Vista, a long waterline, a broad stern, and plenty of firmness through the bulges to ensure form stability at early heel angles. Because the boat would be offered in two transom styles, traditional and reverse transoms, I started with the longer model, the traditional transom, and designed the sheer to balance on that model. It is easy to get a nice sheer for the reverse transom this way, but if you start with the reverse transom and then lengthen the boat for the traditional transom, the sheerline can become unbalanced and have an awkward look.

The real beauty of the new design was that it would be very close to the older 44/48 model in terms of available interior volume; therefore, the weight of the finished boat would be similar. In the 44/48 we had been optimistic with the displacement. As time went on, it became apparent that owners would put everything under the sun on these boats, and while the yard in China did beautiful joiner work, it was a heavy style of building. We were ending up with

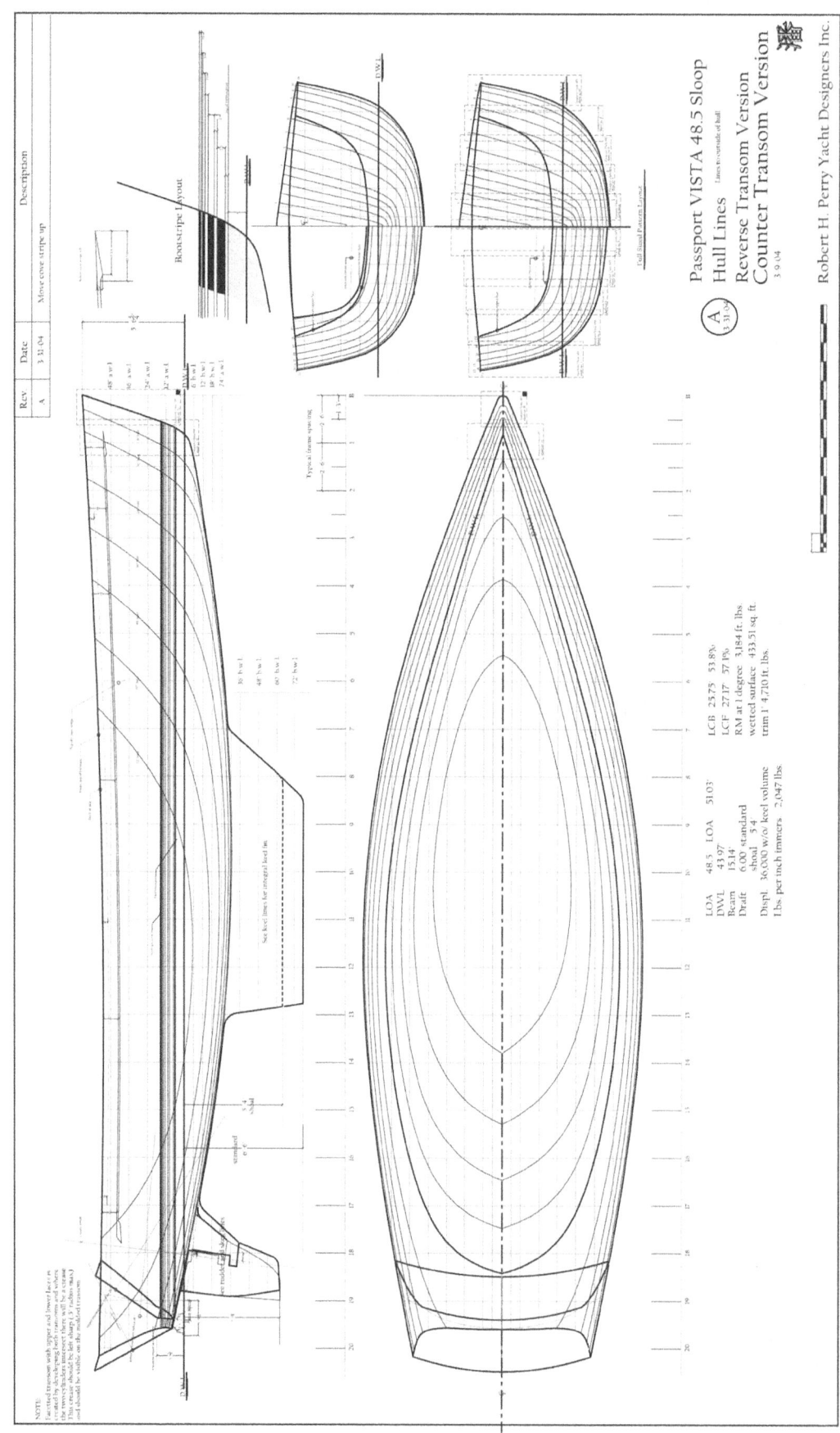

*Passport's Vista 485 has a reverse transom, and the 515 model has the traditional transom. Note the change in sectional shape from the older Passport 456/470, along with additional displacement and sailing length. I went to a partial skeg in this series.*

## Passport Yachts

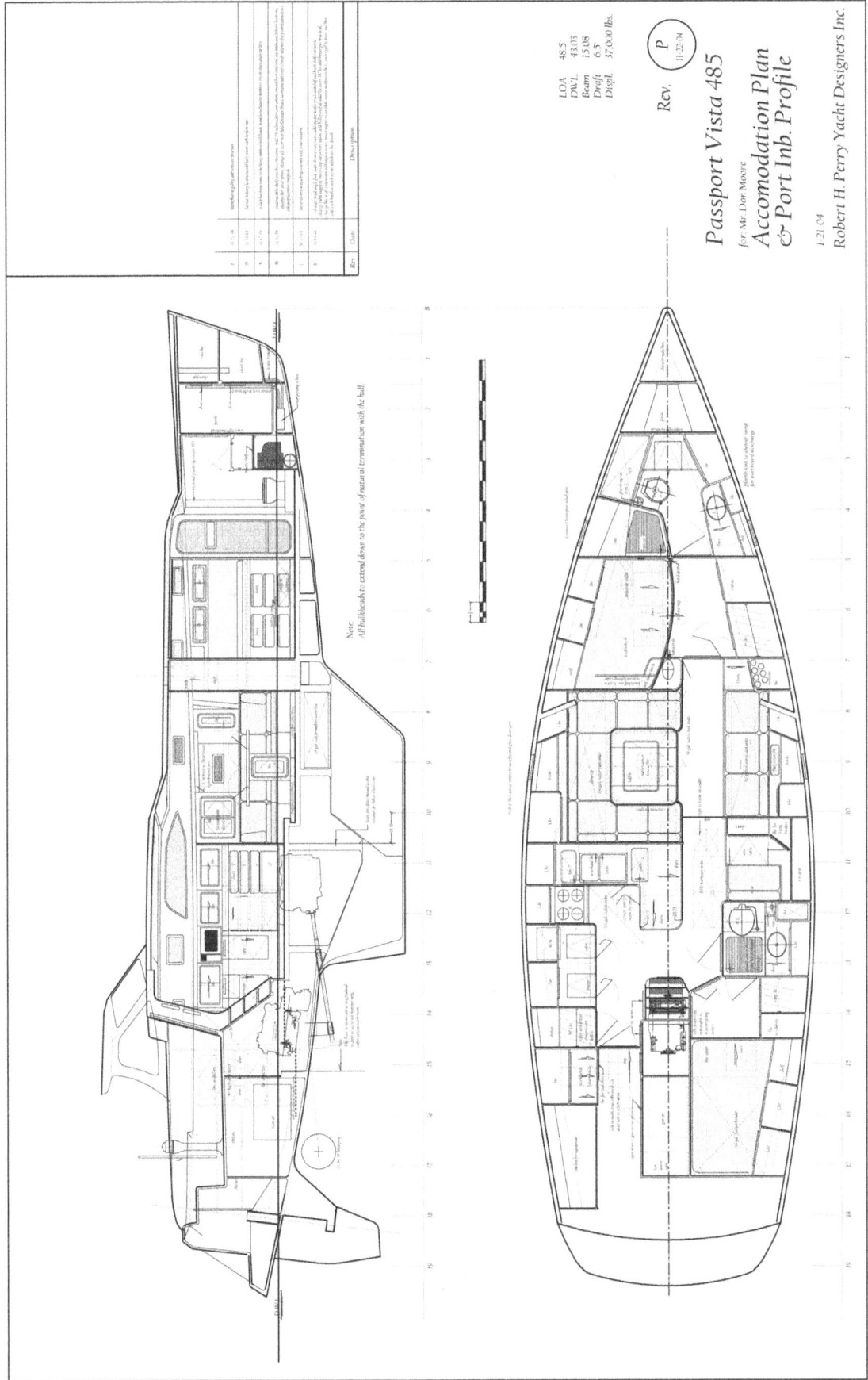

*I worked closely with Thom and his client, Don Moore, to come up with the first of the new Passport Vista 485 interiors. This layout was based mostly upon the experience Don had had with his previous 43-footer.*

# Yacht Design According to Perry

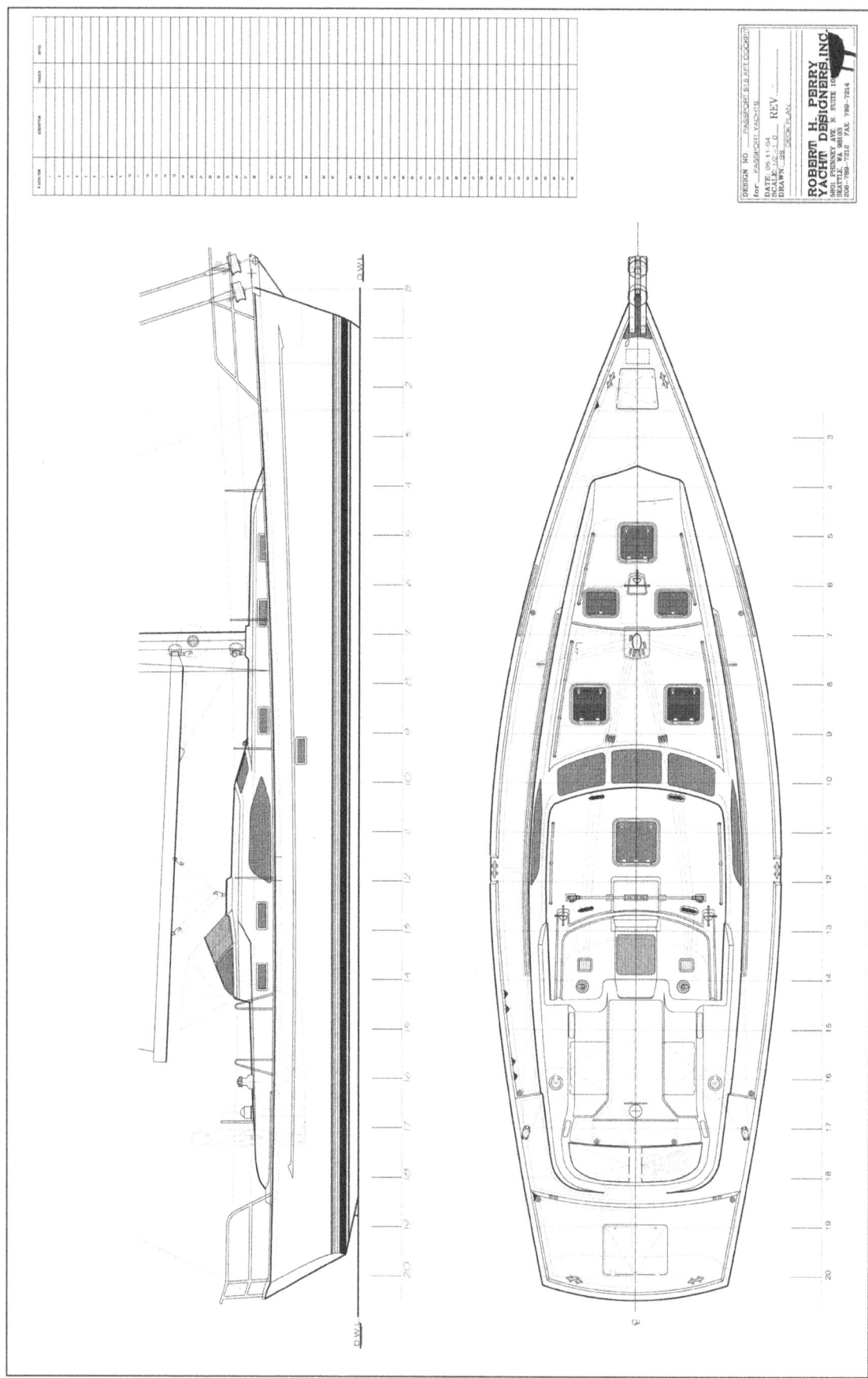

This Passport Vista 515 shows my preferred deck lines: crisp and well defined rather than Euro or overly "blobular."

heavy boats. They still sailed very well, but when you sink a hull four inches, you do end up with a different shape going through the water than the designer originally intended. The new Vista model gave me a chance to add displacement so that the boats as built and outfitted would be at my designed waterline. You can give two boatyards identical sets of plans, and the finished boat can vary widely in displacement due to each yard's style of building. The same goes for owners. One owner may be happy with 400 amp-hours of batteries, while the next may want 1200 amp-hours along with wind generators, solar cells, and every electrical device ever conceived for a sailing yacht. Over the years I have learned that wiring alone is heavy.

We have now launched three of the new Vista models, two with center cockpits and one with an aft cockpit. They are spot-on designed displacement and sail beautifully. Thom was nervous about the new rudder configuration with the half skeg. All previous Passports had full skegs. But full skegs make the rudder-design job difficult for the designer. Marrying the right rudder foil to a constant thickness on the aft edge of the skeg compromises the rudder foils. I can do it, and I have done it a hundred times, but given my choice, I prefer a spade rudder or a half skeg. Sailing trials proved the rudder to be perfect. I made a believer out of Thom.

Center-cockpit Passport Vistas are outselling the aft-cockpit model, but I prefer the aft-cockpit version. Don Moore, the owner of the first aft-cockpit model, has a lot of miles on his new boat already, and we worked very closely on the design of his boat. We have kept in close contact and talk to each other frequently. This gives me valuable feedback outside of the sales effort chain. Don is happy with his new boat. When the owners are happy, I am happy. At this stage, there is every indication that we have another successful Passport model on our hands.

## According to Perry
# DRAFT

One of the most frequent questions I'm asked is, "Will reducing the draft have a negative effect on performance?" Yes. Emphatically!

I wish that designing a good, fixed, shoal-draft keel was as easy as writing convincing ad copy. Shoal-draft keels are a real problem if you're after good upwind performance. That's why the one thing all of today's high-performance boats share in common is generous draft and a high-aspect-ratio fin. The first things you lose with a shoal keel are keel span, aspect ratio, and VCG. A low-aspect-ratio keel will, by simple geometry, be less efficient.

There is an optimal sweep angle for every aspect ratio, and as the aspect ratio decreases, that optimal sweep angle increases. This increase, combined with my preferred nearly vertical trailing edge, puts more chord length at the root and less at the tip; in other words, you wind up with more volume in the top of the keel fin and less in the bottom, and this compounds the difficulty of keeping the VCG low in a low-aspect keel.

If you counter this by making the sweep angle less than what is optimal for a low-aspect keel, you will achieve a longer tip chord and presumably a lower VCG, but that longer tip will increase drag disproportionately to the small increase in lift it provides. There are also pragmatic considerations favoring greater sweep angles. With more sweep in its leading edge, a keel will be less likely to snag weed and lines and may suffer less damage in a catastrophic grounding.

The fact that a molded fin must be released from its hull mold puts further restrictions on its shape and distribution of volume. The fin must be tapered, in section, in order to release, and this rules out a bulb or any increased thickness in the tip foil. You could get around this with a two-piece mold that splits open for release, but you would still have to slide the ballast slug down into that cavity in multiple pieces. It can all be done, but it is not the type of operation most production boatbuilders care to undertake. A tapered ballast slug slides easily and quickly into a tapered fin shape.

The best way to counter the VCG problem in a molded or "integral" keel is by trying to keep the lead in the lower portion of the fin and using the upper portion for a deep sump. Many integral keels use iron ballast at 450 pounds per cubic foot, but you have more placement options and can achieve a lower VCG when you use lead at 700 pounds per cubic foot.

Then too, if you fix draft, any portion of the keel span given over to bulb shape development reduces the effective span even further, since the bulb geometry intrudes into the span of the fin. Wings or "winglets" extending outward from the keel tip or bulb can help increase the apparent aspect ratio of a keel and increase the efficiency of a shoal-draft keel, but they can also bury themselves like a Bruce anchor if you ground the boat in mud or sand. Wings pasted on randomly may just add wetted surface, and additional wetted surface is never good. Wings, like keels, must have a high-aspect ratio to be efficient, and this makes them structurally vulnerable. In a heeled condition, effective, high-aspect wings can actually increase the working draft of a boat, but I don't consider wings a practical solution for a cruising design where occasional grounding is a probability.

One possible way to improve the performance of a shoal keel is to use a centerboard or daggerboard in combination with the keel, but this adds complexity and maintenance issues, and I always try to keep my cruising boats as simple as possible. Centerboards can add effective lateral plane, but most cruising sailors do not want the hassle of dealing with a vulnerable, maintenance-challenged, moveable appendage. The typical centerboard trunk, housed in the keel fin, takes up valuable volume that could otherwise be given to lead ballast, and this either further raises the VCG of this already compromised keel or requires an extra-wide keel foil. A relatively high-aspect board hung below a thick lump of a stub keel operates in disturbed, turbulent water. This vortex coming off the tip of the fin further reduces the board's effectiveness. On the positive side, a pivoting centerboard can be adjusted so as to move the boat's center of lateral resistance aft and thereby relieve excessive weather helm and increase helm balance options.

Recently I designed a ballasted lifting keel that retracts upward into a trunk within the hull. You can imagine the possible problems associated with this type of keel. It can be extremely effective, but it is very expensive and may require more than a normally acceptable amount of maintenance. *Icon's* lifting keel (Chapter 16) was designed to reduce the draft from 13.8 feet in high-performance mode to 8.5 feet for normal "marina" depths. This could hardly be considered a shoal-draft solution, but you can see how a similar design could be employed to produce a restricted-draft boat. If you were to give a 60-footer a slightly longer keel chord length with a keel-up draft of 6 feet and a keel-down draft of 10 feet, you might have the ultimate shoal keel, cost and durability considerations aside. Short of such solutions, however, it's safe to say that you need to reduce your performance expectations when you reduce your draft.

The bottom line is this: With today's relatively high-powered boats of medium to light displacement, there's no substitute for draft. As a designer, I'll fight for every inch of draft the client and his or her intended area of operation will allow. I ask my clients to think carefully about draft. Given an owner-imposed draft limit, I will do my best to design an effective keel using whatever technology best fits the design and cost parameters.

Once the draft and keel geometry have been decided, it remains to be decided how the ballast keel will be attached to the hull. I'm often asked to compare boats with integral or internal ballast to those with bolt-on, externally mounted keels. As a designer, I always prefer a bolt-on keel. Casting a lead keel gives me the freedom of designing any shape I like. If the keel is to be a monocoque part of the molded GRP hull, the keel shape will have to be pulled from the mold. This restricts its geometry, as discussed above.

Then, too, an internally ballasted keel will need to be bigger than an externally ballasted keel. You need to add the thickness of the GRP skin, then add something for a working tolerance so that the lead fits inside the envelope. The result is a thicker fin than is probably optimal. Of course, you can add chord length to get a thicker foil, but that results in added wetted surface.

The benefits of a molded keel fin with internal ballast are that there are no keel bolts, and the space above the lead often provides a convenient bilge sump area. As mentioned before, you might even be able to place a tank above the ballast. An internally ballasted keel is also, by nature, a longer, lower-aspect fin and thus not as likely to suffer impact damage in a grounding as a higher-aspect, bolted-on keel.

The downside of an internally ballasted keel is that if you hit the bottom hard, you could put a hole in your fin. More often than not, this hole will be in the ballasted region of the fin. Because most internal-ballast slugs are encapsulated in fiberglass, no water will intrude into the hull. Should the impact damage occur in a part of the fin that does not contain encapsulated ballast, however, you would be left with a hole in your hull through which seawater would be entering, and that's never a good thing. Either way, a penetrating impact in your keel fin needs to be immediately addressed.

If you hit bottom with a bolt-on keel, you might only put a fist-sized "ding" or depression in the lead without affecting hull integrity. Performance might be reduced by a small degree, but you could sail all summer and do a putty repair during the winter haulout. The downside of a bolt-on keel in a hard grounding is that the impact focuses the loads where the trailing edge of the keel meets the hull. This same problem exists with molded-in keels, but not, as I said, to the same degree. In both cases, special care must be taken by the designer to beef up the floors and structure in the area directly above this intersection at the trailing edge. I usually double up the transverse floor right above the trailing edge of the keel.

Keel bolts themselves are seldom a problem. I use far more bolts than necessary to sustain the static weight of the keel, and I give them substantial backing plates to spread the loads over a wide area of this extra-thick, heavily reinforced area of the hull. Of course, periodical inspection of keel bolts is recommended maintenance.

A cruising boat's keel poses a challenge to the designer, but it should not be a challenge to the owner.

## Chapter Ten
# NIGHT RUNNER

If the success of a design is measured by the owner's satisfaction with the boat, then *Night Runner* has to be one of my most successful creations. The origins of *Night Runner* date back to when I was 15 years old.

I sailed in every race series in Seattle. Weekdays it was small-boat racing on Lake Washington, and weekends it was big-boat racing on Puget Sound out of Shilshole Bay Marina. In the summer this meant racing two or three days a week, depending upon whom I was crewing with and the race schedules. In the winter it meant the Hot Buttered Rum and Windjammer series in big boats on Puget Sound. I would arrive at the marina early and treat myself at the dockside restaurant to the Fisherman's Breakfast. It included everything, took two plates, and, as I recall, cost a whopping $3.50 in 1963. But I had a job in a meat market and got paid on Saturday, so I was usually flush, at least on Sunday.

As I worked my way through my two plates of breakfast one cold Sunday morning, I looked out to the water and noticed a salty-looking, 35-foot cutter sailing down the waterway with one man at the long tiller and no crew in sight. It was a great-looking boat, and it was evident that the skipper was going to dock it under sail, single-handed. He did. I was impressed, so after finishing my breakfast, I walked down to the dock and introduced myself.

The skipper's name was Frank Paine. The cutter was *African Star*, an Atkin Tally Ho Major built locally by Rupert Broome, the legendary Seattle rigger. It would be hard to imagine a more handsome or salty cutter anywhere at anytime. I was enthralled, and I asked Mr. Paine what he was going to do with the boat. He said he had a circumnavigation planned. Of course, I inquired about the crew for the voyage, and he replied that he was going to do it single-handed. "That way the cook always gets along with the crew," he said. I asked if he would consider taking me with him, and he said no, but after a few moments he relented a bit, saying, "I'll take you as far as Hawaii." My heart leapt. "But first we need to do a get-acquainted cruise together to make sure we can get along." I was up for that, so we made a plan to meet in two weeks at the boat at six o'clock on a Friday evening to go cruising for the weekend.

My father dropped me off at the marina on a cold and rainy Friday night, and I went immediately to *African Star* only to find the boat locked up and no Captain Paine in sight. No problem. I'd wait. I had my seabag and my sleeping bag rolled in a garbage sack, so I made myself as comfortable as you can be in a bare cockpit, with no dodger, on a chilly, miserable night. The hours went by and still no Captain Paine. I was cold, wet, and discouraged. Around nine o'clock, I called my dad and asked him to come and get me. I never saw nor heard from Frank Paine again.

In time, *African Star* was bought by Seattle Admiralty law attorney Doug Fryer, who began racing the boat. Doug had a huge, ugly, yellow spinnaker

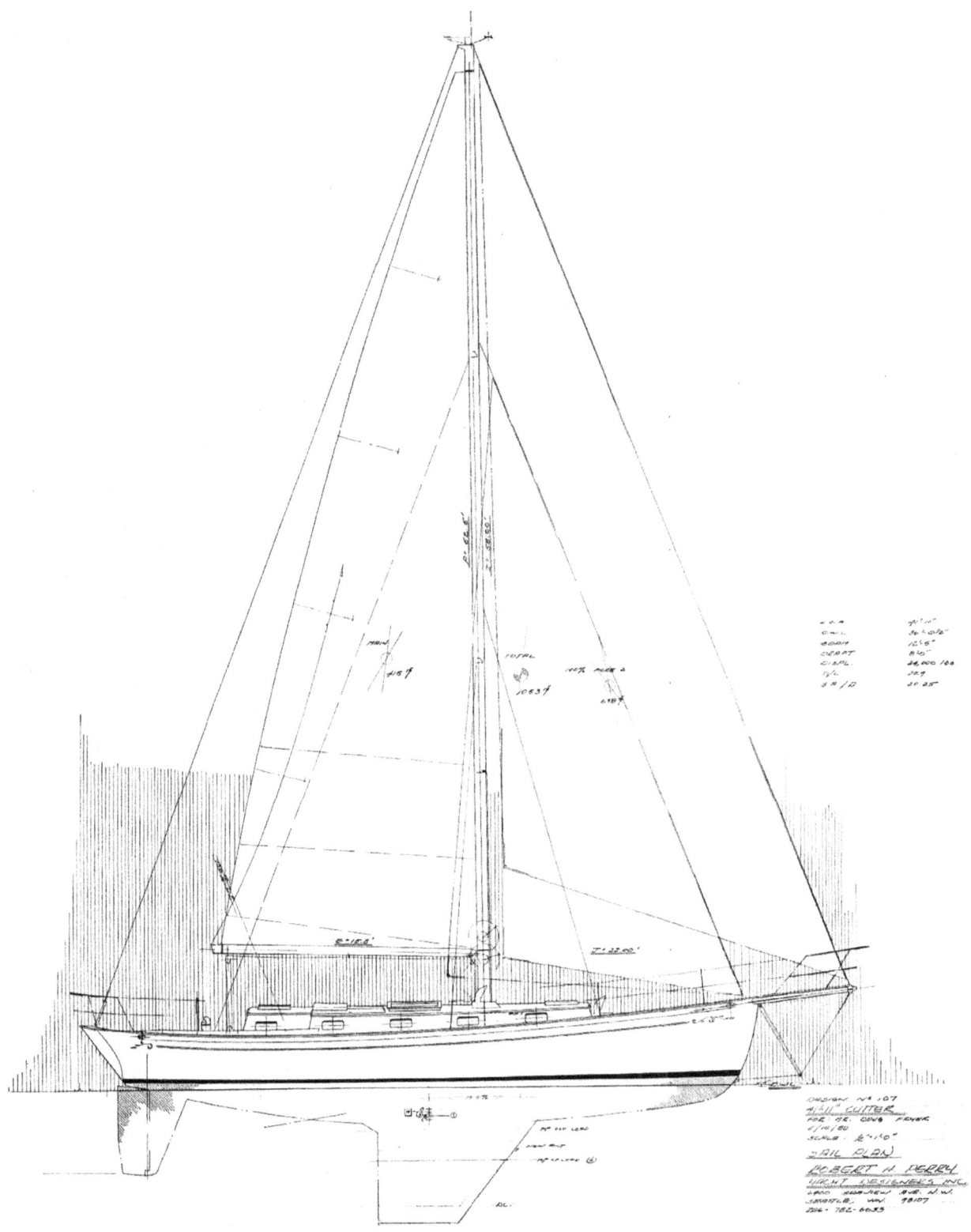

I've hit a few home runs but I have only hit a very few with the bases loaded. *Night Runner* goes down in the book as a grand slam. When asked "What is your favorite design?" I am reluctant to answer, but always in the back of my mind I am thinking of *Night Runner*. That dolphin striker is needed to get the headstay loaded sufficiently to keep that big genoa luff straight.

# Night Runner

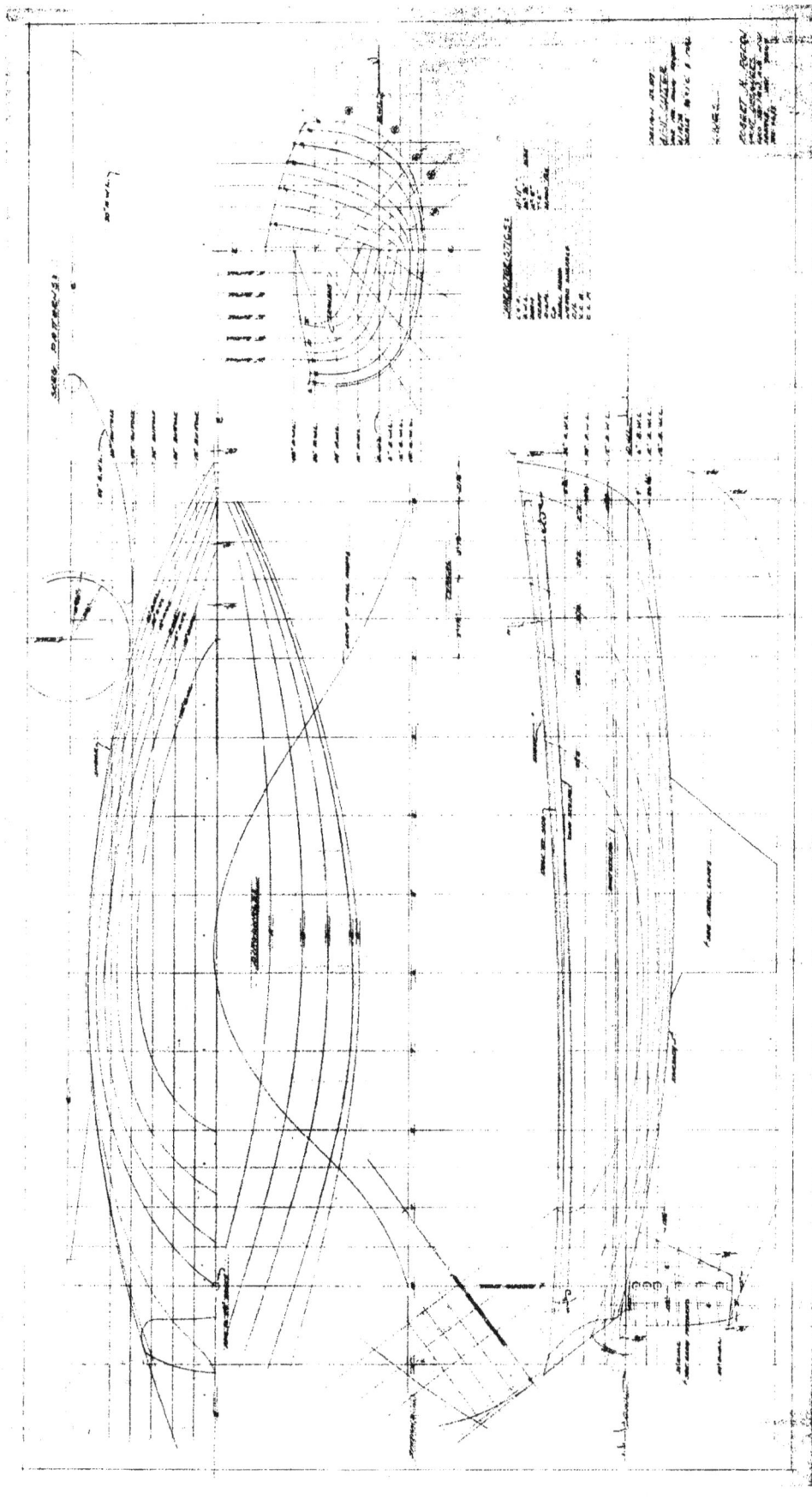

*I always felt that Night Runner's hull was like that of a big dinghy. There is no deadrise, and there is a hint of tumblehome amidships. The buttocks are straight and the diagonals well balanced. Night Runner has one of the nicest feels when pressed of any boat I have sailed.*

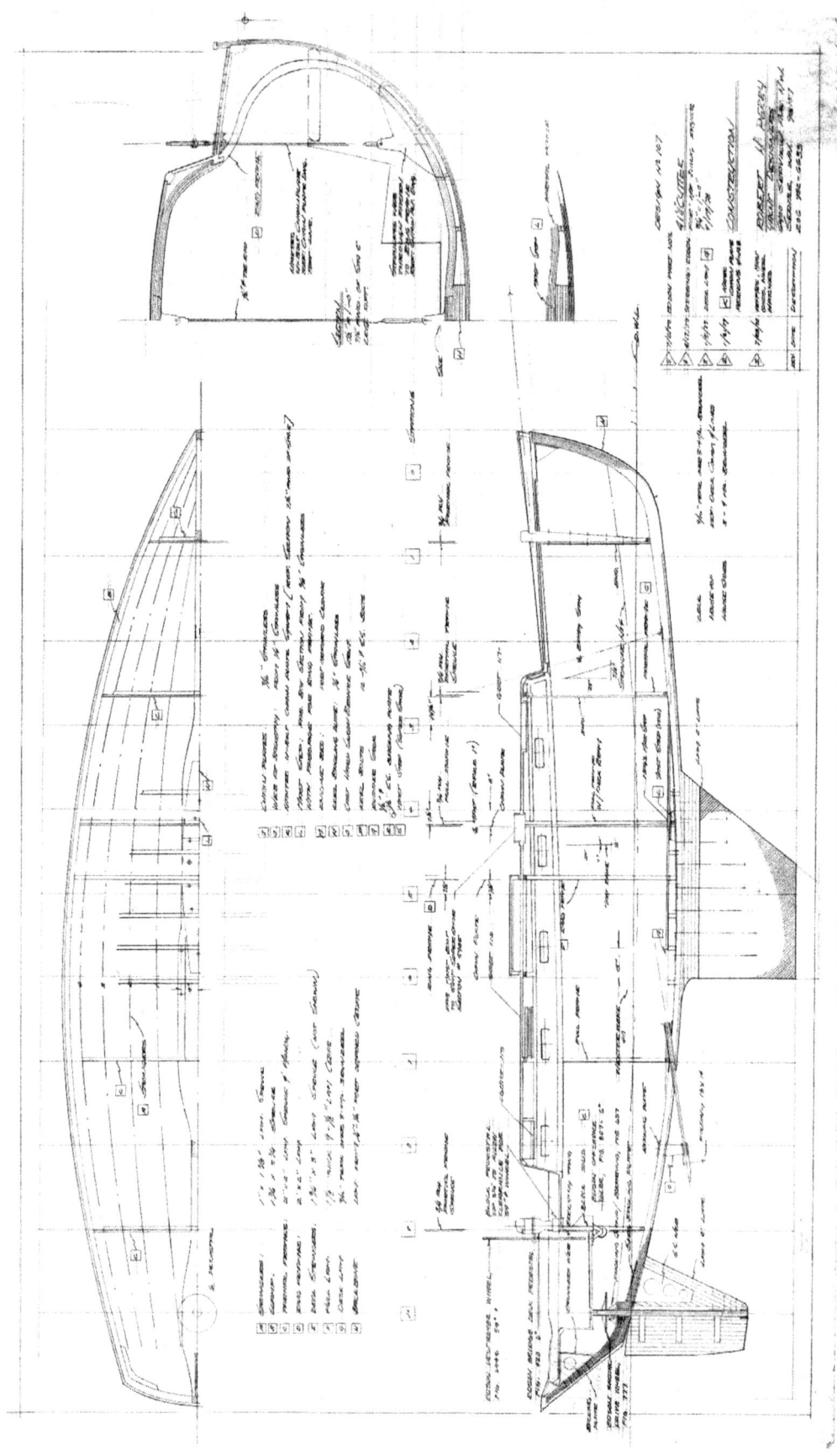

Night Runner's construction drawing shows in section the laminated ring frames that tied the keel, hull, and deck together.

with a green star on it, and the rule of thumb was that at the end of the race, if you could see that spinnaker, *African Star* had beaten you on corrected time. Doug and his crew of stalwart mates won a lot of local races in that old, full-keeled wooden cutter. For many years, *African Star* was a fixture on the Seattle bigboat racing scene. In time I met Doug and told him my Frank Paine story. Doug said that Paine had lost the boat in a divorce. I felt badly for him and imagined what the loss of his boat and dream must've felt like. Still, in Doug's capable hands, the boat had never looked better.

Many years later, in 1977, I was comfortably ensconced in my Shilshole Bay office and business was good. Doug came in one afternoon and said he wanted to build a new boat. "Great," I said. Then Doug explained that he wanted to build a version of Bruce King's *Unicorn* ketch, but he was concerned about the boat's handling characteristics off the wind. This was based on the stories of the King-designed Ericson 39's challenging off-the-wind handling personality. And this was due to the fact that the Ericson 39 was an IOR boat with pinched ends, exacerbated, in Doug's opinion, by an extremely distended bustle. This design feature was a carryover from the design work being done on 12-meters at the time—which were still being used for America's Cup competition. An effort was being made to squeeze volume into the ends to increase the prismatic coefficient of the boat to offset the deep midsection that the 12-meter rule required. It was a common shape in those IOR days, but Bruce King had carried it to an extreme in the Ericson 39. We certainly all went through a "bustle era," myself included. I recalled racing an Ericson 39 while I was in Boston and being handed the wheel on a blustery day. I soon noticed that most of the crew were staring at me as I "snake-waked" my way down the bay, trying to keep the 39 on course. I was soon relieved at the helm, but I never forgot that the Ericson 39 could be a demanding boat to steer off the wind.

The last thing I wanted to do was to be given the job of "fixing" a Bruce King design. I told Doug that I had little interest in that project and asked him what he was doing building a custom boat from someone else's custom design. "That's like using his toothbrush," I said. Custom boats are highly personal projects, and I told Doug that he needed a boat drawn for his own personal style. Doug asked what I had in mind, and I told him to come back in three days, when I would present him with a preliminary design. It was a deal. No money was involved, but I was confident that I could draw something that Doug would like. At that precise instant, however, I had no idea what that would be.

As I stood before the drawing board staring down at that big sheet of blank paper, an idea came to me. Make Doug's new boat as modern as possible under the water without resorting to IOR shapes, but topsides, give him something with which he was familiar—something I knew he liked. I drew a 41-foot, 24,000-pound-displacement, fin-keeled, skeg-hung-rudder version of *African Star*. Above the waterline the boat looked like a drawn-out big sister to *African Star*; that is, extremely traditional. Below the waterline, though, the boat looked like a modern two-tonner without the IOR influence. Given that the Bruce King boat Doug liked was a clipper-bowed, wineglass-transom, Herreshoff-type boat, I realized that I had taken a different tack. But the more I refined the preliminary drawing, the better I liked it. One of the primary attributes of any designer has to be confidence.

Tuesday afternoon arrived and so did Doug in his lawyer's suit. Doug is not tall, but he is solidly built and has a very deep, resonant voice and a shiny bald head. Doug gives the impression of carefully controlled power and ability. (I chose him for my lawyer when the inevitable time came that I needed one.) I unrolled the drawing of the preliminary sail plan and Doug stood in silence for a couple of minutes, then turned to me and said with a big smile, "I like it."

"Of course you do, Doug," thought I, "it looks just like your current boat." We made arrangements for the design fee and were off to produce a new design for Doug. The boat would be built at Cecil Lange's yard in Port Townsend using the cold-molded wood process that was so popular at the time.

The hull shape I had in mind was based upon a big International 14. The boat would have some tumblehome because it looked good. I would try to do a pretty transom without introducing so much hollow in the garboards that it would slow the boat down. I wanted the run to be straight and on the full side. I gave the hull an arc-like midsection that went tangent at the centerline so that there was no deadrise through the middle of the boat. I did this expressly because I wanted to use multiple veneer layers in the cold-molding process, and I wanted to wrap those veneers across the middle of the boat so

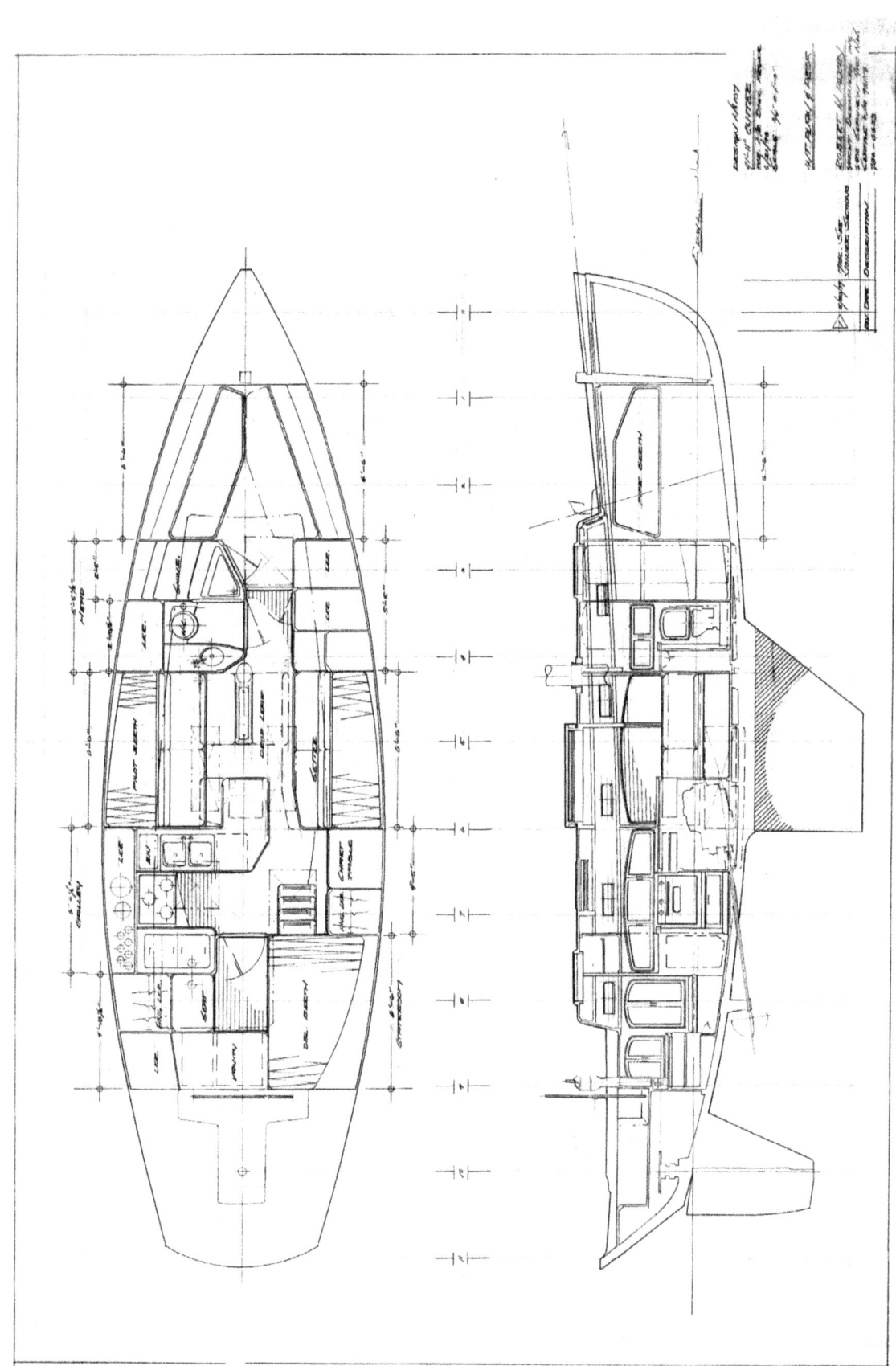

I got the idea for Night Runner's layout from an old Phil Rhodes design. It offers a real aft cabin that does not intrude on the cockpit area. The pilot berths to port and starboard have seen a lot of use by tired and happy crew members over the years.

Night Runner *at the dock at Shilshole showing her cabin trunk painted white. I preferred paint to the all-varnish look, but I would have gone with a sea-mist green on the trunk sides.*

*A classic Steve Davis rendering of* Night Runner's *sail plan. Nobody does it better than Steve.*

that there would be no "seam" where the veneers butted on centerline. I felt that this would make for the strongest boat. But it was labor-intensive, as it required the planks to be spiled or shaped from gunwale to gunwale.

In an effort to cut costs, Cecil Lange reduced my layers of veneer in half and butted them on centerline despite my drawings. This required spiling only one side of the boat and producing the mirror image for the other side. This would eventually cause a problem, and years later Doug apologized for having given Cecil the OK to make the skin-layer change. Clearly this set up a rift between Cecil and me, and that rift is as ripe today as it ever was after that change. Cecil was not a man to be questioned about boatbuilding, and I had raised some serious questions during the building of *Night Runner*. These questions concerned Cecil's cavalier lofting practices and the fact that, after launching, the discontinuous skins needed refastening to the keelson.

Shape-wise, the hull was beautiful and very dinghy-like. I gave *Night Runner* a deep, Peterson-esque keel fin and a rudder hung on a deep skeg. While the boat was built at Cecil's yard, 90 percent of the work was done by Bob Lange, Cecil's son.

I can remember driving to the yard one day to check the lofting. It was atrocious—extremely unfair. Clearly someone overseeing the lofting (Cecil) did not have any idea how to go about resolving the lines in full size to match the lines drawn at 3/4"=1'0" scale on paper. Lofting is a demanding, zero-tolerance process, and it must be done correctly if the finished product is to bear any resemblance to the original design. I found myself in the uncomfortable position of having to lecture the 65-year-old Cecil, a craggy New Zealand boatbuilder, on the basics of lofting. I told Cecil to call me when he had done it right and I would come back up. As I prepared to drive away, Cecil came over to the car and told me that he wasn't going to draw more lines on the floor "just to draw lines on the floor." Clearly he still did not get it. Cecil would eventually fair up *Night Runner*'s hull by using battens on the mold frames. It can be done this way, but it does not ensure that the fairing changes will be in accord with what the designer has drawn. I was a 30-year-old "kid" at the time. What did I know? Well, I sure knew how to loft.

Night Runner *in her element going through Race Rocks during a Swiftsure Race, in the day when genoas were big sails and winches were always too small.*

Looking back, maybe there is some sort of weird justice at work. After all, I am challenged with tools. I can't build anything. But I have seen more than one skilled boatbuilder break out into a sweat the moment I handed him a pencil and asked him to sketch the detail he was describing. Lofting is all about pencils, long battens, and drawing the boat full size.

The cabin trunk always looked odd to me—just not quite right. When a local sailing magazine did a feature on Cecil, they made a big deal of his "Old World" approach to boatbuilding. Given that *Night Runner* was under construction at the time, they went into the shop, where Cecil showed them how he struck the cabin trunk top lines "by eye" using a string. His explanation to the article's author was that because there weren't enough dimensions on the drawing he had to do it by eye.

Upon reading this, I called my friend Cecil and asked him what that was all about. I explained that the drawing of the deck lines, which he had in his possession, was covered in dimensions. Coming from the world of production boatbuilding and molded fiberglass decks, the one thing my office was extremely good at was designing deck structures. I'll paraphrase here, but Cecil's reply was something like, "I know, Bob, but they expected me to give them a show, so I did it that way." His way meant that the sensitivity of changing cambers in the housetop and the gentle spring to the housetop centerline that I drew were lost. But I got over it. Despite the fact that the house shape is Cecil's and not mine, *Night Runner* is still a great-looking boat.

The boat was finished in time for the summer's racing schedule, and I crewed on the boat that season. We did quite well, coming second in class in the Swiftsure race after being edged out by a new Baltic 42. *Night Runner* had a couple of nicknames that I know about. I never cared for "Night Crawler," but due to its all-varnished hull and deck work, I didn't mind "The Mayflower." When *Night Runner* just kept on winning races, I couldn't have cared less what people called it.

There is not a race in the Pacific Northwest that Doug has not raced *Night Runner* in, and he has won almost all of them at some time. I think it is safe to say at this time that *Night Runner* is a boat that is a lot of fun to race. One reason might be because *Night Runner* is a beautifully balanced boat on the helm. The feel on the helm is delicate. It almost always requires just two fingers, and you can dial in or out weather helm as you might need it.

My favorite moment racing *Night Runner* was when I was watch captain on the Swiftsure and we were just leaving the Straits. The wind died as it usually does there in the late afternoon, and we dropped our big genoa and hoisted what we used to call a "banana," a high-clewed, 110 percent drifter. We began to move, close reaching, as you can't point high with the full banana. As we did so, we began to increase our own apparent wind speed. We passed boat after boat with most of them fighting for steerage, let alone boat speed. I remember passing a Valiant 40 that was doing circles. We walked through the fleet. I made the perfect call to shift from the drifter to the number-one genoa as the breeze began to fill gently, and soon we were close reaching to the mark at five-plus knots without another boat in our class in sight. We were the first PHRF boat to round the mark. I was very happy.

Doug finishes each race with what we began calling "ritual rums." Doug uses 151-proof rum "because it's lighter," i.e., he doesn't have to carry as many bottles to achieve the desired effect on a cold, wet, racing crew. A jigger of 151-proof rum mixed with a dollop of hot-buttered rum mix, and even a sixth-place finish begins to look good and sail folding goes a whole lot easier. We all looked forward to those rums as we motored back to the marina after racing.

Doug is a delight to race with. He is always in the same great mood, just happy to be out there sailing, whether he is in first place or last place. I think that everyone who has crewed for Doug has enjoyed the experience. During my first race on *Night Runner*, our bowman managed to tie a half hitch around the outboard end of the spinnaker pole in our first three jibes. The bowman was a regular member of Doug's crew, so I tried to be patient. Finally I lost it and explained to the bowman, in a less-than-courteous way, the correct way to change spinnaker guys. Walking down the dock after the race, another regular for Doug's crew said, "Gee, that's the first time somebody has yelled at anyone on the crew." In fact, I had crewed on boats where most of the communication was yelling. You did not yell when you crewed for Doug. Before the end of that race the bowman was executing flawless jibes.

Doug raced *Night Runner* in the Single-Handed TransPac race. Doug cruised *Night Runner* around Cape Horn. Doug has taken *Night Runner* to just about every anchorage in the Pacific Northwest all the way to Alaska. I can remember almost any Friday afternoon driving up the hill on my way home from my office near the marina and seeing *Night Runner* leaving the marina and heading north. I think it's accurate to say that of all the boats I have drawn, *Night Runner* has the most miles under its keel.

Cruising back from Cape Horn in 1995, *Night Runner* lost its skeg off the coast of Mexico. The rudder stayed on but the skeg was gone. Doug called to get me to mail him a copy of the skeg drawing. I asked how the boat handled without a skeg. He said, "Better."

I am frequently asked, "What is your favorite design?" I try my best not to give an answer, but when pressed, I usually say *Night Runner*.

## According to Perry
# RIG DIMENSIONS AND TYPES

In my 39 years of yacht designing, I've seen a lot of changes in cruising boat rigs. Today, a sloop with an inner forestay (often mistakenly referred to as a cutter) is assumed by most sailors to be the ultimate cruising rig, but I think that a closer look must be taken at all the options so that an understanding can be reached of their respective strengths and weaknesses. The ways in which each rig can be optimized for maximum performance must also be investigated. I know that by attacking some myths, I'm going to tread on a few toes.

Let me begin by establishing a common vocabulary for this discussion. There are universally accepted terms for describing rig dimensions, and these are mandatory if you are going to discuss rig options with a sailmaker, a rigger, or a sparmaker.

*I* is the height of the foretriangle and can be measured a number of ways. I measure I from the sheer (i.e., the intersection of the deck with the hull side at the mast) to the intersection of the forestay or headstay on the mast. For the sake of convenience, some sailors measure upward from the centerline of the cabin trunk rather than the sheer, but this can result in a significant on-paper reduction in rig height. For masthead-rigged boats (i.e., for those in which the headstay reaches the top of the mast), I is the height of the mast. For a fractional rig, the top of I is where the forestay attaches to the mast. In relating your I dimension to a sailmaker or sparmaker it would be wise to describe exactly what method you used to determine the base of I.

*ISP* is the height of the highest spinnaker halyard sheave measured above the base of I. On a fractionally rigged boat, you may have a spinnaker halyard sheave above the top of I (i.e., above the headstay attachment). On a masthead-rigged boat, ISP is always the same as I.

*J* is the horizontal length of the base of the foretriangle from the landing point of the headstay or forestay on the deck or bowsprit to the front side of the mast.

*E* is the length of the foot of the mainsail measured from the back side of the mast to the aftermost position of the mainsail clew.

*EY* is the length of the foot of a mizzen sail.

*P* is the hoist of the mainsail measured from the top of the boom at the mast to the uppermost position of the mainsail head.

*PY* is the hoist of the mizzen.

*LP* is the luff perpendicular, a line from the clew of the jib that meets the jib luff on a perpendicular. *LP* is expressed as a percentage of J. Thus a 130 percent genoa has a luff perpendicular that is 130 percent of the foretriangle base (i.e., J). You can have a variety of genoa shapes all with the same LP depending upon the height of the clew.

The *CE* is the center of effort of an individual sail or of the entire rig. In practice, this is not quite as predicted by the little symbols you commonly see on published sail plans indicating the two-dimensional centroids of the various sails. Although these centroids are often used by designers to derive a sail

*According to Perry: Rig Dimensions and Types*

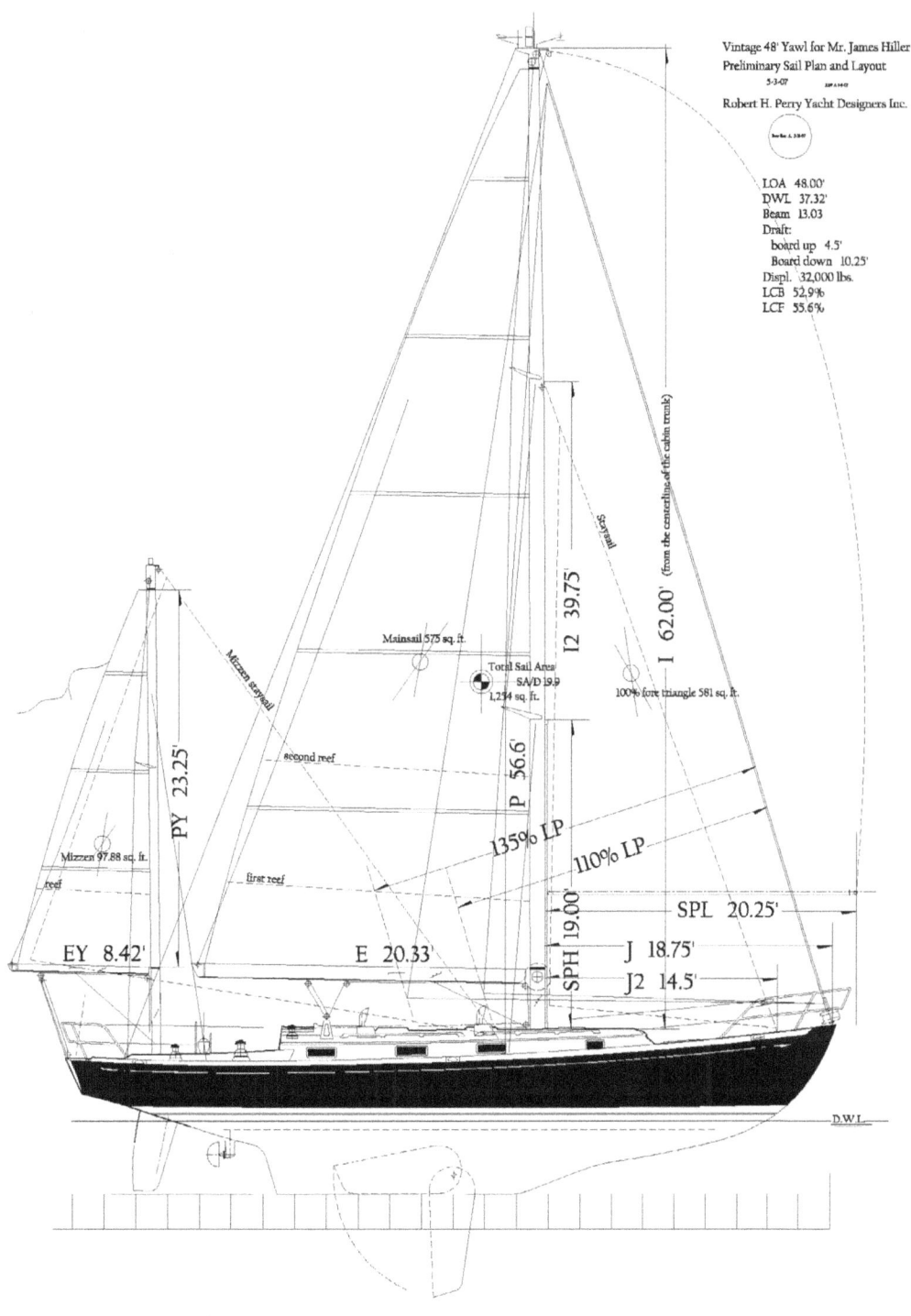

Here is the 48-foot yawl pictured in "According to Perry: Comparing Sailboats," page 10. *The principal rig dimensions are as follows:*

**J** = *foretriangle base to headstay*
**J2** = *foretriangle base to inner forestay*
**I** = *foretriangle height (here taken from centerline of cabin trunk to masthead)*
**I2** = *inner foretriangle height*
**P** = *length of mainsail hoist*

**PY** = *length of mizzen hoist*
**E** = *length of mainsail foot*
**EY** = *length of mizzen foot*
**SPH** = *height of lower spreaders*
**SPL** = *length of spinnaker pole*

plan's overall center of effort for purposes of calculations, the true CE under actual sailing conditions will almost never conform to a two-dimensional centroid. Rather, it will depend on the distribution of draft in the sail and will move as the sheets are eased and the sail moves outboard. A more accurate term for this living, breathing center of effort might be *center of pressure*.

*Weather helm* is a boat's tendency to turn up into the wind (head up) when you let go of the helm. This is common and, to some degree, a healthy and desirable attribute, conveying through the wheel or tiller a constant tactile sense of your boat's balance and overall trim health. A boat with moderate weather helm will naturally want to climb to windward when sailing on the wind, and that, too, is a good thing. On the other hand, excessively beamy boats can have excessive weather helm, as can boats in which the rig's center of pressure is too far aft of the boat's center of lateral resistance. Excessive weather helm is not good; it must be countered with excessive rudder angle, leading to an increase in rudder pressure, which wears out the helmsman and slows down the boat.

*Lee helm* is a boat's tendency to turn away from the wind (fall off) when you let go of the helm and is caused by the rig's center of pressure being too far forward. This is fortunately rare (it is found most frequently on very narrow boats) and is considered indicative of poor design or possibly a rig-tuning problem. It is difficult at best to steer a lee-helmed boat to weather. Lee helm occurs primarily in light air and can disappear as the wind builds and the boat heels.

Now let me go over the basic rig types.

## Sloop

This is a boat with one mast carrying a headsail (or headsails) and a mainsail. A sloop can have a jib and a staysail, but this does not make it a cutter. It's just a sloop with two headsails. A masthead sloop has the headstay going to the masthead. A fractional sloop has the headstay landing on the mast below the masthead. This is usually expressed as a fraction of the mast height, as in a *seven-eighths rig* or a *three-quarters rig*. Masthead or fractional, one headsail or three, a sloop is still a sloop based on the location

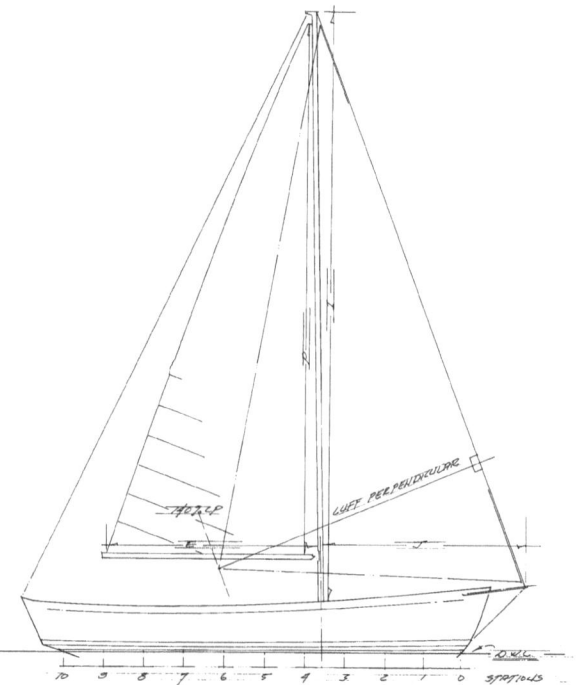
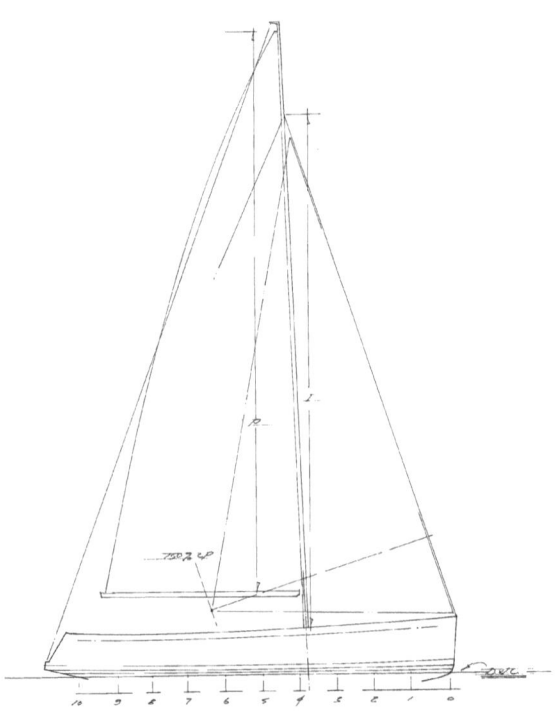

*The masthead-rigged sloop on the left has a fairly short rig and a bowsprit to add foretriangle area. You could add a staysail on an inner forestay, but that would not make this sloop into a cutter because the mast is between stations 3 and 4. The fractional sloop on the right has a higher-aspect rig but still has the mast between stations 3 and 4.*

# According to Perry: Rig Dimensions and Types

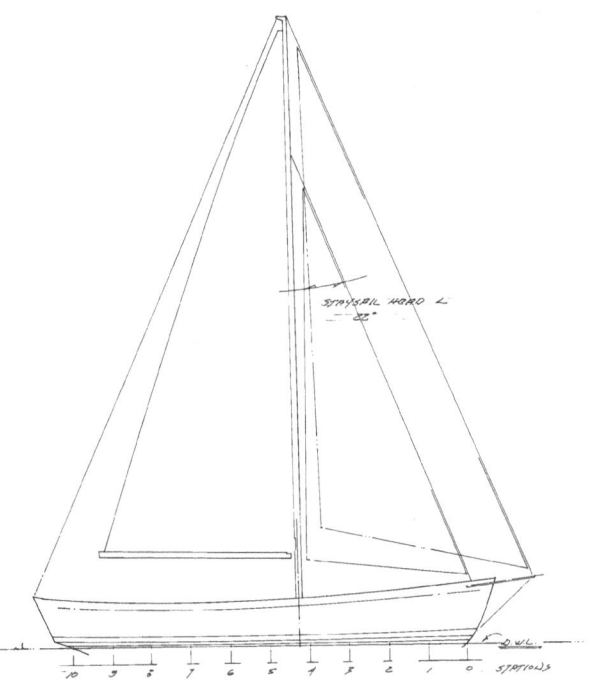

*This cutter has its mast aft of station 4.*

of the mast, which is generally around station 3.2 to station 4 in the ten-station waterline scheme discussed earlier.

## Cutter

A cutter has one mast, like a sloop, but the mast is farther aft, which is to say at or aft of station 4. This fine distinction is further blurred if the boat has a bowsprit, even to the point of becoming a matter of judgment in the eye of the beholder. I would consider a boat with its mast at station 3.75 and a five-foot bowsprit to be a cutter. In short, the real difference between a sloop and a true cutter is in the relative sizes of their foretriangles—larger in the latter than in the former. A Valiant 42 is a good example of a true cutter. Again, although a double-headsail sloop is commonly called a cutter, I think this is misleading. I prefer to call it "a sloop rigged as a cutter" or just "a sloop with staysail option."

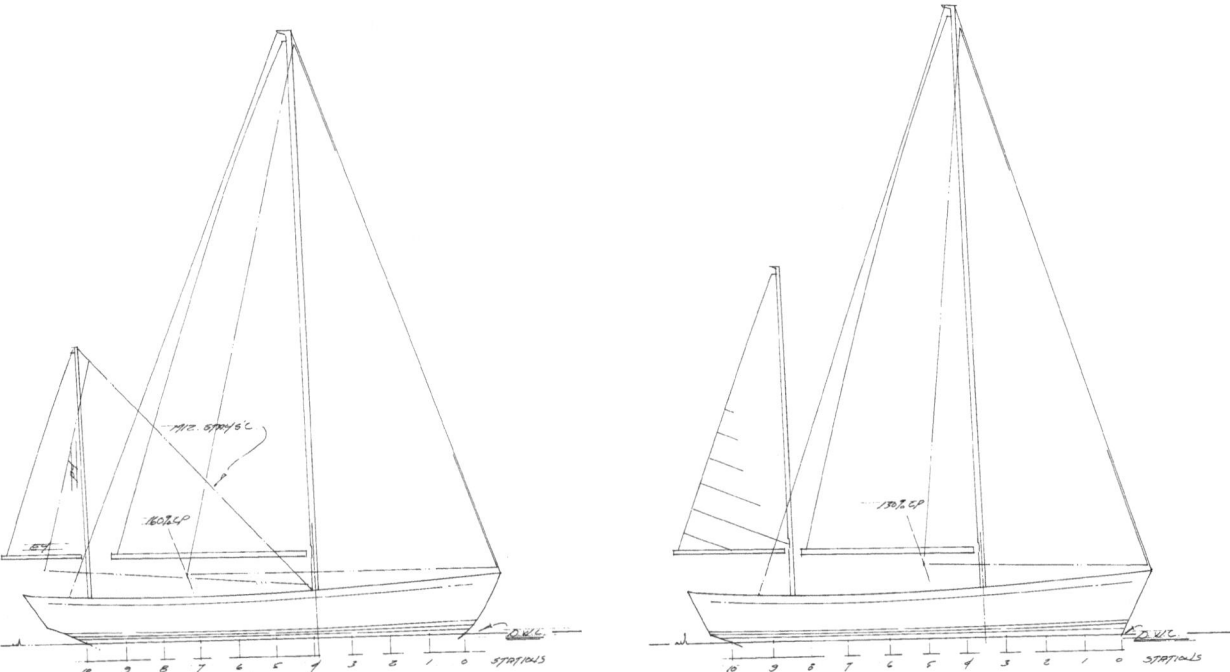

*A yawl (left) has a relatively smaller mizzen than a ketch (right). The yawl was really a creature of the CCA rating rule, whereas the ketch is the more practical of the two rigs.*

## Ketch and Yawl

A ketch has two masts, the after of which is shorter and is called the mizzen. Ketches are often confused with yawls, and the old distinctions between the two no longer universally apply. We used to say that a yawl carries its mizzenmast aft of the helm or rudderpost, but boat shapes and helm locations have changed too much for these old rules to work reliably. The real difference between a ketch and a yawl is in the relative size of the mizzen sail, which is larger on a ketch. Any center-cockpit boat with a short mast located aft would be a yawl by the old rule, but if the mizzen is large, it's a ketch.

Yawls experienced their heyday during the 1950s and early 60s, when the Cruising Club of America (CCA) rating rule was in use. The CCA rule did not penalize any sail area for sails "set flying" from the mizzenmast off the wind. Thus, to remain competitive in off-the-wind races, you had to be able to carry a complement of mizzen staysails and mizzen spinnakers. In those days where this sail area was free, unmeasured sail area, the yawl ruled.

## Schooner

Schooners (see, for example, *Jakatan* in Chapter 17) are lovely rigs, possibly the most picturesque of them all. A schooner can have as many as seven masts, with the shortest being the foremost, but most schooners have only two. Unfortunately, with its biggest sail well aft, a schooner can be a tricky boat to trim for helm balance. You can fly a fisherman's staysail between the masts, but this sail is not a very efficient shape (although it does add a lot of sail area up high, where the wind is more stable). If you replace the foresail of a schooner with a jiblike staysail, you have a staysail schooner.

The problem with a schooner—or any boat with multiple sails—is that the apparent wind is different for each sail. For instance, even if the jib or genoa is trimmed optimally, you may need to overtrim the aftmost sail to get good sail shape. This can aggravate helm balance and add heeling pressure. This is especially critical on a schooner, where the largest sail is all the way aft.

## Catboat

Cat rigs have become popular today primarily through the Nonesuch and Freedom series of production boats. There is also a rich yachting history of the famous Cape Cod catboats. The cat rig certainly has its place, especially on smaller cruising boats in which simplicity is a primary goal, but cat rigs lack versatility. Tom Wylie's cats are special boats and deserve attention, but most of his cats offer spinnakers for off-the-wind performance. In my book that makes them something other than textbook catboats.

The cat rig has also been adapted to ketches. With two masts, the forward of which (the mainmast) is taller, with no headsails, you have a cat ketch. This type was popularized by the early Freedom models and remained mainstream for a while. I'm not sure why it died out. I sailed two different Freedom cat ketches. One sailed wonderfully and the other quite poorly. I attribute this difference in performance to overall design and not the cat ketch rig.

Catboats don't allow their skippers an easy way to "shift gears" and keep the rig effective through a wide range of wind speeds and directions. A study of PHRF ratings of various catboats can easily prove this out. For all their subjective faults, PHRF ratings remain the best way to compare boat speeds and put a quick end to dockside arguments. Nevertheless, a nice, gaff-headed catboat like a Beetle Cat is one of my favorite boats to sail. Traditional Cape Cod catboats like the Beetle Cat are notorious for weather helm, but that's just part of the fun of sailing them. It is not unusual to see a short bowsprit mounted on a Cape Cod catboat with a tiny jib flown from the bowsprit. This can do wonders to help balance the catboat's big mainsail. A true Cape Cod catboat is one of my very favorite traditional models.

Each rig has its advantages, and I don't think we can point to any one of them as the "ultimate cruising rig." The benefits of each will depend largely upon the sailor's sailing style and experience, and where he or she sails. A laid-back approach to sailing might favor a catboat or schooner, while a performance-oriented approach might favor a sloop.

The sloop rig is generally considered the most weatherly (closest pointing) of the rigs. The ketch suffers upwind because the mizzen operates in the backwind of the mainsail and jib, and many ketch sailors lower the mizzen when on the wind. Note that some modern Whitbread-type racing ketches step the mizzen much farther aft than in the traditional ketch, which opens up the slot behind the main and allows the mizzen to get cleaner air.

Still, the chief advantage of a ketch is its ability to fly downwind and reaching staysails off the mizzenmast and to break the total sail area down into three smaller sails. Some ketch aficionados also like to sail under "jib and jigger" (i.e., jib and mizzen) in heavy air. This is a convenient and comfortable combination, especially on a beam reach, but not one that will allow a boat to sail optimally upwind. This is due to the lower apparent wind angle seen by the mizzen. Offshore in a big sea, however, you may find yourself falling off to ease the motion of the boat, and in this case, your optimal upwind apparent wind angle may be in excess of 40 degrees. At this angle of attack, the mizzen is less affected by the jib's backwind, and the jib-and-jigger combo will work admirably.

A cutter likewise suffers from backwind problems upwind when both jib and staysail are carried, but the cutter comes into its own when reaching or when sailing in heavy air under reefed mainsail and staysail. In moderate to light air, if you are after an apparent wind angle of less than 34 degrees, you will find your cutter more close-winded without the staysail provided you have a reasonably low-clewed genoa.

A mainsail and a high-clewed Yankee headsail, while popular and traditional, do not make an efficient combination for beating. The two sails have to work in concert upwind, like one big foil. Think of the genoa as the leading edge of the foil and the mainsail as the trailing edge. That's partially what makes a sloop efficient. A cutter flying a high-clewed Yankee alone with its mainsail leaves a big hole where the staysail would normally be, with no sail to smooth and guide the flow of air into the mainsail.

Upwind efficiency is not simply about boat speed. It's about velocity made good (VMG) toward an imaginary target dead to weather. If you hoist a mainsail, jib, and staysail, then chase a maximum boat speed upwind, you will end up falling off to a close reach and watching your boat speed climb while your VMG falls. Having raced Valiants on numerous occasions under all possible sail combinations and conditions, I can assure you that a good genoa-style headsail—i.e., one with a relatively low clew—and mainsail make the best combination for upwind work.

The only sort of cutter that might perform better upwind with both headsails is an older design with a full hull entry and a wide sheeting angle (the angle between the boat's centerline and a line drawn from the jib tack to the sheeting position). This hypothetical boat probably has a less-than-optimal keel—perhaps like a Westsail 32 with a full keel—so its weatherliness is reduced by hull form even before any rig considerations. If the sheeting angle is in excess of 10 degrees, you might possibly be able to fly both jib and staysail effectively upwind, but you will not point high. The sheeting angle is affected both by the chainplate location and the location of the jib track, and this may be the determining factor in how far in you can sheet your jib. If the angle from the jib tack to the chainplate is in excess of 15 degrees, you might find it advantageous to fly both jib and staysail. Boats have personalities, and you must get to know what makes your boat come alive.

On the other hand—and here's a tough one—if you are having trouble determining the correct upwind trim for your main and jib, throwing a staysail into the mix is probably going to ensure failure. A good rule of thumb for most modern boats is to reserve the staysail for heavy air when the jib is down or for apparent wind angles in excess of 40 degrees.

The schooner is the least weatherly rig of all, and "schooner" and "upwind performance" seldom appear in the same sentence. The problem with a schooner, as discussed earlier, is that the biggest sail, the mainsail, operates in the backwind of the jib and foresail, and this decreases the apparent wind angle on the mainsail and forces the skipper to sheet it in hard, further exacerbating any weather helm. Schooner sailors like the aesthetics of the rig, and for good reason. They will rave about a schooner's off-wind performance, which is true, and they will extol its many possible sail combinations in response to changing wind conditions, which might be true. But the real reason they sail a schooner is because they like the way it looks.

## Chapter Eleven
# LOON

It's one thing to wrap a race boat around the specific objective points of a measurement rule. In many ways that's simple. But in designing a custom cruising boat, the design must be wrapped around the individual who commissions it. It must be a unique expression of the client's approach to life on the water. In short, the boat ideally will reflect the character of the client in almost every way. In my design number 180, *Loon*, I think I achieved that end.

Sandy Bill came to my office with his son-in-law Steve Brower. Sandy was an orthopedic surgeon and had been the head of Seattle's Children's Orthopedic Hospital for more than 30 years. He was not a man to waste his time with idle musings, so I immediately took his request for a new cruising boat seriously. The builder, Steve Brower, had a solid wooden boatbuilding background from Maine. The boat would be built on Lopez Island in the San Juans where Sandy and Steve lived. The boat would be constructed from cold-molded timber.

Sandy wanted a double-ender about 40 feet LOA—something in which he could take his grandkids cruising. Sandy and his wife also liked to cruise with another couple, Bill and Mary Black. Bill Black was one of the first people to buy a Valiant 40, so he will remain, in my eyes, a hero forever. Sandy envisioned rafting the new boat up to the Blacks' Valiant 40. But Sandy's wife, Sally, had bad knees. Sandy claimed this was due to the fact that she, a weaver, raised sheep and spent too much time chasing them around the pasture to shear them. My first decision regarding this design was to make the freeboard amidships of the new boat identical to that of the Valiant 40 so that Sally could climb from boat to boat with ease when they rafted up.

The inspiration for the new boat was a yacht that Sandy had owned many years ago. It was a fabulous-looking canoe yawl designed by Bill Garden. That boat had extremely low freeboard, short ends, very narrow beam, and as much personality as you could pack into 41 feet. Unfortunately, it was a dog under sail. It was also wet, excessively tender, and a challenge to sail. That said, I can think of few better-looking boats. Despite the performance idiosyncrasies, the boat must have left an impression on Sandy, too, because he wanted the new boat to be a double-ender with a canoe-like stern. My preference would have been for a Valiant-type stern. That shape drew the buttocks out as far as possible before rounding them off into a pointed stern. Double-enders with pinched-in, pointed sterns give up too much sailing length and form stability aft.

But Sandy was adamant. He had such a nice, kind, and persuasive manner. Plus, I needed the work. It was during a time in the history of the office, in the mid-1980s, just after the "luxury tax" days, when business was down and I was working alone. Not that I'm complaining, for I liked to work alone. I could puff on my pipe without worrying about bothering anyone. What I missed was another creative mind with whom I could share my ideas. I

# Loon

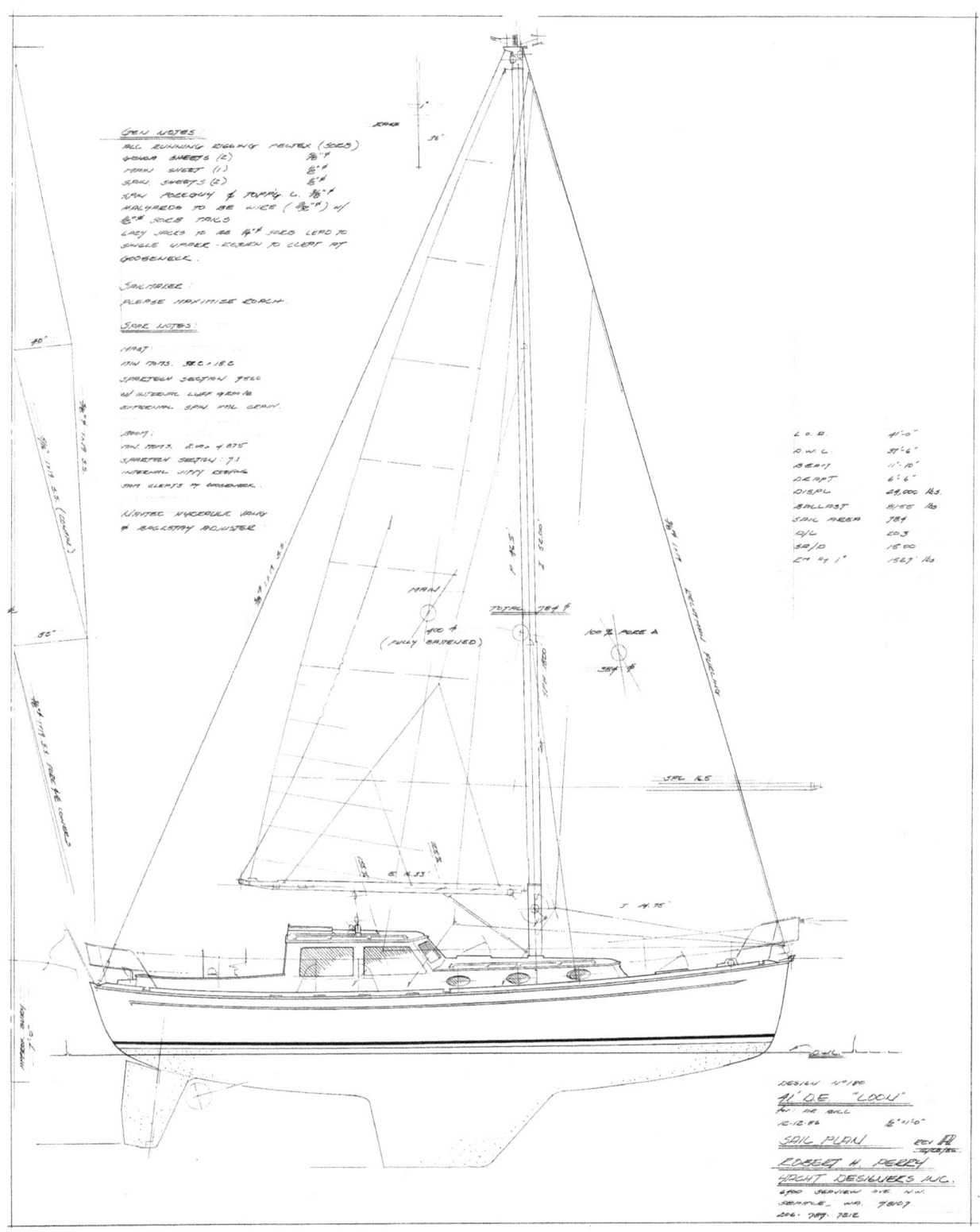

Loon *was a highly personal design for an experienced client. I tried to avoid all the Pacific Northwest's Bill Garden-esque clichés in this design to make it truly a unique work.*

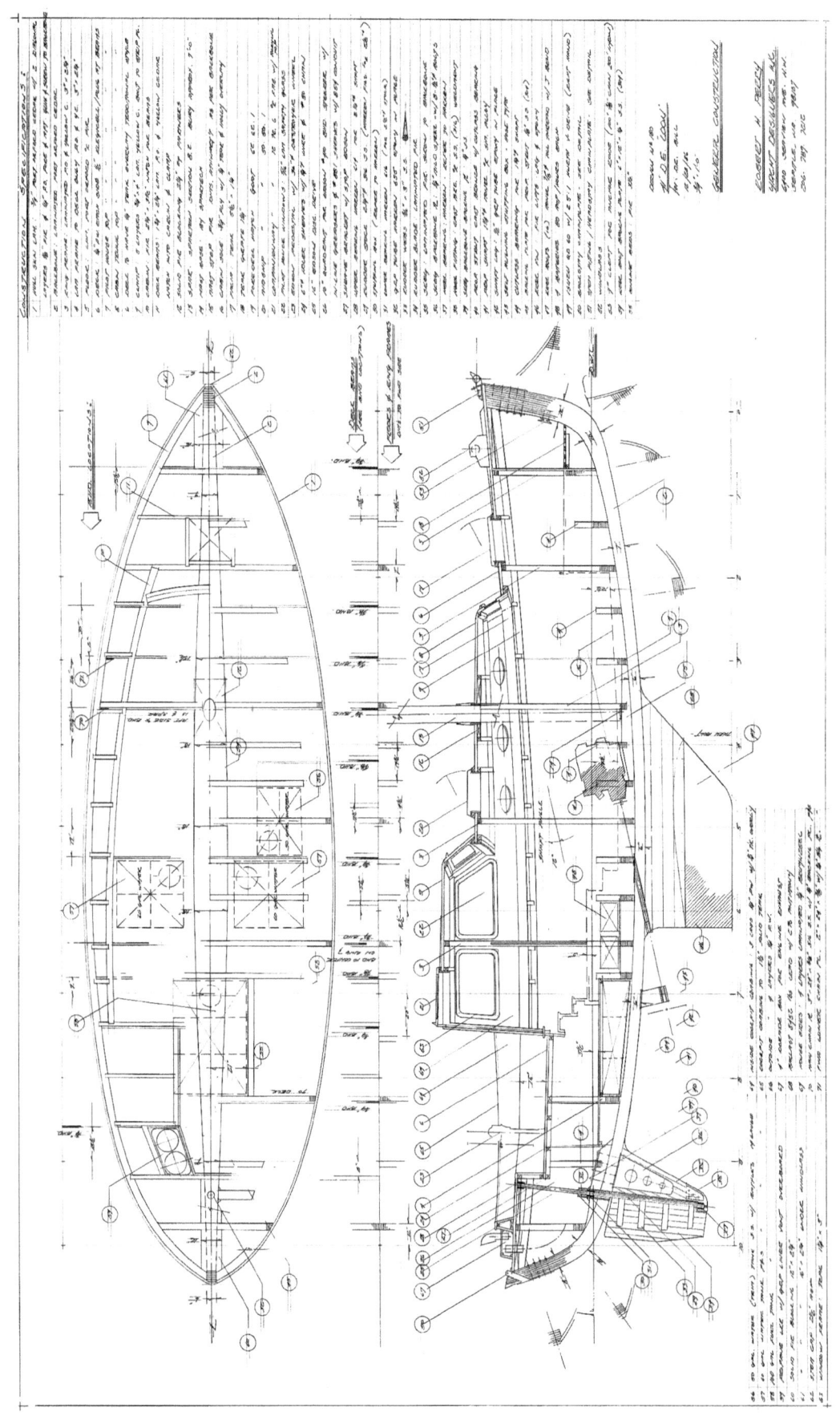

Loon shows very strong construction with a thick backbone and a series of laminated ring frames.

have seldom lacked self-confidence, though, so I enjoyed the quiet time in the office with only my dog for company, as long as I had a good design challenge.

So I wanted this job badly. Not just for the work—it was an opportunity to design a really personal cruising boat for a local client. I'll also have to admit to a certain degree of satisfaction in getting an ex-client of Bill Garden's and having a chance to show him what I could do. I agreed to a ridiculously low design fee. I think it was $6,500. There was no way I was going to let something like money stand between me and this commission. Several years later, when Sandy stopped by the office for a visit, I mentioned that, considering the fact that *Loon* had cost $350,000 to build, my design fee had been miscalculated and he really owed me $25,000.

Now, it could have been my imagination, and Sandy and I never discussed it further, but I'll swear today that no sooner had I said $25,000 than I saw Sandy reach for his checkbook in his back pocket. There was absolutely no doubt in my mind that he was going to write me a check for $25,000, and I could have used that money. I had done a good job and Sandy loved the boat. Of course, with a reflex, I protested, "No, no, no. A deal is a deal." That's exactly what I said, and Sandy's hand moved away from the checkbook as we went on to discuss something else. If the day ever comes when I forget *Loon*, I will still remember in vivid detail that day when at least I imagined that Sandy was ready to write that check. After Sandy died, I called his wife to offer condolences. In an effort to explain to her what Sandy meant to me, I repeated that story. Her reply was, "That was Sandy."

When I got the commission for *Loon*, I'd just started using my first lines program for my computer. I had done a couple of boats on it already and was getting rather proficient at manipulating the electronic battens. I was proud of my ability to control the shape-producing functions of the program. I had resisted lines-fairing programs for several years, although I had a computer in my office almost right from the start. It helped with the IOR and various calculating design chores like hydrostatics, foil development, and rig design. It just took me a while to give up drawing lines by hand. I miss that today, but the accuracy and speed of the computer are seductive and addictive. I had been through the preliminary phase of the design for *Loon*, and now I was developing the hull lines. As I sat there, the door opened and in walked my old chum Laurie Davidson, the New Zealand designer now famous for his work with America's Cup yachts. Laurie had friends in Seattle and it was his style to drop by the office from time to time unannounced.

Laurie was quickly fascinated by the computer's ability to fair hull shape changes quickly. It was his first exposure to this type of program. He pulled up a stool, and the two of us sat there for an hour playing with the hull shape potentials of *Loon*. The final hull shape I came up with relied heavily on the time I had spent playing with the lines with Laurie. I'm kind of proud of that. *Loon* has medium displacement with a D/L lower than that of a Valiant 40 at 203 due to the fact that, despite the identical displacement, *Loon* has three feet more DWL. I removed almost all of the bow overhang to get this extra DWL and to help compensate for the pointy stern that I knew would do the boat no good with regard to sailing length. I did my best with the stern, but I worked just as hard to make it pretty as I did to make it fast.

Achieving Sandy's aesthetic goals aft was easy as long as I accepted the fact that there was just not going to be much boat back there. The sectional shapes were Laurie's, and they had no deadrise amidships. They had a U-shaped entry much like that in a racing yacht. Of course, I had to eventually introduce deadrise as I went aft to get the stern character I wanted. Draft was moderate at 6'6".

In the end, *Loon* proved an able and well-balanced sailing boat. If there was a flaw to the design, it was the installation of a 60-horsepower Isuzu engine; with that much horsepower there was not enough "beef" in the stern to prevent it from squatting and locking into a hull speed of 7.75 knots. Adding revolutions per minute at 7.756 knots resulted in *Loon* sucking up a huge quarter wave. I had warned Sandy of this the first day we met. Even with the sharp shaft angle of 15 degrees (which should have helped), *Loon* was a squatter under power. That's the bad news. The good news is that for a 41-foot, medium-displacement boat, a cruising speed of 7.75 knots was just fine, and *Loon* was a good-looking boat.

Sandy had a rustic house on the shores of a craggy bay on Lopez Island. There was a long dock out front, and that's where he kept *Loon*. The location was perfect. I can remember looking at *Loon* at

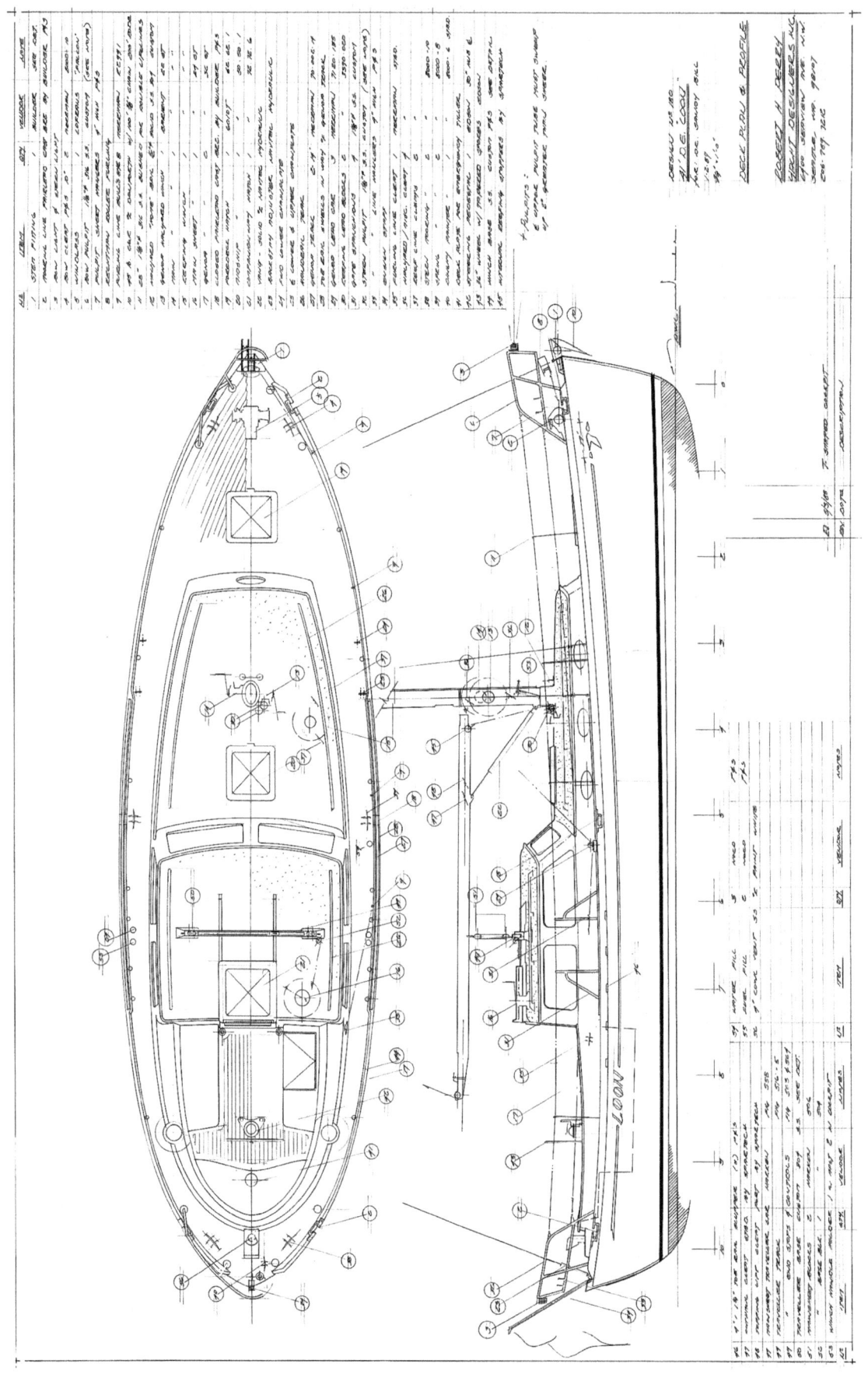

Loon's look is clean and tidy, with moderate proportions. Note that the side decks are minimal to give more volume to the pilothouse.

# Loon

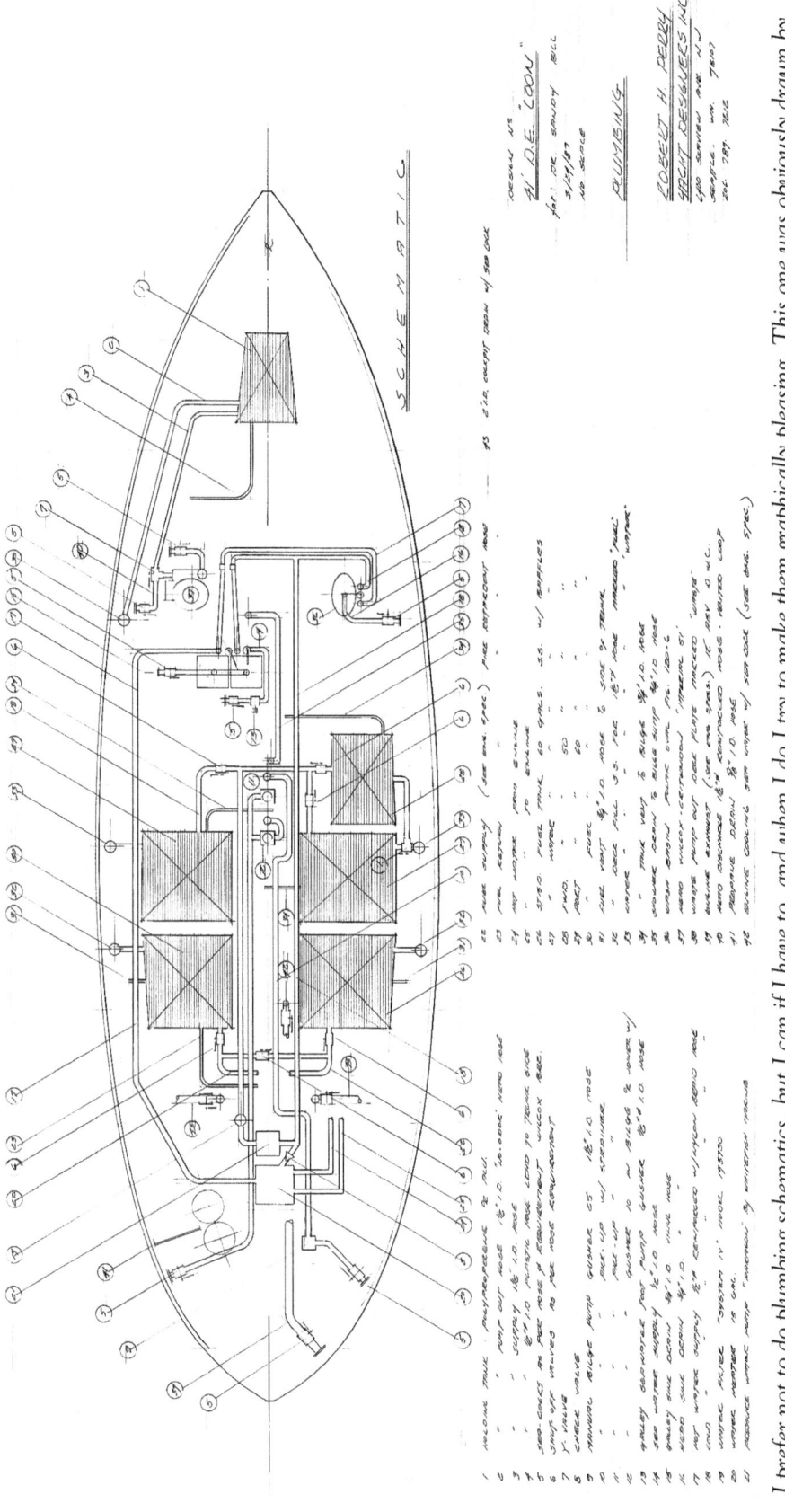

I prefer not to do plumbing schematics, but I can if I have to, and when I do I try to make them graphically pleasing. This one was obviously drawn by hand.

*I love this photo. It says to me, "Here is a yacht that complements its surroundings." Loon is pictured here lying at Sandy Bill's own dock in the San Juan Islands.*

that dock and thinking that the boat was a complement to the beauty of her surroundings. With Sandy at the wheel looking like he just stepped out of the pages of an Eddie Bauer catalog, the picture was complete and perfect. It's good to like your own designs.

Loon's interior was designed around enough berths for the grandchildren and inside steering. Face it: It rains a lot in the Pacific Northwest, but our cruising season is long, especially when you already live in the San Juan Islands. I tucked the engine under the cockpit by using a V-drive gearbox and, as with the Valiant 40, this made room for a nice pilothouse with a steering station, wet locker, quarter berth, and dinette. The galley was snug, and adjacent to it was another settee berth and large hanging locker. You need lots of locker space for foul-weather gear in the Pacific Northwest, and if you are going to put wet gear in a locker, it better be big enough to allow air circulation to dry the gear. I drew a small head compartment with the basin across the passageway, old style. This worked but is not attractive to today's cruisers. There are more large lockers and V berths forward. It's an unusual layout but was designed with specific parameters.

When I drew the construction plan for *Loon*, I was in a reactionary phase. I knew it. I admitted it to myself. I had good reason. My 50-foot, cold-molded *Pachena*, a gorgeous boat built to perfection by Bent Jespersen in Sidney, British Columbia, had gone on the rocks. The owner had, for the first time, let someone else deliver the boat. His professional captain and his son were bringing the boat down the west side of Vancouver Island when inexplicably they turned hard to the left and drove *Pachena* onto the rocks at what we estimated had to be full speed, sails up on a beam reach, probably around 10 knots. The captain and crew died. The boat may have hit a migrating whale. The impact may have caused the captain to tumble forward and crack his head open on the cabin-trunk overhang aft. The son, now panicking, turned the boat toward the closest land and, full throttle, he hit the rocks. The son drowned, tangled in kelp. We will never know the complete story. I can tell you for sure that it was damned depressing for me.

*Pachena* had an in-the-mast furling system. This means that the mast was very heavy. When *Pachena* hit the rocks, the impact tore the backstay pin through the masthead backstay crane, and the mast came down. As the mast came down, it acted kind of like a can opener and pried the deck, almost intact, off of the hull. The hull was now unsupported at the sheer and it broke up, except for the heavily reinforced area around the floors and keel, which stayed intact. There was no doubt in my mind that nothing I could have done could have saved that crew, but I was disturbed that the deck and hull came apart in basically two intact pieces, initially at least. I had used numerous scantling rules to arrive at the scantlings for *Pachena*, along with the extensive experience of Bent Jespersen, the builder of *Pachena*. We knew that the boat was strong given even very hard use. It was not up to being run on the rocks at 10 knots, though. Today it still pains me to write about it.

I vowed to do it differently the next time. Now it was the next time, and I designed *Loon* to have a series of laminated yellow-cedar ring frames that were three inches broad and contoured to wrap around the hull onto the cabin trunk side then over the top of the cabin. The hull and deck were joined by five of these ring frames. They were labor-intensive to build and they looked beautiful when in place and varnished. Steve Brower's workmanship was museum-quality. The heavy backbone, 12 inches thick at the stem, was made of laminated Port Orford cedar. The hull skin was $1\frac{1}{8}''$ thick with $3/4''$ strip-planked Port Orford, covered with two diagonal layers of $1/8''$ fir and over that another $1/4''$ layer of Port Orford. With this heavy construction we still got a ballast/displacement ratio of 34 percent, and I kept the lead low on the bottom half of the keel fin. I did not want Sandy to have another tender boat.

The stability characteristics of *Loon* were similar to those of the Valiant 40. I had learned a thing or two when I designed *Pachena*. Today I see *Loon* at the Perry Rendezvous each year. *Loon* is on her third owner now and is a much-loved boat. I was never too keen on the big carved loons that grace the bow. They make dramatic ends for the cove stripe, but to my eye they are a wee bit too dramatic. Still, I marvel at *Loon*'s good looks, and the owners have all remarked at the number of sailors who row by and ask, "What kind of boat is that?"

## *According to Perry*
# SHORTENING SAIL

Racers reef to increase boat speed, but cruisers generally reef to improve helm balance, to prevent the boat from being overpowered by a rising wind, or just to smooth things out for the night watch. Keeping your boat on its feet and reducing sail area until the sails can be properly sheeted rather than carried half-flogging should both increase boat speed and help preserve the comfort of the crew by reducing heel angle. (It also helps preserve the shape your sailmaker originally cut into your sails.) Think of reefing as a performance- and safety-enhancing technique.

Most boats begin to develop excessive weather helm when they are overly pressed. To combat this, the first sail reduction should be to put a reef in the main. Of course, this should be done after flattening (i.e., depowering) the main and genoa with increased halyard tension for both sails and for the mainsail more outhaul tension. Sheet leads for the genoa may also need to be moved as the wind picks up. Moving the leads aft will free the leech, allowing it to spill some wind. If you have the option you might also find it advisable to move your jib leads outboard, as high seas will prevent you from pointing high anyway.

The current trend in cruising sloops and cutters includes a roller-furled genoa with a luff perpendicular when fully unfurled of approximately 140 percent and a staysail that is usually hanked to a removable inner forestay. The typical cruiser will roll up all or part of the genoa first to reduce sail area quickly. The next step sees the genoa totally rolled up and the staysail hoisted. Simply furling the genoa and hoisting a staysail is like shifting from fifth gear down to first in one move. I would prefer to see the first step in sail shortening to be a reef in the mainsail in order to preserve helm balance and reduce heeling pressure.

In a masthead-rigged boat, the best way to preserve headsail efficiency through a wide range of wind speeds is to carry an inventory of hanked-on or luff-groove-extrusion headsails—say a 150 percent genoa, a 120 percent genoa, a 100 percent working jib, and a storm headsail. For pure cruising boats, hanked-on headsails offer some conveniences as they are always attached to the headstay by their hanks, while a luff-groove-style headsail will be only attached at head and tack when lowered. Changing these jibs is apparently too much work for today's average cruiser. Nowadays, roller furling is popular and, along with it, roller reefing. Having cruised both with furling gear and with an inventory of hanked-on jibs, I have to admit that the convenience of roller reefing is hard to resist, especially once a boat gets above 30′ LOA.

One of the benefits of a fractional rig is that it reduces the need for a broad headsail inventory. The mainsail is the bigger sail in a fractional rig, so it's natural that your initial reefing reflex will be to reef the main. It's easier to control a boomed sail in a breeze than it is to corral a flailing genoa on a heaving foredeck. A tall, fractional rig can get by with one non-overlapping headsail. The caveat is that you will have to be more diligent about reefing the main, and you will need to learn how to depower and flatten the main to keep the boat on its feet as the first move prior to tucking in a reef.

Years ago in Seattle, a dealer imported a fleet of fractionally rigged Scandinavian boats called Aphrodite 101s. These came with non-overlapping headsails. It was thought that the boats would need more horsepower in Seattle's light air, so a genoa was built for one boat and trials were set up against a boat with the standard jib to evaluate the genny's advantage. As it turned out, the genny conferred no speed advantages, and the fleet stayed with blade-type working jibs. The moral of the story might be that jib overlap on many boats can be seductive but misleading. In the old days of the CCA it was not uncommon to see genoa LPs of 160 percent or even greater, with the genoa essentially sheeting just short of the transom. Today I advise most cruisers to buy genoas with an LP not exceeding 135 percent.

You can rig a self-tacking traveler for a blade-type boomless jib, but it will need to be longer/wider than you might think. If it's too short, you will never achieve the sheeting angle required to correctly trim the sail in a variety of wind speeds. The only fully successful self-tacking jib system I have designed had the jib traveler spanning the entire beam of the boat at the mast. The sheeting angle for a self-tacking jib must be no less than 10 degrees or you will end up with a curl in the jib that will constantly pour backwind onto your mainsail. This poses a problem in heavy air, when the better sheeting angle would be outboard. This is slow and increases the heeling moment of the rig.

You also need a long traveler so that the jib lead can move outboard when the sheets are eased, at which point the lead should move forward as well. This is impossible with a self-tacking track system unless you have and take advantage of an aluminum clew board with three alternative sheet attachment points, but I have yet to see cruisers actually use these additional cringles. Face it, most of us are looking for the easiest way, and switching the jib-sheet attachment each time you bear off is not the easiest way, even though it may be effective.

I'm from the old school. I believe that you need at least two headsails on any sloop or cutter in addition to the staysail. I have a two-headsail inventory on my own fractionally rigged boat, and I hank on my jibs the old-fashioned way, which makes jib changes easy. I realize that changing jibs in a breeze is no fun, but a full-hoist, 100 or 95 percent, blade-type jib with a clew no higher than the top lifeline is far more efficient than a partially rolled-up genoa.

I prefer low-clewed headsails, and my rule of thumb is that no clew should be higher than I can easily reach from the deck. The trick is to anticipate a headsail change so that it can be done in relative comfort and safety before the breeze really pipes up. In my latest designs, I have increased both the I dimension (from mast base to headstay attachment on mast) and the relative size of the mainsail in order to reduce the need for overlapping headsails. The days of 160 percent gennies are gone. The typical cruising boat of today should carry a genoa with an LP no greater than 135 percent. Keep in mind that the relative size of the genoa based on LP will be a function of the size of the J dimension. A 40-footer with an 18-foot J dimension (i.e., the base of the foretriangle) will carry a 140 percent genoa equal in size to a 157 percent genoa on a 40-footer with a J of 16 feet.

One way of adding a heavy-air staysail with a good aspect ratio is to pull the staysail stay as far forward on the deck as possible. This imitates a fractional rig and allows the center of effort of the staysail to stay well forward. This is commonly referred to as a Solent stay, and it's my preferred rig on any boat longer than 40 feet. I like this stay to be removable (although you often see it fixed), and you have to find a landing point on deck where you can support the stay adequately from below while avoiding conflicts with the windlass and other foredeck paraphernalia. A heavy-air sail flown from a Solent stay keeps sail area forward and makes for a better steering boat. Upwind, especially, this staysail may make the boat far easier to balance, as it reduces weather helm. Sailing with too much weather helm is like sailing with the parking brake on, not to mention the wear and tear it inflicts on the helmsman or autopilot.

A well-thought-out mainsail reefing system is essential. Conventional slab reefing can work fine if the leads are correct and you can get the appropriate lines to winches. I find it amazing that race boats are so frequently far better set up for easy reefing than cruising boats.

As a general rule, I'm not in favor of single-line slab reefing. There is generally too much friction in that single line for efficient reefing. Separate, properly led lines for the luff and leech, combined with a knowledge of the proper sequence of events to adjust them, is the key to easy reefing.

In-mast mainsail furling is popular these days, but not at my house. The typical mainsail designed for in-mast furling gives up as much as 20 percent of its area due to the lack of a headboard, the lack of roach, and the requisite hollow leech. This sort of mainsail is generally without battens, which means that you will inevitably end up with a tight leech that is hooked to weather—what we sarcastically call a "speed cup." This type of mainsail is also prone to a "catcher's mitt" shape, with the maximum draft pulled well aft despite your best efforts to move the draft forward. This does a lot more to increase heeling and weather helm than it does to increase drive. I know there are batten systems designed to work with in-mast furling, but I have yet to talk to a sailor who said they work.

In-mast furling systems also require large-dimensioned, heavy mast sections that increase the boat's windage and decrease its stability. This is slow. The vertical mast slot can also whistle and howl in a breeze at the dock if it is not fitted with a "whistle-stopper strip." I don't even want to talk about furling systems that roll up the main on a stay just aft of the mast. They may be convenient, but they certainly are not efficient, as the main luff inevitably falls away from the mast and loses the benefit of the mast as a leading edge.

I recognize the appeal and necessity of mainsail roller-furling systems, especially on larger cruising boats, but if you want the convenience of rolling your mainsail up in increments as the wind pipes up, you should investigate an in-the-boom furling system such as the Leisure Furl system developed ten years ago in New Zealand, or the Schaefer Marine system. These give you a normal main with full battens, generous roach, and controllable draft. In fact, when this mainsail is up, you can't distinguish it from a normal mainsail. This is the type of system I would want if I had a boat longer than 40 feet. The only fly in this ointment is the need to control the angle of the boom when you lower the mainsail so that the main rolls up neatly and squarely in the boom. This can be done several ways. You can use a boom gallows as a visual check (as in, "The boom needs to be six inches above the gallows before I roll up the main"). Or you can use a rigid vang that holds the boom at the prescribed angle. You could also use a preset and marked boom topping lift to get this required angle.

To give in-mast furling its due, it probably is the easier system to use, but to me the attendant loss of efficiency and stability are unacceptable. Once again, individual sailing style will play a big part in deciding exactly how you shorten sail.

## Chapter Twelve
# YONI

As a teenager dreaming of yacht design, I never put limits on the types of boats I would create. Racing yachts appealed to me just as much as cruising yachts. Within the world of cruising boats there was a wide array of various traditions I could follow. In 1994, I'd just finished the 61-foot cruising sled *White Eagle*, which displaced a mere 35,000 pounds, and now I was about to get my chance at something different.

Big John Carson, a broker friend of mine and a very good sailor, came by the office one day and told me about an ex-client of his who was interested in a custom boat. John asked if I would be interested in talking to the fellow. Work was a bit slow at the time and I was working with one helper, and one good design job at a time could keep us comfortably busy. I needed a new commission and told Big John I was very interested. Two days later Big John arrived at the office and introduced me to a dentist, Daryl Dahlgard. Daryl was tough. He had concrete ideas of the boat he had in mind down to LOA, displacement, and hull form. It was going to be a boat about as different from *White Eagle* as you could possibly imagine: 13 feet shorter in overall length but heavier by 4,000 pounds. We sparred a bit over design approaches and elements of what made a good offshore cruising boat. Then, after about 30 minutes, when things seemed on the verge of stalling, Daryl pulled out his checkbook and wrote me a generous retainer. I'd landed a nice big fish.

The question comes up from time to time, "What makes a boat a cruising boat?" My answer is simple: A cruising boat is any boat in which you go cruising. The choice of D/L and hull form is subjective. While one sailor is smitten by the idea of surfing down big swells under spinnaker at 16 knots, another might be attracted to a boat that has a more limited envelope of performance and will live 99 percent of its lifetime within the 1.34 S/L ratio at hull speed.

Given the right conditions, of course, you can always push a heavy boat beyond hull speed, but it's hard work on the skipper, and it's often hard on the boat itself. While a long and light boat can accelerate in the puffs and surf, the heavy boat is limited to hull speeds or a bit more, and the shock loads on the rig when a big puff hits can put a strain on the rig and hardware. But the fact is, you can reduce sail and not push your heavy boat hard and still do hull speed all day long, comfortably. The light boat will take a lot of attention from its crew to stay at optimal super-hull-speed performance levels, and most cruising couples will not have the energy to sustain this type of sailing for long. So they reduce sail, and before long they are back at hull speed, too. The heavy boat will be stiffer than the light boat, and it will be a softer and more comfortable ride in a seaway. It just boils down to a matter of personal sailing style. This is what custom design is all about. I don't take sides in the light-displacement versus heavy-displacement

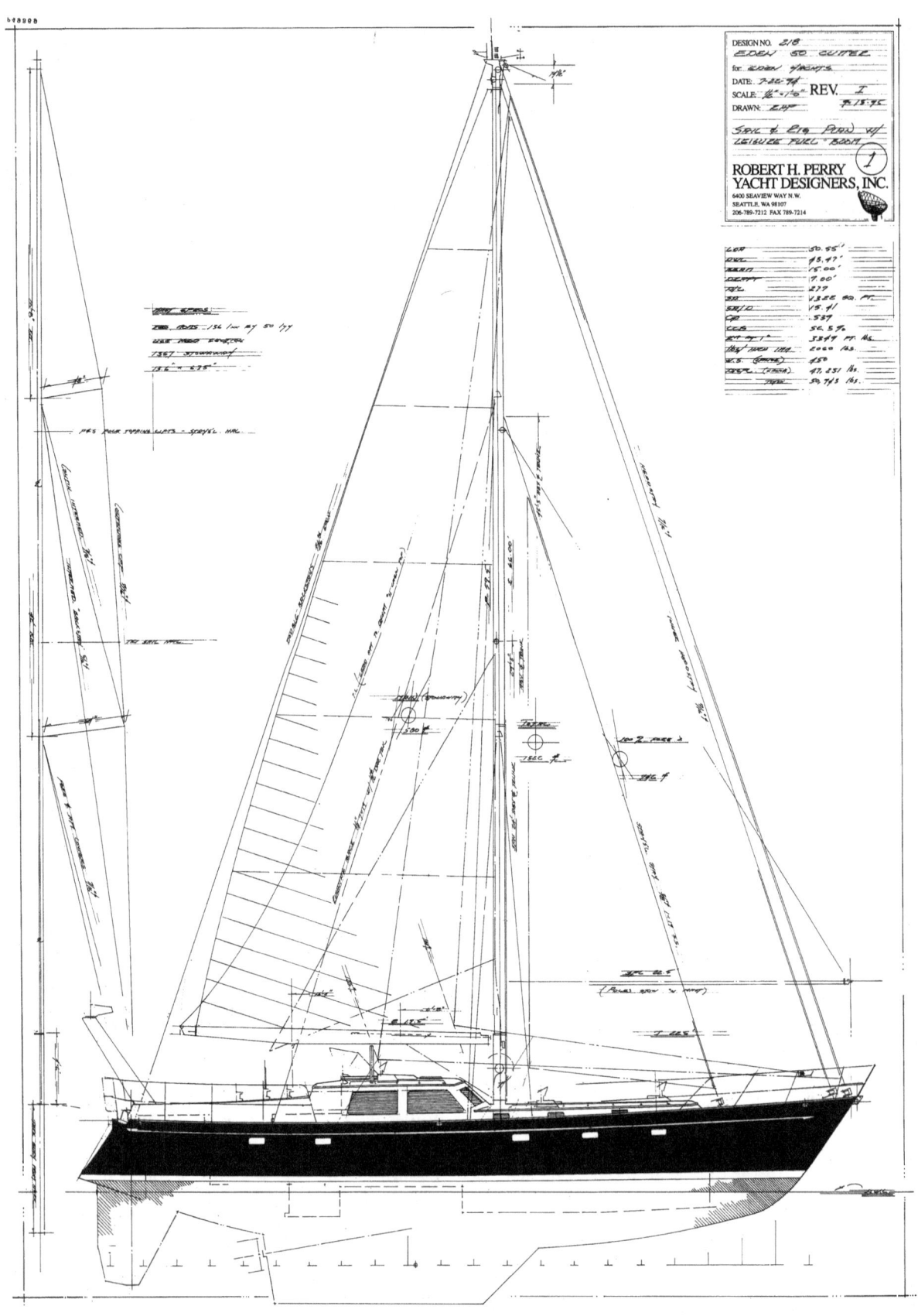

*Yoni* has the mast placement of a true cutter and a tall rig to drive its 50,000-pound displacement.

# Yoni

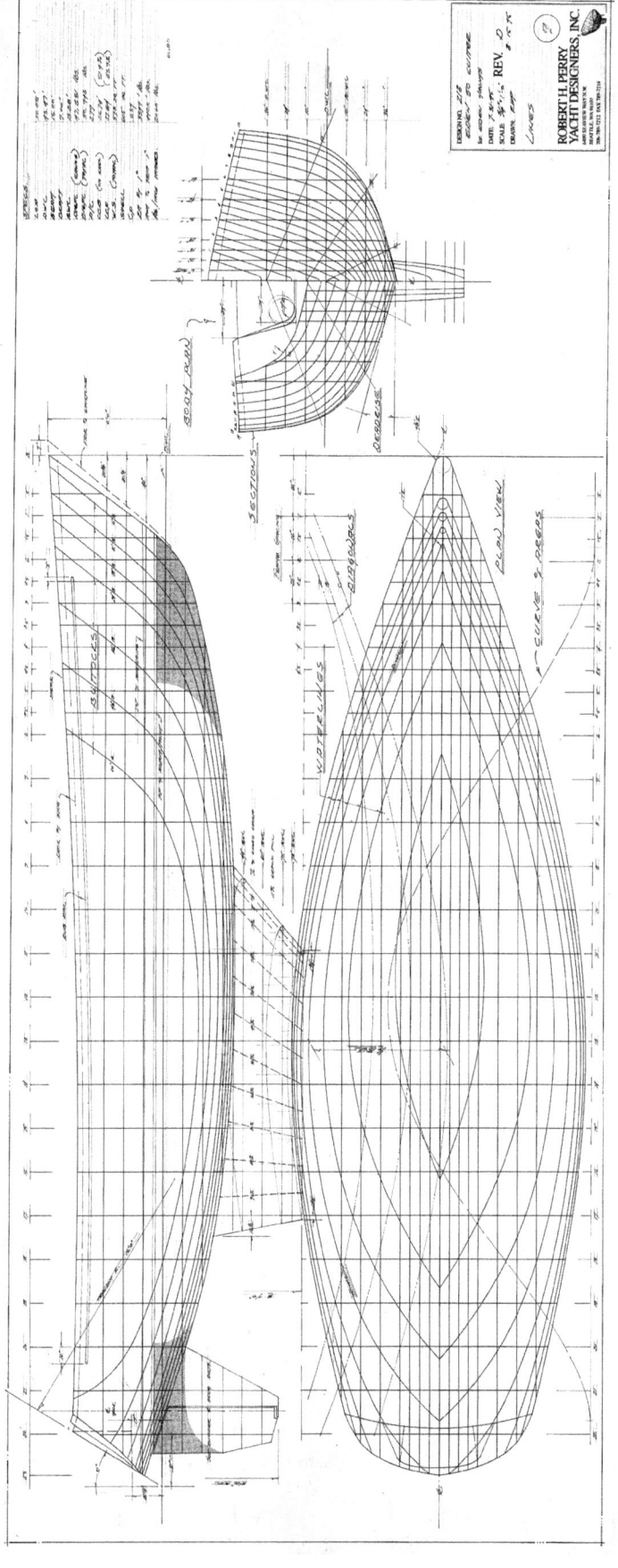

These lines were the product of several models built so that Daryl, the client, could get a better grasp of the small changes we were making in the hull shape. Yoni shows high deadrise and balanced waterlines.

argument. I approach each design honestly, understanding the idiosyncrasies of the type, and I do all I can to design a boat that will be the best of the breed.

Daryl's new boat would optimally be built in steel. There was also the possibility we'd go with aluminum if we couldn't find a good local steel builder. It would be 47 feet LOA and heavy enough to get a ballast-to-displacement ratio of at least 40 percent with a D/L in the 280 range. The boat would have inside steering and a cutter rig. There would be an owner's stateroom aft, one head, and a raised dinette in the pilothouse. The hull form would borrow from the Ted Hood–designed Little Harbor series. These were heavy boats with lots of deadrise and considerable fore-and-aft rocker. I wanted short ends to maximize the DWL and reduce the D/L, and Daryl wanted enough freeboard so we could have a flush deck forward of the pilothouse.

Over the next six months the design came together. Daryl sent me to the boatyard to measure the deadrise angles on a Little Harbor that was hauled out. I did not need to do this, but Daryl, as I would slowly learn, loved to address each component of the design in close detail before making up his mind. Daryl took Wednesdays off from his dental practice and would spend those days at my office sitting right next to me watching me draw and often directing the pen or pencil. "That must drive you nuts," my friends would say. It did not. Daryl and I became fast friends. We shared a love of good live music and attended several great concerts. I invited Daryl to my own musical get-togethers, where he would bring the best wines and sit and at least pretend to be entertained. Daryl was a confirmed bachelor who enjoyed dining out, and he prided himself on getting the very best seats for the musical acts that came through Seattle.

"Do you want to go and see B.B. King?" asked Daryl.

"Sure, Daryl," said I.

It was fun, most of the time, to have Daryl working closely with me on this project. The only difficulty was that a client often does not understand the natural sequence of design evolution, and there were days when I would dance between the deck plan and the plumbing layout without getting very far in either area, as ideas occurred to Daryl. Daryl loved it. He was the ideal client. He gave me the design budget to allow me to do my best work. He was always appreciative of my efforts. If I want to impress a new client or show some kid how the "real men" drew without computers, I will pull out Daryl's drawings. I don't think I ever drew better. Those drawings took a lot of time, but Daryl never grumbled. Apart from the hull and keel lines, the drawings were all hand-done, pencil and pen on Mylar. My helper did the weight study. I did every drawing myself.

I finished the design for the 47-footer and Daryl showed up on Wednesday to pick up the fat, bound set of plans.

"Here's your last bill, Daryl," I said.

"Here's your check, Bob, but it's not your last. I want to start again. I want to make the boat bigger this time," said Daryl.

That's exactly how it happened. On the day I completed the first commission, Daryl asked me to start a second, a 50-footer that would employ the 47-footer as a prototype design. I was delighted. Daryl explained that if he built the first boat we designed, it would be the same as marrying his first high-school girlfriend. He knew now how the design process worked and he wanted to go through it again. His ideas had evolved during the design of the 47, and he realized he needed more boat to get what he wanted. And clearly he was having fun with the process.

As before, Daryl knew exactly what he wanted. This time it was a 50,000-pound boat with 20,000 pounds of ballast. He even knew exactly where he wanted the mast. I'm used to clients telling me what to do, but they usually leave the displacement, ballast, and mast location up to me. I had no problem with the 50,000 pounds. It would be a heavy boat. I had no problem with the 20,000 pounds of ballast, but this meant that the new boat would be aluminum, because I could not get the ballast-to-displacement ratio as dictated by the client with steel. It also would be very stiff. I did have a problem with Daryl telling me where to put the mast. I wanted it forward. Daryl wanted it aft, cutter style. I could have insisted, but I knew from experience that insisting to Daryl did not work. Daryl had done his homework, and his research told him to give the boat a 22.5-foot J measurement. It complicated my job somewhat, as I knew it would require an effort to get the keel far enough aft to balance a rig that far aft. But I did it and it worked well.

When I started drawing the hull lines, Daryl finally admitted that he was having some difficulty in

# Yoni

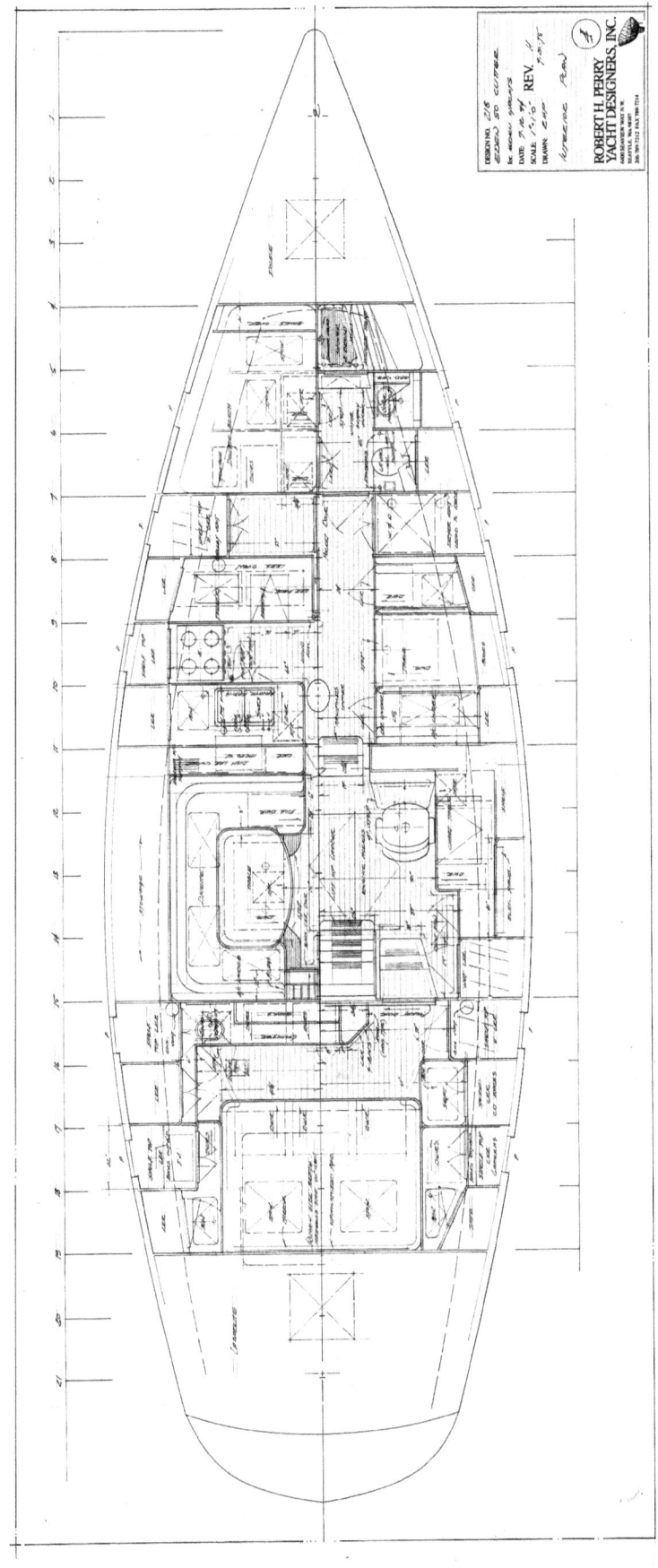

Yoni's aft cabin is tucked under an extended bridgedeck so as not to intrude upon the cockpit. Note that the head is well forward.

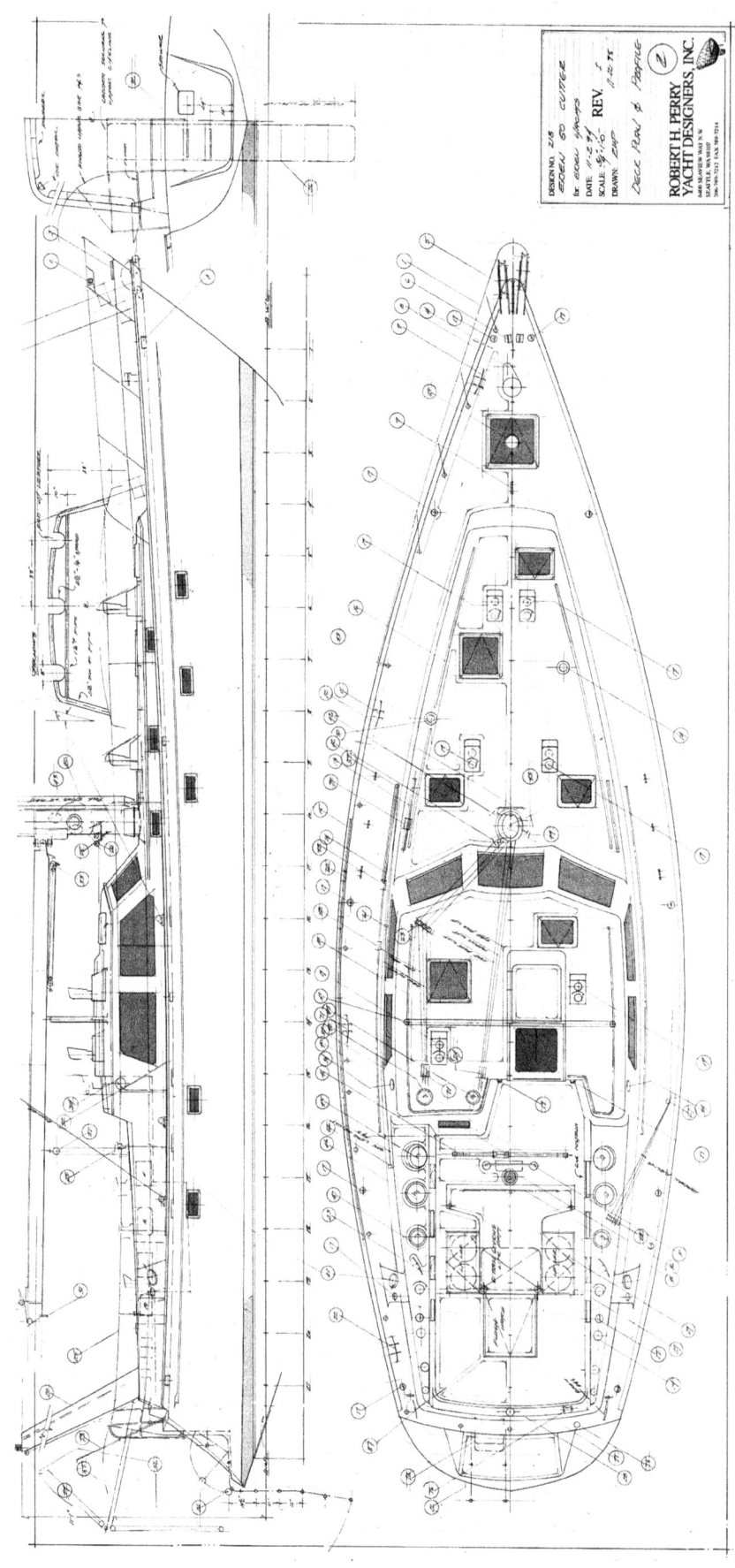

Yoni's deck plan shows a reversed T-shaped cockpit that puts the helmsman forward. The flush hatch in the uncluttered deck area directly aft of the cockpit leads down to the machinery area.

# Yoni

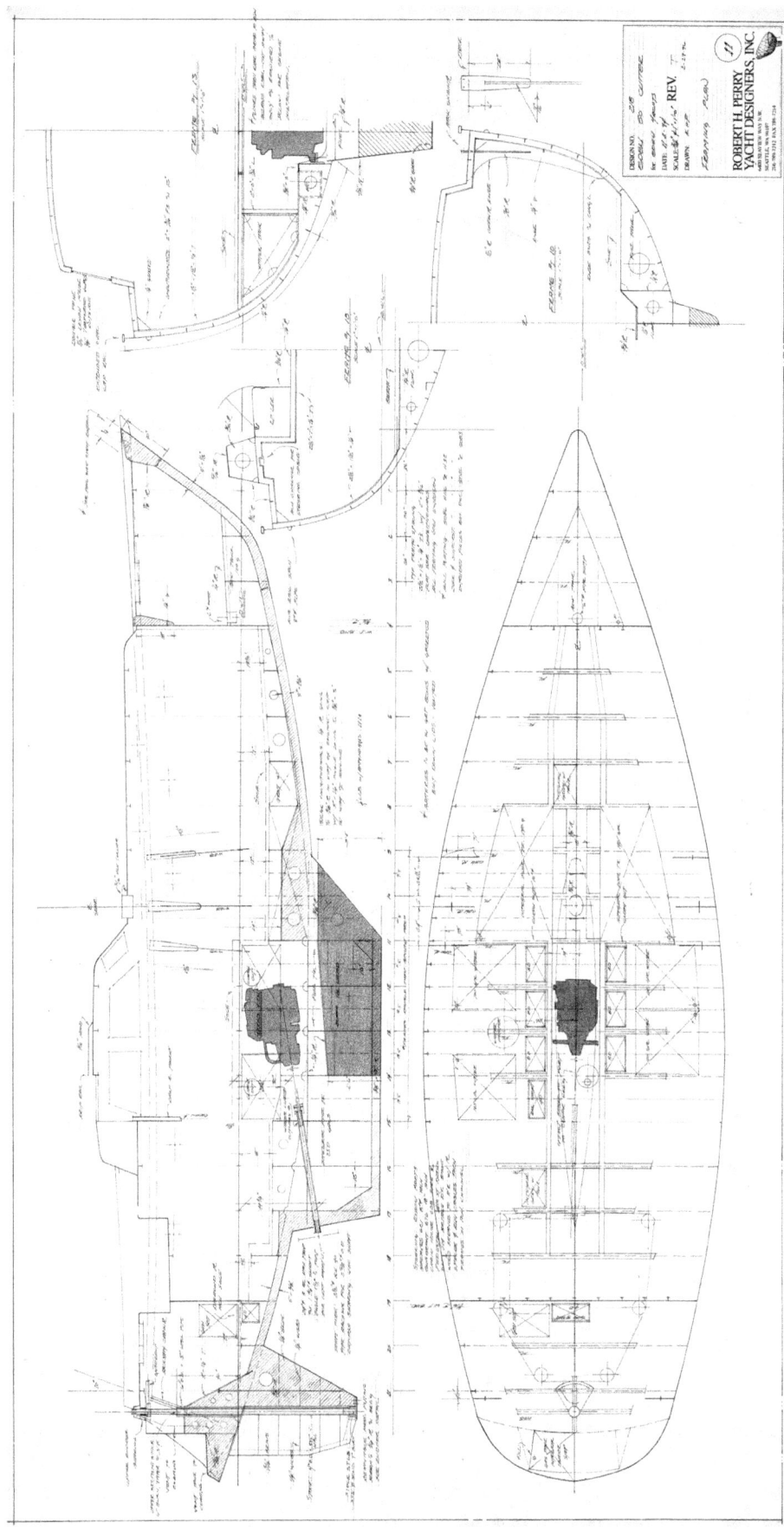

Yoni's aluminum construction was designed to be strong and durable, with 1/4-inch plating used in the topsides above the DWL.

deciphering the exact contours of the line drawings. He understood lines, but like with most clients, it was hard for him to translate a two-dimensional lines plan into a three-dimensional mental image. It was especially difficult given the nuanced level at which we were working. I was drawing the lines with the AutoYacht program, as I had for years, and the thought came to me after receiving a computer numeric controlled-cut half model of *Stealth Chicken* that maybe we could get CNC models of Daryl's hulls done showing the various hull-shape changes we were examining. Daryl liked the idea, and we discovered that we could get full models, cut at a scale of 1″=1′0″, and in foam, on the CNC machine for about $150 a hull.

I sent the CNC company the drawings of the four hulls we were considering as a computer file, and in a week I had four big models. Daryl really liked being able to hold the hulls in his hands and rotate them to get a real feel for the subtle changes in each. Daryl thought we were really close to the hull shape he wanted, but he wanted even more changes carved by the CNC machine. This time the hulls were so similar I told Daryl that I couldn't even tell the difference anymore, and I was sure the water was not going to be able to tell the difference. We called it quits with our foam models and chose a final hull form.

The general hull shape was similar to that of the Hood designs Daryl had admired. The forefoot was deep and sharply V-ed. There was moderate flare to the topsides forward. The beam at the waterline (BWL) was broad for stability and there were 12 degrees of deadrise amidships. This deadrise flattened out slightly toward the stern. I like to keep some deadrise at the transom. I don't think deadrise aft is a fast shape (although Bill Lee and the late Carl Schumacher might disagree with me), but I do think some deadrise at the stern helps prevent the boat from slapping in a chop when it's tied to the dock. Deadrise aft might also help a boat stay directionally stable, because it takes a lot of effort to drag that corner through the water at any yaw angle. *Yoni* has a D/L of 277. That's heavy by *Starbuck* or *White Eagle* standards, but it's close to the 260 of the Valiant 40, and I considered it textbook "moderate."

As just mentioned, the new boat would be *Yoni*, Sanskrit for "abode." Maybe Daryl enjoyed the double entendre. (I think he did, but he wouldn't admit it.) Daryl certainly seemed to enjoy poking the dog with a stick from time to time. When Daryl did your teeth you got a steady stream of music through headphones, all blues, nothing but the blues. Daryl had this theory about the blues and people's reactions to it in the dental chair. I had Daryl for a dentist until he retired and I think he was right. Nothing cheers you up like the blues, and we can all use some cheering up when our teeth are being probed and drilled.

*Yoni*'s layout was unusual. The owner's stateroom was all the way aft, tucked under the big cockpit area. The double berth was a standard queen-sized latex mattress. After careful consideration, we went with an athwartships berth aft because Daryl felt that this orientation of the berth made for the most comfortable sea berth. Below this berth were six big drawers for clothing. There was a sink in the stateroom, but the head was all the way forward. Daryl had a beautiful house and said he walked that far in his house to get to the head, so it wouldn't be a problem on the boat. It was my job to remind the design client about resale value, and I counseled Daryl about the effect the forward head might have on resale, but I lost that argument. One head would be plenty. This was a boat for a small crew to take offshore. With that in mind we used every available cubic inch for stowage. *Yoni* had a lot of lockers and drawers.

Daryl and I fought over the "mini-dinette" adjacent to the galley. I thought this should have been where we put the refrigerator and freezer in my typical "there is no such thing as a galley that is too big" mindset. I lost that argument, too. Daryl felt there would be times at the dock when he wanted to eat without people looking in his big windows and seeing him. The pilothouse is ideal. I raised the pilothouse dinette two steps above the sole. I had done several boats where I raised the dinette one step, and I had learned that one step was not enough. In fact, in some cases, raising the dinette one step resulted in putting the seated eye level even with the lower sill of the pilothouse windows. This was the kiss of death. Not being able to see out at all was better than *almost* being able to see out. It's terrible to sit there and think to yourself, "If only the designer had been smart enough to raise this seat another six inches." It's really terrible when you are the designer. With two steps up into *Yoni*'s dinette, your eye is level to the middle of the window when seated.

On the starboard side of the pilothouse we have an expansive navigation center, an inside steering station, and a swivel chair that works for both the wheel and the chart table. (There's a big wet locker aft of the navigation station. There's no point in cramming wet foul-weather gear into a small locker; it just won't dry without room for air to circulate. No wet locker should be narrower than 24 inches.) There is a handy bank of lockers and drawers right next to the companionway steps to port for signal flags, an air horn, sunscreen, binoculars, and other items you frequently need on deck in a hurry. There is a double berth forward to port for guests.

*Yoni*'s deck plan shows deep bulwarks for security, a low coach roof running forward that puts the handrail at a convenient height, and deep cockpit coamings around a small, T-shaped well; the large-diameter wheel was located in the forward end of the well. This is backward for most designs in that the wheel is usually aft, but we wanted the wheel close to the companionway for safety and shelter. The mainsheet traveler is on the bridge deck, which rules out a dodger. With inside steering, however, we reasoned a dodger would be redundant. The companionway hatchboard drops down into a drained pocket. The board is counterweighted, window-sash style, so you feel very little weight of the board. In addition, it lowers and raises effortlessly. With the companionway notched into the aft bulkhead of the house, you could sit there with your legs inside the boat and feel very secure. Aft of the small cockpit well is a huge lounging area for sunbathing. The lazarette hatch is flush, and with cushions covering that entire area, you could comfortably sleep out there in warm weather.

The lazarette is huge and is used as a machinery room for pumps and mechanical equipment. This way you had a comfortable and well-accessed area with reasonable headroom to make working on your systems at least tolerable. With the large lazarette hatch open, there is lots of headroom and good light and ventilation. Twin cockpit seat lockers allow for four 20-pound propane bottles to be carried. *Yoni* was all about staying self-sufficient for long periods of time. There is an arch over the transom to hold antennae, and the arch has a davit system built into it. There is a deep swim step cut into the transom. My rule of thumb for swim steps is that they have to be big enough for one person to stand on while helping another person out of a dinghy. A boarding ladder extends well below the surface of the water to make boarding easy with a load of diving gear.

Yoni *under sail*.

*Yoni* has eight opening hatches and six dorade vents. Daryl and I worked together to design a dorade vent that could be shut off from inside the boat to ensure water tightness in a storm. *Yoni*'s bow pulpit extends aft to where the forward cabin trunk starts. You were secure on this foredeck. The winches are all clustered around the helm position so a single-handed sailor seldom has to leave the cockpit.

The rig was a straight cutter with two headsails on the stem. The inner headsail was a relatively high-clewed, 110 percent working jib, and the outer headsail was a 125 percent genoa with the clew at the upper lifeline. With 50,000 pounds of boat, I knew I needed a large rig if we were going to get any light-air performance. I gave *Yoni* an I of 66 feet and a SA/D of 15.41. By today's standards that is not a high SA/D, but there is only so much rig height you can put above a deck while keeping the rig-to-hull relationship in proportion. If *Yoni* had weighed 40,000 pounds, I would have given it the same sail area but I would have had a much higher SA/D. A quick check of the Hood series of cruising boats told Daryl and me that we were in the right ballpark for rig size. Having sailed *Yoni* in light and medium-light air, I can tell you with assurance that this boat moves very well. We used a Leisure Furl boom, and the mainsail roach just misses the twin backstays. The standing rigging arrangement is very traditional with fore and aft lowers, cap shrouds, intermediate backstays, and runners for the staysail hounds. When the wind lets up, you can rely on an 85-horsepower Perkins driving a 24-inch-diameter Max Prop propeller.

*Yoni* was built as strong as possible. Aluminum construction gave us the benefit of making the entire hull and deck structure essentially monocoque. The topsides plating is 1/4 inch thick down to about 30 inches before the garboards. The garboard plating is 5/16 inch, and the keel fin is 3/8-inch plating. There is a 3/4-inch-thick plate shoe on the bottom of the keel. Thick hull plating like this is expensive in that you buy your aluminum by the pound. However, it's easier and quicker to fair and is strong and puncture-resistant. *Yoni* has 1/4″ × 2.5″ × 1.5″ T frames on 26-inch centers. The floors are 1/4-inch plating, and the chainplate knees are 1/2-inch plating. They extend well down the hull sides. Twenty-thousand pounds of lead ballast is encapsulated with a 1/4-inch cap plate. Frames and floors are on 13-inch centers through the mast-step area and extend aft to about the 60 percent chord of the keel fin. There is a 3/8-inch-thick backbone plate running the length of the hull, increasing to 7/8 inch thick at the stem/headstay attachment area. The beauty of working with 50,000 pounds of all-up displacement was that we could be very generous with the structure of *Yoni*. You simply could not find a stronger 50-footer.

The aluminum work for *Yoni* was all done by New Zealander Brian Riley, working in Sidney, British Columbia. Brian is a genius with aluminum and a joy to watch at his trade. Like wood, aluminum is a pretty material in its raw state. You can't say that of fiberglass or steel. But aluminum looks shiny and bright during construction. You can see each individual piece of structure; nothing is hidden. Weight studies are easy for the designer because what you see is what you get with aluminum. Brian built a magnificent shell for *Yoni*. The oval caprail was a custom extrusion. Daryl did not want a teak cap, but I wanted the aesthetic look of a teak cap. Therefore, we made an extruded cap-like shape out of aluminum. By most standards, *Yoni* is a "gold plater."

All of the finish work was done by Eric Jespersen's yard in Sidney, British Columbia. Jespersen's is one of my all-time favorite yards to work with. Eric learned his trade from his dad, Bent. Bent is one of those magicians with wood and has a wonderful feel for how boats should go together and how they should look. Bent still hovers around the shop, although he tells people he is retired. It's a bit like having a walking boatbuilding encyclopedia on hand. Needless to say, the quality of work done to finish *Yoni* was spectacular. About 25,000 total hours went into this project. Daryl spent as much time at the yard as he could. It was obvious that he enjoyed this part of the process immensely. Clearly, the gang at Jespersen's knew they had a most-appreciative client, so everyone contributed ideas to make *Yoni* the best possible boat. Daryl put no budget on the building process. The only thing I would add to *Yoni* today would be a bow thruster.

At *Yoni*'s launch, I stood nervously watching as the boat was lowered into the water. "How do you know where it will float?" is a question I am asked frequently. I explain that it is a combination of understanding the hull shape, the materials used, the builder's building style, and a very careful weight-estimate spreadsheet. *Yoni* floated perfectly. I acted nonchalant and smiled. Bent smiled, too. He knew I was either lucky or good, and based upon the roll of plans I had produced for *Yoni*, I think he knew I was good. There is nothing that pleases me more than seeing a new design float on its lines at launch.

When I look at *Yoni* today, I see the ultimate offshore cruising boat. If you are after a self-sufficient boat that is weatherly, stiff, very strong, handsome, and supremely comfortable, then *Yoni* has to be at the top or near the top of your list. If I were heading over the horizon tomorrow, this would be the boat I'd want to sail.

## *According to Perry*
# MASTS

One day while finishing a lengthy weight study for a 70-foot cruising-boat design, I was surprised to see that the vertical center of gravity (VCG) for the boat had moved 12 inches higher since an earlier iteration. Upon double-checking my figures, I discovered that I had inadvertently double-entered the weight of the mast with its in-the-mast mainsail furling system. Rig weights can have the biggest effect of any design component on VCG.

Next to increasing draft, reducing rig weight is probably the most immediate and effective way of increasing the performance of a boat. Experts sometimes argue the supposed benefits of a heavy rig on a boat's roll motion and its resistance to rollover, but this is really a tangent to the main issue. I think we can all agree that nobody likes a tender boat. One well-known builder actually told me that he wanted a high rig weight so that he could "slow the boat's motion down" when it was anchored in an exposed anchorage! Such notions aside, I have never had the luxury of working to raise a VCG. I put every effort into lowering a boat's VCG.

When I talk to groups, one of the most frequent questions I hear is, "What do you think of deck-stepped versus keel-stepped masts?" The short answer is that either type can be as strong as the other, but the two require different engineering. Rig loads are a combination of the size of the boat's rig and the boat's stability. For a given rig size, the stiffer (more stable) the boat, the greater the rig loads will be.

Mast stiffness is measured in moments of inertia around the longitudinal (fore-and-aft) and transverse axes of the mast. Moments are measured in inches to the fourth power, but designers just talk about moments, as in, "You might want to increase the moments for that mast." The higher the moments, the stiffer (less flexible) the mast extrusion is. Moments depend upon mast section dimensions, sectional shape, wall thickness, and mast material. A mast of given moments will be stiffer if it is stepped on the keel, because it has one fixed end (the mast step and the partners at the deck) and one so-called "pin end" (the masthead). The same mast stepped on deck will have two pin ends. If you are after a given amount of mast stiffness, you are going to have to increase the moments for a deck-stepped mast by about 10 percent. Still, technically, both masts can be equally strong.

A deck-stepped mast doesn't intrude in the accommodations, and it doesn't invite mast leaks at the partners. If you are after an absolutely dry bilge, a deck-stepped mast is the way to go. My own 26-footer has a deck-stepped mast. However, for cruising boats longer than 30 to 35 feet, I think that the advantage goes to the keel-stepped mast, especially if you contemplate offshore cruising. If you ever lose your rig or break your mast, the keel-stepped spar will leave a stump sticking out of the deck that will extend about 40 to 60 percent of the way to the lower spreader. On any boat this can provide the base for an effective jury rig. If the mast is deck-stepped, the entire length will go over the side in the same situation, and you are going to have to build your jury rig from scratch (i.e., the deck up). This was illustrated a few years ago when the Transpac fleet suffered several dismastings. Keel-stepped rigs made it to Hawaii with far more effective jury rigs.

The great yacht designer and author Douglas Phillips-Birt once said that nowhere in the design process is science more applicable than in spar design. But the equally great designer and author L. Francis Herreshoff took the opposite view, opining that nowhere in the design process is art more applicable. My own view is closer to that of L. Francis—spar design and moments selection are far from a hard science. In my office, we design rigs based on engineering calculations, then compare our results with existing rigs and our past experiences. The next step is to solicit input from several sparmakers on rig engineering for the specific design. One sailor may want a flexible spar, while another may want a rigid one, and the final spar selection will be a combination of objective engineering results and client preferences.

One of those preferences is for the size of the safety factor. A rig built exactly to the strength recommended by the engineering calculations—without any added tolerance for unforeseen, transitory forces—has a safety factor of 1. A rig made twice as strong as that has a safety factor of 2. Safety factors for rig design can vary from 1 to 4, depending on the use of the boat. For instance, if you were racing for the America's Cup, you would want the lightest rig possible, and safety factors would be reduced to the minimum. If anything breaks, the tender will tow you home and the syndicate will replace it. A circumnavigator might prefer a bulletproof rig with safety factors of 4 to ensure that his or her rig will survive anything. The rig would be heavy, but it would be very strong.

A skilled racing crew can keep a noodle up safely, so a racing boat can lower the safety factors for spar moments, reducing the rig's weight and increasing the ability for the crew to shape the bend of the spar to suit the mainsail shape and the conditions. A flexible spar requires a diligent crew that understands mast bend. For the cruiser it's a different story. Nothing can spoil your day like a broken mast. Keep in mind that mast breaks are usually a function of a broken fitting and not a spar section failure, although a weak section in an extrusion has brought more than one mast down. I've been involved in three dismastings, and I fervently hope to avoid them in the future. With this in mind, I adhere to a safety factor of 4 for most cruising masts. It's comforting and appropriate for a cruiser to be able to take his or her rig for granted. I will reduce the safety factor on custom designs in keeping with the owner's experience, sailing style, and mast stiffness preferences. An ex-racer turned cruiser may want a flexible mast that can be bent to increase control over sail shape as was done while racing.

Obviously, a carbon-fiber mast, weighing approximately half what an equivalent aluminum section would weigh, will enhance stability and reduce a boat's pitching moment. Indeed, it can change a boat's entire sailing personality. On a 45-footer with a 60-foot I dimension and an aluminum mast section weighing six pounds per foot, changing to a carbon stick will reduce the rig weight by 180 pounds. This is the approximate equivalent of adding 1,000 pounds of ballast five feet below the waterline! Consider the effect on pitching of putting a 180-pound crew member up the mast. Re-rigging a vintage Valiant 40 with a taller carbon-fiber stick yielded tremendous advantages in speed and motion comfort.

The biggest drawback of a carbon spar is cost. On one 60-footer I designed recently, the cost of the carbon spars and rigging was more than $150,000. There is also the issue of durability. Aluminum is a forgiving material and will stand far more abuse than carbon fiber. Carbon will bend a tiny amount, then snap. You can modify an aluminum rig by drilling new holes just about anywhere, within reason, without jeopardizing the integrity of the spar. Carbon spars must be built to a designed hardware layout with heavily reinforced sections of additional carbon where the hardware goes. You do not have the option of drilling and tapping new hardware to a carbon spar as you feel the need to change the rig. The tensile strength of carbon relies upon long strands, and structural integrity is reduced when those strands are cut. While a carbon spinnaker pole can be wonderfully light, it is not as durable as an aluminum pole. You can drop your aluminum pole onto the pulpit and perhaps put a small ding in your pulpit, but a carbon pole could be dented or nicked, and that would reduce the strength of the pole. In short, aluminum spars can be abused to some degree, while carbon spars cannot. Now balance the advantage of durability against the advantage of a light pole while you stagger and sway around the foredeck in a seaway trying to connect your pole to the mast.

The final choice for how you set up your mast—including the number of shrouds and spreaders (see "According to Perry: Rigging" on page 202), chainplate locations, and your preferences for rig and sail type—will depend on your style of sailing. A light, bendy mast will require more rigging and spreaders than a stiff, heavy spar, and the more spreaders and stays you have, the harder it will be to tune the rig. Factors controlling weight aloft may be mitigated by practical cruising considerations. The competent designer can make any system work, but some systems require more interaction from the sailor and a higher skill level than others.

## Chapter Thirteen
# A Pair of Chickens

It was 1992. The International Offshore Rule (IOR) was dead, having died a natural death, as most handicap rules eventually do. The IOR had some fatal flaws, and while these flaws were addressed through various iterations of the rule, the damage had been done early. By the time the problems were mitigated, interest in the IOR for the family big-boat racer had waned to the point that fleets were shrunken down to a few boats owned by skippers willing to pay anything to win. It was a racing environment that precluded the sailor who wanted a dual-purpose racer/cruiser that could be campaigned competitively over several seasons. PHRF fleets flourished, but hardcore racers, even the family variety, have never truly warmed up to the often arbitrary nature of PHRF.

PHRF had started as a true handicap rule where the rating of the boat was to be determined by a panel of knowledgeable sailors without the use of measurement formulae. In that no forlumae were used to determine the basic rating of the boat, there were no ways for a designer to "design around" the PHRF rule. The PHRF racer would have its rating adjusted as the true speed of the boat was revealed through a season of races.

I'll digress here a moment to discuss the infamous IOR rule and its role in contemporary yacht design. The flaws in the IOR were genetic and basically centered around the rule's method of measuring sailing length and the penalties for stability. Sailing length was established by placing two girths in the bow and two girths in the stern, then measuring the distance between the forward and aft girths (LBG). These girths were a function of beam; therefore, the beamier the boat, the bigger the girths. The bigger the girths the closer they were together, making the LBG shorter. This is why, when you look at an old IOR boat, you see a hull with a lot of beam but pinched ends. The ends were pinched in order to get the girths closer together on the hull and reduce LBG. In the ends specifically, the closer the two girths, the finer the boat appeared to the rule, and this meant less "power" in the ends. Pinched ends resulted in boats that were fine forward and aft.

This fineness in the stern meant that when the boat was at hull speed, usually downwind, there was not enough boat in the water aft to add any form stability. With a bow wave and a stern wave and a big trough in between, the IOR boat would have to heel enough to begin immersing the wide-beamed midsection before it picked up any initial stability. This was aggravated by the fact that the IOR penalized initial stability by measuring stability at low heel angles. Any stability beyond the rule's allowed minimum would result in a penalty coefficient being applied to $L$, the rule's measurement of sailing length. As a result, we ended up with tippy, tender boats that were hard to handle off the wind. On the positive side, the basic IOR shape was a good shape for light to medium air, especially upwind. Today, many cruising sailors avoid the old IOR type, but in most cases these boats can make very good cruising craft,

## A Pair of Chickens

Bruce Anderson *wanted a boat he could race, but it had to have a nice sheer. I love clients like that. This is the original sail plan of* Stealth Chicken, *showing the original keel profile.*

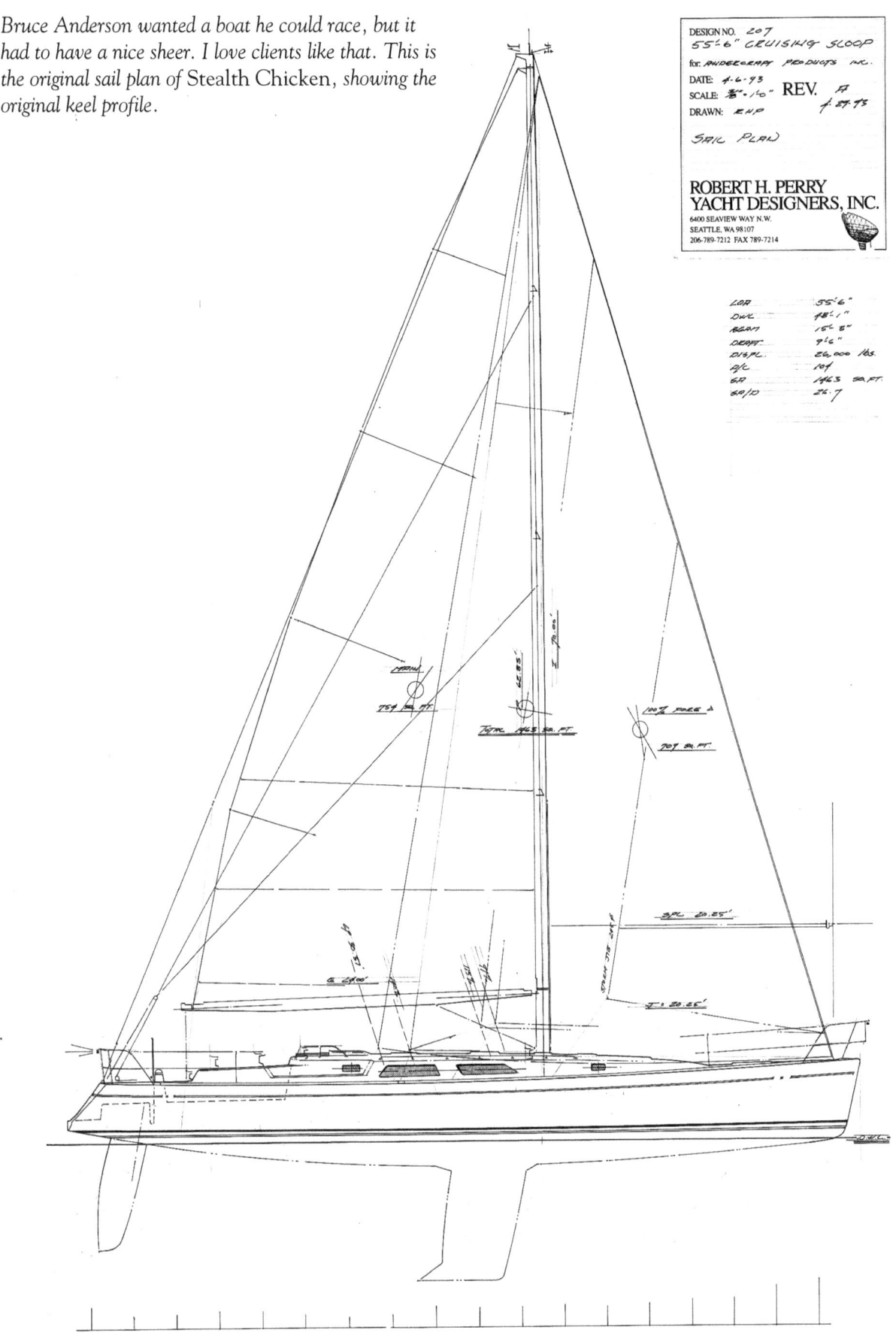

# YACHT DESIGN ACCORDING TO PERRY

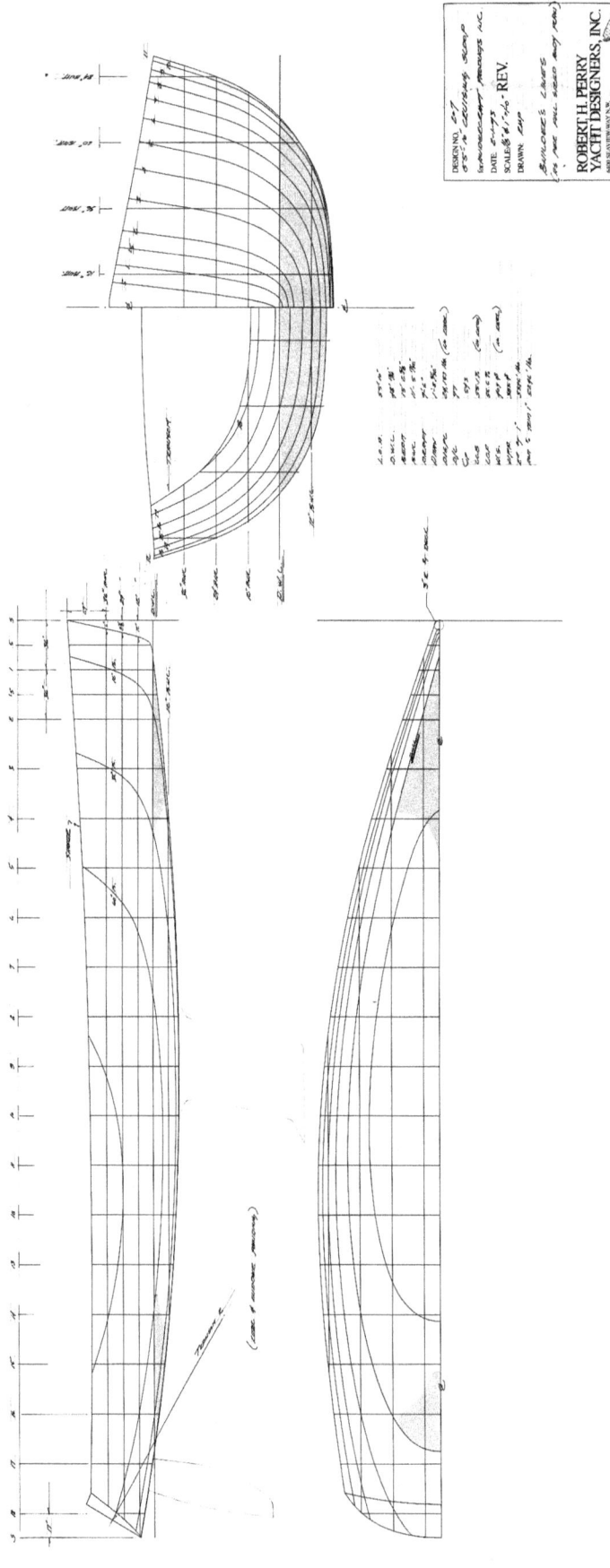

Chicken's lines show a dish-like midsection and a narrow BWL. Chicken's bow is full compared with the race boats of today.

## A Pair of Chickens

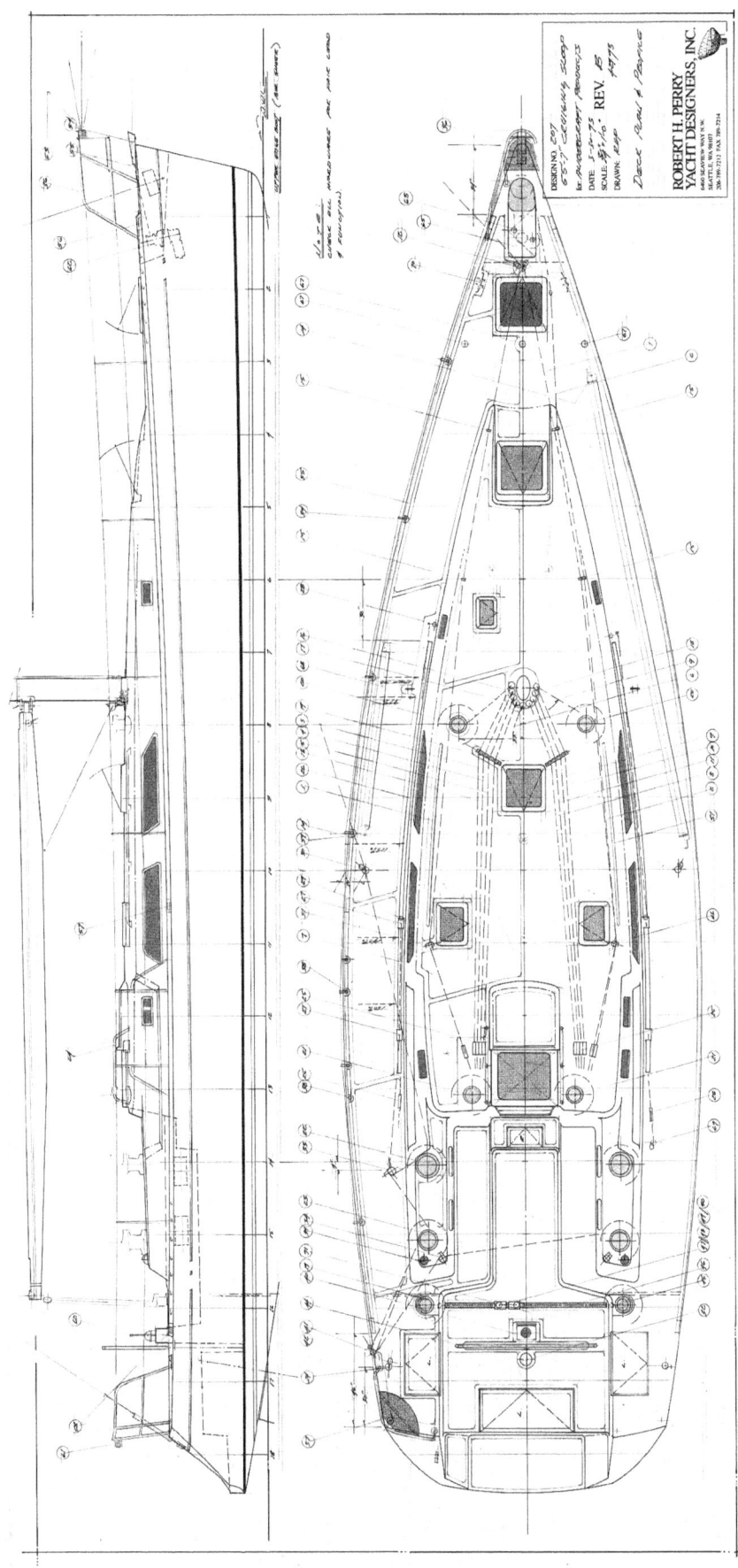

I used some of the old styling tricks that C&C invented to make the long cabin trunk of Chicken appear shorter. Note how the cabin trunk sides are cut away aft of the long windows. Chicken's deck is a pure hybrid racing-cruising layout with high seat backs forward in the cockpit and a flush deck aft.

and their bad habits only manifest themselves when the boats are pushed really hard—harder than most cruisers are inclined to sail their boats.

The IOR was replaced by a very new type of rule, the International Measurement System (IMS). Today, most of the rules under which we race are derivatives of the IMS type of rule. The IOR measured the boat at a series of designated points on the hull and used a set of simple formulae well spelled out and easy to target for the designer so that the boats became wrapped around the measurement points of the rule. This resulted in what we used to call "connect-the-dots" hull shapes, the dots being the IOR's measurement points. This did result in some very weird hulls that clearly showed the shape humping and bumping as it was manipulated to hit a measurement point and then try to return to a normal hull shape. There was even a C&C boat modified with small cones on each measurement point to exaggerate those dimensions. The mavens of the rule plugged that hole quickly. If it sounds silly, it should.

The new IMS was a rule based upon a series of formulae or codes that would be kept secret from the designers so that the designers could not take advantage of loopholes. Sailing length was measured by using a "black box" and wand to take off the entire hull shape of the boat. Humps and bumps would not work in this system. This rule would look at the entire hull form, then measure sailing length by a series of second-moment lengths to replicate the sailing length of the boat at various heel angles. The data from the black box would be used to produce velocity-prediction program (VPP) polar diagrams that described a boat's true performance at varying wind angles in a variety of wind speeds. VPP data have proven very accurate. Most designers use VPP data when designing any new boat today. We can thank computers for this. Polar plots of performance are available for almost any production boat built today. Of course, the old saying "garbage in, garbage out" goes for polars, too, and the sailor looking for data had better make sure that the input was accurate. Push a button here, push a button there, and all of a sudden the design in question is stiffer and faster, at least on paper.

Under this IMS rule, hulls got broader aft and bow overhangs disappeared in order to minimize the second-moment lengths. Stability was measured at bigger angles of heel, and draft was penalized much less than it was under the IOR. The IMS boats had much longer sailing lengths for their LOA, they had plenty of draft, and they were stiff. The masthead rig was dominant in the early stages of the IOR. Sail area was measured favoring large foretriangles and small, ribbon-like mainsails designed to IOR minimum dimensions. Rig dimensions under the IMS became far more complex and accurate in reflecting the potential of the rig. Foretriangle and mainsail areas were weighted differently than under the old IOR. This led to fractional rigs, which are more efficient and easier to handle for a number of reasons. In short, IMS boats were more fun to sail and much faster for their LOA compared with the contorted IOR types.

All this is a prelude to a phone call I received one day from a fellow named Bruce Anderson, who asked me if I was interested in designing a 56-foot IMS boat that would combine race-boat speed with cruising comfort.

I replied, "I'm the guy who designed the Baba 30. What makes you think I can design an IMS boat?"

"Well, can't you?" Bruce said.

"Of course I can. I'm just surprised that someone else thinks I can."

Bruce said confidently, "I do," and we were off on another exciting design project.

Bruce's previous boat had been a custom Alan Andrews boat called *Chicken Lips*, and the new boat was to be *Stealth Chicken*. It was the time of the first Gulf War and stealth technology was the rage. Lynn Bowser and Westerly Marine, who'd built the previous *Chicken*, would build this boat as well. Westerly remains one of my favorite yards. The people are easy and pleasant to work with, and they do an excellent job. Lynn and his crew have a lot of remarkable boats to their credit.

Because the access to the code that drove the IMS was not available, the only way I had to determine the best shape for an IMS design was to look at the boats that were successful at that time. There was a large fleet of mid-50-footers in Southern California that were racing as a fleet, and over time they had evolved into a distinct shape that the IMS seemed to favor. I began collecting measurement certificates for the better boats designed by Alan Andrews and Neson/Marek and comparing the numbers. It helped a lot that my client, Bruce, was an astute observer of hull shapes and had spent a lot of time analyzing the various boats.

# A Pair of Chickens

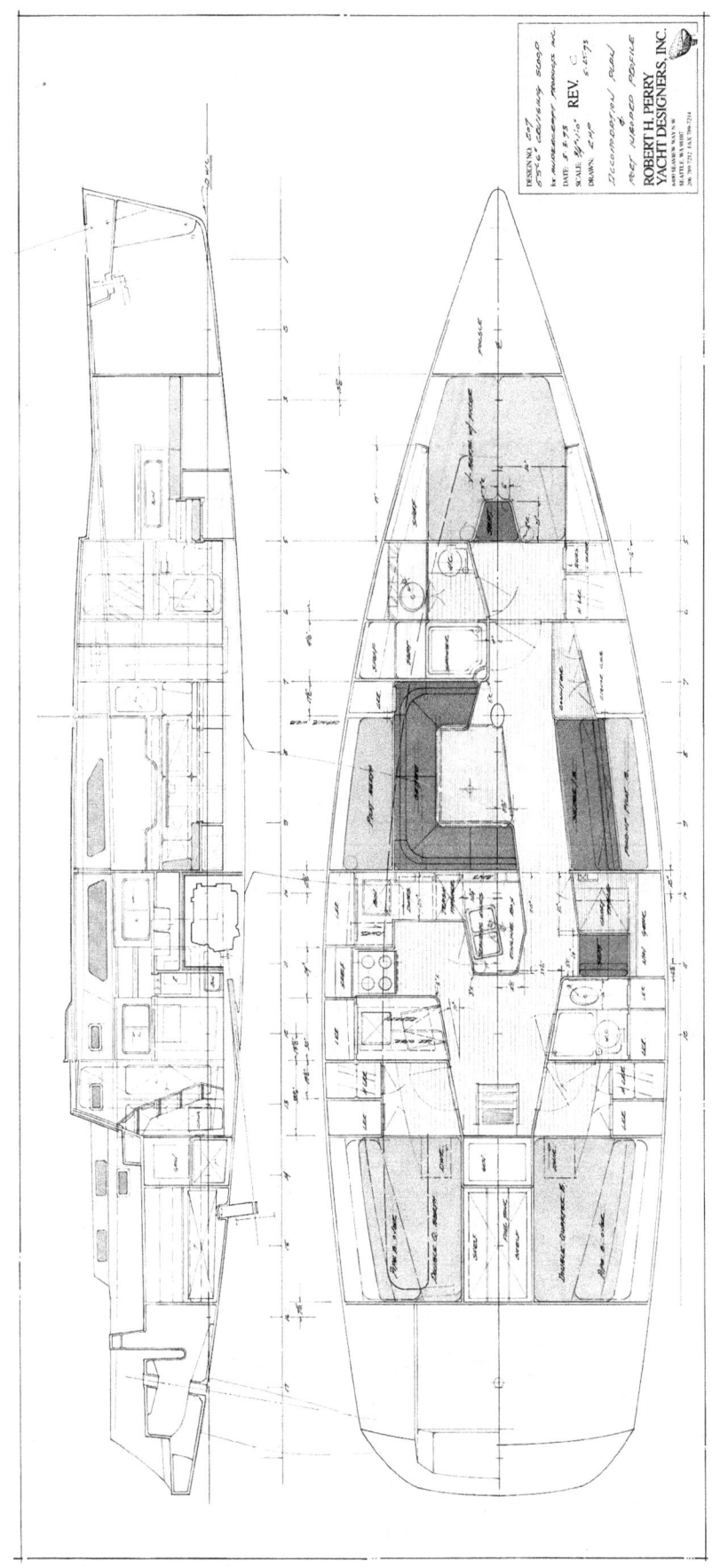

Racing considerations were set aside when I did Chicken's interior. There are pilot berths port and starboard, but the rest of the layout is pure "cruise." Note the large galley.

# Yacht Design According to Perry

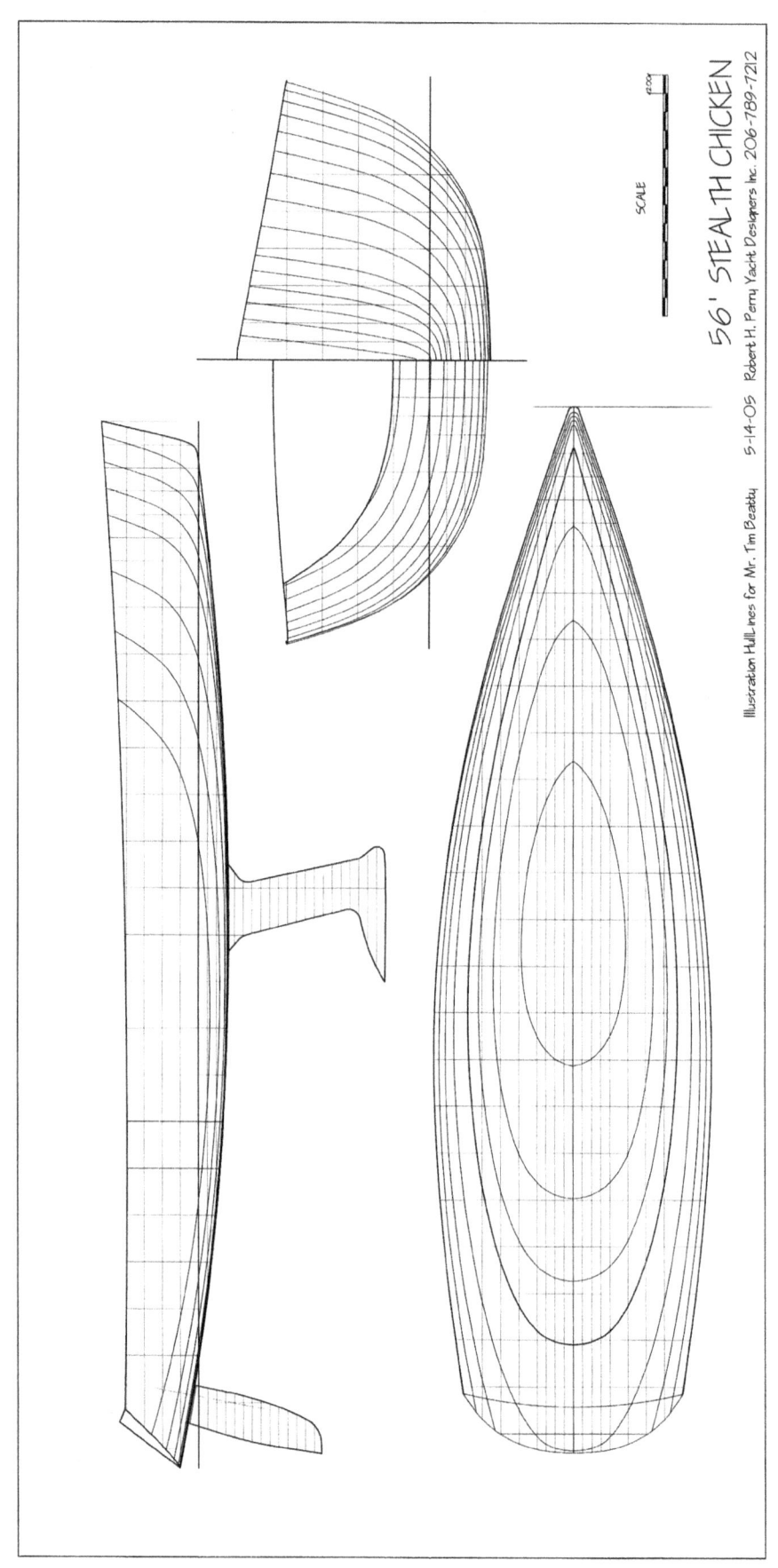

Illustration Hull Lines for Mr. Tim Beatty    5-14-05    Robert H. Perry Yacht Designers Inc. 206-789-7212

56' STEALTH CHICKEN

*Bruce wanted to sink the bow and reduce displacement with a new keel while retaining the same keel bolt pattern. Our solution was this forward-swept keel, similar to the one we had used on Amati. The rudder is big, and I tried to talk Bruce into a newer, smaller, faster one, but he refused, saying, "I can drive the boat out of anything with that rudder!"*

*Stealth Chicken* would be a moderately narrow boat with a L/B of 3.68 and a D/L of 112, making it on the light side of medium displacement. The hull shape featured the signature IMS near plumb bow and arc-like sections to reduce wetted surface. I kept the BWL relatively narrow, and, in retrospect, I probably should have taken some of the fullness out of the topsides. With a very deep, 9'6" keel and a ballast-to-displacement ratio of 38 percent, we had all the stability we needed without trying to capture additional form stability in the topsides. Fullness in the topsides probably just added drag when the boat heeled.

There was no deadrise to the hull. I like a nice tangent at centerline for racing boats. It has never made any sense to me to smooth out the bottom with the most expensive hard bottom paint, then to design in a big "corner" running the length of the boat. Given the yaw angle at which sailboats operate whenever they're not sailing directly downwind, it can't be fast to drag a corner through the water. Maybe in the case of light-displacement, chine-form hulls you could make an argument depending upon where the chine was and the nature of the target performance, but in a medium-displacement racing boat I prefer no deadrise. Bruce wanted a strong spring to the sheer, so he had come to the right designer. *Stealth Chicken*'s sheerline is pronounced, and this separates it from the rest of the Southern California racing fleet. At the launch party, Bruce had decals made and applied to the side of the cabin trunk that read "Baba 56." It was our private joke.

*Stealth Chicken*'s interior layout was designed for comfortable cruising with the option of sleeping an offshore racing crew. We had folding pipe berths over double quarter berths to port and starboard and pilot berths in the saloon. The galley was big in my general style, and the forward head had a shower stall that would work as a mini-bathtub. This layout was very comfortable for cruising. Bruce wanted an in-the-counter blender for mixing margaritas and a refrigerated "beverage box" in the cockpit.

I don't remember why we went with the masthead rig for *Stealth Chicken*. Maybe it was just force of habit for Bruce. I'm sure it was his call. But the rig was big, with a SA/D of 26.7. The tall stick was balanced by a keel with plenty of plan form and a huge rudder. Later on, after designing *Starbuck*, I begged Bruce to let me design him a new, smaller rudder for *Stealth Chicken*, but he was so happy with the performance of *Stealth Chicken* under pressure that he would not let me touch his rudder. The big rudder, with a 13 percent thickness ratio, was effective in driving the boat out of near-broaches when pushed hard under spinnaker. Today, I am certain we could have reduced the plan form by at least 30 percent and we could have reduced the thickness ratio to 10 percent. The boat would have been faster but also more demanding to drive.

Eventually we did redesign the keel to reduce the overall weight of *Stealth Chicken*. The challenge there was to make it lighter to improve *Stealth Chicken*'s light-air performance and acceleration off the line. At the same time, we wanted to induce some bow-down trim in order to get the yacht's fat fanny out of the water to reduce wetted surface.

"And by the way, I want to bolt the new keel on using the existing keel bolt pattern," said Bruce. That was the rub. Given the original keel position, the only way we could use those bolt holes and move the LCG of the keel forward was to use forward sweep on the keel fin. You see very few boats with forward-sweeping keel fins. After some research, though, we thought it was possible and that it may have some advantages in terms of stall angles.

What convinced me to do it was the fact that *Cassiopeia*, the big Laurie Davidson Seattle sloop, had just undergone a similar keel change, and Laurie had designed a forward-sweeping fin. I went down to the boatyard to look at *Cassiopeia*'s new keel. It was magnificent and beautifully sculpted. It just looked right. As I stood there admiring the keel, it came to me in a flash. Of course this keel is forward-swept. Laurie was given the exact same design directive that I had been given. *Cassiopeia* was a boat with a big, broad transom, and it was known to be a heavy boat. I was certain that Laurie had been asked to reduce the ballast weight, induce some bow down trim, and maintain the same keel bolt pattern for pragmatic reasons. I admired Laurie's work immensely, so if it was good enough for him, then I could do it, too.

The new keel worked very well. It achieved all of our goals. The odd drawback to the new keel was that the forward sweep demanded a kelp cutter to clear the keel of weeds. Under power, however, with the kelp cutter removed, water would shoot up through the vacated cutter hole like a fountain. I went on to use forward sweep again in *Amati* (see Chapter 15). In that instance, designing from

*I was proud to see this photo of* Chicken *featured in a North Sails advertisement. Most of the sailing world does not know I can do a race boat when asked. This photo shows the cabin trunk sculpting I used to make it visually interesting.*

scratch, I used the forward sweep by choice, thinking it was the better geometry. Today I don't know. *Amati* is a fine boat and sails very well, but I don't see any other designers using forward sweep. Are they telling me something? It could be that forward sweep moves the center of pressure forward on the fin and can lead to more weather helm than you might want.

Bruce raced and cruised *Stealth Chicken* for more than eight years. He won his share of races and competed in just about every offshore event in Southern California, including several Transpacs from Los Angeles to Honolulu. It was always rewarding to come into the office on a Monday morning and get a phone call from Bruce: "Well, you're a rock star and a hero again." That was music to my ears. There is nothing like a satisfied client. Of course, the highpoint in Bruce's satisfaction with the boat came the day he received a phone call from another Southern Californian racer with an offer to buy *Stealth Chicken*. The offer was generous and very close to what Bruce had paid for the boat initially eight years earlier. The new owner loves *Stealth Chicken* and continues to race the boat vigorously. However, the sale left Bruce with an empty coop. We toyed around with various preliminary design ideas for a couple of years while Bruce tried to make up his mind on exactly what the next boat should be. Then Bruce bought a Santa Cruz 50 and began campaigning it. He called his new 50-footer *Chicken Little*. Bruce campaigned the boat for three years.

It's just so much fun to get that call, "I want to do a new boat." It's even more fun when the caller is a repeat client with whom you have enjoyed working. So it was very satisfying to hear Bruce's voice on the other end. His ideas had changed over the nine years since we'd first talked. The new boat would be a cruising boat that Bruce would race from time to time. Bruce knew he wanted something less than 60 feet, and he specified a hard dodger for protection from the sun when cruising the coast of Mexico.

I designed the new *Chicken* to have more displacement than *Stealth Chicken*. I knew it would have a lot of cruising gear onboard, and while you can reduce hull weight by using high-tech construction, there is nothing you can do about the weight of cruising gear. I had to take into account a trash compactor, an ice maker, a washer and dryer, a dishwasher, a watermaker, copious tankage, a generator, and a 120-horsepower Yanmar diesel. This boat would be loaded for cruising.

## A Pair of Chickens

*Free Range Chicken* shows a tall fractional rig. I favored a shorter one, but Bruce wanted the horsepower for occasional racing. Hard dodgers are always aesthetically challenging, but this one looks pretty good to my eye. The aft support doubles as the support for the mainsheet traveler.

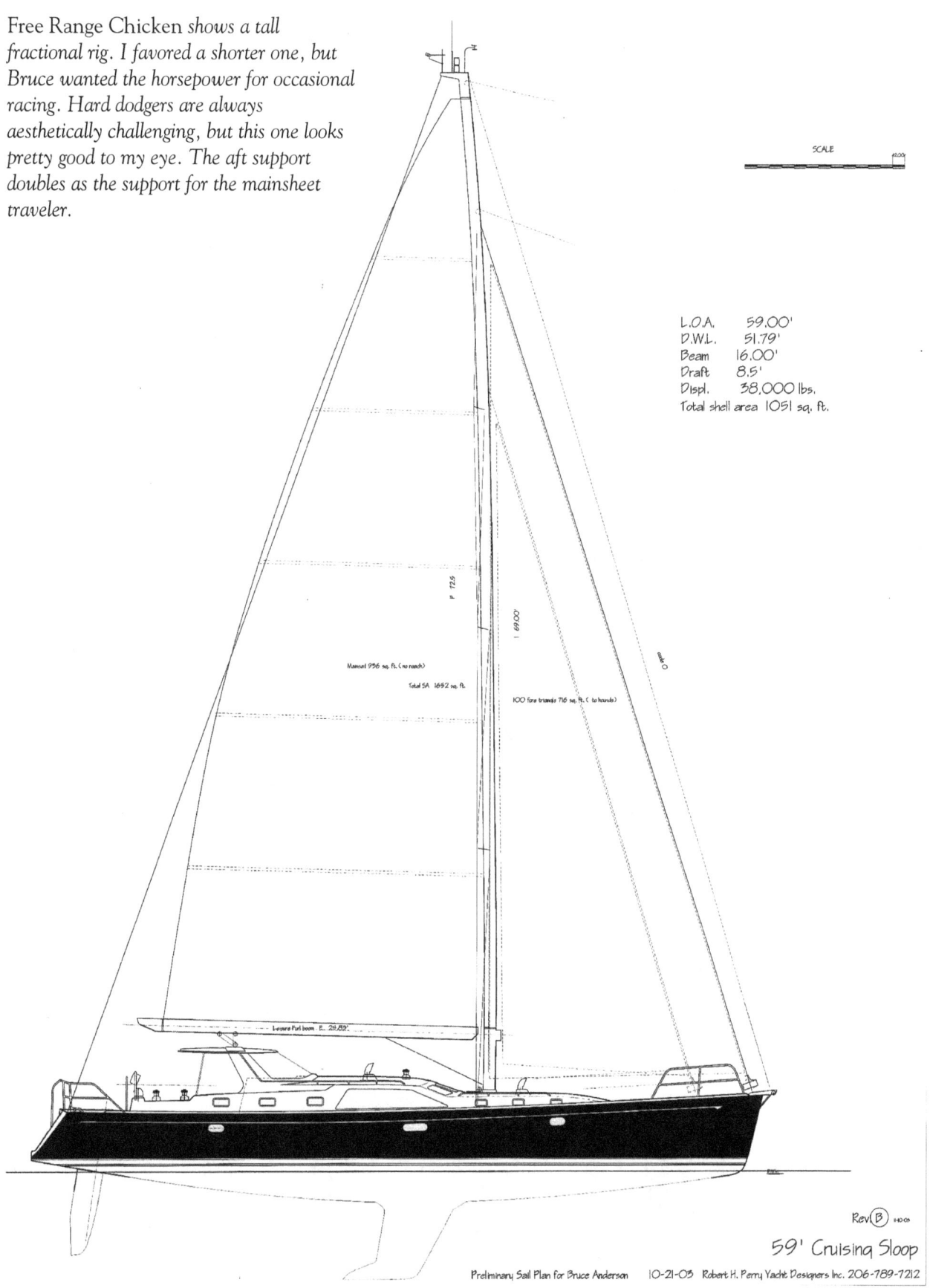

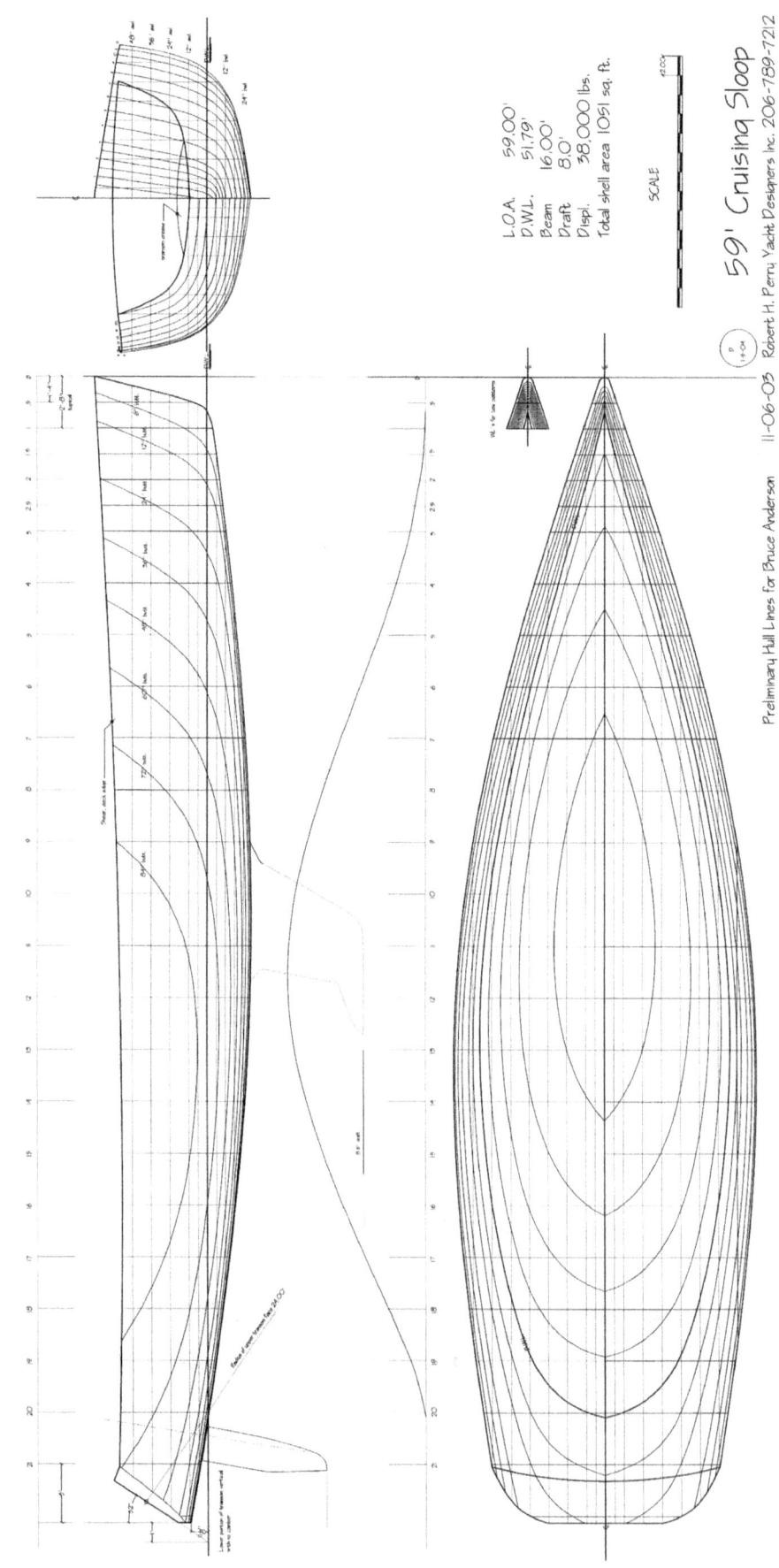

Free Range Chicken's lines show a harder turn to the bilge than Stealth Chicken's, in addition to a broader stem and more deadrise.

Whereas *Stealth Chicken* was drawn almost entirely by me, with most of the drawings done by hand except for the hull, the keel, and the rudder lines, the new boat—to be called *Free Range Chicken*—was designed in collaboration with my associate from 2000 to 2007, Ben Souquet. Ben did all of the engineering and made sure that the promises I made during the preliminary phase of the design could be kept when the boat was built. The design work coming out of the major design offices is seldom the work of one man, regardless of the name on the title block.

I decided to give the new *Free Range Chicken* some deadrise. Cruising boats should have deadrise. It provides a natural bilge sump so that any bilge water will collect in one place instead of just rolling around the entire bilge. The *Free Range Chicken* has more BWL for greater initial stability. Cruisers like stability. The bilges are firmer than those of *Stealth Chicken*, and I carried this firm bilge turn to the transom to keep the stern from squatting and help with speed under power. The entry is sharper than that of *Stealth Chicken*, and there is less fullness to the topsides, especially forward. The new boat had 3.7 feet more DWL than the old boat. Again, Bruce wanted a strong spring to the sheer, but I gave the new boat less sheer spring than *Stealth Chicken* had. Looking at the finished boat, it was obvious that there was still plenty of spring to this sheer.

In the interest of cruising convenience, we went with a modest draft of 8.5 feet with an all-lead keel fin. The fin is more durable than a two-part fin and bulb arrangement. Cruisers will, sooner or later, hit the bottom, and when they do, there is nothing like a big chunk of lead to absorb the shock. The rudder is made completely of carbon and had 17 percent balance.

The layout of *Free Range Chicken* was based on what we knew worked in *Stealth Chicken*, but this time there was no effort made for a racing crew. We do have a quarter pipe berth over the starboard double quarter berth, but there are no pilot berths. The mini-dinette can be converted to a sea berth, as can the port settee. *Free Range Chicken* is a boat designed for a couple to cruise in comfort.

We went with a raised saloon configuration for better light and air. We had plenty of opening ports. I like opening ports in cruising boats. You can never have too much ventilation. I separated the head area from the shower stall forward. I have done this a few times, and it seems better than combining the two areas. There was a counter or long desk forward of the port settee, and this was a computer work space so that you could do some business while you were off cruising.

The focal point of this layout was the big galley. So much of cruising centers around eating that I remain convinced that the heart of the cruising-boat layout has to be the galley. When the cook is happy, the crew will be happy. I have "rules" for galley design, and I used all of them in this galley. The sinks have counter space on each side, as did the range. The refrigerator is both top-loading and front-loading. The counter wraps around to help keep the cook secure. There is a trash compactor right at the bottom of the companionway, which the crew could get to easily without disturbing the cook. Westerly Marine also built *Free Range Chicken* and did a great job with the interior finishing details.

This time we went with a fractional rig. By now we had all learned that the fractional rig, with its big main and small jib, was easier to handle than the masthead rig, with its bigger headsails. We chose the Leisure Furl system for the mainsail. It's hard to manhandle a mainsail this big with a crew of two. Just flaking the sail on top of the boom can be a challenge for husband and wife. The Leisure Furl system, with the sail rolling up paper-towel style inside the boom, solves this problem. But the rig is really big. In fact, I tried to convince Bruce to go with a smaller rig, but he was planning to race the boat from time to time, so he wanted the taller mast with a SA/D of 23.4. We used the hard dodger to fashion a support beam that would carry the mainsheet to reduce cockpit clutter. It's a good-looking boat. If I had seen something in the design that looked odd, I would have changed it. Simple as that.

I've sailed *Free Range Chicken*, and the boat sails very well. Three weeks after the boat was launched, Bruce entered the Puerto Vallarta race. He was entered in the big-boat cruising class and the only other entrant in that division was a brand-new J/65. *Free Range Chicken* beat the J-boat on corrected time and even managed to sail boat for boat with it for almost three days.

"Well, you are a rock star and a hero again," said Bruce. I would hope you could imagine the pride and satisfaction I get from projects like this. It was music to my ears.

# Yacht Design According to Perry

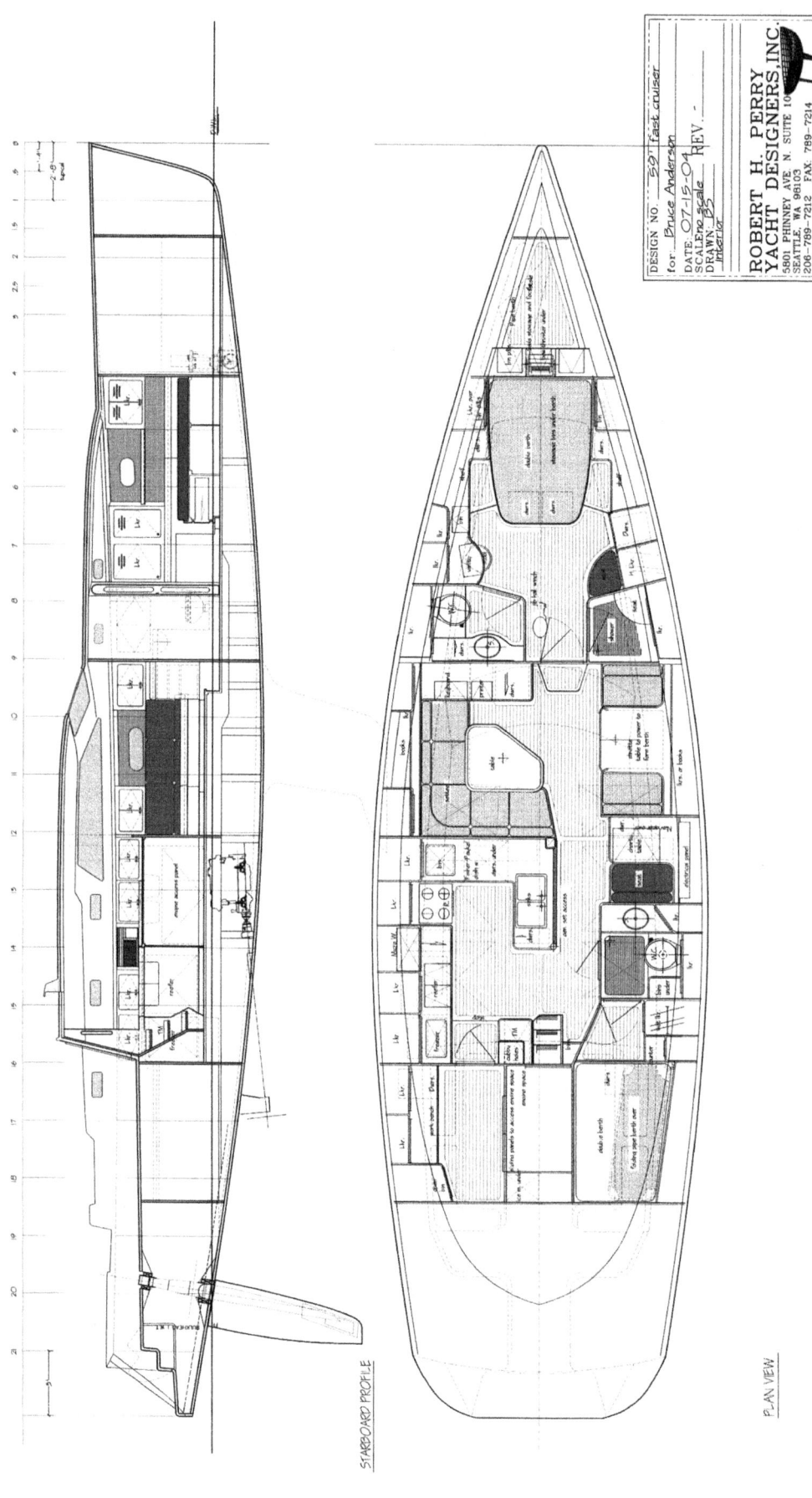

I consider Free Range Chicken's interior one of my best. It is designed to keep a couple comfortable for long cruises. Note the workroom aft of the galley and the computer center forward of the dinette. As usual, the galley is huge.

## A Pair of Chickens

Free Range Chicken *during her first day of sailing trials off Newport Beach, California. Note the small LP jib and the Leisure Furl boom.*

*Here we are during sailing trials, telling each other what a great job we did with the new* Chicken.

## *According to Perry*
# RIGGING

We introduced the concept of rig safety factors in "According to Perry: Masts." Having chosen a safety factor, you can decide how many spreaders you want and whether you want them in-line or swept.

The old Valiants had single-spreader rigs, which required a stiff and relatively heavy mast section. Adding a second set of spreaders, as in the modern Valiant 42, reduces the length of the unsupported sections between masthead, spreaders, and deck, and this enables you to reduce the mast's transverse moments and therefore its weight without reducing the safety factor. Adding spreaders will not do anything for the fore-and-aft moments, and in choosing an extrusion to handle these, you will probably end up with a mast that is overly stiff in the transverse moment, but there is nothing wrong with that. In order to reduce fore-and-aft moments, you would need to add an inner forestay or a babystay, thus reducing the length of the unsupported panels in the fore-and-aft axis. However, most cruisers do not want to deal with pulling a genoa around and over additional forestays.

Today, most extrusions are designed for at least two-spreader rigs. Three spreaders will further reduce your transverse-moment needs but will also add tuning complexity and windage. Once you go to three or more sets of spreaders, you will want to look at discontinuous rigging, which reduces the number of wires reaching the deck chainplates but also adds tuning challenges.

Let's take a moment to examine continuous versus discontinuous rigging. Continuous rigging is simple. All stays extend all the way to the deck, and the tuning can be done at deck level. For a single- or double-spreader rig, continuous rigging is the way to go.

With three sets of spreaders, however, you have to deal with cap shrouds (V1), lower diagonals (D1), intermediate diagonals (D2), and upper diagonals (D3). This means that you will have four wires (or rods; see below) landing on each shroud chainplate, and this necessitates a huge chainplate (or multiple chainplates) just to provide enough clevis-pin holes and material area for the various shrouds and their loads. This large chainplate is cumbersome and usually intrudes on the available deck space. One way to avoid this, and to save weight at the same time, is to go with discontinuous rigging. This means that the cap shroud and the upper diagonal shroud (D3) will terminate at the upper spreader tip in a special fitting, below which a single wire takes the load of the two wires (or rods) above it. In this way, you reduce the number of wires landing on the chainplate, and you also save weight and windage aloft by reducing the number of rods or wires. In this triple-spreader example you end up bringing only two wires to the chainplates at the deck instead of four wires.

The disadvantage of discontinuous rigging is that you have to go aloft in a bosun's chair in order to tune the rig, making adjustments to the turnbuckles located at each spreader tip. This would be extremely

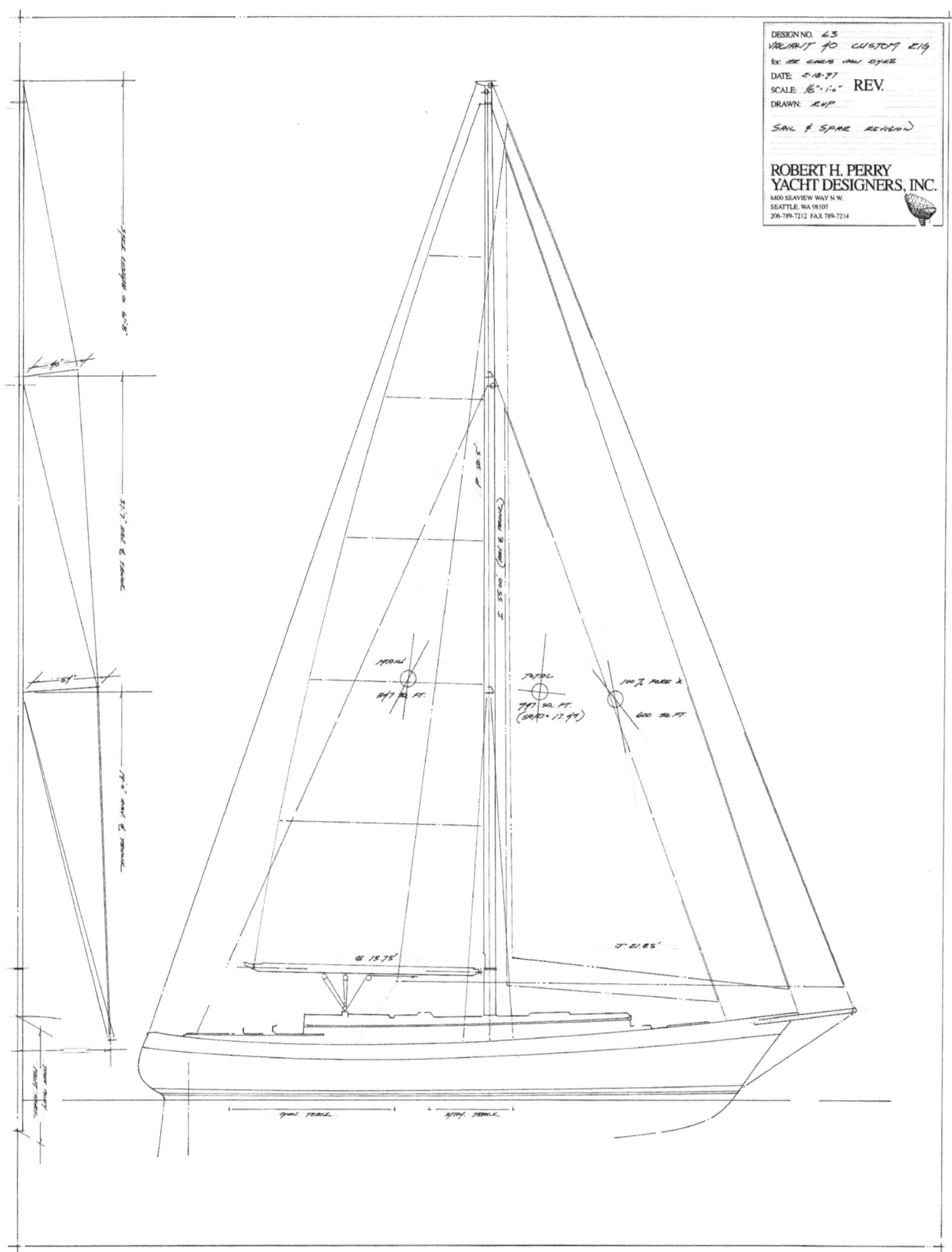

This double-spreader custom rig for a Valiant 40 increased the I dimension from 48 to 55 feet and sail area (with 100 percent foretriangle) from 761 to 947 square feet.

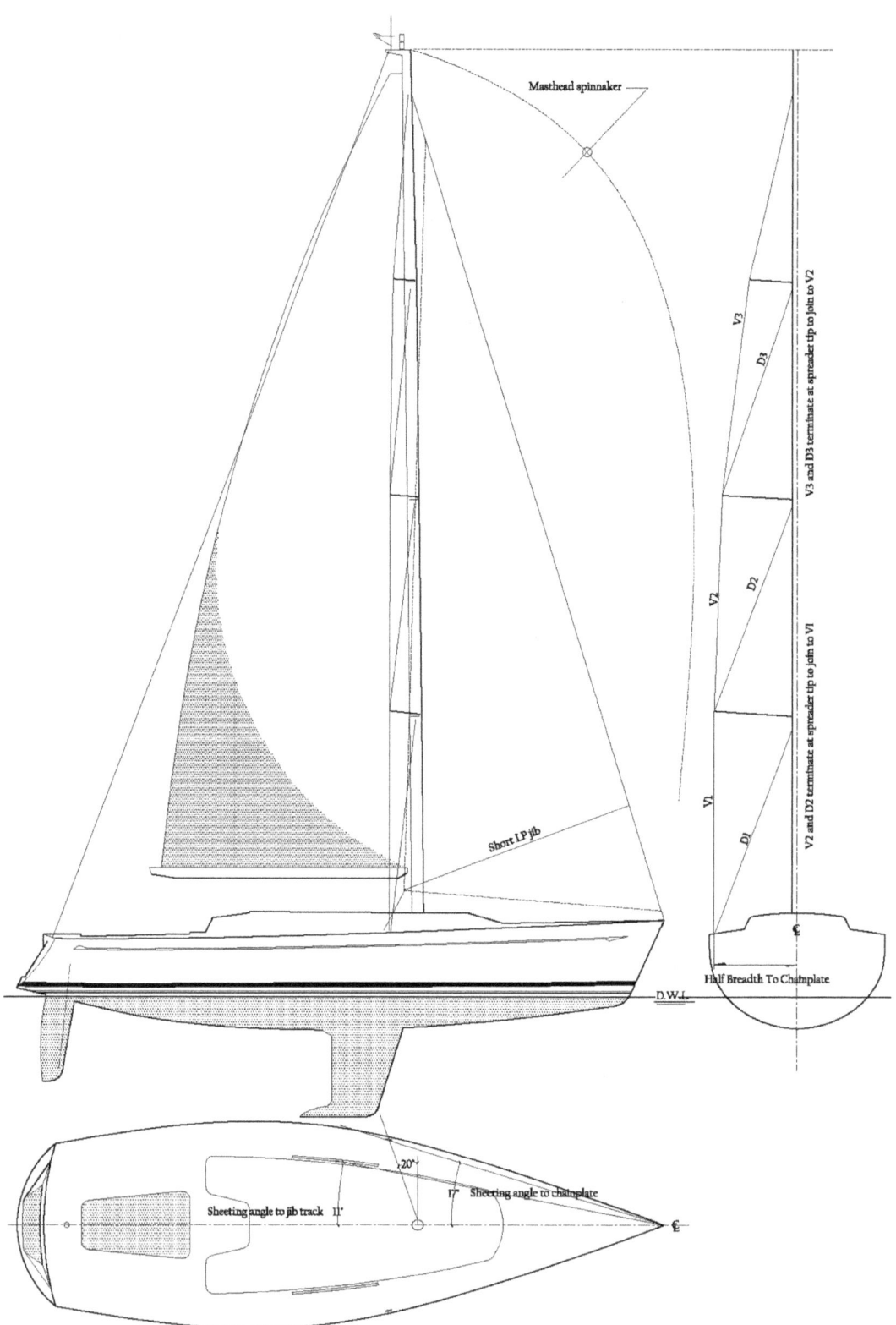

A triple-spreader rig with 20 degrees of spreader sweep and discontinuous rigging. D3 (the upper diagonal shroud) and V3 (the cap shroud segment) both transfer their load to V2 (the next lower cap shroud segment) at the intermediate spreader tip, and D2 and V2 transmit their loads to V1 at the lower spreader tip. This reduces the number of shroud landings on the deck chainplate from four to two. Sweeping the spreaders aft obviates the need for aft lower shrouds and enables a non-overlapping jib to sheet inside the shrouds.

inconvenient for a cruiser, but then again, cruisers seldom have three-spreader rigs.

To recap, a two-spreader rig enables you to stay with continuous rigging and do all your tuning from the deck. Another advantage of a two-spreader rig is that if you want to fly a heavy-air staysail, the second (i.e., upper) spreader provides the ideal mast location for landing the staysail stay. There the stay is well supported by the shrouds and is low enough to give the right aspect ratio to the staysail. You should avoid staysails with a head angle (the angle between luff and leech) of less than 22 degrees.

Having decided on the number of spreaders, you then need to choose whether they should be in-line with the centerline of the mast (i.e., perpendicular to the boat's fore-and-aft centerline) or swept aft—and, if the latter, to what degree. Until the mid-1990s, almost all cruising boats had one forward-leading lower, one aft-leading lower, and an in-line upper shroud on each side. This worked well with stout mast sections, and the fore-and-aft support provided by the lowers eliminated the need for running backstays or a forward babystay. If you wanted to carry a heavy-air staysail, you fitted (or at least should have fitted) running backstays to oppose the load of the staysail stay. Although many cruising-boat mast sections are strong enough to support staysail stay loads without the use of running backstays, I recommend runners for any boat going offshore. Runners make it easier to keep the luff of the staysail straight.

On a lot of cutters, the "intermediate uppers" that run from the staysail hounds (i.e., where the staysail stay hits the mast) to a chainplate on the deck just aft of the aft lower shroud on each side do nothing to help with the staysail. I used to include intermediate uppers in all my cutters until I realized that they did not have enough aft-directed vector to be effective. All this stay does is add to the compression load on the rig, which is already considerable; in many cases, the compression load of the rig equals the displacement of the boat. (You can reduce the compression load by moving your chainplates outboard, but this will result in wider sheeting angles, which can be a problem if you are using overlapping genoas.) Running backstays led well aft do a far better job of supporting the staysail stay than intermediate uppers do, and runners can also greatly reduce "pumping" in boats with lighter spar sections.

The problem with forward- and aft-leading lowers is that, combined with the cap shroud, they require three separate chainplates along with their accompanying below-deck bulkheads or knees for attachment to the hull. The forward lower can also interfere with jib and staysail sheeting angles, although most staysails should be set up to sheet inside the shrouds. The aft lower will limit how far out you can let your boom. You can improve this by moving the aft lower forward to share a double chainplate with the cap (i.e., upper) shroud, but then the lower provides less aft support to the mast. This may require runners and some mast "pre-bend" to keep the mast from pumping in a lumpy sea.

There is nothing mysterious about pre-bend. To achieve it, you push the butt of the mast aft on the mast step (most mast butt plates allow this movement), and you push the mast forward at the partners (where the mast exits the deck or cabin trunk). By tensioning the backstay, you can then induce a gentle curve in the mast between the partners and the masthead. This pre-bend will prevent the mast from pumping aft but may encourage it to pump forward. This is when you would need runners to prevent a pre-bent mast from just bending more and reducing headstay tension when you apply more backstay tension. Runners and an adjustable backstay enable you to pull the bent mast aft "in one piece" and thereby increase headstay tension. Just pumping up the tension on the backstay can actually reduce headstay tension as bending the mast can reduce the vertical height.

If your objective is to replace the aft and forward lower shrouds with a single centerline lower, you are certain to need either mast pre-bend with runners or a babystay forward with runners. Pre-bend is the better way to go if your spar section is flexible enough to allow it.

If you want to eliminate the need for runners, pre-bend, and a babystay, you can sweep your spreaders aft. This will require chainplates at least 15 degrees aft of the centerline of the mast. In some cases, chainplates are as far aft as 30 degrees, although 19 to 22 degrees seems more typical of performance-oriented designs. Now you can tune your mast with some pre-bend, and the vectors of the swept spreaders will prevent any additional mast bend at all. Once it is set up, this rig is foolproof, but it is a more difficult rig to set up and tune properly. The swept

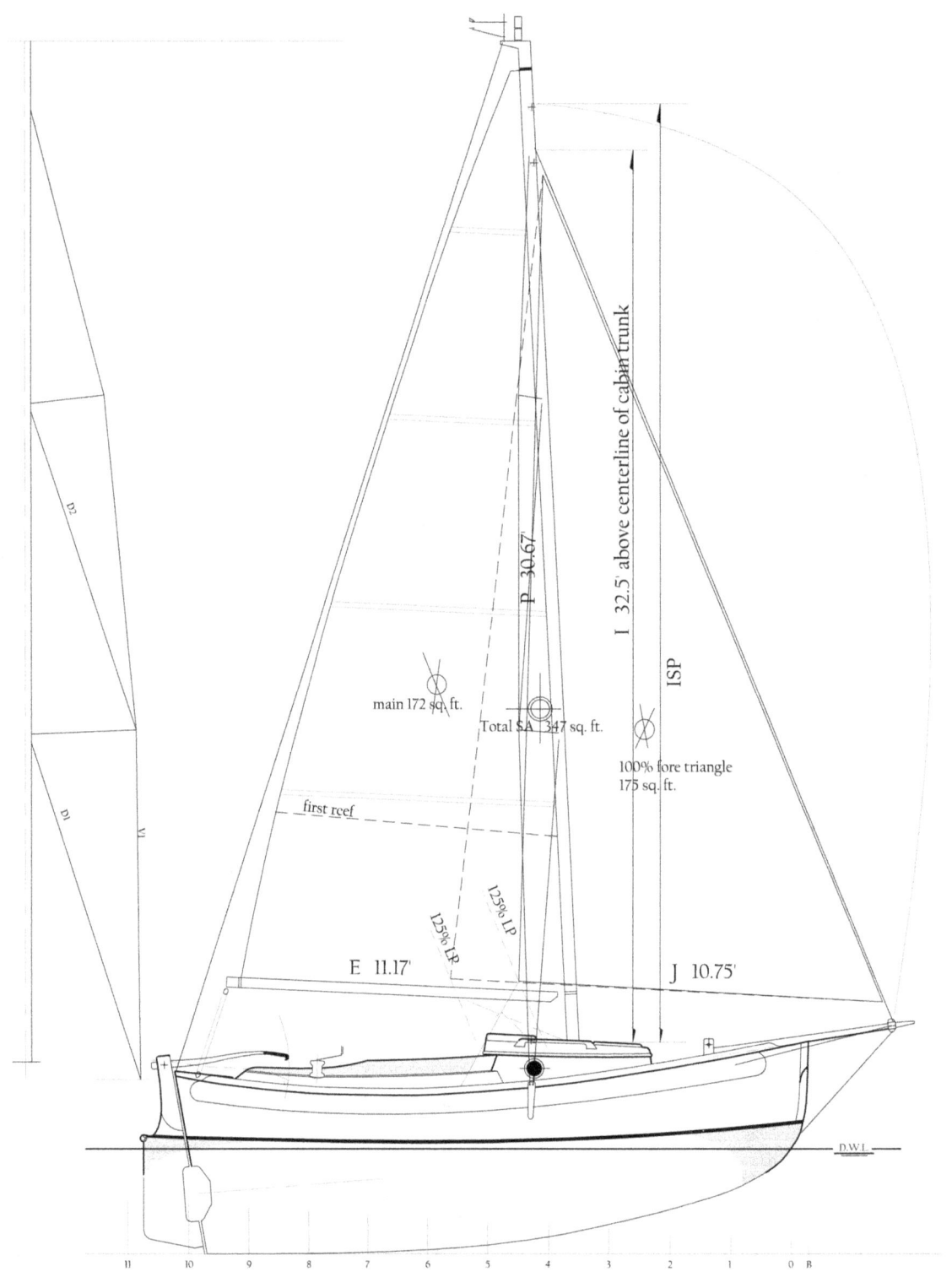

### BCC 22' Daysailer
Robert H. Perry Yacht Designers Inc.

*Double-spreader fractional rigs with swept-back spreaders gracing two very different sloops. The traditional, full-keeled 22-foot daysailer above is in sharp contrast with the ultralight Flying Tiger sport boat (at right), which is 10 meters (32.66 inches) long overall yet weighs just 4,300 pounds. Flying Tiger has a D/L of 81 and an off-the-chart SA/D of 68.75.*

## According to Perry: Rigging

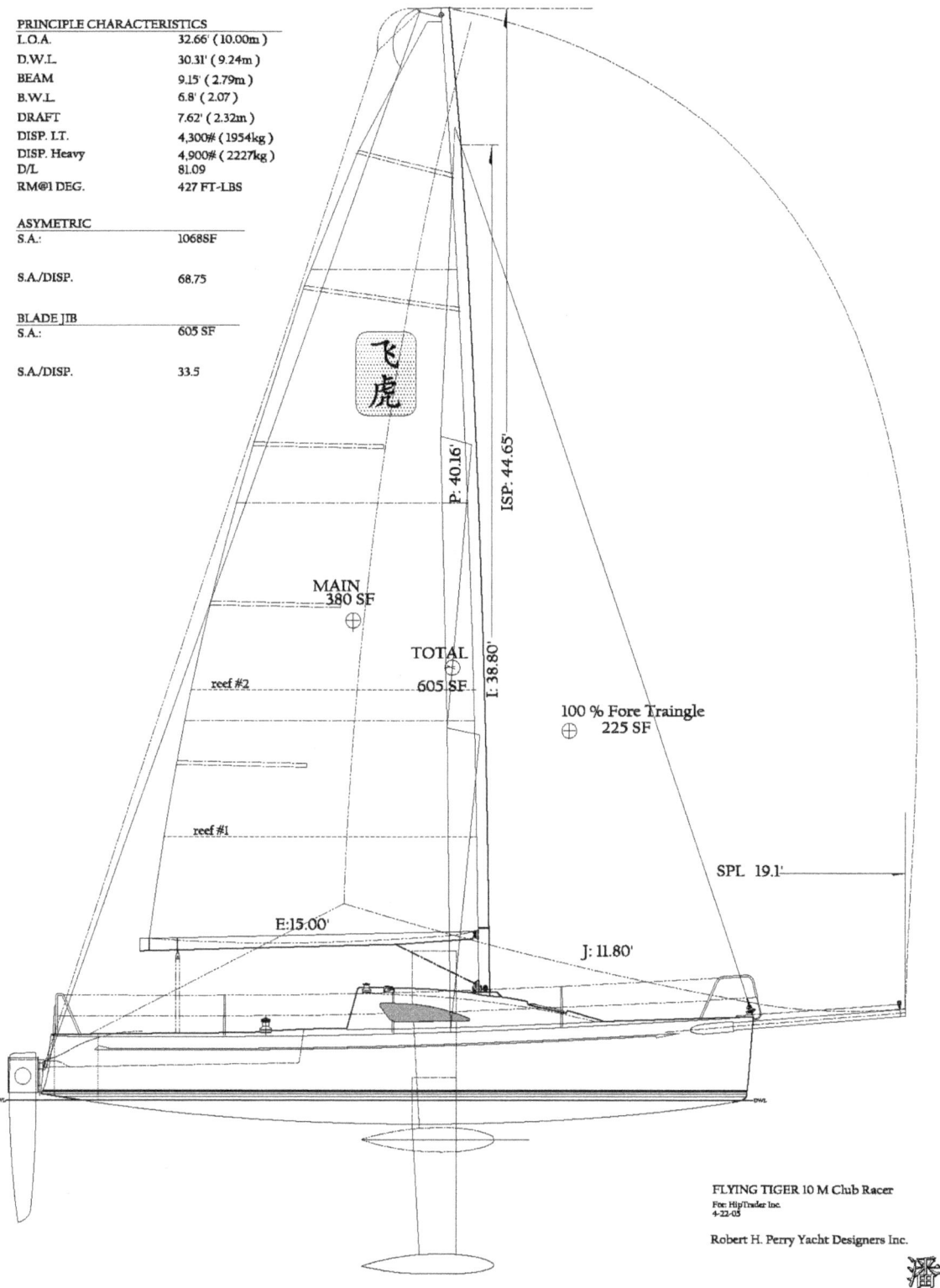

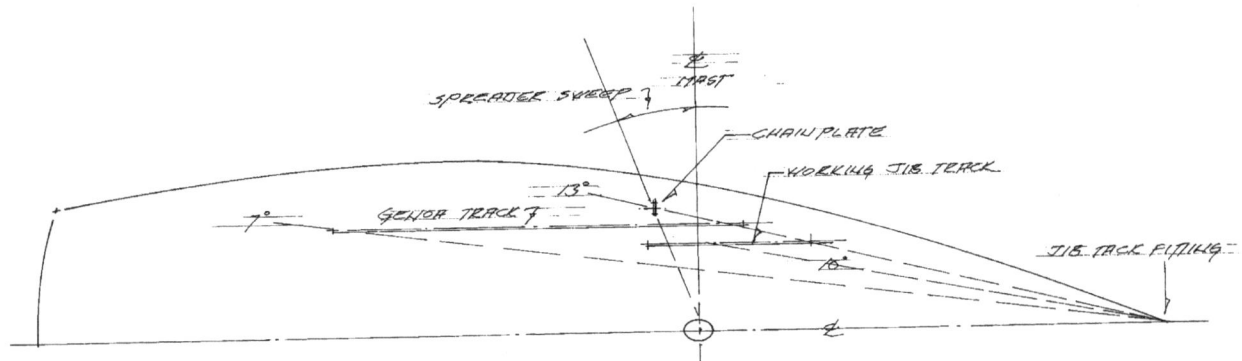

*This half-breadth drawing shows swept spreaders with the working jib sheeting inside the shrouds and the genoa sheeting outside. The dashed lines are at 7, 10, and 13 degrees from the centerline.*

spreaders will impale the mainsail when the mainsheet is eased, so you will need to get used to jibing from one broad reach to the other downwind rather than trying to run at apparent wind angles in excess of 150 degrees. Jibing downwind is faster anyway, with the higher boat speed more than compensating for the greater distance sailed. If you look at the current fleet of performance cruising boats—the J boats, the Bavarias, the Alerions, Tartan, Malo, Hanse, the Jeaneaus, the Beneteaus—you will see that swept spreaders have become almost universal. Sweeping the spreaders reduces the number of chainplates and makes a boat cheaper to build. In my opinion, this, more than anything else, accounts for the current popularity of swept spreaders on production boats.

Sweeping the spreaders aft can also allow you to carry a bigger headsail without its interfering with the shrouds. This means that you can forget about the sheeting angle past the chainplates. Now your jib is going to sheet inside the shrouds. You can take your chainplates out to the rail if you like, reducing the compression load on the spar and permitting yourself a lighter mast with its resulting benefits to stability.

Finally, the choice of rod or wire rigging, like so many other choices, depends on the type of boat, the skipper's performance expectations, and cost. I suspect that the records would show Navtec rod rigging to be every bit as reliable as wire if it is sized correctly. Given the choice I would always go with Navtec rod. On the other hand, offshore cruisers often like to use a terminal such as a Norseman fitting that they can service and replace if necessary while cruising in remote areas, and this eliminates rod. They also sometimes like to carry extra lengths of rigging for repairs or replacement, and this, too, eliminates rod.

The advantage of rod is its lack of stretch. If you set up rod rigging on a new boat, you can tune the rig and maybe come back in a few weeks and tune it again—but that's it. New wire rigging will require several tunings before it is stable. Rod is also smaller in diameter for a given safe working load, so it imposes less windage.

Probably the biggest disadvantage of rod for the cruiser is its cost, which can be twice that of wire. However, starting with Valiant 40 hull number 4 (if memory serves), almost all of the Valiants had Navtec rod rigging.

Today we have gone a step beyond rod and are seeing exotic racing boats with aramid (of which Kevlar is the leading brand) or PBO synthetic-fiber rigging. Fiber rigging is extremely light and can cut the weight of a rod rigging package in half. It is also UV sensitive, so it comes with a protective sheathing that must stay intact if the rigging is to maintain its strength. However, it is ultra-expensive. A PBO backstay for a 56-footer of mine cost $5,000, and the life expectancy of synthetic-fiber rigging is generally estimated at two to five years.

*Chapter Fourteen*

# Two California Cruising Sleds: *Starbuck* and *Foxfire*

When the caller to the office identified himself as Bill Clute, I already knew the name. It was mid-1995. Bill was a well-known California racing sailor who'd registered major victories in the days of the IOR, including San Francisco's Big Boat series and the prestigious Southern Ocean Racing Conference (SORC) on the East Coast. I was a little surprised he was calling me, but I did recall hearing that he owned a Tayana 52 of my design. Bill said that he had enjoyed cruising the Tayana 52, but now he wanted a faster boat that broadened his cruising range. This sounded good to me, so we arranged a meeting. Bill had already decided he would build the boat at Dencho Marine, Dennis Choate's well-known Long Beach yard. We would hold the meeting at the yard with Dennis present.

Bill told me that after years of racing he had just completed Long Beach Race Week and was watching his crew load the boat with supplies for the return trip to Newport Beach, a relatively short trip. After watching cart after cart of food and drinks go down the dock, and considering what it had cost him to put his crew up in a hotel and feed them during the regatta, Bill turned to his sailing friend and said, "There has to be a cheaper way of enjoying sailing."

Bill's friend was the famous sailmaker Lowell North, the founder of North Sails. Lowell said, "There is. Buy one of those and go cruising," and pointed to a Tayana 52 that was moored at the same dock as Bill's IOR racer. Lowell had owned a Tayana 52—he'd purchased it from the famous holder of land-speed records, Craig Breedlove—and he knew the boat well. So Bill bought a Tayana 52. With his wife, Heather, they went cruising in Mexico and loved it.

We had our meeting at Dencho in the heart of the Long Beach industrial area. The area and yard are less than picturesque, but there is an extraordinarily good Mexican restaurant within an easy walk. The Dencho yard was compact and busy and had the reputation of producing competitive racing yachts built to a budget. Unfortunately, in the days of the IOR, this meant that many of the boats had been almost disposable in nature as the IOR went through its many iterations. The winning boat one summer could be made obsolete by rule changes the next. There was simply no point in building monuments to boatbuilding skills and quality. The key was to build the new racer quickly and cheaply. This gave Dencho the unfortunate reputation of building "throwaway" boats. This didn't bother me, though. I was thrilled at the chance to work with Dennis Choate, and Bill was confident that Dennis could do a good job.

There have been many times in my career as a yacht designer that I have landed commissions that whirled me away to a fantasyland where the details of everyday life were totally swept up in the combination of owner, builder, boat, and design. Call it Zen-like, if you need a term for it. Over the next two

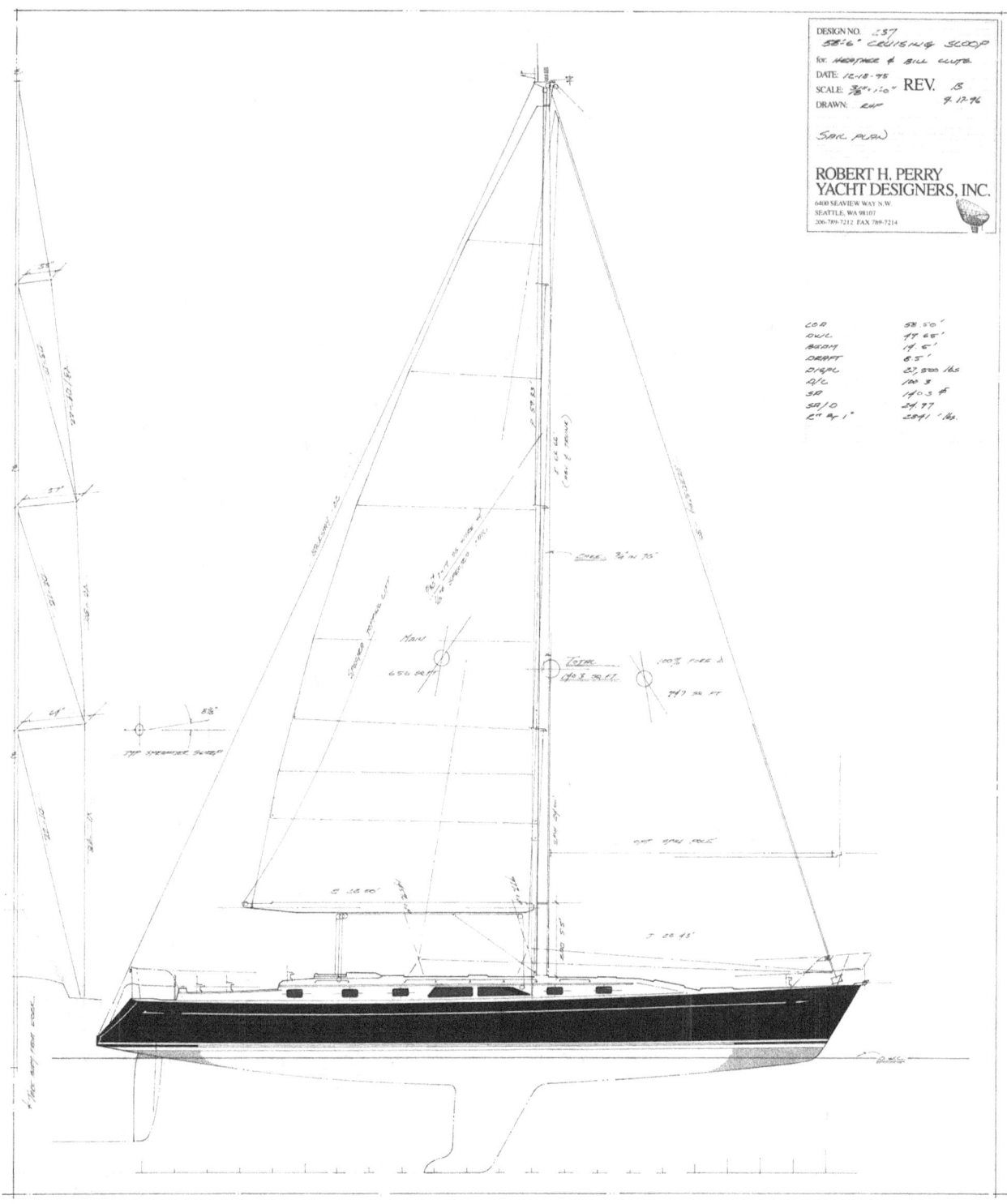

*This is one of my favorite profiles, drawn for a client who shared many of my ideas on what made the perfect cruising boat. Starbuck is an ultimate fast cruising boat for a couple.*

years, I would travel frequently to California, make some good new friends, eat some fantastic Mexican food, and produce two great boats.

At that first meeting at Dencho, Dennis let me know loud and clear what sort of boat he had in mind for Bill.

"But *I'm* the designer!" I cried.

"Never mind that," said Dennis. "Just design what I tell you to design and we'll get along fine."

I was given no option if I wanted the job, as it was clear that Dencho was as much a part of this project as was Bill Clute. As time went by, Dennis and I butted heads numerous times, and in the end, after doing four boats with Dennis, our designer/builder relationship died a natural death. I had my priorities and business model, and Dennis had his. Once Dennis landed the job to build a new boat, the designer became an obligatory accessory to the project. I preferred the "indispensable component" role. I could handle this most of the time, due to my respect for the experience Dennis had building fast boats. But I did think that oftentimes my experience producing cruising-boat designs gave me an edge in deciding a detail or feature of the boat. I won very few arguments with Dennis.

During one debate, after questioning a change that had been made without consulting me, I was told, "You are not welcome in the yard." I showed up anyway and Dennis acted like he had never said it. That was pretty much what working with Dennis was like. One day I was the golden boy, the next day I was told to stay away from the project. There was really no option for the client and me but to shrug off the whims of Dennis with, "Well, that's just Dennis." I look back with respect for Dennis's talent and humor at his quirks.

Dennis explained the hull shape he wanted for Bill's new, light, 59-foot cruising boat. The boat would be narrow, with a L/B of 4.07, and light, with a D/L of 100. This was, in fact, very light for a fully found cruising boat. You can save weight with careful lamination components in the hull and deck, but you can't save weight on the necessities of cruising. However, I had already done a boat like this, *Stealth Chicken*, so I knew I could do it again. Bill's boat would be a derivative of *Stealth* in terms of type and size. Dennis wanted dishlike sections to the hull with a narrow BWL. It was during the days of the IMS boats, but Dennis did not want an IMS-type plumb stem. Dennis wanted some rake to the bow, and this proved to be a very good idea as it kept the ground tackle away from the stem. There would be moderate stern overhang and a broad transom. These were broad parameters, and I felt I had pretty much a free hand to design the hull within those guidelines. The resultant hull shape is very sweet, and the big half model looks great on my wall.

When Dennis got the hull lines, he called me and said, "I don't like the way the forefoot knuckle is above the DWL. Get that knuckle under the DWL."

I explained that, with the shape I'd drawn, the natural termination of the entry area was best carried forward with the knuckle being above the DWL. Plus, it looked cool, fast, and contemporary, and it was a feature of almost all the IMS boats. But Dennis would not build it that way, so I redesigned the boat to get the knuckle right at the DWL. This satisfied Dennis.

The keel would be a one-piece lead fin drawing 8.5 feet. There would be sweep to the fin to allow kelp to be shed, and the keel tip would have a bulb to get the VCG of the lead as low as possible. With a light, narrow boat, we had to do all we could to get the overall VCG of the boat low for stability.

I sent Dennis the rudder drawing and got a phone call from him. "I'm not going to build that rudder," he said.

"Why not?" I asked.

"It's too big."

"It's about the same size as the rudder on *Stealth Chicken*."

"Fine, but I'm not going to build it."

I drew a smaller rudder. The phone rang. "I'm not going to build that rudder either," said Dennis. "It's still too big."

I flew down to Dencho. Dennis showed me to a big plywood door that led to a little shop within the big shop. This was where Dennis built custom surfboards. Dennis was a dedicated surfer. On that door was lofted rudder upon rudder, a blur of lines showing the outlines of all the rudders that Dennis had built over the years.

Dennis proceeded to walk me through the various rudder designs: "This one was too small. This one was too big. This one had too much balance area. This one did not have enough balance."

Textbooks and colleges are great, but a door like this, with a well-laid-out evolutionary trail of rudder design and rudder improvement, was priceless. I would have been a fool not to pay attention

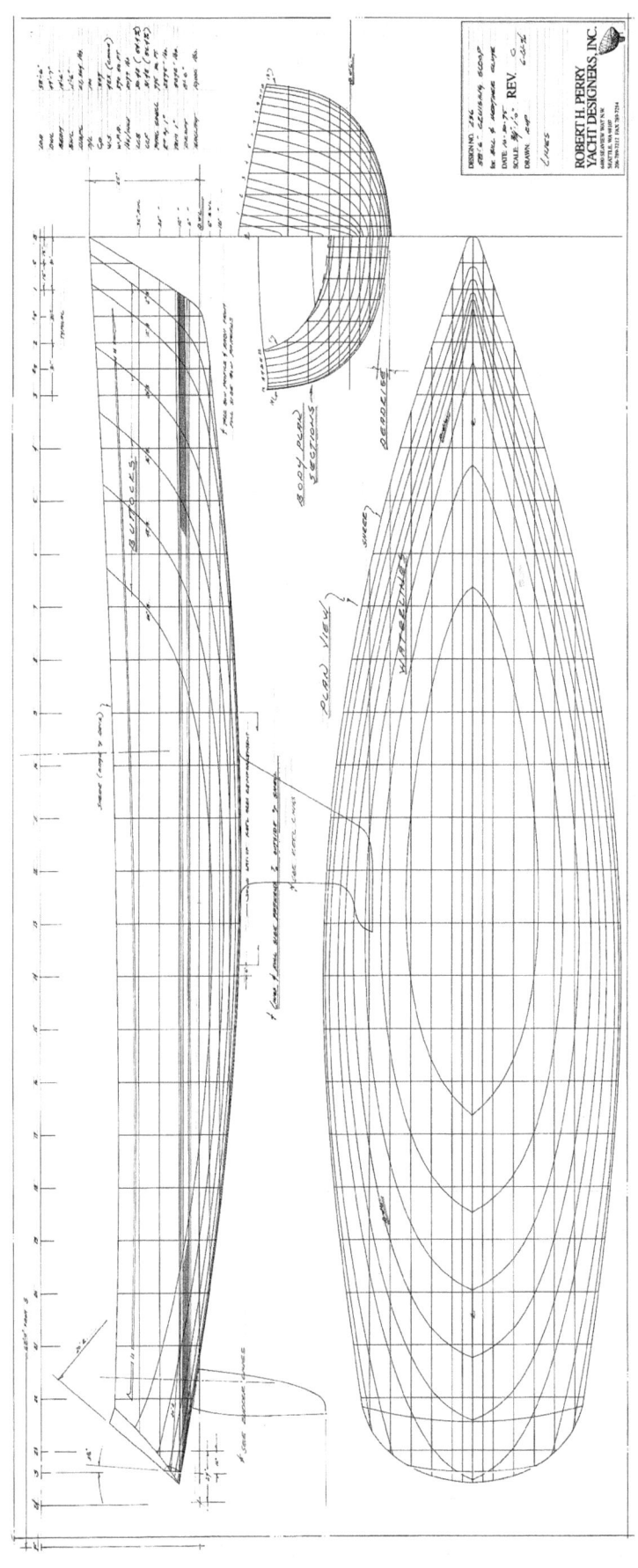

Starbuck's lines reflect Dennis Choate's directives. Note the dish-like midsection, moderately narrow BWL, and forefoot knuckle pushed below the DWL. This is an extremely clean and undistorted hull.

## Two California Cruising Sleds

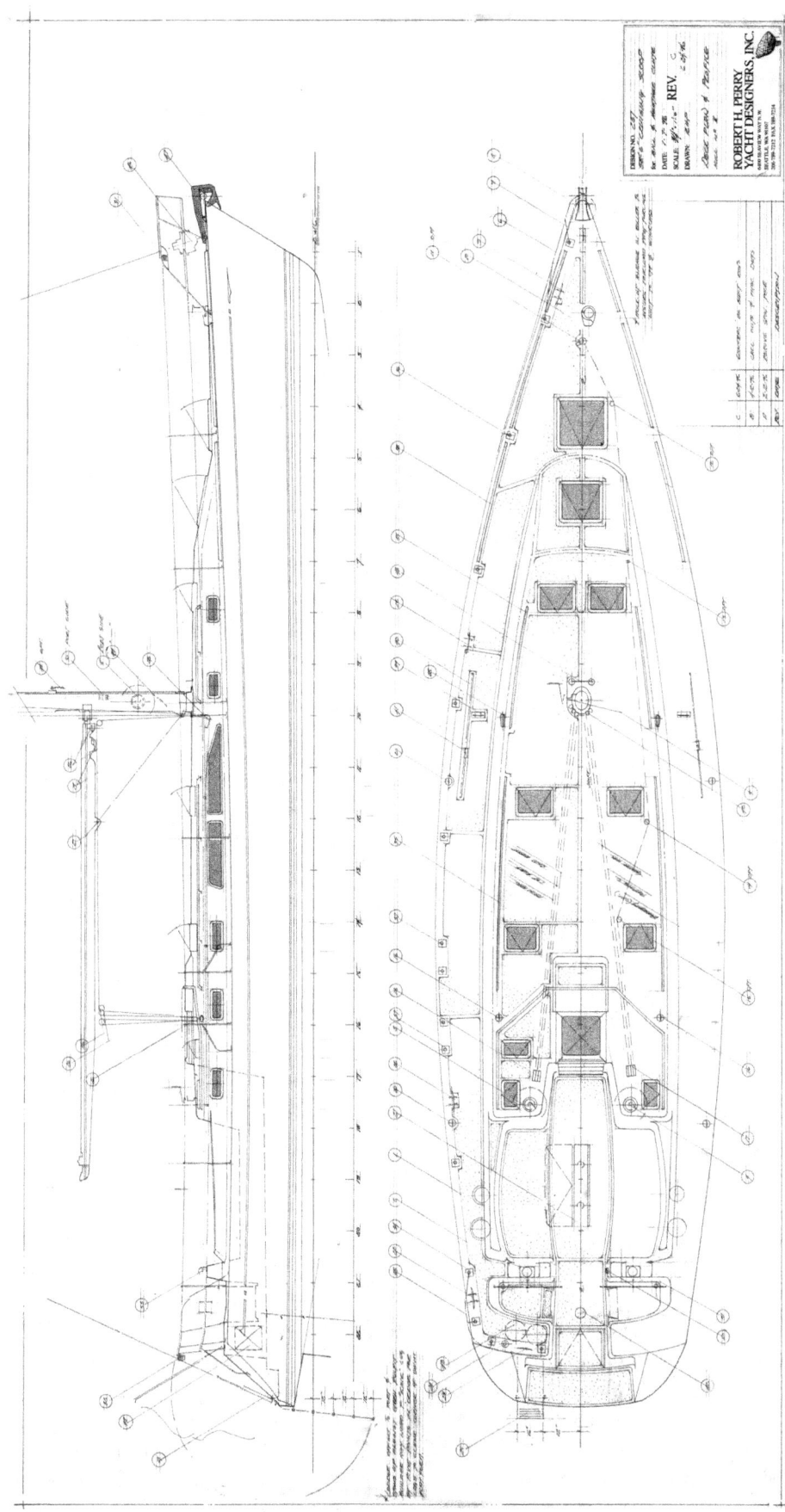

Starbuck's many deck hatches make for good live-aboard ventilation. The side decks are broad, and the twin-wheel cockpit has deep seats. The step at the transom is precisely at the height of the boat's original dock.

and learn from the extensive experience Dennis had with building big, fast, spade rudders. I took some dimensions and drew a new rudder for Bill's boat, and Dennis gave it his seal of approval. The rudder design proved to be perfect. It's fun to learn.

When I made my first trip to see the hull right-side up and off the plug, Dennis greeted me at the door to the shop and said, "You are going to like what I did with the bow." The hair rose up on the back of my neck, but I kept my mouth shut, remembering another time when a builder had called me and said, "You are going to like what I did with the bootstripe." I did not like that bootstripe, and I remain skeptical when builders announce they have changed a major component of any of my designs. But I really liked the bow Dennis had shaped. Using the full-sized patterns I had provided, Dennis had built a bow with the forefoot knuckle clearly above the DWL, just the way I'd originally drawn it. Dennis was proud of his bow and I praised it, then kept my mouth shut.

Bow profiles must be the natural termination of the waterline and sectional shapes you have established in the entry area. It's tempting to draw the bow profile first and is often necessary when you are in the preliminary stage of the design. The bow profile is necessary to establish the balance of the sheerline. Once the hull form starts taking shape, however, the exact bow and forefoot shape will establish itself as a function of the rest of the entry. You often see bow profiles that have little to do with the rest of the bow shape, and this can create a most ungainly looking bow. Yves-Marie Tanton taught me how to shape bows when we both worked for Dick Carter. When it came to hand-drawing hull lines, Yves-Marie was a master, and the IOR rule with its "connect the dots" demands on the designer was the perfect vehicle to allow Yves-Marie to perfect his craft.

*Starbuck* is a great boat. It is beautiful, with low freeboard and a long, low cabin trunk and a long cockpit. The cabin lines are a derivative of the Tayana 52 cabin trunk, with a wedge to the forward end and the companionway indented into the aft bulkhead to allow for headroom in the quarter cabins. The cockpit is big, with twin wheels aft and deep cockpit seats. I'd cruised one of my own CT 54s in the Caribbean for two weeks, which was an instructive experience. I'd designed the CT 54 when I knew little, but I must have known something about cockpit seats because I made them 30 inches deep, front to back. The typical seat—including the chair in your office—is 18 inches deep, front to back. This is a good dimension for a seat on which you will sit to work or eat, but it does not work in most cockpits. When you sit in the cockpit, you often sit with your feet tucked up underneath you or, when relaxing, you often lie on the seats or sprawl. You seldom sit 90 degrees to centerline. I compromised on *Starbuck*'s seats and made them 22 inches deep. Bill Clute trusted me on this dimension and it proved to be a good decision.

*Starbuck* has a layout designed for a couple to cruise with occasional guests. We have mirror-image quarter cabins and two heads; the aft one includes a shower stall. There is the typical big, wraparound Perry galley. *Starbuck*'s center-counter console is directly over the engine. Dennis did not like my banks of drawers in this console, so he substituted a large, cavernous, general-stowage area that I don't think was an improvement at all. It was top opening, chart-table style, and you had to clear it all out before you could get at anything stowed below. It was easier and cheaper to build, but to give Dennis his due, it probably made accessing the engine a lot easier.

The owner's cabin features a Pullman-style double to starboard, and big hanging lockers and a vanity to port. The owner's head is forward. Forward of the head area is a bathtub. (One of my favorite photos from this project during construction is Heather trying out the bathtub.) The fo'c's'le is big and includes a workbench. The interior was finished in white paint and teak trim and is light and airy. Heather did the beautiful varnishing job herself, earning a lot of respect from Dennis's work crew in the process. The Clutes have lived aboard for more than seven years and have always been happy with this layout. They would not think of moving ashore. Note that the transom swim step is precisely at the dock level where the Clutes kept *Starbuck*, making it very easy to get onboard when the boat was moored and the stern was snug up to the dock.

*Starbuck*'s rig is big with a beefy carbon spar built at Dencho and a masthead configuration sail plan. The mainsheet was intended to be double-ended so that you could adjust it from either side of the boat, but, for some strange reason, the boat ended up being rigged with two independent mainsheet systems. I always felt this was potentially danger-

## Two California Cruising Sleds

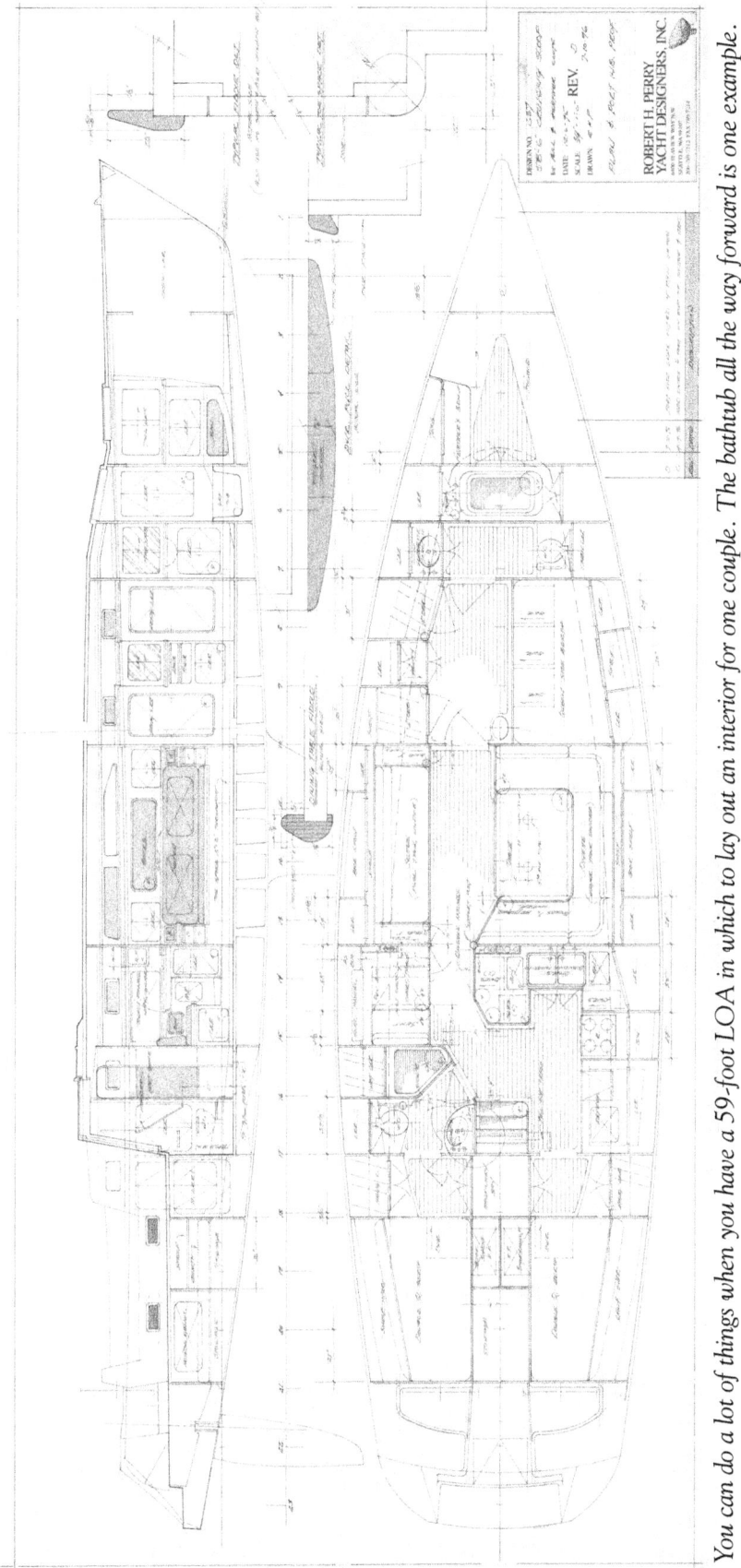

You can do a lot of things when you have a 59-foot LOA in which to lay out an interior for one couple. The bathtub all the way forward is one example.

ous, as you had two sheets to ease if you were knocked down. The working jib is 110 percent, and no overlapping genoas are carried. *Starbuck* is a fast boat and, when it was new, did 10 knots easily under power. There is a 100-gallon cruising fuel tank under the cockpit to allow *Starbuck* to motor upwind on the trip home from Mexico. A smaller fuel tank is located under the cabin sole for normal use.

Just about the time when *Starbuck*'s hull was finished, along came Denny Howarth. Denny had already had a very nice Alan Andrews design built for him at Dencho, and now he wanted a boat like *Starbuck*. *Foxfire* would be bigger, roomier, more comfortable, and faster than his current boat. Denny's experience with his previous boat had filled him full of ideas on the nature of the new boat. I suggested we save some money and use the Clutes' hull plug, but Denny had ideas of is own. He wanted a shorter and beamier boat, with an LOA of 56 feet and a beam of 15 feet, making for a yacht with a L/B of 3.73, still on the narrow side of moderate. The changes were subtle, and *Starbuck*'s hull would have worked, but it is always fun for the designer to get the chance to design a new hull. I appreciated Denny's unique approach.

The sectional shape of Denny's boat is similar to the Clute boat, but there is a little more rocker to deal with the same displacement as *Starbuck* on the new shorter DWL. *Foxfire*'s bow is almost identical to the Clutes' bow, and the stern overhang is about the same. I cut the transom off at less of an angle to capture some of the room on deck that I lost due to the shorter LOA. I gave Dennis a series of closely spaced, full-sized waterline bow patterns to help him get the bow just the way I wanted it. When I made my first visit to the yard to check the plug, the bow looked fine, but I noticed my roll of Mylar bow patterns over in the corner. I may be mistaken, but I'm fairly certain they had never been unrolled. No problem. Dennis has a very good eye and the bow was just what I wanted. *Foxfire* has a keel similar to that of *Starbuck*, and I didn't need coaching to get the rudder "right" this time. Both *Starbuck* and *Foxfire* share prismatics of .52, but *Foxfire* has a D/L of 114. Both boats have their LCBs at 54 percent and LCFs at 56 percent.

*Starbuck*'s cockpit was near ideal, and I knew I needed the same cockpit length in *Foxfire*. Denny would have nothing to do with my 22-inch-deep cockpit seats.

"Okay," I said one Friday. "But the next time you go out sailing, do me a favor and just watch how people sit in the cockpit."

The phone rang early Monday morning. It was Denny. "You're right. Make the cockpit seats 22 inches deep."

Denny was lucky. He had the Clutes' boat to use as his prototype right in the same yard, a mere 40 feet away. Denny wanted a hard dodger, and he also wanted his interior flipped with the galley to starboard instead of to port, like in *Starbuck*. There is a workroom to port instead of another guest cabin aft. You access the starboard quarter cabin through the aft head. Denny's navigation station is fore and aft with a pull-out chair. Denny has a shower stall in the forward head instead of a bathtub. The main cabin features a deep, sofalike settee to starboard. I always try to make one of the main saloon settees deep. It works better for lounging and makes a better, more comfortable sea berth. Denny, a contractor, did much of the interior finish work on *Foxfire* himself. It was fun to watch low-level competition develop between the *Starbuck* and *Foxfire* projects.

While *Starbuck* has a sail-drive unit, Denny wanted a traditional shaft-and-strut prop installation. He coupled this with a 100-horsepower Yanmar. As with *Starbuck*, the engine is located under the centerline galley counter that can be removed for access. It's really too much horsepower for a boat this size. Denny can hit 9.5 knots effortlessly at a comfortable cruising rpm, but applying more power only results in *Foxfire* pulling up a huge quarter wave. Cruisers today love big engines. The long, light, cruising sleds do very well under power. Their flat runs and light displacement don't let the hull dig much of a hole in the water, and they can easily achieve speed under power in excess of the standard 1.34 times the square root of the DWL.

*Foxfire* has a fractional rig with a big mainsail on a Leisure Furl boom. The day Denny and I went sailing together, the Leisure Furl boom proved its worth. The two of us had no problem at all handling the boat. Two things helped with this: electric winches and the fact that Denny had his Navtec vang sized precisely so that when the hydraulic pressure was released, the boom assumed the correct angle to the mast. This ensures that the mainsail rolls up evenly inside the boom. I've pushed this same idea at other clients who want Leisure Furl booms, but they just don't seem to see the wisdom and would

## Two California Cruising Sleds

Foxfire *came right after* Starbuck, *but it has a fractional rig, a hard dodger, windows in the hull, and a little less LOA.*

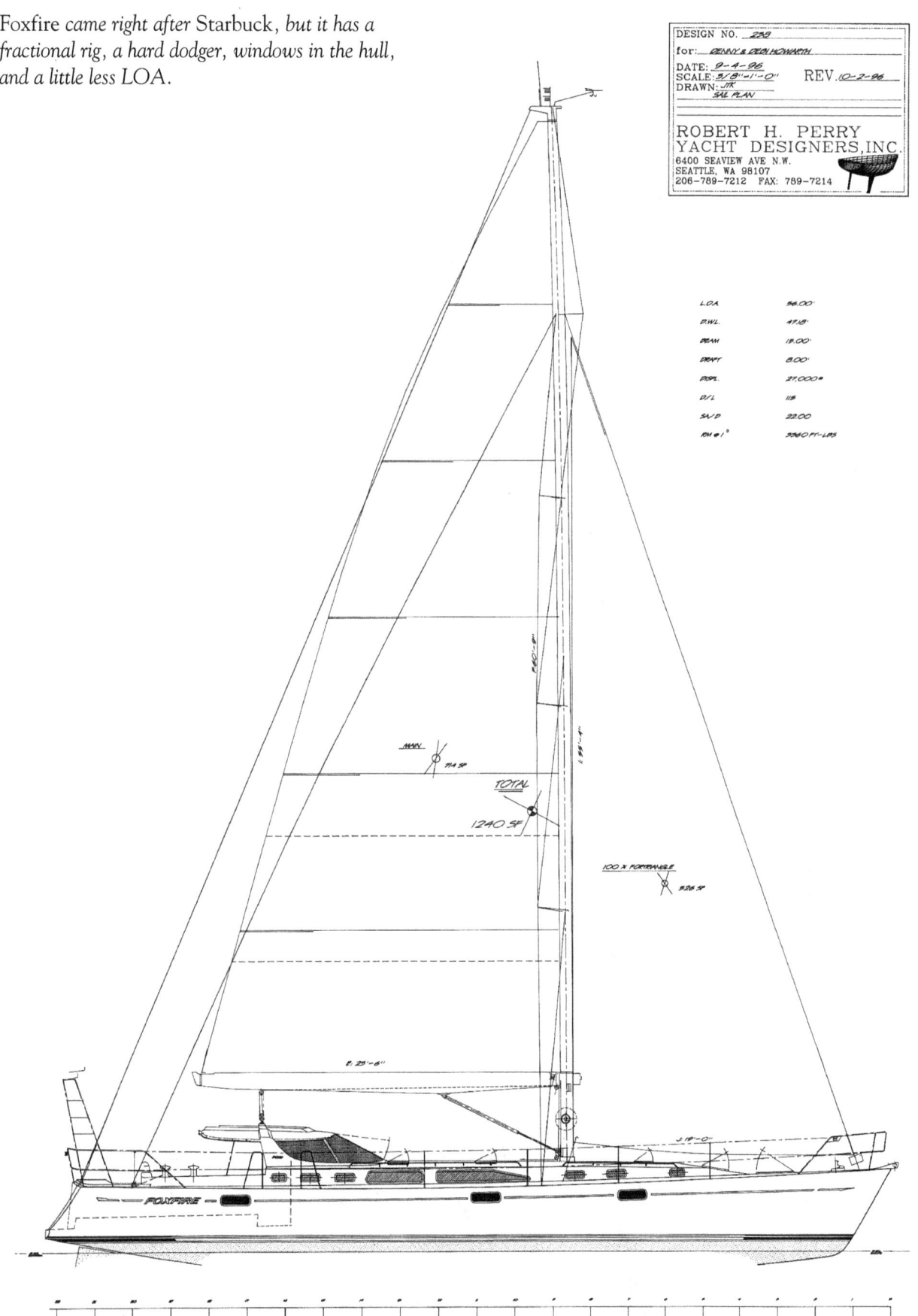

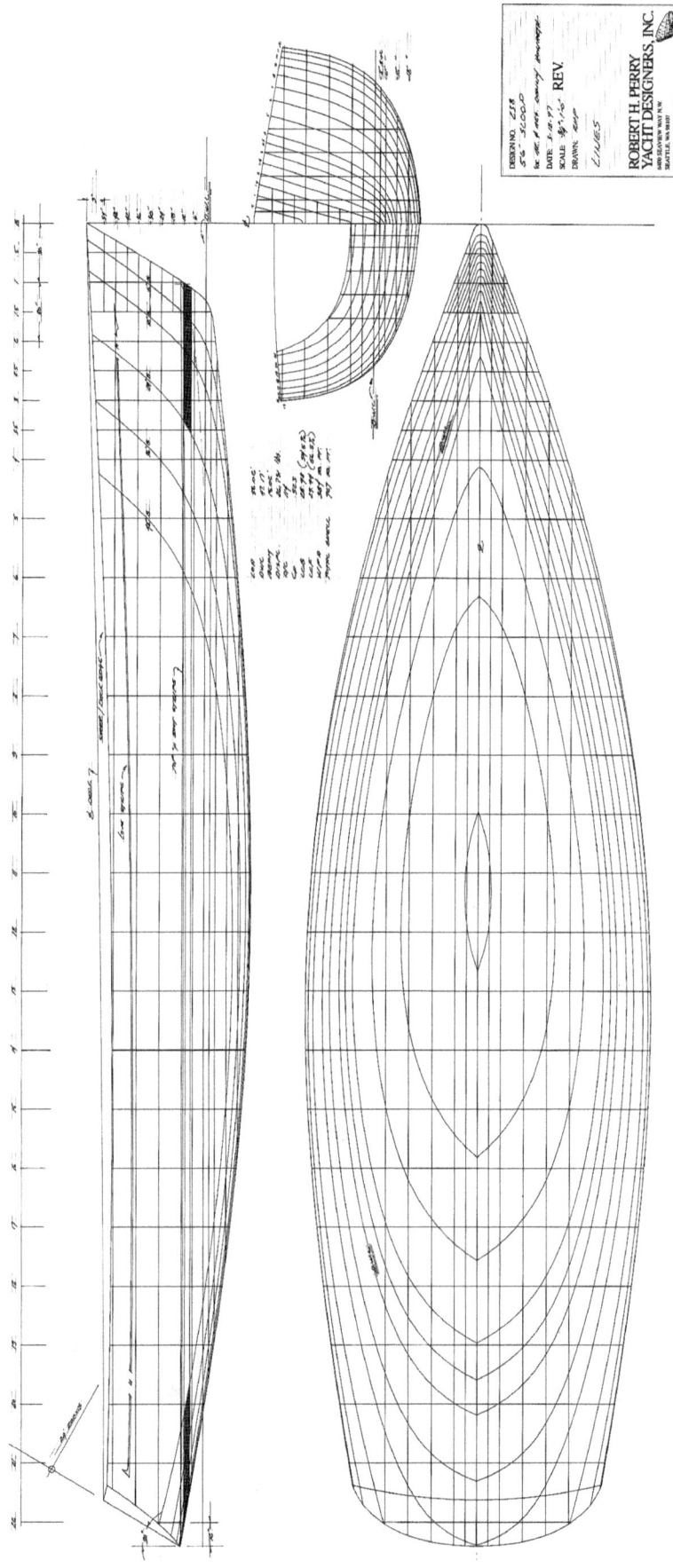

*With Starbuck behind me, I didn't need Dennis Choate's prodding to design a hull for Foxfire we both would like. This hull, too, is very clean and owes its overall proportions to no measurement rule.*

Foxfire *is an aggressive cruising boat but still "pure cruise," as shown in this photo taken by Denny.*

prefer to wrestle with less precise methods of getting the boom at the right angle. Denny got it right the first time. I think many cruisers are not confident with hydraulic vangs. If you want to maximize your boat's performance, a hydraulic vang and backstay adjuster are musts.

I spoke to Denny Howarth recently while preparing to write this chapter. I love it when a client says, "My boat has to be one of your very best designs." Denny loves cruising his big, fast boat. "I just blow by the other boats," he says. I wish he would race it from time to time, but Denny has given up racing. You can't miss *Foxfire* as you enter California's Oxnard Harbor.

I did two more nice boats with Dencho, a beautiful 75-foot power yacht for Mike Campbell, and a very modified version of an Alan Andrews 70-footer, *Elysium*, where we added beam and gave the boat a center-cockpit deck configuration. Then, suddenly, communication with Dennis Choate ceased. It puzzles me to this day.

The designer/builder relationship has to be almost intimate. It requires constant honest communication and the ability from both parties to bring their best to the project while respecting the ideas of the other. Over the time span of my Dencho projects, my relationship with Dennis began to approach the adversarial. When my son Max turned

*The Howarths taking shelter from the brutal Southern California weather behind their hard dodger.*

Foxfire *at rest looks like it can go very fast when pressed. I like the moderate overhangs. Note the Leisure Furl boom and skookum stem fitting.*

21, I asked Dennis Choate if he would build Max a surfboard. He did. It's beautiful and remains one of Max's most prized possessions. Bumps in the road aside, today I miss the fast pace of working with Dennis, the good Mexican food, and the friendly, combative exchange of ideas. But who knows, maybe we'll do another great boat one day.

## According to Perry
# THOUGHTS ON BOWS

Probably the most prominent feature of any design is its bow. Because the subject is so central, I'll consider it not just in this design essay but also in the next two, "According to Perry: More on Bows" and "According to Perry: Real-World Bow Evaluations."

In this and the next essay, I'll examine the aesthetics of bow shapes and how they enhance or detract from the overall look of a boat. Curves in one two-dimensional plane have to work in concert with curves in the other two-dimensional planes. If they do not, the resultant shape will appear forced and unnatural. Any such evaluation is highly subjective, but it's a topic that must be explored.

On the other hand, it makes little sense to consider aesthetics apart from function. Bows that work well will look good or should look good. Bows that do not work well should not look good. If they do, it's time to consider the trade-offs and look again.

As we discuss aesthetics, therefore, we will also be considering the seakeeping characteristics of various bow shapes—although I use the term *seakeeping* with some reservation. I don't think that a boat's seakeeping ability can be wholly determined by the first 15 percent of its length, assuming radical shapes are avoided, nor am I absolutely sure I could arrive at a universal definition of seakeeping.

Finally, in "According to Perry: Real-World Bow Evaluations," we'll use a sophisticated velocity-prediction program (VPP) to compare the impact of four bow shapes on a parent hull, measuring their contributions to performance in terms of speed through the water. I will at all times try to keep this complex and engaging subject as simple as possible. By the time you finish these essays, I hope we will have dispelled some myths and given you a good grasp on bows.

Curvaceous clipper bows festooned with gilt-trimmed trail boards look romantic, but try whacking off the part of the clipper bow that's not adding to sailing length and then weighing what you have cut off. Weight is the enemy. But hang on there, sometimes the entire goal of the design exercise is aesthetics. Sometimes a nostalgic look, not optimized velocity made good, is exactly what the designer is after. You say you want a pretty bow? Look at the work of L. Francis Herreshoff, whose graceful clipper bows are as lovely as they come.

When you look at a bow shape, ask yourself whether the objective of the shape is to take advantage of a mathematical feature in a race handicapping rule. Often the bows you see are artifacts of the way *measured length* (i.e., sailing length) is determined within various rating rules.

Consider, for example, boats from the mid-1970s and early '80s, when the International Offshore Rule (IOR) still ruled the racing scene. The IOR used predetermined girth lengths based on B max in the bow and stern to measure LBG, or length between girths, and LBG was the most important component of the formula used to determine L, which was intended to approximate the boat's sailing

# Yacht Design According to Perry

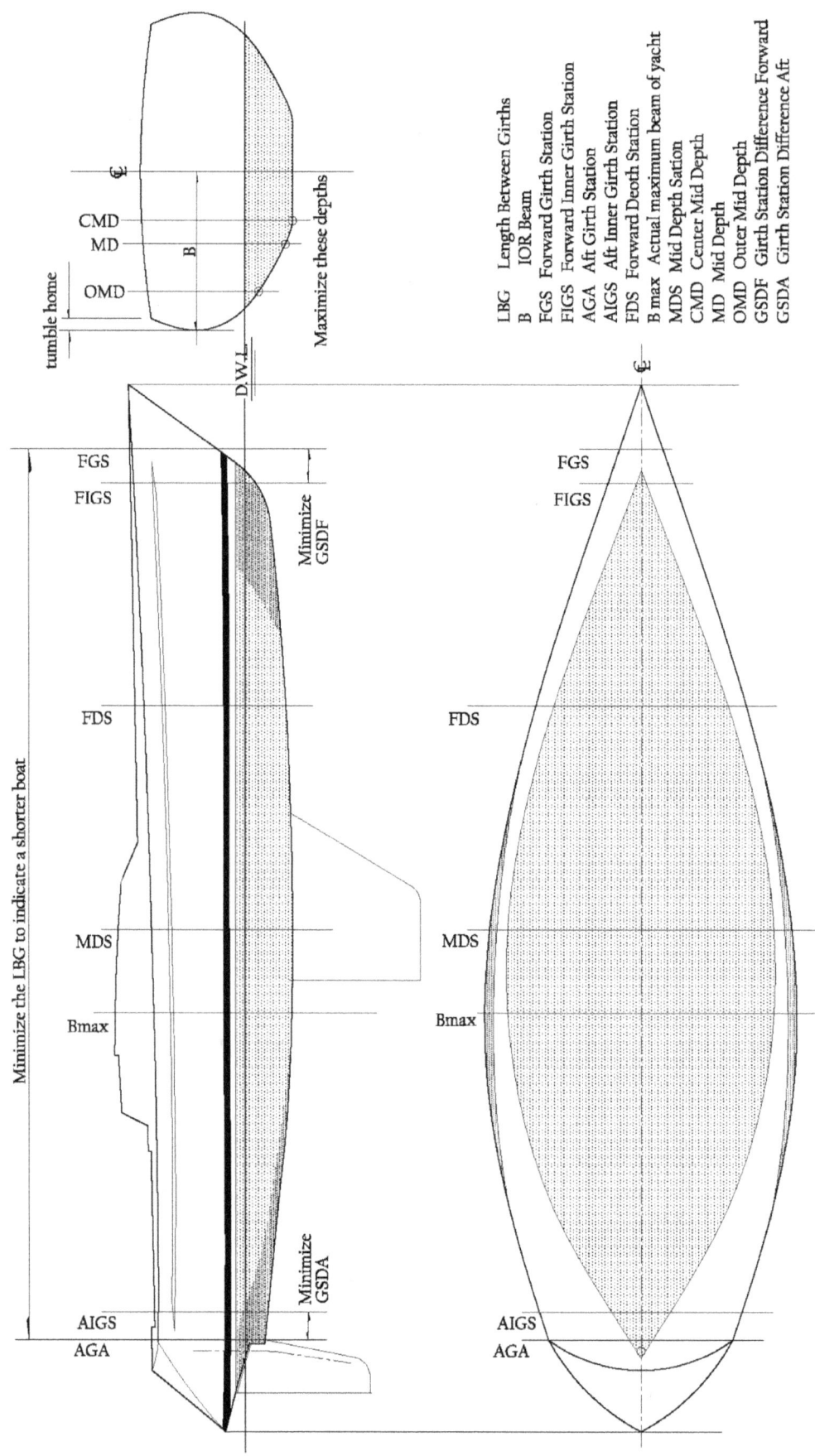

A classic IOR shape from the mid-1970s showing the locations of the major measurement stations and points. Note the flat-bottomed sectional shape inboard of CMD and the "pumpkin seed" waterplane.

length. This encouraged designers to reduce the actual girth measurements in both ends so as to reduce the measured LBG. The result was a dramatic shape effect, especially at the stern where lines were contorted in order to move the girths closer together.

The IOR bow showed no flare and very straight sides. There were two predetermined girth measurements forward, FGS and FIGS, and the closer together these two girth stations were spaced, the better it was for your rating. Much as closely spaced depth contours on a nautical chart indicate rapid shoaling, tightly compressed forward girth stations indicate to the rule that the front of the boat is dwindling rapidly to its forward terminus. This is why you see overhang on IOR bows—because it helped compress the two girth stations. Fine bows fared much better than full ones under the IOR. While the typical IOR bow may or may not be the perfect bow for a cruising boat, it certainly optimized boat speed while minimizing rated speed within the framework of the rule. In my opinion, the IOR bow may not have been far from the ideal. It's important to understand the basics of how the IOR worked, because this rule influenced almost all the production cruiser/racer shapes of the day.

More recently, America's Cup boats adopted the Davidson bow, drawn by Laurie Davidson and first seen on *Kiwi Magic* during the 2000 Cup competition. America's Cup boats have a single girth station in each end located where a waterline 200 millimeters (7.9 inches) above the flotation plane intersects the profile of the boat. The length of this 200-millimeter waterline becomes L in the rule and has huge impacts on all other aspects of the design. The job for an America's Cup designer is to maximize the potential sailing length of the boat while minimizing the measured L. The illustration on the next page shows that by introducing a knuckle in the bow profile, Davidson shaved precious inches off L while preserving the static DWL and theoretical hull speed.

When you watch an America's Cup boat throwing that big, characteristic radial spray pattern off its bow each time it hits a wave, maybe, like me, you ask yourself, "Isn't there a way to make that bow finer and give it a cleaner entry?" Yes, there is, and it was tried on a number of the older America's Cup boats. The long-overhang Peterson bow *sans* knuckle (named after California designer Doug Peterson) provided a clean entry, but it also picked up measured sailing length. The alternative approach—usually called the dinghy bow, and championed by the early Farr America's Cup designs—effectively cut the bow off with a plumb stem just forward of the girth station. This saved weight and provided a fine angle of entry to the topsides. It was fast in light air and flat water, but unfortunately it was slower in a chop. The additional volume forward allowed by a Davidson or Peterson bow just proved a faster all-around bow.

Perhaps this is because that additional volume forward extends the sailing length. You can think of this as "free length" under the America's Cup measuring rule. It is also generally acknowledged that the additional volume forward in the Peterson and Davidson bows reduced pitching in a chop. Most likely both of these concepts are true to some degree.

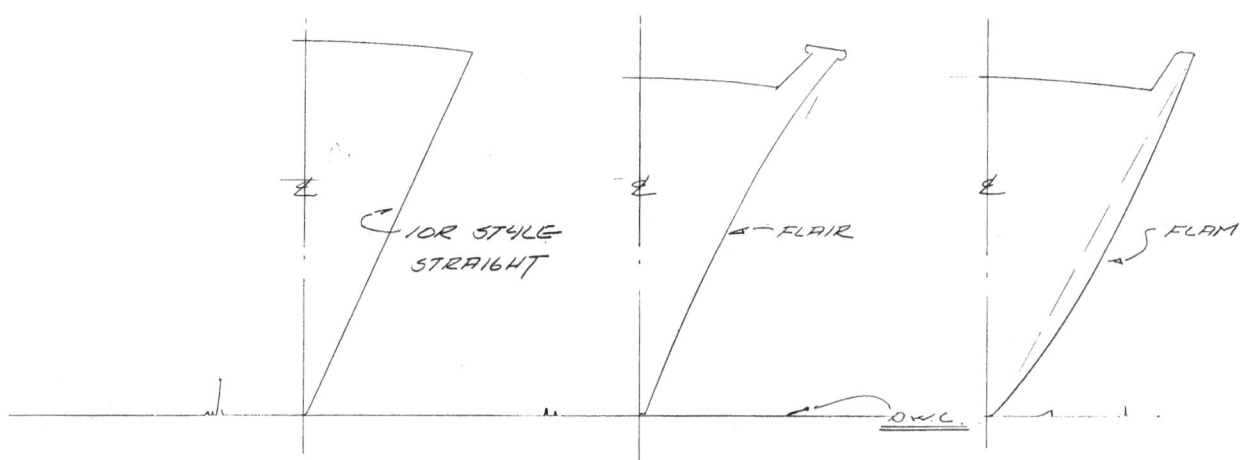

*A comparison of bow shapes at station 0, showing flare, flam, and the IOR-style straight-sided shape.*

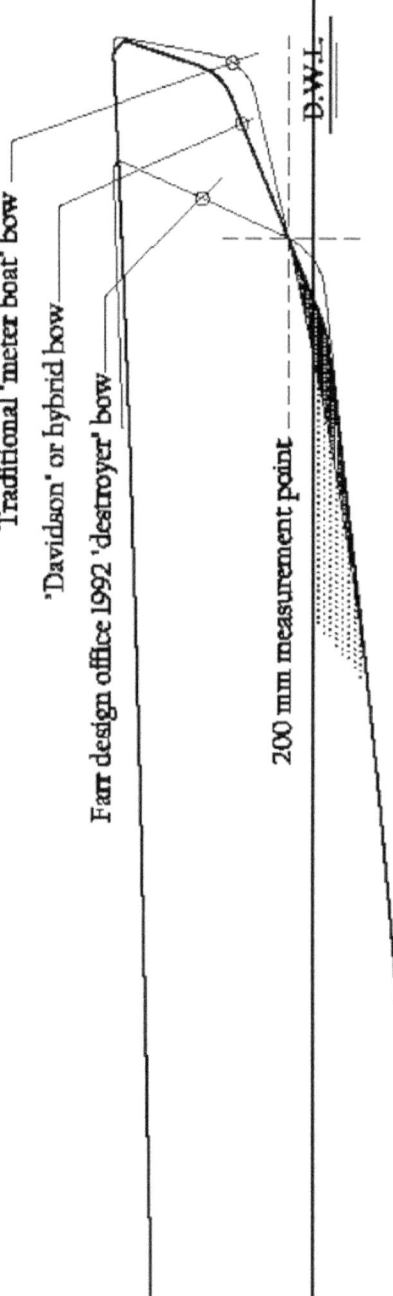

Bows do not always reflect the "shape of speed"—sometimes they are shaped by a rule. A contemporary America's Cup designer must decide how to deal with the bow measurement point 200 millimeters (7.9 inches) above the waterline; the choices made here will affect the distribution of volume forward. The Peterson bow (labeled here as the traditional meter boat bow) provided a clean entry at the cost of a higher sailing-length measurement. The Davidson bow avoids this with a second knuckle just below the waterline. The Farr destroyer or dinghy bow cuts the bow off plumb, improving speed in light air and flat water but slowing it in a chop. (Many thanks to the Farr design office for providing a drawing of their destroyer bow.)

At any rate, it has clearly worked; the influence of the Davidson bow can clearly be seen on all America's Cup class boats.

Keep in mind that if you were to remove all rule restrictions on forward girths, you could very well end up with scowlike bow sections, such as those seen on some of the later Cruising Club of America (CCA) boats. For example, have you ever studied the bow sections of a Cal 40 or a Bermuda 40? They are very full. The half angle of entry for the Cal 40, a speedster in its day, is 24 degrees. Clearly there was an effort to push volume forward in these designs so as to lengthen their effective sailing lengths. The problem is that they are just too full forward, presenting a big surface to oncoming waves. This slows them down on the wind and makes them less weatherly. America's Cup boats are extremely narrow, with a L/B around 6.5; therefore, they have no problem keeping the half angle of entry less than 13 degrees.

That's more than enough about bows for now. We'll resume this discussion in "According to Perry: More on Bows."

## Chapter Fifteen
# AMATI

I met Paul Scott at our local espresso stand. (Hey, it's Seattle.) He was singing an ad-libbed but well-composed counterpoint part to the piece on the shop's radio, so I asked, "Are you a musician?"

Paul told me he was a classical cellist and that his wife, Lorrie, was a classical pianist.

"Cool," I said. "Do you want to play some cowboy music some time?"

Paul said sure, and that was the start of our friendship. Then he realized that I was "that Bob Perry," and he told me he was a sailor. Paul and Lorrie had an Ultimate 20, a high-performance ultra-light-displacement (ULDB) design from Jim Antrim. When you got Paul and Lorrie, you also got Mac, their faithful West Highland white terrier.

Paul and I alternated our conversations between music and boats. Paul had a degree from Harvard in ethnomusicology and, in addition to being an accomplished cellist, was Seattle's premier piano technician. I'd throw music questions at Paul and he'd throw boat questions back. It was a good trade. The friendship flourished, aided by the fact that Paul and Lorrie lived three blocks from my Ballard house and they both liked my cooking.

Before long, Paul brought up the subject of a custom boat. His birthday was coming up, and Lorrie loves to indulge Paul. I'd never designed a boat for a personal friend before. I had become personal friends with a lot of my clients through the design/build process, but this would be a first where the friendship preceded the design process. I felt an obligation, in this case, to walk Paul and Lorrie carefully through all the potential pitfalls of a custom project. I was not very convincing, apparently, because they decided to proceed with the project.

Paul is a student of high-performance sailing craft. When he was younger he raced Finn dinghies and sailboards. He was intently aware of all the advances in yacht design, and this is what he wanted to drive his new cruising-boat project. This cruising boat certainly would not be your father's cruising boat. By most sailors' standards, the new boat, named *Amati* (after the famous cello maker), would look like a race boat. Yet Paul and Lorrie had no intention of racing the boat. Their idea of a perfect sail was to take their Ultimate 20 out in the summer evenings after work and leisurely sail around Puget Sound. In our area, this invariably means you will be sailing in very light air, around five to eight knots on most summer evenings. The new boat had to be fast in those conditions. It also had to be easy to handle, comfortable for two-week-long cruises, and safe for Mac.

Paul and Lorrie's interior requirements were modest, so I did not need much boat to solve that part of the equation. But there is nothing like LOA for boat speed, so I made *Amati* 40 feet on deck, with minimal bow overhang, and with a DWL of 35.6 feet. I cut the transom off plumb in order to maximize the deck area. Any rake to the transom would have reduced the LOD, and for cruising comfort and lazarette volume, I wanted as much as

# Amati

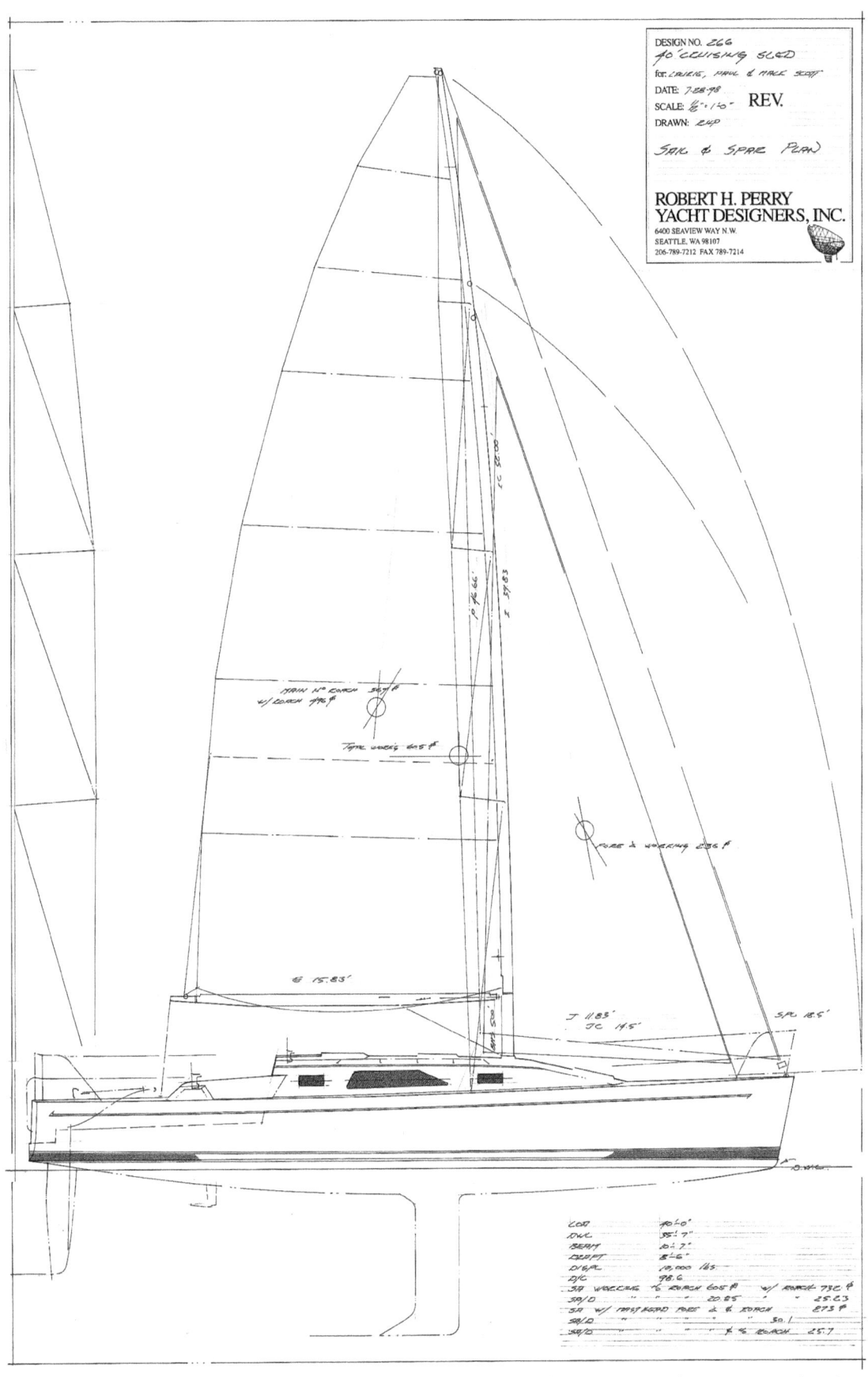

*The ultrasimple and clean Amati showing the keel with a slight forward rake. Paul and Lorrie wanted a "big dinghy," and that's what they got.*

# Yacht Design According to Perry

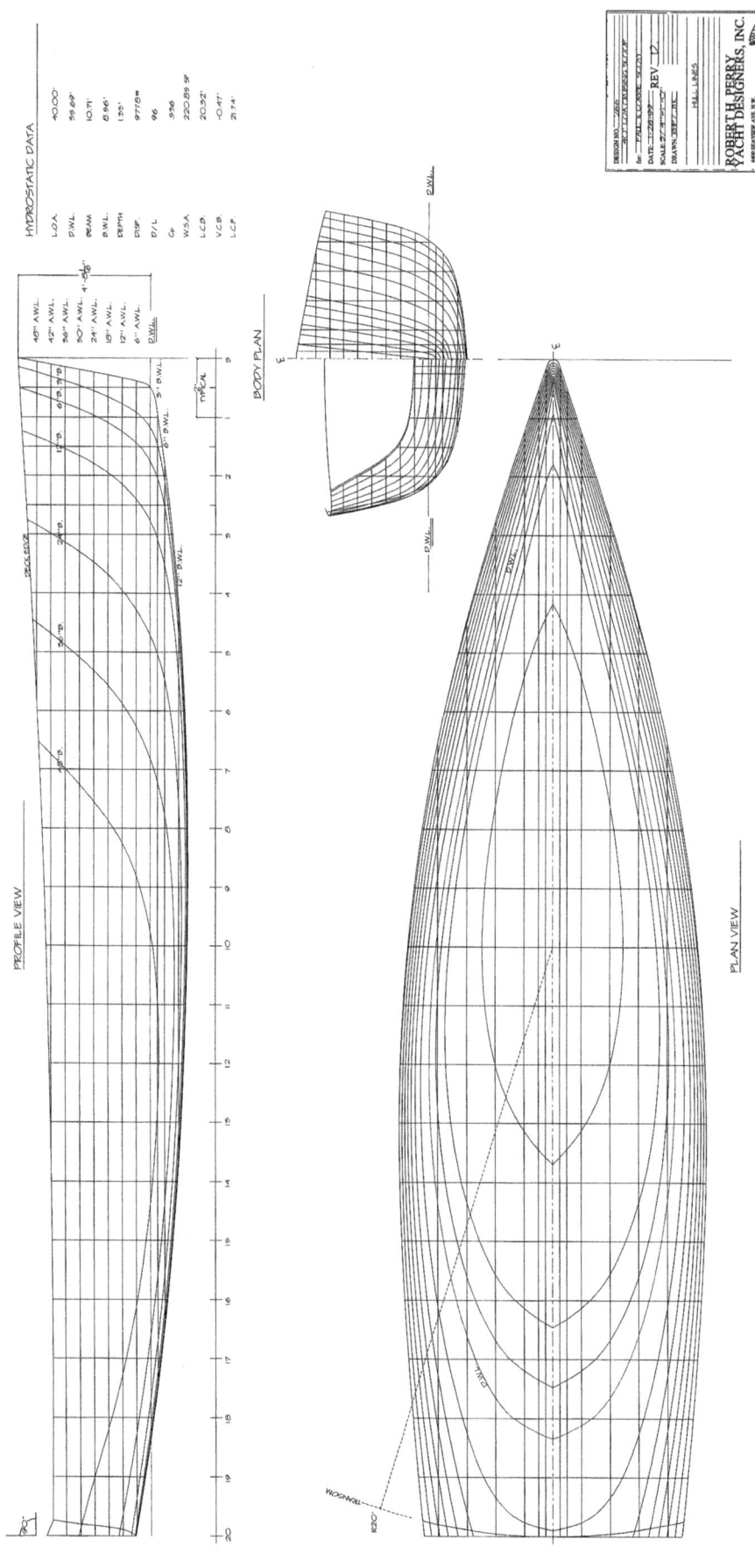

Amati's lines show low displacement with flat buttocks, broad stern, vertical transom, and minimal overhangs.

possible. It's interesting today, six years later, to note that many of the high-powered TransPac 52s also have plumb transoms. This feature may not be pretty but it does work.

I did not need beam for interior volume, so I kept the L/B to 3.73 with a 10.71-foot beam. I kept displacement low at 10,000 pounds in cruise condition for a D/L of less than 100. We don't have a draft problem in Seattle, so *Amati* draws 8.5 feet with a fin and bulb keel with a forward sweep on the fin of four degrees. We had just done the forward-sweeping keel for *Stealth Chicken* and were happy with its performance. *Amati* has a firm turn to the bilge to help with initial stability and give us the beam we need right at the interior settee level. There is a slight hollow to the entry and four degrees of deadrise running the length of the hull. I like deadrise in cruising boats because it makes for an easier bilge to drain to a sump pump. Flat bottoms do not work well when it comes to collecting bilge water in one spot. *Amati*'s prismatic is .536. *Amati*'s hull form could be characterized as a big dinghy. That's exactly what Paul wanted.

The rig is big for a cruising boat, with a SA/D of 22.46. The working jib is not self-tacking, but there is so little overlap to it that it's a breeze to tack anyway. If you remove the overlap of jibs, tacking them is easy; only genoas are hard to tack. I think there is too much preoccupation today with self-tacking jibs due to the fact that so many cruisers have sailed with big, overlapping genoas all their lives, and they do not know how easy it is to tack a 100 percent jib. *Amati* has a "fat head" mainsail with lots of roach. There are running backstays and check stays, but because we have strong sweep to the spreaders, the standing backstay is not needed most of the time. Therefore, it seldom interferes with the roach of the main. The mainsheet traveler bridges the cockpit well and puts the mainsheet right at the hand of the helmsman, dinghy style, just the way Paul likes it.

The cockpit is a long, narrow trough open to the transom. I chose the well width so that Paul and Lorrie could brace their feet to leeward when the boat heels. There are cockpit coamings forward for security for the crew and to provide a comfortable place to sit and read when on the hook. *Amati*'s cabin trunk is narrow and the side decks are broad. The engine is accessed through a hatch in the cockpit sole. The engine area is totally isolated from the rest of the boat. We have a Yanmar with a saildrive that drives *Amati* at almost eight knots. There is a small step in the cockpit sole at the transom at the specific height required so that Lorrie can sit there and drag her toes in the water while sailing. Paul thought this was important. Such details are what custom boats are all about.

The idea for *Amati*'s interior was to keep it simple. Paul and Lorrie needed a comfortable, large double berth, and the rest of it was left to me. What we ended up with was the layout of a 28-footer stretched out to 40 feet. Privacy is a non-issue with Paul and Lorrie. They would not be cruising with anyone else. Therefore, I stretched the head across the entire beam of the boat, and they walk through the head to get to the forward cabin with its large dressing area and big lockers. This makes for a spacious head, in a style that was common 40 years ago. The main cabin settees are long and deep for comfortable lounging.

The galley is where I had one of my all-time, very best ideas. The most expensive part of the galley to build is the icebox. Often, it's also the dirtiest place on the boat. Furthermore, cavernous, top-loading iceboxes are hard to load efficiently. Most of us can remember finding a sandwich from the last summer in the bottom of our icebox at some time.

I designed into *Amati* two slots that extended aft under the galley counter to each side of the companionway. These slots are sized exactly for two large Igloo coolers. The coolers slide in and out for access, can be taken home to clean, and can then be loaded for the next cruise. It may not qualify as an elegant solution, but it has worked very well for Paul and Lorrie. A complex refrigeration system was never a consideration for this design.

The saloon table drops down from a locker forward that holds wineglasses and bottles. The table is supported by wires from the overhead. This leaves the space below the table free of any obstructions. A subtle touch that I used in the main cabin was to angle the settee fronts back from the top. This provides for a more natural way of sitting and increases the available cabin sole area.

*Amati* was built by my good pal Steve Rander and his crew at Schooner Creek Boatworks in Portland, Oregon. Steve has had a lot of experience building light cruising boats, and his preferred method of building is wood-veneer skins over a foam core. For *Amati*, this meant 1/4-inch Port Orford cedar veneers and a layer of six-ounce unidirectional

# Yacht Design According to Perry

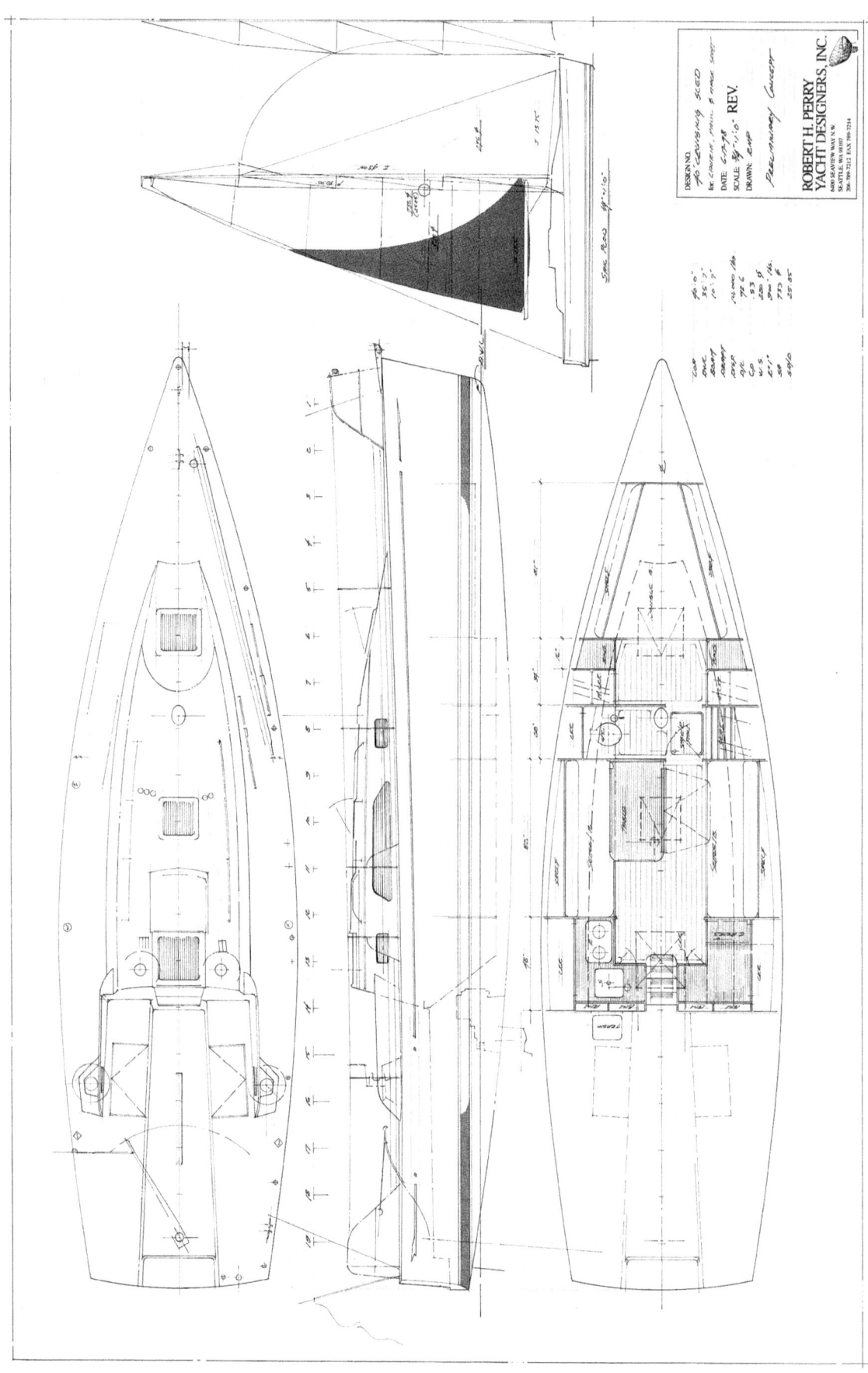

*This drawing shows how a design begins. This is a first-round preliminary sketch intended to identify the important components of the design before proceeding to working drawings. I take pride in the fact that I hit the target on this design early in the design process. The finished Amati is close to this sketch.*

# Amati

*Compare this Lorrie Scott photo of* Amati *clearing the locks in Seattle with the preliminary sketch.*

E-glass sandwiched around 3/4-inch Klegecell foam for the hull. The wood veneers are covered for protection with two layers of six-ounce E-glass cloth on the inside. The outermost skin has an additional layer of six-ounce unidirectional E-glass. At the launching party, the crew at Schooner Creek presented Paul with their custom-built, laminated mahogany and carbon-fiber tiller with the tiller end carved exactly like the head of a cello neck. This was a surprise to Paul but so fitting.

*Amati* is a rocket of a cruising boat. You can sail *Amati* fast very easily. You can reduce sail quickly and punch through heavy weather with a snug "masthead" rig with the head of the main at the jib hounds well supported by the runners. Paul and Lorrie like to cruise up to my beach office north of Seattle and tie up to my mooring. They can sit on my lawn and admire their boat. When we have the big Perry Rendezvous each summer, we get about 50 boats, and a lot of them are bigger and fancier than *Amati*, but *Amati* is the boat that sailors admire the most—they quickly recognize the wisdom in *Amati*'s priorities. *Amati* just looks and feels right.

## According to Perry
# MORE ON BOWS

Today there is a trend toward plumb or nearly plumb stems. There is certainly nothing new or unusual about this. The old Falmouth punts and Blackwater smacks in England had plumb stems, as did the English Channel cutters. These stems might seem to bear little in common with an overhanging IOR bow, yet they, too, were rule-induced in that a plumb stem minimized a boat's taxed value because LOA was reduced while volume was maintained. To our eye today, these bows look very traditional, and it's hard to think of them as rule-beaters.

Any "box-type" racing rule (i.e., any rule that specifies the box dimensions within which a boat must fit) or any other rule that fixes LOA will inevitably produce boats with plumb stems. Why is that inevitable? Because hull speed is a function of DWL. This means that anytime a rule measures sailing length by limiting overall length, the designer is going to make the DWL as close as possible to the LOA. To see the results in box-rule boats, look at International 14 dinghies, TransPac 52s, or Open 60s.

For the most part, however, the plumb stems of today's production cruiser/racer types are artifacts of the short-lived but influential IMS. The IMS was the first rule that tried to measure the entire shape of a hull, not just its dimensions at prescribed stations and points. To do this, the hull shape was digitized with the use of a black box and a "wand." Sailing length was then measured by a series of second-moment lengths at various heel angles to determine the potential benefits derived by immersing topsides and overhangs as the boat heeled. It was the way in which these second-moment lengths were weighted in the rule that encouraged the plumb stems seen today on many production models. Shapes developed for racing migrate to cruising boats because they work, because they simply look fast or stylish, or both.

While rules can have a huge effect on the shape of the bow of a cruising sailboat, there is also no getting around the fact that your hull speed will be approximately 1.34 times the square root of your DWL. The constant, 1.34, will vary depending upon a number of factors, for example L/B and prismatic coefficient, and can be as low as 1.1, but it seldom goes much above 1.34 in what is called displacement, or non-planing, hulls. Of course, almost any boat, if it is well trimmed and pushed hard in a strong breeze by a good skipper, can go faster than this theoretical hull speed, but for our calculations, 1.34 works. If you are after boat speed, therefore, you must maximize your DWL.

Theoretically, and discounting the effects of overhang, the greatest wave-making resistance a boat will experience is when the distance between the crests of the bow and stern waves is close to the DWL length. Overhangs, however, may allow a heeled boat to pick up sailing length as these overhangs are immersed. This is one reason why most sailors report speeds under sail in excess of theoretical hull speeds.

Clients usually come to a designer with an overall length in mind. They don't usually think about DWL unless they have a specific speed under power in mind. If I were to get a request for a medium D/L cruising boat that must do nine knots under power, I would know that I'll be looking for a DWL of around 46 feet. Then I could attach a pair of ends to this DWL and come up with an LOA. But this is unusual. Clients are generally LOA-oriented: "I want a 56-footer," they might say. I must then decide how much of that 56 feet will be consumed in overhangs, forward and aft. If the client is speed-hungry, I will be inclined to straighten the bow so as to add DWL forward.

In addition to adding boat speed through more DWL, a plumb stem confers another advantage for a cruiser working on a fixed LOA. Even if I hold the target displacement static—say 30,000 pounds for our hypothetical 56-footer—I can greatly increase the usable interior volume forward for accommodations if I add DWL forward. If I am working toward a target D/L rather than a target displacement, the advantage of added DWL is even greater, since it will mean that I can add displacement. The resultant plumb-stemmed 56-footer is a bigger boat than the raked-stem 56-footer. I will get more square feet of cabin sole forward and more beam up in the areas of the bunk flats and countertops. In short, I can get more interior into the plumb-stemmed boat even if I keep the original displacement. More volume forward will also dampen pitching.

Are there downsides to a plumb stem? You bet. A plumb-stemmed boat will generally have a finer bow with more nearly vertical topsides than a boat with overhang, and this will make it wetter. While a typical overhanging bow will provide a half-angle of entry of around 22+ degrees, the half-angle of entry on one of my conservative plumb-stemmed cruising boats is 17 degrees. While this fine entry does wonders for helping the hull cut effortlessly through the water, it provides little resistance to immersion. With almost-vertical topsides, it's easy to bury this bow in a seaway. That's why, in my Saga series of plumb-stemmed boats, I flared the plan view of the deck forward and introduced some concavity and beam into the bow sections in order to add volume forward.

If you want to see this concave, flared shape carried almost to an extreme, look at the bow of my Valiant 40 design (Chapter 3). This is probably the

*The Saga 48* Altair *under sail. A plumb stem requires a bowsprit for anchor handling.*

driest bow I have ever drawn. The downside is that it is not the most effective bow when you are driving to weather in a steep chop. As you add flare above the DWL to any bow, you increase the half angle of entry above the DWL. For pragmatic seakeeping considerations, the "fastest" bow may not be the most desirable. Wetness aside, I think it's always faster to go through waves than over them. Energy expended to prevent the bow from burying is energy lost to forward motion.

From a pragmatic perspective, the plumb stem has other drawbacks. A cruiser will need some way to get the anchor roller out and away from the stem to avoid banging up the topsides when the anchor is raised. I have designed bowsprits of various geometries to accomplish this, and they also make a nice place for the tack of an asymmetric spinnaker and for a well-thought-out, dual-anchor roller system. However, they are expensive, can be heavy, and are often unattractive. This begs the question, "Then why not just eliminate the bowsprit and extend the bow out to do the same job?" There are certainly advantages to this. A dry bow is one advantage, as is the additional deck area you gain at the bow.

The answer is complex and mostly subjective. The client may be LOA-oriented and may not see the bowsprit as LOA, so I can effectively, with a bowsprit, give him a 61-foot boat with a length on deck of 56 feet. Then, too, extending the bow with overhang will change the entire look of the boat. A plumb stem is a strong styling element. It gives a boat a purposeful, pugnacious look, and this aesthetic influence will be felt in the entire look of the boat. An overhanging bow gives a boat a more delicate, classic look, and that may not be what the client is after.

I recently went through this exercise with a client, and after evaluating both bow types, he went back to the plumb stem because it gave him the look he wanted. Ironically, a raked stem without a bowsprit can be lighter and less expensive than a complex, welded, stainless-steel bowsprit with bobstay and bobstay tang. Racing boats do not have to deal with the weight and complexity issues of welded bowsprits, as they usually avoid serious ground-tackle components and resort to internally stowable carbon-fiber, pole-type bowsprits for the tacks of their asymmetric chutes.

## Chapter Sixteen
# THREE CRUISING SLEDS: *WHITE EAGLE*, *MOBISLE*, AND *ICON*

I knew the name Tullus Gordon. I'd read it on the side of a building near my office for years: Tullus Gordon Construction Company. Mr. Gordon—Tully—called me one afternoon and said that he was interested in building a custom boat. We scheduled a meeting and got together to talk about cruising boats. Tully wanted a big, fast, 60-foot cruising boat. Tully had done a lot of racing in the 1960s and had also been a commercial fisherman. He knew boats and he thought he knew what he wanted.

I showed him *Stealth Chicken*. It was close to what Tully had in mind, so we called Bruce Anderson, *Chicken*'s owner, and we arranged for Tully to fly down and take a sail on the boat. Tully got lucky, as Bruce invited Tully to crew on the boat in the upcoming Ensenada race. Tully accepted the invitation and, while I waited anxiously, off he went. Upon returning to Seattle, Tully came by the office and was ecstatic. He had loved *Stealth Chicken* and particularly enjoyed steering the boat when charging along at more than 15 knots. We discussed the options, and it was decided to go ahead on a design for a new boat based upon the concept of *Chicken*.

We would stretch the boat to 61 feet LOA, keep the beam modest, and add a hard dodger for protection from Seattle's rain. The primary issue for Tully, who is 6'3", was headroom. His oldest son is 6'5" and his younger son is closer to 6'7". I would have a target minimum headroom of 6'9" in this design. This meant that I had to raise the freeboard so that the height of the house was in proportion to the freeboard of the hull. I couldn't just raise the house height six inches. That would have looked odd.

I started with *Chicken*'s hull and added the freeboard I needed. I kept beam at 16.04 feet for a L/B of 3.81, and I gave the bow slightly more rake. The forefoot knuckle was just above the DWL, and there was a slight amount of deadrise at the transom. I had a D/L of 91.7 on a light ship displacement of 30,099 pounds. Ready to cruise, I figured a displacement of 34,000 pounds. The prismatic was right in the middle at .547. The LCF was at 56.8 percent and the LCB at 55.2 percent of the DWL. The keel fin was an aluminum weldment with an external lead bulb weighing 9,417 pounds. The fin would double as a fuel tank. Tully's boat, *White Eagle*, would be just what he was after: a big, fast, cruising boat.

But cruising boats are generally designed around their accommodations. In this case, we worked forward from the cockpit layout. I used a twin-wheel layout to open up the cockpit to the swim step. In order to reduce the height of the hard dodger, I sunk the forward end of the cockpit sole down one step and extended the hard dodger well aft over the seats. This feature worked out extremely well. This was a big, two-level cockpit that would never feel cramped.

Down below, I chose to go with a bigger standard of minimal acceptable tolerances so that the boat would feel spacious to the taller-than-normal Gordon clan. There were twin staterooms aft, but we dedicated the port quarter stateroom to a workshop that had full access to the engine under the cockpit

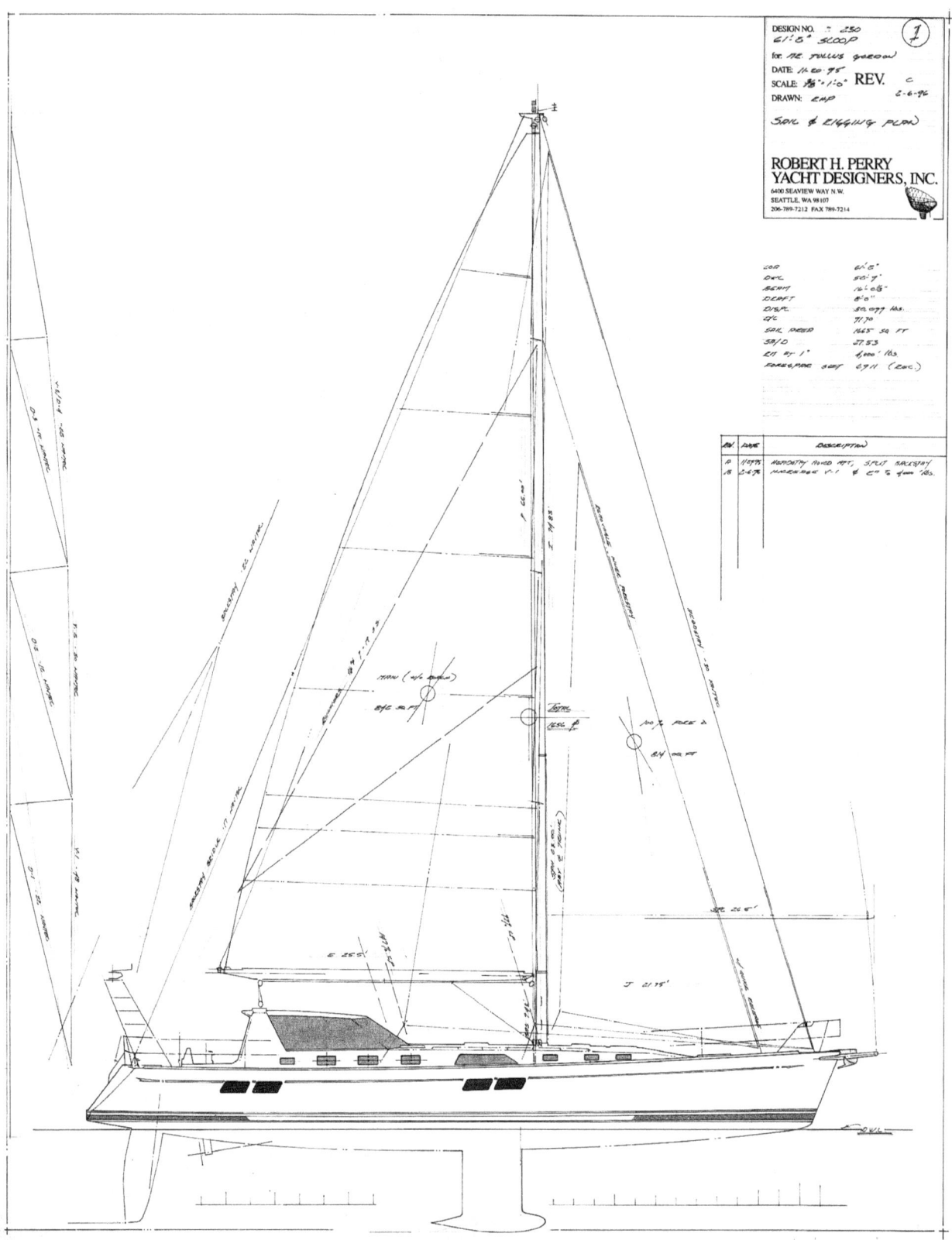

White Eagle, *one of my all-time favorite designs, was a development of* Stealth Chicken.

## Three Cruising Sleds

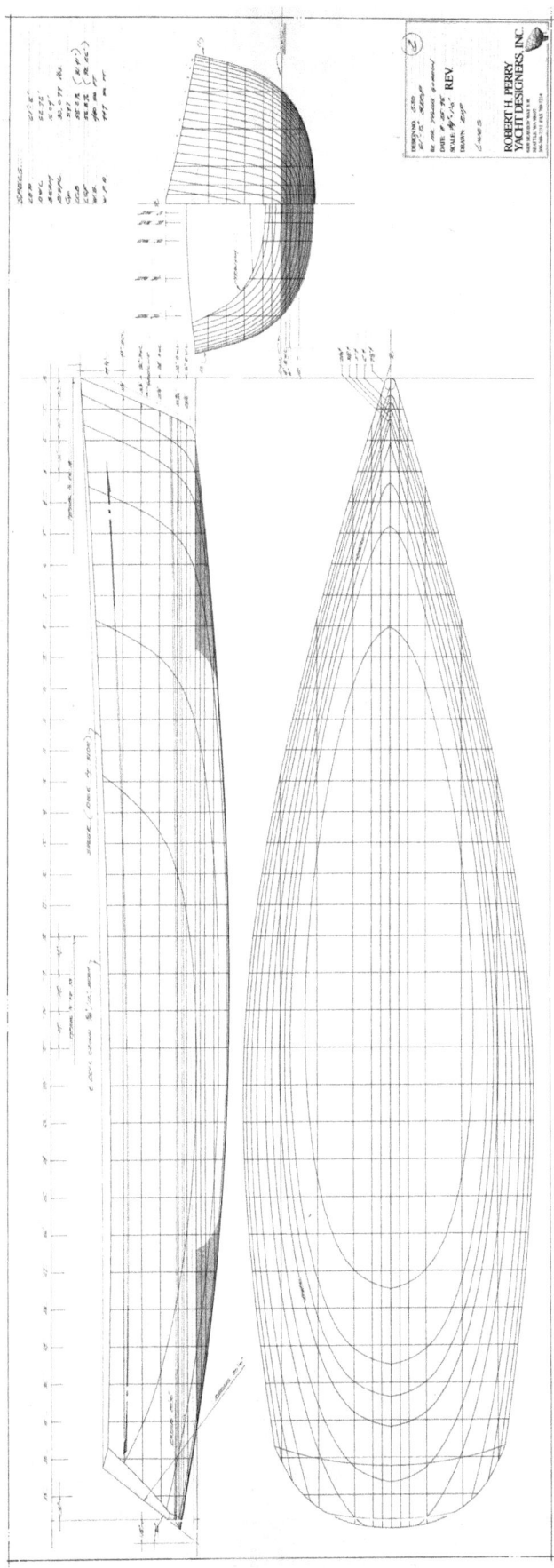

White Eagle's lines are similar to Stealth Chicken's, but with more freeboard, a slightly finer bow, and a little more overhang forward.

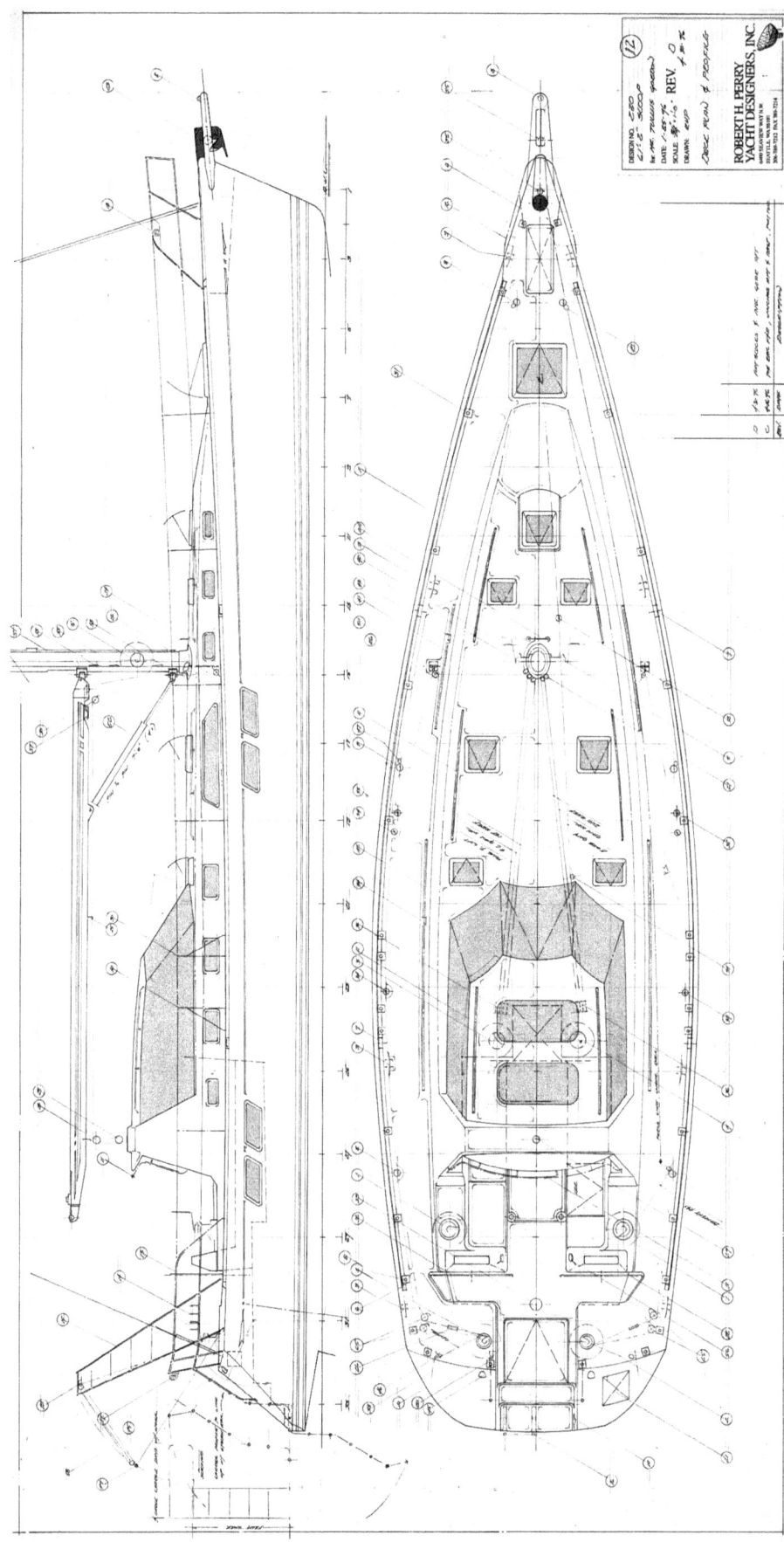

*Tully would often sit by my side for hours while I hand drew the details for White Eagle, and the result was drawings that I am proud of today. This is perhaps the best cockpit I ever designed.*

## Three Cruising Sleds

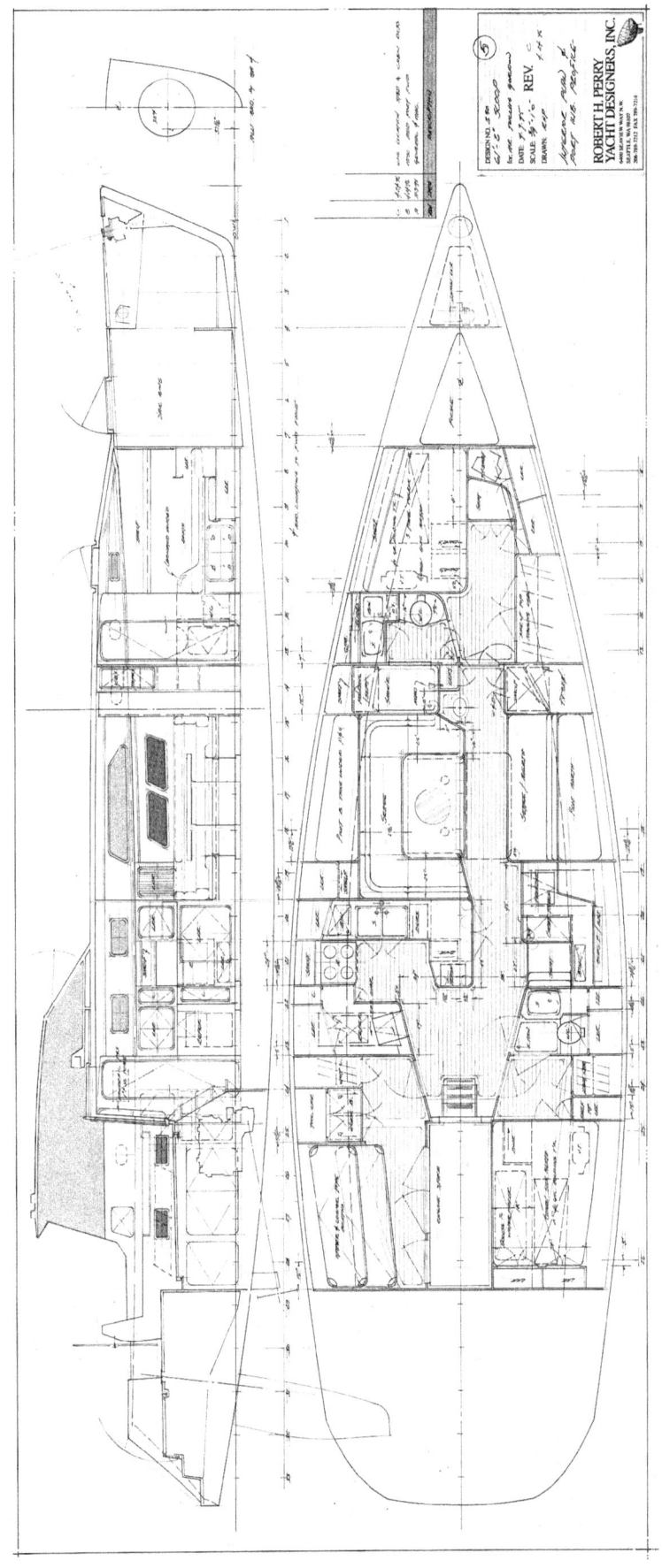

White Eagle's layout was organized around the ergonomic requirements of a crew—Tully and his sons—taller than 6 feet, 5 inches. All the spaces are generous, including my signature huge galley.

White Eagle *moored in front of my house. I look at my own work with a critical eye, but I can't see a single thing I would change on this boat. OK, maybe that stern arch. And maybe that sail cover.*

sole. The starboard stateroom had direct access to the aft head.

The galley was big; as it must be clear by now, that's just the way I do them. It wrapped around the cook and had a centerline leg that was all stowage and drawers. The 8'9" dinette was huge. Opposite the dinette, there was a deep settee. Pilot berths for the grandchildren flanked the dinette and settee. The navigation station was also big. Actually, everything was big in this layout. You could go below and the boat would just open to you and feel right. You weren't really aware of the headroom, but you felt like you were in a spacious interior. Well, okay, I admit it: The owner's stateroom forward was less than spacious. But it was adequate, with a 6'9" berth like all the other berths in the boat. Still, it was the one space on board that felt tight to me. I suspect that's because there was so much elbow room in the rest of the layout.

The rig was tall and also based upon *Chicken's* rig. It was a masthead type with a provision for a staysail to be used in heavy air. I designed the rig tall so that it could be sailed with a 100 percent jib most of the time. Tully bought a genoa, but I prefer sailing the boat with the non-overlapping jib. It's just a lot easier and you go just about as fast when the wind stays over eight knots. The SA/D was 27.53, and that was more than enough for any cruising boat. Primary, main halyard winches, and winches for the double-ended mainsheet were electric.

Tully and I investigated several yards before choosing Jim Betts's yard in Truckee, California. Jim wanted to build the hull in aluminum and use a composite foam-and-carbon sandwich for the deck. I liked this idea. It gave us the strength of aluminum where we wanted it along with a very lightweight deck structure. This was a combination that Jim had used on several boats and it was his preferred way of building. Jim's a genius with shaping aluminum, a true artist. The hull and deck of *White Eagle* are beautiful. Jim took a five-foot piece of aluminum mast section, split it down the middle, and tapered it and welded it into the bow sections to serve as a short bowsprit on which to tack the asymmetrical chute. We incorporated the anchor rollers into this tapered sprit and it looks great.

Unfortunately, Jim was not as good at the interior of a cruising boat. Jim came from the world of racing yachts and he was just not used to the complexity of accommodations and systems in a modern cruising boat. Soon Jim and Tully were at each other and the contract was being questioned. I made several trips to Truckee to act as "referee," but to no avail. Tully soon realized that the only way to complete the project was to move to Truckee, rent an apartment, and work daily in the boatyard. It was not a happy time for anyone involved. Eventually the boat was finished, and now she lives happily, floating merrily on her designed lines in Seattle. *White Eagle* is a gas to sail. It's powerful and quick and will get you up Puget Sound in no time.

Building difficulties aside, I have fond memories of this project. Tully was fun to work with and would spend a lot of time in the office just watching me draw. I got this commission when work was slow and I needed a project. I did 95 percent of the drawings myself, by hand. Only the hull and appendages were drawn on the computer. I was so proud of this boat that for the first three months of its life in Seattle, I would show up every Saturday morning and wash the boat down myself. Tully liked that. *White Eagle* was moored in a prominent spot at Shilshole Bay Marina, and I wanted it to sparkle. Tully had a decal made for the side of the dodger that read "Perry 61." I liked that.

I met Dave Rutter when he was considering a 52-foot project with which I was involved. My job was to

## Three Cruising Sleds

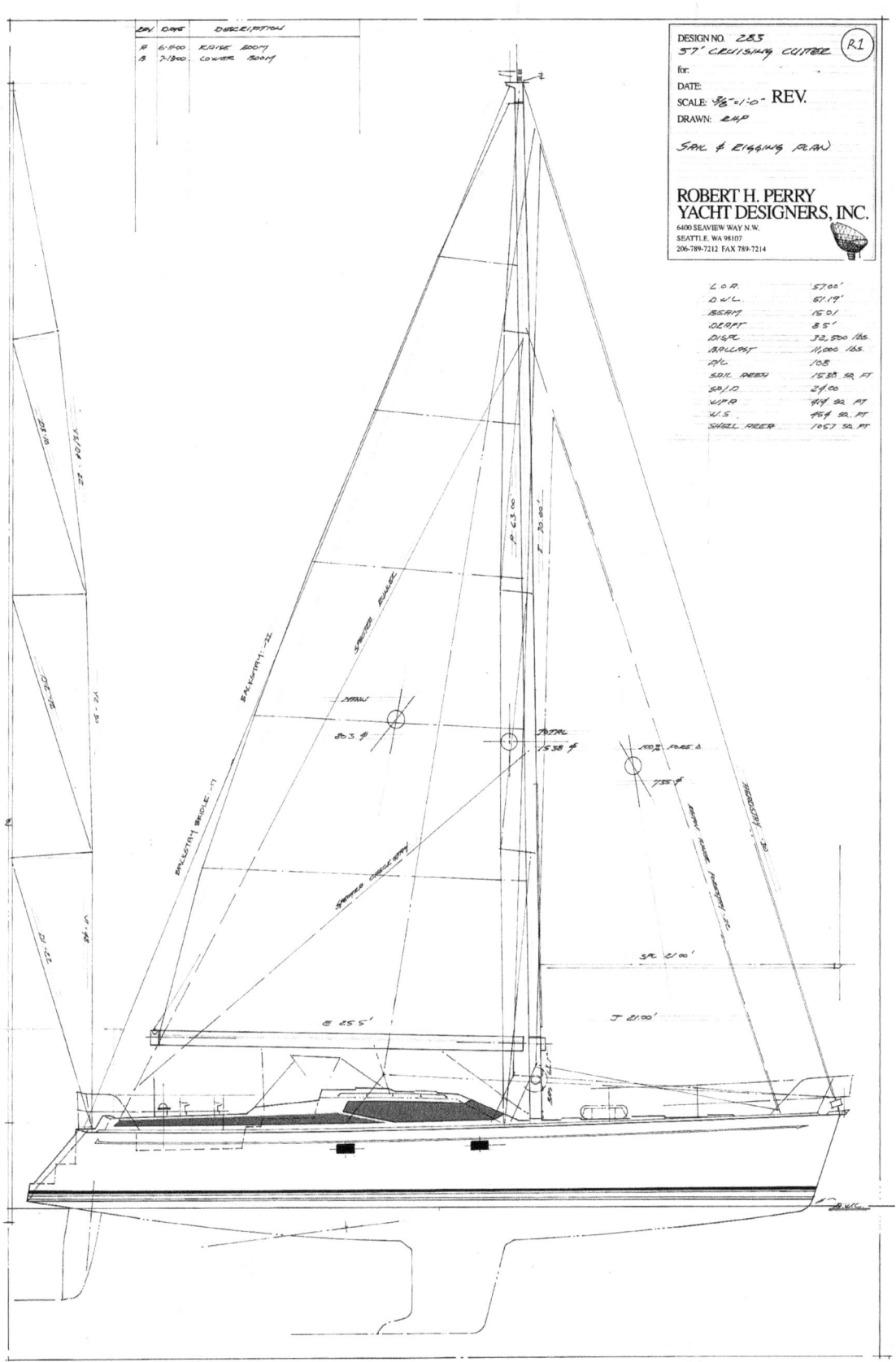

Mobisle is a couple's cruising boat with an aggressive rig for good light-air performance. I like the clean, stretched-out look of this design. I worked hard to get the E dimension reduced, but Dave wanted off-the-wind power.

# Yacht Design According to Perry

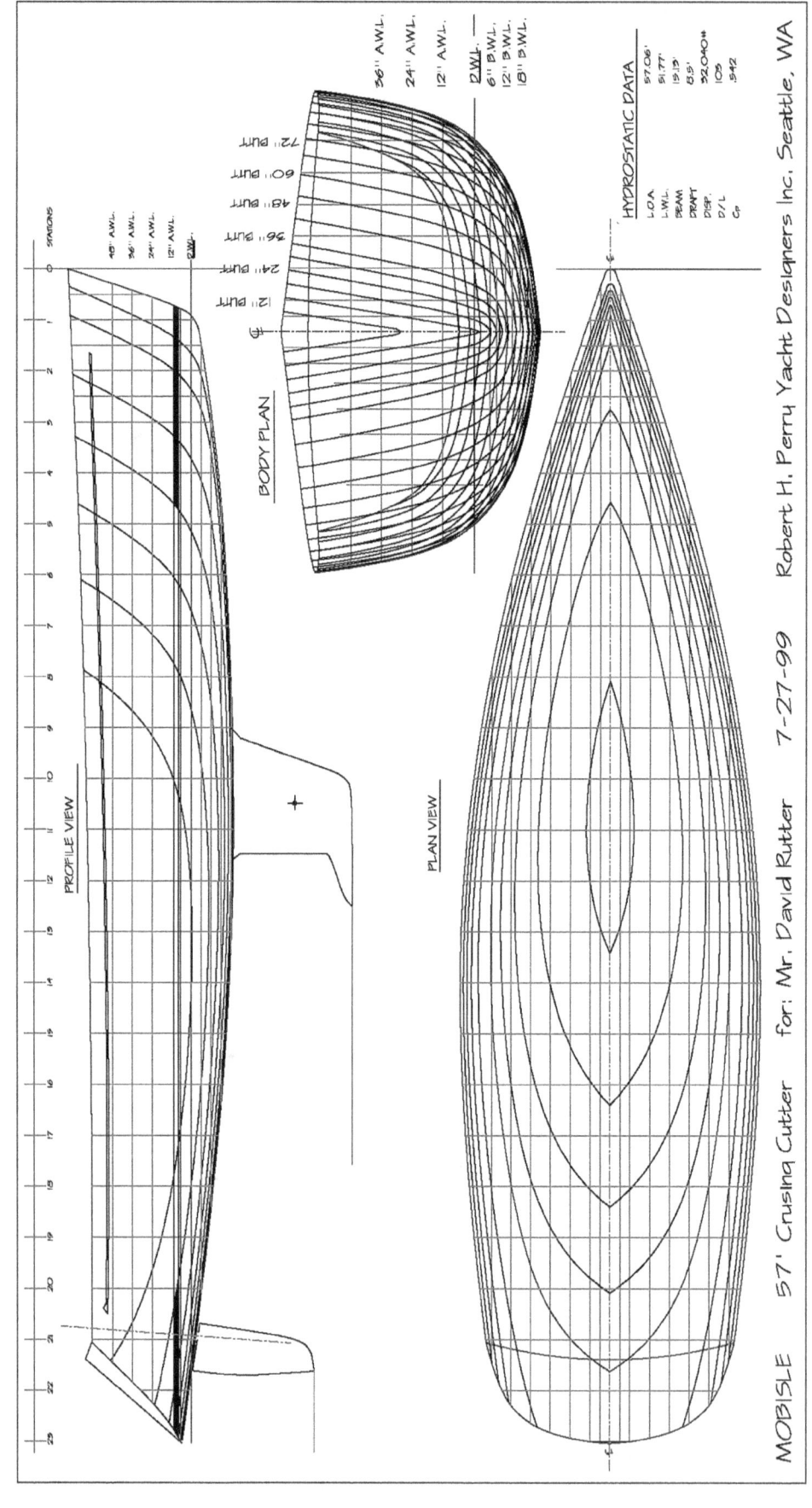

MOBISLE  57' Cruising Cutter  for: Mr. David Rutter  7-27-99  Robert H. Perry Yacht Designers Inc, Seattle, WA

Mobisle's lines are a development of Starbuck and Foxfire, with more deadrise, more BWL, and less bow overhang. I really like this hull.

redesign an older S&S design to make it more marketable. This is never a fun job. However, the 52 was classic S&S, and it was well built and seemed to me to be the right boat for Dave and his wife, Gay—but not to Dave. Dave always felt that there was something not right with the boat. He put the brakes on the 52 project and announced that he thought he should do a custom boat. Now you're talking, Dave.

Dave wanted a bigger boat with more room so that he and Gay could live aboard and do some extended cruising. The problem for me was that while Dave and Gay had done some chartering, they had never owned a boat before and their sailing experiences were limited.

Dave was an intelligent guy—intelligent enough to be retiring at a very early age—and he knew what he wanted. Owners like Dave, who may start on the steep side of the learning curve, oftentimes devote themselves to acquiring knowledge and they move up the curve quickly. I decided with Dave that the right boat for him would be a development of my *Starbuck* design that I'd done for Bill and Heather Clute. Both couples had similar requirements in a boat, and *Starbuck* had proven to be a highly successful design.

Dave wanted a boat designed for just a couple. There would be no concessions for a crew or guest accommodations. He also wanted a boat with a flush deck forward, so I gave the boat enough freeboard to get the headroom I needed for his 6'3" frame. I raised a small house aft so that we could get some windows in the boat and let in some light and air. The boat was named *Mobisle*. (Dave came from the mobile phone industry.) We chose Westerly Marine, the builder of both Chickens, to build the boat.

*Mobisle* has a layout designed around the owner's stateroom aft and the large workshop forward. If Dave and Gay have guests aboard, they sleep in the workshop with its upper and lower berths. There is a large head forward to port and a shower stall to starboard. There is another head aft, accessed from the owner's cabin. The galley is big, and the reefer unit is on the port side, while the rest of the galley is to starboard. The dinette is small, although comfortably big enough for two. This bothered me when I was designing the boat, but it's just what Dave wanted. I think, foot for foot, *Mobisle* has more locker space than any other boat I have designed.

The hull form of *Mobisle* shows a much firmer turn to the bilge than that of *White Eagle*. I asked Dave early on in the project if he wanted deadrise to the hull, and he said he did. When Dave and I visited the yard for the first time together, and Dave saw the hull upside down, he remarked that he didn't realize that the bottom would be V-ed.

I said, "You told me you wanted deadrise, Dave."
"What's deadrise?" he asked.

I explained that boats like his needed deadrise to provide a natural bilge sump. *Mobisle* has a D/L of 107 and a L/B of 3.8. The keel and rudder are similar to those of *Starbuck*—the keel is an all-lead, swept fin with a bulb tip. *Mobisle* is a true cruising sled, designed to go fast with the emphasis on off-the-wind speed.

*Mobisle* has a big rig. I think, given Dave's experience, the rig is probably too big and too demanding, but try as I might, Dave wouldn't let me shorten it. After the boat was launched and sea-trialed, I wanted to take 24 inches off the foot of the main to make the boat more forgiving to balance. Of course, that would reduce off-the-wind horsepower, and Dave would not agree to the change. *Mobisle* is rigged with a staysail for heavy air.

Today, *Mobisle* has a lot of miles under her keel. Dave called me from New Zealand after crossing the Pacific, en route to more adventures up the coast of Australia. He was having trouble with his Leisure Furl. I had a trip to New Zealand scheduled, so while I was there, I stopped in to see Dave. *Mobisle* looked pristine—beautiful. Dave was in good shape, too. It made me feel good to know that *Mobisle* had taken Dave so far, so safely.

In 2000, Dick Robbins already had a great boat. He owned the restored, S&S-designed, Palmer Johnson–built *Charisma*. It's hard to imagine a more beautiful or better-kept boat. *Charisma* was a heavy IOR design with a very short rig, tiny cockpit, and a very good PHRF rating. It's also hard to imagine a boat more opposite to *Charisma* than the boat Dick would ask me to design for him next.

Dick Robbins is an energetic fellow who could spend his time in front of the fire playing his classical guitar, but Dick is also a bit of an adventurer. He comes out of a manufacturing background that brought him to the top of his field in the world. Dick built tunneling equipment; he dug the Chunnel, so

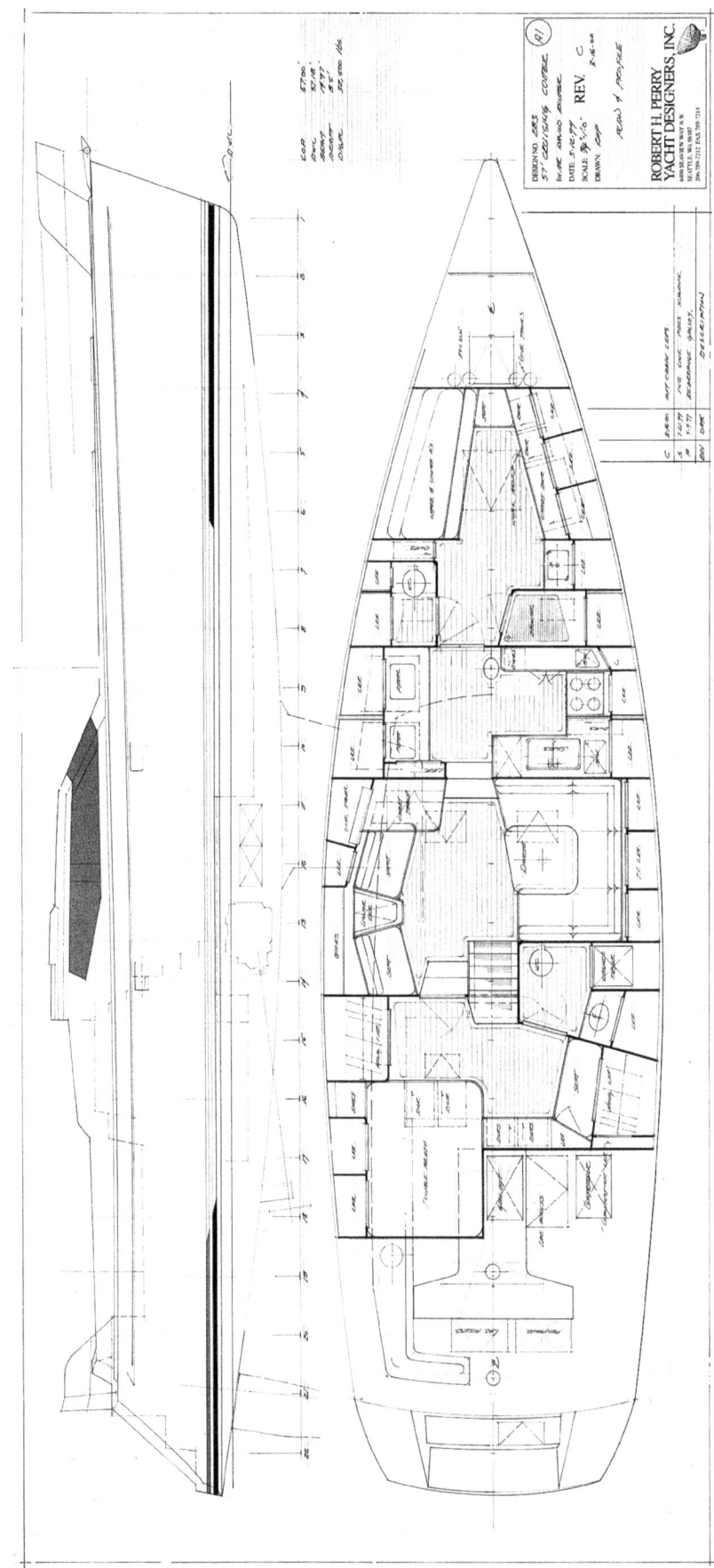

*Mobisle's interior was designed to accommodate Dave and Gay, with little regard to potential guests. Note the huge workshop in the fo'c's'le and the small dinette.*

Mobisle *under sail*.

to speak. Dick also had a dedicated crew that had campaigned Charisma on the West Coast, earning more than their fair share of wins. This group included Charisma's paid captain, Jim Roser, and sailmaker Doug Christie. Jim and Doug were pushing for a new boat and Dick liked the idea. I can thank Doug and Jim for pushing Dick my way.

The new boat, Icon, would be the ultimate cruising sled. Icon would be cruised all over the Pacific and would race in the premier races on the West Coast.

"We want a boat we can race in Puget Sound, so we need light-air boat speed," said Jim Roser. "We also want to race the legendary heavy-air Sydney–Hobart race. Oh yeah, and we want a boat that a couple in their 60s can cruise comfortably."

"I can do that," I said.

We began the hull design by looking at water ballast to help with stability. We knew the boat would be very light—27,700 pounds light—so we knew we needed to get some stability from somewhere. We quickly found that the tanks for water ballast would interfere with the interior layout Dick wanted. Icon would be a very narrow boat, with a L/B of 4.43, but water ballast works best when you have a beamy boat so that you can get that ballast well out to weather for righting moment. We chose to go with a lifting keel: with the keel up, draft would be 8.67 feet, and with the keel down, it would be 13.67 feet. The bulb was lead, and the fin was forged stainless steel. The keel was gunbarrel drilled so that hydraulic cylinders could be built into it for raising and lowering. This was a very, very expensive keel.

The hull form was designed to be the ultimate light-air boat with a fine, hollow entry, low freeboard, narrow BWL, and no deadrise. The stern was broad to help Icon surf when off the wind. The exact beam at the top of the deck at the transom, however, was a function of the room I needed for the cockpit layout. The slight spoon shape to the bow profile was a feature requested by Dick. This boat was very light with a D/L of 68.

Icon's interior was a convertible layout. Designed for cruising comfort, the interior could be taken apart easily and reduced to a racing layout with berths for a racing crew. In the cruise mode, there was a large galley aft and a skipper's stateroom to port extending a large double berth under the cockpit. There was a small head aft. The dinette to starboard was large and terminated forward against the wall of the lifting keel trunk. The small, minimum dinette to port converted to upper and lower berths for racing. The owner's cabin forward was spacious and included a head with shower and a washer/dryer. This cabin converted to crew berths and sail stowage area for racing. There was a large fo'c's'le area that had folding pipe berths.

Our sailmaker advisor, Doug, wanted a big rig. We looked at the boats that were winning the races Icon would sail, and we could easily see that we were

# Yacht Design According to Perry

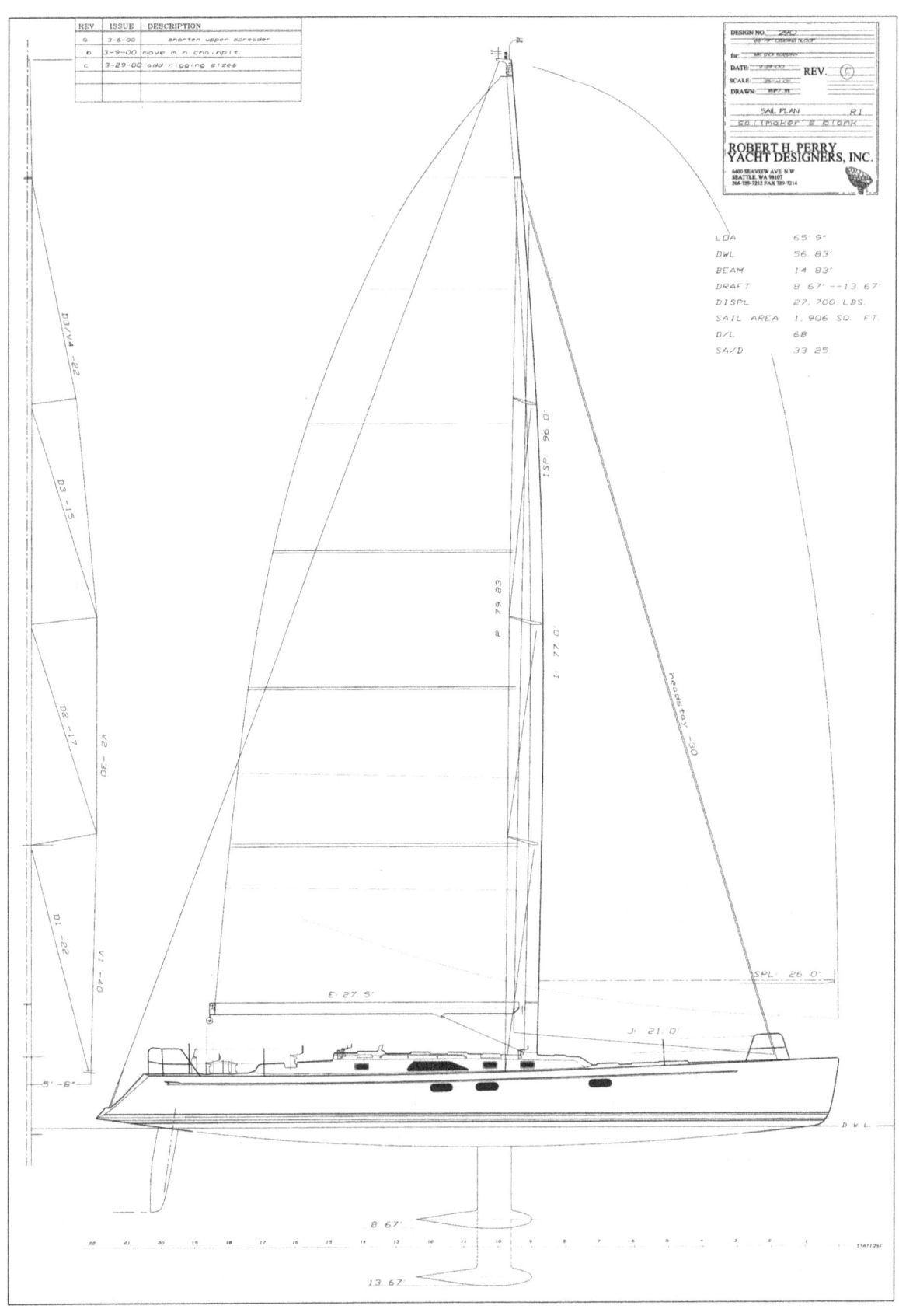

Icon's triple-spreader carbon rig shows what a SA/D of 33.25 looks like without headsail overlap—a tall mast with a lot of mainsail roach.

## Three Cruising Sleds

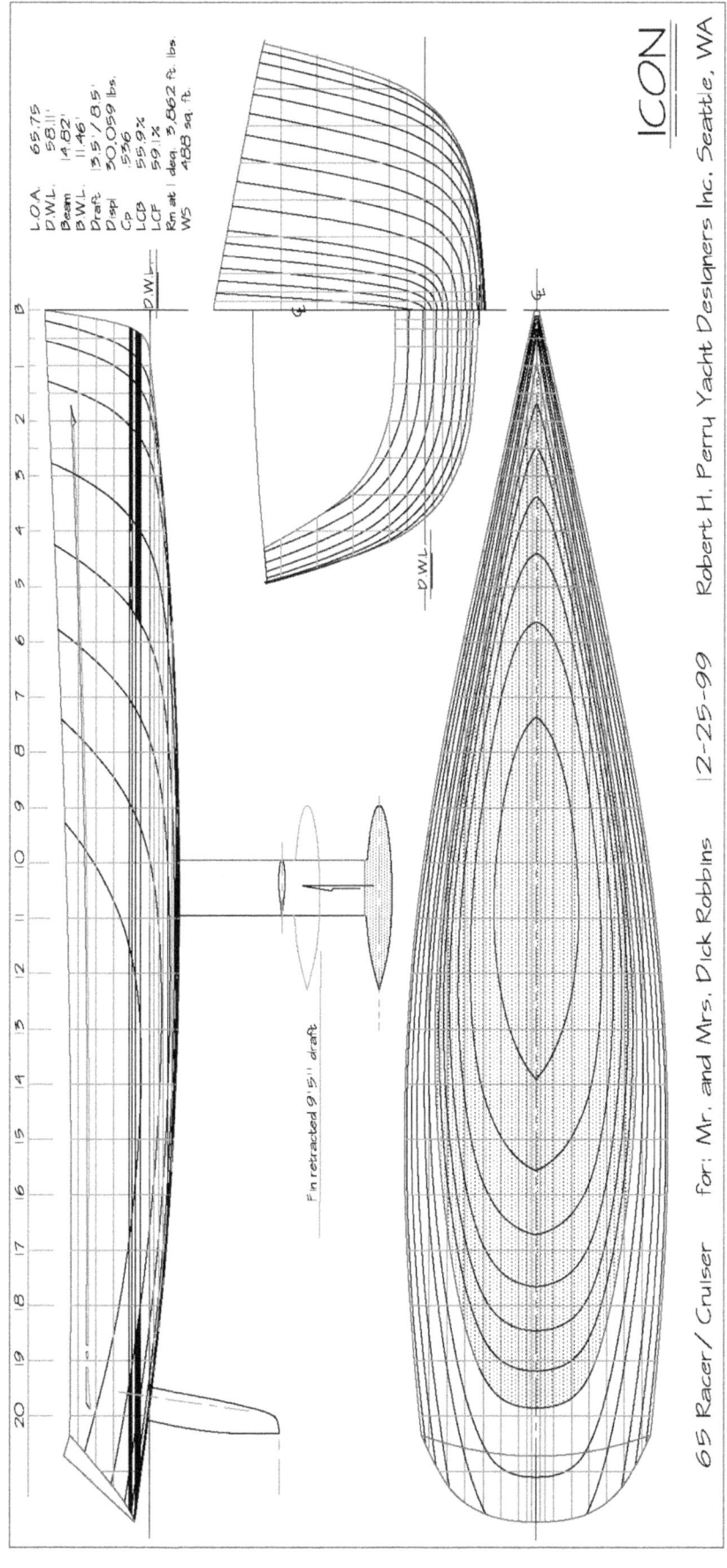

65 Racer/Cruiser   For: Mr. and Mrs. Dick Robbins   12-25-99   Robert H. Perry Yacht Designers Inc. Seattle, WA

Like her sail plan, Icon's lines are shaped for light-air speed, with a L/B of 4.43 and a D/L of just 68. The entry is fine, the freeboard low, and the BWL narrow, and the boat has no deadrise. The draft increases by 5 feet when the lifting keel is lowered.

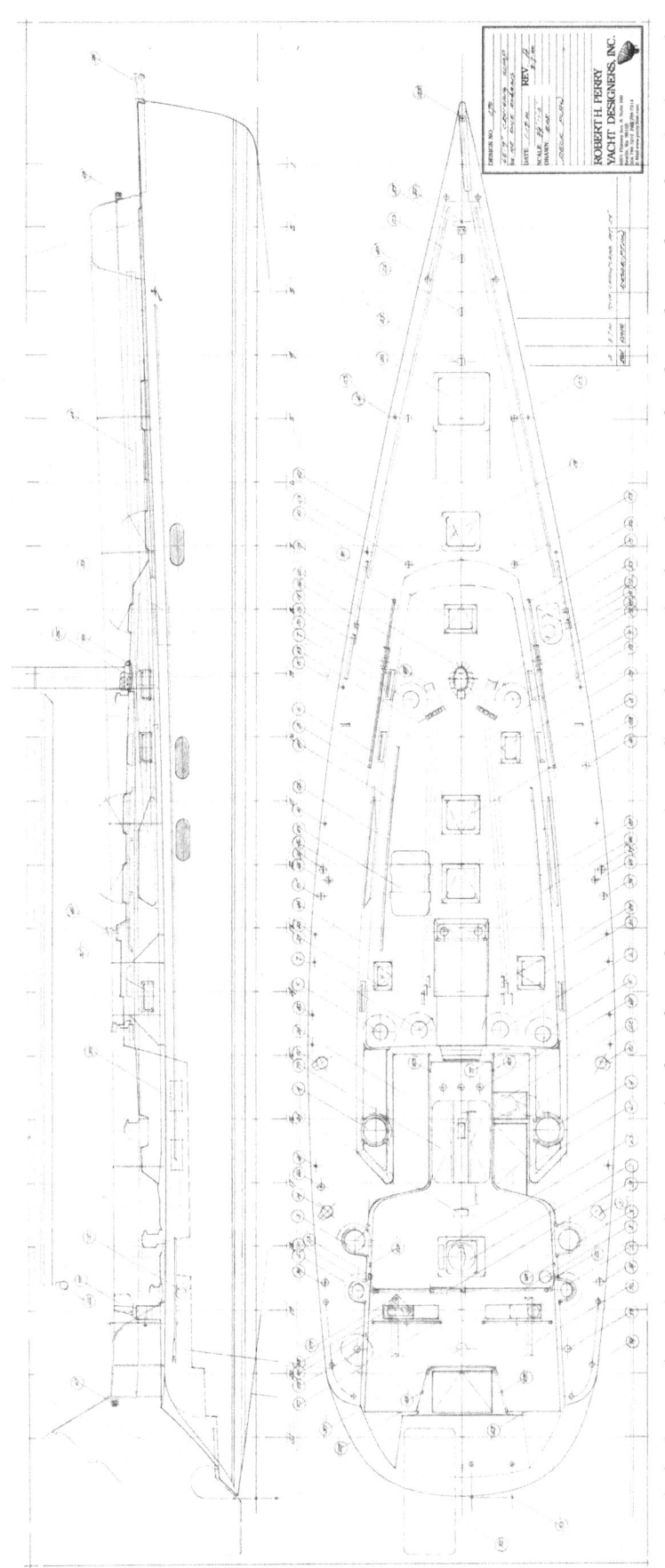

Icon's deck plan combines features for cruising (such as the cockpit coamings forward) and racing (such as the twin pedestal winches in the cockpit for fast sail trimming).

involved in an "arms race." Rigs were getting bigger and bigger. Spinnakers were getting huge. The only thing getting smaller was the size of the headsail. *Icon* would carry no overlapping headsails. *Icon*'s SA/D was a whopping 33.25. If you wanted light-air boat speed, you needed sail area. If you wanted to surf and plane, you also needed sail area. Suffice it to say, we had plenty of sail area on a beautiful, carbon rig. I flew to New Zealand to sea-trial *Icon*. Those sails were among the most rewarding I have ever had. *Icon* was very close-winded and quick while being very easy on the helm.

*Icon*'s deck plan featured components designed for cruising married to the efficiency of a racing deck. There were cockpit coamings forward for comfort and twin pedestal winches in the cockpit for fast sail trimming. The cockpit was open to the transom. The short house came from *Charisma*, to some degree, and it contributed to the overall good looks of *Icon*.

I find *Icon* very beautiful. It has the look of a "big, little" boat. By this, I mean that it's long, but it's lean, and the freeboard is low. It has the look of a big dinghy. Martin Marine in New Zealand did a wonderful job building *Icon* out of the most high-tech materials available at the time, including epoxy resin, Nomex honeycomb core, and carbon-fiber skins. *Icon* was vacuum-bagged and baked in an oven at 150 degrees three times. My youngest son, Spike, touring New Zealand after graduating from high school, stood the night watch during the first bake. The phone at home rang in the middle of the night. "Dad," said Spike, "you'll never guess what I am doing right now."

Icon *under sail with her code zero headsail (top) and reaching with her huge spinnaker (above).*

*Icon* marked a turning point in my office. I was charging along, happy to be producing the nicest hand-drawn drawings I'd ever done. I'd look at these drawings and think, "I am getting really good at this." They were pencil and ink on Mylar—gorgeous. Then the builders at Martin Marine in New Zealand called. I'll paraphrase: "We don't want no stinking hand drawings! We want everything on AutoCAD so we can convert the drawings to metric scale."

"I knew that," thought I.

This changed everything. My helper at the time, Tim Kernan, was full-time AutoCAD, but I had been resisting and was not ready to change yet. But now I had no choice. I had been fooling around with AutoCAD for about three years, and now I would have to make the transition overnight. I need to thank Martin Marine for kicking me in the butt and making me finally join the world of twenty-first-century computer-aided drafting. I had done hulls, keels, and rudders on the computer for more than twenty years, but I had fallen in love with my own hand drafting. Even when I had computer-generated shapes, I combined those with hand detailing and lettering. I'm sure that Frank Sinatra liked the sound of his voice in the shower, too. Today, I could never go back to hand drafting. I am now addicted to the accuracy and convenience of computer drafting. Of course, my eyesight is not what it was thirty years ago, either. I wear thick glasses now. AutoCAD has a "zoom" feature that I like. I see just fine when I use it. The *Icon* design work was completed with my new engineer, Ben Souquet.

*Icon* has done some serious cruising. It has taken Dick and his wife, Bonnie, from New Zealand to race-cruise in Australia; across the Pacific to cruise the coast of Australia; to the Pacific Northwest; back to Hawaii in the Pacific Cup; and on to the Marshall Islands and Mexico. When *Icon* wasn't cruising, she was racing and being lovingly cared for by Jim and Robin Roser. *Icon* has won races and proven a threat on any racecourse. I particularly liked it when *Icon* won her first Swiftsure Race with my oldest son, Max, aboard. *Icon* also holds the record for our unusual Around the County Race.

*Icon* has also proven to be an exciting handful for a couple to cruise. The rig is enormous, and the boat is a lot of boat to get on and off a crowded dock when there is a crosswind. We put a "pad" in the hull forward for a retracting bow thruster, and I am pushing for that today to make *Icon* easier to cruise. I also pushed hard for a Leisure Furl boom. We could cut some of that rig off, but Dick does not want to compromise the speed of the boat.

*Icon* was and remains my ultimate cruising sled and one of my most rewarding projects.

## According to Perry
# REAL-WORLD BOW EVALUATIONS

To finish the discussion of bows begun in the previous two design essays, let's subject three bows on a fixed LOA to a quantitative evaluation. Specifically, we'll use a velocity-prediction program (VPP) to show what impact each bow will have on speed through the water. The bow shapes will be:

1. An IOR-type raked bow, which, for our purposes, will serve as the "parent model" conventional bow
2. A spoon profile
3. A plumb stem

I am also going to throw in an evaluation of a longer boat to show the effect of LOA on speed.

First, the ground rules. It is of paramount importance to establish exactly what we mean by the *bow*. The bow certainly is far more than a two-dimensional profile shape. It is, in fact, a three-dimensional shape describing a distribution of volume. It is also necessary to understand just how much of the front end of the boat is being called the bow. There is no hard rule for this, but as I push and pull on these illustrative bows, the resultant volumetric changes in the first 10 percent of LOA will have to be faired to as far aft as 20 percent of LOA if the boats are to retain reasonable lines. At some point as I move aft, the bow becomes the forward quarters, but I can't point to a spot on the hull and say, "Eureka! It's right there." In short, you cannot just replace the first 12 feet of a 56-footer with a different bow and obtain any meaningful results.

Said another way, in modifying the bow, I am to some degree changing the entire forward end of the boat. I have tried to keep these changes to a minimum for the sake of comparison. I have retained LOA and maximum beam, and certainly from their midship sections aft, these examples are identical. While the sectional shapes of the variations on the parent hull may not be what I would consider ideal, I have restrained myself from "correcting" them in order to keep the models more comparable and keep the focus on the bow shapes.

I am also going to keep the rigs, sail inventories, rudders, keels, and VCGs of my test boats identical. I have made small adjustments to the waterplane areas of the boats to ensure similar displacements. (Interestingly, these small changes resulted in differences in limits of positive stability of up to three degrees.)

I have chosen to make the comparisons in terms of boat speed differentials because I think this is the easiest way to grasp the numbers. I am using actual speeds through the water and not velocities made good, as I think many of us find it easier to relate to actual speeds.

For fun, I added 56 inches of forward overhang to the plumb-bowed model to see what would happen. I expected the longer LOA to be faster, but, in fact, the differences are smaller than I expected.

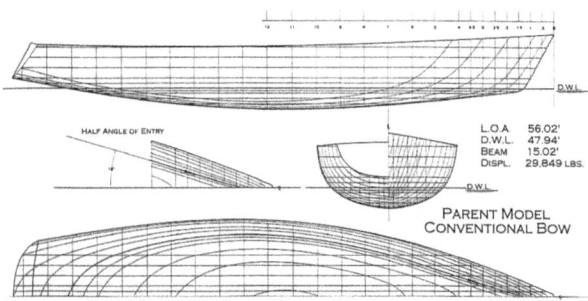

The "parent bow model" is a conventional IOR-inspired bow.

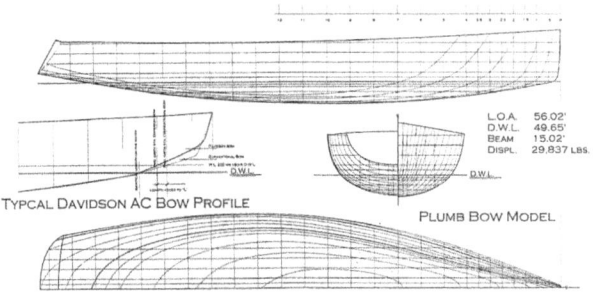

The plum-bow model proves faster, but is also wetter and requires special anchor-handling provisions.

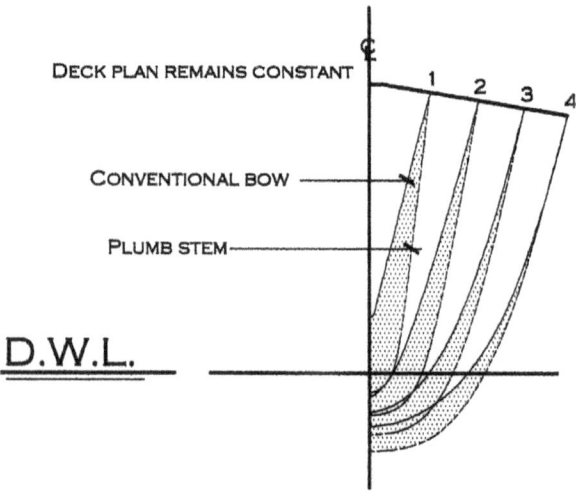

The shaded areas show the additional volume forward allowed by a plumb stem.

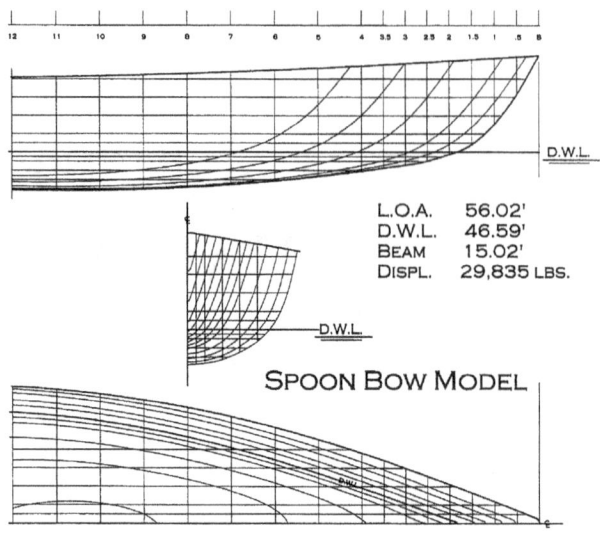

A spoon bow resembles a long bow in profile, but the half-angle of entry is much fuller, as can be seen in the half-breadth, and a bow this full will make the boat less weatherly.

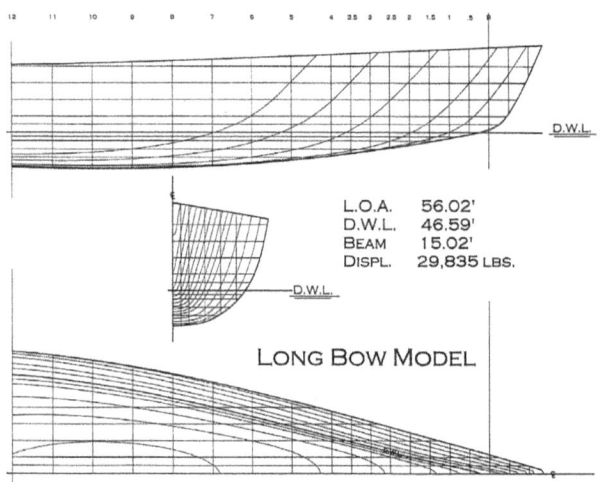

The long-bow model is finer than the spoon bow.

### VPP Comparison Chart

| Condition, True Wind Speed | Parent Hull | Plumb Bow | Spoon Bow | Long Bow |
|---|---|---|---|---|
| Opt. Upwind in 6 knots | 5.80 kts. | 5.83 kts. | 5.69 kts. | 5.89 kts. |
| Opt. Downwind in 6 knots | 5.46 kts. | 5.54 kts. | 5.38 kts. | 5.62 kts. |
| Opt. Upwind in 10 knots | 7.2 kts. | 7.3 kts. | 7.15 kts. | 7.38 kts. |
| Opt. Downwind in 10 knots | 7.50 kts. | 7.64 kts. | 7.42 kts. | 7.76 kts. |
| Opt. Upwind in 16 knots | 7.93 kts. | 8.01 kts. | 7.84 kts. | 8.1 kts. |
| Opt. Downwind in 16 knots | 8.70 kts. | 8.84 kts. | 8.62 kts. | 8.88 kts. |
| Opt. Upwind in 20 knots | 8.08 kts. | 8.15 kts. | 7.99 kts. | 8.18 kts. |
| Opt. Downwind in 20 knots | 9.7 kts. | 9.85 kts. | 9.63 kts. | 9.88 kts. |
| ILC Overall Rating | 593.1 | 587.1 | 599.2 | 584.3 |

The VPP comparison chart shows the speed advantage of the plumb-bow model over the parent model and the spoon bow, together with the ratings assigned by the International Level Class (ILC).

(Blue Water Sailing)

On a 24-hour run in 20 knots of wind, the plumb-bowed 56-footer will put 3.6 nautical miles on the parent model and 5.28 miles on the spoon-bowed model. The results are virtually the same in 10 knots of breeze. I did not make a similar chart for reaching, but the plumb-bowed model's maximum reaching speeds will put it 7.2 nautical miles ahead of the spoon-bowed model in 24 hours.

These speed differences may look impressive when extrapolated over 24 hours, but in absolute terms they're quite modest—just 0.15 to 0.30 knot. Whether such differences matter to you is a question only you can answer. If you're a competitive sailor, you know that a 0.2-knot improvement is significant. It will gain you almost half a mile on a two-hour beat to weather, and in a race, a half mile is huge. The bottom line is that small differences in bow shape add up to make some boats faster—I won't say "better"—than others.

This is the point at which I should tell you emphatically that one of these bows is "the ideal," but I won't. You should find sufficient data in the performance spreadsheet and in what I've said above and in the previous two design essays to balance the factors and decide for yourself.

Pragmatically speaking, a conventional (i.e., IOR-type) bow looks good. It's cheap, it's dry, and it keeps the anchor off the stem. The plumb stem is faster, may offer more interior volume forward for accommodations, and looks up to date, but it is also wet and complicates anchor handling. Spoon bows are dry and can be pretty, but they give up a lot of DWL.

At the end of the day, I don't see how your choice of a bow type can be an isolated decision. Rather, it must be based upon the overall character of the boat and the aesthetic as well as practical goals of the design.

*Chapter Seventeen*

# DESIGNING *JAKATAN*: A CUSTOM 40'6" SCHOONER

When Jeff Hawkins called to say he was interested in having a 40-foot schooner designed, my first question was, "Why?" I explained that the schooner rig is inefficient and that most modern cruising sailors consider the cutter rig far superior. Jeff understood all that, but he was drawn to the look of schooners in general and to the San Francisco Bay scow schooners in particular. A designer can argue performance issues all day, but few arguments will trump a client's aesthetic preferences. I agreed to design the schooner.

I'm including the schooner in this book not because it's typical of my office's design output—it isn't—but because this unusual one-off project offers a great opportunity to synthesize the elements of the book. Foregoing chapters have explored some of the stories behind my boats, and between-chapter design essays have looked at critical aspects of a designer's work. What I'll try to do here is weave those separate strands together into a living, breathing design overview. Come to think of it, the schooner, which Jeff Hawkins has named *Jakatan*, is typical of my work in one respect, and that is that every project is unique.

As I have said in previous chapters, a primary part of any custom project is a clear understanding of how the client will use the boat. This can be tricky. The client might say, "One day I'd like to sail to Europe," when in reality the boat will spend its entire life on the West Coast. I was lucky with Jeff. Jeff daysails on San Francisco Bay, has a favorite place he likes to cruise to and anchor, and at some point may venture as far south as Mexico. That's it. Simple.

So the boat would be designed first and foremost for daysailing on blustery San Francisco Bay and cruising up the Sacramento River delta. Jeff is married and has two teenage daughters who enjoy cruising, so the boat would need to be stiff and roomy. Given that the return trip downriver to San Francisco Bay is typically dead upwind, Jeff likes to motor home; therefore, the boat would need to have good speed under power. It went without saying that we would have to do everything possible to marry Jeff's preference for a schooner rig with a good-performing hull. Another constraint was imposed by Jeff's request for a 5.5-foot draft, the same as his current boat, which would enable him to cruise the same areas. We started with a short list of design parameters:

LOA: 40 feet
Draft: 5.5 feet
Rig: Gaff-rigged schooner with a one-halyard system (see below for more on this)
Accommodations: Comfortable cruising interior for four, with a big holding tank and headroom for a 6'4" owner
Extras: Dinghy davits

The first thing I do with any new custom design is to advise the client that the LOA should be left to "float" while the other parameters are addressed.

## Designing Jakatan

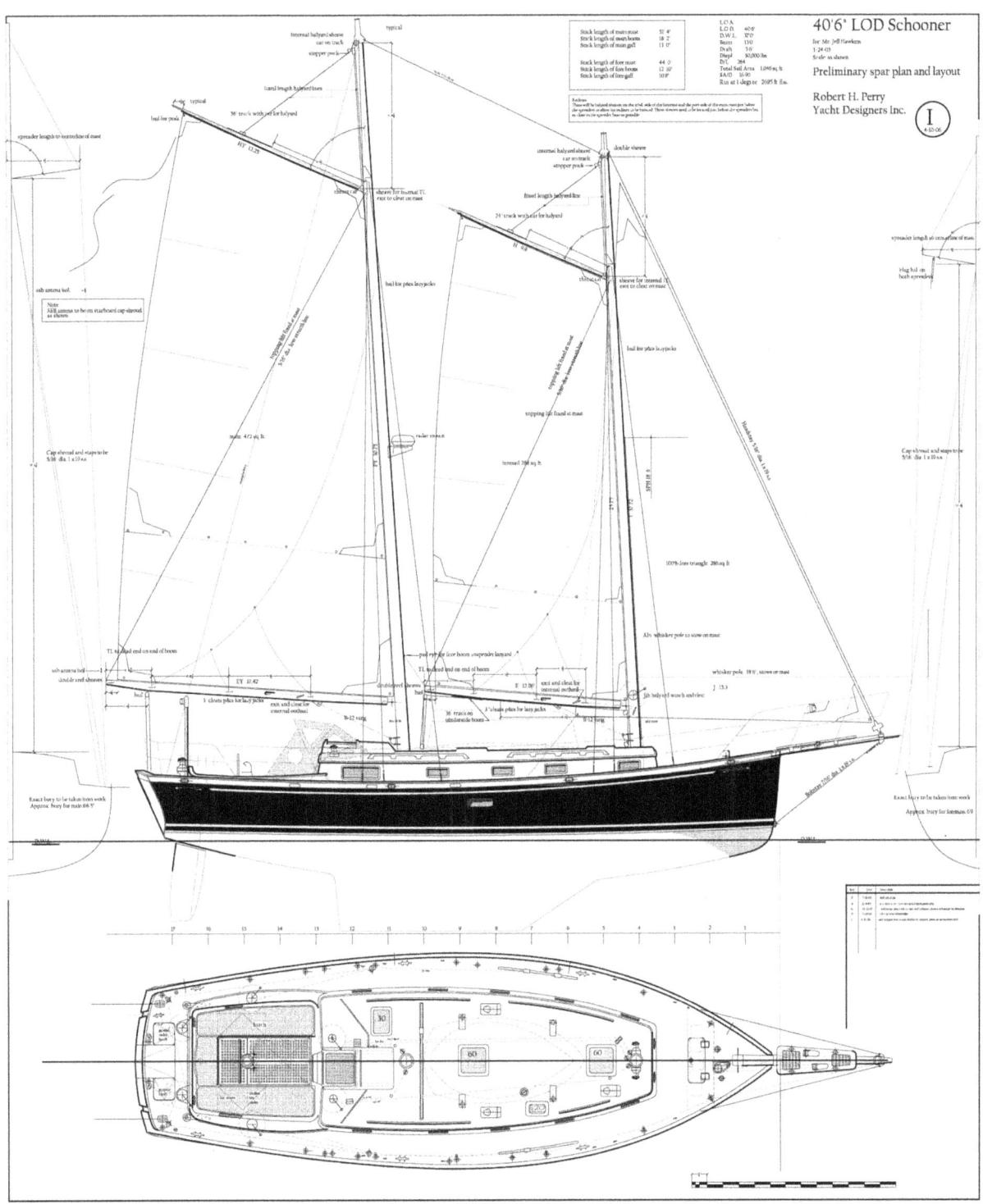

Jakatan *reflects a discerning client's requirements coupled with an unbounded quest for a boat that was neither traditional nor contemporary. The droop of the gaffs was requested by the client to echo the look of the old San Francisco Bay scow schooners. Note the single-halyard detail.*

# Yacht Design According to Perry

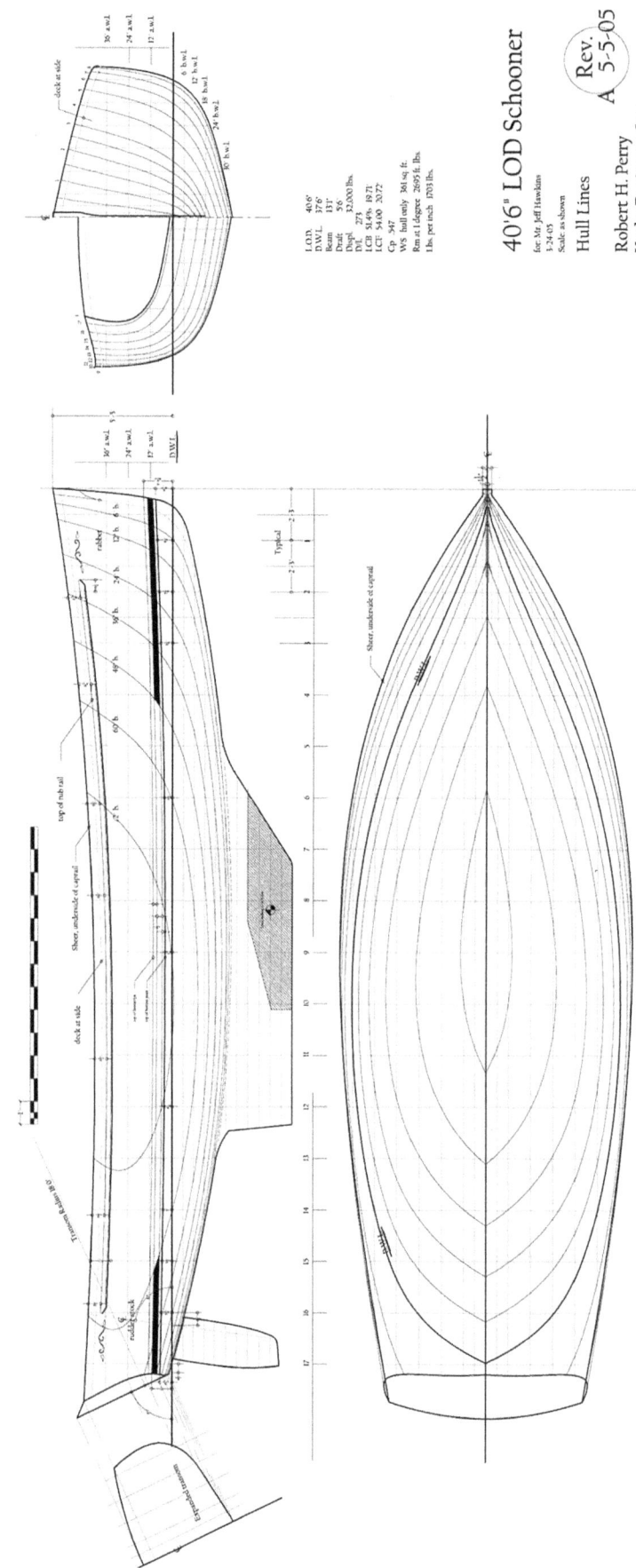

*I like this big, beefy hull with its muscular forefoot, plenty of beam forward, and a hint of tumblehome at the transom. The spade rudder provides an element of excitement in what could be mistakenly seen as a traditional hull form.*

The "size" of the boat is more a function of displacement than LOA, and additional length is relatively cheap as long as the rest of the boat stays the same. At the end of the project, most of my clients say, "I should have made it bigger." I felt that Jeff was being too rigid with his 40-foot LOA, but he was adamant that we stay at that length.

I hand-drew a sketch of a 40-foot schooner and mailed it to Jeff. I liked it. It had attractive (and relatively efficient) peaked-up gaffs, a long DWL, and a traditional look, although it did not lean hard on any specific traditional type. Jeff also liked the sketch—just not quite as much as I did. He was concerned about headroom, and he wanted me to drop the gaffs to get more of the scow schooner look. I did a second hand-drawn sketch, which Jeff approved of enough to have confidence to proceed.

The next step was a face-to-face meeting with the client, and that meant that Jeff would have to fly to Seattle. To make this meeting as productive as possible, I suggested that I produce some more preliminary drawings so that we could progress beyond the "arm-waving" stage when Jeff was in the office. With hard prints in front of us, we could make some critical decisions to accelerate the process. Some clients can tell you exactly what they want. Others only know what they want after seeing what they don't want. Usually it's a combination of both, and that requires drawings.

I usually start the design process with a sketch of what we have in mind. In this case, I'd already progressed through two hand sketches. I had done these to scale using old-fashioned ship's curves and splines. Now the trick was to transfer the feel and look of the sketch to the computer. I always begin by crafting a set of hull lines so that I have a well-defined shape to use when the time comes to lay out the interior. (On the other hand, you have to bear in mind the requirements for interior accommodations while you work on the lines, a subject we'll come back to below.) Usually I already have a hull in my computer library of designs that I can use as a starting point for a new boat. I may have to adjust the scale of length-to-beam and canoe-body depth, but I can get a quick start by using an existing hull shape. If I don't have a starting point on hand, I will do a quick hand-drawn set of lines and input that shape into the computer. For Jeff's schooner, I chose to start with the lines of the 41-foot *Amati* (see Chapter 15). Jeff's hull would essentially be *Amati* on steroids.

The next job was to establish a displacement goal for the new design. A boat should be as light as possible, but low displacement translates to low interior volume, and for this boat I needed the opposite. Displacement also enhances stability, and with draft limited to 5.5 feet, I was going to have to add displacement to get the stability the boat would need for comfortable sailing on San Francisco Bay. Any displacement beyond what would be required to build the basic boat would go into ballast, and in this case I wanted a 40 percent ballast-to-displacement ratio. Working backward through a preliminary weight study, I determined that I would need an overall displacement of 32,000 pounds.

After half an hour of pushing and pulling *Amati*'s hull lines around on the computer, there was nothing left of the parent model. The 10,000-pound *Amati* had been transformed into the 32,000-pound *Jakatan*.

Next we needed to get the desired midsection shape, define the ends of the boat, and hit appropriate targets for the prismatic coefficient (Cp), longitudinal center of buoyancy (LCB), and longitudinal center of flotation (LCF). Since I was after good speed under power, I made the designed waterline as long as possible by minimizing the overhangs and starting with a straight, nearly plumb stem and a transom with its lower apex just above the DWL. This gave me a DWL of 37'6" and a D/L of 273, making the boat a textbook medium-displacement cruiser. Eventually I managed to talk Jeff into giving me an additional six inches of LOA to work with. (I tried for an additional 24 inches, but Jeff was resolutely LOA-sensitive. In a moment of generosity he gave me the additional six, and I greedily accepted.)

I kept the Cp at the upper end of the middle range at 0.547. I never include the volume of the keel in this calculation. You can if you like, but to gain any valuable record of design progression over time, you have to do it the same way on each design, and I've always excluded keel volume for the Cp of fin-keeled boats.

The LCB was 53.3 percent of the DWL aft of the cutwater, which might suggest a volume-aft design, but I pulled the beam at the deck forward and kept the hull full above the DWL. I needed volume forward for accommodations. That's always the case, of course, but in most instances I'm also trying to keep the entry fine and the beam on deck narrow forward to help the boat sail to weather. But with the specified (and inherently inefficient) schooner rig, regardless of what I did with the entry, *Jakatan* was not going to be a close-winded boat. Hard on the wind with all sails drawing, this boat might achieve an apparent wind angle of 35 degrees, compared with the 28 degrees you would expect from a high-performance sloop. Thus, I settled for a full bow, but I kept the half-angle of entry at 19 degrees by incorporating some plan-view hollow forward in the DWL.

I did add some complexity to the bow's sectional shape by giving the stem profile a slight spoon curvature instead of the dead-straight stem I had started with. This improved the look of the boat and also enabled me to fill out the forward sections above the DWL. This combination of entry angle, beam at deck, and stem profile resulted in shapely bow sections that show a hint of flare back to station 2.

It was easy work, relatively speaking, to torture hull shapes like this when lines were hand-drawn, but the computer prefers smooth, simple, predictable hull shapes. Still, with patience and skill, and by using the same batten tricks you use when drawing by hand, you can convince the computer to do your bidding. If you have ever wondered why so many hull shapes look the same today, maybe you can blame it on computer fairing programs.

I also wanted a full bow for purely aesthetic reasons. I was after a traditional look—not a specific traditional type but a hybrid of sorts, one that would recall a boat from the 1940s or 1950s. Jeff was very much against a "replica" approach to styling. He wanted a unique boat, but one that had the look of an older vessel. Those boats did not have fine entries, and they certainly were not fine in the bow at deck level. *Jakatan* carries its maximum deck-level beam at station 5.2 (i.e., 52 percent of the DWL aft of the cutwater), substantially farther forward than the typical modern sloop, which would be at station 6.0. Pulling the beam forward also increased the room on deck and contributed to the boat's traditional look. The result is not as exaggerated as the proverbial "cod's head and mackerel tail" plan-view shape of the nineteenth century, but it comes a lot closer to that than a modern design. I carried the beam aft and used a broad transom to gain cockpit volume and space on deck aft.

For a sectional shape, I chose a midships deadrise angle of 12 degrees, flattening out to 8.5 degrees at the transom. This provided powerful stern sections to add to sailing length and also flattened the buttocks aft to improve speed under power. I added some tumblehome in the topsides aft, starting at about station 6, to give the transom a more complex and attractive shape. By the time you get to the transom, the tumblehome is pronounced, adding to the traditional look. One of the other benefits of tumblehome is that it puts the rubrail where it will actually come in contact with the pier. I kept the entry V-shaped to soften the ride through a chop when the boat is under power. The flare in the forward sections should keep the ride dry when punching through a chop, despite the lack of forward overhang.

Once you hit your target numbers with a shape that is pleasing to the eye and promises to do what you want, you can move on, but it may take days to get the hull you really want. When we drew hull lines by hand, it would take a solid week to get a well-crafted and fair set of hull lines. Of course, there were designers who could whip out a set of lines in a day, but I have seen plenty of these that I would not consider well crafted. They worked all right, but they left too much discretion in the hands of the yard loftsman who translated them from small-scale drawings into full-sized patterns. If you wanted to be certain that the shape you drew was the shape that would be built, you took the extra time to develop perfectly faired lines. It was so arduous that in some cases, if you were 90 percent through the process when you thought of a change, you might find the change impossible to make due to the time involved with a builder waiting for finished lines. You would just mentally file the desired change away for use on the next set of lines.

Things are different now. With computer programs for hull lines, you can come up with a perfectly fair set of hull lines in well less than an hour. Of course, it probably isn't and shouldn't be the hull you want to end up with, but it will be close. This allows the designer to tweak the lines for days or weeks, even making major changes. If you use a velocity-prediction program (VPP), this may be the time to run a check on the potential performance of your preliminary design. In my office, however, we usually wait until we have an accurate vertical center of gravity (VCG) before doing VPPs, because the effect of the VCG on stability will ripple through the entire VPP. This is an instance in which a cruising-boat designer might follow a different sequence of design steps from a designer working to a rating rule

## Designing Jakatan

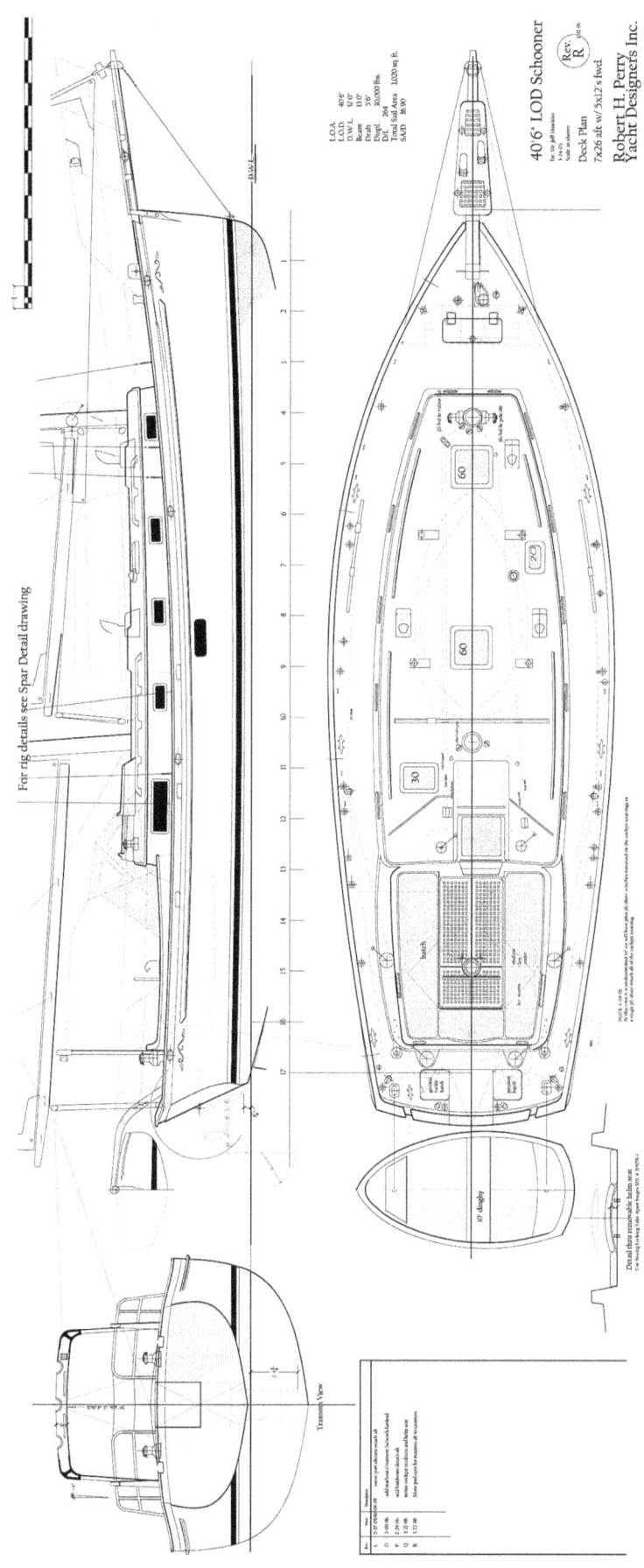

*I really enjoyed doing these drawings for an appreciative and knowledgeable client. He gave me the room to do my best work.*

or a box rule. In the latter cases, VPP work will start with the first set of preliminary lines. I often use VPP data to evaluate and possibly modify the keel fin and draft, but I seldom use these data for determining the hull form of my cruising designs. The success of a cruising boat never comes down to fraction-of-a-knot differences in boat speed.

The computer gives the designer the power to change hull shapes quickly. In designing *Jakatan*, I raised the sheer, added beam, changed the shape of the stem, and finally added six inches to the LOA, as noted above. In real time, I think I spend as much time on a finished set of computer-drawn lines as I would on a finished set of hand-drawn lines. The difference is that the computer lines have a higher degree of refinement and accuracy. From the computer, the lines can be lofted full size on the office plotter, and the full-sized patterns can be mailed to the builder. Alternatively, a builder may take the computer file via e-mail and send it out via e-mail to a shop that does CNC cutting, in which case there is never a need for full-sized patterns at all. You can even take it another step and e-mail the computer file to a company that does three-dimensional CNC work, producing either a full-sized male plug or a full-sized female mold for the hull. Today's skilled loftsman spends no time on his knees and all of his time at the keyboard.

The biggest practical advantages of creating hull shapes on a computer are not only accuracy of translation into full-sized patterns, but also the freedom the computer gives me to make changes to the hull shape all the way through the design process up until the minute I have to fire off that e-mail with the computer file. After all, the hull shape that looks good to you on Friday afternoon may not look as good on the following Monday.

I designed *Jakatan*'s appendages next. Despite the rig's archaic geometry, I did not want a full-keeled boat. There is no point in leaving any amount of boat speed on the drawing board. I wanted a fin keel and a spade rudder. Working with only 5.5 feet of allowable draft, I couldn't make the fin deep, so I had to make it long. I did this for several reasons. First, I believe that cruising boats should be able to sit on their keels when hauled out. Second, the longer the keel and the thicker the foil, the lower on the fin the lead can be placed, yielding a lower VCG of the ballast. I also wanted to pull as much keel area aft as possible to help balance the schooner rig, which, with its center of effort pulled aft by the mainsail, would otherwise develop too much weather helm. At the same time, however, I needed to keep enough ballast forward to control fore-and-aft trim. It's purely a balancing act, and you go through it to some degree on every design. It seems I always want to get the keel aft and the ballast forward. In the end, however, you want a boat that floats on its lines and has a docile, forgiving helm.

We used a NACA section 63-A010 foil for the keel. This designation tells you that the foil has a 10 percent thickness ratio. I used to go as high as 12 percent, and now I sometimes go as low as 9 percent. It depends on what I am trying to do with the ballast, the aspect ratio of the fin, and the overall nature of the design. The sweep angle of the leading edge is 53 percent. With a low-aspect-ratio fin like *Jakatan*'s, you need more sweep than you would use on a deep, high-aspect-ratio fin. Adding sweep to the low-aspect fin helps keep the flow attached to the fin, providing better lift for drag. It also helps shed kelp and lobster-pot warps.

Rudders are easier to design than keels. I like to get the rudder as far aft as possible and make it big and deep. Nobody has ever called the office to complain that their rudder was too big. If draft is restricted, as it was in this case, the rudder geometry may be compromised by the keel draft. I like to keep the tip of the rudder six inches above the bottom of the keel so that it is protected in grounding situations and during haulouts, but I'll go as little as three inches in some cases. *Jakatan*'s rudder has the full six inches of offset.

I prefer to keep the centerline of the rudderstock nearly perpendicular to the hull profile at the rudder. This helps avoid rudder binding problems and makes for a nice, tight fit between the rudder and the hull at low rudder angles. The designer should do his best to have the hull provide some end-plate effect for the rudder, because this improves the apparent aspect ratio of the rudder plan form. With deadrise, you are limited in how much end plate you can achieve, but on a flat-bottomed boat you should be able to keep the top of the rudder blade snug to the hull at angles approaching 30 degrees of helm.

*Jakatan*'s rudder is built as a monocoque carbon-fiber piece. This means that the carbon-fiber stock and blade are bonded together with epoxy to become, in effect, one unit. The rudderstock is tapered above and below the bearing and sleeved where it enters the bearing. We used a NACA 0012 for the top of the rudder, fattening it to a 13.4 percent thickness ratio to give us room for the required rudderstock diameter. The thickness ratio at the bottom of the rudder blade is 12 percent. On a racing boat, this thickness ratio may be as low as 9 percent, but a rudder that thin requires a deft hand on the tiller to prevent it from stalling.

I prefer spade rudders because they steer a boat more efficiently than keel-attached or skeg-hung rudders and because they permit some blade area forward of the rudderstock centerline so as to reduce helm pressure. Spade rudders are also much better for good handling characteristics in reverse under engine power. With the schooner rig presenting so much sail area aft, I wanted the rudder to be shaped with at least 15 percent of its blade area forward of the stock, and we wound up with 16 percent.

A spade rudder experiences twisting and bending loads that you do not get with a skeg-hung rudder, which only sees twisting moments, so the required stock diameter for a spade rudder is large. This does require some modification of the optimal blade-thickness ratio to give you enough volume within the blade to surround the rudderstock. For cruising boats, a nice, thick rudder will be more forgiving in heavy going.

The next step is to start laying out the interior from the hull lines. This can be done two-dimensionally with AutoCAD, or you can work in three dimensions with a program like Rhino or AutoCAD 3D. If you take advantage of all the computer tools available for the job, you can provide a builder with full-sized patterns for every component of the interior. Some builders like to build that way, and others prefer to work the old-fashioned way, taking their own patterns from the work as it progresses. *Jakatan*'s layout was drawn in AutoCAD 2D. This required a plan view, inboard profiles, and joiner sections. Joiner sections should be taken wherever the area needs additional definition for the builder.

The interior must be addressed in detail before you finalize the hull lines. In this regard, cruising boats are designed from the inside out. Put another way, I need a good idea of what I am going to do inside the boat when I draw the hull lines. When I draw that first bulkhead, usually the forward bulkhead in an aft-cockpit design, I will have a pretty good mental image of what is going to follow. In this case, Jeff wanted a large double berth, Pullman-style, for his wife and himself. One head, with shower stall attached, would be sufficient. One daughter would sleep on a settee berth and the other would get a quarter berth. There would be a fireplace, a large dinette, a navigation station, and a comfortable galley. There would have to be sufficient space in the forepeak and the lazarette for copious amounts of cruising gear.

There are no hard rules when it comes to layouts. I use a few benchmark dimensions to make sure that what I draw is ergonomically correct, but beyond that, the client's wish list and the designer's imagination determine the interior layout. One fixed point in the layout of a boat this size is the engine location. The interior will develop from there aft, and forward it will develop from where you place that forward bulkhead. It should be obvious, looking at this layout, that the placement of the two schooner masts had a lot of influence over exactly how things were laid out. Suffice it to say, I worked carefully around the two 8-inch-plus-diameter spars to minimize their impact on the efficiency of the layout.

The engine location is determined by the hull shape and by how much volume you need for the interior. Of course, I would always like to put the engine right in the middle of the boat, directly over the LCB, but unless you want your dining table to be the top of the engine box, this location is just not practical. Racing boats do it all the time, but cruisers have different priorities. I like to put the engine as far aft as possible while accommodating prop-tip clearance, shaft angle, and engine-access issues. I used a Volvo engine with a saildrive unit for *Jakatan*. I like the efficiency of a saildrive, and it freed me from prop and shaft limitations in placing the engine.

With the ends of the layout more or less defined, you can start placing your accommodation components. I like my berths to be 6'9" long. You can get by nicely with 6'6", but the added three inches give a little extra room for the pillow. In *Jakatan*, the quarter berth is 6'6", the settee berth is 6'9", and the double berth forward is 6'9". The double features an angled backrest/headboard for sitting up and reading in bed, and this is topped off with a shelf exactly wide enough for a box of Kleenex. There are stowage bins under the shelf. The settee berth is wide with a contoured bottom and seat back for seated comfort. I like at least one settee on a boat to be deep, front to back. You can sit comfortably on an 18-inch seat if you are

# Yacht Design According to Perry

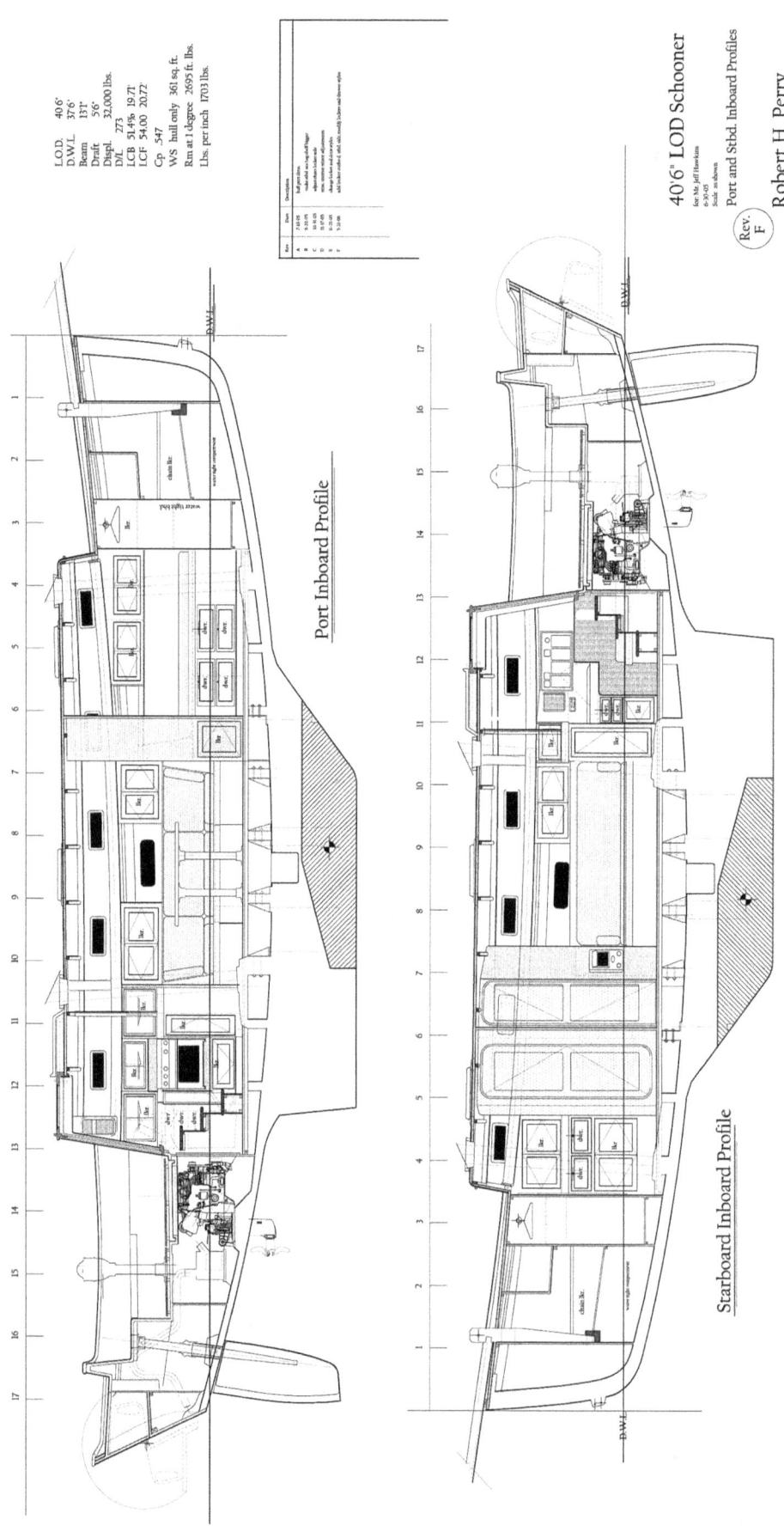

Jakatan is laid out for a family of four. Note the saildrive engine aft. These efficient engines are a designer's dream, eliminating the need for shaft alignment.

eating at the table or sitting up straight, but—as mentioned in a previous chapter—if you really want to slouch and relax, you need 22 inches of depth.

I've seen so many bad dinettes that I've developed definite theories about dinette design. It's imperative that all the people who will cruise on a boat have room to sit and eat together. Too many designs sleep eight but feed six or fewer. The dinette has to be big enough to allow 24 inches of "bottom space" per diner. That's generous, but I'm a generous kind of guy. And now that we have room for our fannies, we need room for our feet. I wear a size 14 shoe, so I need 15 inches of space for my two flippers. Some dinettes have a total foot space of about 28" × 24", and that's not enough. *Jakatan*'s foot space is 36" × 34" for four diners. There is a pullout, piano-stool-style seat for the occasional fifth diner. I also like to put a small shelf area around the perimeter of the seat back. This gives the dinette a more finished and detailed look and is a good place to rest your drink if you are playing cards or Monopoly. *Jakatan*'s dinette measures 7'3" in length through the middle. You will spend most of your time below at this table, so it should not be cramped.

I am sometimes asked to draw heavily radiused corners on dinettes. I have done it, but I won't anymore. I have designed circular dinettes and then sat at them, and they do not work—or rather, they work only as long as you are sitting up at the table, erect and eating. If you want to relax and hunch down a bit, they do not work. My theory is that the human body seeks corners. We like to be nestled in a corner, safe and secure, cradled on two sides. If you put big radii in the corners of the dinette, they will look sexy on the drawing, but in real life they will deprive you of a comforting corner. There is not a single corner in a round dinette.

Galleys are hard to design. Every client will have a specific wish list for his or her galley, but there are some fixed issues. You need 24 inches for the gimbaled range. I prefer a two-sink arrangement, and I prefer deep sinks. I like counter space on both sides of the sinks and on both sides of the range. You need drawers, lockers, and a well-thought-out place for garbage. In *Jakatan*, we used the volume under the companionway steps for trash, creating a two-bin arrangement that is accessed through a hinged trap in the front of the steps. One bin is for biodegradable trash, while the other is for recyclables. The companionway steps are removable to gain access to the engine, but the lowest step is fixed in place so that you can sit on it while pondering why your engine isn't starting. There is a fire extinguisher located under this fixed step.

The chart table is a compromise. A table should hang over its seat by three inches, but in this case that would have made a head knocker for whoever was sleeping in the big quarter berth. We chose to cut the front of the chart table back to avoid this problem. Despite Jeff's background in the high-tech industry, he does not like the look of electronic equipment. In *Jakatan*, we were very discreet with instrument placement to avoid that fighter-jet-cockpit look that some navigation centers get. The locker directly ahead of the chart table was originally drawn as a wet locker but gradually transitioned into a pantry locker.

I'm not a fan of large head areas. It's not a place you spend much time, so why devote much space to it? You need 24 inches for shoulder width at the toilet, and you need 22 inches between the front of the toilet bowl and the door or bulkhead opposite. I know that 22 inches is a good dimension because I once took my tape measure into the head of a Boeing 747 and took a series of measurements. I reasoned that the airline industry must have paid hundreds of thousands of dollars for the data, so I might as well take advantage of the research. Today you probably couldn't get a tape measure through airport security.

The head should always be mounted as far outboard as possible, and today's fancy electric heads with house-sized bowls take up a lot of space. The shower stall, ideally, should be 28" × 24" or larger. *Jakatan*'s shower stall is 32 inches long athwartships, but with an odd shape—partly under the cabin trunk and partly under the side deck. It's tight, but it will work. The angled face of the aft bulkhead on the head was a perfect place to hang the fireplace. Yacht interiors are like Chinese puzzles. When you are done with the layout, every cubic inch has been allocated.

Despite all the effort put into designing and redesigning the interior layout, you have to expect some adjustments once the boat is under construction. These were minimal for *Jakatan*, but when I was in the yard with the owner and we had an interior area like the galley mocked up in door skins, it was easy to see how some areas could be fine-tuned to take better advantage of the available space. It's also at this stage that workers at the yard will often come up and say, "Hey, did you ever think of putting this there?" and they often have excellent ideas. Pride of authorship aside, I will use any good idea. After all, in the end, I get the credit anyway (or the blame). *Jakatan*'s basic layout stayed intact through the building process, but we made adjustments to shelving and locker divisions to improve efficiency.

A designer works in what's called a classic design spiral (see page 9), visiting and revisiting the various design components as each modifies the others. Rig issues are considered while the hull lines are being drawn, based upon what has been identified in the preliminary sketches. *Jakatan*'s rig started with the spar placement, then we played around with the proportions of the mainsail and foresail until they had the look Jeff wanted. As mentioned, I wanted peaked-up gaffs, but Jeff wanted the gaffs lower. I wanted shorter gaffs, but Jeff wanted them longer. Given that such choices for a schooner rig are 85 percent a matter of aesthetics, I went with Jeff's recommendations. They did not interfere with the basic proportions I had set early in the process. I wanted a medium-sized rig for windy San Francisco Bay, so we have a SA/D of 16.9. I did not want a rig that would require frequent reefing. I wanted *Jakatan* to be able to carry all sail in 20 knots of true wind.

The biggest rig challenge was devising the one-halyard system Jeff wanted for the gaff rig. Normally a gaff sail has two halyards: throat and peak. The throat halyard controls luff tension, while the peak halyard controls the leech tension and the angle of the gaff. Two halyards give you a lot of control over the shape of a gaff sail, but Jeff did not want to have to pull on two halyards to hoist each sail. He wanted one halyard to do both jobs.

This is a nice idea, but it turned out to be difficult to execute. The closest we could get was a single-halyard system that will achieve a good-setting sail through carefully calculated geometry plus some on-site fine-tuning. Adjustments to luff and leech tension were designed into the spar systems, although these adjustments can only be made when the sails are down. There will be times when Jeff will want a flatter sail and times he will want a fuller sail, but he won't be able to make those refinements without lowering sail. On the other hand, the rig is simple, and that was one of Jeff's prime goals from day one. We worked hard with Chris Johnson at Hall Spars to make this work. All the spars are carbon fiber and were designed to convert readily to a two-halyard sys-

Jakatan *during initial sailing trials proving, despite a plethora of nay-saying, that Jeff's idea of a single-halyard gaff system does in fact work well.* Jakatan *is quick, powerful, and a joy to drive. What looks like reefs at the booms are really the Stack Pack–style sail covers.*

tem should the single halyard have proved ineffective. The spars are round and tapered.

The deck design and layout for a typical 40′6″ sloop is pretty simple, but the deck design and layout for a 40′6″ schooner is not. To begin with, the two masts restrict what you can do with deck structures. Add to this the fact that this deck needed all the features and conveniences of a modern sloop coupled with the added complexity of the two-stick rig. *Jakatan*'s cabin trunk goes far enough forward to allow good headroom in the owner's stateroom, and forward of the cabin trunk is a flush hatch in the deck for access to a self-draining fender and line locker. The long bowsprit butts into a single samson post.

The aft end of the cabin trunk and companionway come close to interfering with the mainmast. This took careful planning and in the end was one of those features that only worked one way. We have a long cockpit—the well is almost six feet long. There is an engine access hatch in the cockpit sole below a teak grate, and there are long cockpit seat hatches for access to the huge lazarette. We have a shallow line and winch handle locker in the starboard cockpit seat. There's a removable, contoured helm seat.

The dinghy davits are carbon fiber, weigh nine pounds each, and slide into sockets so they can be removed easily if Jeff chooses not to take a dinghy.

The cockpit coaming top is varnished teak, wide enough to sit on comfortably but not so wide that it's difficult to step over. The engine and autopilot controls are recessed into the cockpit seat back. The cabin trunk top is dotted with hatches and dorade vents to ensure good light and ventilation below. A roughly ten-foot-long hard dinghy can be carried on the cabintop when the boat goes offshore.

Probably the most interesting aspect of this deck is its transom door. In a contemporary design with a reverse transom, it's easy to mold in a recess for a swim step, which just about everyone wants. They make sense. In the design of *Jakatan*, however, we did not have that luxury due to the traditional transom rake. The solution was for a section of the transom to hinge down to provide an opening in the stern. That seems like an easy request to satisfy until you consider that *Jakatan*'s transom has camber to it. In short, the transom is a section of a cylinder cut through the hull of the boat at a prescribed angle. This is typical of most transoms. The designer can control the amount of camber, but there must be some. You can get by without transom camber on small boats or on racing boats, but an uncambered transom on *Jakatan* would look like a barn door. Needless to say, hinging this cambered section of transom is harder than hinging a flat plate. It requires offset hinges so that the door portion will not bind against the transom as it is lowered. To make it even more difficult, I combined a section of the aft deck area with the door so that when the door was lowered, the deck section would become a swim step.

When the transom door is lowered, a deep well opens at the stern for boarding. On each side of this well are hatches with flush hatch lids. The port hatch is for the stern ground tackle system and outboard gasoline tank stowage. The starboard hatch is for propane bottles. It is this precise area of the boat that made me ask Jeff for extra LOA. We have not an inch to spare here.

When we began the project, Jeff and I kicked around various methods of building the boat, but he kept coming back to wood. Jeff had grown up around wooden boatbuilding and liked the idea of a wooden boat. I knew two local builders who worked in wood: Schooner Creek in Portland, Oregon, run by Steve Rander; and Jespersen's Boatyard in Sidney, British Columbia, once run by Bent Jespersen and now operated by his capable son Eric. Bent pretends to be retired but is always around. In fact, he just finished restoring an old six-meter sloop with Eric. We sent plans to both yards and made plans to visit them. I had worked with both of them previously and liked the idea of working with a yard to which I could travel easily. Jeff also wanted a yard that he could visit in one day from his home in San Francisco. This eliminated East Coast yards. After an estimating and bidding process, Jeff compared the yards and their bids and decided to go with Jespersen's. I had done two boats with Bent and Eric, and I knew their work to be top-notch. Schooner Creek has had to be content with the two other Perry boats they have under construction as of this writing.

But today's wooden boat is not your grandfather's plank-on-frame, stick-built boat. Today we build with wood veneers that are vacuum-bagged in epoxy over a core. The result is a light, thick, very strong sandwich that avoids the seams of old-fashioned plank-on-frame construction. For the designer raised on monocoque (i.e., one-piece) fiberglass construction, the wooden-boat structural design is a challenge. In short, there are a lot of pieces.

I have a simple way of starting a project like this with Jespersen's. I schedule a day with Eric and Bent, and I take a big, blank notebook and a long list of questions. In a perfect world, the designer would tell the builder exactly what to do everywhere, but I'm not that designer and this is not that world. Because Bent has built countless wooden boats, it would have been foolish not to tap into his data bank early in the project. I knew generally how the boat should be built, but I needed to know how Bent and Eric would prefer building it. It does work both ways.

For *Jakatan*, we specified a foam core, even though the Jespersens hadn't built a foam-cored boat before. Their previous boats had been veneers laid over a strip-planked core, but my engineer specified foam in order to lighten the sandwich weight, which would enable us to increase the ballast. The veneer skins were laid over the foam and vacuum-bagged in place, and Eric was ecstatic about how the process went and the integrity of the resulting sandwich laminate. I kept cornering Bent and asking questions. Eric came up with a good way to do the chainplates so they wouldn't interfere with the interior. Eric's number-one shipwright, Michel, is always good for a bag full of great ideas, and at times, when faced with a problem, we'd just say, "Give it to Michel, he'll figure it out." My removable companionway steps cum garbage bin cum recycling center was refined and executed by Michel without trampling the initial concept. It's a full team effort.

From the inside out, *Jakatan*'s hull layers are:

3 layers of 5/32" red cedar oriented
    0 degrees, 45 degrees, and 45 degrees
3/4" Corecell foam
3 layers of 5/32" red cedar, oriented
    45 degrees, 45 degrees, and 0 degrees
6 oz. fiberglass cloth

All these layers are set in West epoxy and vacuum-bagged.

The backbone, stem, and keelson are laminated Honduras mahogany. The stem is shaped in old-fashioned, plank-on-frame style, flared out above the DWL from a marked rabbet line to a square facing at its top. There is a 1" × 4" hull clamp running the length of the hull-to-deck joint. The hull and deck cores are removed and blocked solid at their edges with red cedar. The bulwark is laminated Douglas fir, faced inside and out with plywood and edged with an oval-topped teak cap. The keel deadwood is laminated Honduras mahogany built up in three-inch lifts.

There are nine athwartship floors, each cut from four-inch-thick Honduras mahogany. These floors are doubled at the mast steps. The thirteen one-inch-diameter Aquamet keel bolts are secured at the top in cast bronze brackets that hang off of the floor timbers.

Eric's suggestion for the chainplates involved laminating to the inner hull side and notching into the clamp a block of Honduras mahogany about four inches thick. Then we recessed into this block a stainless plate that was drilled and tapped. The actual chainplate strap was then bolted to this plate. This moves the chainplates far enough inboard to keep the waterway inside the bulwark clear.

From the outside in, the deck and house side layers are:

2 layers of 6 oz. plain-weave E-glass cloth
A layer of 6 mm Okoume plywood with
    scarfed joints
3/4" H80 Divinycell foam core
An inner layer of 6 mm Okoume plywood

All layers are sealed in West epoxy.

From the outside in, the coach roof layers are:

2 layers of 6 oz. plain-weave E-glass cloth
6 mm Okoume plywood
3/4" H80 Divinycell foam core
2 layers of 1350 13 oz. unidirectional
    E-glass at 90 degrees
One layer of 1/4" Alaska yellow cedar
    planking with V grooves
Laminated faux deck beams capped in
    mahogany

If there is one part of the design process I like the least, it is arranging the tankage. In a perfect world, we would design the tanks into the boat before we laid out the interior, but that's never going to happen. Tanks end up where there is space available. One of Jeff's primary requirements for *Jakatan* was that it have a large holding tank. On Jeff's previous boat, his holding tank was small. This becomes a limiting factor in the duration of a cruise. *Jakatan* has a 50-gallon holding tank under the starboard settee. We have two fuel tanks for a total of 110 gallons of fuel, and two water tanks for a total of 130 gallons of water.

*Jakatan*'s topsides are painted dark green, with a white sheerwale and broad white bootstripe. The sheer is accented with a rubrail capped by a stainless, half-oval rubbing strip. The carbon spars are buff-colored with white tips.

Jeff and I visited the yard once a month during construction. It was a long day of travel for both of us. Jeff would spend most of his day in the airport and in the air, while I would spend mine in my car and on the ferry to Vancouver Island. Given all the travel time, we would each get about three hours of solid working time at the yard during each visit. This was just about enough to catch up on the progress made since the last trip and to go over areas that we were still refining.

I loved these trips. It's wonderfully gratifying to see a boat coming together with such careful workmanship and attention to detail. Jeff was like a kid in a candy store when he was at the yard. He was a very happy client. He had given me the design budget my office needed to do its very best work. He was demanding but appreciative and always open to ideas. Client, designer, and yard were focused on the same goal: to make *Jakatan* a beautiful, capable, and unique custom cruising boat. We sailed *Jakatan* for the first time in mid-April 2007, leaving the dock in Sidney, British Columbia, with bright sunshine and a wispy five knots of breeze. Soon after motoring out of the tight marina, we were reaching eight-plus knots under power on our way to the fuel dock. There we filled *Jakatan*'s tanks in order to check her cruising trim.

To my relief, the impact of the two masts on the feel of the layout is minimal—less noticeable, in fact, than a single mast right in the middle of the saloon.

After hoisting sail amid a variety of corny schooner jokes, we began chasing wind patches. The boat moved well in light air, and once we adjusted the halyard pick point on the foresail gaff in order to correct the foresail shape, it was apparent that our single-line halyard system was working as hoped. Subsequent wind speeds ranged from six to 20 knots, but we never felt the need to alter the gaff angles again. This single-halyard system had been my primary point of concern with the rig, and all credit goes to Jeff for pushing this detail through.

Soon the breeze began to fill from the north, bringing with it dark clouds, and before long we were rolling along in 15 to 20 knots of wind. *Jakatan* was a real kick to sail in a breeze, stable and slow to heel. As hoped, she could carry all sail without problem. Pressing the boat hard, we never managed to immerse even the bottom edges of the hull windows.

We executed a series of crash jibes down the bay to see if we could break anything. The banging of the foresail traveler car on its end stop was a bit unnerving—something we can cure with a single-line traveler control to restrain the car—but other than that, the boat came through each jibe effortlessly. Upwind, the foresail and mainsail are self-tending, and the minimal-overlap jib is easy to tack.

Both upwind and down, *Jakatan* romped along at around eight knots. Reaching, she hit nine knots. When a puff hit, the bow would lift gently and the boat would accelerate, feeling not at all like its 30,000-plus pounds. Sheeting the mainsail hard induced some weather helm, but not too much. We could always drive the boat without having to fight the helm. Reefing lines had not been led for this initial sail, so we could not see the effect a reef would have on helm feel. We didn't need a reef, though. We all agreed that there was too much fullness in the mainsail and foresail above the gaff throats, and that stiffer upper battens would maintain a better sail shape near the gaffs. Fine-tuning the rig of a new schooner was pretty much new territory for all of us.

It was a great sail. All aboard had a chance to take the wheel, each of us trying to outdo the others for top speed. I was relieved to see how well *Jakatan* sailed to weather. Jeff clearly enjoyed the ride, and he single-handed *Jakatan* through a series of jibes just to get a feel for what it will be like when he sails alone or with family.

I wish I had the words to convey the feeling I get at times like this. The dreams I had when I was 14 years old seemed close at hand as I felt *Jakatan* surge and lift in the puffs while responding to my hands on the wheel. This is exactly why I wanted to be a yacht designer.

# Acknowledgments

I want to thank all the designers who have shared their knowledge of boats with me through the years.

I also want to thank all the talented young designers who have passed through my office over the decades. They have enriched my professional life and left their stamp on hundreds of my designs. After so many years I don't trust myself to remember every name accurately, so I'm not going to try, but I am truly grateful for their innumerable contributions to my body of work.

Last but not least, I want to thank my old dog Piper. Every working day for $15\frac{1}{2}$ years she faithfully accompanied me to the office. She was a lousy draftsman but the best of company, and she loved boats.

# *Index*

Numbers in **bold** indicate pages with illustrations

## A

*African Star* (Fryer's boat), 149, 153
*Aggressive* (Carter design), 20
*Airloom* (Roth's boat), 95
*Airmail* (Carter design), 20
aluminum construction, **181**, 184, 240
aluminum spars, 186–87
*Amati*, **226–31**
    bow profiles, **61**
    design based on, 257
    hull lines, **228**
    interior layout, 229, **230**
    keel, 120, 122, 195–96, **227**, 229
    sail plan, **227**, 229
    sheerline, **61**
    transom, **61**, 74, 226, 229
America's Cup 12-meters, 17, 73, 153, 186, 223–25, **224**
anchor-roller systems, 233
Anderson, Bruce
    *Chicken Lips*, 192
    *Chicken Little*, 196
    *Free Range Chicken*, 196–**201**
    *Stealth Chicken*, **189–96**, 235
Andrews, Alan, 192, 216, 219
Angleman, Hugh, 45
Annapolis Boat Show, 26, 30–31
Antrim, Jim, 226
Aphrodite 101, 173

aramid rigging, 208
Archer, Colin, 75–76
Arnold, Phil, 45
Artese, Joe, 45
Atkin, William, 19, 23, 76, 149
AutoCAD (ACAD), 42–43, 249, 250, 261
Auto Yacht, 42

## B

Baba 30, 88–92, **91**, 93, 94
Baba 35 (Flying Dutchman 35), **92–93**, 94
Baba 40, **93–95**
Baba 56 (*Stealth Chicken*), 195
Babson, Bob, 44, 45
backstays, 205
ballast, 58, 81, 107, 118, 146, 147
ballast-to-displacement ratio (B/D), 13–14
Baltic 42, 156
Bavaria 36, 16
beam
    hull design and, 40
    initial stability and, 85–**86**
    IOR designs, 188
    maximum beam (B max), **11**, 18, 40
    minimum, designing for, 107
    weather helm and, 107, 160
beam at the waterline (BWL), 17–18, 40
Beetle Cat, 162
Beily, Leif, 45
Beneteau designs, 16
Benford, Jay, 6–9, 25

# INDEX

Benford, Robin, 8
Berg, Bob
    Baba 40, 93, 95
    Babo 30, 88–89
    interior layouts by, 88, 95
    Tayana 37 (CT 37), 78, **82**, 88
Bermuda 40, 61, 225
berths, 55, 57, 261
Betty, Jim, 240
Bill, Sally, 164, 167
Bill, Sandy, 164, 167
Black, Bill, 164
Black, Mary, 164
"black box and wand" sailing length rules, 192, 232
Blum, Bernie, 112–13, **115**
BOC Challenge, 30
body plan, 37, **38**
*Bolero*, 19, 20
bolt-on keels, 147–48
bow overhang, 62, **223**, 232–34
bow profiles
    aesthetic considerations, 221
    CCA designs, 225
    clipper bows, 221
    cruising boats, 41
    Davidson bow, 223–25, **224**
    definition of bow, 251
    design of, **61**–62, 214
    entry half-angle, 62, 233
    flare, **223**, 233
    hull speed and, 251–53, **252**
    IMS designs, 62, 195, 232
    IOR designs, 62, 188, 221–**23**, **252**–53
    Peterson bow, 223–**24**
    plumb stems, **61**, 62, 232–34, **233**, **252**–53
    raked stems, 234
    rules for, 61–63
    seakeeping characteristics, 221, 233
    spoon bows, **61**–62, **252**–53
    tumblehome in, **61**
    Valiant 40, 20, 41, 233
bow pulpits, 11, 15
Bowser, Lynn, 192
bowsprits, 11, 233, 234
box-rule boats, 62, 192, 232
Breedlove, Craig, 209
Brewer, Ted
    Hans Christian 54 (CT 54), work on, 8, 64, 65
    Perry's work for, 9
    on quality of Perry's work, 65
    SA/D and D/L article, 20, 81–82
Brewer bite, 77
Bristol, John, 133
Bristol Bay double-enders, 75
Broome, Rupert, 149

Brotman, Jeff, 19
Brower, Steve, 164, 171
Buffiou, Chuck, 51
Burns, Dennis, 23
bustle, 47, **50**, 153
buttocks
    hull-lines plans, 37, **38**
    stern design and, 19–20
    Stevens 53 motorsailer, **39**

## C

C&C 99, 16
C&C deck styling, **191**
Cabo Rico series (Paine design), 118, 119
Cal 35, 55
Cal 40, 61, 225
California rococo-style interior, **53**, 55
Calkin 50, 102
Campbell, Mike, 220
canoe sterns
    advantages of, 76
    canoe stern 45-footer, **11**
    design of, 19–20
    tumblehome canoe stern, 20, **61**
Cape Cod catboats, 162
carbon-fiber spars, 186–87
Carson, John, 175
Carter, Dick
    *Aggressive*, 20
    *Airmail*, 20
    design career with, 8–9, 47
*Cassiopeia* (Davidson design), 195
Catalina 387, 16
catboats, 162
cat ketches, 162
centerboards, 147
center-cockpit boats, 46, 133, **135**, **140**, **141**
center of buoyancy (CB), 18, 84
center of effort (CE), 158, 160
center of pressure, 84
chainplates, 202, 205, 208, 265, 266
Chance, Britton, 115
*Charisma* (S&S design), 243, 245
chart table, 263
*Chatelain* (Berg's boat), 88
Chen, C.S., 65–66, 70
Chen, C.T., 65–66, 70, 78
Chen, Peter, 81
Chen, S.T., 65–66, 70
Chen, Wayne, 65–66, **69**–70
Chen, Y.P., 81
Cheoy Lee, 102–117
    Cheoy Lee 35 Lion (Robb design), 102
    CL 35, 102–**6**, 112

CL 43, 112–13, **115**, **116**
CL 44, 107, **108–12**
CL 48, 107, 112, **113**, **114**, **115**
design career and business relationship with, 102, 105–6, 107, 113, 115
Golden Wave 42, 113, 115, **117**
interest in, 102
weight study for, 102
Chesapeake 32 (Rhodes design), 102
Chicken designs. *See Stealth Chicken* and *Free Range Chicken*
*Chicken Lips* (Andrews design), 192
*Chicken Little* (Santa Cruz 50), 196
chines, 195
Choate, Dennis, 209, 211, 212, 214, 219–20
Christie, Doug, 245
Chu, Tsai Wan, 137
Cirrus 5.8, 17
Clark, Dennis, 5
clipper bows, 221
Clute, Bill, 209, 211, 214
Clute, Heather, 209
cockpit seats, 214, 216
cold-molded construction
 *Loon*, 164
 *Night Runner*, 153, **155**
 *Pachena*, 170
Cole, Bob, 112
Columbia 30, 17
comparing sailboats
 computer-generated hydrostatic calculations, 18, 42
 dimensions for specific boats, 16–17
 terms and ratios for, 10–15, **11**, **12**, 17–18
computer design software. *See also* AutoCAD
 benefits of, 18, 42–43, 250
 development of, 42
 hull-lines plans, 37, 38, 42, 258, 260
 limitations of, 258
 resistance to, 41–42, 249–50
 sheerline development, 61
computer numeric controlled (CNC) machines, 37
computer numeric controlled (CNC) models, 182
continuous rigging, 202
Corinthian Junior Yacht Club, 5
Costa Mesa, California, 45
Crealock, Bill, 19, 23
cruising boats
 B/D for, 14
 bow shape, 41
 ($C_p$) for, 15
 comparing dimensions, 16–17
 deadrise on, 40–**41**, 199, 229, 243
 design elements and sailing styles, 175, 178, 188, 192
 draft, 122

keels, 260
racing boats as, 20
SA/D for, **12**, 13
sailing rigs for, 162–63
spar safety factors, 186
stiff boats, 28, 53, 85–**86**
transoms, 73
Cruising Club of America (CCA)
 bow profiles, 61–62, 225
 designs following rules of, 23
 rating rules (1960s), **11**
 yawls, popularity of, 162
cruising keels, 99
cruising sleds. *See also Icon*
 *Foxfire*, 216–20, **217**, **218**, **219**, **220**
 *Mobisle*, **121**, 122, **241–43**, **244–45**
 under power, 219
 *Starbuck*, 195, 209–**16**
 *White Eagle*, 175, 235–**40**
CT 37 (Tayana 37), **78**–83
CT 48, 70, **71–72**
CT 54 (Hans Christian 54), 8–9, 47, 64–**66**, **67**, 214
CT 56, 70
CT 65, 66–**70**
CT Yachts, 64–72
cutter rigs, 127, **161**, 163

# D

Dabney, Stanley, 25
Dabney, Sylvia, 25
daggerboards, 147
Dahlgard, Daryl, 175, 178, 182, 183, 184
*Dandelion* (Horder's boat), 102
Davidson, Laurie, 167, 195, 223–25
Davidson bow, 223–25, **224**
Davies, Charlie, 45
Davis, Steve, 155
davits, 15, 264
Day, George, 81
deadrise
 benefits of, 182
 on cruising boats, 40–**41**, 199, 229, 243
 initial stability and, **85**
 on racing boats, 195
 at the stern, 74, 182
deck construction. *See also* hull-to-deck joints
 *Jakatan*, 266
 *White Eagle*, 240
deck-stepped spars, 105, 115, 185–86
Dencho Marine, 209, 211, 216, 219
Deng, Sea Dog, 67–69
designed waterline (DWL), **11**, 17, 40, 62, 232–33
designer/builder relationships
 Cheoy Lee, 102, 105–6, 107, 113, 115

*271*

designer/builder relationships *(cont.)*
    Dencho Marine, 211, 219
    Jespersen's Boatyard, 265
    Passport Yachts, 123, 124
    reenergizing boatbuilder's business, 52
    Ta Chaio, 66, 69–70
designer/client relationships, 178, 226, 266–67
designing boats. *See also* computer-design software, hull design
    client's use of boat and, 164, 178, 245, 250, 254
    design spiral, **9**, 264
    ownership of designs, 65, 76
    process for, 254, 257–58, 260–61, 263–65
    to reenergize boatbuilder's business, 52
    rewards of, 267
diagonals, **21**, 37
dinette design, 182, 263
dinghy bow, 223–**24**
directional stability, 120, 122, 182
discontinuous rigging, 202, **204**, 205
displacement, 13, 257
displacement-to-length ratio (D/L), 10
dolphin striker, **150**
double-enders
    appeal of, 75, 98
    design of, 164
    drawback of, 98
    loss of popularity of, 98
    offshore boats as, 75–76
downwind sailing, 163, 208
draft, 122, 146–48
drafting. *See aslo* AutoCAD, computer-design software
    freehand, **32**, 42, **57**

## E

Edwards, John, 8, 64–65, 75–76, 78
eel farm, 123
Eickholt, Will "The Flying Dutchman," 77–78, 80–81, 88
Ellis, Tim, 88
*Elysium* (Andrews design), 219
engine location
    *Amati*, 229
    Cheoy Lee designs, **105**, 112
    *Foxfire* and *Starbuck*, 214, 216
    Freeport 36, 55, 57–58
    *Jakatan*, 261, **262**
    *Loon*, 167, 170
    Passport designs, **127**
entry half-angle, 62, 233
EO 36, 76
*Eric* (Atkin design), 23
Ericson 39, 153
Ericson Yachts, 45

Errol Flynn casement windows, 45
Esprit 37, 31–32, **34**, 35–36
Evergreen State College, 6

## F

fairing hull shapes
    computer fairing programs, 41–42, 167, 258
    diagonals for, 37
    lofting, 155–56
    sheerlines, 61
Farr 50, 16
Farr 52, 17
Farr bow profiles, 223–**24**
ferro-cement boats, 7, 8
fiberglass boats, plank lines on, 65
fiber rigging, 208
Fiji, 3
fin keels
    comparison points, **100**
    for cruising boats, 260
    full keels vs., 122
    high-aspect, 120, 146
    molded fin, 146, 147
    with spade rudders, 120, 260
    types of, 101
fitting out, weight added during, 145
Flying Dutchman 35 (Baba 35), **92**–93, 94
*Flying Tiger*, 206, **207**
fore-and-aft rocker, 39–40, 41
forestays, 202
form stability, 84–85
forward depth station (FDS), 47, 51
forward girth measurements, 62
Fox, Uffa, 5
*Foxfire*, 216–20, **217**, **218**, **219**, **220**
fractional-rigged boats, 158, **160**, 172–73, 199
frames, stations located on, 39
Frank, Vic, 7, 8
freeboard, 85, 127, 133
Freeman, Mrs. Harvey, 23
Freeport 36, 55–58, **56**, **57**
Freeport 37, 57
Freeport 41 (Islander 40), 45–**47**, 52
*Free Range Chicken*, 196–**201**
Frers, German, 61
Friendship 40, 16
Fryer, Doug
    *African Star*, 149, 153
    *Night Runner*, 153, 156–57
Fuqua Industries, 58
furling systems
    in-boom furling systems, 174, 199, **201**, **220**
    in-mast furling systems, 170, 174
    roller-furling, 172, 174

## G

gaff system, single-halyard, **264**, 267
galley design, 195, 199, **200**, 229, **230**, 263
*Ganbare* (Peterson's boat), 9, 55
Garden, Bill
    *Bolero* design, 19, 20
    designs of, 19, 45, 61, 75
    influence of on Perry's designs, 64, 66, 164, 165
    *Oceanus*, 5, 75, 98
    *Seal*, 76
    *Teak Bird*, 102
    visit with, 4–5
    *Walloon*, 102
genoas, 158, 172, 173
Gibson, Don, 66–67, **69**, 70
Golberg, Joe, 5, 58
Golden Wave 42, 113, 115, **117**
Gordon, Tullus, 235, 240
Goring, Craig, **82**
Grand Harbor yard, 133
Grant, Gary, 95
*Gull*, 75
Gurney, Alan, 45, 47

## H

Haida 26, 20
Hai Yang yard, 124
half-angle of entry, 62, 233
half models, 37, 60–**61**
half-stations, 39
Hallberg-Rassy designs, 16
Hall Spars, 264
Hammond, Roland "Buster," 44, 45, 57, 59
Hand, William, 112
Hans Christian 34, 47, 76, 77
Hans Christian 36, 76–77
Hans Christian 54 (CT 54), 8–9, 47, 64–**66**, 67
Han Sheng Yacht Building Company, 137
Hawkins, Jeff, 254, 257, 258, 261, 264, 266
Hazen, George, 41
head, 263
headsails
    clew location, 173
    fractional-rigged boats, 172–73
    inventory, 172–73, 173
    jib sheeting angle, 163, 172
    roller-furler systems, 172
    self-tacking traveler for jib, 173
heeled center of buoyancy (CB), 18
heeling force, 84
Heg, Jim, 88
Herreshoff, L. Francis, 186, 221
Hetron resin, 26
*Holger Danske* (Nielsen design), 19–20, 76
Hong Kong, visit to, 106–7
Hood, Ted, 178, 182
Hoosenally, Hebtee, 106–7
Horder, Gary, 102
Howarth, Denny, 216, 219
Hoyt, Peter, 123
hull design. *See also* bow profiles; computer design software; deadrise; designing boats; keels; transoms
    development of, 37
    evaluation of, 39–**41**
    fore-and-aft rocker, 39–40, 41
    midsectional shape, 40–**41**
    plank lines on, 65
    pounding and, 41
    rules for, 61–63
    "size" components, 257
    stability and, 84–**87**
    weight of boat and, 141, 145
hull-lines plans
    computer-generated, 37, 42, 258, 260
    evaluation of, 39–**41**
    hand-drawn lines, 42, 249–50, 258
    patterns made from, 37, 42
    views shown, 37–**39**
hull speed
    bow profiles and, 251–53, **252**
    ($C_p$) and, 14–15
    DWL and, 232–33
    weight of boat and, 175, 178
hull-to-deck joints
    laminated ring frames, **152**, **166**, 170–71
    *Loon*, 170–71
    *Pachena*, 170
    Passport designs, 124
Humphreys, Rob, 61
Hungarian three-hat cold remedy, 45
Huntingford, Stan, 123
hydraulic vang, 219
Hylas 66, 16

## I

iceboxes, 229
*Icon*
    bow profiles, **61**
    characteristics, **11**, 245
    client's sailing styles, 245, 250
    deck plan, **248**, 249
    handling of, 250
    hull lines, **247**
    interior layout, 245
    keel, 147, 245, **246**
    response to hand-drawn plans for, 42, 249

*Icon (cont.)*
  sail plan, 245–**46**, **249**
  sheerline, **61**
initial stability, 53, **85–86**, 188
interior layouts
  berths, 55, 57, 261
  California rococo-style, **53**, 55
  designing of, 261, 263–64
  dinette design, 182, 263
  galley design, 195, 199, **200**, 229, **230**, 263
  head, 263
  head-forward arrangements, 55, 57, 131
  trends in, 107, 112, 131
International 14 dinghy class, 62
International Measurement System (IMS)
  basis for, 192
  bow profiles, 62, 195, 232
  design characteristics of boats under, 47, 192
  velocity-predicting programs (VPPs), 63
International Offshore Rule (IOR)
  bow profiles, 62, 188, 221–**23**, **252**–53
  bustle, 153
  design characteristics of boats under, 9, 188, 192, 209, 214
  end of, 59, 188
  flaws of, 188
  initial stability, 53
  Islander 28 design for, 47, **50**, 51
  LBG measurement, 188, 221–23, **222**
  sail plans, 55
  sectional shapes, 20, 188
  stern treatment encouraged by, 23, 188
iron ballast, 107, 118, 146
Islander 28
  bustle, 47, **50**
  designing of, 9
  dimensions, 16
  hull lines, **49**
  interior layout, **50**
  IOR design and, 47, **50**, 51
  keel, **51**
  launch of, 51
  L/B of, 52
  sailing, **52**
  sail plan, **48**
  success of, 51
Islander 32, 52–**55**
  interior layout, **53**, **54**, 55
  keel, 55
  weather helm, 53, 55
Islander 34, 58, **59**
Islander 36, 45, 52
Islander 40 (Freeport 41), 45–**47**, 52
Islander 41, 47
Islander Yachts
  closing of, 58
  design career with, 59
  engineering and in-house design, 45
  management of, 44–45
Island Packet designs, 16

## J

*Jakatan*, **254**–67
  basis for design of, 257
  bow profile, 257–58
  characteristics, 254, 257–58, 260
  deck plan, **255**, **259**, 264–65
  hull lines, **256**
  interior layout, 261–64, **262**
  keel, 260
  rudder, **256**, 260–61
  sailing, 267
  sail plan, **255**, **264**, 267
  tank arrangement, 266
  transom, 258, 265
  wood construction, 265–66
J/Boats, 16, 17, 86, 199
Jespersen, Bent, 170, 184, 265
Jespersen, Eric, 184, 265, 266
jib-and-jigger sail combination, 163
jibing downwind, 208
jib self-tacking traveler, 173
jib sheeting angle, 163, 172, 205, **208**
Johnson, Chris, 264
Johnson, Ned, 32
Johnson, Palmer, 243
Johnstone, Rodney, 86
Jones, Hugh, 82

## K

keel bolts, 147–48
keels
  *Amati*, 120, 122, 195–96, **227**, 229
  aspect ratios, **100**, 101, 118, 146
  Baba designs, 94
  bolt-on keels, 147–48
  Brewer bite, 77
  bulbs at tip, 120
  Cheoy Lee designs, 107, 112
  for cruising boats, 99, 260
  draft and keel design, 146–48
  fin keels, **100**, 101, 120, 122, 146, 147, 260
  Flying Dutchman 35 (Baba 35), 94
  foil types and thickness ratios, 99, 101, 118
  forward-swept keels, **194**, 195–96, **227**, 229
  full keels, 77, 118–**19**
  function of, 99
  hybrid keels, **121**, 122

Islander designs, **51**, 55
lifting keels, 147, 245, **246**
modified full keels, 118, **119**
NACA foil, 77, 98, 107, 260
Passport designs, 127
sailing-area specific keels, 99
stability and, 99, 119–20, 122
sweep angle, 146
Tashiba designs, 98, 118
Tayana 37, 94, 119
terms and definitions, **100**
trim and, 94
types of, **119**
Valiant designs, 20, **21**, 23, 28
weather helm and, 99, 196
wing keels, **58**, 146–47
keel-stepped spars, 105, 115, 185–86
kelp cutter, 120, 195
Kernan, Tim, 249
ketches, 7–8, **161**, 162–63
Kibby, Mr., 4, 5
King, Bruce, 153
King Dragon yard, 123–24, 133
*Kiwi Magic* (Davidson design), 223
Kuo, B.K., 98

# L

Lafitte 44, 106
*Lakemba*, 3
Lange, Bob, 155
Lange, Cecil, 153, 155–56
Lapworth, Bill, 55
lead ballast, 118, 146, 147
Lee, Bill, 40, 131, 182
lee helm, 99, 160
Leisure Furl system, 199, **201**, 220
length at waterline (LWL), 17. *See also* designed
    waterline (DWL)
length between girths (LBG), 62, 188, 221–23, **222**
length on deck (LOD), **11**, 15, 17
length overall (LOA)
    client's focus on, 233, 257
    comparing sailboats, **11**, 15, 17, 18, 40
    transom design and, 73
length-to-beam ratio (L/B), 10
length waterline (LWL), **11**
lifting keels, 147, 245, **246**
limit of positive stability (LPS), 86
Lin, Basil, **78**
Lindsay, Mark, 9
Little Harbor series (Hood), 178, 182
Lo, Big, **124**
load waterline, 17. *See also* designed waterline
    (DWL)

lofting, 37, 42, 155–56
*Lonestar* (Valiant 47), 30
Long Beach Boat Show, 23, 25
longitudinal center of buoyancy (LCB), 15
longitudinal center of flotation (LCF), 15
longitudinal center of gravity (LCG), 84
*Loon*, 164–71
    construction drawing, **166**
    deck plan, **168**
    design elements requested by owner, 164
    design inspiration, 164
    at the dock, 167, **170**
    engine for, 167, 170
    fee for, 167
    hull-to-deck joints, 170–71
    interior layout, 170
    Laurie Davidson's work on, 167
    plumbing schematics, **169**
    sail plan, **165**
    stability of, 171
Luders, Bill, 104
luff perpendicular (LP), 158
*Lurline*, 3
luxury tax, 58–59, 164

# M

Ma, Willie, 77
The Magic Machine, 25
mainsails
    in-boom furling systems, 174, 199, **201**, 220
    in-mast furling systems, 170, 174
    shortening, 172–74
Mao Ta 36, 77
Mao Ta yard, 77
Mariner Polaris 36, 76
Marine Weight Control, 6
*Mariposa*, 3
Martin Marine, 249
masthead-rigged boats, 158, **160**
masts. *See* spars
McClear, Frank, 112
McCormick, Hank, 44–45, 55, 57, 58
McNabb, Daryl, 27
*Merrimack*, 4
meter-boat rule, 17. *See also* America's Cup 12-meters
midsectional shape, 40–**41**, 47
Miller, Don, 4, 5
*Mobisle*, 121, 122, **241**–43, **244**–45
models. *See* half models
moment, 18, 84
moments of inertia, 185
Moody 47, 16
Moore, Don, 143, 145
Mosely, Steve, 45, 57

motorsailers
    CL 43, 112–13, **115**, **116**
    SA/D for, 11
    Stevens 53 motorsailer, **39**, **40**
Mudd, Roger, 107

# N

National Advisory Committee for Aeronautics (NACA) keel foil, 77, 98, 107, 260
Navtec rod rigging, 208
Nelson, Ricky, 31–32
Ni, Bengt, 76, 77
Nielsen, K. Aage, 19, 20, 61, 76
*Night Runner*, **149**–57
    cabin trunk, 156
    cold-molded construction, 153, **155**
    construction drawing, **152**
    cruising in, 157
    design elements, 153
    dolphin striker, **150**
    as favorite boat, 150, 157
    hull lines, **151**
    interior layout, **156**
    lofting, 155–56
    nicknames, 156
    origin of design, 149, 153
    racing in, **156**–57
    sail plan, **150**
Nordhavn powerboats, 137
Nordic Yachts, 31, 32, 58–59
    Nordic 40, 32
    Nordic 44, 32, **38**, 106
Norseman 447, 92, 94, 106
North, Lowell, 209
North Sails, 58, 209

# O

*Oceanus* (Garden's boat), 5, 75, 98
Oldham, Ben, 127, 131
One-Ton North Americans, 9
Open 40 class, 17, 62
Open 60 class, 62
O'Steen, Jim, 81
Outbound 44, 16
overhang
    aft, 73
    bow, 62, **223**, 232–34
Oyster 62, 16

# P

*Pachena*, 170, 171
Paine, Chuck, 9, 42, 118, 119
Paine, Frank, 149, 153
Panda 40, 95
Passport 37, 131, **132**
Passport 40, 123, **125**, **126–27**, **128**, 131
Passport 41, 127, **130**, 131
Passport 42 (Huntington design), 123
Passport 43, 127, 131
Passport 44, 131
Passport 44/47, 137, **138–41**
Passport 47, **129**, 131, 133, **134**, **135**
Passport 49, 133, **135**
Passport 50, 133, **136**, **137**
Passport 456, **138–39**, **141**
Passport 470, **138–41**
Passport Vista 485/515, 137, 141, **142–44**
Passport Yachts, 123–145
    dealers, 125, 127, 133
    design career and business relationship with, 123, 124
    inquiry from, 123
    yards building boats for, 123–24, 133, 137
Pathfinder diesel, 57–58
PBO synthetic-fiber rigging, 208
Pedrick, Dave, 112, 115
performance. *See also* hull speed
    draft and, 146–47
    rig weight and, 185
    velocity-predicting programs (VPPs), 42, 63, 192, 251, 252, 258, 260
performance cruiser, 23
Performance Handicap Rating Fleet (PHRF)
    basis for handicaps, 62–63, 188
    catboat ratings, 162
    designing for, 188
    popularity of, 188
    SA/D and, 13
Perkins 4-108 diesel, 55, 57
Perry, Max, 220, 250
Perry, Robert H., **8**
    with Basil Lin, **78**
    drawing interest of, 4–5
    education of, 4, 5, 6
    racing introduction, 5
    sailing introduction, 4, 5
    on Tayana 37, **82**
    teaching career, 6
    voyage to America, 3–4
    with Wayne Chen and Don Gibson, **69**
    with Wendel Renkin, **124**
    working alone, 164, 167
Perry, Spike, 249
Perry 61 (*White Eagle*), 240
Perrywinkle dinghies, 34
Peterson, Doug, 9, 55
Peterson 40, 58

Peterson bow, 223–24
Phillips-Birt, Douglas, 186
PHRF. See Performance Handicap Rating Fleet (PHRF)
Pierce, Dooley, 20
pilothouse boats. See also *Loon*; *Yoni*
    Baba 40, 95
    CT 54, **67**
    Flying Dutchman 35, **92**
    Tashiba 31, 98
    Tashiba 36, 98
    Tashiba 40, 98
    Valiant 40, 30–31, **32**, **33**, **34**
planar sheer, 60–**61**
plank lines, 65
plan view, 37, **38**
plumb stems, **61**, 62, 232–34, **233**, **252**–53
point of vanishing stability, 86
pounding, 41
pounds-per-inch immersion, 15
powerboats, demand for, 133, 137
pre-bend, 205
prismatic coefficient ($C_p$), 14–15
profile view, 37, **38**
propellers, 119
Pullman-style double berths, 55, 57
pumpkin seed waterplane, **222**

# R

racing boats
    B/D for, 13–14
    cruising on, 20
    deadrise, 40, 195
    SA/D for, 11, 13
    spar safety factors, 186
    transoms, 73, 74
    VCG for, 15
    weight of boat, 127, 131
raked stems, 234
Rander, Steve, 229
reefing systems, 172, 173–74
Renkin, Caroline, **124**
Renkin, Wendel, 123–25, **124**, 131, 133
reserve buoyancy, 62
reverse sheer spring, 60
reverse transoms, **11**, 73, 265
Rhino, 42
Rhodes, Philip, 61, 102, 104, 105, 156
Richards, Ray, 20
*Ricky Nelson* (Esprit 37), 31–32, **36**
rigging
    chainplates, 202, 205, 208, 265, 266
    continuous vs. discontinuous, 202, **204**, 205
    dimensions and types, 158–163
    materials for, 208

    shrouds, 202, **204**, 205
    spreaders, 202–**8**
righting arm, 15, 18, **85**, **86**
righting moment (RM), 18, 84, **85**
rigs—dimensions and types, 158–163
Riley, Brian, 184
ring frames, laminated, **152**, **166**, 170–71
ritual rums, 156–57
Robb, Arthur, 102
Robbins, Bonnie, 250
Robbins, Dick, 243, 245, 250
rod rigging, 208
Rohrer, Scott, 5
roller-furler systems, 172, 174
roller-reefing systems, 172
Roser, Jim, 245, 250
Roser, Robin, 250
Roth, Tim, 95
Rothman, Nathan, 7, 8, 19, 34
*Ruby* (Valiant 40), **25**
rudders
    design of, 119, 145, 211, 214, 260–61
    DWL and, 17
    Passport designs, 145
    plywood door lofting, 211, 214
    spade rudders, 120, **256**, 260–61
    surface-piercing rudder blade, 11
rums, ritual, 156–57
Rutter, Dave, 240, 243
Rutter, Gay, 243

# S

S&S designs, 243
Sabre designs, 16
safety factors, 186
Saga series, 16, 233
sail area, calculating, **12**, 13
sail area–to-displacement ratio (SA/D), 10–13, **12**, 81–82
sailing length, 188, 192, 221, 223, 225
sailing rigs
    terms for dimensions, 158–60, **159**
    types of, 158, **160**–63
sail plans
    48-foot keel-centerboard, **12**
    *Amati*, **227**, 229
    Babo 30, **90**
    Cheoy Lee designs, **104**, **109**–11, **113**, **117**
    Esprit 37, **35**
    *Foxfire*, **217**
    *Free Range Chicken*, **197**
    geometry for, 4
    *Icon*, 245–**46**, 249
    IOR requirements, 55

sail plans *(cont.)*
    Islander designs, **46, 48**
    *Jakatan*, **255**
    *Loon*, **165**
    *Mobisle*, **241**
    *Night Runner*, **150**
    Passport designs, **125, 129, 130, 132, 134, 136**
    *Starbuck*, **210**
    *Stealth Chicken*, **189**
    Tashiba 36, **96**
    Tayana 37, **79–80**
    Valiant designs, **22, 27, 29**
    *White Eagle*, **236**
    *Yoni*, **176**
sails. *See also* furling systems; headsails
    inventory, 173–74
    shortening, 172–74
    terms and dimensions, 158–60, **159**
Santa Cruz designs, 17, 196
Schock boats, 44
Schooner Creek Boatworks, 229, 231, 265
schooners, 4, 162, 163. See also *Jakatan*
Schrader, Mark, 30
Schumacher, Carl, 182
Scorpio 72 (CT 65), **70**
Scott, Lorrie, 226, 229, 231
Scott, Paul, 226, 229, 231
seakeeping characteristics, 221, 233
*Seal* (Garden design), 76
sectional shapes, 20, 39–40, **41**, 84–85, 167
sections, 37, **38**
Shannon, Graham, 41–42
sheerline
    degree of spring, 60
    examples of, **61**
    influence of on design, 60
    nonplanar sheer, 61
    planar sheer, 60–**61**
    reverse spring, 60
    spring, 60
Shilshole Bay Marina, 5, 25
shrouds, 202, **204**, 205
Slocum 43, 123
sloop rigs, 158, **160**–61, 162, 163
Solar 42 (Huntington design), 123
Solent stay, 173
Souquet, Ben, 199, 250
South Coast Marine yard, 137
Southerly 110, 16
spade rudders, 120, **256**, 260–61
spars
    broken masts, 185–86
    compression load on, 205
    deck-stepped vs. keel-stepped, 105, 115, 185–86
    design and moments, 185, 186
    fore-and-aft moments, 202
    in-boom furling systems, 174, 199, **201**, 220
    in-mast furling systems, 170, 174
    materials for, 186–87
    pre-bend, 205
    rig weight and performance, 185
    safety factors, 186
    sailing style and rig setup, 187
    single-halyard gaff system, **264**, 267
    stiffness of, 185
speed cup, 174
spoon bows, **61**–62, **252**–53
spreaders, 202–**8**
spring, 60
The Springfield Rifle, 5, 6
stability
    B/D and, 13–14
    boat size and, 86
    BWL and, 40
    components of, 84–**85**, **86**, **87**
    directional stability, 120, 122, 182
    form stability, 84–85
    initial stability, 53, **85**–**86**, 188
    keels and, 99, 119–20, 122
    righting moment and, 18
    ultimate stability, 86
stability curve, 18
*Starbuck*, 209–16
    characteristics, 211
    deck plan, **213**
    design based on, 243
    hull lines, **212**
    interior layout, 214, **215**
    rudder, 195, 211, 214
    sail plan, **210**
static stability numbers, 86
stations, 37–**39**
staysails, 163
staysail stay, 173
*Stealth Chicken*, **189**–96
    characteristics, 195, 211, 235
    CNC model of, 182
    deck plan, **191**
    hull lines, **190**
    interior layout, **193**, 195
    keel, **194**, 195
    performance of, **196**
    rudder, **194**, 195
    sail plan, **189**
Stevens, Curt, 133
Stevens 53 motorsailer, **39**, 40
Strange, Albert, 19
Sunlight 30, **87**
surface-piercing rudder blade, 11
Swan designs, 16, 17

Swiftsure Race, 250
swim platforms and steps, 73, 98, 183, 265
Synergy 1000, 17

## T

Ta Chaio, 64–72
    CT 54 (Hans Christian 54), 47, 64–65, **67**
    CT sales in U.S., 70
    design career with, 70
    dispute with Edwards, 65, 76
    workers at, 67–69
Taiwan-built boats. *See also specific boatyards*
    business deals with, 77
    contracts for, 65
    Edwards idea for, 8
    U.S. builders' arrangements with, 133, 137
Tally Ho Major (*African Star*), 149, 153
Tamsui Miracle yard, 123
Tanton, Yves-Marie, 9, 47, 49, 214
Tartan designs, 16
Tashiba 31, 98
Tashiba 36, **96**–98
Tashiba 40, 95, 98
Ta Shing yard, 88–98
    location of, 88
    quality of building by, 88, 93
    Taswell boats, 98
Tayana 37, **78**–83
    ballast, 81
    deck modifications, 82–83
    interior layout, **81**
    keel, 94, 119
    sail plans, **79**–**80**
    stability of, 93
    weather helm, 82
Tayana 52, 209
Ta Yang yard, 78, 81
*Teak Bird* (Garden design), 102
Tissier, Michel, 70
tracking ability, 120, 122
transom doors, 57, 265
transoms
    crown shaping, 64–65
    cruising boats, 73
    design of, **11**, **61**, 73–74, 226, 229, 265
    IOR designs, 23, 188
    Passport designs, 127, 131, 137, 141
    racing boats, 73, 74
    reverse transoms, **11**, 73, 265
TransPac 52, 62, 229
Transpac race, 186, 196
transverse center of buoyancy (TCB), **86**
Tripp, Bill, Sr., 74
tumblehome
    advantages of, 47
    at the bow, **61**
    at the stern, 20, **61**, 258

## U

Ultimate designs, 17, 226
ultimate stability, 86
ultralight displacement (ULDB) movement, 40
*Unicorn* (King design), 153
Uniflite, 23, 26, 31, 32
Union 36, 76
Union Mariner 36, 76
Union yard, 76, 77
Universal 36, 76
upwind sailing, 162–63, 173

## V

Vacanti, Dave, 42
Valiant 32
    custom prototype, 28, 30
    design elements, 28
    house design, 30
    interior layout, **28**
    keel, 28
    *Practical Sailor* review of, 28
    sail plan, **27**
    weather helm, 28
Valiant 39, 32
Valiant 40
    advertising campaign, 25–26
    bow design, 20, 41, 233
    building of, 23, 26–27
    business side of, 25
    bustle, 47
    designing of, 9
    D/L of, 20
    hull lines, **21**
    inspiration for design elements, 23
    interior layout, **24**, **32**
    introduction of, 23, 25
    keel, 20, **21**, 23
    LPS of, 86
    naming of, 23
    number built, 26, 27
    performance of, 23, 32
    pilothouse version, 30–31, **32**, **33**, **34**
    rigging, 208
    rudder, 20, 23
    sailing, **25**, **26**, 27–28, 30–31
    sail plan, **22**
    sales team, 25
    sectional shape, 20
    spreaders, 202, **203**

stern design, 19–20, 23
success of, 34
waterline, 23
Valiant 42, 16, 202
Valiant 47, **29**, **30**
Valiant 50, 30, **31**
Valiant Yacht Corporation, 28
vang, 219–20
V-berths, 57
velocity made good (VMG), 163
velocity-predicting programs (VPPs)
accuracy of, 192
basis for, 63
bow evaluation with, 251, 252
use of data when designing, 42, 192, 258, 260
vertical center of gravity (VCG), 15, 18, 84, **85**, 185, 258
*Victory*, 47
Vietnam War, 5–6

# W

Wagner, Thom, 127, 133, 135, 137, 143, 145
*Walloon* (Garden design), 102
watch-buying mission, 106
waterlines
asymmetrical, 73
designed waterline (DWL), **11**, 17, 40, 62, 232–33
hull-lines plans, 37, **38**
stations, 37–**39**
waterplane, 15, 17, **222**
weather helm
beam and, 107, 160
characteristics, 160, 173
hull design and, 73
Islander 32, 53, 55
keels and, 99, 196
sail reduction and, 172
Tayana 37, 82
Valiant 32, 28
weight of boat
fitting out, weight added during, 145
hull design and, 141, 145
hull speed and, 175, 178
racing and, 127, 131
weight study, 102
Wertheimer, Brian, 5
Westerly Marine, 192, 199, 243
Westsail
hull and keel design, 81
location of, 45
Westsail 32
dimensions, 16
D/L of, 20
fore-and-aft rocker, 41
rudder, 17
success of, 19
*White Eagle*, 175, 235–**40**
*Windwalker* (CT 45), **67**
Windward Passage, 47
wing keels, **58**, 146–47
wire rigging, 208
Worstell, Rich, 26–27

# Y

yacht design. *See* designing boats
yawls, **11**, **12**, **161**, 162
*Yoni*, 175–84
aluminum construction, **181**, 184
basis for design of, 178
CNC models of, 182
deck plan, **180**, 183
design elements, 182
design elements requested by owner, 178
hull lines, **177**
interior layout, **179**, 182–83
launch of, 184
number of hours to complete, 184
rig, **183**–84
sail plan, **176**
Young Sun 35, 77